W9-CRT-154

CRIMINAL LAW AND PROCEDURE
Fourth Edition

The West Legal Studies Series

Your options keep growing with West Legal Studies

Each year our list continues to offer you more options for every area of the law to meet your course or on-the-job reference requirements. We now have over 140 titles from which to choose in the following areas:

Administrative Law	Family Law
Alternative Dispute Resolution	Federal Taxation
Bankruptcy	Intellectual Property
Business Organizations/Corporations	Introduction to Law
Civil Litigation and Procedure	Introduction to Paralegalism
CLA Exam Preparation	Law Office Management
Client Accounting	Law Office Procedures
Computer in the Law Office	Legal Research, Writing, and Analysis
Constitutional Law	Legal Terminology
Contract Law	Paralegal Employment
Criminal Law and Procedure	Real Estate Law
Document Preparation	Reference Materials
Environmental Law	Torts and Personal Injury Law
Ethics	Will, Trusts, and Estate Administration

You will find unparalleled, practical support

Each book is augmented by instructor and student supplements to ensure the best learning experience possible. We also offer custom publishing and other benefits such as West's Student Achievement Award. In addition, our sales representatives are ready to provide you with dependable service.

We want to hear from you

Our best contributions for improving the quality of our books and instructional materials is feedback from the people who use them. If you have a question, concern, or observation about any of our materials, or you have a product proposal or manuscript, we want to hear from you. Please contact your local representative or write us at the following address:

West Legal Studies, 5 Maxwell Drive, P. O. Box 8007, Clifton Park, New York 12065

For additional information point your browser at
www.westlegalstudies.com

THOMSON

DELMAR LEARNING

CRIMINAL LAW AND PROCEDURE
Fourth Edition

Daniel E. Hall, J.D., Ed.D.

THOMSON

DELMAR LEARNING

Australia Canada Mexico Singapore Spain United Kingdom United States

THOMSON

DELMAR LEARNING

WEST LEGAL STUDIES

CRIMINAL LAW AND PROCEDURE 4E
Daniel E. Hall, J.D., Ed.D

Career Education Strategic Business Unit:
Vice President,
Dawn Gerrain

Director of Editorial:
Sherry Gomoll

Acquisitions Editor:
Pamela Fuller

Developmental Editor:
Melissa Riveglia

Editorial Assistant:
Sarah Duncan

Director of Production:
Wendy A. Troeger

Production Manager:
Carolyn Miller

Production Editor:
Betty L. Dickson

Technology Manager:
Joseph Saba

Director of Marketing:
Donna J. Lewis

Channel Manager:
Wendy E. Mapstone

Cover Design:
Dutton and Sherman Design

Library of Congress Cataloging-in-Publication Data

Hall, Daniel (Daniel E.)
    Criminal law and procedure / Daniel E. Hall.—4th ed.
        p. cm.
    Includes index.
        ISBN 1–4018–1559–6
        1. Criminal law—United States.
2. Criminal procedure—United States.
3. Legal assistants—United States—Handbooks, manuals, etc. I.Title.
KF9219.3.H32 2003
345.73—dc21   2003046287

NOTICE TO THE READER

To Stace and Grace

Contents

Preface   *xiii*

Table of Cases   *xxi*

PART 1

Criminal Law

CHAPTER 1

Introduction to the Legal System of the United States   3

FEDERALISM   4

SEPARATION OF POWERS   7

THE STRUCTURE OF THE COURT SYSTEM   9

THE DUTIES AND POWERS OF THE JUDICIAL
    BRANCH   14

COMPARING CIVIL LAW AND CRIMINAL LAW   16

WEB LINKS   20

KEY TERMS   20

REVIEW QUESTIONS   20

REVIEW PROBLEMS   21

END NOTES   21

CHAPTER 2

Introduction to Criminal Law   23

THE DISTINCTION BETWEEN CRIMINAL LAW AND
    CRIMINAL PROCEDURE   24

THE POWER OF GOVERNMENT TO REGULATE
    BEHAVIOR   24

THE PURPOSES OF PUNISHING CRIMINAL LAW
    VIOLATORS   27

    Specific and General Deterrence   27

    Incapacitation   28

    Rehabilitation   28

    Retribution   29

SOURCES OF CRIMINAL LAW   30

    The Common Law   30

    Statutory Law   37

    Ordinances   37

    Administrative Law   38

    Court Rules   41

    The Model Penal Code   43

    Constitutional Law   43

WEB LINKS   45

KEY TERMS   46

REVIEW QUESTIONS   46

REVIEW PROBLEMS   46

END NOTES   47

CHAPTER 3

The Two Essential Elements   49

MENS REA   50

    Mens Rea and the Common Law   50

    Strict Liability   56

    Vicarious Liability   61

    Current Approaches to Mens Rea   62

    Proving Mens Rea   64

    Motive   65

ACTUS REUS   66

    Voluntariness   66

    Thoughts and Statements as Acts   66

    Personal Status as an Act   68

    Possession as an Act   69

Omissions as Acts   70

Causation   72

WEB LINKS   79

KEY TERMS   79

REVIEW QUESTIONS   79

REVIEW PROBLEMS   80

END NOTES   81

C H A P T E R   4

Crimes Against the Person   83

STUDYING CRIMES   84

HOMICIDE   85

Homicide and the Common Law   86

Statutory Approaches to Homicide   90

Manslaughter   98

The Model Penal Code Approach to
    Homicide   101

Life, Death, and Homicide   101

Suicide   102

Corpus Delicti   104

ASSAULT AND BATTERY   105

Aggravated Assault and Battery   106

MAYHEM   107

SEX CRIMES   107

Rape   108

Nonforcible Rape   109

Sodomy   110

Rape Shield Laws   111

Incest   111

Sex Offenses Against Children   111

Megan's Laws, Commitment, and Castration   113

KIDNAPPING AND FALSE IMPRISONMENT   114

Kidnapping   114

Parental Kidnapping   115

False Imprisonment   117

STALKING   117

CIVIL RIGHTS AND HATE CRIMES   118

WEB LINKS   120

KEY TERMS   120

REVIEW QUESTIONS   120

REVIEW PROBLEMS   120

END NOTES   121

C H A P T E R   5

Crimes Against Property and Habitation   123

ARSON   124

BURGLARY   125

THEFT CRIMES   126

Introduction to Theft Crimes   126

Larceny   128

Embezzlement   130

False Pretenses   131

Receiving Stolen Property   135

Robbery   136

Extortion   137

Consolidated Theft Statutes   139

Identity Theft   140

The Model Penal Code Consolidation   143

Destruction of Property   144

Computer Crimes   145

WEB LINKS   149

KEY TERMS   149

REVIEW QUESTIONS   150

REVIEW PROBLEMS   150

END NOTES   151

C H A P T E R   6

Crimes Against the Public   153

DEFINING A "CRIME AGAINST THE PUBLIC"   154

CRIMES AGAINST PUBLIC MORALITY   155

Prostitution and Solicitation   155
Deviate Sexual Conduct   155
Indecent Exposure and Lewdness   158
Obscenity   158
Regulating the Internet   161

CRIMES AGAINST THE PUBLIC ORDER   167
Introduction   167
Riot and Unlawful Assembly   167
Disturbing the Peace   168
Incitement/Advocacy of Unlawful
    Conduct   168
Threats   170
Vagrancy and Panhandling   170
Crimes Involving Firearms   173
Drug and Alcohol Crimes   175

CRIMES AGAINST THE ADMINISTRATION
    OF GOVERNMENT   180
Perjury   180
Bribery   183
Tax Crimes   184
Obstruction of Justice   186
Contempt   187

CRIMES AGAINST SOVEREIGNTY
    AND SECURITY   189
Treason   189
Sedition & Espionage   191
Terrorism   191

CRIMES AGAINST THE ENVIRONMENT   200
Clean Water Act   202
Clean Air Act   202
Comprehensive Environmental Response,
    Compensation and Liability Act   202
Resource Conservation and Recovery Act   203
Occupational Safety and Health Act   203
Toxic Substances Control Act   203
Federal Insecticide, Fungicide, and
    Rodenticide Act   204

Emergency Planning and Community Right-to-
    Know Act   204
Endangered Species Act   204
Marine Mammal Protection Act   204
WEB LINKS   205
KEY TERMS   205
REVIEW QUESTIONS   205
REVIEW PROBLEMS   206
END NOTES   207

CHAPTER   7

Parties and Inchoate Offenses   209

PARTIES TO CRIMES   210
INCHOATE CRIMES   211
    Attempt   211
    Conspiracy   214
    Solicitation   218

WEB LINKS   218
KEY TERMS   219
REVIEW QUESTIONS   219
REVIEW PROBLEMS   219
END NOTES   220

CHAPTER   8

Factual and Statutory Defenses   221

"DEFENSE" DEFINED   222
AFFIRMATIVE DEFENSES   222
INSANITY   223
    M'Naghten   224
    Irresistible Impulse   225
    Durham   225
    The Model Penal Code Test   225
    Guilty But Mentally Ill   226
    Procedures of the Insanity Defense   226
    Disposition of the Criminally Insane   227
    Insanity at the Time of Trial   229

DURESS AND NECESSITY   230

USE-OF-FORCE DEFENSES   231

Self-Defense   231

Defense of Others   233

Defense of Property and Habitation   233

Imperfect Self-Defense   234

Arrests   234

INFANCY   238

INTOXICATION   239

MISTAKE   239

ENTRAPMENT   240

ALIBI AND CONSENT   241

STATUTES OF LIMITATION   241

WEB LINKS   242

KEY TERMS   243

REVIEW QUESTIONS   243

REVIEW PROBLEMS   243

END NOTES   244

C H A P T E R   9

Constitutional Defenses   245

INTRODUCTION   246

DOUBLE JEOPARDY   246

SELF-INCRIMINATION AND IMMUNITY   247

DUE PROCESS AND EQUAL
    PROTECTION   249

VAGUENESS AND OVERBREADTH   251

EX POST FACTO AND BILLS OF
    ATTAINDER   251

FIRST AMENDMENT AND RELIGION   252

FIRST AMENDMENT AND SPEECH   259

PRIVACY AND OTHER UNENUMERATED
    RIGHTS   266

WEB LINKS   271

KEY TERMS   271

REVIEW QUESTIONS   271

REVIEW PROBLEMS   272

END NOTES   272

P A R T   I I

Criminal Procedure

C H A P T E R   1 0

Introduction and Participants   275

CRIMINAL PROCEDURE DEFINED   276

A COMMON-LAW, ADVERSARIAL, AND
    ACCUSATORIAL SYSTEM   276

THE DUE PROCESS MODEL   278

THE PARTICIPANTS   279

Law Enforcement Officers   279

Prosecutors   280

Judges   287

Defense Attorneys   288

Victims   292

LIABILITY OF GOVERNMENTS AND
    THEIR OFFICIALS   293

WEB LINKS   295

KEY TERMS   295

REVIEW QUESTIONS   295

REVIEW PROBLEMS   295

END NOTES   296

C H A P T E R   1 1

The Constitutional Aspects of Criminal Procedure   297

INTRODUCTION   298

INCORPORATION   298

EXPANSION OF RIGHTS   300

EXCLUSIONARY RULE   300

Exclusionary Rule and Exceptions   303

FRUIT OF THE POISONOUS TREE   303

STANDING   304

STATE CONSTITUTIONS AND THE "NEW
    FEDERALISM"   305

WEB LINKS   309

KEY TERMS   310
REVIEW QUESTIONS   310
REVIEW PROBLEMS   310
END NOTES   310

CHAPTER 12
Searches, Seizures, and Arrests 311

THE FOURTH AMENDMENT   312
Privacy   312

PROBABLE CAUSE   319
SEARCHES AND SEIZURES   328
The Warrant Requirement   328
Exceptions to the Search Warrant
Requirement   334

ARREST   362
Defining Arrest   362
The Warrant Preference   363
Arrests in Protected Areas   365
Search Incident to Arrest and the Protective
Sweep   369
Executing Arrest Warrants   371
Illegal Arrests   372
Analyzing Fourth Amendment Problems   372

WEB LINKS   375
KEY TERMS   376
REVIEW QUESTIONS   376
REVIEW PROBLEMS   376
END NOTES   377

CHAPTER 13
Interrogation and Other Law
Enforcement Practices 379

INTERROGATIONS, CONFESSIONS, AND
ADMISSIONS   380
Miranda   380

Sixth Amendment   389
Voluntariness Requirement   390

ELECTRONIC SURVEILLANCE   390
Title III of the Omnibus Crime Control Act   390

PRETRIAL IDENTIFICATION PROCEDURES   393
Lineups and One-Man Showups   393
The Fairness Right   394
Photographs   396
Scientific Identification Procedures   396
Exclusion of Improper Identifications   401

WEB LINKS   402
KEY TERMS   402
REVIEW QUESTIONS   402
REVIEW PROBLEMS   403
END NOTES   403

CHAPTER 14
The Pretrial Process 405

INTRODUCTION   406
DISCOVERY AND INVESTIGATION
OF CRIMINAL ACTIVITY   406
ARREST   406
THE COMPLAINT   406
INITIAL APPEARANCE   411

PRETRIAL RELEASE AND DETENTION   411
Types of Release   411
Eighth Amendment   412
Detention   412
PRELIMINARY HEARING   413
THE FORMAL CHARGE   416
Indictment and Grand Jury   416
Information   421

ARRAIGNMENT   421
PRETRIAL ACTIVITY   422
Discovery   422

Motion Practice   427

Pretrial Conference   429

EXTRADITION AND DETAINERS   429

REMOVAL   431

WEB LINKS   431

KEY TERMS   431

REVIEW QUESTIONS   432

REVIEW PROBLEMS   432

END NOTES   432

CHAPTER 15
Trial   435

TRIAL RIGHTS OF DEFENDANTS   436

The Right to a Jury Trial   436

The Right to a Public Trial   437

The Right to Confrontation and
Cross-Examination   442

The Presumption of Innocence/Burden
of Proof   442

The Right to Speedy Trial   443

The Right to Counsel   445

TRIAL PROCEDURE   450

Voir Dire   450

Preliminary Instructions   450

Opening Statements   451

The Prosecution's Case in Chief   451

The Defense Case   452

Rebuttal   452

Closing Arguments   453

Final Instructions   453

Jury Deliberations and Verdict   453

JNOV/New Trial   454

WEB LINKS   454

KEY TERMS   455

REVIEW QUESTIONS   455

REVIEW PROBLEMS   455

END NOTES   455

CHAPTER 16
Sentencing and Appeal   457

SENTENCING   458

Sentencing Procedure   458

Forms of Punishment   460

Habitual Offender Statutes   489

POSTCONVICTION REMEDIES   491

Appeal   491

Habeas Corpus   492

WEB LINKS   496

KEY TERMS   496

REVIEW QUESTIONS   496

REVIEW PROBLEMS   496

END NOTES   497

APPENDIX A
The Constitution of the United States of America   499

APPENDIX B
Selected Excerpts from the Model Penal Code   509

Glossary   543

Index   551

Preface to the Fourth Edition

Like its three previous editions, *Criminal Law and Procedure*, 4th Edition, is a comprehensive text covering both substantive criminal law and criminal procedure. The importance of constitutional law to these fields is emphasized, as are practical insights. This book has been designed for use in undergraduate programs in both legal studies and criminal justice.

Organization of the Text

Because the first three editions were so well received, I have retained the original organization, content, and pedagogy in this edition. This remains a combination textbook and casebook. The cases are edited and the text written with the undergraduate student in mind. It is my hope that the writing level of this book will challenge undergraduate students without overwhelming them.

All of the pedagogical features of the earlier editions have been retained, including highlighted definitions, glossary of terms, table of cases, and a thorough index. The distinction between chapter questions and chapter problems continues in this text, the former testing content knowledge and the latter testing the students' problem solving and analytical skills.

With the diverse audience of students and instructors who use this text in mind, I have designed two general methods of use. The first is as a combination text and casebook. The second method is to omit the cases and use the text alone. Both methods are possible because I do not use any case to exclusively teach a point of law. Instead, the cases are used to illustrate a point in practice and to develop the cognitive skills of students. Accordingly, if time doesn't permit it or the educational goals of an instructor are focused elsewhere, the cases may be omitted without losing substantive content.

The first half of the text covers substantive criminal law, while the second half of the text discusses both the constitutional dimensions of criminal procedure and the practical dimensions of the criminal justice process.

Key Features

Writing Style that challenges but does not overwhelm undergraduate students.
Key Terms that are bolded on first use and clearly defined in the margin.
Cases that reinforce content and promote the development of case analysis skills.

Sidebars that can be used to spark class discussion and student interest in issues involving the criminal justice system and criminal law.

Figures that reinforce textual material and help illustrate important ideas.

Web Links that highlight Websites that are germane to chapter materials.

Review Questions that call for content-related answers to reinforce and retain chapter concepts.

Chapter Problems that are intended to develop critical thinking and problem solving skills.

Changes to the Fourth Edition

I have added new material and updated existing material to keep abreast of changes in both the law and the criminal justice disciplines. The changes and additions include the following:

- Recent developments in Fourth Amendment law are discussed, including the authority of law enforcement officers to arrest for misdemeanors; to stop, search, and seize vehicles; to use thermo imaging to detect criminal activity in private areas; and to rely on anonymous tips to conduct searches.
- A new section on terrorism, treason, and national security crimes has been added.
- The previous edition's discussion of racial profiling has been expanded to include a sidebar on racial profiling in the context of the terrorist attacks on the United States on September 11, 2001.
- A discussion of recent attempts by the government to regulate virtual child pornography, including an excerpt of the Supreme Court decision in *Ashcroft v. Free Speech Coalition* (2002).
- The previous editions' sections on cyberstalking, identity theft, and other computer crimes have been expanded.
- The previous edition's discussion of the death penalty has been expanded to include a discussion of the growing moratorium movement and the 2002 Supreme Court decision in *Atkins v. Virginia* concerning the execution of the mentally retarded.
- A sidebar explaining the differences between common law and civil law jurisdictions has been added.
- The discussion of corporate crime has been expanded to include the recent Enron and Arthur Andersen cases.
- A new section on crimes involving firearms has been added.
- An explanation of the source and nature of the Uniform Crime Reports and National Crime Victimization Survey data has been added.
- All the data, including crime, courts, and law enforcement, has been updated.
- New illustrations and charts have been added to facilitate the students' understanding of the readings.
- A note about case excerpts: To this author, there are three objectives of including judicial opinions in a textbook. The first is doctrinal: to teach the law. The second is purely cognitive: to develop a reader's analytical,

and more specifically, legal reasoning skills. The third is to develop the reader's familiarity with the language and structure of legal writing. I consider all of these purposes when selecting cases, knowing that not every case will accomplish all three objectives. In addition, the importance and impact of a case, its age, the clarity of its language, and my ability to successfully edit it are considered. I have taken some liberties in my editing. Because successive ellipses become a distracting Pac-Man game, many citations and footnotes were redacted without any indication in the text. The reader is advised to consult the appropriate official reporter for the complete text.

Please share any ideas you have for improvement of this book with either the publisher or myself.

Ancillary Materials

- An **Instructor's Guide** is available for this text. The Instructor's Guide includes an outline of the material, answers to chapter questions and chapter problems, and a test bank of true/false and multiple choice questions.
- A **computerized test bank** including true/false and multiple choice questions will be offered to qualified adopters on CD-ROM. The platforms supported include Windows™ 98, ME, 2000, XP or a more recent version, and Macintosh® System 8.5 or a more recent version including OS X in classic mode.

- **On-line Resource™**—The On-line Resource™ can be found at *http://www.westlegalstudies.com* in the On-line Resource™ section of the Website.
- **Web page**—Come visit our Website at *http://www.westlegalstudies.com*, where you will find valuable information such as hot links and sample materials to download, as well as other West Legal Studies products.
- **WESTLAW®**—West's on-line computerized legal research system offers students "hands-on" experience with a system commonly used in law offices. Qualified adopters can receive ten free hours of WESTLAW®. WESTLAW® can be accessed with Macintosh and with IBM PC and compatibles. A modem is required.
- **Strategies and Tips for Paralegal Educators,** a pamphlet by Anita Tebbe of Johnson County Community College, provides teaching strategies specifically designed for paralegal educators. A copy of this pamphlet is available to each adopter. Quantities for distribution to adjunct instructors are available for purchase at a minimal price. A coupon on the pamphlet provides ordering information.
- **Survival Guide for Paralegal Students,** a pamphlet by Kathleen Mercer Reed and Bradene Moore covers practical and basic information to help students make the most of their paralegal courses. Topics covered include choosing courses of study and note-taking skills.
- **West's Paralegal Video Library**—West Legal Studies is pleased to offer the following videos at no charge to qualified adopters:
  - *The Drama of the Law II: Paralegal Issues Video*
    ISBN: 0-314-07088-5

- *The Making of a Case Video*
  ISBN: 0-314-07300-0
- *ABA Mock Trial Video—Product Liability*
  ISBN: 0-314-07342-6
- *Arguments to the United States Supreme Court Video*
  ISBN: 0-314-07070-2

Please note the Internet resources are of a time-sensitive nature and URL addresses may often change or be deleted.

Contact us at westlegalstudies@delmar.com

Acknowledgments

I would like to thank the acquisitions editor, Pamela Fuller and the developmental editor, Melissa Riveglia, in seeing this project through to fruition.

I was fortunate to have good reviewers whose insightful, substantive comments led to an improved text. Some of the reviewers went so far as to detail where I could find content they wanted added, what cases they believed would illustrate a concept, and what kind of illustration should be added to summarize an area of law or distill challenging material. I very much appreciate these efforts.

Marty Campbell
Northeast Kansas Technical College
Atchison, Kansas

Robert Diotalevi
Florida Gulf Coast University
Fort Myers, Florida

Craig Hemmens
Boise State University
Boise, Idaho

Robert Morse
Brown Mackie College
Olathe, Kansas

Kathryn L. Myers
St. Mary of the Woods College
St. Mary of the Woods, Indiana

Michael Rayboun
University of West Florida
Pensacola, Florida

Gary Schmidt
Williams Woods University
California, Missouri

Kenneth Whiteside
Hickey College
St. Louis, Missouri

About the Author

A native of Indiana, Daniel E. Hall is Executive Director of the Hamilton Campus and Professor of Political Science at Miami University. He was formerly chairperson of the Department of Criminal Justice at The University of Toledo and Associate Professor of Criminal Justice and Legal Studies at the University of Central Florida. He earned his B.S. at Indiana University, J.D. at Washburn University, and Ed.D. at the University of Central Florida. In addition to experience practicing criminal law, he has thirteen years of experience teaching criminal law and procedure in higher education. He has authored several books in the public law area, including:

Administrative Law, Second Edition, (Prentice Hall 2002)
Constitutional Law (West 1997)
Criminal Procedure and the Constitution (West 1997)
Survey of Criminal Law, Second Edition (West 1997)
California Criminal Law and Procedure (West 1998) with co-author William
   Raymond, Jr.

   In addition, he has published several articles in law reviews and academic journals outside of law.
   Daniel is married to Stacey Lynn Hall, and they live in Ohio with their daughter, Grace Kathryn, and their golden retriever Atticus.

Table of Cases

A

Aguilar v. Texas, 323, 329, 378
Ah Sin v. Whitman, 285
Alabama v. Shelton, 446–447
Allen v. United States, 453
Appollomedia v. Reno, 122
Apprendi v. New Jersey, 497
American Library Association v. Pataki, 166
Argersinger v. Hamlin, 446, 447, 455
Arizona v. Fulminante, 390
Arizona v. Hicks, 377
Arizona v. Washington, 272
Ashcroft v. Free Speech Coalition, 162–166
Atkins v. Virginia, 244, 467–471
Atwater v. City of Lago Vista, et al., 358, 366–369
Austin v. United States, 481–483,484–485, 486

B

Baldwin v. New York, 455
Barclay v. Florida, 264–265
Barker v. Wingo, 443, 445,455
Barnes v. Glen Theater, Inc., 158
Batson v. Kentucky, 456
Bazeley's Case, 151
Bearden v. Georgia, 498
Beck v. Ohio, 377
Beckwith v. United States, 383
Bell v. Wolfish, 362
Berkemer v. McCarty, 384
Betts v. Brady, 448, 455
Bivens v. Six Unknown Named Agents, 377
Blockburger v. United States, 272
Bolling v. Sharpe, 284
Bond v. United States, 319, 355, 356
"John Cleland's Memoirs of a Woman of Pleasure" v. Attorney General of Massachusetts (Book), 165
Booth v. Maryland, 459, 460, 461, 463, 464
Bordenkircher v. Hayes, 284
Bowers v. Hardwick, 121, 156–157, 270

Bouie v. City of Columbia, 77
Boykin v. Alabama, 419
Brady v. Maryland, 296, 425, 426
Brandenburg v. Ohio, 207
Briggs v. Maryland, 146–148
Broadrick v. Oklahoma, 164
Brooks v. Tennessee, 455
Brown v. Allen, 493
Brown v. Mississippi, 403
Brown v. Texas, 377
Browning-Ferris Industries of Vt., Inc. v. Kelco Disposal, Inc., 482, 484
Burch v. Louisiana, 455
Burdeau v. McDowell, 310
Burgett v. Texas, 456
Burns v. Reed, 296

C

California v. Acevedo, 358, 359
California v. Ciraolo, 377
Callins v. Collins, 385, 464, 497
Camara v. Municipal Court of City and County of San Francisco, 353
Capitol News Co. v. Metropolitan Government, 207
Carroll v. United States, 357, 358, 377
Carson v. United States, 53–55
Casey v. Planned Parenthood, 267, 268–269, 270
C.E. Carlson, Inc. v. SEC, 286
Chambers v. Mahoney, 378
Champlinsky v. New Hampshire, 207
Chandler v. Miller, 353
Cheek v. United States, 185–186
Chimel v. California, 345, 346–347
Church of Lukumi Babalu Aye, Inc. v. Hialeah, 253–256
City of Indianapolis v. Edmond, 352–357
City of Little Falls v. Edwin George Witucki, 168, 169–170
Coates v. Cincinnati, 272
Cohen v. California, 169
Coker v. Georgia, 468, 497
Colorado v. Bertine, 356, 359, 378
Commonwealth v. Edmunds, 302, 308–309
Commonwealth v. Hughes, 115, 116
Commonwealth v. Ludwig, 310
Commonwealth v. Redline, 121
Commonwealth v. Schnopps, 99
Commonwealth v. Triplett, 310
Commonwealth v. Wright, 377
Connally v. General Construction Co., 272

Coolidge v. New Hampshire, 338, 339, 340, 377
Cooper v. Oklahoma, 229
Cumbie v. Singletary, 455
Cuyler v. Sullivan, 447

D

Daubert v. Merrell Dow Pharmaceuticals, 397
Davis v. United States, 403
Dawson v. Delaware, 264–265
Delaware v. Cannon, 497
Delaware v. Prouse, 353, 354, 357, 358, 359–360
Department of Human Resources v. Smith, 252, 256, 310
Douglas v. California, 272, 492
Douglas v. Wainwright, 440
Dunaway v. New York, 369
Durham v. United States, 225
Dusky v. United States, 244

E

Eddings v. Oklahoma, 497
Edmond v. Goldsmith, 352
Edwards v. Arizona, 387, 388
Eisenstadt v. Baird, 270
Elledge v. Dugger, 441
Enmund v. Florida, 468, 497
Escobedo v. Illinois, 380
Estelle v. Williams, 455
Estes v. Texas, 437

F

Faretta v. California, 449
Fay v. NOIA, 498
Florida v. J.L., 324–326
Florida v. Royer, 342
Florida v. Wells, 356
Florida v. White, 359
Ford v. Wainwright, 244, 469, 471, 497
Foucha v. Louisiana, 229
Frisbie v. Collins, 375, 378, 430
Frye v. United States, 396–397
Furman v. Georgia, 461, 464, 466

G

Gargliano v. State, 147
Gebhard v. State, 82
Gerstein v. Pugh, 432

Gideon v. Wainwright, 446, 448, 449, 498
Ginsberg v. New York, 166
Godfrey v. Georgia, 470
Goldschmitt v. State, 498
Gore v. United States, 486–487
Graham v. Connor, 235, 236–237
Gregg v. Georgia, 464, 470
Griffin v. Wisconsin, 497
Griswold v. Connecticut, 266, 267, 310

H

Heckler v. Chaney, 284
Helms v. American Security Co., 47
Hensley v. Municipal Court, 498
Herrera v. Collins, 498
H.J., Inc. v. Northwestern Bell Telephone Co., 134
Horton v. California, 340
Hudson v. Palmer, 378
Hughey v. United States, 497
Hurtado v. California, 310
Hyde v. United States, 220

I

Illinois v. Gates, 323
Illinois v. Krull, 377
Illinois v. Perkins, 403
Illinois v. Wardlow, 341, 377
Indianapolis v. Edmonds, 358

J

Jackson v. Bishop, 497
Jackson v. Indiana, 244
Jacobellis v. Ohio, 159
John Doe Corp. v. John Doe Agency, 433
Johnson v. Louisiana, 455
Johnson v. Zerbst, 446
Jones v. Cunningham, 498
Jones v. United States, 318, 378

K

Kansas v. Hendricks, 82, 114
Katz v. United States, 312, 313–314, 315–316, 317, 390
Keeler v. Superior Court, 33, 34–36, 102
Keller v. State Bar of Cal., 164
Kehrli v. Sprinkle, 497
Ker v. California, 371
Ker v. Illinois, 433

King v. Cogdon, 66, 67
Kirby v. Illinois, 394
Knowles v. Iowa, 359, 378
Kois v. Wisconsin, 165
Kyllo v. United States, 314, 315–316

L

Labelle v. State, 95–96, 121
Lambert v. California, 81
Little Falls, City of v. Witucki, 168, 169–170
Locket v. Ohio, 461, 464, 470
Loving v. Virginia, 272

M

Manson v. Braithwaite, 404
Manual Enterprises, Inc. v. Day, 207
Mapp v. Ohio, 300, 301, 302–303
Marbury v. Madison, 15
Marsillett v. State, 47
Martin v. Bissonette, 440
Maryland v. Buie, 345, 369, 370–371
Maryland v. Craig, 455
Maryland v. Dyson, 358, 378
Maryland v. Wilson, 358, 378
Massiah v. United States, 403
McCleskey v. Kemp, 466
McDonald v. United States, 377
McKane v. Durston, 498
McKeiver v. Pennsylvania, 455
Mempa v. Rhay, 479
Michael M. v. Superior Court, 121
Michigan State Police v. Sitz, 352, 353, 354
Michigan v. Chesternut, 384
Michigan v. DeFillippo, 377
Michigan v. Jackson, 389
Michigan v. Long, 308, 344, 370, 377
Michigan v. Mosley, 403
Michigan v. Sitz, 358
Michigan v. Summers, 377
Michigan v. Tyler, 353
Miller v. California, 159–160, 163, 166
Mincey v. Arizona, 347–348
Minnesota v. Carter, 316–319, 321–322, 323
Minnesota v. Dickerson, 343–345
Minnesota v. Johns, 317
Minnesota v. Murphy, 384
Minnesota v. Olson, 316, 317, 318–319, 377

Minnick v. Mississippi, 387–388
Miranda v. Arizona, 300, 380, 381–382, 383–385, 387, 388
M'Naghten's Case, 224
Monell v. Department of Social Services, 296
Monge v. California, 272
Mooney v. Holohan, 432
Morissette v. United States, 57, 58

N

Nardone v. United States, 310
New York v. Belton, 377
New York v. Burger, 318, 322, 353, 377
New York v. Ferber, 162–163, 166, 207
New York v. Quarles, 403
Nieto v. Sullivan, 440
North v. Walsh, 433
North Carolina v. Butler, 389
N.O.W. v. Scheidler, 151

O

O'Connor v. Ortega, 318
Oliver v. United States, 377
One 1958 Plymouth v. Pennsylvania, 498
Oregon v. Haas, 404
Osborne v. Ohio, 160, 165–166, 440
Oyler v. Boles, 282, 284

P

Papachristou v. City of Jacksonville, 172
Payne v. Tennessee, 460, 461–464
Payton v. New York, 366, 367, 369
Pennsylvania v. Bruder, 384, 403
Pennsylvania v. Mimms, 358, 378
Penry v. Lynaugh, 467, 469
People v. Belge, 289–290
People v. Dioguardi, 138–139
People v. Disbrow, 310
People v. Herdan, 385
People v. Murray, 213, 214
People v. Richards, 151
People v. Superior Court, 122
People v. Alicia Troiano, 59–60
People v. Warner-Lambert Co., 74–75
People v. Woody, 272, 310
Percer v. State, 76
Pervear v. Commonwealth, 497
Phillips v. United States, 498

Pierson v. Ray, 296
Pillsbury v. Conboy, 272
Plymouth v. Pennsylvania, 498
Porth v. Templar, 497
Posters 'N' Things, Ltd. v. United States, 180, 207
Powell v. Alabama, 445, 446, 448

R
R.A.V. v. City of St. Paul, 262–263
Rakas v. Illinois, 318–321
Rawlings v. Kentucky, 318
Reno v. ACLU, 162
Rex v. Higgins, 220
Rex v. Scofield, 220
Reynolds v. United States, 272
Rhode Island v. Innis, 385–386
Richards v. Wisconsin, 335–337
Richardson v. United States, 137
Richmond Newspapers, Inc. v. Virginia, 433
Riverside, County of v. McLaughlin, 411, 413, 416
Robinson v. California, 68, 207
Roe v. Wade, 102, 267, 268, 269, 272, 310
Rogers v. Tennessee, 76–78
Rosenberger v. Rector and Visitors of Univ. of Va, 164
Roth v. United States, 159, 207
Rummel v. Estelle, 468, 487

S
Santobello v. New York, 419
Schechter Poultry Corp. v. United States, 47
Schmerber v. California, 377, 398–399, 404
Schneckloth v. Bustamonte, 377
Scott v. Illinois, 446, 447
Scott v. United States, 404
Seling v. Young, 114
Shadwick v. Tampa, 377
Sherman v. United States, 244
Silverman v. United States, 314
Simmons v. United States, 304, 433
Skinner v. Railway Labor Executives' Association, 353
Smith v. Illinois, 455
Smith v. Maryland, 317, 404
Solem v. Helm, 486, 487
Sparf v. United States, 456
Stack v. Boyle, 432
Stanley v. Georgia, 156–157, 207
Stansbury v. California, 382–385

State v. Baldwin, 141–142
State v. Blanding, 385
State v. Borucki, 244
State v. Corn, 121
State v. David Fierro, 102, 103
State v. Haines, 214, 215–216
State v. Hartman, 385
State v. Hodges, 256, 257–258
State v. Johnson, 244
State of Illinois v. Gerry Lockett, 126, 127
State v. Losey, 89–90
State v. McJimpson, 142
State v. Santiago, 310
State v. Snowden, 91, 92, 93
Stealgald v. United States, 378
Stewart v. Corbin, 455
Stoner v. California, 377
Stoval v. Denno, 394

T

Taylor v. Alabama, 378
Tennessee v. Garner, 235, 237
Terry v. Ohio, 325, 341, 342, 343, 344–345, 362, 370
Texas v. Gregory Lee Johnson, 259–261
Thomas v. Commonwealth of Kentucky, 170, 171–172
Touby v. United States, 39, 41–43
Treasury Employees v. Von Raab, 353
Trop v. Dulles, 468
Tucker v. Fireman's Fund Inc. Co., 147
Tyler v. Berodt, 404

U

Union Pacific Railroad v. Botsford, 272
United States v. Armstrong, 282–286
United States v. Arvizu, 177
United States v. Aulicino, 438
United States v. Avery, 456
United States v. Bajakajian, 483–487
United States v. Bassford, 377
United States v. Batchelder, 284
United States v. Berrios, 285, 286
United States v. Birkenstock, 81
United States v. Brantley, 207
United States v. Brawner, 244
United States v. Brignoni-Ponce, 350, 351, 359
United States v. Broadhurst, 377
United States v. Brooks, 441

United States v. Calandra, 432
United States v. Calley, 230, 231
United States v. Cardiff, 272
United States v. Carr, 321
United States v. Chemical Foundation, Inc., 284
United States v. Clipper, 325
United States v. Consuelo-Gonzalez, 476, 477–478
United States v. Conway, 321, 322
United States v. Cox, 432
United States v. Darden, 439
United States v. DeLuca, 437, 438–441
United States v. DeBerry, 325
United States v. Diecidue, 432
United States v. DiRe, 358, 378
United States v. Doe, 438
United States v. Dotterweich, 82
United States v. Dreitzler, 272
United States v. Dunn, 348
United States v. Edmond, 438
United States v. Fares, 286
United States v. Farmer, 440
United States v. Goodwin, 284
United States v. Gordon, 319, 320–323
United States v. Green, 497
United States v. Greenwood, 286
United States v. Grimaud, 39–40
United States v. Guglielmi, 207
United States v. Havens, 310
United States v. Hernandez-Cuartas, 378
United States v. Jackson, 437, 497
United States v. Jacobsen, 377
United States v. James Daniel Good Real Property, 481
United States v. Kampbell, 377
United States v. Knowles, 81
United States v. Krout, 438
United States v. Leon, 307, 308, 309, 327–328, 329
United States v. Lewis, 174
United States v. Llerla Plaza, 404
United States v. Locascio, 456
United States v. Ludwig, 326–327
United States v. Mandujano, 432
United States v. Marion, 455
United States v. Martin Linen Supply Co., 272, 456
United States v. Martinez-Fuerte, 352, 353, 354, 355, 356
United States v. Matlock, 338
United States v. Mendenhall, 377, 384
United States v. Mezzanatto, 284

United States v. Miller, 173
United States v. Mitchell, 286
United States v. Moore, 96
United States v. Newman, 456
United States v. Ortiz, 378
United States v. Paccione, 438, 439
United States v. Parham, 286
United States v. Peete, 286
United States v. Place, 354, 377
United States v. Pompanio, 81
United States v. Ramsey, 377
United States v. Riggio, 438
United States v. Robinson, 345
United States v. Rogers, 497
United States v. Ross, 378, 438, 439
United States v. Scheffer, 401
United States v. Sherlock, 440
United States v. Sturgill, 171
United States v. Son Myong Moon, 186, 187
United States v. Toscanino, 374–375, 433
United States v. Turpin, 354
United States v. Tutino, 438
United States v. Wade, 394–395
United States v. Watson, 363
United States v. Watts, 460, 497
United States ex rel. Lujan v. Gengler, 378

V

Vermont v. Tonzola, 244
Vernonia School Dist. 47J v. Acton, 353
Virginia v. Black, 272

W

Walder v. United States, 310
Washington v. Glucksberg, 104
Wayte v. United States, 284
Webster v. Reproductive Health Services, 272
Weeks v. United States, 310
Weems v. United States, 468
Whack v. State, 147
Whren v. United States, 355, 356, 357, 358
Williams v. Florida, 244, 455
Williams v. Illinois, 480
Wilson v. Arkansas, 335, 336, 367, 369
Wilson, Ex parte, 432
Wing Wong v. United States, 497
Winston v. Lee, 399

Wisconsin v. Mitchell, 263–266
Woods v. Kuhlmann, 439, 440
Wooley v. Maynard, 164
Wyoming v. Houghton, 359

Y

Ybarra v. Illinois, 377
Yick Wo v. Hopkins, 284, 285
Young v. Callahan, 443, 444

Z

Zemel v. Rusk, 272
Zurcher v. Stanford Daily, 377

PART

I

Criminal Law

CHAPTER 1 Introduction to the Legal System of the United States

CHAPTER 2 Introduction to Criminal Law

CHAPTER 3 The Two Essential Elements

CHAPTER 4 Crimes Against the Person

CHAPTER 5 Crimes Against Property and Habitation

CHAPTER 6 Crimes Against the Public

CHAPTER 7 Parties and Inchoate Offenses

CHAPTER 8 Factual and Statutory Defenses

CHAPTER 9 Constitutional Defenses

CHAPTER 1

Introduction to the Legal System of the United States

CHAPTER OUTLINE

Federalism

Separation of Powers

The Structure of the Court System

The Duties and Powers of the Judicial Branch

Comparing Civil Law and Criminal Law

CHAPTER OBJECTIVES

In this chapter, you should:

- become familiar with the basic constitutional structure of state and federal governments with an emphasis on how structure impacts criminal justice.

- become familiar with both civil and criminal law with an emphasis on their differing objectives and procedures.

- examine the third branch of government, the judiciary, in greater detail than the executive and legislative, including the structure of U.S. courts and the authorities and duties of courts in criminal justice.

FEDERALISM

Before one can undertake learning criminal law or criminal procedure, a basic understanding of the legal system of the United States is necessary. This can be a complex task, as criminal law and procedure are significantly influenced by federal and state constitutional law, the common law, and statutory law at both the federal and state levels. It will be easier to understand how these areas of law affect criminal law if we first explore the basic structure of American government.

The United States is divided into two sovereign forms of government—the government of the United States and the governments of the many states. This division of power is commonly known as **federalism.** It is also common to refer to this division as the vertical division of power, as the national government rests above the state governments in hierarchy in those areas where the constitution grants supremacy to the federal government. The framers of the Constitution of the United States established these two levels of government in an attempt to prevent the centralization of power, that is, too much power being vested in one group. The belief that "absolute power corrupts absolutely" was the catalyst for the division of governmental power.

federalism

A system of political organization with several different levels of government (for example, city, state, and national) co-existing in the same area with the lower levels having some independent powers.

SIDEBAR

At trial, a *sidebar* is a meeting between the judge and the attorneys, at the judge's bench, outside the hearing of the jury. Sidebars are used to discuss issues that the jury is not permitted to hear. In this text, sidebars will appear periodically. These features contain information relevant to the subject being studied.

In theory, the national government, commonly referred to as the *federal government*, and the state governments each possess authority over citizens, as well as over particular policy areas, free from the interference of the other government (dual sovereignty).

Determining what powers belong to the national government, as opposed to the states, is not always an easy task. The framers of the Constitution intended to establish a limited national government. That is, most governmental powers were to reside in the states, with the national government being limited to the powers expressly delegated to it in the federal Constitution. This principle is found in the Tenth Amendment, which reads, "The powers not delegated to the United States by the Constitution, nor prohibited to it by the States, are reserved to the States respectively, or the people."

What powers are delegated to the United States by the Constitution? There are several, including, but not limited to the power:

1. To coin money, punish counterfeiters, and fix standards of weights and measures.
2. To establish a post office and post roads.
3. To promote the progress of science and useful arts by providing artists and scientists exclusive rights to their discoveries and writings.

4. To punish piracy and other crimes on the high seas.
5. To declare war and raise armies.
6. To conduct diplomacy and foreign affairs.
7. To regulate interstate and foreign commerce.
8. To make laws necessary and proper for carrying into execution other powers expressly granted in the Constitution.

The last two of these powers—the regulation of interstate commerce and the making of all necessary and proper laws—have proven to be significant sources of federal power. Also important is the Supremacy Clause of Article VI, which provides that

> This Constitution, and the Laws of the United States which shall be made in Pursuance thereof; and all Treaties made, or which shall be made, under the Authority of the United States, shall be the supreme Law of the Land; and the Judges in every State shall be bound thereby, any Thing in the Constitution or Laws of any State to the Contrary notwithstanding.

Simply stated, the Supremacy Clause declares national law, if valid, to be a higher form of law than state law. Of course, if the national government attempts to regulate an area belonging to the states, its law is invalid and the state law is controlling. But if the national government possesses **jurisdiction** and a state enacts a conflicting law, the state law is invalid. This is not a common issue in criminal law, because state and federal laws rarely conflict; rather, they are more likely to be parallel or complementary. In such cases, a state and federal government have **concurrent jurisdiction** (see Exhibit 1.1).

Keep in mind that the United States Constitution is the highest form of law in the land. It is the national constitution that establishes the structure of our

jurisdiction
The geographical area within which a court (or a public official) has the right and power to operate. Or, the persons about whom and the subject matters about which a court has the right and power to make decisions that are legally binding.

concurrent jurisdiction
Two or more courts having the power to adjudicate the same class of cases or the same matter.

STATE JURISDICTION	CONCURRENT JURISDICTION	NATIONAL JURISDICTION
1. States may regulate for the health, safety, and morals of their citizens	1. Those acts that fall into both federal and state jurisdictions	1. Crimes that are interstate in character
2. Those acts that involve a state government, its officials and property	Example: Bank robbery of a federally insured institution	2. Crimes involving the government of the United States, including its officials and property
Example: Murder; rape; theft; driving under the influence of a drug; gambling		Example: Murder of a federal official or murder on federal land; interstate transportation of illegal item; interstate flight of a felon

EXHIBIT 1.1
Federal and State Criminal Jurisdiction

government. You will learn later the various duties of the judicial branch of government. One duty is the interpretation (determining what written law means) of statutes and constitutions. The highest court in the United States is the United States Supreme Court; as such, that Court is the final word on what powers are exclusively federal or state, or concurrently held. However, once the Supreme Court decides that an issue is exclusively under the control of state governments, then each state has the final word on that issue.

During the past 200 years, the Supreme Court has differed in its approach to federalism. Two general models can be identified, though. *Dual federalism* refers to an approach under which the states and federal government are viewed as coequals. Under this approach, the Tenth Amendment is interpreted broadly and the Commerce Clause and the Necessary and Proper Clause are read narrowly. The Tenth Amendment is interpreted as an independent source of state powers, staking out policy areas within which the national government cannot encroach.

Another model, *cooperative federalism*, provides that the national government is supreme. Under this approach, the Commerce and Necessary and Proper Clauses are construed broadly. The Tenth Amendment becomes a truism, that is, it reserves to the states only those powers the national government does not possess.

Another characteristic of cooperative federalism is increased interaction between the states and federal government (and local forms of government) in an effort to effectively regulate and administer laws and programs. This aspect of cooperative federalism is a product of the political branches, the executive and legislative. The increased cooperation between state and federal law enforcement agencies to fight the war against drugs is a good example of cooperative federalism.

The Court has vacillated between the two models. The dominant approach today is cooperative federalism. This is not to say that the states are powerless. In fact, one policy area over which the states have maintained considerable control is criminal law. More than 90 percent of all crimes fall within the jurisdiction of the states, not the federal government. However, the sphere of federal government power in criminal law is increasing. This is because more acts are taken in, or are committed using an item that has traveled in, interstate commerce. Acts that have traditionally been state-law crimes may today be federal crimes as well, if there is an interstate component to the act. For example, carjacking, which is the state crime of robbery, if committed with a gun that has travelled in interstate commerce, is also a federal crime.

Regardless of the expansion of federal jurisdiction, most crimes continue to fall within the exclusive jurisdiction of the states. This is because one of the responsibilities of the states is to regulate for the health and safety of its citizens. This is known as the **police power.** Most murders, rapes, and thefts are state-law crimes. A few policy areas belong exclusively to the federal government. Punishing counterfeiters is an example.

Many crimes fall within the jurisdiction of both state and federal governments. In these situations, state and federal authorities share jurisdiction to bring charges against the accused. Drug dealers are subject to federal law if they

police power
The government's right and power to set up and enforce laws to provide for the safety, health, and general welfare of the people.

transport or sell drugs in interstate commerce and are also subject to the laws of the states where the transaction occurred. Robbing a federally insured bank, interstate transportation of a crime victim, and violating a person's civil rights (i.e., police brutality) are other examples. Which government will bring charges in these situations is more a political question than a legal one. It is not a violation of double jeopardy for an individual to be tried and punished by both federal and state governments, even for the same act.

Note that local governments have not been mentioned so far. This is because the Constitution does not recognize the existence of local governments. However, state constitutions and laws establish local forms of government, such as counties, cities, and districts. These local entities are often empowered by state law with limited authority to create criminal law. These laws, usually in the form of ordinances, are discussed in Chapter 2.

The result of this division of power is that the states (as well as other jurisdictions, such as the District of Columbia), the federal government, and local governments each have a separate set of criminal laws. For this reason, you must keep in mind that the principles you will learn from this book are general in nature. It would be both impossible and pointless to teach the specific laws of each jurisdiction of the United States.

SEPARATION OF POWERS

Another division of governmental power is known as **separation of powers.** This is the division of governmental power into three branches, the executive, legislative, and judicial, making a horizontal division of power, just as federalism is the vertical division (see Exhibit 1.2). Each branch is delegated certain functions that the other two may not encroach upon. The executive branch consists of the president of the United States, the president's staff, and the various administrative agencies that the president oversees. Generally, it is the duty of the executive branch to enforce the laws of the federal government. In criminal law, the executive branch investigates alleged violations of the law, gathers the evidence necessary to prove that a violation has occurred,

separation of powers
The division of the federal government (and state governments) into legislative (law making), judicial (law interpreting), and executive (law carrying-out) branches.

	LEGISLATIVE BRANCH	EXECUTIVE BRANCH	JUDICIAL BRANCH
The Government of the United States (Federal Government)	United States Congress	President of the United States	Federal Courts
State Governments	State Legislatures	Governors	State Courts

EXHIBIT 1.2
Division of Governmental Power

and brings violators before the judicial branch for disposition. The president does this through the various federal law enforcement and administrative agencies.

The legislative branch consists of the United States Congress, which creates the laws of the United States. Congressionally created laws are known as **statutes.** Finally, the judicial branch comprises the various federal courts of the land. That branch is charged with the administration of justice. A more comprehensive discussion of the judicial branch follows later in this chapter.

statute
A law passed by a legislature.

In a further attempt to diffuse governmental power, the framers designed a system of checks and balances that prevents any one branch from exclusively controlling a function. Several checks can be found in the Constitution.

For example, Congress is responsible for making the law. This function is checked by the president, who may veto legislation. The president is then checked by Congress, which may override a veto with a two-thirds majority. The president is responsible for conducting foreign affairs and making treaties, and is the Commander-in-Chief of the military. Congress, however, must approve treaties and declare war, and it establishes the rules that regulate the military.

Through the power of judicial review, the judiciary may invalidate actions of the president or Congress that violate the Constitution. In contrast, the political branches select federal judges through the nomination (president) and confirmation (Senate) process. Unpopular judicial decisions may be changed either by statute, if the issue is one of statutory interpretation, or by constitutional amendment, if the issue is one of constitutional interpretation.

Keep in mind that two levels of government exist, excluding local entities. Even though the United States Constitution does not establish three branches of government for the many states (the United States Constitution only designs the structure of the federal government), all state constitutions do, in varying forms, model the federal constitution. The result is a two-tiered system with each tier split into three parts.

What should be gleaned from this is that the legislatures are responsible for defining what acts are criminal, what process must be used to assure that a wrongdoer answers for an act, and what punishment should be imposed for the act.

It is the duty of the executive branch to enforce and implement the laws created by the legislature, as well as to enforce the orders of courts. For example, if a state legislature prohibits the sale of alcohol on Sundays, it is the duty of the appropriate state law enforcement agencies, such as the police or alcohol, firearm, and tobacco agents, to investigate suspected violations and take whatever lawful action is necessary to bring violators to justice. Law enforcement, in the criminal law context, is accomplished through law enforcement agencies and prosecutorial agencies. At the federal level, there are many law enforcement agencies. The Federal Bureau of Investigation, Drug Enforcement Administration, United States Marshal Service, and Department of the Treasury name only a few. State law enforcement agencies include state departments of investigation, state police departments, and local police departments. These and other enforcement agencies are responsible for investigating criminal conduct and for gathering evidence to prove that a criminal violation has occurred. When the law enforcement agency has completed its investigation, the case is turned over to a prosecutor. The prosecutor is the attorney responsible for representing the people. The prosecutor files the formal criminal charge, or conducts a grand jury, and then sees the prosecution through to fruition. In the federal system, the prosecutor is called a United States Attorney. In the states and localities, prosecutors are known as district attorneys, county attorneys, state attorneys, city attorneys, or, simply, prosecutors.

Finally, the judicial branch is charged with the administration of justice. The courts become involved after the executive branch has arrested or accused an individual of a crime. This is explored further in the next section of this chapter. Lawyers, legal assistants, and law enforcement officials are likely to have significant contacts with state and federal courts; therefore, it is important to understand the structure of the court system.

THE STRUCTURE OF THE COURT SYSTEM

Within the federal and state judiciaries, a hierarchy of courts exists. All state court systems, as well as the federal court system, have at least two types of courts, trial courts and appellate courts. However, each state is free to structure its judiciary in any manner; hence, significant variation is found in the different court systems. What follows are general principles that apply to all states and the federal system.

Trial courts are what most people envision when they think of courts. Trial courts are where a case begins, where witnesses are heard and evidence is presented, often to a jury as well as to a judge. In the federal system, trial courts are known as United States District Courts. The United States is divided up into 94 judicial districts, using state boundaries to establish district limits. Each state constitutes at least one district, although larger states are divided into several districts. For example, Kansas has only one district, and the federal trial court located in Kansas is known as the United States District Court for the District of Kansas. California, in contrast, is made up of four districts, the Northern, Eastern, Central, and Southern Districts of California.

trial court
A court that hears and determines a case initially, as opposed to an appellate court; a court of general jurisdiction.

The court system is actually many court systems comprised of the federal system and the many state systems. As of 2000, there were 29,000 state court judges in the United States sitting in 16,300 state courts. A total of 92 million cases were filed in state courts in 2000. Of these, 56 million were traffic cases, 15 million were civil cases, 14 million were criminal cases, 5 million were domestic cases, and 2 million were juvenile cases.

Source of state statistics: National Center for State Courts. http://www.ncsconline.org

Source of federal statistics: Administrative office of vs courts http://www.vscourts.Gov In 2001 there were 1 supreme court, 13 appellate courts and 94 district courts in the federal system. The district courts had 250,907 cases filed, of which 50,673 were criminal. The courts of appeals had over 57,000 cases filed for their hearing.

appellate court
A higher court that can hear appeals from a lower court.

record on appeal
A formal, written account of a case, containing the complete formal history of all actions taken, papers filed, rulings made, opinions written, etc.

State trial courts are known by various names, such as district, superior, county, and circuit courts. Despite variations in name, these courts are very similar.

Appellate courts review the decisions and actions of trial courts (or lower appellate courts, as discussed later) for error. These courts do not conduct trials, but review the **record** from the trial court and examine it for mistakes, known as trial court error. Usually, appellate courts will hear argument from the attorneys involved in the case under review, but witnesses are not heard nor other evidence submitted. After the appellate court has reviewed the record and examined it for error, it renders an opinion. An appellate court can reverse, affirm, or remand the lower court decision. To *reverse* is to determine that the court below has rendered a wrong decision and to change that decision. When an appellate court *affirms* a lower court, it is approving the decision made and leaving it unchanged.

In some cases, an appellate court will remand the case to the lower court. A *remand* is an order that the case be returned to the lower court and that some action be taken by the judge when the case is returned. Often this will involve conducting a new trial. For example, if an appellate court decides that a judge took an action that prevented a criminal defendant from having a fair trial, and the defendant was convicted, an appellate court may reverse the conviction and remand the case to the trial court for a new trial with instructions that the judge not act in a similar manner.

In the federal system and many states, there are two levels of appellate courts, an intermediate and highest level. The intermediate level courts in the federal system are the United States Courts of Appeal.[1] There are eleven judicial circuits in the United States, with one court of appeal in each circuit. Additionally, there is a court of appeal for Washington, D.C. and for the Federal Circuit. Therefore, there are thirteen United States Courts of Appeal in total (see Exhibit 1.3). Appeals from the district courts are taken to the circuit courts. The highest court in the country is the United States Supreme Court. Appeals from the circuit courts are taken to the Supreme Court. Also, appeals of federal issues from state supreme courts are taken to the United States Supreme Court. Although appeal to a circuit court or a state supreme court is generally a right anyone has, the Supreme Court is not required to hear most appeals, and it does not. In recent years, the Supreme Court has denied review of approximately 97 percent of the cases appealed.[2] Therefore, the States' Supreme Courts and federal circuit courts are often a defendant's last chance to have his or her case heard.

Many states also have intermediate-level appellate courts, as well as a high court, although a few states have only one appellate court. Most states call the high court the supreme court of that state and the intermediate level court the court of appeals. An exception is New York, which has named its highest court the Court of Appeals of New York and its lower-level courts supreme courts.

In states that have only one appellate court, appeals are taken directly to that court. New Hampshire is such a state, so appeals from New Hampshire's trial courts are taken directly to the Supreme Court of New Hampshire. Note that in most instances a first appeal is an appeal of right. That means that one has a right to appeal, and the appellate court is required to hear the case. However, second

EXHIBIT 1.3

The Thirteen Federal Judicial Circuits

appeals are generally not appeals of right, unless state law has provided otherwise. To have a case heard by the United States Supreme Court and most state supreme courts, the person appealing must seek *certiorari*, an order from an appellate court to the lower court requiring the record to be sent to the higher court for review. When "cert." is granted, the appellate court will hear the appeal, and when certiorari is denied it will not.

Finally, be aware that a number of **inferior courts** exist. These are courts that fall under trial courts in hierarchy. As such, appeals from these courts do not usually go to the intermediate level appellate courts, as described earlier, but to the trial-level court first. Municipal courts, police courts, and justices of the peace are examples of inferior courts. An appeal from one of these courts is initially heard by a state trial-level court before an appeal is taken to a state appellate court. The federal system also has inferior courts. The United States Bankruptcy Courts are inferior courts, as appeals from the decisions of these courts go to the district courts, in most cases, and not to the courts of appeals. Only after the trial court has rendered its decision may an appeal be taken to an appellate court.

Many inferior courts in the state system are not **courts of record.** No tape recording or stenographic recording of the trial or hearing at the inferior court is made. As such, when an appeal is taken to the trial level court, it is normally *de novo.* This means that the trial-level court conducts a new trial, rather than reviewing a record as most appellate courts do. This is necessary because there is no record to review, because the inferior court is not a court of record. Federal district courts do not conduct new trials, as all federal courts, including bankruptcy courts, are courts of record. State inferior courts have limited jurisdiction; for example, municipal courts usually hear municipal ordinance violations and only minor state law violations. The amount of money that a person may be fined and the amount of time that a defendant may be sentenced to serve in jail are also limited. Generally, no juries are used at the inferior court level.

Exhibit 1.4 is a basic diagram of the federal and state court systems. The appellate routes are indicated by lines drawn from one court to another. Later in this book you will learn how the appeals process works and how the federal and state systems interact in criminal law. Note where this diagram is located so that you may refer to it later.

Most state trial courts are known as **courts of general jurisdiction.** Courts of general jurisdiction possess the authority to hear a broad range of cases, including civil law as well as criminal. In contrast, **courts of limited jurisdiction** hear only specific types of cases. You have already been introduced to one limited jurisdiction court, municipal courts. Inferior courts, such as municipal courts, are always courts of limited jurisdiction. Some states employ systems that have specialized trial courts to handle domestic, civil, or criminal cases. These may be in the form of a separate court (e.g., Criminal Court of Harp County), or may be a division of a trial court (e.g., Superior Court of Harp County, Criminal Division). Appellate courts may also be limited in jurisdiction to a particular area of law, such as the Oklahoma Court of Criminal Appeals.

certiorari

(Latin) "To make sure." A request for *certiorari* (or "cert." for short) is like an appeal, but one that the higher court is not required to take for decision. It is literally a writ from the higher court asking the lower court for the record of the case.

inferior court

A court with special, limited responsibilities, such as a probate court.

court of record

Generally, another term for trial court.

court of general jurisdiction

Another term for trial court; that is, a court having jurisdiction to try all classes of civil and criminal cases except those that can be heard only by a court of limited jurisdiction.

court of limited jurisdiction

A court whose jurisdiction is limited to civil cases of a certain type, or which involve a limited amount of money, or whose jurisdiction in criminal cases is confined to petty offenses and preliminary hearings.

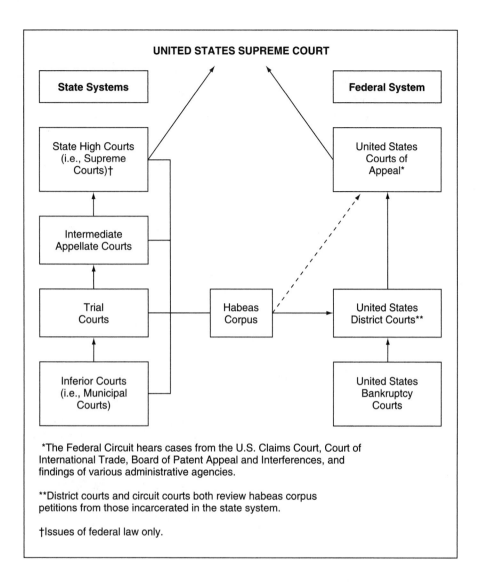

EXHIBIT 1.4
State and Federal Court Structures

The federal government also has special courts. As previously mentioned, a nationwide system of bankruptcy courts is administered by the national government. In addition, the United States Claims Court, Tax Court, and Court of International Trade are part of the federal judiciary, and each has a specific area of law over which it may exercise jurisdiction. Often those cases over which they have jurisdiction are exclusive of district courts. However, the jurisdiction of those courts is outside the scope of this book, as they deal only with civil law. Criminal cases in federal court are heard by district courts, and criminal appeals are heard by the United States Courts of Appeals.

THE DUTIES AND POWERS OF THE JUDICIAL BRANCH

Of the three branches of government, attorneys and other legal professionals have the most interaction with the judicial branch. For that reason, we single out the judicial branch for a more extensive examination of its functions.

First, it must be emphasized that all courts, local, state, and federal, are bound by the United States Constitution. The effect of this is that all courts have a duty to apply federal constitutional law. This is important in criminal law because it allows defendants to assert their United States constitutional claims and defenses in state court, where most criminal cases are heard. Of course, defendants may also assert applicable state defenses as well.

As previously stated, the judicial branch is charged with the administration of justice. The courts administer justice by acting as the conduit for dispute resolution. The courts are the place where civil and criminal disputes are resolved, if the parties cannot reach a resolution themselves. In an effort to resolve disputes, courts must apply the laws of the land. To apply the law, judges must **interpret** the legislation and constitutions of the nation. To *interpret* means to read the law in an attempt to understand its meaning. This nation's courts are the final word in declaring the meaning of written law. If a court interprets a statute's meaning contrary to the intent of a legislature, then the legislature may later rewrite the statute to make its intent more clear. This has the effect of "reversing" the judicial interpretation of the statute. The process is much more difficult if a legislature desires to change a judicial interpretation of a constitution. At the national level, the Constitution has been amended twenty-six times. The amendment process is found in Article V of the Constitution and requires not only action by the federal legislature but also action by the states. To amend a constitution is simply a more cumbersome and time-consuming endeavor than amending legislation.

The judicial branch is independent from the other two branches of government. Often people think of the courts as enforcers of the law. Though this is true in a sense, it is untrue in that the judicial branch does not work with the executive branch in an attempt to achieve criminal convictions. It is the duty of the courts of this nation to remain neutral and apply the laws in a fair and impartial manner. The United States Constitution establishes a judiciary system that is shielded from interference from the other two branches. For example, the Constitution prohibits Congress from reducing the pay of federal judges after they are appointed. This prevents Congress from coercing the courts into action under the threat of no pay. The Constitution also provides for lifetime appointments of federal judges, thereby keeping the judicial branch from being influenced by political concerns, which may cause judges to ignore the law and make decisions based on what is best for their political careers. Judicial independence permits courts to make decisions that are disadvantageous to the government, but required by law, without fear of retribution from the other two branches.

The need for an independent judiciary is most important when considering the power of **judicial review.** Judicial review is a power held by the judicial branch, which permits it to review the actions of the executive and legislative

interpret
Studying a document *and* surrounding circumstances to decide the document's meaning.

judicial review
A higher court's examination of a lower court's decision.

branches and of the states and declare acts that are in violation of the Constitution void. Hamilton wrote of the power of judicial review, and of the importance of an independent judiciary, in the *Federalist Papers*, where he stated:

> Permanency in office frees the judges from political pressures and prevents invasions on judicial power by the president and Congress.

* * *

> The Constitution imposes certain restrictions on the Congress designed to protect individual liberties, but unless the courts are independent and have the power to declare the laws in violation of the Constitution null and void these protections amount to nothing. The power of the Supreme Court to declare laws unconstitutional leads some to assume that the judicial branch will be superior to the legislative branch. Let us look at this argument.
>
> Only the Constitution is *fundamental* law; the Constitution establishes the principles and structure of the government. [To a]rgue that the Constitution is not superior to the laws suggests that the *representatives of the people* are superior *to the people* and that the Constitution is inferior to the government it gave birth to. The courts are the arbiters between the legislative branch and the people; the courts are to interpret the laws and prevent the legislative branch from exceeding the powers granted it. The courts must not only place the Constitution higher than the laws passed by Congress, they must also place the intentions of the people ahead of the intentions of the representatives . . . [emphasis in original].

The landmark case dealing with judicial review is *Marbury v. Madison*, 1 Cranch 137, 2 L. Ed. 60 (1803). Chief Justice Marshall wrote the opinion for the Court and determined that, although the Constitution does not contain explicit language providing for the power of judicial review, Article III of the Constitution implicitly endows the power in the judiciary. It is now well established that courts possess the authority to review the actions of the executive and legislative branches and to declare any law, command, or other action void if such violates the United States Constitution. The power is held by both state and federal courts. Any state or federal law that violates the United States Constitution may be struck down by either federal or state courts. Of course, state laws that violate state constitutions may be stricken for the same reason.

The power to invalidate statutes is rarely used, for two reasons. First, the judiciary is aware of how awesome the power is, and this causes courts to be reluctant to use it. Second, many rules of statutory constructions exist, which have the effect of preserving legislation. For example, if two interpretations of a statute are possible, one that violates the Constitution and one that does not, one rule of statutory construction requires that the statute be construed so that it is consistent with the Constitution. Although rarely done, statutes are occasionally determined invalid. In the chapter on defenses, you will learn many constitutional constraints on government behavior. These defenses often rely on the power of the judiciary to invalidate statutes or police conduct to give them teeth.

COMPARING CIVIL LAW AND CRIMINAL LAW

The difference between civil law and criminal law appears obvious, and great differences do exist. Yet, most students are surprised at the similarities that can be found.

The source of most of the dissimilarities between criminal law and civil law is the differing objectives of the two. The purpose of criminal law is twofold. First, it is intended to prevent behavior that society has determined to be undesirable. A second purpose of criminal law is to punish those who take the acts deemed undesirable by society. Arguably, there is only one purpose, to prevent antisocial behavior. Under this theory, punishment is only used as a tool to achieve the primary goal of preventing antisocial behavior. In any event, prevention and punishment are essential reasons why we have criminal law and a criminal justice system.

CRIMINAL AND CIVIL LAW COMPARED

	CRIMINAL LAW	CIVIL LAW
Purposes	Punishment and deterrence	Compensation and deterrence
Remedies	Fines, restitution, imprisonment, counseling, rehabilitation, injunctions, capital punishment	Damages and equitable relief
Parties	Government and defendant	Private plaintiff and defendant
Standard of Proof	Beyond a reasonable doubt	Preponderance of evidence
Burdens	Government bears burden of proof	Plaintiff bears burden of proof

In contrast, civil law has as its primary purpose the compensation of those injured by someone else's behavior. It is argued that the real purpose of civil law is the same as that of criminal law. By allowing lawsuits against individuals who have behaved in a manner not consistent with society's rules, civil law actually acts to prevent undesirable behavior. However, prevention of bad behavior may be more the consequence of civil law than the purpose. To understand this you must know something about civil law.

Many definitions of civil law exist. The *American Heritage Dictionary of the English Language* (1980) defines it as "The body of law dealing with the rights of private citizens." *Black's Law Dictionary,* Fifth Edition (1979) defines civil law as "Laws concerned with civil or private rights and remedies, as contrasted with criminal laws." This author prefers a negative definition similar to the latter, such as, all law except that which is criminal law. Whatever definition you accept, many areas of law fall under the umbrella of civil law. Two of the largest categories of civil law are contract law and tort law.

Contract law is a branch of civil law that deals with agreements between two or more parties. You probably have already entered into a contract. Apartment leases, credit card agreements, and book-of-the-month club agreements are all contracts. To have a **contract,** two or more people must agree to behave in a specific manner. Generally, there must be mutuality of consideration for an agreement to be enforceable. That is, all the parties must both acquire a benefit and suffer a detriment. For example, when you agree to lease an apartment, you gain the use of the apartment during the lease period and your landlord loses the right to use the property. The flip side is that the landlord gets your money, in the form of rent, and you lose the value of that rent. You promise to pay rent at a specified time, and the landlord promises to give you the use of the premises during the rental period. In contract law, the duties and obligations of the parties are created by the parties themselves and appear in the form of a contract. If you violate your obligation to your landlord under the contract (i.e., you move out earlier than the contract allows), you have committed a civil wrong called a breach of contract. The landlord may sue you for your breach and receive **damages.** *Damages* are monetary compensation for loss.

Tort law is a branch of civil law that is concerned with civil wrongs, but not contract actions. You have likely seen television ads for personal injury attorneys. These attorneys are practicing in the tort law area. A civil wrong, other than a breach of contract, is known as a **tort.** Torts are different from contracts in that the duty owed another party in contract law is created by the parties through their agreement. In tort law, the duty is imposed by the law. For example, at a party you are struck and injured by a beer bottle heaved by an intoxicated partier: a tort has been committed. The partier is known as a *tortfeasor,* which is the term used to describe one who commits a tort. Yet, why does that partier owe you a duty to not strike you with a flying beer bottle? You have not entered into a contract with the partier whereby he has promised not to harm you in this manner. The answer is that the law imposes the duty to act with caution when it is possible to injure another or cause injury to another's property. This duty is imposed upon all people at all times. The law requires that we all act reasonably when conducting our lives.

When a person fails to act reasonably and unintentionally injures another, that person is responsible for a **negligent** tort. Automobile accidents and medical malpractice are examples of negligent torts. When a person injures another intentionally, an **intentional** tort has occurred. Many intentional torts are also crimes, and this is an area where civil law and criminal law have much in common. If at that fraternity party you make a partier angry, and as a result he intentionally strikes you with the bottle, then he has committed both a crime and an intentional tort. Although criminal law may impose a jail sentence (or other punitive measures), tort law normally seeks only to compensate you for your injury. So, if you suffered $1,000 in medical bills to repair your broken nose, you would be entitled to that amount, but the partier cannot be sentenced to jail or otherwise be punished within the civil tort action. A separate criminal charge may be filed by the government.

contract

An agreement that affects or creates legal relationships between two or more persons. To be a *contract*, an agreement must involve: at least one promise, consideration, persons legally capable of making binding agreements, and a reasonable certainty about the meaning of the terms.

damages

Money that a court orders paid to a person who has suffered damage (a loss or harm) by the person who caused the injury (the violation of the person's rights).

tort

A civil (as opposed to a criminal) wrong, other than a breach of contract.

negligence

The failure to exercise a reasonable amount of care in a situation that causes harm to someone or something.

intentional

Determination to do a certain thing.

strict liability

The legal responsibility for damage or injury, even if you are not at fault or negligent.

compensatory damages

Damages awarded for the actual loss suffered by a plaintiff.

punitive damages

Damages that are awarded over and above compensatory damages or actual damages because of the wanton, reckless, or malicious nature of the wrong done by the plaintiff.

The final type of tort is the **strict liability** tort. In these situations liability exists even though the tortfeasor acted with extreme caution and did not intend to cause harm. An example of a strict liability tort is blasting. Whenever a mining or demolition company uses blasting, it is liable for any injuries or damages it causes to property, even if the company exercises extreme caution.

Damages that are awarded (won) in a lawsuit to compensate a party for actual loss are **compensatory damages.** Compensatory damages do just what the name states—compensate the injured party. However, another type of damages exists, **punitive damages.** Contrary to what you have learned so far, punitive damages are awarded in civil suits and are intended to prevent undesirable behavior by punishing those who commit outrageous acts. Punitive damages are often requested by plaintiffs in lawsuits, but are rarely awarded. Do not worry if the idea of punitive damages confuses you because it appears to be a criminal law concept. They are penal in nature and many lawyers argue that punitives should not be allowed because a person can end up punished twice, once when convicted and sentenced by a criminal court and again by a civil court if punitives are awarded. Yet, punitive damages have been upheld in most instances by the Supreme Court. A note of caution: Do not get the concept of punitive damages mixed up with restitution or fines, which are discussed in the chapter on punishment.

Finally, a few other differences between criminal law and civil law should be mentioned. First, in civil law the person who brings the lawsuit (the plaintiff) is the person who was injured. For example, you go to the grocery store to do your shopping and request the assistance of a checkout person who recently was divorced from a spouse who looks very much like you. The checker immediately becomes enraged and vents all of his anger for his ex-wife on you by striking you with a box of cereal, which he was checking. He has committed a possible assault and battery in both tort law (these are intentional torts) and criminal law. However, in tort law you must sue the checker yourself to recover any losses you suffer.

This is not true in criminal law. The government, whether national, state, or local, is always the party that files criminal charges. Often you will hear people say that they have filed criminal charges against someone. This is not true. What they have usually done is file a complaint; the government determines whether criminal charges are to be filed. This is because a violation of criminal law is characterized as an attack on the citizens of a state (or the federal government), and, as such, a violation of public, not private, law. Because it is public, the decision to file, or not file, is made by a public official, the prosecutor. So, in our example, you have to contact either the police or your local prosecutor to have a criminal action brought against the checker. Civil cases are entitled Citizen v. Citizen; in criminal law, it is Government (i.e., *State of Montana*) *v. Citizen.* In some jurisdictions criminal actions are brought under the name of the people. This is done in New York, where criminal cases are entitled *The People of the State of New York v. Citizen.*

There is no difference between a criminal action brought in the name of the state and a criminal action brought in the name of the people of a state. All prosecutions at the national level are brought by the United States of America. Note that governments may become involved in civil disputes. For example, if the state of South Dakota enters into a contract with a person, and a dispute concerning that contract arises, the suit will either be *Citizen v. South Dakota* or *South Dakota v. Citizen.*

ABOUT CASE NAMES, TITLES, AND CAPTIONS Cases filed with courts are given a case title, also known as a case name. The title consists of the parties to the action. In civil cases the title is *citizen v. citizen,* for example, *Joe Smith v. Anna Smith.* In criminal actions the title is *the government v. citizen.* For example, *United States of America v. Joe Smith* or *State of New Mexico v. Anna Smith.*

Cases also have captions. The caption appears at the top of the title page of all documents filed with a court and includes the case name, the court name, the case number, and the name of the document being filed with the court. The illustration in Exhibit 1.5 is an example of both a criminal case caption and a civil case caption.

SIDEBAR

IN THE UNITED STATES DISTRICT COURT FOR
THE DISTRICT OF MARYLAND
NORTHERN DIVISION

UNITED STATES OF AMERICA
_____Plaintiff,

v.   Case No._____

JOHN D. CRIMINAL,
_____Defendant

IN THE UNITED STATES DISTRICT COURT FOR
THE DISTRICT OF MARYLAND
NORTHERN DIVISION

JOHN I. CITIZEN
_____Plaintiff,

v.   Case No._____

JANE Q. SMITH,
_____Defendant

EXHIBIT 1.5

Simple Caption— Criminal Case and Civil Case

The two fields also differ in what is required to have a successful case. In civil law one must show actual injury to win. If, in our example, the box of cereal missed your head and you suffered no injury (damages), you would not have a civil suit. However, a criminal action for assault or battery may still be brought, as no injury is required in criminal law. This is because the purpose of criminal law

culpable
Blamable; at fault. A person who has done a wrongful act (whether criminal or civil) is described as "culpable."

is to prevent this type of conduct, not to compensate for actual injuries. To turn this around, there are many instances in which a person's negligence could be subject to a civil cause of action, but not to a criminal action. If a person accidently strikes another during a game of golf with a golf ball, causing injury, the injured party may sue for the concussion received, but no purpose would be served by prosecuting the individual who hit the ball. No deterrent effect is achieved, as there was no intent to cause the injury. In most cases, society has made the determination (through its criminal laws) that a greater amount of **culpability** should be required for criminal liability than for civil. Criminal law is usually more concerned with the immorality of an act than is tort law. This is consistent with the goals of the two disciplines, as it is easier to prevent intentional acts than accidental ones. These concepts will be discussed later in the chapter on mens rea.

 WEB LINKS

Courts and Prosecutors
What follows are a few of the excellent sites providing statistical data on United States courts and prosecutors:

- *http://www.albany.edu/sourcebook/1995/ind/COURTS.ind.html* (United States Department of Justice, Bureau of Justice Statistics)
- *http://www.ncsconline.org* (National Center for State Courts)
- *http://www.communitycourts.org* (community courts page)

KEY TERMS

appellate court
certiorari
compensatory damages
concurrent jurisdiction
contract
court of general jurisdiction
court of limited jurisdiction
court of record
culpable

damages
federalism
inferior court
intentional
interpret
judicial review
jurisdiction
negligence
police power

punitive damages
record on appeal
separation of powers
statute
strict liability
tort
trial court

REVIEW QUESTIONS

1. What is the primary duty of the executive branch of government in criminal law?
2. Define the phrase "court of record."

3. Define jurisdiction and differentiate between a court of general jurisdiction and a court of limited jurisdiction.

4. What are the goals of criminal law? Civil law?
5. Who may file a civil suit? A criminal suit? How are these different?
6. What are compensatory damages? Punitive damages?

7. Should punitive damages be permitted in civil law? Explain your position.
8. Define culpability.

REVIEW PROBLEMS

1. In 1973 the United States Supreme Court handed down the famous case, *Roe v. Wade,* 410 U.S. 113 (1973), wherein the Court determined that the decision to have an abortion is a private decision that is protected from government intervention, in some circumstances, by the United States Constitution. Suppose that a state legislature passes legislation (a state statute) that attempts to reverse the *Roe* decision by prohibiting all abortions in that state. Which is controlling in that state, the statute or the decision of the United States Supreme Court? Explain your answer.

2. Same facts as in problem 1, except the state supreme court has determined that the state constitution protects the life of fetuses from abortion, except when the life of the mother is endangered. Which is controlling when a mother seeks to have an abortion and her life is not endangered to any greater amount than the average pregnancy, the state constitutional provision protecting fetuses or the decision of the United States Supreme Court? Explain your answer.

3. Assume that the United States Supreme Court has previously determined that regulation of traffic on county roads is a power reserved exclusively for the states. In reaction to this opinion, the United States Congress enacts a statute providing that the regulation of county roads will be within the power of the United States Congress from that date forward. Your law office represents a client who is charged with violating the federal statute that prohibits driving on all roads while intoxicated. Do you have a defense? If so, explain.

END NOTES

1. 28 U.S.C. § 41 *et seq.*
2. According to the Office of the Deputy Clerk, Supreme Court of the United States, there were 7,692 cases on the Supreme Court docket in 1998. The Court granted review and rendered decisions in 138 cases, 1.8% of the total.

CHAPTER 2

Introduction to Criminal Law

CHAPTER OUTLINE

The Distinction Between Criminal Law
and Criminal Procedure

The Power of Government to Regulate
Behavior

The Purposes of Punishing Criminal
Law Violators

Specific and General Deterrence

Incapacitation

Rehabilitation

Retribution

Sources of Criminal Law

The Common Law

Statutory Law

Ordinances

Administrative Law

Court Rules

The Model Penal Code

Constitutional Law

CHAPTER OBJECTIVES

In this chapter, you should:

- learn the objectives of criminal law and
begin thinking critically about these
objectives.
- learn the various sources of criminal law.
- learn how to brief a judicial opinion and
begin developing your case analysis skills.

- be challenged to begin thinking about
the tension between social control and
freedom.
- be introduced to the history of the United
States legal system.

THE DISTINCTION BETWEEN CRIMINAL LAW AND CRIMINAL PROCEDURE

In all areas of legal study, a distinction is made between substance and procedure. Substantive law defines rights and obligations. Procedural law establishes the methods used to enforce legal rights and obligations. The substance of tort law tells you what a tort is and what damages an injured party is entitled to recover from a lawsuit. Substantive contract law defines what a contract is, tells us whether it must be in writing to be enforceable, who must sign it, what the penalty for breach is, and other such information. The field of civil procedure sets rules for how to bring the substance of the law before a court for resolution of a claim. To decide that a client has an injury that can be compensated under the law is a substantive decision. The question then becomes how this injured client gets the compensation to which he or she is entitled. This is the procedural question. Procedural law tells you how to file a lawsuit, where to file, when to file, and how to prosecute the claim. Such is the case for criminal law and procedure.

criminal law
Branch of the law that specifies what conduct constitutes crime and establishes appropriate punishments for such conduct.

criminal procedure
The rules of procedure by which criminal prosecutions are governed.

Criminal law, as a field of law, defines what constitutes a crime. It establishes what conduct is prohibited and what punishment can be imposed for violating its mandates. Criminal law establishes what degree of intent is required for criminal liability. In addition, criminal law sets out the defenses to criminal charges that may be asserted. Alibi, insanity, and the like are defenses and fall under the umbrella of criminal law.

Criminal procedure puts substantive criminal law into action. It is concerned with the procedures used to bring criminals to justice, beginning with police investigation and continuing throughout the process of administering justice. When and under what conditions may a person be arrested? How and where must the criminal charge be filed? When can the police conduct a search? How does the accused assert a defense? How long can a person be held in custody by the police without charges being filed? How long after charges are filed does the accused have to wait before a trial is held? These are all examples of questions that criminal procedure deals with. As you will learn in later chapters, many of the rules of criminal procedure have their roots in both the United States and state Constitutions. Of course, statutory law is also important in this context. Do not worry if you cannot always distinguish between a procedural question and a substantive one. There is considerable overlap between the two concepts.

The first half of this text is devoted to criminal law and the latter half to criminal procedure. In the remainder of the book, the phrase "criminal law" is used often. This, in most cases, refers to general criminal law, including both substantive criminal law and criminal procedure.

THE POWER OF GOVERNMENT TO REGULATE BEHAVIOR

Freedom and liberty are two concepts that pervade the American political being. Most of us have learned that the longing for freedom of religious thought caused the English Puritan emigration from England to what was to become

Plymouth, Massachusetts, in 1620. Later, the desire for freedom from the oppressive crown of England was the catalyst for the Declaration of Independence and the American Revolution. Finally, the fear that all governments tend to abuse their power led to the creation of a constitution that contains specific limits on governmental power and specific protections of individual rights. But what exactly is freedom? Liberty?

Freedom generally means the ability to act without interference. In a political and legal sense, it means the ability to act free from the interference of government. However, even in the most free societies personal behavior is limited. This is because the actions of every member of society have the potential, at times, to affect other members. The total absence of government is anarchy and few people believe that freedom results from anarchy. Without government, there would be little control over behavior. No system would exist to punish those who intentionally injure others. No system would exist to allow someone injured by the negligence of another to recover his or her losses. There would be no deterrence to wrongful behavior, other than fear of retribution from the victim. The strong and cunning would prey on the weak and unintelligent; the licentious on the decent. Although it is true that to live in such a world would be living free from government interference, it cannot be reasonably considered freedom. If women are in constant fear of sexual assault, they are not free. If people are hesitant to own property for fear of it being taken by others, they are not totally free. To prevent anarchy, people establish governments. The people then vest their governments with certain authorities, so that the government can control the behavior of all people.

The forefathers of the United States did this when they met in Philadelphia to draft the Constitution of the United States. Some characterize the relationship between a democratic form of government and its people as a contract. The people relinquish some freedoms in an effort to secure other freedoms. The preamble to the United States Constitution recognizes this principle. It states "We, the People of the United States, in order to form a more perfect union, establish justice, insure domestic tranquility, provide for the common defense, promote the general welfare, and secure the blessings of liberty to ourselves and our posterity, do ordain and establish this Constitution for the United States of America." The concept is also found in the Declaration of Independence, where Thomas Jefferson penned "that all Men are created equal, that they are endowed by their Creator with certain unalienable Rights, that among these are Life, Liberty, and the Pursuit of Happiness—That to secure these Rights, Governments are instituted among Men, deriving their just Powers from the Consent of the Governed."

So the contract is formed. The people are to receive the benefits of an organized, fair government. The government is to establish laws designed to protect the people from one another and from other nations. In exchange, the people agree to comply with the laws created by their government. Some would argue that the duty extends to require the people to participate in the activities of the government. You have probably heard people speak of a "duty" to vote. Clearly, this is the rationale for requiring individuals to sit as jurors.

Every government is different. Some governments permit little or no political participation by the people. Others permit more. In those nations where the people are active participants, the rights and duties of individuals can vary significantly. This is because values can vary significantly from culture to culture. Hence, what one society believes to be an important freedom and protects from government interference may not be so valued by other societies.

In nearly all nations, however, governmental involvement in the affairs of people is continually increasing. This is due in part to the fact that people are increasingly less independent. That is, members of society now depend on one another to provide goods and services that were once commonly self-provided. In addition, the staggering increase in world population has caused people to have much more contact with each other than they did 100 years ago. The greater the population, contact between, and dependence of people on one another, the greater the number of conflicts that will arise requiring government intervention. As the population and dependence of people increase, so does the likelihood that one person's action may affect another. A person who lives alone in a forest far from other people can scream loudly in the middle of the night without bothering anyone. He or she could dispose of trash in any manner desired. If that same person lived in the middle of a city, the scream could wake people, and the improper disposal of trash could cause the spread of disease, as well as create an unpleasant environment. As the number of contacts between members of a society increases, so does the number of conflicts requiring government intervention. Even if the parties involved do not desire legal intervention to resolve their conflict, society will sometimes intervene through its government to prevent unacceptable behavior. For example, society has decided that duels are not an acceptable method of resolving disputes, even if two individuals wish to use this method. The government will try to prevent such behavior from occurring. If the duel is not discovered until after the fact, then the parties involved may be punished for participating.

As the need for government involvement in the private lives of citizens increases, it becomes more difficult to protect individual rights, also known as **civil liberties.** Although we the people have bestowed upon our government certain powers that have the effect of limiting our behavior, we have also specifically created "civil rights," which the government may not encroach upon. Many of these rights are contained in the first ten amendments to our Constitution, which are commonly known as the **Bill of Rights.** As the world becomes more populated and complex, the balance between permissible government involvement in the private lives of its citizens and impermissible encroachment upon those citizens' civil liberties becomes harder to maintain. As that line becomes thinner, the duty of the defense lawyer and legal assistant to be zealous in preparation of their defenses increases.

As previously discussed, the attempt to control people's behavior is achieved through both civil law and criminal law. Generally, society reserves only those acts that are perceived as serious moral wrongs or extremely dangerous for sanction under criminal law. Those acts that are accidental or are not serious breaches of moral duty are usually not criminal, but may lead to civil liability. Beliefs about what acts should be considered under each category are

civil liberties
Political liberties guaranteed by the Constitution and, in particular, by the Bill of Rights, especially the First Amendment.

Bill of Rights
The first ten amendments (changes or additions) to the U.S. Constitution.

very subjective and often change because a problem intensifies or because the public perceives an increased problem, even though the situation may not be any different than years before.

For example, the 1980s saw an increased effort to stop people from driving while under the influence of alcohol. Many states enacted new laws increasing the penalty for violating their D.U.I. statutes. In addition, a few states limited police discretion by requiring that violators be arrested. The practice once exercised by many police departments of taking drunk drivers home was stopped by legislative command. At one time, it can be argued that civil law was as much of a deterrent to driving under the influence as was criminal. Fear of civil liability for causing property damage or personal liability was as great as fear of criminal liability, because of the inconsistent and often minor penalties that followed convictions for driving under the influence. However, as public concern over alcohol-related automobile accidents increased, the focus turned to criminal law to prevent such behavior. Increased penalties, consistent arrest policies, and mandatory alcohol treatment for those convicted are now common. The extensive media coverage that particular cases have received, such as the Larry Mahoney accident,[1] have increased the public awareness that one who drives while intoxicated risks arrest, conviction, and punishment, as well as civil liability for injuries to property and person. What this example teaches is that society determines what acts will be treated as criminal based on public perceptions of morality, the importance of deterrence, and the danger posed to the public by the acts in question. Do not forget that criminal acts are often the subject of civil suits. This is not always true, as you learned in Chapter 1, when the general purposes of civil law and criminal law were discussed.

THE PURPOSES OF PUNISHING CRIMINAL LAW VIOLATORS

You have already learned that the general goal of criminal law is to prevent behavior determined by society to be undesirable. The criminal justice system uses punishment as a prevention tool. Many theories support punishing criminal law violators. Although some people focus on one theory and use it as the basis for punishment, a more accurate approach, in this author's opinion, is to recognize that many theories have merit and that when a legislature establishes the range of punishment applicable to a particular crime, many theories were involved in motivating individual legislators. It is unlikely that every member of a legislature will be motivated by the same objective. It is also unlikely that an individual legislator will be motivated by one theory only. Rather, all of the following objectives influence legislative decision making to some degree.

Specific and General Deterrence

Specific deterrence seeks to **deter** individuals already convicted of crimes from committing crimes in the future. It is a negative reward theory. By punishing Mr. X for today's crime, we teach him that he will be disciplined for future

deter
To discourage; to prevent from acting.

criminal behavior. The arrest and conviction of an individual show that individual that society has the capability to detect crime and is willing to punish those who commit crimes.

General deterrence attempts to deter all members of society from engaging in criminal activity. In theory, when the public observes Mr. X being punished for his actions, the public is deterred from behaving similarly for fear of the same punishment. Of course, individuals will react differently to the knowledge of Mr. X's punishment. Individuals weigh the risk of being caught and the level of punishment against the benefit of committing the crime. All people do this at one time or another. Have you ever intentionally run a stoplight? Jaywalked? If so, you have made the decision to violate the law. Neither crime involves a severe penalty. That fact, in addition to the likelihood of not being discovered by law enforcement agents, probably affected your decision. Presumably, if conviction of either crime was punished by incarceration (time in jail), then the deterrent effect would be greater. Would you be as likely to jaywalk if you knew that you could spend time in jail for such an act? Some people would; others would not. It is safe to assume, however, that as the punishment increases, so does compliance. However, one author observed that it is not as effective to increase the punishment as it is to increase the likelihood of being punished.[2] It is unknown how much either of these factors influences behavior, but it is generally accepted that they both do.

Incapacitation

Incapacitation, also referred to as restraint, is the third purpose of criminal punishment. Incapacitation does not seek to deter criminal conduct by influencing people's choices, but prevents criminal conduct by restraining those who have committed crimes. Criminals who are restrained in jail or prison, or in the extreme, executed, are incapable of causing harm to the general public. This theory is often the rationale for long-term imprisonment of individuals who are believed to be beyond rehabilitation. It is also promoted by those who lack faith in rehabilitation and feel that all criminals should be removed from society to prevent the chance of repetition.

Crimes that are caused by mental disease or occur in a moment of passion are not affected by deterrence theories, because the individual does not have the opportunity to consider the punishment that will be inflicted for committing the crime before it is committed. Deterrence theories are effective only for individuals who are sufficiently intelligent to understand the consequences of their actions, who are sane enough to understand the consequences of their actions, and who are not laboring under such uncontrollable feelings that an understanding that they may be punished is lost.

Rehabilitation

Rehabilitation is another purpose of punishing criminals. The theory of rehabilitation is that if the criminal is subjected to educational and vocational programs, treatment and counseling, and other measures, it is possible to alter the individual's behavior to conform to societal norms. Another author noted that:

> To the extent that crime is caused by elements of the offender's personality, educational defects, lack of work skills, and the like, we should be able to prevent him from committing more crimes by training, medical and psychiatric help, and guidance into law-abiding patterns of behavior. Strictly speaking, rehabilitation is not "punishment," but help to the offender. However, since this kind of help is frequently provided while the subject is in prison or at large on probation or parole under a sentence that carries some condemnation and some restriction of freedom, it is customary to list rehabilitation as one of the objects of a sentence in a criminal case.[3]

The concept of rehabilitation has come under considerable scrutiny in recent years, and the success of rehabilitative programs is questionable. However, the poor quality of prison rehabilitative programs may be the cause of the lack of success of these programs.

Retribution

Retribution, or societal vengeance, is the fifth purpose. Simply put, punishment through the criminal justice system is society's method of avenging a wrong. The idea that one who commits a wrong must be punished is an old one. The Old Testament speaks of an "eye for an eye." However, many people question the place of retribution in contemporary society. Is retribution consistent with American values? Jewish or Christian values? The question is actually moot, as there are few instances in which retribution stands alone as a reason for punishing someone who did not comply with the law. In most instances society's desire for revenge can be satisfied while fulfilling one of the other purposes of punishment, such as incapacitation.

It has also been asserted that public retribution prevents private retribution.[4] That is, when the victim (or anyone who might avenge a victim) of a crime knows that the offender has been punished, the victim's need to seek revenge is lessened or removed. Therefore, punishing those who harm others has the effect of promoting social order by preventing undesirable conduct by victims of crimes. Retribution in such instances has a deterrent effect, as victims of crimes are less likely to seek revenge. This is a good example of how the various purposes discussed are interrelated.

Finally, consider a sociological note. Do not become so focused on criminal law as a method of social control that you forget the many other methods of control that exist.

> The criminal law is not, of course, the only weapon which society uses to prevent conduct which harms or threatens to harm these important interests of the public. Education, at home and at school, as to the types of conduct that society thinks good and bad, is an important weapon; religion,

with its emphasis on distinguishing between good and evil conduct, is another. The human desire to acquire and keep the affection and respect of family, friends and associates no doubt has a great influence in deterring most people from conduct which is socially unacceptable. The civil side of the law, which forces one to pay damages for the harmful results which his undesirable conduct has caused to others, or which in inappropriate situations grants injunctions against bad conduct or orders the specific performance of good conduct, also plays a part in influencing behavior along desirable lines.[5]

SOURCES OF CRIMINAL LAW

Criminal law is actually a body of many laws emanating from many sources. Today most American criminal law is a product of legislative enactment. That has not always been so. Further, administrative regulations now make up a much larger percentage of the criminal law than in the past. It is vital to successful legal research that you understand the sources of criminal law. As you read this section, you will begin to see why an understanding of the functions of the three branches of government is important to an understanding of all criminal law.

The Common Law

common law
The legal system that originated in England and is composed of caselaw and statutes that grow and change, influenced by everchanging custom and tradition.

The oldest form of criminal law in the United States is the **common law.** The common law was developed in England and brought to the United States by the English colonists.

> The common law, as it exists in this country, is of English origin. Founded on ancient local rules and customs and in feudal times, it began to evolve in the King's courts and was eventually molded into the viable principles through which it continues to operate. The common law migrated to this continent with the first English colonists, who claimed the system as their birthright; it continued in full force in the 13 original colonies until the American Revolution, at which time it was adopted by each of the states as well as the national government of the new nation.[6]

stare decisis
(Latin) The doctrine that judicial decisions stand as precedents for cases arising in the future.

precedent
Prior decisions of the same court, or a higher court, which a judge must follow in deciding a subsequent case presenting similar facts and the same legal problem, even though different parties are involved and many years have elapsed.

But what exactly is this common law? Simply stated, the common law is judge-made law. It is law that has been developed by the hands of the judges of both England and the United States. To comprehend how common law developed, you must understand the concepts of precedence and **stare decisis.** When a court renders a legal decision, that decision becomes binding on itself and its inferior courts, whenever the same issue arises again in the future. The decision of the court is known as a **precedent.** The principle that inferior courts will comply with that decision when the issue is raised in the future is known as "stare decisis et non quieta movera" (a Latin phrase meaning "stand by precedents and do not disturb settled points"). The Supreme Court of Indiana expressed its view of stare decisis:

> Under the doctrine of stare decisis, this Court adheres to a principle of law which has been firmly established. Important policy considerations militate in favor of continuity and predictability in the law. Therefore, we are reluctant to disturb long-standing precedent which involves salient issues. Precedent operates as a maxim for judicial restraint to prevent the unjustified reversal to a series of decisions merely because the composition of the court has changed.[7]

During the feudal years in England, there were few formal criminal laws. Rather, local customs and practices developed into rules that governed the behavior of people. The concepts of fairness, justice, and equity were the guiding principles behind these rules. Eventually the courts began to recognize these rules. With that recognition came judicial decisions enforcing them. As precedent, each of those decisions began to establish a body of law, both civil and criminal in nature. The whole of those decisions is known as the common law.

> The common law, as frequently defined, includes those principles, usages, and rules of action applicable to the government and security of persons and property which do not rest for their authority upon any express or positive statute or other written declaration, but upon statements of principles found in the decisions of courts. The common law is inseparably identified with the decisions of the courts and can be determined only from such decisions in former cases bearing upon the subject under inquiry. As distinguished from statutory or written law, it embraces the great body of unwritten law founded upon general custom, usage, or common consent, and based upon natural justice or reason. It may otherwise be defined as custom long acquiesced in or sanctioned by immemorial usage and judicial decision. . . .
>
> In a broader sense the common law is the system of rules and declarations of principles from which our judicial ideas and legal definitions are derived, and which are continually expanding. It is not a codification of exact or inflexible rules for human conduct, for the redress of injuries, or for protection against wrongs, but is rather the embodiment of broad and comprehensive unwritten principles, inspired by natural reason and an innate sense of justice, and adopted by common consent for the regulation and government of the affairs of men.[8]

As stated, the common law is fluid and dynamic, changing to meet societal values and expectations. As one court stated, "The common law of the land is based upon human experience in the unceasing effort of an enlightened people to ascertain what is right and just between men."[9]

What happened historically is that courts defined crimes, as there was usually no legislative enactment that determined what acts should be criminal. As time passed, established "common-law crimes" developed. First the courts determined what acts should be criminal, and then the specifics of each crime developed; that is, what exactly had to be proved to establish guilt, what defenses were available, and what punishment was appropriate for conviction.

Although there is great similarity between the common laws of the many jurisdictions, differences exist because judicial decisions of one state are not binding precedents on other states and because customs and practices vary among communities. However, courts may look outside their jurisdictions for opinions to guide them in their decision making if no court in their jurisdiction has addressed the issue under consideration. Each state, as a separate and sovereign entity, has the power to decide whether to adopt the common law, in whole or in part, or to reject it.

Initially, the thirteen original states all adopted the common law. Most did so through their state constitutions. Today, only Louisiana has not adopted the common law in some form. However, for reasons you will learn later, approximately half of the states no longer recognize common-law crimes.[10] Even in those states, though, the civil common law and portions of the criminal common law (i.e., defenses to criminal charges) continue in force. Most states have expressly adopted the common law either by statute or constitutional authority. Many states adopted only parts of the common law.

Generally, there is no federal common law; rather, federal courts, in civil cases, apply the common law of the states in which they sit. For example, a United States district court in New Jersey will apply New Jersey common law. Even though this may appear strange to you, it is common practice for federal courts to apply state law. Further discussion of this topic is beyond the scope of this text.

Finally, be aware that common law has been modified and even abolished in some jurisdictions. The modifications to, and nullifications of, common law have come about in many different manners. In some instances, courts have decided that the common law must be changed to meet contemporary conditions. In extreme situations, parts of the common law have been totally abolished. Because legislatures are charged with the duty of making the laws, they have the final word, unless there is a state constitutional provision stating otherwise, on the status of the common law. Some legislatures have expressly given their judiciaries the authority to modify the common law, often with limitations. State legislatures are free to modify, partially abolish, or wholly abolish the common law as long as their own state constitution or the United States Constitution is not violated by so doing. The common law normally is inferior to legislation. This means that if a legislature acts in an area previously dealt with by common law, the new statute controls, absent a statement by the legislature to the contrary. For example, assume that under common law adultery was a crime in State Y. The legislature of State Y can change this by simply enacting a statute that provides that adultery is not criminal. The legislature may also amend the common law by continuing to recognize common-law adultery, but change the penalty for violation. If a state constitution, statute, or judicial decision has not abrogated the common law, presume that it continues in effect.

The Principle of Legality.   The question of whether common-law crimes should continue to exist is debatable. Those who favor permitting common-law crimes claim that it permits courts to "fill in the gaps" left by the legislatures when those bodies either fail to foresee all potential crimes or simply forget to include a crime that was foreseen. You should question whether the judicial branch should be actively second-guessing or cleaning house for the legislative branch. There appears to be a separation of powers issue when the judicial branch begins to behave in such a manner. However, few people want intentionally dangerous or disruptive behavior not to be criminalized.

Those who oppose a common law of crimes point to the concept embodied in the phrase "nullum crimen sine lege," which means, "there is no crime if there is no statute." Similarly, "nulla poena sine lege" has come to mean that "there shall be no punishment if there is no statute." These concepts, when considered in concert, insist that the criminal law must be written, that the written law must exist at the time that the accused took the act in question, and that criminal laws be more precise than civil laws.[11] This is the *principle of legality.*

The legality principle is founded on the belief that all people are entitled to know, prior to taking an act, that an act is criminal and that punishment could result from such behavior. This is commonly referred to as *notice.* The idea is sensible, as it appears to be a rule consistent with general notions of fairness and justice. Does it appear fair to you to hold an individual criminally accountable for taking an act that he or she could not have known was prohibited? The legality principle remedies the notice problem by requiring that written law be the basis of criminal liability, not unwritten common law. Understand that the law imposes a duty on all people to be aware of written law; thus, all people are presumed to be aware of criminal prohibitions. The *Keeler* case discusses the legality principle.

HOW TO BRIEF A CASE Decisions of courts are often written and are called *judicial opinions* or cases. These cases are published in law reporters so they may be used as precedent. Many cases appear in this text for your education. Your instructor may also require that you read other cases, often from your jurisdiction. The cases included in your book have been edited, citations have been omitted, and legal issues not relevant to the subject discussed have been excised.

Most judicial opinions are written using a similar format. First, the name of the case appears with the name of the court, the cite (location where the case has been published), and the year. When the body of the case begins, the name of the judge, or judges, responsible for writing the opinion appears directly before the first paragraph. The opinion contains an introduction to the case, which normally gives you the procedural history of the case. This is followed by a summary of the facts that led to the dispute, the court's analysis of the law that applies to the case, and the court's conclusions and orders, if any.

Most opinions used here are from appellate courts, where many judges sit at one time. After the case is over, the judges vote on an outcome. The majority vote wins, and the opinion of the majority is written by one of those judges. If other judges in the majority wish to add to the majority opinion, they may write what is known as a *concurring opinion.* Concurring opinions appear after

SIDEBAR

majority opinions in the law reporters. When a judge who was not in the majority feels strongly about his or her position, he or she may file a dissenting opinion, which appears after the concurring opinions, if any. Only the majority opinion
is law, although concurring and dissenting opinions are often informative.

During your legal education you may be instructed to "brief" a case. Even if
your instructor does not require you to brief cases, you may want to, as many
students understand a case better after they have completed a brief. Here are
suggestions for reading and understanding cases.

1. Read the case. On your first reading, do not take notes; simply attempt to
   get a feel for the case. Then read the case again and use the following
   suggested method of briefing.
2. State the *relevant* facts. Often cases read like little stories. You need to weed
   out the facts that have no bearing on the subject you are studying.
3. Identify the issues. *Issues* are the legal questions discussed by the court.
4. State the applicable rules, standards, or other law.
5. Summarize the court's decision and analysis. Why and how did the court
   reach its conclusion? Note whether the court affirmed, reversed, or
   remanded the case.

 CASE

KEELER V. SUPERIOR COURT

Supreme Court of
California

2 Cal. 3d 619, 470 P.2d
617 (1970)

In this proceeding for writ of prohibition we are
called upon to decide whether an unborn viable
fetus is a "human being" within the meaning of
the California statute defining murder. We
conclude that the legislature did not intend such
a meaning, and that for us to construe the
statute to the contrary and apply it to this
petitioner would exceed our judicial power
and deny petitioner due process of law.

The evidence received at the preliminary
examination may be summarized as follows:
Petitioner and Teresa Keeler obtained an
interlocutory decree of divorce on September 27,
1968. They had been married for sixteen years.
Unknown to petitioner, Mrs. Keeler was then
pregnant by one Ernest Vogt, whom she had met

earlier that summer. She subsequently began living
with Vogt in Stockton, but concealed the fact from
petitioner. Petitioner was given custody of their
two daughters, aged 12 and 13 years, and under
the decree Mrs. Keeler had the right to take the
girls on alternate weekends.

On February 23, 1969, Mrs. Keeler was driving
on a narrow mountain road in Amador County
after delivering the girls to their home. She met
petitioner driving in the opposite direction; he
blocked the road with his car, and she pulled over
to the side. He walked to her vehicle and began
speaking to her. He seemed calm, and she rolled
down her window to hear him. He said, "I hear
you're pregnant. If you are you had better stay
away from the girls and from here." She did not
reply, and he opened the car door; as she later
testified, "He assisted me out of the car . . . [I]t
wasn't rough at this time." Petitioner then looked
at her abdomen and became "extremely upset."
He said, "You sure are. I'm going to stomp it out
of you." He pushed her against the car, shoved
his knee into her abdomen, and struck her in the

face with several blows. She fainted, and when she regained consciousness petitioner had departed.

Mrs. Keeler drove back to Stockton, and the police and medical assistance were summoned. She had suffered substantial facial injuries, as well as extensive bruising of the abdominal wall. A Caesarian section was performed, and the fetus was examined in utero. Its head was found to be severely fractured, and it was delivered stillborn. The pathologist gave as his opinion that the cause of death was skull fracture with consequent cerebral hemorrhaging, that death would be immediate, and that the injury could have been the result of force applied to the mother's abdomen. There was no air in the fetus' lungs, and the umbilical cord was intact. . . .

The evidence was in conflict as to the estimated age of the fetus; the expert testimony on the point, however, concluded "with reasonable medical certainty" that the fetus had developed to the stage of viability, i.e., that in the event of premature birth on the date in question it would have had a 75 percent to 96 percent chance of survival.

An information was filed charging petitioner, in count I, with committing the crime of murder. . . .

Penal Code section 187 provides: "Murder is the unlawful killing of a human being, with malice aforethought." The dispositive question is whether the fetus which petitioner is accused of killing was, on February 23, 1969, a "human being" within the meaning of the statute. If it was not, petitioner cannot be charged with its "murder". . . .

* * *

We conclude that in declaring murder to be the unlawful and malicious killing of a "human being" the Legislature of 1850 intended that term to have the settled common law meaning of a person who had been born alive, and did not intend the act of feticide—as distinguished from abortion—to be an offense under the laws of California.

* * *

The People urge, however that the sciences of obstetrics and pediatrics have greatly progressed since 1872, to the point where with proper medical care a normally developed fetus prematurely born. . . is "viable". . . since an unborn but viable fetus is now fully capable of independent life. . . . But we cannot join in the conclusion sought to be deduced: we cannot hold this petitioner to answer for murder by reason of his alleged act of killing an unborn—even though viable—fetus. To such a charge there are two insuperable obstacles, one "jurisdictional" and the other constitutional.

Penal Code section 6 declares in relevant part that "No act or omission" accomplished after the code has taken effect "is criminal or punishable, except as prescribed by this code. . . ." This section embodies a fundamental principle of our tripartite form of government, i.e., that subject to the constitutional prohibition against cruel and unusual punishment, the power to define crimes and fix penalties is vested exclusively in the legislative branch. Stated differently, there are no common law crimes in California. . . . In order that a public offense be committed, some statute, ordinance or regulation prior in time to the commission of the act, must denounce it.

* * *

Applying these rules to the case at bar, we would undoubtedly act in excess of the judicial power if we were to adopt the People's proposed construction of section 187. As we have shown, the Legislature has defined the crime of murder in California to apply only to the unlawful and malicious killing of one who has been born alive. We recognize that the killing of an unborn but viable fetus may be deemed by some to be an offense of similar nature and gravity; but as Chief Justice Marshall warned long ago, "It would be dangerous, indeed, to carry the principle, that a case which is within the reason or mischief of a statute, is within its provisions, so far as to punish a crime not enumerated in the statute, because it is of equal atrocity, or of kindred character, with those which are enumerated.". . . Whether to thus extend liability for murder in California is a determination solely within the province of the Legislature. For a court to simply declare, by judicial fiat, that the time has now come to prosecute under section 187 one who kills an unborn but viable fetus would indeed be to rewrite the statute under the guise of construing it. . . . to make it "a judicial function". . . "raises very serious questions concerning the principle of separation of powers."

The second obstacle to the proposed judicial enlargement of section 187 is the guarantee of due process of law. . . .

The first essential of due process is fair warning of the act which is made punishable as a crime. "That the terms of a penal statute creating a new offense must be sufficiently explicit to inform those who are subject to it what conduct on their part will render them liable to its penalties, is a well-recognized requirement, consonant alike with ordinary notions of fair play and the settled rules of law."

◆

Due Process Clause

The *due process clauses* of the Fifth and Fourteenth Amendments to the U.S. Constitution require that no person be deprived of life, liberty, or property without having notice and a real chance to present his or her side in a legal dispute.

Do not forget that *Keeler* is an opinion of the California Supreme Court; therefore, it is not the law of all the land. It is the law in California, though, and similar decisions have been made elsewhere.

Also note that the court determined that the common law violates "ordinary notions of fair play" and that no warning or notice was given to Keeler that his act could be defined as murder. As the court noted, these requirements are embodied in the **Due Process Clauses** of the United States Constitution and the constitutions of the many states. Due process, in both civil and criminal law, requires that individuals be put on notice of impending government action, be given an opportunity to be heard and to present evidence, and often the right to a jury trial. Due process is founded upon principles of fair play and justice. However, the United States Supreme Court has determined that states may, under some circumstances, use the common law to define criminal conduct. The court in *Keeler* based its decision on the California Constitution's Due Process Clause. You should remember that the California Supreme Court is the final word on California law, and *Keeler* teaches you that the California Constitution provides more protection than the United States Constitution in this regard. Still, the United States Constitution places limits on the use of the common law by the states to create crimes. This is done primarily through the Due Process Clause and the provision prohibiting ex post facto laws. You will learn more about the Due Process and Ex Post Facto Clauses later in this book when we examine defenses to criminal charges. If states, such as California in the *Keeler* case, want to increase a defendant's rights beyond what the United States Constitution protects, they may do so through their own statutes or constitutions.

Other Uses of the Common Law.   Even in those jurisdictions that have abandoned use of the common law to create crimes, the common law continues to be important for many reasons.

First, many statutes mirror the common law in language. That is, legislatures often simply codify the common law's criminal prohibitions. Hence, when a question arises concerning whether a particular act of a defendant is intended to fall under the intent of a criminal prohibition, the case law handed down prior to codification of the common law may continue to be helpful after codification. The result is that the crime remains the same, but the source of the prohibition has changed. It is also possible for a legislature to change only part of a common-law definition and leave the remainder the same. If so, prior case law may be helpful when considering the unaltered portion of the definition.

Second, many of the concepts developed at the common law continue to be recognized today. For example, the distinction between felonies and misdemeanors continues today. Although jurisdictions vary in definition, a felony is a serious crime usually punishable by more than one year in prison. A misdemeanor is less serious and usually is punishable by one year or less in jail.

Third, legislatures occasionally enact a criminal prohibition without establishing the potential penalty for violation. In such cases courts will often look to the penalties applied to similar common law crimes for guidance.

Fourth, in addition to defining crimes, the common law established many procedures that were used to adjudicate criminal cases. These procedures most often dealt with criminal defenses. What defenses could be raised, as well as how and when, were often answered by the common law. For example, the various tests to determine if a defendant was sane when an alleged crime was committed were developed under the common law. If a legislature has not specifically changed these procedural rules, they remain in effect, even if the power of courts to create common-law crimes has been abolished.

Statutory Law

As you have already learned, the legislative branch is responsible for the creation of law. You have also learned that legislatures possess the authority to modify, abolish, or adopt the common law, in whole or in part. During the nineteenth century, the codification of criminal law began. This effectively displaced the role of the judiciary in defining crimes. Today, nearly all criminal law is found in criminal codes.

Although the power of the legislative branch to declare behavior criminal is significant, there are limits. The constitutions of the United States and of the many states contain limits on such state and federal authority. Most of these limits are found in the Bill of Rights. For example, the First Amendment to the federal Constitution prohibits government from punishing an individual for exercising choice of religion. If a legislature does enact law that violates a constitutional provision, it is the duty of the judicial branch to declare the law void. This is the power of judicial review, previously discussed in Chapter 1. For now, you need only understand that legislatures do not have unlimited authority to create criminal law. Individual (civil) rights limit legislative power to make conduct criminal, and the judicial branch acts to protect individuals from unconstitutional legislation.

Ordinances

The written laws of municipalities are **ordinances.** Ordinances are enacted by city councils and commonly regulate zoning, building, construction, and related matters. Many cities have criminal ordinances that mirror state statutes,

ordinances
A local or city law, rule, or regulation.

but apply to those acts that occur within the jurisdiction of the city. For example, many cities have assault and battery ordinances, just as their states have assault and battery statutes. Traffic and parking violations may also be criminal, although some cities pursue these as civil violations, which permits the state to pursue the criminal charge.

Ordinances may not conflict with state or federal law. Any ordinance that is inconsistent with higher law may be invalidated by a court. States limit the power of cities to punish for ordinance violations, and most city court trials are to the bench, not to a jury.

Administrative Law

It is likely that at some time in your life you have had to deal with an administrative agency. Agencies are governmental units, federal, state, and local, which administer the affairs of the government. Although often lumped together, there are actually two types of agencies, social welfare and regulatory. The two names reflect the purposes behind each type. Social welfare agencies put into effect government programs. For example, in Indiana the State Department of Public Welfare administers the distribution of public money to those deemed needy. In contrast, state medical licensing boards are regulatory, because their duty is to oversee and regulate the practice of medicine in the various states. Both regulatory and administrative agencies receive their power from the legislative branch.

regulation
A rule that is put out by a local government or an administrative agency to regulate conduct.

Because legislatures do not possess the time or the expertise to write precise statutes, they often enact a statute that is very general and in that statute grant one or more administrative agencies the authority to make more precise laws. Just as legislative enactments are known as statutes (or codes), administrative laws are known as **regulations** or rules. The extent to which a legislature may delegate its law-making authority has been a continuing source of debate. It is argued that legislatures may not grant such an important legislative function to agencies. This is believed to be a violation of the principle of separation of powers, because agencies usually fall under the control of the executive branch, and the legislative branch is not permitted to delegate its powers to the executive branch, or vice versa.

SIDEBAR

FINDING ADMINISTRATIVE REGULATIONS Federal administrative rules are found in the Code of Federal Regulations (C.F.R.). New rules that have not yet been added to the C.F.R. may be found in the *Federal Register*. Each state has its counterpart publications. For example, in Florida they are the Florida Administrative Code and the *Florida Administrative Weekly*, respectively.

Despite this, the United States Supreme Court has determined that agencies may create regulations that have the effect of law, including criminal prohibitions. The Court's opinion on how much authority may be given administrative agencies has undergone a few changes over the years. In 1911 the United States Supreme Court handed down the opinion in the *Grimaud* case.

Grimaud is the law today. Agencies may be delegated penal rulemaking authority. However, the Supreme Court has said that although Congress may delegate to an agency the authority to make criminal laws, it may not delegate the responsibility of establishing penalties to an agency, with the possible exception of small fines. Congress must either set the precise penalty or set a range from which an agency can further determine the appropriate penalty.

An interesting question concerns how much guidance Congress must give an agency in its delegation. Because Congress is delegating its power to create law to an agency, it is expected to give the agency some guidance as to what it wants. This limits the discretion of the agency and prevents it from becoming a substitute legislature.[12] Normally, Congress must provide an intelligible principle or sufficient standards to guide an agency.[13] It takes little congressional guidance to satisfy these tests. Because of the special nature of criminal law (i.e., the deprivation to liberty that may result from a criminal conviction) defendants have argued that Congress must be more specific, or give an agency less discretion, when delegating the authority to create penal rules, as opposed to nonpenal rules. The Supreme Court refused to answer that question in *Touby v. United States.*

In conclusion, an agency may be delegated the authority to declare acts criminal. Congress must provide at least an "intelligible principle," and possibly

 CASE

UNITED STATES V. GRIMAUD

United States Supreme Court

220 U.S. 506 (1911)

The defendants were indicted for grazing sheep on the Sierra Forest Reserve without having obtained the permission required by the regulations adopted by the Secretary of Agriculture. They demurred on the ground that the Forest Reserve Act of 1891 was unconstitutional, in so far as it delegated to the Secretary of Agriculture power to make rules and regulations and made a violation thereof a penal offense.

* * *

From the various acts relating to the establishment and management of forest reservations it appears that they were intended "to improve and protect the forest and to secure favorable conditions to water flows.". . . It was also declared that the Secretary "may make such rules and regulations and establish such service as will insure the objects of such reservation, namely, to regulate their occupancy and use to prevent the forests thereon from destruction; *and any violation of the provisions of this act or such* rules and regulations shall be punished," as is provided in [the statute].

Under these acts, therefore, any use of the reservations for grazing or other lawful purpose was required to be subject to the rules and regulations established by the Secretary of

Agriculture. To pasture sheep and cattle on the reservation, at will and without restraint, might interfere seriously with the accomplishment of the purposes for which they were established. But a limited and regulated use for pasturage might not be inconsistent with the object sought to be attained by the statute. The determination of such questions, however, was a matter of administrative detail. What might be harmless in one forest might be harmful to another. What might be injurious at one stage of timber growth, or at one season of the year, might not be so at another.

In the nature of things it was impracticable for Congress to provide general regulations for these various and varying details of management. Each reservation had its peculiar and special features; and in authorizing the Secretary of Agriculture to meet these local conditions Congress was merely conferring administrative functions upon an agent, and not delegating to him legislative power.

* * *

It must be admitted that it is difficult to define the line which separates legislative power to make laws, from administrative authority to make regulations. This difficulty has often been recognized [as] referred to by Chief Justice Marshall . . . : "It will not be contended that Congress can delegate to the courts, or to any other tribunals, powers which are strictly and exclusively legislative. But Congress may certainly delegate to others, powers which the legislature may rightfully exercise itself." What were these non-legislative powers which Congress could exercise but which might also be delegated to others was not determined, for he said: "The line has not been exactly drawn which separates those important subjects, which *must* be entirely regulated by the legislature

itself, from those of less interest, in which a general provision may be made, and power given to those who are to act under such general provisions to fill up the details."

From the beginning of the Government various acts have been passed conferring upon the executive officers power to make rules and regulations—not for the government of their departments; but for administering the laws which did govern. None of these statutes could confer legislative power. But when Congress had legislated and indicated its will, it could give to those who were to act under such general provisions "power to fill up the details" by the establishment of administrative rules and regulations, the violation of which could be punished by fine or imprisonment fixed by Congress, or by penalties fixed by Congress or measured by the injury done.

* * *

It is true that there is no act of Congress which, in express terms, declares that it shall be unlawful to graze sheep on a forest reserve. But the statutes, from which we have quoted, declare, that the privilege of using reserves for "all proper and lawful purposes" is subject to the proviso that the person shall comply "with the rules and regulations covering such forest reservation." The same act makes it an offense to violate those regulations.

* * *

The Secretary of Agriculture could not make rules and regulations for any and every purpose. As to those here involved, they all regulate matters clearly indicated and authorized by Congress.

more, when making this type of delegation. Congress may not delegate the authority to set a penalty to an agency, although it may allow the agency to set the penalty for a violation from within statutory guidelines.

Court Rules

Just as administrative agencies need the authority to "fill in the gaps" of legislation because statutes are not specific enough to satisfy all of an agency's needs, so do courts. The United States Congress and all of the state legislatures have enacted some form of statute establishing general rules of civil and criminal procedure. However, to fill in the gaps left by legislatures, courts adopt **court rules,** which also govern civil and criminal processes. Although court rules deal with procedural issues (such as service of process, limits on the length of briefs and memoranda, and timing of filing) and not substantive issues, they are important. Of course, court rules may not conflict with legislative mandates. If a rule does conflict with a statute, the statute is controlling. One exception to this rule may be when the statute is unconstitutional and the rule is a viable alternative, but discussion of that issue is best left to a course on constitutional law and judicial process.

> **rules of court**
> Rules promulgated by the court, governing procedure or practice before it.

Most court rules are drafted under the direction of the highest court of the state and either become effective by vote of the court or after being presented to the state legislature for ratification. In the federal system, the rules are drafted by the Judicial Conference under the direction of the Supreme Court and then presented to Congress. If Congress fails to act to nullify the rules, they become law. Of course, Congress may amend the rules at will. Many jurisdictions also have local rules, that is, rules created by local courts for practice in those courts. The rules cannot conflict with either statutes or higher court rules. In the federal system, district courts adopt local rules. Being familiar with the rules of the courts in your jurisdiction is imperative. If you are not, you may miss important deadlines, file incomplete documents, or have your filings stricken.

 CASE

TOUBY V. UNITED STATES

United States Supreme Court

500 U.S. 160 (1991)

Petitioners were convicted of manufacturing and conspiring to manufacture "Euphoria," a drug temporarily designated as a schedule I controlled substance pursuant to § 201(h) of the Controlled Substances Act. We consider whether § 201(h) unconstitutionally delegates legislative power to the Attorney General and whether the Attorney General's subdelegation to the Drug Enforcement Administration (DEA) was authorized by statute. . . .

[T]he Controlled Substances Act (Act) . . . establishes five categories or "schedules" of controlled substances, the manufacture, possession, and distribution of which the Act regulates or prohibits. Violations involving schedule I substances carry the most severe penalties, as these substances are believed to pose the most serious threat to public safety. Relevant here, § 201(a) of the Act authorizes the Attorney General to add or remove substances, or to move a substance from one schedule to another. . . .

When adding a substance to a schedule, the Attorney General must follow specified procedures. First, the Attorney General must request a scientific and medical evaluation from the Secretary of

Health and Human Services (HHS), together with a recommendation as to whether the substances should be controlled. A substance cannot be scheduled if the Secretary recommends against it. . . . Second, the Attorney General must consider eight factors with respect to the substance, including its potential for abuse, scientific evidence of its pharmacological effect, its psychic or physiological dependence liability, and whether the substance is an immediate precursor of a substance already controlled. . . . Third, the Attorney General must comply with notice-and-hearing provisions of the Administrative Procedure Act . . . which permit comment by interested parties. . . . In addition, the Act permits any aggrieved person to challenge the scheduling of a substance by the Attorney General in a court of appeals. . . .

It takes time to comply with these procedural requirements. From the time when law enforcement officials identify a dangerous new drug, it typically takes 6 to 12 months to add it to one of the schedules. . . . Drug traffickers were able to take advantage of this time gap by designing drugs that were similar in pharmacological effect to scheduled substances but differing slightly in chemical composition, so that existing schedules did not apply to them. These "designer drugs" were developed and widely marketed long before the Government was able to schedule them and initiate prosecutions. . . .

To combat "designer drug" problem, Congress in 1984 amended the Act to create an expedited procedure by which the Attorney General can schedule a substance on a temporary basis when doing so is "necessary to avoid an imminent hazard to the public safety.". . . Temporary scheduling under § 201(h) allows the Attorney General to bypass, for a limited time, several of the requirements for permanent scheduling. The Attorney General need consider only three of the eight factors required for permanent scheduling. . . . Rather than comply with the APA notice-and-hearing provisions, the Attorney General need provide only a 30-day notice of proposed scheduling in the Federal Register. . . . Notice also must be transmitted to the Secretary of HHS, but the Secretary's prior approval of a

proposed scheduling is not required. . . . Finally . . . an order to schedule a substance temporarily "is not subject to judicial review."

Because it has fewer procedural requirements, temporary scheduling enables the government to respond more quickly to the threat posed by dangerous new drugs. A temporary scheduling order can be issued 30 days after a new drug is identified, and the order remains valid for one year. During this 1-year period, the Attorney General presumably will initiate the permanent scheduling process. . . .

The Attorney General promulgated regulations delegating to the DEA his powers under the Act, including the power to schedule controlled substances on a temporary basis. Pursuant to that delegation, the DEA Administrator issued an order scheduling . . . "Euphoria" as a schedule I controlled substance. . . .

While the temporary scheduling order was in effect, DEA agents, executing a valid search warrant, discovered a fully operational drug laboratory in Daniel and Lyrissa Touby's home. The Toubys were indicted for manufacturing and conspiring to manufacture Euphoria. They moved to dismiss the indictment on the grounds that § 201(h) unconstitutionally delegates legislative power to the Attorney General. . . . The United States District Court for the District of New Jersey denied the motion to dismiss . . . and the Court of Appeals for the Third Circuit affirmed. . . . We granted certiorari . . . and now affirm.

The Constitution provides that "all legislative Powers herein granted shall be vested in a Congress of the United States." From this language the Court has derived the nondelegation doctrine: that Congress may not constitutionally delegate its legislative power to another Branch of government. "The nondelegation doctrine is rooted in the principle of separation of powers that underlies our tripartite system of Government." . . .

We have long recognized that nondelegation does not prevent Congress from seeking assistance, within proper limits, from its coordinate Branches. . . . Thus, Congress does not violate the Constitution merely because it legislates in broad terms, leaving a certain degree of discretion to executive or judicial actors. So long as Congress "lay[s] down by legislative act an intelligible principle to which the person or body authorized to [act] is directed to conform, such legislative action is not a forbidden delegation of legislative power.". . .

Petitioners wisely concede that Congress has set forth in § 201(h) an "intelligible principle" to constrain the Attorney General's discretion to schedule controlled substances on a temporary basis. . . . Petitioners suggest, however, that something more than an "intelligible principle" is required when Congress authorizes another Branch to promulgate regulations that contemplate criminal sanctions. They contend that regulations of this sort pose a heightened risk to individual liberty and that Congress must

therefore provide more specific guidance. Our cases are not entirely clear as to whether or not more specific guidance is in fact required. . . . We need not resolve the issue today. We conclude that § 201(h) passes muster even if greater congressional specificity is required in the criminal context.

Although it features fewer procedural requirements than the permanent scheduling statute, § 201(h) meaningfully constrains the Attorney General's discretion to define criminal conduct. . . .

It is clear that in § 201(h) and 202(b) Congress has placed multiple restrictions on the Attorney General's discretion to define criminal conduct. These restrictions satisfy the constitutional requirements of the nondelegation doctrine.

The Model Penal Code

On occasion the **Model Penal Code** will be referenced in this text. Actually entitled *Model Penal Code and Commentaries,* it was drafted by a group of individuals expert in criminal law while working for the American Law Institute, which is a private organization. The intent of the drafters of the Code was to draft a consistent, thoughtful code that could be recommended to the states for adoption. The code itself is not law until adopted and made into law by a legislature.

According to one source, by 1985 thirty-four states had "enacted widespread criminal-law revision and codification based on its provisions; fifteen hundred courts had cited its provisions and referred to its commentary."[14] The Model Penal Code has been included in this text, in edited form, as Appendix B. You should refer to that as the Code is discussed in following chapters.

Model Penal Code

A proposed criminal code prepared jointly by the Commission on Uniform State Laws and the American Law Institute.

Constitutional Law

Finally, constitutional law is included in this list of sources of criminal law, not because it defines what conduct is criminal, but because of its significant impact on criminal law generally. In particular, the United States Constitution, primarily through the Bill of Rights, is responsible for establishing many of the rules governing criminal procedure. This has been especially true in the past few decades. You will become more aware of why this is true as you learn more about criminal law and procedure. Pay close attention to the dates of the cases included in this text; it is likely that many were handed down in your lifetime.

IMPORTANT DATES IN THE HISTORY OF THE CONSTITUTION OF THE UNITED STATES

May 25, 1787	Constitutional Convention opens in Philadelphia.
September 17, 1787	Constitutional Convention closes, and Constitution is sent to the states for ratification.
December 6, 1787	Delaware is the first state to ratify the Constitution.
June 21, 1788	New Hampshire is the ninth state to ratify and thereby provides the requisite number of ratifying states to adopt the Constitution for the entire United States.
May 29, 1790	Rhode Island is the thirteenth (last) state to ratify the Constitution.
December 15, 1791	Bill of Rights is ratified.
July 28, 1868	Fourteenth Amendment is ratified.

Although it is common to associate the study of constitutional law with the study of the United States Constitution, do not forget that each state also has its own constitution with its own body of case law interpreting its meaning. Even though the dominant source for defending civil liberties has been the United States Constitution, it is possible that a shift to state constitutions will occur, as the current Supreme Court is expected to be more conservative on criminal issues, which means it is less likely to extend constitutional protections. Remember, the United States Constitution is the highest form of law, and the states may not decrease the individual protections secured by it. States may, however, increase civil liberties through state law. Most state constitutions mirror the federal constitution, often verbatim. In spite of this, state courts are free to interpret their constitutional provisions as providing more protection than their federal counterparts, even if identical in text.

SOURCES OF CRIMINAL LAW

SOURCE	COMMENT
CONSTITUTIONS	The United States and every state have a constitution. The United States Constitution is the supreme law of the land. Amendment of the federal Constitution requires action by both the states and the United States Congress.
STATUTES	The written law created by legislatures, also known as codes. State statutes may not conflict with either their own constitution or the federal constitution. State statutes are also invalid if they conflict with other federal law, and the

	federal government has concurrent jurisdiction with the states. Statutes of the United States are invalid if they conflict with the United States Constitution or if they attempt to regulate outside federal jurisdiction. Legislatures may change statutes at will.
COMMON LAW	Law which evolved, as courts, through judicial opinions, recognized customs, and practices. Legislatures may alter, amend, or abolish the common law at will. In criminal law the common law is responsible for the creation of crimes and for establishing defenses to crimes.
REGULATIONS	Created by administrative agencies under a grant of authority from a legislative body. Regulations must be consistent with statutes and constitutions and may not exceed the legislative grant of power. The power to make rules and regulations is granted to "fill in the gaps" left by legislatures when drafting statutes.
ORDINANCES	Written law of local bodies, such as city councils. Must be consistent with all higher forms of law.
MODEL PENAL CODE	Written under the direction of the American Law Institute. It was drafted by experts in criminal law to be presented to the states for adoption. It is not law until a state has adopted it, in whole or part. More than half the states have adopted at least part of the Model Penal Code.
COURT RULES	Rules created by courts to manage their cases. Court rules are procedural and commonly establish deadlines, lengths of filings, etc. Court rules may not conflict with statutes or constitutions.

 WEB LINKS

Findlaw

http://www.findlaw.com is an excellent Web site that contains both state and federal statutory law, administrative law, and case law. In addition, Findlaw provides information on law schools, law firms, professional development, and legal news.

KEY TERMS

Bill of Rights
civil liberties
common law
criminal law
criminal procedure

deter
Due Process Clause
Model Penal Code
ordinances
precedent

regulation
rules of court
stare decisis

REVIEW QUESTIONS

1. What are civil liberties? Give two examples of civil liberties that are protected by the Constitution of the United States.
2. What is the common law? How do the concepts of stare decisis and precedent relate to the common law?
3. The common law is different in every state. Why?
4. What does the Latin phrase "nullum crimen sine lege" translate to? Explain the significance of that phrase.
5. Explain how the common law can violate the principle of legality.
6. State three uses the common law has in criminal law in those jurisdictions that do not permit common-law creation of crimes.
7. What is the source of most criminal law today? Where does that law come from?
8. What is an ordinance?
9. What is a regulation?
10. What is a court rule?
11. Place the following sources of law in order of authority, beginning with the highest form of law and ending with the lowest. Notice that both state and federal sources of law are included: United States Code, state constitutions, federal administrative regulations, ordinances, United States Constitution, state administrative regulations, state statutes.

REVIEW PROBLEMS

1. In theory, people can increase their "freedom" by establishing a government and relinquishing freedoms (civil liberties) to that government. Explain why this paradox is true.
2. List the various purposes for punishing criminal law violators.
   Using your answers from question 2, determine if the goals of punishment can be achieved if prosecution is sought for the following acts (numbers 3–6):
3. John, having always wanted a guitar, stole one from a fellow student's room while that student was out.
4. Jack suffers from a physical disease of the mind that causes him to have violent episodes. Jack has no way of knowing when the episodes will occur. However, the disease is controllable with medication. Despite this, Jack often does not take the medicine, as he finds the injections painful and inconvenient.

One day, when he had not taken the medicine, Jack had an episode and struck Mike, causing him personal injury.

5. Same facts as in question 4, except there is no treatment or medication that can control Jack's behavior. He was diagnosed as having the disease years prior to striking Mike and has caused such an injury before during a similar violent episode.

6. Unknown to Kevin, he has epilepsy. One day while he was driving his automobile, he suffered his first seizure. The seizure caused him to lose control of his car and strike a pedestrian, inflicting a fatal injury.

END NOTES

1. In May, 1988, Larry Mahoney, while driving under the influence of alcohol, struck a school bus, causing it to burst into flames. At the time he hit the bus he was traveling in the wrong direction on an interstate highway. Twenty-four children and three adults died in the fire. On December 22, 1989, a Kentucky jury convicted Mr. Mahoney of second-degree manslaughter and other lesser offenses, and recommended that he be sentenced to sixteen years in prison.

2. *See* E. Puttkammer, *Administration of Criminal Law*, 16–17 (1953).

3. Schwartz and Goldstein, *Police Guidance Manuals* (University of Virginia Press, 1968), Manual No. 3, at 21–32, reprinted in *Cases, Materials, and Problems on the Advocacy and Administration of Criminal Justice* 173 by Harold Norris (unpublished manuscript available in the Detroit College of Law library).

4. *See* Note, 78 *Colum. L. Rev.* 1249, 1247–59 (1978); LaFave and Scott, *Criminal Law* 26 (Hornbook Series, St. Paul: West, 1986).

5. LaFave and Scott at 23.

6. 15A Am. Jur. 2d *Common Law* 6 (1976).

7. *Marsillett v. State*, 495 N.E.2d 699, 704 (Ind. 1986) (citations omitted).

8. 15A Am. Jur. 2d *Common Law* 1 (1976).

9. *Helms v. American Security Co.*, 22 N.E.2d 822 (Ind. 1986).

10. T. Gardner, *Criminal Law: Principles and Cases*, 4th ed. (Criminal Justice Series; St. Paul: West, 1989).

11. P. Robinson, *Fundamentals of Criminal Law* (Boston: Little, Brown, 1988).

12. *See Schechter Poultry Corp. v. United States*, 2nd edition, 295 U.S. 495 (1935).

13. *See* D. Hall, *Administrative Law* ch. 5 (Prentice Hall 2002).

14. J. Samaha, *Criminal Law*, 3d ed. (St. Paul: West, 1990).

The Two Essential Elements

CHAPTER OUTLINE

Mens Rea

    Mens Rea and the Common Law

    Strict Liability

    Vicarious Liability

    Current Approaches to Mens Rea

    Proving Mens Rea

    Motive

Actus Reus

    Voluntariness

    Thoughts and Statements as Acts

    Personal Status as an Act

    Possession as an Act

    Omissions as Acts

    Causation

CHAPTER OBJECTIVES

In this chapter, you should:

- learn about the two basic elements of most crime, mens rea and actus reus.
- be challenged to think about what it means to have a guilty mind.
- learn the historic and contemporary approaches to characterizing a guilty mind.
- continue to develop your case analysis and legal reasoning skills.
- learn element analysis.

MENS REA

Nearly every crime consists of two essential elements, the mental and the physical. This chapter begins by addressing the mental part and concludes by examining the physical.

It is common to distinguish between acts that are intentional and those that occur accidentally. Everyone has had an experience where they have caused injury to another person or another person's property accidentally. The fact that the injury was accidental and not intended often leads to a statement such as, "I'm sorry, I didn't mean to hurt you." In these situations people often feel a social obligation to pay for any injuries they have caused, or to assist the injured party in other ways, but probably do not expect to be punished criminally. As the late Supreme Court Justice Holmes stated, "Even a dog distinguishes between being stumbled over and being kicked." As this statement implies, to make such a distinction between accidental and intentional acts that injure others appears to be natural and consistent with common notions of fairness. The criminal law often models this theory; that is, people are often held accountable for intentional behavior and not for accidental, even though the consequences may be the same. However, this is not always so. Under some circumstances accidental behavior (negligent or reckless) may be the basis of criminal liability.

Mens rea is the mental part, the state of mind required to be criminally liable. It is often defined as "a guilty mind" or possessing a criminal intent. It is best defined as the state of mind required to be criminally liable for a certain act. It is sometimes the case that no intent whatsoever is required to be guilty of a crime, although most criminal laws require intent of some degree before criminal liability attaches to an act.

Mens rea is an important concept in criminal law. It is also a confusing one. This is in large part because of the inconsistency and lack of uniformity between criminal statutes and judicial decisions. One author found seventy-nine words and phrases in the United States Criminal Code used to describe mens rea.[1] Often when courts or legislatures use the same term they do so assuming different meanings for the term. For this reason, the drafters of the Model Penal Code attempted to establish uniform terms and definitions for those terms. The Model Penal Code approach is examined later. First, you will learn how the common law treated mens rea.

Mens Rea and the Common Law

One principle under the common law was that there should be no crime if there was no act accompanied by a guilty mind. The Latin phrase that states this principle is "actus non facit reum nisi mens sit rea." Today, under some statutes, no intent is required to be guilty of a crime. Despite this, the principle that "only conscious wrongdoing constitutes crime is deeply rooted in our legal system and remains the rule, rather than the exception."[2]

Many terms have been used to describe a guilty mind. Malicious, mischievous, purposeful, unlawful, intentional, with specific intent, knowing, fraudulent, with

mens rea

(Latin) A state of mind that produces a crime.

an evil purpose, careless, willful, negligent and reckless are examples of terms and phrases used to describe the mental state required to prove guilt.

General, Specific, and Constructive Intent. One common distinction is between *general intent* and **specific intent.** The distinction turns on whether the defendant intended to cause the consequences of the act. If the defendant had a desire or purpose to cause the result of the act, then the defendant possessed specific intent. If the defendant only intended the act, and not the result of that act, then the defendant possessed general intent. For example, Don Defendant throws a large rock at Vern Victim, inflicting a fatal wound. If Defendant only intended to injure Victim, not kill him, then he possessed general intent. However, if Defendant threw the rock hoping it would kill Victim, then he possessed specific intent. The distinction between general and specific intent is often an important one, as many statutes require specific intent for a higher-level crime and general for a lower. In this example, many state statutes would allow Defendant to be charged with first-degree murder if he intended to kill Victim, but only second-degree murder if he only intended to injure Victim.

> **specific intent**
> An intent to commit the exact crime charged, not merely a general intent to commit some crime or merely a generally guilty mind.

If a defendant intends to cause the result, then the fact that the means used to achieve the result are likely to fail is irrelevant. For example, assume Defendant desires to cause the death of Victim. One day, while walking down a street, Defendant notices Victim far away. Defendant picks up a rock and hurls it toward Victim, hoping it will strike Victim and kill him, although because of the distance he does not expect the rock to strike its intended target. However, all those afternoons practicing his baseball pitch paid off, and the rock hit Victim in the head, killing him instantly. The fact that Defendant threw the rock with an intent to kill is enough to establish Defendant's specific intent. The fact that the act is unlikely to be successful is no defense.

Specific intent may also be proved, in some jurisdictions, by showing that the defendant possessed knowledge of a particular fact or illegality. This requirement of knowledge is known as *scienter.* In jurisdictions that require such knowledge, if an individual violates a criminal law while believing that the act engaged in is lawful, then specific intent is lacking, and only general intent can be proven.[3] Scienter often does not require proof of subjective knowledge (what was actually in the defendant's mind), but can be established if the prosecution can prove that the defendant should have known the fact in question.

> **scienter**
> (Latin) Knowingly; with guilty knowledge. [pronounce: si-*en*-ter]

Often without scienter no crime exists to punish. Consider the crime of receiving stolen property. If an individual received stolen property, but did so without knowledge that it was stolen, then no crime has been committed. For some crimes that require scienter, the absence of scienter may leave a general-intent crime. If a man strikes a person whom he believes is obstructing traffic, he has committed an assault. If he knew, or should have known, that the person was a police officer attempting to direct traffic, then he may be accountable for the higher crime of assault on a police officer. However, if the police officer was not wearing a uniform and did not announce himself as an officer, then the defendant is liable only for simple assault. Possession of burglary tools and obstruction of justice are also examples: the former requiring knowledge of the tools' character and the latter requiring knowledge of obstruction.

constructive

Inferred, implied, or presumed from the circumstances.

At common law, specific intent could be found in a third type of situation, whenever **constructive** intent could be proven. That is, although the defendant does not intend to cause the result, it is so likely to occur that the law treats the act as one of specific intent. If John fires a handgun at close range at Sally, aiming at her torso, and kills her as a result, it is possible that he could be charged with the specific-intent crime of first-degree murder, even though he only intended to injure her. This is because the possibility of killing someone under those circumstances is significant. However, this may not be true if he aimed at her leg and the weapon discharged improperly, causing the bullet to strike her in the torso. This is because the likelihood of killing someone with a gunshot to the leg is much less than with a gunshot to the upper body. The bullet entered Victim's torso as a result of the malfunction of the gun; it was not Defendant's desire to shoot her in the upper body. As to the amount of probability necessary to prove constructive intent, only "practical or substantial" probability is required, not absolute.[4]

Specific intent can be found in a fourth situation, whenever a defendant intends a result beyond the act taken. This refers to situations when a criminal act is uncompleted. For example, if a man attacks a woman intending to rape her, but she is able to free herself and escape, he may be charged with assault with intent to rape. To prove this charge, the prosecution must show that he assaulted the victim with the specific intent of raping her. Proving that the defendant had a specific intent to assault her is not enough to sustain the intent-to-rape charge, although it would justify a conviction for assault, a lesser crime. Another example is the crime of breaking and entering with the intent to burglarize. Again, the prosecution must prove that the defendant intended to steal from the home after the entry and did not complete the burglary for some reason. Proving that the defendant broke in and entered, but had no intent to steal, will support a conviction for breaking and entering, but not intent to commit burglary.

General intent is much easier to define, as it is simply the desire to act. In most situations, if the prosecution can show that a defendant intended to take the act prohibited, then general intent is proved. Generally, no desire to cause a particular consequence is required. So, if you fire a gun without a desire to kill someone, but the bullet does kill a person, you possess a general intent and may be prosecuted for a general-intent homicide.

Some jurisdictions require more than simply a desire to act to prove general intent. In those states some level of negligence must be proven. Consider the following two examples: Rural Defendant has lived on a farm for more than twenty years. Defendant's nearest neighbor is over three miles away, and Defendant routinely target shoots in his backyard. He has never encountered anyone in the area where he shoots, and everyone who lives in the community knows of his practice. One day, while target shooting, he accidently shoots and kills a trespasser he did not know was on his property. In the second example, Metro Defendant likes to hunt on weekends. One weekend Metro and his friend were hunting, and Metro lost sight of his friend. Eager to capture his first deer of the season, Metro fired into a bush in which he observed some movement. It was Metro's friend that was in the bush, and Metro's gunshot inflicted a fatal wound.

In both examples the defendants had no desire to harm the individuals shot, and both possessed the intent to fire the weapon. A strict construction of general and specific intent results in both committing a general-intent murder. However, in some jurisdictions Rural may be free from liability because he appears to have been less reckless or negligent than Metro, who should have considered the possibility that it could have been his friend he was firing at.

This discussion has not exhausted the many definitions and distinctions that exist for specific and general intent. In the *Carson* case, it appears that the Court of Appeals for the District of Columbia has created a hybrid general-specific intent for the crime of cruelty to children.

 CASE

JANET A. CARSON, APPELLANT V. UNITED STATES, APPELLEE

556 A.2d 1076, 1989 D.C.
App. LEXIS 57 (1989)

On June 4, 1985, Janet Carson arrived home from work at about 3:45 P.M. and was informed by one of her children that a fuse needed replacement. While looking for a fuse, appellant noticed that eight dollars were missing from her dresser drawer. She called her children—thirteen-year-old Cornell, six-year-old Everett, five-year-old Angelica and eight-year-old Charmaine Schmidt—to her bedroom; each child denied knowing anything about the missing money. At that point she went downstairs, and as she returned upstairs she picked up an electrical cord; she later testified that she routinely used the cord to discipline the children. She again asked the children about the missing money, and they again denied any knowledge of the money's disappearance. Appellant then whipped each of the children several times.

The next day at the school attended by Everett, Angelica, and Charmaine, school officials noticed marks and bruises on the children. Detective Harmon of the Metropolitan Police Department went to the school and took the three children to Children's Hospital. Everett's abrasions were cleaned and bandaged; the other two children received no treatment.

Appellant was subsequently charged with three counts of cruelty to children. . . . [Ms. Carson was convicted and sentenced to thirty days on each count, which was suspended to one year's probation. She appealed the conviction and this is the opinion of the appellate court.]

Before considering appellant's claim that the evidence was insufficient to support her conviction, we must first determine the mens rea required for conviction under D.C. Code § 22–901. We conclude that the offense is a general intent crime, which also requires a showing of malice. . . .

Section 22–901 provides in pertinent part:

Any person who shall torture, cruelly beat, abuse, or otherwise willfully maltreat any child under the age of 18 years . . . shall be deemed guilty of a misdemeanor, and, when convicted thereof, shall be subject to punishment by a fine of not more than $250, or by imprisonment for a term not exceeding 2 years, or both.

The [D.C. Jury Instructions] define the elements of the offense as follows:
1. That the defendant tortured, cruelly beat, abused or otherwise maltreated a child;
2. That at the time of the incident, the child was under the age of 18 years; and
3. That the defendant acted willfully, that is, with an evil intent or with bad purpose to maltreat the child. It is not enough that you find that the defendant exercised bad judgment or acted unreasonably. Rather, it is necessary that you

find that the defendant was motivated by an evil intent or state of mind in committing the acts which constitute the offense.

* * *

Judicial interpretation of D.C. Code § 22–901 has been limited . . . [T]he United States Court of Appeals for the District of Columbia held that the terms "abuse" and "willfully mistreat" as used in the statute "call for something worse than good intentions coupled with bad judgment," and incorporate "the requirement of an evil state of mind." . . . The cases would seem to teach that cruelty to children is something more than a general intent crime and something less than a specific intent crime.

* * *

In other contexts, this court has equated the terms "evil intent" and "malice." This court has noted that a showing of bad or evil purpose is "necessary to distinguish the mental state required for malice-based offenses from that involved in crimes the conviction for which demands proof no more than general intent or criminal negligence." Thus, if cruelty to children requires proof of something more than general intent, that something more would seem to be malice.

* * *

Having determined the mens rea required for conviction of cruelty to children, we must now determine whether the government's proof was sufficient to establish the requisite mens rea in this case. Appellant concedes that the record supports the trial court's finding of general intent. However, she argues that the government failed to prove that she acted with malice. She argues that according to her undisputed testimony, she was motivated not by an evil intent, but rather by a "concern for [her] children's welfare and upbringing." At first blush, the record supports her argument as to motivation.

The government argues, however, that to find malice "all that is required [is] a conscious disregard of a known and substantial risk of the harm. . . ."

Malice is a rather slippery concept, not amenable to precise definition. . . . Simply put, we believe that a parent acts with malice when a parent acts out of a desire to inflict pain rather than out of genuine effort to correct the child, or when the parent, in a genuine effort to correct the child, acts with a conscious disregard that serious harm will result.

* * *

In this case, appellant's testimony regarding her motive was not directly contradicted. The government relied basically on the nature of the wounds and the manner of the punishment to establish malice. The government introduced pictures of the injuries sustained by the children and also pointed to the ages of the children, and the fact that appellant used an electrical cord to whip the children as evidence that appellant acted with evil intent, or at least as evidence that appellant acted with a conscious disregard that serious harm (of the nature which would flow from an evil intent) would result.

From our perspective in this court, we cannot conclude that the evidence justifies the inference that appellant acted out of a desire to inflict pain. . . .

The trial court also noted that appellant had "high standards" for her children—"she didn't want them to steal; she didn't want them to use drugs." The court found that appellant had worked hard to make a good life for herself and her children. She had left the welfare rolls and become a policewoman, "supporting all those children on her own." We echo the trial court's sentiment that appellant had a genuine and deep-felt love and concern for her children.

Further, we do not believe that the punishment was so excessive or the manner so egregious as to lead to the conclusion that appellant acted with a conscious disregard of the serious harm which would result. The mother testified that the whippings lasted perhaps a minute. As to the manner of discipline, reasonable people might disagree as to whether whipping with an electrical cord is in itself offensive or no more offensive than the use of commonly employed devices or methods used to exact discipline. We would only note that appellant testified that because the children were jumping around and that because she was eight months pregnant and therefore awkward, the cord made contact on the children's bodies where it otherwise may not have done so.

However, when the manner of punishment, the length of punishment, the nature of the injuries and the ages of the children are viewed as a whole, we cannot say that the trial court was plainly in error in concluding that appellant acted with conscious disregard of the harm which resulted. . . .

Conviction AFFIRMED.

Malum in Se and Malum Prohibitum.   Often crimes are characterized as either malum in se or malum prohibitum. If a crime is inherently evil, it is malum in se. If a crime is not evil in itself, but is only criminal because declared so by a legislature, then it is malum prohibitum. Murder, rape, arson, and mayhem are examples of crimes that are malum in se. Failure to file your quarterly tax report or to get the proper building permit are both crimes malum prohibitum.

The distinction between malum in se and malum prohibitum is used throughout criminal law, but the importance of the distinction is in how it affects intent. Crimes malum in se are treated as requiring an evil intent, and crimes malum prohibitum are not. Some crimes may be both malum in se and malum prohibitum, depending upon the degree of violation. For example, speeding "a little over the limit may be malum prohibitum, but speeding at high speed malum in se."[5] Whether an act is malum prohibitum or in se often determines what crime may be charged. This usually revolves around the issue of foreseeability of harm. In the preceding example, speeding slightly over the limit is not likely to cause another's death, whereas racing through a city thirty miles over the speed limit can foreseeably cause a fatal accident. If while driving four miles over the speed limit the defendant strikes and kills a pedestrian who walks into the driver's path from behind another car, the act is likely to be determined malum prohibitum, and no resulting manslaughter charge will follow. However, the same may not be true if the driver is traveling thirty miles over the speed limit at the time the accident occurs.

Although some jurisdictions no longer distinguish between crimes malum in se and malum prohibitum, many still do. What crimes fall into each category is determined by judicial decision. Thus the case law in your jurisdiction must be researched to determine where the crime in question falls.

Transferred Intent.   Whenever a person intends a harm, but because of bad aim or other cause the intended harm befalls another, the intent is transferred

transferred intent

The principle that if an unintended illegal act results from the intent to commit a crime, that act is also a crime.

from the intended victim to the unintended victim. This is the doctrine of **transferred intent.** If John Defendant observes a neighbor burning the American flag and in anger shoots at him, missing him but killing William, the doctrine of transferred intent permits prosecution of Defendant as if he intended to kill William.

There are limits on the doctrine of transferred intent. First, the harm that actually results must be similar to the intended harm. If the harms are substantially different, then the intent does not transfer. For example, if A throws a baseball at B's window, hoping to break it, and the ball instead hits C in the head and kills him, it cannot be said that the intent to break the window transfers to C and that A can be punished for intentionally killing C. A may be criminally liable for a lesser crime, such as involuntary manslaughter, depending upon the amount of negligence involved, but he is not responsible for intentionally causing C's death.

A second limitation on the doctrine is that the transfer cannot increase the defendant's liability. Another way of stating this is that any defenses the defendant has against the intended victim are transferred to the unintended victim. For example, A shoots at B in self-defense, but hits C, inflicting a fatal wound. Because A had a valid defense if B had been killed by the shot, then A also has a defense as to C. In this case A has committed no crime. In some situations a defense may only limit a person's criminal liability to a lesser charge. You will learn later that certain defenses negate specific intent, but not general intent. One such defense is intoxication. Assault is a general-intent crime, whereas assault with an intent to kill is a specific-intent crime. Intoxication may be a defense to the higher assault with an intent to kill, but not assault. So, if A, while intoxicated, hurls a knife at B, but hits C, A may be charged with assault, because intoxication would be no defense if he hit B. A would have a defense against the specific intent crime of assault with intent to kill, so the same defense is available for harm to C.

Strict Liability

strict liability

Guilt of a criminal offense even if you had no criminal intention (mens rea).

strict liability crimes

Crimes or offenses in which mens rea or criminal intent is not an element. Such offenses include regulatory crimes, petty offenses, and infractions.

At the beginning of this chapter it was noted that some acts are criminal although no mens rea accompanies the prohibited act. These crimes are proven simply by showing that the act was committed, and no particular mental state has to be proved at all. This is **strict liability,** or liability without fault, and is an exception to the common-law requirement that there be both an evil mind and an evil act to have a crime. The term *strict liability* is not used in all jurisdictions. Further, the term also has a tort meaning. Do not confuse criminal liability without fault with tort strict liability. However, for convenience, the phrase "strict liability" is used in this text.

Strict liability crimes usually are minor violations, punished by fines and not incarceration. However, strict liability is permitted for felonies and may be punished with incarceration.

Most traffic violations, such as running a stoplight and speeding, are examples of strict liability crimes. Statutory rape is treated as a strict liability crime in most states; therefore, the accused adult cannot claim that he or she had a mistaken belief that the minor was above the statutory age when the two had sexual intercourse. There are many other strict liability crimes in every state, and legislatures are increasingly using the strict liability standard when declaring acts illegal.

It is common for crimes that are malum prohibitum to be strict liability, whereas crimes malum in se usually require proof of some mental state. It is also generally true that violation of crimes malum prohibitum is not punished as severely as violation of crimes malum in se.

Crimes with strict liability are often termed "public offenses" or "regulatory offenses." The term *regulatory* is often used because the criminal prohibition has either been established by an administrative agency through rulemaking, is enforced by an administrative agency, or is part of a comprehensive regulatory scheme established by a legislature.

In many cases, strict liability laws deal with potential, rather than actual, harms. For example, a murder statute can only be applied after someone has been murdered. However, many strict liability offenses deal with violations and no harm. For example, running a stoplight, speeding, or failing to have adequate fire extinguishers in your business may or may not result in an injury. Regardless of whether harm results, you are liable for the offense. This is considered regulatory because the purpose is to induce compliance (using the easy proof standard) with the law, rather than to punish for caused harm. Increased compliance is a result of an awareness by people that violation alone means liability; hence, they are more cautious and less likely to engage in the prohibited conduct. Of course, this argument can be made to justify making all crimes strict liability. The idea of not requiring any intent for acts to be criminal is contrary to American values of fairness and justice, and this is probably the reason why the strict liability standard has not been extended to all crimes.

Strict liability is only available for crimes defined by legislatures. With little restriction, legislatures may define an act as criminal without requiring proof of intent. However, in jurisdictions that continue to recognize common-law crimes, mens rea must be an element.

Many have alleged that liability without fault is violative of the Constitution, but the United States Supreme Court has upheld strict liability statutes in most instances.[6] Despite this, if a legislature declares that a crime that has traditionally required proof of specific intent or purpose has no mens rea requirement, the due process question should be raised. This is especially true if the crime can be punished with a significant jail sentence.

In the *Morissette* case, the defendant entered federal property, a military bombing range, and collected spent bomb casings, which had been on the site for years. The casings were exposed to the weather and were rusting when the defendant removed them. The defendant was charged with converting (stealing) the casings. The defendant was convicted at the trial level, and the United States Supreme Court reversed the conviction.

CASE

MORISSETTE
V.
UNITED STATES
342 U.S. 246 (1952)

The contention that an injury can amount to a crime only when inflicted by intention is no provincial or transient notion. It is universal and persistent in mature systems of law as belief in freedom of the human will and a consequent ability and duty of the normal individual to choose between good and evil. A relation between some mental element and punishment for a harmful act is almost as instinctive as the child's familiar exculpatory "But I didn't mean to," and has afforded the rational basis for a tardy and unfinished substitution of deterrence and reformation in place of retaliation and vengeance as the motivation for public prosecution. . . .

Crime, as a compound concept, generally constituted only from concurrence of an evil-meaning mind with an evil-doing hand, was congenial to an intense individualism and took deep and early root in American soil. As the states codified the common law of crimes, even if their enactments were silent on the subject, their courts assumed that the omission did not signify disapproval of the principle but merely recognized that intent was so inherent in the idea of the offense that it required no statutory definition.

However, [some crimes fall into a] category of another character, with very different antecedents and origins. The crimes there involved depend on no mental element but consist only of forbidden acts or omissions. . . . The industrial revolution multiplied the number of workmen exposed to injury from increasingly powerful and complex mechanisms, driven by freshly discovered sources of energy, requiring higher precautions by employers. Traffic of velocities, volumes and varieties unheard of came to subject the wayfarer to intolerable casualty risks if the owners and drivers were not to observe new cares and uniformities of conduct. Congestion of cities and crowding of quarters called for health and welfare regulations undreamed of in simpler times. Wide distribution of goods became an instrument of wide distribution of harm when those who dispersed food, drink, drugs, and even securities, did not comply with reasonable standards of quality, integrity, disclosure and care. Such dangers have engendered increasingly numerous and detailed regulations which heighten the duties of those in control of particular industries, trades, properties, or activities that affect public health, safety or welfare.

. . . Many violations of such regulations result in no direct or immediate injury to person or property but merely create the danger or probability of injury which the law seeks to minimize.

* * *

Stealing, larceny, and its variants and equivalents, were among the earliest offenses known to the law that existed before legislation [common law]. . . . State courts of last resort, on whom fall the heaviest burden of interpreting criminal law in this country, have consistently retained the requirement of intent in larceny-type offenses. If any state has deviated, the exception has neither been called to our attention nor disclosed by our research.

We hold that the mere omission from [the conversion statute] of any mention of intent will not be construed as eliminating that element from the crimes denounced.

legislative history

The background documents and records of hearings related to the enactment of a bill.

Strict Liability and Statutory Construction. The problem addressed by the Supreme Court in *Morissette* occurs often: What is the mens rea requirement when a statute does not provide for such? That decision depends on many factors. First, the **legislative history** of the statute may indicate whether the crime was intended to have a mens rea requirement. The statements of members of legislatures while debating the law (before it became law and was a bill), reports of committees of Congress, and other related materials may indicate whether the legislature intended a mens rea requirement. Second, courts look to whether the crime existed under the common law. If so, the mens rea used under the common law may be adopted by the court. Other factors include the seriousness of the harm to the public; mens rea standards for other related crimes; the punishment imposed upon conviction; the burden that would be placed on the prosecution if mens rea were required; and rules of statutory construction.

Generally, the greater the potential harm to the public and the more difficult it is for prosecution to prove mens rea, the more likely a court is to find that strict liability is to be imposed.[7] Although not a significant factor, the amount of penalty can play a role. The greater the penalty, the more likely that some intent will be read into the statute. Also, courts will look to other related statutes for guidance. If a state legislature has consistently required proof of intent for all crimes of larceny and theft, then if a new statute is enacted dealing with a particular theft (i.e., theft of computer information), and that law does not specify the mental state that must be proven, then the court will fill in the missing element with intent.

Finally, courts have rules that must be followed when interpreting a statute. These are known as *canons of* **statutory construction.** You previously learned one of these rules; that is, whenever a statute can be construed as either constitutional or unconstitutional, it must be read as constitutional. Some jurisdictions follow the rule, either by judicial rule (canon) or by statute, that if a criminal statute does not specifically impose strict liability, then the court is to impose a mens rea requirement. *Troiano* is a case from New York, a jurisdiction where such a rule is applied. See Exhibit 3.1 for examples of other canons that are applied in criminal cases.

statutory construction
Determining the meaning of a statute.

 CASE

PEOPLE V. ALICIA TROIANO

552 N.Y.S.2d 541, 1990
N.Y. Misc. LEXIS 90
(1990)

[Defendant was charged with having insufficient brakes on her car and the following facts were stipulated to by the parties:]

On May 1, 1987 at approximately 11:35 P.M. the defendant was involved in a two-car accident. . . . Defendant was the owner and operator of a 1972 Oldsmobile station wagon. . . . The driver of the other vehicle died as a result of injuries suffered in that accident. The decedent failed to yield the right of way at a stop sign at that intersection. The decedent's blood alcohol level was .10%. Both vehicles were impounded. The defendant's vehicle was inspected by Al Stern of Al's Towing Corporation and as a result of that inspection the instant charge was brought. [Mr. Stern testified that the defendant's right rear brake was insufficient under state law guidelines.]

The defendant testified that she had not experienced any problems with the braking system of the car. She did not hear any squeaks or other noises. She did not notice any leaking of brake fluid and was able to stop properly at a stop sign just minutes before the accident. Further, the car had been inspected in September, 1986 and had a proper inspection sticker affixed to the windshield.

The defense also called Mr. Troiano, defendant's husband, who had been employed as an automobile mechanic until 1983. Following Stern's inspection, Mr. Troiano towed the vehicle in question back to his house. He pulled off all four wheels and examined the brake shoes and lining and found the brake lining on the right rear wheel to be a little more than 1/16 of an inch at its thinnest point and, consequently adequate.

* * *

[The statute] provides in pertinent part, "every motor vehicle, operated or driven on the highways of the State, shall be provided with adequate brakes. . . ."

The court will first deal with the question of whether the statute is one of strict liability. The plain language of [the brake statute] does not require a mens rea or a culpable mental state as an element of the crime and in reliance thereon the People have made no attempt to make a prima facie showing that defendant knew or had reason to know of the defect.

"Culpable mental state" means intentional, knowing, reckless or criminally negligent conduct. . . . If the commission of a particular offense or some material element thereof does not require a culpable mental state on the part of the actor, such an offense is one of "strict liability."

It is a well-known principle of statutory construction that absent the legislature's clear indication of an intent to impose strict liability, a statute should be construed to require mens rea. . . . [The court determined that the defendant had to have had knowledge of the defect to be liable and that no such showing had been made. Accordingly, defendant's motion for dismissal was granted.]

EXHIBIT 3.1

Examples of Canons of Construction That Apply in Criminal Cases

CANON	DESCRIPTION
Narrow Construction	Criminal statutes are to be narrowly construed by courts.
Ambiguous Language	Ambiguous language in a statute is to be construed in the defendant's favor or if it is too ambiguous, the statute is void.
Legislative Prerogative	Courts are to be mindful that the source of penal law should be legislatures, not courts. Criminal statutes are to be narrowly construed. This is also known as the Rule of Lenity.
Constitutionality Presumption	Statutes are presumed constitutional and if a court can construe a statute as constitutional or unconstitutional without causing an unfairness to the defendant, the statute is to be construed as constitutional.
Plain Meaning	The plain meaning of a statute shall be enforced unless the result is absurd. If absurd, the court may turn to other evidence (e.g., legislative intent) to assist in interpreting the statute.

Vicarious Liability

The term **vicarious liability** refers to situations in which one person is held accountable for the actions of another. Under vicarious liability, there is no requirement of mens rea, as there is for strict liability, and additionally there is no requirement for an act, at least not by the defendant. The person who is liable for the actions of another need not act, encourage another to act, or intend any harm at all. As is true with vicarious liability in tort law, this situation is most common between employers and employees.

Employers may be liable for the actions of their employees when criminal laws relating to the operation of the business are violated. For example, the owner of a business may be prosecuted for failure to comply with product safety regulations, even though that was a duty delegated to an employee and the owner had no knowledge that the products manufactured were substandard. Vicarious liability is often imposed on those who market food and drugs.[8] This is because of the significant public welfare interest in the quality of these products.

Corporate Liability. **Corporate liability** is a form of vicarious liability. Under the common law, corporations could not be convicted of crimes. However, this is no longer the law.

Corporations, partnerships, and other organizations can be held criminally accountable for the acts of their employees and agents. The agent must be working within the scope of his or her employment for the company to be liable. If an employee of Burger King strikes an enemy while on break in the parking lot of the store, the company is not liable for battery. However, if officers of a corporation send employees into a workplace knowing that it is dangerous and represent to the employees that it is safe, the company may be liable for battery to the employee, or even manslaughter, if death results.

The Model Penal Code provides for corporate liability when the agent is acting within the scope of employment. In addition, it must be shown that the corporation had a duty under the law to take some act, and the act was not done or the act taken by the agent was authorized, requested, commanded, performed, or recklessly tolerated by the board of directors or other high management.[9]

Obviously, companies cannot be incarcerated, so fines are usually imposed. In some instances, **injunctions** may be imposed or a company's status may be altered, suspended, or terminated. Finally, note that corporate liability does not free the agent from criminal liability. In most cases the agent or employee remains criminally liable for his or her act.

The 2002 Enron debacle is an example of corporate crime. As a result of misrepresentations about Enron's financial status by Enron officers and Enron's accounting firm, Arthur Andersen, investors were not aware of Enron's financial distress. Employees and investors lost millions of dollars when the company went bankrupt in December 2001.

In addition to criminal charges against Enron officials, Enron's accounting firm, Arthur Andersen, was charged with obstruction of justice for destroying Enron documents and computer files that were sought by federal authorities. The government alleged that Andersen employees destroyed files containing unfavorable information about Enron that had not been made available to investors.

---

vicarious liability
Legal responsibility for the acts of another person because of some relationship with that person.

corporate liability
The liability of a corporation for the acts of its directors, officers, shareholders, agents, and employees.

injunction
A judge's order to a person to do or to refrain from doing a particular thing.

Andersen, a top five accounting firm, had 85,000 employees and offices the world over at the time of its indictment. Many commentators were critical of the indictment, asserting that the focus of corporate crime should be the responsible individuals, not companies. A conviction of Andersen, it was alleged, could lead to more than a fine (as provided for by statute). Andersen faced demise by losing its Securities and Exchange status and its corporate status. This would result in 85,000 unemployed individuals, most of whom were not parties to the crime. Ultimately, Andersen was convicted of obstruction of justice and was sentenced to five years probation and a $500,000 fine. The terms of its probation included additional fines if it committed new crimes and it was required to obtain approval before it sold its assets.

Current Approaches to Mens Rea

The Model Penal Code and States of Mind.   The drafters of the Model Penal Code chose to reject most of the common-law terms when they addressed mens rea. The result is that the Model Penal Code recognizes four states of mind: purposeful; knowing; reckless; and negligent (see Exhibit 3.2).[10]

To act **purposely,** a defendant must have a desire to cause the result. *Purposely* most closely equates with what the common law called specific intent.

To act **knowingly,** a defendant must be aware of the nature of the act and be practically certain that his or her conduct will cause a particular result, which is not the defendant's objective. The difference between purposeful acts and

purposely
Intentionally; knowingly.

knowingly
With full knowledge and intentionally; willfully.

EXHIBIT 3.2

Mens Rea under the Model Penal Code

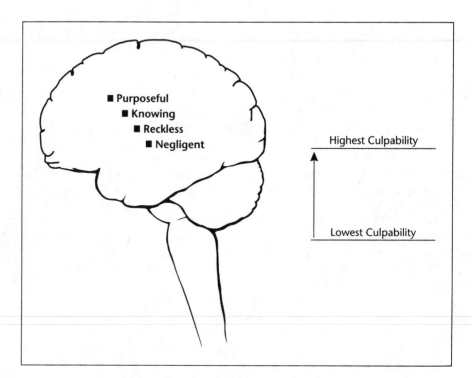

- Purposeful
- Knowing
- Reckless
- Negligent

Highest Culpability

Lowest Culpability

knowing acts is that to be purposeful, one must act intending to cause the particular result. To act knowingly, the defendant must be practically certain (nearly 100 percent positive) that the result will occur, but the defendant is not taking the act to cause that result. For example, if a legitimate moving company owner leases a van to an illegal drug dealer knowing that the van will be used to transport drugs across the country, then the owner has acted knowingly. He has not acted with purpose because it is not his objective to transport the contraband.

The third state of mind recognized by the Model Penal Code is **recklessness.** A person acts recklessly when he or she consciously disregards a substantial and unjustifiable risk that the result will occur. The difference between a knowing act and a reckless act is in the degree of risk. "A person acts 'knowingly' with respect to a result if he is nearly certain that his conduct will cause the result. If he is aware only of a substantial risk, he acts 'recklessly' with respect to the result."[11] The Code says that the risk taken must be one that involves a "gross deviation from the standard of conduct that a law-abiding person would observe in the actor's situation."[12]

The final state of mind is negligence. The definition of negligence is similar to recklessness; that is, there must be a "substantial and unjustifiable risk" taken by the defendant. However, a person acts negligently when there is no conscious awareness of the risk, when there should have been. To act recklessly one must take a risk that amounts to a "gross deviation from the standard of conduct that a law-abiding person would observe in the actor's situation." When a defendant has acted negligently, he or she has failed to perceive (be aware of) the risk altogether, and that failure is a gross deviation from a law-abiding person's standard.

Element Analysis. So far the discussion of culpable states of mind has been limited to one state of mind for each individual crime. For example, under the common law a specific intent to kill must have been proven to establish first-degree murder. This was true of all offenses under the common law; that is, only one state of mind had to be shown. This was true even if the crime had many different elements.

Elements are the parts of a crime. The prosecution must prove all the elements of a crime beyond a reasonable doubt to gain a conviction. For example, the common-law elements of larceny were: (1) The taking and carrying away (2) of personal property (3) of another (4) with an intent to steal. The prosecution has the burden of proving all four elements. If the prosecution fails to prove any element, the defendant must be acquitted. At common law, only one mental state had to be proved: intent to steal. Additionally, the prosecution had to show that the other four elements occurred without reference to mental state. This is known as offense analysis, as the entire offense is thought of as requiring one mental state.

The Model Penal Code, as well as some specific statutes, recognize that the various acts of a crime may involve differing mental states. As such, each element of a crime may have a different mens rea.[13]

Assume that state law prohibits: (1) Notary publics (2) from notarizing documents (3) of known blood relatives (4) of the third degree or closer (degrees define closeness of family relationship). Under the Code, the first two elements

recklessness

Indifference to consequences; indifference to the safety and rights of others. Recklessness implies conduct amounting to more than ordinary negligence.

element

A basic part. For example, some of the *elements* of a cause of action for battery are of an intentional, unwanted physical contact. Each of these things ("intentional," "unwanted," etc.) is one "*element.*"

appear to require no mental state—just the act of a notary notarizing a document. Hence, it would be no defense for the notary to claim that he was signing the document as a witness and not as a notary. The third element requires specific knowledge that the person for whom he notarizes the document is a blood relative. If the notary can prove that there was no reason for him to have known of the relationship, then his knowledge is negated. The last element is likely to be treated as a negligence element. It would be a valid defense for the notary to show that he made a reasonable error as to the degree of the relationship. Attempt to apply element analysis when examining Penal statutes in your state or in your criminal law class.

Proving Mens Rea

At trial the prosecution has the burden of establishing that the defendant possessed the required mental state when the act was committed. Proof of intent can be troublesome to prosecution, especially when the prosecution has to prove subjective intent. *Subjective intent* refers to the motives, intentions, and desires that were in the defendant's mind at the time the act took place. Subjective intent is a defendant's actual intent.

Objective intent is not the defendant's actual intent; rather, it is a legal imposition upon the defendant of what he or she should have known or believed at the time the act occurred. Generally, the law imposes a reasonable person standard. That means that the defendant is expected to have known or believed what a reasonable person would have known at the time of the act. Objective intent is easier to prove than subjective intent. This is because the prosecution does not have to probe directly into a defendant's mind to prove that an intent to harm existed; rather, all that has to be shown is that the defendant should have known that the harm would result.

In most cases defendants do not admit to committing the acts in question. Even when defendants do admit to some acts, they commonly deny intent. For crimes that require intent, admission of the act is not enough to sustain a conviction. The question is, how does a prosecutor gain a conviction for a crime that requires a showing of intent when the defendant denies possessing the required intent? The answer is by using **inferences.**

inference

A fact (or proposition) that is *probably* true because a true fact (or proposition) leads you to believe that the *inferred* fact (or proposition) is also true.

An *inference* is a conclusion that a judge or jury is permitted to make after considering the facts of a case. Imagine that a man walks up to another man and strikes him in the head with a hammer, using great force in his swing. The wound is fatal, and the attacker is charged with first-degree murder. To sustain a first-degree murder charge in this jurisdiction, it must be shown that the man intended to cause the victim's death. The defendant disavows such intent, admitting only that he intended to hit and injure the victim. In such a case the jury would be permitted to infer the defendant's intent to kill the victim from the seriousness of the act. In a jurisdiction that uses the objective standard, the jury could conclude that a reasonable person would have known that the blow from a hammer would cause the victim's death, and the subjective intent of the defendant would not matter.

A **presumption** is a conclusion that must be made by a judge or jury. Most people have heard of the presumption of innocence in criminal law. This presumption is a *rebuttable presumption.* Rebuttable presumptions are conclusions that must be made by a judge or jury, unless disproven by the facts. Hence, defendants are innocent until proven guilty. *Irrebuttable presumptions* are conclusions that must be made by the judge or jury and cannot be disproved. Regardless of what the evidence shows, an irrebuttable presumption stands as a fact.

presumption

A *presumption of law* is an automatic assumption required by law that whenever a certain set of facts shows up, a court must automatically draw certain legal conclusions.

Motive

The reason a person commits a crime is **motive.** More particularly, the reason that leads a person to a desired result or particular action is motive.

motive

The reason why a person does something.

Motive is different from mens rea. Motive leads to mens rea. Motive is concerned with why people act. Mens rea, in contrast, is concerned with whether a person intended to act. For example, greed is a motive for many acts. A bank robber's motive for robbing a bank is greed (or even, possibly, the challenge). The robber's mens rea is neither greed nor the emotional thrill resulting from the risk; rather, it is the intent to take money using force or threat. Said another way, the robber's mens rea (intent) is used to satisfy his or her motive (greed).

Motive is not an element of crimes. Therefore, prosecutors do not have to prove motive to be successful in a prosecution. As a practical matter, however, the trier of fact will want to know why the defendant committed the alleged crime. In many crimes, the motive will be apparent. Greed is easily understood and is imputed by juries to accused thieves. In other crimes, such as murder, there may be no apparent motive, and the prosecutor must establish the defendant's reason for committing the crime. Was the murder motivated by greed (e.g., to gain an inheritance), or by passion (e.g., in revenge for infidelity), or by some other emotion? Usually, the prosecutor will prove motive, but in a case in which the defendant has pleaded insanity, the defendant bears the burden of providing either that there was no motive (e.g., the defendant did not want this to happen, but a mental disease or defect made her do it), or that the motive was the product of insanity (e.g., he believed the decedent was Godzilla).

A bad motive does not make an otherwise lawful act criminal. Conversely, a good motive does not excuse the commission of a crime. The issue is simply whether the prosecution has proven, beyond a reasonable doubt, that all the elements of the crime were committed.

Motive plays a role at sentencing. A good motive may justify a mitigation of sentence, whereas a bad motive may act in the reverse.

In some instances, a good motive may prevent charges from being filed at all. Police and prosecutors do not pursue some cases, even though a crime has been committed, when a person acted with good intentions. Conversely, law enforcement officials may pursue a case more passionately if the defendant acted from an evil motive.

ACTUS REUS

Earlier in this chapter you learned the Latin phrase "actus non facit reum nisi mens sit rea." The phrase expresses the common-law requirement that two essential elements must be present to have a crime: a guilty mind and a guilty act. **Actus reus** is the physical part of a crime; it is the act engaged in by the accused. An act is a physical movement. If Mrs. X shoots and kills Mrs. T, the act is pulling the trigger of the gun.

The Model Penal Code states that a "person is not guilty of an offense unless his liability is based on conduct that includes a voluntary act."[14]

actus reus

(Latin) An act. For example, an "*actus reus*" is a "wrongful deed" (such as killing a person) which, if done with mens rea, a "guilty mind" (such as "*malice aforethought*"), is a crime (such as *first degree* murder).

Voluntariness

To be held criminally liable for one's actions, those actions must be voluntary. To be voluntary, an act must occur as a result of the actor's conscious choice. The person accused must have acted freely, or no liability attaches. The Model Penal Code requires that acts be voluntary and specifically lists the following as being involuntary:

1. reflexes and convulsions;
2. bodily movements during unconsciousness or sleep;
3. conduct during hypnosis or resulting from hypnotic suggestion; and
4. other movements that are not a product of the effort or determination of the actor.[15]

Do not confuse the concepts of mens rea and actus reus. All that is required to have an act is a choice by the defendant to act. No evil intent is required to have an act; that is a question of mens rea. Say that Jim chooses to swing his arm. As a result he hits Tom. What intent is required to prove battery and whether Jim possessed that intent are questions of mens rea. For actus reus, all that need be known is whether Jim voluntarily chose to swing his arm. His swing would be involuntary if Bill grabbed Jim's arm and moved it, causing it to strike Tom.

In the *Cogdon* case, a woman was acquitted of murdering her daughter because it was determined that her acts were not voluntary.

No defense of insanity was raised in this case. If it had been, the analysis would have been different. In most jurisdictions one cannot claim lack of a voluntary act if insanity is also claimed. In those situations the rules of the insanity defense apply.[16] See Chapter 8 for a complete discussion of insanity as a defense.

Thoughts and Statements as Acts

Thoughts alone are not acts that can be made criminal. People may think evil thoughts, but if there is no act furthering such a thought, there is no crime.

Generally, people are also free to speak. The First Amendment to the United States Constitution protects freedom of speech. When the First Amendment

CASE

KING V. COGDON

Supreme Court of
Victoria (1950)[17]

Mrs. Cogdon was charged with the murder of her only child, a daughter called Pat, aged 19. Pat had for some time been receiving psychiatric treatment for a relatively minor neurotic condition of which, in her psychiatrist's opinion, she was now cured. Despite this, Mrs. Cogdon continued to worry unduly about her. Describing the relationship between Pat and her mother, Mr. Cogdon testified: "I don't think a mother could have thought any more of her daughter. I think she absolutely adored her." On the conscious level, there was no doubt [of] Mrs. Cogdon's deep attachment to her daughter.

To the charge of murdering Pat, Mrs. Cogdon pleaded not guilty. Her story, though somewhat bizarre, was not seriously challenged by the Crown, and led to her acquittal. She told how on the night before her daughter's death she had dreamt that their house was full of spiders and that these spiders were crawling all over Pat. In her sleep, Mrs. Cogdon left the bed she shared with her husband, went into Pat's room and awakened to find herself violently brushing at Pat's face, presumably to remove the spiders. This woke Pat. Mrs. Cogdon told her she was just tucking her in. At the trial, she testified that she still believed, as she had been told, that the occupants of a nearby house bred spiders as a hobby, preparing nests for them behind the pictures on their walls. It was these spiders that in her dreams had invaded their home and attacked Pat. There had also been a previous dream in which ghosts had sat at the end of Mrs. Cogdon's bed and she had said to them, "Well, you have come to take Pattie." It does not seem fanciful to accept the psychological explanation of these spiders and ghosts as the projections of Mrs. Cogdon's subconscious hostility towards her daughter; a hostility which was itself rooted in Mrs. Cogdon's own early life and marital relationship.

The morning after the spider dream she told her doctor of it. He gave her a sedative and, because of the dream and certain previous difficulties she had reported, discussed the possibility of psychiatric treatment. That evening Mrs. Cogdon suggested to her husband that he attend his lodge meeting, and asked Pat to come with her to the cinema. After he had gone, Pat looked through the paper, not unusually found no tolerable programme, and said that as she was going out the next evening she thought she would rather go to bed early. Later while Pat was having a bath preparatory to retiring, Mrs. Cogdon went into her room, put a hot water bottle in the bed, turned back the bedclothes, and placed a glass of hot milk beside the bed ready for Pat. She then went to bed herself. There was some desultory conversation between them about the war in Korea, and just before she put out her light Pat called out to her mother, "Mum, don't be so silly worrying about the war, it's not on our front step yet."

Mrs. Cogdon went to sleep. She dreamt that "the war was all around the house," that the soldiers were in Pat's room, and that one soldier was on the bed attacking Pat. This is all of the dream that she could later recapture. Her first "waking" memory was of running from Pat's room, out of the house to the home of her sister who lived next door. When her sister opened the front door Mrs. Cogdon fell into her arms crying, "I think I've hurt Pattie."

In fact Mrs. Cogdon had, in her somnambulistic state, left her bed, fetched an axe from the woodheap, entered Pat's room, and struck her two accurate forceful blows on the head with the blade of the axe, thus killing her.

* * *

At all events the jury believed Mrs. Cogdon's story . . . [Mrs. Cogdon] was acquitted because the act of killing itself was not, in law, regarded as her act at all. . . .

applies, speech may not be made criminal. There are, however, limits to First Amendment protection of speech. Inciting riots, treason, solicitation, conspiracy, and causing imminent harm to others are examples of speech that may be prohibited. You will learn more about the First Amendment protection of speech later.

Personal Status as an Act

Generally, a person's status cannot be declared criminal. Illness, financial status, race, sex, and religion are examples of human conditions. Some conditions are directly related to illegal behavior. For example, being addicted to illegal narcotics is a condition that cannot be punished. This is because status is generally believed not to be an act. However, using and selling prohibited narcotics are acts and may be punished.

Vagrancy is one area over which there is a split in legal opinion. Some courts have held that vagrancy may be prohibited; others have determined that vagrancy is a condition and does not constitute a crime. One author noted that there is a "growing body of authority" holding such statutes unconstitutional.[18]

In *Robinson v. California*, 370 U.S. 660 (1962), the United States Supreme Court was called upon to review a California statute that made it a crime "either to use narcotics, or to be addicted to the use of narcotics." The Court reversed Robinson's conviction and in the opinion stated:

> This statute, therefore, is not one which punishes a person for the use of narcotics, for their purchase, sale or possession, or for antisocial or disorderly behavior resulting from their administration. It is not a law which even purports to provide or require medical treatment. Rather, we deal with a statute which makes the "status" of narcotic addiction a criminal offense, for which the offender may be prosecuted "at any time before he reforms." California has said that a person can be continuously guilty of this offense, whether or not he has ever used or possessed any narcotics within the state, and whether or not he has been guilty of any antisocial behavior there.
>
> It is unlikely that any State at this moment in history would attempt to make it a criminal offense for a person to be mentally ill, or a leper, or to be afflicted with a venereal disease. A State might determine that the general health and welfare require that the victims of these and other human afflictions be dealt with by compulsory treatment, involving quarantine, confinement, or sequestration. But, in the light of contemporary human knowledge, a law which made a criminal offense of such a disease would doubtless be universally thought of to be an infliction of cruel and unusual punishment in violation of the Eighth and Fourteenth Amendments. . . .
>
> We cannot but consider the statute before us as of the same category. . . . We hold that a state law which imprisons a person thus afflicted as a criminal, even though he has never touched any narcotic drug within the State or been guilty of any irregular behavior there, inflicts a cruel and unusual punishment in violation of the Fourteenth Amendment. . . .

While personal status may not be criminalized, it may be subject to the regulatory authority of the state. Individuals who are mentally ill and who pose a danger to themselves or others may be civilly committed, for example. This includes the commitment of sexual predators.[19] This topic is discussed more fully in Chapter 4.

Possession as an Act

Possession of certain items, such as narcotics, burglary tools, or dangerous weapons, may be made criminal. Possession is not, strictly speaking, an act. Possession does not involve an active body movement; rather, possession is a passive state of being. Even so, most possession laws have been upheld.

Jurisdictions differ in what is required to prove possession. Some require that actual possession be shown, whereas others allow proof of constructive possession. Constructive possession is used to extend criminal liability to those who never exercised actual possession, but had dominion and control over the contraband. A person who is the owner and driver of a car may never possess the cocaine that his passenger is using, but the law says that the driver is in constructive possession because the dominion and control over the auto belong to the driver. In essence, the law imposes a duty on people to remove illegal items from the area over which they have dominion and control. Failure to comply with such a duty is treated as an act and can lead to criminal liability.

One problem with crimes of possession is the possibility of convicting people who had no knowledge of the existence of illegal items in an area under their dominion and control. An owner of a house has dominion and control over the guest room, but may not be aware that a guest has brought illegal items into the room. Most jurisdictions have remedied this problem by requiring knowledge of the presence of the goods. The Model Penal Code also uses such a test. The Code states that possession is an act as long as the "possessor knowingly procured or received the thing possessed or was aware of his control thereof for a sufficient period to have been able to terminate his possession."[20] Under the Code, possession can be actual or constructive. However, if constructive, the possessor must have known of the items for a period of time long enough to permit the possessor to terminate possession. So, if the owner of the house only discovered the cocaine minutes before the police arrived to search the premises, no possession could be found on the owner's behalf.

Finally, one person or many people can be in possession of items. Using the preceding example, assume that two or more people jointly owned the home in question. All of the owners could be liable, if it was determined that all had constructive possession and adequate time to remove the cocaine from the house. It is possible that fewer than all of the owners knew of the cocaine, and, as such, did not have constructive possession. Each person who is alleged to have dominion and control (constructive possession) must be examined individually, and separate decisions as to their individual liability must be made.

Omissions as Acts

Generally, only acts are prohibited by criminal law. Rarely does criminal law require a person to act. However, in some situations people have a duty to act, and failure to act is criminal. An **omission** is a failure to act when required to do so by criminal law.

It is often the case that a person who may have a moral duty to act does not have a legal duty to act. In most instances people do not have a legal duty to assist one another in times of need. It would not be criminal in most jurisdictions for an excellent swimmer to watch another drown. Nor would it be criminal to watch another walk into a dangerous situation, such as a bank robbery in progress, if the observer had no connection with the criminal event. There are exceptions to this rule. To be liable for a failure to act, a person must have a "duty" to act. The duty to act can come about in many different ways.

Duty Imposed by Statute.   First, criminal statutes may impose a duty to act. The following are examples of duties imposed by statutes: businesses that store or dispose of toxic materials are required to file certain documents; taxpayers are required to file tax returns; and those involved in automobile accidents are required to stop at the scene of the accident.

Under the common law, in most instances, people had no duty to assist others whose lives were in danger. Today criminal statutes may impose liability for failure to assist someone in danger. A few states have enactments that directly change the common-law rule and require people to assist others who are in danger. However, even in those jurisdictions, rescue need not be attempted if the rescuer's life would thereby be endangered.[21] Imposing criminal liability for not rescuing someone in danger of losing life or limb continues to be the exception and not the rule. However, no legal reason prevents all jurisdictions from requiring people to rescue one another when there is no danger associated with the rescue.

At common law, several exceptions to the "no duty to assist people in danger" rule evolved. Many of these are discussed in the following paragraphs. Bear in mind that many legislatures have codified one or more of these exceptions. In those instances, the duty is imposed by statute and not the common law.

Duty by Relationship.   A duty to assist another can be created by the existence of a personal relationship. The most common examples are parent to child and spouse to spouse. In such personal relationships, a level of dependence exists that gives rise to criminal liability for failure to assist the party who is in danger. There is no bright-line rule for determining if a duty is owed. The more that one party becomes dependent upon another party or the parties become dependent upon one another, the more likely that a duty to assist is created.

Generally, any time a joint enterprise is undertaken by two or more parties, it can be assumed that a duty to assist one another during that enterprise is created. For example, if two people decide to go river rafting, they must rescue one another during that rafting trip, provided that the rescuer is not endangered by attempting the rescue.

In the parent-child relationship, a parent can be guilty of manslaughter if the child dies as a result of the parent's failure to seek medical attention for the child when he or she is sick, or for failing to pull the child out of a pool when the child is drowning. The same would be true of a spouse. If a wife permitted her husband to die when she could have saved his life by summoning medical attention, she could be criminally liable. In addition, it has been held that employers owe a duty to assist their employees. For example, the master of a ship must attempt to rescue a seaman who has fallen overboard.[22]

Duty by Contract.   A duty to act can be created in a third way, by contract. For example, physicians are hired to care for the health of their patients. If a doctor watches as a patient slowly dies, doing nothing to save the patient's life when there were measures that could have been taken, the doctor is liable for homicide. The same is true of a lifeguard. The lifeguard is hired to save those who are drowning, and if a lifeguard sits and watches a swimmer drown when the swimmer could have been saved, the lifeguard is liable for homicide.

Remember, the general rule is that people owe no duty to rescue others. So, if an expert swimmer happens to be on the beach when another person is drowning, the expert swimmer can watch the person drown without risking criminal liability.

Assumption of Duty.   Even though the general rule is that people do not have a duty to rescue strangers, it is possible, either expressly or by one's actions, to make an *assumption of duty*. The assumption is express if it is stated orally or in writing. Assumption is different from duty premised on contract, in that assumptions are gratuitous. If Sidney is at a pool and agrees to care for another's child, then Sidney has assumed the duty expressly. If the child falls into the pool, and Sidney takes no action to save the child, Sidney is liable for murder if the child drowns.

It is possible through one's actions to assume the duty to rescue someone. Assume that Sidney is now at a lake. One person, David, is swimming, and three other people are relaxing on the beach. David begins to scream for help. Sidney jumps up and dives into the water to rescue David. Halfway out to David, he changes his mind and returns to shore. By the time he returns to shore, it is too late for someone else to make the swim to David, and David dies. In this case, Sidney assumed the duty of the rescue by beginning the rescue attempt. However, whether Sidney is liable for murder depends on what condition the drowning person was left in after Sidney changed his mind. If Sidney's actions caused the other three people on the beach to fail to attempt a rescue, then Sidney's actions left David in a worse condition than he would have been in had Sidney not begun the rescue. However, if Sidney's actions did not prevent anyone else from attempting a rescue, then Sidney's action did not put David in a worse situation, and Sidney is not liable for murder, even if the other person fails in the rescue attempt.

Finally, note that we can easily change this last example into an express assumption. All that has to be added is a statement by Sidney to the others on the beach that he will swim out and rescue David. Such a statement, if it caused others to forgo a rescue attempt, is an express assumption of duty.

Creating Danger.   Any time a person creates the circumstance that endangers a stranger, a duty to save the stranger is created. This is true whether the danger was caused intentionally or negligently. So, if an arsonist sets fire to a house that is believed to be empty and is discovered not to be, the arsonist must attempt to save anyone inside. If not, the arsonist is also a murderer. The same would be true of a negligently caused fire. If an electrician begins a fire in a home and does nothing to warn the inhabitants, the electrician is also liable for murder.

Causation

Some acts are criminal even though the prohibited result does not occur. For example, it is a crime to lie when testifying in court (the crime of perjury). Assume that the purpose of the lie is to deceive the jury and change the outcome of the case. Even if no juror, or anyone else for that matter, believes the lie, and the purpose is not achieved, it is a crime. Causation is not an issue in such crimes.

For crimes that do require a particular result, the act must be the "cause" of the result. In criminal law, two forms of causation exist: factual and legal. If either of these "causes" is missing, then a defense as to the intent of the crime exists. Even if so, the actor may be convicted of a lower, non-intent crime.

An act is the *cause in fact* of the result if the result would not have occurred unless the act occurred. This is known as the *sine qua non* test, which means that "but for" the conduct the harm would not have resulted.

Legal cause must also be proved. Legal causation focuses on the degree of similarity between the defendant's intended result and the actual result. It also examines the similarity between the intended manner used to bring about a result and the actual manner that caused the result. Generally, the greater the similarity between the purpose and the result, and the manner intended and the manner that actually caused the result, the more likely that the defendant is the legal cause. Legal cause is also commonly referred to as **proximate cause.** *Proximate* means nearly, next to, or close. In the context of criminal causation, it refers to the relationship between the act and the result. The result must be a consequence of the act, not a coincidence. A happening is proximately caused by an act if a reasonable person would have foreseen and expected the result. This is called **foreseeability.**

Most problems raised in this area involve legal causation, not factual causation. This is because, to prove factual causation, it must be shown that the defendant's action set into motion the events that led to the prohibited result. The question that should be asked is, had the defendant not acted, would the result have happened? If the answer is no, then the defendant is the factual cause. Determining legal causation is more troublesome, however.

Let us examine a few examples. Hank shoots Mark intending to kill him. Mark dies from the gunshot wound. Hank is the factual cause of the murder because it was his conduct that caused Mark to die. To state it another way, "but for" Hank's act Mark would not have died. Hank is also the legal cause of Mark's death because the resulting death is identical to Hank's intention.

Now assume that Hank intended only to injure Mark, not to kill him. Accordingly, he shot Mark in the arm. Mark then contacted a hospital, which

legal cause

The proximate cause of an injury; probable cause; cause that the law deems sufficient.

proximate cause

The "legal cause" of an accident or other injury (which may have several actual causes). The *proximate cause* of an injury is not necessarily the closest thing in time or space to the injury and not necessarily the event that set things in motion because "proximate cause" is a legal, not a physical concept.

foreseeable

The degree to which the consequences of an action *should* have been anticipated, recognized, and considered beforehand. *Not* hindsight.

dispatched an ambulance. The paramedics who arrived to assist Mark negligently administered a dangerous medication, which caused his death. Hank continues to be the factual cause of Mark's death, because if he had not injured Mark the medical attention that ended Mark's life would not have been necessary. However, Hank is not the legal cause of Mark's death. This is because the result greatly differs from Hank's intent. There is not enough similarity between Hank's purpose when he shot Mark (to cause an injury) and the resulting harm (Mark's death).

Note that it is common for legal cause to be lacking when an **intervening cause** exists, as it does in the previous example. An *intervening cause* is a happening that occurs after the initial act and changes the outcome. Intervening causes act to block the connection between an act and the result, because the intervening cause changes what would have been the result if the result had flowed freely from the act. Intervening causes can negate or lower criminal liability for the particular result. However, lower crimes may continue to be punishable. In the preceding example, the intervening cause is the negligent medical care of the paramedics. Hank's intent was not to cause Mark's death, and, as such, he was not the legal cause of Mark's death. Of course, Hank may also have a mens rea defense.

intervening cause
A cause of an accident or other injury that will remove the blame from the wrongdoer who originally set events in motion.

Assume that Hank shot Mark intending to kill him, but because Hank is a poor shot he only injured Mark. As before, the paramedics who treat Mark negligently administer the wrong medication and cause his death. Again, Hank is the factual cause of Mark's death. Whether he is the legal cause is debatable. Even though the intended result occurred, it occurred in a manner entirely unintended. If the manner in which the result occurs differs significantly from the manner that was intended, the defendant may not be liable. This appears consistent with common notions of fairness—why should Hank be liable for murder when at least part of the blame belongs to the paramedics? Courts are split on this issue. Some would find that Hank is liable for intent murder, whereas others would hold Hank liable for a lower murder.

If a victim suffers the intended injury while attempting to avoid the injury, the defendant is liable for the crime, even though the manner is entirely different than intended. So if Mark is struck and killed by a bus while running from Hank, who intends to stab Mark to death, Hank is considered both the legal and factual cause of Mark's death. There is a limit to this theory; that is, there must be some nexus between the unintended manner and the act. If a reasonable person would not have expected the result to occur, the defendant is not liable. So, if Mark was not killed by a passing bus, but rather by a hit on the head by a piano accidentally dropped by movers, Hank is not the legal cause of his death. This is true even though Mark would not have happened to be under the piano if he were not running from Hank.

In the rare instance where two events happen simultaneously, and both could be the legal cause of the outcome, then both are treated as the legal cause. This is true even if only one event was the actual cause. For example, if two people shoot a victim at the same moment, then both are liable for murder. However, it is possible that only one actually caused the death. If it is not possible to determine which bullet was the actual cause of death, then both people are liable. If it can be determined which bullet was responsible for killing the victim, then the other party is relieved of responsibility for murder (although not attempted murder).

Even though the preceding examples dealt with purposeful crimes, remember that the principle applies to all crimes that require a particular result. The result need not be one that comes about purposefully or intentionally. Crimes of recklessness and negligence may require a specific result to be criminal. Reckless homicide requires that the behavior that is reckless actually cause a death.

The Model Penal Code also requires that the conduct in question be the actual result or cause of the result. Also, under the Model Penal Code, if a particular result is necessary to prove a crime, then the "element is not established unless the actual result is a probable consequence of the actor's conduct." Further, the Code states that the crime is not proven if the actual result is different from the defendant's purpose, unless:

1. The resulting harm is the same, however it occurred to the wrong person or thing (transferred intent).
2. The actual harm is not as great or serious as intended.
3. The actual harm involves the same kind of injury or harm as intended and is not *too remote or accidental* in its occurrence to have a bearing on the actor's liability.

These apply to all levels of culpability under the Code—that is, purposeful, knowing, reckless, and negligent—and must be adjusted accordingly. So, if the crime is one of recklessness or negligence, then the Code's criteria should be viewed in light of risks and probable results and not purpose.[23]

The phrase "too remote or accidental" is the Code's proximate cause requirement. It is the same as discussed earlier, except that the drafters of the Code chose not to use the phrase "proximate cause." In *People v. Warner-Lambert Co.*, a company and some of its officers were indicted for manslaughter and negligent homicide. The charges stemmed from an industrial accident at one of

 CASE

PEOPLE V. WARNER-LAMBERT CO.

51 N.Y.2d 295, 414 N.E.2d 660 (1980), *cert. denied*, 450 U.S. 1031 (1981)

On the day on which the explosion occurred, Freshen-Up gum, which is retailed in the shape of a square tablet with a jelly-like center, was being produced at the Warner-Lambert plant by a process in which filled ropes of the gum were passed through a bed of magnesium stearate (MS), a dry,

dustlike lubricant which was applied by hand, then into a die-cut punch (a Uniplast machine) which was sprayed with a cooling agent (liquid nitrogen), where the gum was formed into the square tablets. Both the MS (normally an inert, organic compound) and the liquid nitrogen were employed to prevent the chicle from adhering to the sizing and cutting machinery, the tendency to adhere being less if a dry lubricant was used and the punch was kept at a low temperature. The process produced a dispersal of MS dust in the air and an accumulation of it at the base of the Uniplast machine and on overhead pipes;

some also remained ambient in the atmosphere in the surrounding area.

Both MS and liquid nitrogen are considered safe and are widely used in the industry. In bulk, MS will only burn or smoulder if ignited; however, like many substances, if suspended in the air in sufficient concentration the dust poses a substantial risk of explosion if ignited. . . . Liquid nitrogen is highly volatile, is easily ignited and, if ignited, will explode. Among possible causes of such ignition of either liquid oxygen or ambient MS are electrical or mechanical sparks.

* * *

There was proof that an inspection of the plant by Warner-Lambert's insurance carrier in February, 1976, had resulted in advice to the insured that the dust condition in the Freshen-Up gum production area presented an explosion hazard and that the MS concentration was above the [low point where explosion could occur], together with recommendations for installation of a dust exhaust system and modification of electrical equipment to meet standards for dust areas. Although a variety of proposals for altering the dust condition were considered by the individual defendants in consultations and communications with each other and some alterations in the MS application were made, both ambient and settled MS dust were still present on November 21, 1976.

* * *

The issue before us, however, is whether defendants could be held criminally liable for what actually occurred, on theories of reckless or

negligent conduct, based on the evidence submitted to this Grand Jury, viewed in the light most favorable to the People. The focus of our attention must be on the issue of culpability, taking into account the conduct of the defendants and the factors of foreseeability and of causation, all of which in combination constitute the ultimate amalgam on which criminal liability may or may not be predicated.

First, we look at the evidence as to the actual event or chain of events which triggered the explosion—evidence which may only be characterized as hypothetical and speculative. . . . The prosecution hypothesizes that under what it describes as "the most plausible of theories" the initial detonation was attributable to mechanical sparking. . . .

Another explanation for the initial explosion was offered by an expert called by the prosecution who hypothesized that liquid oxygen . . . dripped onto settled MS dust at the base of the Uniplast, became trapped there and then, when subjected to the impact caused by a moving metal part, reacted violently, causing ignition of already dispersed MS.

Viewed most favorably to the People, the proof with respect to the actual cause of the explosion is speculative only, and as to at least one of the major hypotheses—that involving oxygen liquefaction—there was no evidence that the process was foreseeable or known to any of the defendants. In sum, there was no proof sufficient to support a finding that defendants foresaw or should have foreseen the physical cause of the explosion. This being so there was not legally sufficient evidence to establish the offenses charged or any lesser included offense.

Warner-Lambert's plants. The high court of New York dismissed the indictments, finding that the defendants were not the proximate cause of the plant employees' deaths because the explosion that caused their deaths was not foreseeable.

The "Year-and-a-Day Rule."   At common law, a person could not be charged with murder if the victim did not die within one year and one day after the act took place. The rule was one of causation. It was developed to prevent a conviction for murder at a time in history when medical science could not precisely determine the actual cause of a person's death. If a person lived for more than a year and a day after being injured by a defendant's acts and then died, it was assumed that medical science could not pinpoint the exact cause of death and that to hold the defendant liable would be unjust. It is questionable, in light of the advances in medicine, whether the rule should continue to exist. It has been abolished in many states.[24] In Rogers v. Tennessee (2001) the Supreme Court reviewed a conviction in Tennessee that was allowed to stand because the Tennessee courts announced the abrogation of the rule in the case. The court was asked to invalidate the conviction as ex post facto and contrary to due process.

 CASE

ROGERS V. TENNESSEE

532 U.S. 451 (2001)

This case concerns the constitutionality of the retroactive application of a judicial decision abolishing the common law "year and a day rule." At common law, the year and a day rule provided that no defendant could be convicted of murder unless his victim had died by the defendant's act within a year and a day of the act. . . . The Supreme Court of Tennessee abolished the rule as it had existed at common law in Tennessee and applied its decision to petitioner to uphold his conviction. The question before us is whether, in doing so, the court denied petitioner due process of law in violation of the Fourteenth Amendment.

Petitioner Wilbert K. Rogers was convicted in Tennessee state court of second degree murder. According to the undisputed facts, petitioner stabbed his victim, James Bowdery, with a butcher knife on May 6, 1994. One of the stab wounds penetrated Bowdery's heart. During surgery to repair the wound to his heart, Bowdery went into cardiac arrest, but was resuscitated and survived the procedure. As a result, however, he had developed a condition known as "cerebral hypoxia," which results from a loss of oxygen to the brain. Bowdery's higher brain functions had ceased, and he slipped into and remained in a coma until August 7, 1995, when he died from a kidney infection (a common complication experienced by comatose patients).

Approximately 15 months had passed between the stabbing and Bowdery's death which, according to the undisputed testimony of the county medical examiner, was caused by cerebral hypoxia "secondary to a stab wound to the heart.". . .

Based on this evidence, the jury found petitioner guilty under Tennessee's criminal homicide statute. The statute, which makes no mention of the year and a day rule, defines criminal homicide simply as "the unlawful killing of another person which may be first degree murder, second degree murder, voluntary manslaughter, criminally negligent homicide or vehicular homicide." . . . Petitioner appealed his conviction to the Tennessee Court of Criminal Appeals, arguing that, despite its absence from the statute, the year and a day rule persisted as part of the common law of Tennessee and, as such, precluded his conviction. The Court of Criminal Appeals rejected that argument and affirmed the conviction. The court held that Tennessee's Criminal Sentencing Reform Act of 1989 (1989 Act), which abolished all common law defenses in criminal actions in Tennessee, had abolished the rule. The court also rejected *455 petitioner's further contention that the legislative abolition of the rule constituted an *ex post facto* violation, noting that the 1989 Act had taken effect five years before petitioner committed his crime. . . . The Supreme Court of Tennessee affirmed on different grounds. The court observed that it had recognized the viability of the year and a day rule in Tennessee in *Percer v. State*, 118 Tenn.

765, 103 S.W. 780 (1907), and that, "[d]espite the paucity of case law" on the rule in Tennessee, "both parties . . . agree that the . . . rule was a part of the common law of this State." Turning to the rule's present status, the court noted that the rule has been legislatively or judicially abolished by the "vast majority" of jurisdictions recently to have considered the issue. The court concluded that, contrary to the conclusion of the Court of Criminal Appeals, the 1989 Act had not abolished the rule. After reviewing the justifications for the rule at common law, however, the court found that the original reasons for recognizing the rule no longer exist. Accordingly, the court abolished the rule as it had existed at common law in Tennessee. The court disagreed with petitioner's contention that application of its decision abolishing the rule to his case would violate the *Ex Post Facto* Clauses of the State and Federal Constitutions. Those constitutional provisions, the court observed, refer only to legislative Acts. . . .

Although petitioner's claim is one of due process, the Constitution's *Ex Post Facto* Clause figures prominently in his argument. The Clause provides simply that "[n]o State shall . . . pass any . . . ex post facto Law." Art. I, § 10, cl. 1. The most well-known and oft-repeated explanation of the scope of the Clause's protection was given by Justice Chase, who long ago identified, in dictum, four types of laws to which the Clause extends: "1st. Every law that makes an action done before the passing of the law, and which was innocent when done, criminal; and punishes such action. 2d. Every law that aggravates a crime, or makes it greater than it was, when committed. 3d. Every law that changes the punishment, and inflicts a greater punishment, than the law annexed to the crime, when committed. 4th. Every law that alters the legal rules of evidence, and receives less, or different, testimony, than the law required at the time of the commission of the offense, in order to convict the offender."

Strict application of *ex post facto* principles [to courts] would unduly impair the incremental and reasoned development of precedent that is the foundation of the common law system. The common law, in short, presupposes a measure of

evolution that is incompatible with stringent application of *ex post facto* principles. It was on account of concerns such as these that *Bouie* restricted due process limitations on the retroactive application of judicial interpretations of criminal statutes to those that are "unexpected and indefensible by reference to the law which had been expressed prior to the conduct in issue." *Bouie v. City of Columbia*, 378 U.S., at 354, 84 S.Ct. 1697 (internal quotation marks omitted). . . .

We believe this limitation adequately serves the common law context as well. It accords common law courts the substantial leeway they must enjoy as they engage in the daily task of formulating and passing upon criminal defenses and interpreting such doctrines as causation and intent, reevaluating *462 and refining them as may be necessary to bring the common law into conformity with logic and common sense. It also adequately respects the due process concern with fundamental fairness and protects against vindictive or arbitrary judicial lawmaking by safeguarding defendants against unjustified and unpredictable breaks with prior law. Accordingly, we conclude that a judicial alteration of a common law doctrine of criminal law violates the principle of fair warning, and hence must not be given retroactive effect, only where it is "unexpected and indefensible by reference to the law which had been expressed prior to the conduct in issue.". . .

Turning to the particular facts of the instant case, the Tennessee court's abolition of the year and a day rule was not unexpected and indefensible. The year and a day rule is widely viewed as an outdated relic of the common law. Petitioner does not even so much as hint that good reasons exist for retaining the rule, and so we need not delve too deeply into the rule and its history here. Suffice it to say that the rule is generally believed to date back to the 13th century, when it served as a statute of limitations governing the time in which an individual might initiate a private action for murder known as an "appeal of death"; that by the 18th century the rule had been extended to the law governing public prosecutions for murder; that the primary and most frequently cited justification for the rule is that 13th century medical science was incapable of establishing causation beyond a reasonable doubt when a great deal of time had elapsed between the injury to the victim and his death; and that, as practically every court recently to have considered the rule has noted, advances in medical and related science have so undermined the usefulness of the rule as to render it without question obsolete. . . . For this reason, the year and a day rule has been legislatively or judicially abolished in the vast majority of jurisdictions recently to have addressed the issue. . . .

[The Court then discussed the small number of Tennessee cases that mention the the Rule and concluded that in no class did the Supreme Court of Tennessee ever apply the Rule.]

There is, in short, nothing to indicate that the Tennessee court's abolition of the rule in petitioner's case represented an exercise of the sort of unfair and arbitrary judicial action against which the Due Process Clause aims to protect. Far from a marked and unpredictable departure from prior precedent, the court's decision was a routine exercise of common law decisionmaking in which the court brought the law into conformity with reason and common sense. It did so by laying to rest an archaic and outdated rule that had never been relied upon as a ground of decision in any reported Tennessee case.

The judgment of the Supreme Court of Tennessee is accordingly affirmed.

Concurrence. In this chapter you have learned that there are two primary components of crimes, the mental and the physical. Although a showing of mens rea is not required for every crime, there must be a showing of some act or omission for all crimes.

For crimes that have both a mental and a physical element, an additional requirement of concurrence must be proved. *Concurrence* is the joining of mens rea and the act. The mens rea must be the reason that the act was taken. Stated another way, the mental state must occur first and set into motion the act. For example, Doug hates Andy and desires to see him dead. Because of this feeling, Doug waits for Andy to leave the house one night and runs him down with a car. In such a case, Doug's mens rea set into motion the act that caused Andy's death. Now imagine that Doug accidentally kills Andy in an auto accident. After the accident Doug exclaims his happiness over Andy's demise. In this case, the mens rea occurred after the act. It was not the catalyst for the act that killed Andy, and, as such, there was no concurrence.

The mere fact that the mental state happens before the act does not mean that there is concurrence. There must be a connection between the intent and the act; the mens rea must set the act into motion. So if Doug forms the desire to kill Andy today, but takes no action to further the desire, he cannot be charged with murder a year later when he accidentally shoots Andy while hunting.

As stated by the Court of Appeals of Indiana:

Unless statutorily stated otherwise, it is black letter law that in order to constitute a crime "criminal intent" . . . must unite with an overt act, and they must concur in point of time. There must be a criminal act or omission as well as criminal intent. A felonious intent unconnected with an unlawful act constitutes no crime. . . . A person can only be punished for an offense he has committed and never for an offense he may commit in the future. A crime cannot be predicated upon future acts or upon contingencies or the taking effect of some future event.[25]

 WEB LINKS

American Bar Association
The American Bar Association's homepage, *http:www.abanet.org,* has considerable law-related information, including criminal law, legal education, and legal ethics topics. In addition, it contains several links to other sources of information.

KEY TERMS

actus reus
constructive
corporate liability
element
forseeable
inference
injunction
intervening cause
knowingly

legal cause
legislative history
mens rea
motive
omission
presumption
proximate cause
purposely
recklessness

scienter
specific intent
statutory construction
strict liability
strict liability crimes
transferred intent
vicarious liability

REVIEW QUESTIONS

1. In criminal law, causation is broken down into two forms. Name and briefly describe each.
2. Can a person be prosecuted for failing to save a stranger from danger? Why or why not?
3. What is concurrence?
4. What is an omission?
5. The Model Penal Code recognizes four types of mens rea. Name and briefly describe each.
6. What is vicarious liability?
7. What is a rebuttable presumption? An irrebuttable presumption?
8. Can corporations and other associations be guilty of crimes?
9. Distinguish mens rea from motive.

REVIEW PROBLEMS

1–6. Many prisoners in the state and federal correctional systems are held at minimum-security "farms." Only inmates considered not to be dangerous are housed at these facilities because of the minimal security. In fact, in many cases it is possible for inmates to simply walk off. Of course, most do not leave the premises, because to do so results in an increased sentence (either due to a conviction for escape or a decrease in "good time") and a likelihood that the sentence will be spent in prison rather than the more desirable farm. Despite this, prisoners of these facilities do escape. What follows are several different sets of facts involving a ficticious inmate, Spike Vincelli. Read each and discuss the defenses, if any, that Spike may have against a charge of escape. Discuss each in light of the following two statutes:

Statute I:

It shall be unlawful for any person committed to any correctional facility to escape from that facility. Escape is defined as passing beyond the borders of a facility with an intent to never return or being lawfully beyond the borders of the facility and not returning when required to do so with an intent to never return. Violation of this statute constitutes a felony.

Statute II:

It shall be unlawful for any person committed to any correctional facility to leave the premises of the facility. Leaving is defined as passing over the boundary lines of the facility. Violation of this statute constitutes a misdemeanor.

1. On June 21, Spike Vincelli received a telephone call from a hospital informing him that his mother had been involved in a serious accident. That evening Spike left to see his mother, intending to return in the morning.

2. On June 21, Spike Vincelli had his first epileptic seizure. The seizure caused Spike to fall outside the boundary line surrounding the facility.

3. On June 21, Spike Vincelli decided that he was bored with living on the farm. That night he walked off the premises and fled for a friend's house 300 miles away, intending never to return.

4. On June 21, Spike Vincelli became involved in a fight with Ben Ichabod. In a fit of rage, Ben picked Spike up and threw him over the fence surrounding the farm. Spike was caught outside the fence by a guard before he had an opportunity to return.

5. In early April, Spike Vincelli decided that he was going to escape. He developed a plan that called for him to leave in July and meet his brother, who was passing through the area. As part of the plan, Ben Ichabod, a fellow inmate, was enlisted to pick Spike up off the ground and throw him over the fence that surrounded the facility. However, Ben, who is not very bright, threw Spike over the fence on June 21.

6. On June 21, Spike Vincelli became involved in a fight with Ben Ichabod. Ben, in a fit of rage, picked Spike up and threw him over the fence surrounding the facility. While outside the fence Spike became overcome with a sense of freedom and ran from the facility.

7. Fred failed to show up for a date he had made with Penni. Penni, who was angered by Fred's actions, decided to vent her anger by cutting the tires of Fred's automobile. However, Penni did not know what make of automobile Fred drove and mistakenly cut the tires of a car owned by Fred's neighbor, Stacey. Penni is now charged with the "purposeful destruction of personal property." Penni claims that her act was not purposeful because she did not intend to cut the tires of Stacey's car. Discuss this defense.

8. William, an experienced canoeist, was hired by a Boy Scout troop to supervise a canoe trip. While on the trip two boys fell out of their canoe and began to drown. William watched as the boys drowned. Is William criminally liable for the deaths?

9. Sherri, who was near bankruptcy, decided to burn her house down and make an insurance claim for the loss. Sherri started the fire, which spread to a neighbor's house located twenty feet

from Sherri's home. Unknown to Sherri, her neighbor was storing massive quantities of dynamite in the home. The fire at the neighbor's house spread to the room where the explosives were being stored, and the resulting explosion caused such vibrations that a construction worker one block away fell off a ladder and subsequently died from the fall. Sherri is charged with arson and murder. She has pled guilty to arson, but maintains that she is not liable for the death of the worker. Is she correct?

10. The following statute was enacted by State Legislature:

   It shall be unlawful for any person to be a pedophile. Pedophilia is defined as a condition where a person over the age of seventeen years possesses a sexual desire for a person under the age of eight years.

   While attending a group therapy session, Jane admitted that she had sexual interest in boys under eight years of age. A member of the group contacted the local police and reported Jane's statement. Jane was subsequently arrested and charged with violating the quoted statute. Discuss her defenses, if any.

11. Ashley, Amy, and Karen are roommates in college. They occupy a four-bedroom apartment, and all share in the bills and household duties. One weekend a friend of Karen's, Janice, came to visit. Janice arrived on Thursday and was scheduled to stay until Monday. She stayed in the extra bedroom. On Thursday evening Ashley discovered, while she was watching Janice unpack, that Janice had a significant amount of cocaine in one suitcase. Later that night, Ashley discussed this matter with Karen, who stated, "I'm sure she does—why does it matter to you?" Ashley immediately confronted Janice and told her that she would have to remove the cocaine from the premises or Ashley would call the police. Janice picked up the suitcase, carried it to her car, and placed it in the trunk. The next morning, when Karen learned what Ashley had done, she encouraged Janice to bring the suitcase back into the apartment. On Sunday morning the police arrived with a warrant to search the apartment. The search uncovered the suitcase in the extra bedroom. Later, at the police station, the suitcase was opened and the drugs were discovered. All four women were charged with possession. Do Amy, Ashley, or Karen have a defense? The jurisdiction where they live applies the Model Penal Code.

12. In some nations, vicarious criminal liability is much broader than in the United States. For example, parents may be vicariously liable for the criminal acts of their children until the children reach adulthood. Should such laws be adopted in the United States? Explain your answer.

13. Develop your own fact scenarios, one demonstrating specific intent and another demonstrating general intent. Explain why each is an example of specific or general intent.

14. Using the two fact scenarios you created in problem 13, change the facts so that the general-intent crime becomes a specific-intent crime and the specific-intent crime becomes a general-intent crime.

END NOTES

1. J. Goldstein, et al., *Criminal Law: Theory and Process* (New York: Free Press, 1974).
2. 21 Am. Jur. 2d *Criminal Law* 129 (1981).
3. *See United States v. Birkenstock,* 823 F.2d 1026 (7th Cir. 1987); *United States v. Pompanio,* 429 U.S. 10 (1976).
4. LaFave & Scott, *Criminal Law* (Hornbook Series, St. Paul: West, 1986), at 217.
5. LaFave & Scott at 34.
6. *See Lambert v. California,* 355 U.S. 225 (1957), in which the United States Supreme Court found that a strict liability statute was violative of the

due process clause of the United States Constitution.

7. LaFave & Scott at 244–45.

8. *See United States v. Dotterweich,* 320 U.S. 277 (1943).

9. Model Penal Code § 2.07 deals with liability of corporations and unincorporated associations.

10. Model Penal Code § 2.02, General Requirements of Culpability.

11. Kaplan & Weisberg, *Criminal Law* (Boston: Little, Brown, 1986).

12. Model Penal Code § 2.02(2)(c).

13. The Model Penal Code actually recognizes three "objective elements" that may have differing culpability levels. Those are circumstance, result, and conduct. Also, the Code provides, at § 2.02(4), that one mental state shall apply to an entire offense, unless a contrary intent is plain.

14. Model Penal Code § 2.01.

15. *Id.*

16. *Kansas v. Hendricks,* 117 S. Ct. 2072 (1997).

17. From N. Morris, "Somnambulistic Homicide: Ghosts, Spiders, and North Koreans," 5 *Res Judicata* 29 (1951).

18. A. Loewy, *Criminal Law,* 2d ed. (Nutshell Series, St. Paul: West, 1987).

19. LaFave & Scott, at 200.

20. Model Penal Code § 2.01(4).

21. Vermont and Rhode Island impose a duty to rescue. *See* Vt. Stat. Ann. tit. 12, § 519; R.I. Gen. Laws § 11-56-1.

22. *United States v. Knowles,* 26 F. Cas. 800 (N.D. Cal. 1864).

23. Model Penal Code § 2.03.

24. Loewy at 55.

25. *Gebhard v. State,* 484 N.E.2d 45, 48 (Ind. Ct. App. 1985).

CHAPTER 4

Crimes Against the Person

CHAPTER OUTLINE

Studying Crimes

Homicide

    Homicide and the Common Law

    Statutory Approaches to Homicide

    Manslaughter

    The Model Penal Code Approach to
        Homicide

    Life, Death, and Homicide

    Suicide

    Corpus Delicti

Assault and Battery

    Aggravated Assault and Battery

Mayhem

Sex Crimes

    Rape

    Nonforcible Rape

    Sodomy

    Rape Shield Laws

    Incest

    Sex Offenses Against Children

    Megan's Laws, Commitment, and
        Castration

Kidnapping and False Imprisonment

    Kidnapping

    Parental Kidnapping

    False Imprisonment

Stalking

Civil Rights and Hate Crimes

CHAPTER OBJECTIVES

In this chapter, you should:

- learn the elements of historic and contemporary crimes against the person, such as murder, rape, and assault.
- learn the common defenses to charges of crimes against the person, such as self-defense.
- examine contemporary issues concerning death and suicide.
- continue to develop your case analysis and legal reasoning skills.

STUDYING CRIMES

In the next three chapters you will learn about many crimes. It would be impossible to include a discussion of all crimes. The federal government and each city and state have their own unique laws. What follows is a discussion of the major crimes recognized, in some form, in most jurisdictions. The crimes have been categorized as crimes against the person, crimes against property, and crimes against the public. Although it is common to make these distinctions, do not become involved with understanding why these classifications have been made, as they are used only for organizational purposes. In a sense, all crimes are offenses against the public. That is why the public prosecutes crimes, and private individuals may not. Also, any offense "against property" is actually injuring a person, not the property. A stolen television set does not long to be returned to its rightful owner. However, the rightful owner does feel wronged and desires the return of the stolen item. In a sense the classifications are often accurate in that they describe the focus of the criminal conduct. The focus of a thief's act is property; hence, a crime against property. The focus of a rapist's attack is a human; hence, a crime against a person.

element

A basic part. For example, some of the *elements* of a cause of action for battery are an intentional, unwanted physical contact. Each of these things ("intentional," "unwanted," etc.) is one "*element*."

All of the following crimes have been broken into parts. Each part of a crime is an **element** of that crime. At trial, every element of a crime must be proven beyond a reasonable doubt by the prosecution. If any element is not proven beyond a reasonable doubt, the accused must be found not guilty. The rule requires that each element be proved individually. That is, if a crime consists of six elements, and a jury is convinced that five have been proven, but cannot say that the sixth has been proven beyond a reasonable doubt, then there must be a not-guilty verdict. This is true even if the jury was solidly convinced that all the other elements were true and generally believed that the defendant committed the crime. Later you will learn more about the "beyond a reasonable doubt" standard.

merger of offenses

When a person is charged with two crimes (based on the exact same acts), one of which is a lesser included offense of the other. The lesser crime *merges* because, under the prohibition against double jeopardy, the person may be tried for only one of them.

Finally, you may notice that, often, if one crime has been proven, all the elements of a related lesser crime can also be proved. For example, if a defendant is convicted of murdering someone with a hammer, he has also committed a battery of the victim. In such circumstances, the lesser offense merges into the greater offense. This is the **merger** doctrine. Under this doctrine, both crimes may be charged, but if the defendant is convicted of the more serious crime the lesser is absorbed by the greater, and the defendant is not punished for both. If acquitted of the greater charge, the defendant may be convicted of the lesser.

HOMICIDE

Homicide is the killing of one human being by another. Not all homicides are crimes. It is possible to cause another person's death accidentally, that is, accompanied by no mens rea. For example, if a bridge builder lost her balance and fell against a co-worker, causing the co-worker to fall to his death, no crime has been committed, but there has been a homicide.

Criminal homicide occurs when a person takes another's life in a manner proscribed by law. The law proscribes more than intentional killings. Under the Model Penal Code, purposeful, knowing, negligent, and reckless homicides may be punished.

CRIME STATISTICS   There are many different ways to measure crime. Some methods, such as observation and experimentation, are impractical, or even more, immoral! The Federal Bureau of Investigation collects crime data from police departments all over the United States. This data is compiled and reported yearly under the title *Uniform Crime Reports.* Although a good comprehensive source of crime data since 1929, there are flaws in UCR data. The most significant flaw concerns underreporting. Many crimes are not reported to the police. Even when reported, most police agencies only report the most serious offense committed. Hence, many crimes go unreported by individuals and police agencies. Also, because UCR data is aggregate data, no detail about the number of victims, offenders, or offenses per incident are provided. In an effort to remedy some of these problems, there is an on-going effort to redesign the UCR system. This effort, known as the National Incident Based Reporting System (NIBRS), asks local law enforcement officers to move beyond aggregate data to information about each criminal incident.

Since 1991, colleges and universities that receive federal monies have been required to collect statistics on campus crime. The Campus Security Act requires that the collected data be made available to current and prospective faculty, staff, and students.

The second major system of crime data collection is the National Crime Victimization Survey administered by the United States Census Bureau on behalf of the United States Department of Justice. The NCVS is a large random survey of U.S. households. Respondents are asked whether they have been victimized by one or more of the listed violent and nonviolent crimes. The NCVS touts an impressive 95% response rate to its survey. The NCVS has its flaws as well. Some victims, particularly of certain crimes, are reluctant or ashamed to report the crime. Also, some people may not know that they have been victimized (e.g. embezzlement or fraud).

UCR data is often used in this text. For additional information, NCVS data should be examined. Also, most local and state law enforcement agencies and courts have data available that is not provided by either the UCR or NCVS, such as data on arrests and crimes not included in the UCR or NCVS systems.

The FBI's UCR reports can be found in many locations, including:

http://www.fbi.gov/ucr/ucr.htm

NCVS data can be found in many locations, including:

http://www.ojp.usdoj.gov/bjs/

SIDEBAR

Source: National Crime
Victimization Survey

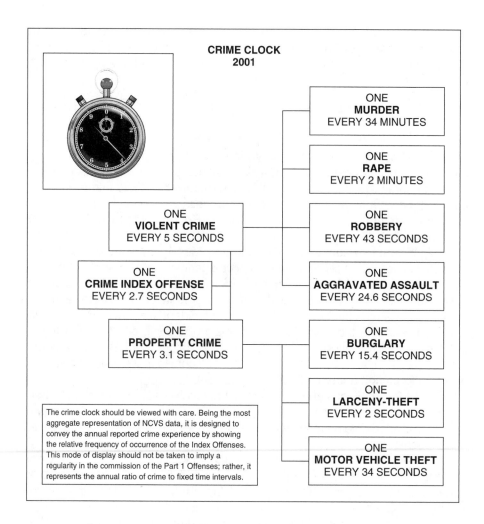

The mens rea part of homicide is important. The determination of what mens rea was possessed by the defendant (actually, what mens rea can be proven by the prosecution) will usually determine what crime may be punished. At common law, various forms of murder were developed. This is where we begin.

Homicide and the Common Law

Initially, at common law, all murders were punished equally: the murderer was executed.[1] Over time, the belief that not all homicides should be punished equally developed. As a result, homicides were divided into murder and manslaughter. Manslaughter was punished by incarceration, not death.

Murder, at common law, was defined as: (1) The unlawful killing of a (2) human being with (3) malice aforethought. It was the requirement of malice aforethought that distinguished murder from manslaughter. Although malice aforethought was defined differently among the states, the following types of homicide became recognized as murder under the common law:

1. When the defendant intended to cause the death of the victim.
2. When the defendant intended to cause serious bodily harm, and death resulted.
3. When the defendant created an unreasonably high risk of death that caused the victim's death, regardless of the defendant's mens rea. This was known as "depraved-heart murder."
4. When the doctrine of felony-murder was applicable.

All criminal homicides that did not constitute murder were treated as manslaughter. Today, nearly every jurisdiction further divides murder into degrees, and most divide manslaughter into voluntary and involuntary. Few jurisdictions rely on the common-law definition of malice aforethought. However, many states continue to recognize felony-murder.

The Felony-Murder Doctrine.

At common law, one who caused an unintended death during the commission (or attempted commission) of any felony was guilty of murder. This became known as **felony-murder**. Under the early common law all felonies were punished by death. Generally, most of the crimes that were felonies under the common law posed a threat to human life. This threat was one justification for the harshness of the rule. However, as the common law developed, many new crimes were created, many of which did not involve serious threat to human life. For this reason the felony-murder doctrine was very harsh, as it applied to all felonies regardless of their relative dangerousness to human life. In time, courts began to limit the application of the rule to specified felonies; specifically, those perceived as posing the largest threat to human life. It was common to apply the rule to rape, mayhem, arson, kidnapping, and robbery.

For example, Andy and Gene decide to rob the First National Bank. They agreed to use whatever amount of violence is necessary to carry out the robbery. During the robbery a bank teller summoned the police by use of a silent alarm. As Andy and Gene were leaving the bank, the police shouted to them, ordering their surrender. Andy then fired a shot from his gun and fatally wounded a police officer. Using the felony-murder rule, both Gene and Andy are criminally liable for the death of the police officer, even though Gene did not fire the weapon or conspire with Andy to kill the officer.

The felony-murder rule acts to impute the required mens rea to the defendant and to create a form of vicarious liability between co-felons. The rule imputes mens rea because it applies in situations of unintended death; however, murder in the first degree is a specific-intent crime. The rationale is that one who engages in inherently dangerous crimes should be aware of the high risk to human life created by the crime. Vicarious liability is also imposed in some states; that is, all the individuals involved in the perpetration of the crime may be criminally liable for the resulting death.

felony-murder rule
The principle that if a person (even accidentally) kills another while committing a felony, then the killing is murder.

Today, most states have felony-murder statutes. Generally, the following must be shown to establish a felony-murder:

1. The defendant must have been engaged in the commission, or attempted commission, of a named felony, and
2. during the commission, or attempted commission, of that felony a death occurred, and
3. there is a causal connection between the crime and the death.

In most jurisdictions the legislature has specified the crimes that must be committed, or attempted, for the rule to apply. A few jurisdictions have limited the application of the rule to crimes that were felonies at common law, and others have limited the rule to felonies that involve a threat to human life.

To satisfy the second requirement, it must be determined when the commission of the crime began and when it concluded. This appears to be an easy task, and is in most cases, but there are instances when it is not clear. Suppose that a robber knew that a large sum of money was being transferred between a bank and an armored car at a particular time and intended to steal the money during that transfer. Also assume that the traffic was heavier than anticipated by the robber on the day of the robbery and, in an effort to arrive at the bank on time, the robber ran a stop sign. While passing through the intersection, the robber struck another vehicle, killing the driver. Was this death during the commission, or attempted commission, of the robbery? What if a police officer were to chase an individual from the scene of a felony and get shot fifteen minutes and one mile away from the scene of the crime? Is this during the commission, or attempted commission, of the felony? It is likely that no felony-murder would be found in the first example, because the death was too far removed from actual commission of the crime. The result would be different if the robber struck and killed the motorist while fleeing from the police immediately after commission of the holdup. This answers the second question. Courts have generally held that deaths that occur during the flight of a felon are "during the commission of the felony." However, the chase must be immediate, and the rule does not apply if there is a gap between the time the crime occurred, or was attempted, and the time the chase begins.

Requirement number three can be troublesome. In many ways this requirement is similar to the causation requirement discussed in Chapter 3 regarding actus reus. That is, the commission, or attempted commission, of the felony must be the legal cause (proximate cause) of the death. The death must be a "consequence, not coincidence" of the act; the resulting death must have been a foreseeable consequence of the act. So, if a patron of a store suffers a heart attack during a robbery, which was precipitated by the crime, the robbers are guilty of felony-murder if the patron dies. However, if a patron who is unaware of an ongoing robbery suffers a heart attack and dies, the robbers are not liable for the death. The mere fact that the death and the crime occurred simultaneously does not mean that the robbers were the legal cause of the death.

In some states, the act that causes the death of the victim need not be taken by one of the perpetrators of the crime. For example, if Gene and Andy become involved in a shootout with the police after they rob the First National Bank, and the police accidentally shoot an innocent bystander, then Gene and Andy are guilty of felony-murder. This is because they began the series of events which led to the death of the bystander. However, if a police officer (or another) kills one of many felons who are jointly involved in the commission of the crime, it is generally held that the other felons are not guilty of felony murder.[2]

Although the felony-murder rule does impose vicarious liability between cofelons, this aspect is limited. If a defendant can prove that he did not commit the act that caused the death; did not authorize, plan, or encourage the act of his co-felon; and had no reason to believe that his cohort would commit the act, he has a defense to felony-murder in some jurisdictions. Note that the rules concerning parties (principals and accomplices) to crimes may create liability independent of the felony-murder rule. (See Chapter 7 for a discussion of parties to crimes.)

Finally, note that in most jurisdictions that continue to recognize felony-murder, the murder is treated as first-degree murder for the purpose of sentencing. Other statutes provide that felony-murders that occur during named felonies are to be treated as first-degree murder and that murders during "all other felonies" are to be treated as second-degree murder. Even if the statute that creates this "all other felony" category does not expressly state that the felony must involve a danger to human life, it is common for courts to impose the requirement.

In the *Losey* case, a defendant appealed his conviction of involuntary manslaughter and aggravated burglary. The Ohio Court of Appeals applied a statute which read, "No person shall cause the death of another as a proximate result of the offender's committing or attempting to commit a felony." The statute named the crime involuntary manslaughter. The case is interesting from a causation perspective. Read the case and decide for yourself if the defendant should be punished for the death that occurred.

 CASE ──◆

STATE V. LOSEY

23 Ohio App. 3d 93,
491 N.E.2d 379 (1985)

Defendant testified that he approached a house located at 616 Whitehorne Avenue shortly after 11:00 P.M. on November 25, 1983; that he knocked at the front door and, upon receiving no response, forced open the door and proceeded to attempt to remove a bicycle. His friend, who had been waiting outside, yelled that a car was slowly approaching. The defendant then placed the bicycle beside the front door and departed, leaving the front door open behind him. James Harper, the owner of 616 Whitehorne Avenue, testified that he heard a noise

at approximately 1:00 A.M. Shortly thereafter, his mother, with whom he resided, appeared at his bedroom door inquiring about the noise. They proceeded together to the living room, whereupon they discovered the open front door and the bicycle standing near the door. James Harper stated that he told his mother to go back to her bedroom while he went to check the rest of the house. After so checking, he returned to the living room and was calling the police when his mother appeared in the hallway looking very upset and then collapsed. He called an emergency squad, which attempted to revive Mrs. Harper for almost an hour when the squadmen pronounced her dead. Prior to the burglary, Mrs. Harper had returned from bingo at approximately 10:00 P.M. that evening and had gone to bed. Based on these facts, the trial court found defendant guilty of aggravated burglary and involuntary manslaughter.

* * *

The doctor's testimony established that defendant's conduct was a cause of Mrs. Harper's death in the sense that it set in motion events which culminated in her death. However, it still must be determined whether defendant was legally responsible for her death—whether the death was the proximate result of his conduct. It is not necessary that the accused be in a position to

foresee the precise consequence of his conduct; only that the consequence be foreseeable in the sense that what actually transpired was natural and logical in that it was within the scope of the risk created by his conduct. . . .

By the same token, in this case, the causal relationship between defendant's criminal conduct and Mrs. Harper's death was not too improbable, remote, or speculative to form a basis for criminal responsibility. Although the defendant did not engage in loud or violent conduct calculated to frighten or shock, his presence was nevertheless detected by Mrs. Harper. . . . [Conviction affirmed.]

Misdemeanor Manslaughter.   Similar to the felony-murder rule, one may be guilty of misdemeanor manslaughter if a death results from the commission of a misdemeanor, not a felony. Conviction of misdemeanor manslaughter results in liability for manslaughter, often involuntary manslaughter, and not murder.

Just as the felony-murder doctrine has been limited in recent years, so has the crime of misdemeanor manslaughter. This is due in large part to the significant increase in the creation of nonviolent crimes by legislatures and administrative bodies. Many states require that the misdemeanor be *malum in se*, and crimes that are *malum prohibitum* cannot be a basis for misdemeanor manslaughter. Requiring that the misdemeanor have a mens rea element is another limitation; that is, strict liability crimes may not be the basis for misdemeanor manslaughter. There is a trend to reject the misdemeanor manslaughter rule (as there is with the felony-murder rule) and require that one of the four types of culpability recognized by the Model Penal Code (purposeful, knowing, negligent, or reckless) be present before imposing liability.

Statutory Approaches to Homicide

first-degree murder
The most serious form of a particular crime that has more than one type. For example, *first-degree* murder includes premeditation or extreme atrocity or cruelty, or is done in the commission of a major felony.

second-degree murder
Murder without premeditation.

Although the common law recognized only one form of murder, most states now divide murder into degrees; most often into first and second degrees. **First-degree murder** is the highest form of murder and is punished more severely than second-degree murder. **Second-degree murder** is a higher crime than manslaughter.

First-and Second-Degree Murder.   For a murder to be of the first degree, the highest crime, it must be shown that the homicide was willful, deliberate, and premeditated. Generally, first-degree murder applies whenever the murderer has as a goal the death of the victim. *Willful,* as used in first-degree murder, is

SIDEBAR

SERIAL AND MASS MURDERERS IN THE UNITED STATES   Few crimes generate as much attention as those committed by serial killers and mass murderers.

Serial killers are individuals who kill over long periods of time. Serial killers tend to follow patterns, such as stalking of victims with similar physical characteristics. Ritual is a common pattern of the serial killer, as is sexual motivation.

It is estimated that there are as many as 50 to 100 serial killers in the United States at any given time. The span of killing by most serial killers is longer than four years. The number of serial murders appears to be increasing. Between 1975 and 1988, the number of victims rose from 29 to 42 yearly. In total, between 1975 and 1988, serial killers accounted for as many as 2,161 murders. Most serial killers have been men.

Unlike serial murderers, mass murderers do not act cryptically. A mass murderer randomly kills many people within a short period of time, often minutes. The murders usually occur in a public place, and it is common for the murderer to commit suicide at the close of the killing. Between 1949 and 1990, mass murderers were responsible for at least 150 deaths. Mass murderers are also usually men.

Sources: Eric Hickey, *Serial Murderers and Their Victims* (Brooks/Cole Publishing 1991); "Serial-Murder Aftershocks," *Newsweek,* Aug. 12, 1991; "Silence of the Wolves," *Newsweek,* Feb. 3, 1992.

a specific-intent concept. To be willful, the defendant must have specifically intended to cause the death.

Deliberate is usually defined as a cool mind, not acting out of an immediate passion, fear, or rage. The term *premeditated* means to think beforehand. Similar to deliberate, it eliminates impulsive acts from the grasp of first-degree murder. It is commonly said that there must be a gap in time between the decision to kill and the actual act. Of course, the length of the gap is the critical issue. Most courts hold that the gap in time must be "appreciable." Again, this term describes little. The fact is that courts differ greatly in how they define *appreciable*. There are many reported cases where a lapse of only seconds was sufficient.[3] Some courts have held that all that need be shown is that the defendant had adequate time to form the intention before taking the act; the length of time is not determinative of the question.[4]

In *State v. Snowden*, the defendant appealed his conviction of first-degree murder, claiming that he lacked premeditation, and, as such, he should have been convicted of second-degree murder, not first.

Decisions such as this obscure the difference between first- and second-degree murder. Do you agree with the Idaho Court that there can be premeditation even if there is "no appreciable space of time between the intention to kill and the act of killing?" Note that the facts of this case did not require mention of the prior case where it was held that "no appreciable" time has to be shown. The fact that the autopsy evidenced that the murder occurred after the victim suffered torture would justify a murder conviction under the statute.

C A S E

STATE V. SNOWDEN

79 Idaho 266, 313 P.2d
706 (1957)

Defendant Snowden had been playing pool and drinking in a Boise pool room early in the evening. With a companion, one Carrier, he visited a club near Boise, then went to nearby Garden City. There the two men visited a number of bars, and defendant had several drinks. Their last stop was the HiHo Club.

Witnesses related that while defendant was in the HiHo Club he met and talked to Cora Lucyle Dean. The defendant himself said he hadn't been acquainted with Mrs. Dean prior to that time, but he had "seen her in a couple of the joints up town." He danced with Mrs. Dean while at the HiHo Club. Upon departing from the tavern, the two left together.

In statements to police officers, that were admitted to evidence, defendant Snowden said after they left the club Mrs. Dean wanted him to find a cab and take her back to Boise, and he refused because he didn't feel he should pay her fare. After some words, he related:

> She got mad at me so I got pretty hot and I don't know whether I back handed her there or not. And, we got calmed down and decided to walk across to the gas station and call a cab.

They crossed the street, and began arguing again. Defendant said: "She swung and at the same time she kneed me again. I blew my top."

Defendant said he pushed the woman over beside a pickup truck which was standing near a business building. There he pulled his knife— a pocket knife with a two-inch blade—and cut her throat.

The body, which was found the next morning, was viciously and sadistically cut and mutilated. An autopsy surgeon testified the voice box had been cut, and that this would have prevented the victim from making any intelligible cry. There were other wounds inflicted while she was still alive— one in her neck, one in her abdomen, two in the face, and two on the back of the neck. The second neck wound severed the spinal cord and caused her death. There were other wounds all over the body, and her clothing had been cut away. The nipple of her right breast was missing. There was no evidence of sexual attack on the victim; however, some of the lacerations were around the breasts and vagina of the deceased. . . .

[M]urder is defined by statute as follows:

> All murder which is perpetrated by means of poison, or lying in wait, torture, or by any other kind of willful, deliberate and premeditated killing, or which is committed in the perpetration of, or attempt to perpetrate arson, rape, robbery, burglary, kidnapping, or mayhem, is murder in the first degree. All other murders are of the second degree.

The defendant admitted taking the life of the deceased.

The principal argument of the defendant pertaining to [the charge of premeditated murder] is that the defendant did not have sufficient time to develop a desire to take the life of the deceased, but rather his action was instantaneous and a normal reaction to the physical injury which she dealt him. . . .

> There need be no appreciable space of time between the intention to kill and the act of killing. They may be as instantaneous as successive thoughts of the mind. It is only necessary that the act of killing be preceded by a concurrence of will, deliberation, and premeditation on the part of the slayer, and, if such is the case, the killing is murder in the first degree.

In the present case, the trial court had no other alternative than to find the defendant guilty of willful, deliberate, and premeditated killing with malice aforethought in view of the defendant's acts in deliberately opening up a pocket knife, next cutting the victim's throat, and then hacking and cutting until he had killed Cora Lucyle Dean. . . .

Note that the statute mentioned in *Snowden* to describe first-degree murder is used by many jurisdictions. Those murders that result from poisoning, follow torture, or are traditional felony-murders are often designated first-degree murder. Second-degree murder is commonly given the negative definition "all murders that are not of the first degree are of the second." Second-degree murders differ from first in that the defendant lacked the specific intent to kill or lacked the premeditation and deliberation element of first-degree murder.

HOMICIDE IN THE UNITED STATES   There was one murder in the United States every 34 minutes in 2001. A total of 15,517 people were murdered or the subject of a nonnegligent manslaughter in 2000. This was 5.5 of every 100,000 persons in the United States. Most people are murdered with guns, primarily handguns. Knives, poisons, fists, and other weapons are also used to commit homicides. Murder constituted 0.1 percent of all crimes in 2000.

Source: *Uniform Crime Reports*, U.S. Department of Justice, Federal Bureau of Investigation, 2001.

Intent to Do Serious Bodily Harm and the Deadly Weapon Doctrine.   One method of reducing a murder from the first degree to the second is by proving that the defendant did not intend to kill, but only intended to cause the victim serious bodily harm. Note that if the defendant intended less than serious bodily harm the crime is either manslaughter or a form of reckless or negligent homicide.

This is an area where inferences are important. Juries (or judges, if the court is acting as the finder of fact) are permitted to view the facts surrounding the murder and determine what the defendant's state of mind was at the time the act occurred. A jury may conclude from the facts that the defendant did intend to cause the death of the victim and convict of first-degree murder. If a jury concludes that the defendant did not intend to cause the death of the victim, but that the defendant did intend to cause serious bodily injury, then the crime is second-degree murder.

A related inference used in murder cases is the *deadly weapon doctrine*. This is a rule that permits juries to infer that a defendant intended to kill his or her victim if a **deadly weapon** was used in the killing. Being an inference, this conclusion does not have to be drawn; this is a decision for the factfinder. If a jury were to conclude that a defendant's use of a deadly weapon indicated that murder was intended, then a first-degree murder conviction would be warranted. So, if Gwen intended only to injure Fred by shooting him, but Fred died as a result of the wound, then a jury could convict Gwen of first-degree murder. Of course, the jury could reject the inference if they believed that Gwen did not intend to kill Fred, and in that case either second-degree murder (if her intent was to inflict serious bodily injury) or manslaughter would be appropriate.

Any device or item may be a deadly weapon if, from the manner used, it is calculated or likely to produce death or serious bodily injury.[5] The Model Penal

deadly weapon
Any instrument likely to cause serious bodily harm under the circumstances of its actual use. Such things as a fan belt used to choke a man and a fire used to burn an occupied house have been called *deadly weapons* by courts.

```
                              CIRCUIT COURT
STATE OF WISCONSIN            CRIMINAL DIVISION            MILWAUKEE COUNTY
- - - - - - - - - - - - - - - - - - - - - - - - - - - - - - - - - - - - - -
STATE OF WISCONSIN, Plaintiff                    INFORMATION

           vs.                               CRIME(S):
                                             See Charging Section Below
Jeffrey L. Dahmer   05/21/60                 STATUTE(S) VIOLATED
924 N. 25th St.                              See Charging Section Below
Milwaukee, WI                                COMPLAINING WITNESS:
                                             Donald Domagalski
                     Defendant,              CASE NUMBER:
                                             F-912542
- - - - - - - - - - - - - - - - - - - - - - - - - - - - - - - - - - - - - -
```

I, E. MICHAEL MC CANN, DISTRICT ATTORNEY FOR MILWAUKEE COUNTY, WISCONSIN,
HEREBY INFORM THE COURT THAT THE ABOVE NAMED DEFENDANT IN THE COUNTY OF
MILWAUKEE, STATE OF WISCONSIN,

COUNT 01: FIRST DEGREE MURDER

COUNT 12: FIRST DEGREE INTENTIONAL HOMICIDE

on or about June 30, 1991, at 924 North 25th Street, City and County of
Milwaukee, did cause the death of another human being, Matt Turner a/k/a
Donald Montrell, with intent to kill that person contrary to Wisconsin
Statutes section 940.01(1).

Upon conviction of each count of First Degree Intentional Homicide and each
count of First Degree Murder, Class A Felonies, the penalty is life
imprisonment.

DATED   E. MICHAEL MC CANN
                                        DISTRICT ATTORNEY

          9/10/91   E. Michael McCann
                                        District Attorney

Part of criminal information in Dahmer serial murder case (only count 12 is shown; the other counts were similar).

Code defines a deadly weapon as "any firearm, or other weapon, device, instrument, material, or substance, whether animate or inanimate, which in the manner it is used or is intended to be used is known to be capable of producing death or serious bodily injury."[6] Under these definitions, some items that are not normally considered deadly may be deadly weapons if their use is calculated to cause serious bodily injury or death. The opposite is also true; some items that are normally considered deadly may not be, if used in a manner that does not pose a threat of serious harm or death. Hence, a bowling ball may be transformed from a recreational device into a deadly weapon when it is used to crush a person's skull. A gun, probably the most obvious example of a deadly device, may not be deemed deadly if used to hit someone over the head. A person's hands and feet are not normally deadly weapons. However, if it can be shown that the victim was significantly smaller than the defendant or that the defendant was especially expert in the use of his or her hands to cause injury, then they may constitute deadly weapons.

In the *Labelle* case, the inference created by the deadly weapon doctrine was used to affirm a trial court conviction of attempted murder.

 C A S E

LABELLE V. STATE

550 N.E.2d 752
(Ind. 1990)

Appellant waived his right to a jury trial and was tried to the court and found guilty of attempted murder. . . and carrying a handgun without a license. . . .

The evidence produced at trial which tended to support the determination of guilt shows that members of the Outlaws motorcycle gang, who refer to themselves as "brothers," sometimes frequent the Beehive Tavern in Indianapolis. On February 2, 1987, appellant was a patron of the Beehive. He asked Oliphant, the bartender and co-owner of the bar, whether the Outlaws had come into the bar before, and Oliphant informed him that they had. Appellant remained at the Beehive until closing time and returned the next night. By 11:00 P.M., at least three employees and several patrons were in the bar. Three members of the Outlaws, including the victim, Allen Mayes, were there shooting pool. Sometime after 11:00, appellant threw a beer can at the stage, whereupon Oliphant asked him to leave, and appellant spat in

his face. Oliphant testified, "[appellant said] that we're going to a funeral[,] to get my brothers together because we were going to a funeral. . . . [Appellant] told me I wasn't worth killing but a few of them—a few people in here were. And he proceeded to walk out the door." Oliphant stated that the three Outlaws were standing by the bar about ten feet from the door as he followed appellant out and that they were in roughly the same place when he came back in. Two or three minutes later, a shot rang out and Mayes was struck in the neck by a bullet and fell to the floor.

Fifteen to twenty minutes after the shooting, appellant was found under a truck which was parked across the street from the Beehive. A crowd which included the victim's two companions stood outside the bar and watched as appellant was being placed under arrest, and one of the Beehive's managers testified that appellant shouted at the two men, "Scumbags, you tell your brothers the angels are on their way[.] I got your brother."

The door to the bar has a diamond-shaped window, which is taped to leave unobstructed only a two- or three-inch peephole. Looking into the bar from the outside, the peephole is approximately five feet, seven inches off the ground. Police found a bullet hole in the taped area to the right of the peephole. . . . [the police] searched the underneath side of the truck and found a .38 caliber revolver on the transmission brace, above the approximate spot appellant's head had been when he was under the truck. . . . [The medical expert] testified that, based on test results, it was his opinion that the bullet in Mayes's neck was from a .38 caliber weapon. . . .

Appellant also claims that there was insufficient evidence of intent to kill to support a conviction for attempted murder. . . . This court held there [in a previous case] that intent may be inferred from the use of a deadly weapon in a manner likely to cause injury or death and upheld the conviction. This Court has repeatedly upheld convictions for murder and attempted murder where the State sought to carry its burden of proof on the issue of intent by producing evidence that the defendant fired a gun in a crowd or at a group of people.

Appellant conceded in his testimony that he did fire a shot at the Beehive, but maintained that he was trying to hit a light over the door to the bar. He testified that he could not see into the bar because of the tape on the window and his distance from the door and that he had no intention of shooting any person, but intended only to aggravate Oliphant. . . .

State of mind can be established by the circumstances surrounding an incident. Appellant questioned the bartender the night before the shooting as to whether the Outlaws frequented the Beehive. . . . The eye-level location of the peephole and the proximity of the bullet hole to it would support an inference that the shot was fired into this inhabited barroom in a manner calculated to strike anyone standing at the bar in the upper body or head. This constitutes utilization of a deadly weapon in a manner likely to cause injury or death. There was sufficient evidence to support the trial court's verdict.

The judgment of the trial court is affirmed.

AIDS and Murder.   Acquired immunodeficiency syndrome (AIDS) and other contagious diseases raise interesting criminal-law situations. First, the transmission of a disease can be criminal. For example, passing AIDS to another, if intentional, is either attempted murder, if the disease is not passed to the victim, or murder, if the disease is successfully passed to the victim.

Second, the unintentional but criminally negligent or reckless passing of such a disease may be criminal under negligent manslaughter statutes. Sharing a needle with another, knowing that it has been used by an HIV-infected individual, falls into this category, as does the passing of the disease by a prostitute who knows of her infection to a client.

Third, due to the nature of the disease, it is often not discovered until long after it is contracted, and death may not occur for many years. This poses problems in jurisdictions that continue to follow the year-and-a-day rule or other similar rules.

Fourth, in some situations, defendants have claimed that, because of the low probability of infecting another person, it is a factual impossibility to commit murder using AIDS. *See United States v. Moore*, 669 F. Supp. 289 (D. Minn. 1987), *aff'd*, 846 F.2d 1163 (8th Cir. 1988), in which a defendant asserted that his conviction for attempted murder (the defendant, who was infected with AIDS, spat on and caused his blood to spray into a victim's mouth and eyes) should be set aside because his acts did not amount to a "substantial step" toward the commission of murder. His conviction was affirmed.

CRIME IN THE UNITED STATES: GUN OWNERSHIP IN THE UNITED STATES In 2000, 533,470 acts of rape, sexual assault, robbery, and aggravated robbery were committed by individuals brandishing firearms. In addition, 66% of all murders, 41% of robberies, and 18% of all aggravated assaults were committed with guns. In 1997, there were approximately 200 million guns in the hands of private owners in the United States (Cook and Ludwig 1997). There are 60 to 65 million gun owners, of which 30 to 35 million own handguns (Johns Hopkins Center for Gun Policy and Research). Despite enough guns in private hands to provide a gun to each American, the concentration of gun ownership is small (Cook and Ludwig 1997). Seventy-four percent of gun owners possessed two or more guns in 1994 (Cook and Ludwig 1997). Most guns are used for recreational purposes, either hunting or target practice.

The Second Amendment of the U.S. Constitution states: " . . . the right of the people to keep and bear arms, shall not be infringed." Who are "keeping and bearing arms"? White, middle-aged, college-educated males from rural or small-town America are most likely to own a gun (Cook and Ludwig 1997). According to Johns Hopkins Center for Gun Policy and Research, 39% of Americans have a gun in their home.

The purchase, sale, and in certain circumstances, the possession and interstate transportation of firearms is regulated by a larger body of laws, state and federal. One of the most significant is the Gun Control Act of 1968 (NRA 1998*).

*Federal law (Brady Handgun Violence Prevention Act) also requires criminal record background checks of firearm purchasers in some circumstances. The Bureau of Justice statistics reports that presale background checks prevent 6,600 firearm sales to convicted and indicted felons and other ineligible purchasers, such as individuals who are under a restraining order to not intimidate an intimate partner or child. Source: Presale Firearm Checks 1997.

Cook, Philip J., Ludwig, Jens. *Guns In America: National Survey on Private Ownership and Use of Firearms.* NIJ May 1997.

http://www.ncjrs.org/txtfiles/165476.txt

Johns Hopkins Center for Gun Policy and Research: National Opinion Research Center.

http://www.code7cafe.com

National Rifle Association. http://nraila.org/gun-laws/fl.html

U.S. Constitution, Amendment 2.

Presale Firearm Checks, Bureau of Justice Statistics, Dept. of Justice, 1997.

SIDEBAR

Fifth, AIDS may be characterized as a deadly weapon, and therefore, a charge of assault may be elevated to assault with a deadly weapon. Similarly, attacks leading to death may be treated as murder under the deadly weapon doctrine.

In most states, preexisting laws (e.g., murder, attempted murder, and intentional transmission of venereal disease) are relied upon to prosecute AIDS-related crimes. However, a few states have enacted statutes specifically directed at the intentional or negligent transmission of AIDS.

Manslaughter

At common law, murder was an unlawful killing with malice aforethought. **Manslaughter** was an unlawful killing without malice aforethought. Just as was the case with murder, the common law did not divide manslaughter into degrees. Whenever the states began codifying homicides, it was common for manslaughter to be divided into degrees, commonly referred to as voluntary and involuntary, although a few jurisdictions used first- and second-degree language. Today, many jurisdictions continue to recognize two forms of manslaughter.

The important fact is that manslaughter is a lesser crime than murder, and, accordingly, is punished less severely. It is a lesser crime because some fact or facts exist that make the defendant less culpable than a murderer in the eyes of the law. The most common fact that mitigates a defendant's culpability is the absence of a state of mind that society has decided should be punished as murder. Even though society has decided that, because of such extenuating circumstances, a defendant should not be punished as a murderer, it has also decided that some punishment should be inflicted.

Provocation. **Provocation** of the defendant by the victim can reduce a homicide from murder to manslaughter. In jurisdictions that grade manslaughter, a provoked killing is treated as the higher manslaughter, whether that be called first-degree or voluntary.

The theory of provocation, also known as "heat of passion manslaughter," is that a defendant was operating under such an anger or passion that it was impossible for the defendant to have formed the desire to kill, which is required for both first- and second-degree murder. The defense of provocation applies to instances in which people act without thinking; the impulsive act being the result of the victim's behavior.

Again, an objective test is used when examining the defense of provocation. To prove provocation, it must be shown that the provoking act was so severe that a reasonable person may have also killed. It does not require that a reasonable person would have killed; only that a reasonable person would have been so affected by the act that homicide was possible. A few states have enumerated the acts that may act to negate intent to kill (and reduce the homicide to manslaughter) in their manslaughter statutes. Any act not included may not be used by a defendant to reduce a murder charge.

Catching one's spouse in the act of adultery is an example of an act that is considered adequate provocation to reduce any resulting homicide to manslaughter. This rule applies only to marriages and not to other romantic relationships. Generally, serious assaults (batteries) may constitute adequate provocation.

If two people are engaged in "mutual combat," then any resulting death may be reduced from murder to voluntary manslaughter. The key to this defense is mutuality. If it can be shown that the victim did not voluntarily engage in the fight, then the defense of mutual combat is not applicable, and the defendant is responsible for murder.

It is widely held that words and gestures are never adequate provocation. This is true regardless of how vile or vicious a statement or gesture is to the defendant. However, some recent cases have distinguished statements that are informational from those that are not. In such situations, if a statement provides information of an act, and that act would be sufficient provocation, if witnessed, then the statement may also be provocation.

In the *Schnopps* case, the trial judge refused to instruct the jury on the alternative of manslaughter, as opposed to murder. The trial judge followed the rule that statements are never adequate provocation. The appellate court reversed the judge, holding that the statements made by the defendant's wife directly before he killed her may have been adequate provocation for a jury to find voluntary manslaughter and not murder.

Usually, when claiming adultery as provocation, one must have actually caught his or her spouse in the act. Also, the general rule is that words are not adequate provocation. What did the court do in the *Schnopps* case? It appears that the court attempted to sidestep those rules, in a manner that would permit the benefit of the defense without changing the rules. It did this by holding that in adulterous situations, an admission of adultery to one's spouse, when uttered for the first time, is as shocking as finding one's spouse engaged in the act.

 CASE

COMMONWEALTH V. SCHNOPPS

383 Mass. 178, 417 N.E.2d 1213 (1981)

Schnopps testified that his wife had left him three weeks prior to the slaying. He claims that he first became aware of the problems in his fourteen-year marriage at a point about six months before the slaying. According to the defendant, on that occasion he took his wife to a club to dance, and she spent the evening dancing with a co-worker. On arriving home, the defendant and his wife argued over her conduct. She told him that she no longer loved him and that she wanted a divorce. Schnopps became very upset. He admitted that he took out his shotgun during the course of this argument, but he denied that he intended to use it. . . . [The defendant and his wife continued to have marital problems for the next few months.]

On the day of the killing, Schnopps had asked his wife to come to their home and talk over their marital difficulties. Schnopps told his wife that he wanted his children at home, and that he wanted the family to remain intact. Schnopps cried during the conversation and begged his wife to let the children live with him and to keep their family together. His wife replied, "No, I am going to

court, you are going to give me all the furniture, you are going to get the Hell out of here, and you won't have nothing." Then, pointing to her crotch, she said, "You will never touch this again, because I have got something bigger and better for it."

On hearing those words, Schnopps claims that his mind went blank, and that he went "berserk." He went to a cabinet and got out a pistol he had bought the day before, and he shot his wife and himself. . . . [Schnopps lived and his wife died.]

Schnopps argues that "[t]he existence of sufficient provocation is not foreclosed absolutely because a defendant learns of a fact from oral statements rather than from personal observation," and that a sudden admission of adultery is equivalent to a discovery of the act itself, and is sufficient evidence of provocation.

Schnopps asserts that his wife's statements constituted a "peculiarly immediate and intense offense to a spouse's sensitivities." He concedes that the words at issue are indicative of past as well as present adultery. Schnopps claims, however, that his wife's admission of adultery was made for the first time on the day of the killing. . . .

Reversed and remanded for new trial on the manslaughter issue.

Finally, the defense will not be available if there was a sufficient "cooling-off" period. That is, if the time between the provocation and the homicide was long enough for a defendant to regain self-control, then the homicide will be treated as murder and not manslaughter.

Imperfect Self-Defense and Defense of Others.   If Gwen harms Sue while defending herself from Sue's attack, Gwen is said to have acted in self-defense. Self-defense, when valid, normally works to negate criminal liability entirely. So, if Gwen kills Sue to avoid serious bodily harm or death, she has committed an excused homicide. What happens if Gwen was incorrect in her belief that her life was endangered by Sue? This is known as an imperfect self-defense and does not negate culpability entirely. It may, however, reduce liability. Thus, Gwen may be liable only for voluntary manslaughter and not murder. For Gwen to be successful in her claim, she must prove that she had a good faith belief that her life was in danger and that the killing appeared to be necessary to protect herself.

A person may also have an imperfect self-defense when an excessive amount of force is used as protection. So, if Gwen was correct in her belief that she needed to use force for her protection, but used excessive force, she receives the benefit of reduced liability. Again, there must be a reasonable, although incorrect, belief that the amount of force used was necessary.

The concept of self-defense is extended to the defense of others. In such situations, one may be privileged to harm another to prevent that person from injuring or killing someone else. Just as with an imperfect self-defense, if one has a mistaken, but reasonable, belief that another is in danger, and kills as a result of that belief, then he or she is responsible for voluntary manslaughter rather than murder. Also, if one uses deadly force when a lesser amount of force would have been sufficient to stay the attack, liability is limited to manslaughter, provided the belief that deadly force was necessary was reasonable under the circumstances.

Involuntary Manslaughter.   The lowest form of criminal homicide in most jurisdictions is involuntary manslaughter, sometimes named second-degree manslaughter. In most instances involuntary manslaughter is a form of negligent or reckless manslaughter.

You have already learned the misdemeanor manslaughter rule. In jurisdictions that recognize the rule, the person who commits the misdemeanor that results in an unintended death is responsible for the lowest form of criminal homicide.

Involuntary manslaughter also refers to negligent homicide, vehicular homicide, and similar statutes that punish for unintended, accidental deaths. The classic vehicular homicide is when a motorist runs a red light, strikes another car, and causes the death of the driver or passenger of that automobile. Some states, such as Illinois, make vehicular homicide a separate crime from involuntary manslaughter and impose a lesser punishment for vehicular homicide.[7]

Be aware that many states now have specific statutes dealing with deaths caused by intoxicated drivers. Often the punishment is greater if the death is the result of a drunk or otherwise impaired driver.

The term *negligent* has a different meaning in criminal law than in civil law. In tort law, any unreasonable act that causes an injury creates tort liability. In criminal law, more must be shown. The risk taken by the defendant must be high and pose a threat of death or serious bodily injury to the victim. In addition, some jurisdictions require that the defendant be aware of the risk before liability can be imposed. Of course, knowledge can be inferred from the defendant's actions. Some jurisdictions do not require knowledge of the risk (scienter).

The Model Penal Code Approach to Homicide

The Model Penal Code states that "A person is guilty of criminal homicide if he purposely, knowingly, recklessly, or negligently causes the death of another human being."[8] The Code then classifies all criminal homicides as murder, manslaughter, or negligent homicide. This is done by taking the four mens rea (purposeful, knowing, reckless, and negligent) and setting them into one of the classifications. There is some overlap; for example, under some conditions a reckless homicide is murder, and under other conditions it is manslaughter. Let us look at the specifics of the Code.

As you would guess, all purposeful and knowing homicides are murder under the Model Penal Code. Additionally, a reckless homicide is murder when committed "under circumstances manifesting extreme indifference to the value of human life." The Code then incorporates a "felony-murder" type rule, by stating that recklessness and indifference to human life are presumed if the accused was engaged in the commission or attempted commission of robbery, rape, arson, burglary, kidnapping, or felonious escape. So, if an accused is involved in one of those crimes, and a death results, then he may be charged with murder under the Code. Note that the Code only creates a presumption of recklessness and indifference, which may be overcome at trial. Murder is the highest form of homicide, and the Code declares it to be a felony of the first degree.

Manslaughters are felonies of the second degree under the Code. All reckless homicides, except those previously described, are manslaughters. Just as was true at common law, the Code contains a provision that reduces heat-of-passion murders to manslaughter. Specifically, the Code states that a homicide, which would normally be murder, is manslaughter when it is "committed under the influence of extreme mental or emotional disturbance for which there is reasonable explanation or excuse. The reasonableness of such explanation or excuse shall be determined from the viewpoint of a person in the actor's situation under the circumstances he believes them to be."

Last, negligent homicides are entitled just that and are felonies of the third degree.

Life, Death, and Homicide

The actus reus of murder and manslaughter is the taking of a human life. Determining when life begins and ends can be a problem in criminal law, especially when dealing with fetuses.

At common law, it was not a crime to destroy a fetus, unless it was "born alive." To be born alive, the fetus must leave its mother's body and exhibit some ability to live independently. Some courts required that the umbilical cord be cut and that the fetus show its independence thereafter before it was considered a human life. Breathing and crying are both proof of the viability of the child.

Today, many states have enacted feticide statutes that focus on the viability of the fetus. Once it can be shown that the fetus is viable, that is, could live independently if it were born, then anyone who causes its death has committed feticide. Of course, this does not apply to abortion. Since the United States Supreme Court decision in *Roe v. Wade*, 410 U.S. 113 (1973), a woman possesses a limited right to abort a fetus she carries. Thus, states may not prohibit abortions that are protected under that decision. The primary purpose of feticide statutes is to punish individuals who kill fetuses without the mother's approval, as occurred in the *Keeler* case (see Chapter 2).

At the other end of the spectrum is death. Medical advances have made the determination of when death occurs more complex than it was only years ago. For a long period of time, a person was considered dead when there was no heartbeat and no breathing. Today, artificial means can be used to sustain both heart action and respiration. That being so, should one be free of criminal homicide in cases where the victim is being kept "alive" by artificial means and there is no reasonable hope of recovery? Should a physician be charged with murder for "pulling the plug" on a patient who has irreversible brain damage and is in a coma? Using the respiration and heart function test, it would be criminal homicide to end such a treatment. However, many states now use brain death, rather than respiration and heartbeat, to determine when life has ended. In states that employ a brain death definition, it must be shown that there is a total cessation of brain function before legal death exists. The importance of defining death is illustrated by the *Fierro* case.

Suicide

Successful suicide was a crime under the common law of England. The property owned by the one who committed suicide was forfeited to (taken by) the Crown. In early American common law attempted suicide was a crime, usually punished as a misdemeanor. Today suicide is not treated as a crime. However, it is possible to restrain and examine individuals who have attempted to commit suicide under civil psychiatric commitment laws.

It continues to be criminal to encourage or aid another to commit suicide. In most situations such a commission is treated as murder. Assisting suicide may be treated as murder, or, as in Michigan, it may be a separate crime that is punished less severely.

The most well-known suicide cases involve Dr. Jack Kevorkian of Michigan. Dr. Kevorkian, a physician, assisted twenty terminally ill persons in committing suicide between 1990 and 1994.

Dr. Kevorkian's license to practice medicine was suspended in 1991 for his behavior, and criminal charges have been filed against him on several

CASE

**STATE V.
DAVID FIERRO**

124 Ariz. 182, 603 P.2d
74 (1979)

The facts necessary for a resolution of this matter on appeal are as follows. Between 8 and 9 o'clock on the evening of 18 August 1977, Victor Corella was given a ride by Ray Montez and his wife Sandra as they were attempting to locate some marijuana. In the vicinity of 12th Street and Pima, Ray Montez heard his name called from another car. He stopped his car, walked over to the other car and saw that the passenger who had called his name was the defendant Fierro. Defendant told Ray Montez that his brother in the "M," or "Mexican Mafia," had instructed the defendant to kill Corella. Ray Montez told defendant to do it outside the car because he and his wife "did not want to see anything."

Montez returned to his car. Defendant followed and began talking with Corella. Corella got out of the car. Montez started to drive away when defendant began shooting Corella. Corella was shot once in the chest and four times in the head. . . . Corella was maintained on support systems for the next three days while follow-up studies were completed which confirmed the occurrence of brain death. The supportive measures were terminated and he was pronounced dead on 22 August 1977. . . .

CAUSE OF DEATH

At the trial, Dr. Hugh McGill, a surgical resident at the Maricopa County Hospital, testified that:

After surgery he was taken to the intensive-care unit. He was evaluated by a neurosurgeon who felt there was nothing we could do for his brain, he had brain death. He remained somewhat stable over the next two or three days. We had follow-up studies that confirmed our impression of brain death and because of that supportive measures were terminated and he was pronounced dead, I believe, on the 22nd. . . .

Defendant initially argues that the termination of support systems by attendant doctors three days after Corella suffered "brain death" was the cause of Corella's death [and as such, he could not be responsible for Corella's death]. . . .

In the instant case, the body of the victim was breathing, though not spontaneously, and blood was pulsating through his body before the life support mechanisms were withdrawn. Because there was an absence of cardiac and circulatory arrest, under the common-law rule he would not have been legally dead. Under the Harvard Medical School test and Proposal of the National Conference of Commissioners on Uniform State Laws he was, in fact, dead before the life supports were withdrawn as he had become "brain" or "neurologically" dead prior to that time. We believe that while the common-law definition of death is still sufficient to establish death, the [brain death test] is also a valid test for death in Arizona.

occasions. The first three cases were dismissed because the statute under which he was charged was held unconstitutional.

The Michigan legislature enacted a law in February 1993 that provided for as much as four years imprisonment and a $2,000 fine for providing the physical means by which another attempts or commits suicide or participates in a physical act by which another attempts or commits suicide. The person charged must have had knowledge that the other person intended to commit suicide.[9]

In 1999 Dr. Kevorkian allowed the news program *60 Minutes* to nationally broadcast his act of assisting Thomas Youk to die. However, Dr. Kevorkian went further than he had in previous cases. Rather than providing a machine to the patient that could assist in death, Dr. Kevorkian administered a lethal injection to Mr. Youk. He then challenged Michigan prosecutors to charge him again. They did and Dr. Kevorkian was convicted of murder and sentenced to ten to twenty-five years in prison.

While Dr. Kevorkian may have gone too far in committing euthanasia, Dr. Kevorkian's first three acquittals suggest that there is public support for physician-assisted suicide. In 1997 Oregon enacted the Death With Dignity Act. This law decriminalizes physician-assisted suicide under certain circumstances. This is the first law of its type in United States history.[10] Whether other states will follow Oregon's lead remains to be seen. It will take individual state action to pave the way for physician-assisted suicide, however, since the Supreme Court handed down *Washington v. Glucksberg* (1997).[11] In *Glucksberg* the Court found that terminally ill patients do not possess a privacy or due process right in having physicians assist them in committing suicide. Accordingly, state action is required to recognize the right.

Corpus Delicti

corpus delicti

(Latin) "The body of the crime." The material substance upon which a crime has been committed; for example, a dead body (in the crime of murder) or a house burned down (in the crime of arson).

Corpus delicti is a Latin phrase that translates as "the body of a crime." Prosecutors have the burden of proving the corpus delicti of crimes at trial. Every crime has a corpus delicti. It refers to the substance of the crime. For example, in murder cases the corpus delicti is the death of a victim and the act that caused the death. In arson, the corpus delicti is a burned structure and the cause of the fire.

A confession of an accused is never enough to prove corpus delicti. There must be either direct proof or evidence supporting a confession.

In murder cases the corpus delicti can usually be proved by an examination of the victim's corpse. After an autopsy a physician will usually be prepared to testify that the alleged act either did, or could have, caused the death. In some instances, the body of a victim cannot be located. Such "no body" cases make the job of the prosecution harder. Even so, if evidence establishes that the person is dead, such as blood stains and discovered personal effects, then murder may be proven. Of course, the prosecution must also show that the defendant caused the death. So, if a defendant confesses to a murder, or makes other incriminating statements, and no other evidence is found, no corpus delicti exists, and the defendant cannot be convicted. However, if blood matching the victim's is discovered where the defendant stated the murder occurred, then a murder conviction can be sustained.

SIDEBAR

CRIME IN THE UNITED STATES: VIOLENT CRIME   Violent crime is at one of its highest levels in United States history. Only during two other periods (1931–1934 and 1979–1981) has violent crime been as high as during the 1990s.

The murder rate (per capita figures) is twice as high in the United States as in Spain, which has the second highest crime rate of industrialized nations. It is four times as high as the Canadian murder rate, eight times as high as England's, and as much as ten times as high as Japan's.

Regrettably, most violence falls on ethnic minorities; the lifetime risk of murder for a black male is 42 per 1,000 people and 18 per 1,000 among Native American males. It is only 6 per 1,000 for white males and 3 per 1,000 for white females.

Violent crime is much higher in urban areas than rural, and the larger a city becomes, the greater its crime rate. The nation's metropolitan areas report 684 violent crimes per 100,000 people while rural counties reported 231 violent crimes per 100,000 people in 1997.

Sources: *Understanding and Preventing Crime* (National Institute of Justice, Feb. 1994); Erika Fairchild, *Comparative Criminal Justice Systems* (Wadsworth Publishing 1993); Source Book, Federal Bureau of Investigation, Department of Justice (1998).

ASSAULT AND BATTERY

Assault and **battery** are two different crimes, although they commonly occur together. As with homicide, all states have made assaults and batteries criminal by statute.

A *battery* is an intentional touching of another that is either offensive or harmful. The mens rea element varies among the states; however, most now provide for both intentional and negligent battery. Of course, negligence in criminal law involves a greater risk than in civil law. To be negligent in criminal law, there must be a disregard of a high risk of injury to another; in tort law, one need only show a disregard of an ordinary risk. The Model Penal Code provides for purposeful, knowing, and reckless batteries. In addition, if one uses a deadly weapon, negligence may give rise to a battery charge. Otherwise, negligence may not provide the basis for a battery conviction.

The actus reus of battery is a touching. An individual need not touch someone with his or her actual person to commit a battery. Objects that are held are considered extensions of the body. If Sherry strikes Doug with an iron, she has battered him regardless of the fact that her person never came into contact with his. Likewise, items thrown at another are extensions of the person who took the act of propelling them into the air. If Doug were to injure Sherry with a knife he threw at her, then he has battered her.

A touching must be either offensive or harmful to be a battery. Of course, any resulting physical injury is proof of harm. The problem arises when one touches another in a manner found offensive to the person being touched, but there is no apparent physical injury. For example, a man who touches a woman's breast without her consent has committed a battery because the touching is offensive. If a person touches another in an angry manner, a battery has been committed, even though the touching was not intended to injure the party and in fact does no harm.

There are two varieties of assault. First, when a person puts another in fear or apprehension of an imminent battery, an assault has been committed. For

assault

An intentional threat, show of force, or movement that could reasonably make a person feel in danger of physical attack or harmful physical contact. It can be a crime or tort.

battery

An intentional, unconsented to, physical contact by one person (or an object controlled by that person) with another person. It can be a crime or a tort.

example, if Gary attempts to strike Terry, but Terry evades the swing by ducking, Gary has committed an assault. The rule does not require that the victim actually experience fear; apprehension of an impending battery is sufficient. Apprehension is simply an expectation of an unwanted event. Also, the threat must be imminent to rise to the level of an assault. A threat that one will be battered in the future is not sufficient. So, if Terry told Gary that he was "going to kick the shit out of him in one hour," there is no assault.

Because an apprehension by the victim is required, there is no assault under this theory if the victim was not aware of the assault. For example, if X swings his arm at Y intending to scare Y, but Y has her back turned and does not see X's behavior, then there is no assault. This is not true of batteries. If X strikes Y, a battery has been committed, regardless of whether Y saw the punch coming.

The second type of assault is an attempted battery. This definition remedies the problem just discussed. Any unsuccessful battery is an assault, regardless of the victim's knowledge of the act. Of course, it must be determined that the act in question would have been a battery if it had been completed.

To prove battery it must be shown that a contact was made. This is not necessary to prove an assault. However, it is possible to have both an assault and a battery. If John sees Henry swing the baseball bat that strikes John, there has been an assault and battery. However, due to the doctrine of merger the defendant will only be punished for the higher crime of battery.

Aggravated Assault and Battery

Under special circumstances, an assault or battery can be classified as aggravated. If aggravated, a higher penalty is imposed. The process of defining such crimes as more serious than simple assaults and batteries varies. Statutes may call such crimes aggravated assault or battery; or may refer to specific crimes under a special name, such as assault with intent to kill; or may simply use the facts at the sentencing stage to enhance (increase) the sentence; or may refer to such as a higher assault, such as felony assault rather than misdemeanor assault. In any event, the following facts commonly aggravate an assault or battery.

The assault is aggravated if the assault or battery is committed while the actor is engaged in the commission of another crime. So, if a man batters a woman while possessing the specific intent to rape her, he has committed an aggravated battery. This is true regardless of whether the rape was completed. If a defendant is stopped before he has committed the rape, but after he has assaulted or battered the victim, there has been an aggravated battery. Hence the crime may be titled "assault with an intent to commit rape" or "assault with intent to murder."

It is also common to make assault and battery committed on persons of some special status more serious. Law enforcement officers or other public officials often fall into this category. Of course, the crime must relate to the performance or status of the officer to be aggravated. For example, if an off-duty police officer is struck by an angry neighbor over a boundary dispute, the battery is not aggravated. Examples of other protected classes of individuals are minors and the mentally disabled.

The extent of injury to the victim may also lead to an increased charge. Usually a battery may be aggravated if the harm rises to the level of "serious bodily injury." Some statutes specifically state that certain injuries aggravate the crime of battery, such as the loss of an eye. Mayhem, a related crime, is discussed next.

CRIME IN THE UNITED STATES In 2000, there were 910,744 aggravated assaults in the United States; that is, 324 aggravated assaults per 100,000 people. This crime accounted for 7.8 percent of all crimes in the United States in 2000.

Source: *Uniform Crime Reports*, U.S. Department of Justice, Federal Bureau of Investigation, 2001.

MAYHEM

Mayhem, originally a common-law crime, is the crime of intentionally dismembering or disfiguring a person. The crime has an interesting origin. In England, all men were to be available to fight for the king. It was a serious crime to injure a man in such a manner as to make him unable to fight. Early punishments for mayhem were incarceration, death, and the imposition of the same injury that had been inflicted on the victim. Originally, only dismemberment that could prevent a man from fighting for the king was punished as mayhem. As such, cutting off a man's leg or arm was punishable, whereas cutting off an ear was not. Of course, causing a disfigurement was not mayhem.

Today, both disfigurement and dismemberment fall under mayhem statutes. Many jurisdictions specifically state what injuries must be sustained for a charge of mayhem. Causing another to lose an eye, ear, or limb are examples, as is castration.

Some states no longer have mayhem statutes, but have chosen to treat such crimes as aggravated batteries.

mayhem
The crime of violently, maliciously, and intentionally giving someone a serious permanent wound. In some states, a type of aggravated assault. Once, the crime of permanently wounding another (as by dismemberment) to deprive the person of fighting ability.

SEX CRIMES

This section deals with crimes that involve sex. Keep in mind that crimes such as assault and battery may be sexually motivated. For example, if a man touches a woman's breast, he has committed a battery (provided that the touching was unwelcome).

The phrase "sex crimes" actually encompasses a variety of sexually motivated crimes. Rape, sodomy, incest, and sexually motivated batteries and murders are included. Obscenity, prostitution, abortion, distribution of child pornography, and public nudity are examples of other sex-related offenses.

Although certain offenses are universally prohibited, other offenses vary among the states. For example, rape is criminal in all states, but prostitution is not.

Rape

rape
The crime of a man imposing sexual intercourse by force or otherwise without legally valid consent.

At common law, the elements of **rape** were (1) sexual intercourse with (2) a woman, not the man's wife (3) committed without the victim's consent and by using force. Many problems were encountered with this definition. First, the common-law definition required that the rapist be a man. Hence, women and male minors could not be convicted of rape. Also, the *marital rape exception* provided that men could not be convicted of raping their wives. Similarly, a man could not be charged with battering his wife if the battery was inflicted in an effort to force sex. This exception was founded upon the theory that when women married they consented to sex with their husbands upon demand. Additionally, many courts wrote that to permit a woman to charge her husband with such a crime would lead to destruction of the family unit. Finally, the last requirement, with force and without consent, led many courts to require victims to resist the attack to the utmost and to continue to resist during the rape.

States have changed the common-law definition of rape to remedy these problems. First, most states have worded their statutes to permit minors and women to be charged with rape. While there are few cases of women actually raping men, or other women, there are several cases where women have been convicted as principals to the crime.[12] The Model Penal Code is gender-neutral as to all sex crimes except rape.[13]

The marital rape exception has been abolished in most states. A few states have retained the rule in modified form, such as Ohio, which provides immunity to a husband except when he is separated from his wife.[14]

Finally, the last requirement has changed significantly. A person need not resist to the extent required under the common law. What is required now is proof that the victim did resist. However, a victim need not risk life or serious bodily injury in an attempt to prevent the rape. So if a woman simply tells a man on a date "I don't want to," there has been inadequate resistance. The result would be different if the man produced a gun and told the woman he would kill her if she resisted.

SIDEBAR

RECIDIVISM BY SEXUAL OFFENDERS   Special legislation dealing with sexual predators can be found as early as 1930. In recent years, states have enacted laws requiring treatment after release from prison, monitoring after release, castration as part of sentences, and civil commitment of offenders after release. One reason sexual offenders receive so much attention is the apparent inability to treat and reform them. The recidivism rate of sexual offenders is much higher than that of other crimes. One study found that rapists and child molesters reported that they had committed five or more sexual offenses for which they had not been arrested. As many as 50 percent of all sexual offenders will reoffend after being released from prison. Within three years of release, 7.7 percent of rapists commit another rape. Nearly one-third of rapists commit some form of violent crime within three years of release.

Contrary to a prevailing myth, the likelihood of a sex offender reoffending does not diminish with age. Some experts believe what is critical is identifying potential sex offenders at an early age. Research has shown that the level of violence committed by sex offenders increases as their acts go undiscovered.

Source: Steven I. Friedland, "On Treatment, Punishment, and the Civil Commitment of Sex Offenders," 70 *U. Colo. L. Rev.* 73 (1999).

So, the elements of rape, under new statutes, are: (1) Sexual intercourse (2) with another against that person's will or without that person's consent and (3) by the use of force or under such a threat of force that a reasonable person would have believed that resistance would have resulted in serious bodily harm or death.

Note that one element has not changed, namely, the definition of sexual intercourse. Generally, the contact must be penis-vagina; anal sex, fellatio, and other acts are usually punished under sodomy statutes. The requirement is the same today as it was under the common law. The "slightest penetration" of the woman's vulva is sufficient. The man need not ejaculate.

Some states grade rape according to the extent of injuries that the victim received and whether the victim knew the rapist. The Model Penal Code punishes rape as a felony in the second degree, unless serious bodily injury occurs or the victim was not a social companion of the rapist, in which case the rape is of the first degree.

CRIME IN THE UNITED STATES In 2000 there were 90,186 reported forcible rapes in the United States. This number includes attempted rapes and assaults with intent to rape; however, nonforcible rapes, such as statutory rape, are not included. Rapes constituted .8 percent of all crimes in the United States in 2000. The actual number of rapes is likely much higher, as rape is believed to be one of the most under-reported crimes.

Source: *Uniform Crime Reports,* U.S. Department of Justice, Federal Bureau of Investigation, 2001.

Nonforcible Rape

Under some circumstances, one may commit a rape even though the other party consented to the sexual contact. So-called **statutory rape** is such a crime. The actus reus of statutory rape is sexual intercourse with someone under a specified age, commonly sixteen. The purpose of the law is to protect those the law presumes are too young to make a mature decision concerning sex. Hence, consent is not relevant. So, a rape has occurred when a girl under sixteen consents to sexual intercourse with a male aged eighteen or older.

statutory rape
The crime of a man having sexual intercourse with a girl under a certain state-set age (whether or not the girl consents.)

In most states, statutory rape is a strict liability crime. The act of having sex with someone below the specified age is proof alone of guilt. No showing of mens rea is required. A few states impose a knowledge requirement. In those states, if the accused can convince the jury that there was reason to believe that the other party was "of age," then the accused is acquitted. For example, if a fifteen-year-old girl tells a boy that she is seventeen, she indeed looks seventeen, and she shows the boy a falsified identification bearing that age, he would have a defense to statutory rape.

In many states, only females are protected by statutory rape laws. If a boy of fifteen years has sex with a girl of seventeen years, the law will not punish her as they would the boy if the ages were turned around. It has been alleged that such treatment is violative of the Equal Protection Clause of the United States Constitution. The United States Supreme Court has rejected that claim by reasoning that one of the goals of such statutes is the prevention of teenage pregnancy. Because females can be impregnated, states have a legitimate interest in prosecuting males who have sex with females who are under the age of consent.[15] Using this analysis a state may prosecute males only, as females cannot impregnate young men or women. However, many acts by adult females (or adult males to young males) may be prosecuted under another law, such as child molestation or criminal deviate conduct.

Similar to statutory rape, having sex with those who are incapable of consenting due to mental or emotional disability is also rape.

Sodomy

sodomy
A general word for an "unnatural" sex act or the crime committed by such act. While the definition varies, *sodomy* can include oral sex, anal sex, homosexual sex, or sex with animals.

Sodomy is defined by Merrian *Webster Online Dictionary* (2003) as "copulation with a member of the same sex or with an animal" or "noncoital and especially anal or oral copulation with a member of the opposite sex." Many statutes now include sodomy in "criminal deviate conduct" statutes. Sodomy is prohibited in most states, and in most jurisdictions fellatio, cunnilingus, bestiality, homosexual activity, anal sex, and sometimes masturbation are included. There is substantial disagreement concerning whether such acts should be prohibited between consenting adults. Those who support sodomy laws usually do so for religious reasons. Those who oppose such laws contend that two adults should be permitted to engage in any sexual conduct they desire, provided that no one is injured. In any event, one practical problem exists; enforcement of sodomy laws is nearly impossible. Determining what sexual acts people engage in privately is not an easy task. Additionally, law enforcement appears to have no incentive to enforce such laws when there appears to be no resulting injury, and there is substantial noncompliance with many sodomy laws, such as fellatio and cunnilingus.

Those who oppose enforcement of sodomy laws between consenting adults do not oppose punishment of those who force acts of sodomy on others. At common law, a man had to have penile-vulva contact to commit rape. If a man forced oral or anal sex on a woman, he committed sodomy. Sodomy was also punished severely. Many states continue to prohibit sodomy, even in marriage. Some prosecutors are using sodomy laws to punish homosexuals for their sexual activity, and the United States Supreme Court has upheld such applications of sodomy laws.[16]

Rape Shield Laws

So-called **shield laws** were enacted in the 1970s and 1980s in an effort to protect rape victims from harassment by defense attorneys at trial. Before such laws existed, defense attorneys often would use evidence of a victim's prior sexual conduct to infer that the victim had consented to the act. It is thought that the humiliation of the rape itself, matched with this treatment at trial, accounted for the nonreporting of many rapes.

In an effort to protect victims from unwarranted abuse at trial, rape shield laws were enacted. Evidence of prior sexual conduct, except with the defendant, is not permitted at trial. Also, evidence of a victim's reputation in the community is inadmissible.

shield laws
A state law that prohibits use of most evidence of a rape (or other sexual crime) victim's past sexual conduct, or that protects the victim's identity.

Incest

Sex between family members is *incest,* which is a crime. Generally, law enforcement is concerned with abuse of children, although it is also a crime for two consenting adult family members to engage in sex. Often, when an adult family member is involved with a child, other statutes, such as child molestation laws, will also apply.

The actus reus of incest is intercourse, or other sexual conduct, between family members. Normally, incest laws parallel marriage laws for a definition of *family.* That is, if two people are permitted to marry under state law, then they are also permitted to engage in sex, regardless of marriage. It is common for states to prohibit marriage of individuals of first cousin affinity and closer.

If the incestuous party is a parent, courts often attempt to seek family counseling and therapy rather than incarceration. However, in extreme situations criminal penalties can be severe, and civil remedies allow removal of the child from the home, as well as termination of parental rights.

Sex Offenses Against Children

Most states have a number of statutes specifically aimed at protecting children from sexual abuse and exploitation. Indiana has five statutes that directly pertain to sexual activity with children. Those statutes are:

Indiana Code § 35-42-4-3 Child Molesting
(a) A person who, with a child under twelve (12) years of age, performs or submits to sexual intercourse or deviate sexual conduct commits child molesting, a Class B felony. However, the offense is a Class A felony if it is committed by using or threatening the use of deadly force, or while armed with a deadly weapon, or if it results in serious bodily injury.
(b) A person who, with a child under twelve (12) years of age, performs or submits to any fondling or touching, of either the child or the older person,

with intent to arouse or to satisfy the sexual desire of either the child or the older person, commits child molesting, a Class C felony. However, the offense is a Class A felony if it is committed by using or threatening the use of deadly force, or while armed with a deadly weapon.

(c) A person sixteen (16) years of age or older who, with a child of twelve (12) years of age or older but under sixteen (16) years of age, performs or submits to sexual intercourse or deviate sexual conduct commits child molesting, a Class C felony. However, the offense is a Class A felony if it is committed by using or threatening the use of deadly force, or while armed with a deadly weapon.

(d) A person sixteen (16) years of age, or older who, with a child twelve (12) years of age or older but under sixteen (16) years of age, performs or submits to any fondling or touching, of either the child or the older person, with intent to arouse or to satisfy the sexual desires of either the child or the older person, commits child molesting, a Class D felony. However, the offense is a Class B felony if it is committed by using or threatening the use of deadly force, or while armed with a deadly weapon.

(e) It is a defense that the accused person reasonably believed that the child was sixteen (16) years of age or older at the time of the conduct.

(f) It is a defense that the child is or has ever been married.

Indiana Code § 35-42-4-4 Child Exploitation

(b) Any person who knowingly or intentionally:

   (1) manages, produces, sponsors, presents, exhibits, photographs, films, or videotapes any performance or incident that includes sexual conduct by a child under sixteen (16) years of age; or

   (2) disseminates, exhibits to another person, offers to disseminate or exhibit to another person, or sends or brings into Indiana for dissemination or exhibition matter that depicts or describes sexual conduct by a child under sixteen (16) years of age; commits child exploitation. . . .

(c) A person who knowingly or intentionally possesses:

   (1) a picture;
   (2) a drawing;
   (3) a photograph;
   (4) a negative image;
   (5) undeveloped film;
   (6) a motion picture;
   (7) a videotape; or
   (8) any pictorial representation;

   that depicts sexual conduct by a child who is, or appears to be, less than sixteen (16) years of age and that lacks serious literary, artistic, political or scientific value commits possession of child pornography. . . .

Indiana Code § 35-42-4-5 Vicarious Sexual Gratification

(a) A person eighteen (18) years of age or older who knowingly or intentionally directs, aids, induces, or causes a child under the age of sixteen (16) to touch or fondle himself or another child under the age of sixteen (16) with intent to arouse or satisfy the sexual desires of a child or the older person commits vicarious sexual gratification. . . .

(b) A person eighteen (18) years of age or older who knowingly or intentionally directs, aids, induces, or causes a child under the age of sixteen (16) to:

    (1) engage in sexual intercourse with another child under sixteen (16) years of age;

    (2) engage in sexual conduct with an animal other than a human being; or

    (3) engage in deviate sexual conduct with another person . . . commits vicarious sexual gratification. . . .

Indiana Code § 35-42-4-6 Child Solicitation

A person eighteen (18) years of age or older who knowingly or intentionally solicits a child under twelve (12) years of age to engage in:

(1) sexual intercourse;

(2) deviate sexual conduct; or

(3) any fondling or touching intended to arouse or satisfy the sexual desires of either the child or the older person; commits child solicitation. . . .

Indiana Code § 35-42-4-7 Child Seduction

(e) If a person who is:

    (1) at least eighteen (18) years of age; and

    (2) the guardian, adoptive parent, adoptive grandparent, custodian . . . of a child at least sixteen (16) years of age but less than eighteen (18) years of age; engages in sexual intercourse or deviate sexual conduct with the child, the person commits child seduction. . . .

Note that statutory rape falls under the child molestation statute in Indiana. Also, the defense of a good faith and reasonable belief that a child is of statutory age is recognized by statute.

The number of people charged with committing sex crimes against children is increasing. Many of those charged are nonbiological guardians. This has led to statutes such as Ind. Code § 35-42-4-7, "Child seduction," which was added to Indiana's sex offenses statutes in 1987.

Megan's Laws, Commitment, and Castration

In New Jersey in 1994 Megan Kanka, a seven-year-old girl, was kidnapped, raped, and murdered by a recidivist sex offender who had been released from prison. In response, New Jersey enacted what has become known as Megan's Law. The statute requires sex offenders to register with local law enforcement agencies. These agencies in turn make the registration information available to the public.

Today, every state has some form of Megan's Law.[17] In some states, registration is required and the information is not generally available. In others, the public may request the information. And in others, law enforcement officials are required to disseminate the information. The rapid adoption of such laws by the states is due in part to the federal government. In 1996 a federal statute became effective that encouraged the states to adopt such laws and threatened loss of federal funds to those states that did not participate.[18]

In addition to registration and notification laws, some states have turned to civil or regulatory law to control sex offenders. Kansas law, for example, provides for the civil commitment of sexual predators who are "mentally abnormal" or suffer a "personality disorder," who lack control over their behavior, and who pose a danger to others. The law may be applied to any individual who meets these standards, regardless of whether charged, convicted, or previously punished. The Supreme Court found this law constitutional in *Kansas v. Hendricks* (1997).[19] A similar Washington state statute was upheld by the Supreme Court in *Seling v. Young* (2001).[20] The Court reasoned that the law is not criminal in nature, it is regulatory, and there is a long history of civil detention of individuals who are both mentally ill and dangerous.

Critics allege that these laws are unconstitutional efforts by states to bypass the criminal justice system by using civil commitment to punish sexual offenders. They also contend that individuals are not being punished for actual behaviors, but for status. While the Supreme Court rejected these claims in the *Hendricks* case, it also emphasized that only individuals who are both mentally ill and dangerous may be committed and that the state must prove these elements in an adversarial hearing by at least clear and convincing evidence.

So-called chemical castration is also used to control sex offenders. Drugs such as Depo-Provera are used to inhibit the sex drive and sexual function of male sex offenders. Actual surgical castration is provided for by Texas law in lieu of taking the drugs. Texas leaves the choice to the offender. Castration is criticized for not addressing the underlying motivation of sex crimes—the need to control others. It is argued that castration will only lead to the commission of some other form of violent crime.[21]

KIDNAPPING AND FALSE IMPRISONMENT

Kidnapping

kidnapping
Taking away and holding a person illegally, usually against the person's will or by force.

Kidnapping was a misdemeanor at common law, although it was regarded as a very serious crime, often resulting in life imprisonment. Felonies were often punished by death at the early common law. Today kidnapping is a felony and carries a harsh penalty in most states. Additionally, if the kidnapping takes the victim across state lines, the crime is a violation of the Federal Kidnapping Act.[22] The federal government, usually the Federal Bureau of Investigation, may become involved in any kidnapping twenty-four hours after the victim has been seized, by virtue of the Federal Kidnapping Act, which creates a presumption that the victim has been transported across state lines after that period of time.[23]

The elements of kidnapping are (1) the unlawful (2) taking and confinement and (3) asportation of (4) another person (5) by use of force, threat, fraud, or deception.

The taking of the victim must be unlawful. Thus, arrests made by police officers while engaged in their lawful duties are not kidnappings. Neither is it kidnapping for a guardian to take a ward from one place to another, so long as the action is lawful. However, when an officer, or other, acts completely without legal authority, he or she may not be shielded from liability.

There must be a taking and confinement. Confinement is broadly construed. If Pat puts a gun to Craig's back and orders him to walk a half mile to Pat's home, there has been a confinement. Generally, there must be a restriction of the victim's freedom to take alternative action.

This taking and confinement must occur as a result of threat, force, fraud, or deception. Of course, Pat's gun in the example is ample threat to satisfy this requirement. Deception may also be used to gain control over the victim. For example, if Jon convinces his estranged wife to enter a house under the pretense of discussing their marital difficulties and then locks the door, he has fraudulently gained control over her.

Finally, there must be an asportation of the victim. *Asportation* means movement. The issue of the amount of movement necessary to meet this requirement is the most controversial question concerning kidnapping as a crime. The Model Penal Code and most states now hold that if the kidnapping is incidental to the commission of another crime, there is insufficient asportation; some courts speak in terms of a movement of a "substantial distance."[24] To be incidental, a kidnapping must simply be a product of an intent to commit another crime. If a bank robber orders a teller to move from her window to the safe to fill a bag with money, four of the elements of kidnapping are present; however, the third element, asportation, has not been established because the movement was only incidental to the robbery. The result may be different if the teller was ordered to move to the safe for the purpose of raping her. The issue of substantial distance was raised in *Commonwealth v. Hughes.* In that case the court focused on whether the movement substantially increased the risk of harm to victim.

Many statutes specifically state that if the acts of asportation and confinement occur in furtherance of named crimes, then there is a kidnapping. Such statutes commonly include kidnapping for ransom, political reasons, rape, and murder. It is also common to upgrade kidnappings for these reasons. One type of kidnapping that is usually graded low is the taking of a child by a parent in violation of a court order.

Parental Kidnapping

With a dissolution of marriage comes the separation of property owned by the couple, as well as a custody order if the couple has children. Often, costly and bitter custody disputes are also the result of divorce. In recent years "childnapping," or kidnapping of one's own child in violation of a custody order, has received much public attention.

CASE

COMMONWEALTH V. HUGHES

399 A.2d 694 (Pa. Super. Ct. 1979)

[The appellant approached the victim, Ms. Helfrich, who was seated on a park bench.] Appellant asked Ms. Helfrich if she wanted to go for a ride or smoke some marijuana with him. When Ms. Helfrich refused, appellant left. Minutes later, the appellant returned, placed a sharp kitchen knife to her throat, and stated, "I think you are going for a ride." Appellant forced Ms. Helfrich to walk to his car one and one-half blocks away and threatened to kill her if she resisted. Once in the car, he drove around the Media area in a reckless manner for approximately two miles and stopped his car in an abandoned lot surrounded by trees. He then forced Ms. Helfrich into the wooded area where he raped her. . . .

"A person is guilty of kidnapping if he unlawfully removes another a substantial distance, under the circumstances, from the place where he is found or if he unlawfully confines another for a substantial period in a place of isolation." . . .

The framers of the Model Penal Code were aware of the experience of other jurisdictions when they drafted the model kidnapping statute. They recognized that "[w]hen an especially outrageous crime is committed there will be a public clamor for the extreme penalty and it is asking too much of public officials and juries to resist such pressures." . . . To combat the undesirable situation of charging kidnapping to obtain a higher permissible sentence, the framers of the Model Penal Code drafted the kidnapping statute restrictively. . . . The drafters made explicit their "purpose to preclude kidnapping convictions based on trivial changes of location having no bearing on the evil at hand."

Drawing from the experience of other jurisdictions, the comments to the Model Code, and the fact that the Pennsylvania statute is similar to the Model Penal Code statute of kidnapping, it is clear to us that the legislature intended to exclude from kidnapping the incidental movement of a victim during the commission of a crime which does not substantially increase the risk of harm to the victim.

Turning to the case at hand, we find that the movement of the victim was not a trivial incident to the other crime charged. Although the victim was removed only a distance of two miles, the wooded area to which she was brought was in an isolated area, seemingly beyond the aid of her friends and police. Under the circumstances, two miles is a substantial enough distance to place the victim in a completely different environmental setting removed from the security of familiar surroundings. (In addition, the movement itself seriously endangered the victim as she was subject to a knife poised at her throat and to the reckless driving of appellant. At one point, appellant drove onto a one-way street in the wrong direction.) . . . Accordingly, the conviction is sustained.

Due to the rise in the number of such acts, new statutes specifically aimed at parental kidnapping have been adopted. The federal government entered this arena in 1980 by enacting the Parental Kidnapping Prevention Act.[25] Although this statute does not concern itself with criminal sanctions for childnapping, it does require that all states respect child custody orders of other states. That is, a person cannot escape a court order concerning custody of the child by kidnapping the child and fleeing to another jurisdiction. Interestingly, the federal government has left the actual punishment of parental kidnapping to the states. The federal kidnapping act specifically excludes such acts from its reach. Thus, kidnapping by a parent must be punished in a state court. This may occur in the state from which the child is taken or in any state where the parent takes the child.

Kidnapping of one's own child is often punished less severely than other kidnappings. This is sensible because many "childnappings" do not create a risk to the child's welfare; rather, they are the result of an overzealous, loving parent or a parent who is trying to hurt the other parent. Obviously, the crime should be punished because of the harm to the custodial parent, but the crime does not have the same evil motive a kidnapping with an intent to rape or murder does.

False Imprisonment

The crime of **false imprisonment** is similar to kidnapping, and in fact all kidnappings involve a false imprisonment. The opposite is not true. Not all false imprisonments are kidnappings. A false imprisonment occurs when (1) one person (2) interferes (3) with another's liberty (4) by use of threat or force (5) without authority. The primary distinction between the two crimes is the absence of asportation as an element of false imprisonment.

Today, some states have one statute that encompasses both false imprisonment and kidnapping. Such statutes are drafted so that the crime is graded, often elevating the crime if the motive is ransom, rape, serious bodily injury, or murder.

false imprisonment
The unlawful restraint by one person of the physical liberty of another.

STALKING

In recent years, **stalking** has been the subject of considerable media, public, and legislative attention. Public awareness of stalking increased when prominent public figures who were the victims of stalkers, including politicians, actors, and law enforcement officials, began to speak out.

Stalking posed unique problems to law enforcement officials, prosecutors, and judges. Before 1990, no state had a law specifically aimed at combatting stalking. Therefore, preexisting criminal laws, such as assault, battery, and threats, as well as the use of restraining orders, were relied upon in dealing with stalkers. But these laws proved ineffective. Often there is no assault, battery, or provable threat until the victim has been injured or murdered. Even when one of these crimes could be proven, sentences were short. Restraining orders also proved to give victims little protection.

In response to the growing public interest in stalking, California enacted the nation's first stalking law in 1990. By 1993, another forty-six states enacted similar laws.[26]

Stalking laws vary in their elements, but most include a list of acts that satisfy the actus reus of the crime. These include following, harassing, threatening, lying in wait, or conducting surveillance of another person. Usually, one act does not amount to stalking; rather, there must be a pattern or scheme of acts. The first statutes had as a mens rea element a specific intent to cause emotional distress, or to invoke fear of bodily injury or death. However, this has proven ineffective, as stalkers, who are often suffering from emotional or mental illness, often do not have a specific intent to cause fear or harm, even though either or both of these are likely to result. Many states, such as Washington,

stalking
The crime of repeatedly following, threatening, or harassing another person in ways that lead to a legitimate fear of physical harm. Some states define *stalking* more broadly as any conduct with no legitimate purpose that seriously upsets a targeted person, especially conduct in violation of a protective order.

have remedied this by lowering the mens rea to actual or constructive knowl-edge. So long as the stalker should have known that the victim would suffer distress or fear, the mens rea satisfies this breed of stalking law. Through these laws, the police may intercede before violence occurs.

Even before stalking laws, many states criminalized harassment. Personal harassment, telephone harassment, and other specific forms of harassment are commonly included in these laws. However, as mentioned earlier, these statutes were not effective in stopping stalkers, primarily because of the short sentences violators usually received.

A new type of stalker has emerged in the recent past, the cyberstalker. Because of the impersonal and seemingly anonymous nature of electronic communications, it is both easier and safer to harass other persons than it has been in the past. In recent years, stalking using another person's identity has increased. Known as "spoofing," this crime has two victims. The individual receiving the messages and the individual whose identity has been stolen.

Both state and federal statutes exist that criminalize cyberstalking. For example, the Communications Decency Act, 47 U.S.C. § 223(a)(1)(A), provides for criminal prosecution of any person who "by means of a telecommunications device knowingly makes, creates, or solicits, and initiates the transmission of any comment, request, suggestion, proposal, image, or other communication which is obscene, lascivious, filthy, or indecent, with the intent to annoy, abuse, threaten or harass another person." Another federal statute, 18 U.S.C. § 875(c), makes it a federal crime to "transmit [] in interstate or foreign commerce any communication containing any threat to kidnap any person or any threat to injure the person of another." Other federal and state laws that were originally intended to apply to telephone harassment may apply as well.

However, anytime speech is criminalized, there is a First Amendment free speech issue. Statute 47 U.S.C. § 223(a)(1)(A) and similar statutes have been challenged as overbroad because they prohibit not only obscene speech, which clearly may be regulated, but also "indecent" speech that is intended to annoy. The jury is still out on this question.[27]

CIVIL RIGHTS AND HATE CRIMES

The federal and state governments have enacted laws criminalizing acts that encroach upon an individual's civil liberties. It is a crime against the United States for two or more persons to conspire to injure, oppress, threaten, or intimidate a person for exercising a federally secured right.[28]

In addition, any person acting pursuant to state law or authority (under color of law) who deprives a person of a federally secured right due to alienage, race, or color is guilty of a federal civil rights crime.[29] Because of the "color of law" requirement, defendants are usually state or local officials. It was under this statute that the police officers who beat Rodney King in Los Angeles were tried and convicted in federal court. In addition to criminal remedies, victims may seek civil remedies under a separate civil rights statute.[30] States have similar civil rights laws.

So-called "hate crimes" laws have become popular in recent years. By 1993, forty-nine states had enacted hate crimes statutes.[31] Although commonly referred to as hate crimes, most of these statutes do not actually declare an act criminal; rather, they are sentence enhancements for crimes in which the motive was the victim's race, ethnicity, religion, or other factor.

CRIME IN THE UNITED STATES   There were 8,152 reported hate crimes in the United States in 2000. Of these crimes, 4,368 were racially motivated, 1,483 were motivated by religious beliefs, 1,330 by sexual orientation, 927 by ethnicity, 36 by disability, and 8 by multiple factors.

Source: Crime in the United States, U.S. Department of Justice, Federal Bureau of Investigation, 2001.

Florida's hate crime law reads as follows:

Evidencing prejudice while committing offense; enhanced penalties
(1) The penalty for any felony or misdemeanor shall be reclassified as provided in this subsection if the commission of such felony or misdemeanor evidences prejudice based on the race, color, ancestry, ethnicity, religion, sexual orientation, or national origin of the victim:
   (a) A misdemeanor of the second degree shall be punishable as if it were a misdemeanor of the first degree.
   (b) A misdemeanor of the first degree shall be punishable as if it were a felony of the third degree.
   (c) A felony of the third degree shall be punishable as if it were a felony of the second degree.
   (d) A felony of the second degree shall be punishable as if it were a felony of the first degree.
   [The statute then provides for civil remedies to victims in subsection 2.]
(3) It shall be an essential element of this section that the record reflect that the defendant perceived, knew, or had reasonable grounds to know or perceive that the victim was within the class delineated herein.[32]

Hate crimes laws have been attacked on First Amendment grounds as violating a person's right to expression. Clearly, a statute that makes a person's beliefs, and the expression of those beliefs, criminal is unconstitutional. But the Supreme Court has upheld statutes that enhance sentences when otherwise prohibited acts are taken because of a prejudicial motive. For example, a state cannot make it illegal to hate a particular ethnic group. Further, with few exceptions (e.g., fighting words), the state may not regulate a person's First Amendment right to express hatred of a particular group. But if the person's beliefs motivate a criminal act, such as a trespass or battery, then the sentence for that crime may be enhanced. See Chapter 9 for a more thorough review of the First Amendment aspects of hate crime legislation.

WEB LINKS

Legislative Information
Washburn Law School maintains a comprehensive site that includes state and federal legislative information. Enter through *http://www.washlaw.edu*. The United States Library of Congress also has legislative information on its page at *http://thomas.loc.gov*.

KEY TERMS

assault	first-degree murder	second-degree murder
battery	kidnapping	shield laws
corpus delicti	manslaughter	sodomy
deadly weapon	mayhem	stalking
element	merger of offenses	statutory rape
false imprisonment	provocation	
felony-murder rule	rape	

REVIEW QUESTIONS

1. What is the primary distinction between first- and second-degree murder?
2. What is felony-murder?
3. What is the difference between an assault and a battery?
4. What is the marital rape exception?
5. John caught his wife having sex with another man. In a fit of rage, he killed his wife. What crime has been committed?
6. What is meant by the phrase "imperfect self-defense"?
7. What is the primary distinction between false imprisonment and kidnapping?
8. Under the common law, if a person cut another's limb off, what crime was committed?
9. Give an example of a nonforcible rape.
10. What was the common-law definition of murder?

REVIEW PROBLEMS

1. State Statute reads: "Any act of 1. sexual intercourse 2. with another person 3. against that person's will and 4. by use of force or under such a threat of force that resistance would result in serious bodily injury or death, is rape." Explain how this statutory definition of rape differs from the common-law definition.
2. On May 5, Mark and Sam, who had been neighbors for three years, argued over Sam's construction of a ditch, which diverted water onto Mark's property. Mark told Sam to stop construction of the ditch or he "would pay with his life." The following day, Mark and Sam met again in Sam's garage. Within minutes Mark became very angry and cut Sam's leg with an axe he found in Sam's garage. After cutting Sam he panicked and ran home. Sam attempted to reach a telephone to call for help, but the cut proved fatal.

Mark has been charged with first-degree murder. He claims that he had no intent to kill Sam; rather, he only intended to hit him on the leg with the dull, flat side of the axe in an effort to scare Sam. Discuss the facts and explain what crimes could be proved and why.

3. On July 1, 1990, Jeff shot Megan during a bank robbery. Megan remained on life-support systems until September 4, 1991. At that time the systems were disconnected and she ceased breathing. On June 15, 1991, her physician had declared her brain dead. It was not until September 4, 1991, that her family decided to stop the life-support system. Jeff is charged with murder. Discuss any defenses he may have.

4. Penelope and Brenda had been enemies for years. One evening Penelope discovered that Brenda had attempted on many occasions to "pick up" Penelope's boyfriend. Penelope told a friend that she was "going to fix Brenda once and for all—that she was going to mess her face up bad." That evening Penelope waited for Brenda outside her home and attacked her with a knife. Penelope slashed her in the face four times and cut off one ear. Brenda reported the event to the police, who have turned it over to the county prosecutor's office. As the office legal assistant, you have been assigned the task of determining what crime can be charged.

5. State Statute reads: "It shall be a felony for any person to purposefully, knowingly, or recklessly cause the death of another person by the use of poison or other toxins." Eddie Farmer spread a toxic insecticide on his crops, which eventually mixed with rainwater and made its way into his neighbor's well. The insecticide was new, but recommended by other farmers who had used it successfully. His neighbor's seven-year-old son, Mikie, died from the poisons in the water. Eddie has been charged with violating the state statute. Is he liable?

6. One evening after a play Tracy was approached by a woman who pointed a pistol at her and ordered her to "give me all your money and jewelry." Tracy removed her jewels and handed them over, but told the robber that her money was in her purse, which was in the trunk of her car. The robber asked her where her car was parked, and Tracy pointed to a car thirty feet away. Tracy was then ordered to go to the automobile, remove the purse, and give it to the robber. She complied, and the woman ran off. The thief was eventually captured and tried for aggravated robbery and kidnapping. She was convicted of both and has appealed the kidnapping conviction. What do you think her argument would be to reverse the kidnapping conviction?

7. Do you believe that prostitution and solicitation of prostitution are victimless crimes? If so, does the threat of AIDS and other communicable diseases change your decision?

8. Make your best argument in support of legalizing (decriminalizing) prostitution.

9. Consider your life experiences. Have you ever committed a technical stalking (such as repeatedly seeking the affection of an uninterested person)?

END NOTES

1. A. Loewy, *Criminal Law,* 2d ed. (Nutshell Series, St. Paul: West, 1987).
2. *See Commonwealth v. Redline,* 391 Pa. 486, 137 A.2d 472 (1958).
3. *See* LaFave & Scott, *Criminal Law* § 7.7 (Hornbook Series, St. Paul: West, 1986).
4. *State v. Corn,* 278 S.E.2d 221 (N.C. 1981).
5. *Labelle v. State,* 550 N.E.2d 752 (Ind. 1990); *see also* LaFave & Scott at § 7.2(b).
6. Model Penal Code § 210.0(4).
7. *See* Ill. Rev. Stat. ch. 38, para. 9–3.
8. The Model Penal Code addresses homicide at § 210.0 *et seq.*
9. Mich. Comp. Laws Ann. § 752.1027.
10. Robert Hardaway, Miranda Peterson, and Cassandra Mann, "The Right to Die and the Ninth Amendment: Compassion and Dying After

Glucksberg and Vacco," 7 *George Mason L. Rev.* 313 (1999).

11. 521 U.S. 702 (1997).
12. *See* 65 Am. Jur. 2d *Rape* 28 (1976).
13. Model Penal Code § 213.
14. Ohio Rev. Code § 2907.
15. *Michael M. v. Superior Court,* 450 U.S. 464 (1981).
16. *See Bowers v. Hardwick,* 478 U.S. 186 (1986).
17. Steven I. Friedland, "On Treatment, Punishment, and the Civil Commitment of Sex Offenders," 70 *U. Colo. L. Rev.* 73 (1999).
18. 42 U.S.C. § 14071.
19. 117 S.Ct. 2072 (1997).
20. 531 U.S. 250 (2001).
21. Jean Peters-Baker, "Challenging Traditional Notions of Managing Sex Offenders: Prognosis is Lifetime Management," 66 *U. Mo. at Kansas City L. Rev.* 629 (1997).
22. 18 U.S.C. § 1201.
23. 18 U.S.C. § 1201(b).
24. Model Penal Code § 212.1.
25. 28 U.S.C. § 1738A.
26. Karen Brooks, "The New Stalking Laws: Are They Adequate to End Violence?," 14 *Hamline J. Pub. L. &Pol'y* 259 (1993).
27. *ApolloMedia v. Reno,* 19F. Supp. 2d 1081 (1998), aff'd, 119 S. Ct. 1450 (1999) and *ACLU v. Reno* 521 U.S. 844 (1997).
28. 18 U.S.C. § 241.
29. 18 U.S.C. § 242.
30. 42 U.S.C. § 1983.
31. *People v. Superior Court,* 15 Cal. App. 4th 1593, 1599 (1993).
32. Fla. Stat. Ann. § 775.085.

CHAPTER 5

Crimes Against Property and Habitation

CHAPTER OUTLINE

Arson

Burglary

Theft Crimes

   Introduction to Theft Crimes

   Larceny

   Embezzlement

   False Pretenses

   Receiving Stolen Property

Robbery

Extortion

Consolidated Theft Statutes

   Identity Theft

   The Model Penal Code Consolidation

   The Destruction of Property

   Computer Crimes

CHAPTER OBJECTIVES

In this chapter, you should:

- learn the elements of historic and contemporary crimes involving property and habitation, such as arson, burglary, and larceny.
- learn how computers and the Internet have given rise to new ways to commit old crimes and how the law is changing to deal with these developments.
- continue to develop your case analysis and legal reasoning skills.

ARSON

Arson is a crime against property. In addition, it is a crime against habitation. Crimes against habitation developed because of the importance of peoples' homes. In England and the United States, the concept that a "man's home is his castle" is one with great influence. A home is not merely property, but a refuge from the rest of the world. As such, special common-law crimes developed that sought to protect this important sanctuary. Arson and burglary are such crimes.

At common law, arson was defined very narrowly. It was the (1) malicious (2) burning of a (3) dwelling house of (4) another. This definition was so narrowly construed that an owner could burn her own property with an intent to defraud her insurer and not be guilty of arson, because she did not burn the dwelling of another.[1] In addition, the structure burned had to be a *dwelling*, which was defined as a structure inhabited by people. This definition did include outhouses and the area directly around the home *(curtilage)*, so long as the area was used frequently by people. However, the burning of businesses and other structures was not arson.

To be a burning, the dwelling must actually sustain some damage, although slight damage was sufficient. If the structure is simply charred by the fire, there is a burning. However, if the structure is only smoke-damaged or discolored by the heat of a fire that never touched the building, there is no arson. Finally, causing a dwelling to explode is not arson, unless some of the dwelling is left standing after the explosion and is then burned by a fire caused by the explosion.

At common law, malice was the mens rea of arson. As was true of murder at common law, *malice* meant evil intent. However, an intentional or extremely reckless burning would suffice.

Today, the definition of arson has been broadened by statute in most, if not all, states. It is now common to prosecute an owner of property for burning his own building, if the purpose was to defraud an insurer or to cause another injury. Be aware that the fraud may constitute a separate offense: defrauding an insurance carrier. Also, the structure burned need not be a dwelling under most statutes, though most statutes aggravate the crime if a dwelling is burned. Although the common law did not recognize explosions as a burning, the Model Penal Code and most statutes do.[2]

The mens rea for arson under the Model Penal Code is purposeful and reckless. If a person starts a fire or causes an explosion with the purpose of destroying the building or defrauding an insurer, a felony of the second degree has been committed. It is a felony of the third degree to purposely start a fire or cause an explosion and thereby recklessly endanger a person or structure.[3] Note that under the Model Penal Code the fire need not touch the structure, as was required by the common law. Setting the fire is enough to satisfy the burning requirement.

Arson is often graded. The burning of dwellings is usually the highest form of the crime. The burning of uninhabited structures is usually the next highest form of arson, and arson of personal property, if treated as arson, is the lowest.

CRIME IN THE UNITED STATES In 2000, there were a total of 75,000 arsons committed.

Source: *Source Book of Criminal Justice Statistics*, U.S. Department of Justice, Federal Bureau of Investigation, 2001.

SIDEBAR

BURGLARY

The (1) breaking and entering (2) of another's dwelling (3) at night (4) for the purpose of committing a felony once inside, was **burglary** at common law. A burglary, or entry of a dwelling, may be for the purpose of theft, rape, murder, or another felony. For that reason, burglary is a crime against habitation, as well as against property and person.

burglary
Unlawfully entering the house of another person at night with the intention of committing a felony (usually theft).

CRIME IN THE UNITED STATES In 2000 there were a total of 2,049,946 burglaries and attempted forcible entries to structures in the United States. This represented 728 burglaries per 100,000 people. Of all the crimes in the United States in 2000, 17.7 percent were burglaries.

Source: *Uniform Crime Report*, U.S. Department of Justice, Federal Bureau of Investigation, 2001.

SIDEBAR

The first element, the actus reus, a breaking, can be satisfied by either an actual break-in or by a constructive breaking. If one enters a dwelling by simply passing through an open door or window (a trespass), there is no breaking. Generally, there has to be some act on the part of the defendant to change the condition of the house so as to gain entry. For example, opening an unlocked door or window is a breaking, while passing through an open door or window is not a breaking. Of course, picking a lock and breaking a window or door are breakings.

A burglar may also gain entry by a constructive breaking. A constructive breaking occurs when one uses fraud or force to gain entry. So, if a burglar poses as a telephone repairworker to gain entry, then the breaking element has been satisfied. The same is true if the owner consents to the burglar's entry under threat or the use of force.

Once the breaking occurs, there must be an entry of the home. The burglar does not need to fully enter the structure; an entry occurs if any part of the burglar's body enters the house. So, the individual who breaks a window and reaches in to grab an item has entered the house.

Modern statutes have eliminated the breaking requirement, although most still require some form of "unlawful entry." Because trespasses, frauds, and breakings are unlawful, they satisfy modern statutory requirements.

The second element required is that the breaking and entry be of another person's dwelling. As with arson, at common law the structure had to be a dwelling. The person who lives in the dwelling does not have to be the owner, only an occupant. As such, rental property is included. Interestingly, at least one court has held that churches are dwellings, regardless of whether a person actually resides in the church, premised on the theory that churches are God's dwellings.[4] The dwelling had to belong to another person, so one could not burglarize his or her own property. No jurisdiction continues to require that the structure be a dwelling. Most statutes now refer to all buildings or other structures.[5] However, if the structure burglarized is a dwelling, most states punish the crime more severely than if it was another type of building.

The third requirement was that the burglary occur at night. Although this is no longer an element of burglary, many states do aggravate the crime if it happens at night.

The fourth element is that the person entering must have as a purpose the commission of a felony once inside. This is the mens rea of the crime. If the person's intent is only to commit a misdemeanor, there is no burglary. If Jay's intent is to murder Mark, there is a burglary. It is not a burglary if Jay's intent is to punch Mark in the nose.

Of course, many breaking and enterings with an intent to commit a burglary are not completed. A burglar may be caught by surprise by someone who was not known to be inside and flee from the property. It also happens that burglars are caught in the act by occupants who return to the building. In any event, what is important is that the intended felony need not be completed. All that needs to be proven is that the accused entered with an intent to commit a felony. As is always true, proving a person's subjective mental state is nearly impossible. Thus, juries are permitted to infer intent from the actions of the defendant. A jury did just that in the *Lockett* case.

Some statutes now provide that intent to commit any crime is sufficient, whether misdemeanor or felony. However, many continue to require an intent to commit either felony or any theft.

In summary, most jurisdictions have changed burglary in such a way that the following elements are common: (1) an unlawful entry (2) of any structure or building (3) for the purpose of committing a felony or stealing from the premises (4) once inside.

As mentioned, burglary may be graded and higher penalties imposed if the act occurred at night; involved a dwelling or was perpetrated at a dwelling that was actually inhabited at the time of the crime; or was committed by a burglar with a weapon.

THEFT CRIMES

Introduction to Theft Crimes

There are many types of theft. It is theft to take a pack of gum from a grocery store and not pay for it; for a lawyer to take a client's trust fund and spend it on personal items; for a bank officer to use a computer to make a paper transfer of funds from a patron's account to the officer's with an intent to later withdraw the money and

CASE

STATE OF ILLINOIS V. GERRY LOCKETT

196 Ill. App. 3d 981,
554 N.E.2d 566 (1990)

Gerry Lockett was charged with residential burglary, convicted after a jury trial, and sentenced to 8 years imprisonment. . . .

At about 3:00 A.M. on November 27, 1987, Allan Cannon entered his apartment, which he shared with his sister. Cannon noticed a broken window in his sister's bedroom. He then saw a man, whom he did not know, standing about six feet away from him in the apartment hallway. The only light came from the bathroom off the hallway. The man said to Cannon, "I know your sister." Cannon fled the apartment to call the police from the nearby El station. Outside his apartment, Cannon saw the man running down an alley. Cannon described the man to police as a dark black man with curly hair, about 5'5", weighing about 200 pounds.

Cannon returned to his apartment and noticed that his bicycle had been placed on his bed, and that his sister's baby clothes, which had been packed in bags, had been thrown all over. Although the apartment was in a general state of disarray, which Cannon admitted was not uncommon, nothing had been taken. . . .

Lockett also argues, without merit, that the evidence could not support an inference of his intent to commit a theft. But when Cannon entered his apartment, he found a broken window and later noticed a rock and broken glass on the floor, indicating that the window had been broken from outside. Cannon also discovered contents of the apartment had been rearranged and thrown about. Even assuming that Lockett was, as he said, an acquaintance of Cannon's sister, and that the Cannons, as defense counsel implied, were less than diligent housekeepers, Lockett's presence, without permission, in the dark, empty apartment, at 3 A.M., supported the jury's inference of intent to commit a theft.

abscond; and to hold a gun on a person and demand that property and money be surrendered. However, they are all fundamentally different crimes.

Some thefts are more violative of the person, such as robbery, and others are more violative of a trust relationship, such as an attorney absconding with a client's money. The crimes also differ in the methods by which they are committed. A robbery involves an unlawful taking. Embezzlement, however, involves a lawful taking with a subsequent unlawful conversion.

Larceny was the first theft crime. It was created by judges as part of the common law. The elements of larceny were very narrow and did not cover most thefts. Larceny began as one crime, but developed into many different crimes. This was not a fluid, orderly development, for two reasons. First, when larceny was first created, well over 600 years ago, the purpose of making it criminal was more to prevent breaches of the peace (fights over possession of property) than to protect ownership of property. Larceny did not prohibit fraudulent takings of another's property. The theory was that an embezzlement or other theft by trick was less likely to result in an altercation (breach of the peace) between the owner and the thief, because the owner would not be aware of the theft until after it was completed. Using this theory, many courts were reluctant to expand the scope of larceny. Second, at early common law, larceny was punishable by death. For this reason, some judges were reluctant to expand its reach.[6]

Eventually, two other theft crimes were created, embezzlement and false pretenses. Despite the creation of these crimes, many theft acts continued to go unpunished because they fell into the cracks that separated the elements of the three common-law theft crimes. Some courts attempted to remedy this problem by broadening the definitions of the three crimes. However, computers, electronic banking, and other technological advances have led to new methods of stealing money and property, posing problems not anticipated by the judges who created the common-law theft crimes. Some states have changed their definitions of larceny, false pretenses, and embezzlement to be more contemporary. Other states have simply abandoned the common-law crimes and have enacted consolidated theft statutes. The common-law theft crimes, modern consolidated theft statutes, and the Model Penal Code approach to theft are discussed here.

SIDEBAR

CRIME IN THE UNITED STATES   The United States Department of Justice includes shoplifting, pocket-picking, purse-snatching, thefts from automobiles, thefts of motor vehicles, and all other thefts of personal property, which occur without the use of force, as larceny for the purpose of the Uniform Crime Reporting Program. That program shows that there were 6,965,957 reported larcenies in the United States in 2000. This represents 2,475 thefts per 100,000 people. In addition, 1,165,559 automobiles were stolen in 2000, or 414 per 100,000 people. In 2000, 60 percent of crime in the United States was theft and 10 percent of that was automobile theft.

Source: *Uniform Crime Reports,* United States Department of Justice, Federal Bureau of Investigation, 2001.

Larceny

larceny
Stealing of any kind. Some types of larceny are specific crimes, such as *larceny by trick* or grand larceny.

At common law the elements of **larceny** were: (1) the trespassory taking (2) and carrying away (*asportation*) (3) of personal property (4) of another (5) with an intent to permanently deprive the owner of possession. The actus reus of larceny was the taking and carrying away of personal property of another. The mens rea was the intent to permanently deprive the owner of possession.

To have had a common-law larceny, there must have been a "taking" of property. A taking alone would not have sufficed; the taking must have been unlawful or trespassory. That is, the property must be taken by the defendant without the owner's consent. This element is only concerned with the method that the defendant used in acquiring possession. For example, if Mandy takes Sean's wallet from his hand, she has committed a taking. However, if Sean were to give Mandy his wallet with the understanding that she is to return it at a specified time, there is no unlawful taking when she does not return it; she lawfully acquired possession of the wallet. Taking property from another without that person's consent was a trespass under the common law, but failing to return property was not.

In an effort to protect employers (masters) from theft by their employees (servants), the theory of *constructive possession* was created. This theory held that when an employee received actual possession of the employer's property as part of the job, the employer maintained "constructive possession" while the employee had custody of the property. If this theory had not been developed, employees would have been free to steal property entrusted to them, as larceny required a trespassory taking. Of course, if an employee took property that was not under his or her care, there was a trespassory taking.

Interestingly, the theory of constructive possession was never extended to other relationships. This led to the creation of a new crime, embezzlement.

Once the taking has been effected, the defendant must carry away the property. This carrying away is called *asportation*. Generally, any asportation, even slight movement, will satisfy this requirement. The term *asportation* is deceiving, as not all property has to be "carried away" to satisfy this requirement. Riding a horse away will satisfy the requirement, as will driving another's automobile. Most states have done away with the asportation requirement by statute.

Third, the item stolen must be personal property. Land and items attached to land (e.g., houses) are considered real property. Theft of such property was not larceny. All other property is personal property. Objects that are movable property are personal property. In the early years of larceny, there was a further requirement that the item stolen be tangible personal property. Tangible personal property includes most items, such as automobiles, books, electronic equipment, and the like. Documents, such as stocks, bonds, and promissory notes, which represent ownership of something, are considered intangible property. It was not larceny to steal intangible personal property. Under modern statutes, most states have broadened theft to include all types of property.

The fourth element is that the personal property taken and carried away must be owned by another. One cannot steal from oneself. However, the rule was extended to prohibit prosecution of a partner for taking partnership assets and joint tenants from taking each other's things; also, because husband and wife were one person under the common law, it was not possible for spouses to steal from one another.

Finally, the mens rea element: It is required that the defendant intend to permanently deprive the owner of possession of the property. In short, to be a thief one must have an intent to steal. If Jack takes Eddie's lawnmower, intending to return the mower when he has completed his mowing, he has not committed larceny, as he did not possess an intent to permanently deprive Eddie of his possession of the mower. Also, the accused must intend to deprive an owner (or possessor) of property to be guilty of larceny. If an accused had a good faith belief that he had lawful right to the property, the requisite mens rea did not exist, and there was no larceny.

Although proving "an intent to permanently deprive the owner of possession" is the common method of proving the mens rea of larceny, it is not the only method. Courts have held that if the property is held so long that it causes the owner to lose a significant portion of its value, a larceny has occurred. Some cases have held that if the property is taken with an intent to subject the property to substantial risk, there is a larceny. Of course, the intent must exist at the time of taking. To illustrate this last method, imagine a thief who steals a plane intending to use the plane in a daredevil show. In such a case the thief is subjecting the property to a substantial risk, and even though the intent was to return the plane when the show was over, there is a larceny.

Embezzlement

The definition of larceny left a large gap that permitted people in some circumstances to steal from others. That gap was caused by requiring a trespassory taking of the property. For various reasons, people entrust money and property to others. The intent is not to transfer ownership (title), only possession. A depositor of a bank gives possession of money to the bank; a client may give an attorney money to hold in a trust account; a stockbroker may keep an account with a client-investor's money in it. In all of these situations the money is taken lawfully; there is no trespassory taking. So, what happens if the person entrusted with the money *converts* (steals) it after taking lawful possession? At the early common law, it was not a crime. However, the thief could have been sued for recovery of the stolen money.

This theory was carried to an extreme in a case in which a bank teller converted money handed to him by a depositor to himself, by placing the money in his own pocket. It was held that there was no larceny, because the teller acquired the money lawfully. The court also determined that there was no larceny under the theory of constructive possession, because the employer (bank) never had possession of the money. If the teller had put the money in the drawer and then taken it, the bank would have had constructive possession, and he would have committed larceny. The result was that the teller was guilty of no crime.[7] Unsatisfied with this situation, the English Parliament created a new crime: **embezzlement.**

The elements of embezzlement are (1) conversion (2) of personal property (3) of another (4) by one who has acquired lawful possession (5) with an intent to defraud the owner.

To prove embezzlement, the prosecution must first show that an act of **conversion** occurred. Conversion is the unauthorized control over property with an intent to permanently deprive the owner of its possession or which substantially interferes with the rights of the owner.

As was the case with larceny, only tangible personal property was included. Today, nearly all forms of personal property may be embezzled. Also, the property had to belong to another. One could not embezzle one's own property.

The element that distinguished embezzlement from larceny was the taking requirement. Whereas larceny required a trespassory taking, embezzlement required lawful acquisition. Accountants, lawyers, bailees, executors of estates, and trustees are examples of those who can commit embezzlement.

To satisfy the mens rea requirement of embezzlement, it must be shown that the defendant possessed an "intent to defraud." Mere negligent conversion of another's property is not embezzlement. Because the mens rea requirement is so high, bona fide claims of mistake of fact and law are valid defenses. If an

embezzlement
The fraudulent and secret taking of money or property by a person who has been trusted with it. This usually applies to an employee's taking money and covering it up by faking business records or account books.

conversion
Any act that deprives an owner of property without that owner's permission and without just cause.

accountant makes an accounting error and converts a client's money, there is no embezzlement. This is a mistake of fact. If a friend you loaned money to keeps the money with the mistaken belief that he is allowed to in order to offset damage you caused to his property last year (when the law requires that he sue you for the damage), there is no embezzlement. This is a mistake of law and negates the intent required, as does a mistake of fact.

Embezzlement is prohibited in all states. Some states have retained the name *embezzlement;* others have named it theft and included it in a consolidated theft statute. Embezzlement, which occurs in interstate commerce, federally insured banks, and lending institutions, or involves officers and agents of the federal government, is also made criminal by the statutes of the United States.[8] Statute 18 U.S.C. § 641 is the embezzlement of public monies, property, and records statute. Violation of that provision, if the property embezzled has a value of $100 or greater, results in a fine of up to $10,000 and ten years in prison. The remainder of that statute deals with embezzlement of nonpublic property that occurs in interstate commerce or by federal officials. The penalties vary for each provision.

False Pretenses

At common law, it was not larcenous to use lies (false representations) to gain ownership of property. For example, if Brogan were to sell Sean a ring containing glass, while representing to Sean that the ring contained a diamond, it was not larceny under the early common law, even though Brogan knew that the ring contained glass. The early judges believed strongly in the concept of *caveat emptor,* which translates as "let the buyer beware."

As it had done with embezzlement, Parliament decided to make such acts criminal. It did so by creating the crime of **false pretenses.** The elements of false pretenses are (1) a false representation of (2) a material present or past fact (3) made with knowledge that the fact is false (4) and with an intent to defraud the victim (5) thereby causing the victim to pass title to property to the actor.

To prove the first element, it must be shown that the actor made a false representation. This representation may be made orally or by writing, or may be implied by one's actions. The law does not require that people disclose all relevant information during a business transaction—*caveat emptor* still exists in that regard. The law does, however, require that any affirmative statements (or implications from actions) be true. So, if a buyer fails to ask if property has a lien against it, there is no false pretense if the seller does not inform the buyer of such. The opposite is true if the buyer inquires about existing liens and encumbrances and is told there are none.

The false representation must be important to the transaction. If the statement is important, the law says that it is *material.* Generally, a representation is material if it would have had an impact on the victim's decision-making had the victim known the truth at the time the transaction took place. For example, if Connie represents to Pam that the lighter in a used car she is selling works, when it does not, she has not committed false pretenses. However, if she states to Pam that the automobile recently had its engine replaced, that would be

false pretenses
A lie told to cheat another person out of his or her money or property. It is a crime in most states, though the precise definition varies.

material and she would be liable for false pretenses if she knew that the statement was untrue.

The fact conveyed by the actor must not only be material, but it must also concern a present fact or past fact. In this context, *present* refers to the time of the transaction. Statements of expected facts, promises, predictions, and expectations cannot be the basis of false pretenses. So, if Aaron buys an automobile from Kathy and promises to pay her in six months, it is no crime if he fails to pay because he loses his source of income during that period. To permit breaches of such promises to be criminal would be the same as having a debtor's prison, which is not recognized in the United States. The same is not true if Aaron made the promise but had no intent of paying the debt. Some states treat this as false pretenses under the theory that his state of mind at the time of the sale was fraudulent. Some states do not treat his action as criminal and place the burden on Kathy to seek her own remedy in a civil cause of action. It is also necessary that the representation be one of fact. Accordingly, opinions are not included. Of course, the line between fact and opinion is often unclear.

It must also be proved that the defendant knew the statement was false. An unintentional misrepresentation is not sufficient to establish this element in most jurisdictions, although most jurisdictions will find knowledge if the lower mens rea standard, recklessness, is proved.

The defendant must have the additional mens rea of "intent to defraud." As with other theft crimes, if one has a bona fide belief that the property belongs to him or her, there is a defense. In addition to intending to defraud the victim, it must also be shown that the victim was defrauded. Hence, if the victim was aware of the falsity of the statement and entered into the bargain anyway, there has been no crime.

Finally, the misrepresentation must be the cause of the victim passing title to property to the defendant. *Title* is ownership. Transferring possession to the defendant is not adequate. However, causing one to transfer possession of property by use of fraud was a type of larceny, known as *larceny by trick*. Just as with larceny and embezzlement, only tangible personal property was included within the grasp of the prohibition at early common law. Today, false pretenses usually includes all property that is subject to the protection of larceny—in most instances, this includes all personal property.

Fraudulent Checks.   Related to the crime of false pretenses is the crime of acquiring property or money by writing a check (draft) from an account that has insufficient funds to cover the draft. The act appears to fall into the category of false pretenses. Some theorize that a check is a promise of future payment, and, accordingly, the check does not meet the "representation of present or past fact" requirement of false pretenses. Courts have rejected that theory and held that at the time one drafts a check, a representation is made that there are adequate funds in the account to pay the amount drafted.

Today, most states have bad-check statutes. Conviction of these laws, for the most part, results in a less serious punishment than conviction on false pretenses.[9] Three common material elements are found in bad-check statutes. First, the mens rea may be proven by showing either an intent to defraud the payee or knowledge that there were insufficient funds in the account. Second, the check must be taken in exchange for something of value; third, there must have been insufficient funds in the account.

Mail Fraud.   Another crime related to false pretenses is mail fraud.[10] Mail fraud is a crime against the United States, because the mail system is run by a federal agency. Using the United States mail system with an intent to defraud another of money or property is mail fraud. The intended victim need not be defrauded; the act of sending such mails with the intent to defraud is itself criminal.

Mail fraud has become increasingly important in recent years, because it often is the foundation of a RICO count.

Racketeer Influenced and Corrupt Organizations Act.   Another federal statute that deals with fraud is the **Racketeer Influenced and Corrupt Organizations Act,** commonly known as RICO.[11] The United States Congress enacted RICO in the early 1970s in an attempt to curb organized crime.

Judicial interpretation of RICO has led to much controversy in recent years. Some people contend that the effect of court opinions has been to extend the prohibition of RICO beyond Congress's original intent. Today, all businesses, not just traditional organized crime, are subject to RICO.

To establish a RICO violation, the United States must prove that the (1) defendant received money or income (2) from a pattern of racketeering activity and (3) invested that money in an enterprise (business), (4) which is in interstate commerce or affects interstate commerce.

The second element is the key to proving a RICO violation. The term *pattern* means two or more acts, referred to as the predicate acts. Those acts must fall into the definition of a "racketeering activity." The statute provides a list of state and federal crimes that are considered to be racketeering. Murder, kidnapping, extortion, and drug sales and transportation are examples of the state crimes included in the list. Mail fraud, wire fraud, white slave traffic, securities fraud, and bribery are a few examples of the federal crimes included. Mail fraud is often the basis of a RICO violation, because the mails are often used by such enterprises.

For example, the Supreme Court announced, in a 1994 decision, that RICO could apply to a coalition of antiabortion groups that were alleged to have conspired, through a pattern of racketeering, to shut down abortion clinics.[12] In that case, extortion, including alleged threats of assault, was used to satisfy this element.

Violation of RICO can result in serious criminal penalties. In addition, victims of such activity may sue civilly and receive treble damages, costs, and attorney fees. RICO also provides for **forfeiture** of property in criminal proceedings. *Forfeiture* is the taking of property and money of a defendant by the government. Many crimes have forfeiture provisions. A forfeiture is not the same as a fine. Both forfeitures and fines are levied as punishment, but the focus of a fine is generally to hurt a defendant's pocketbook. Forfeitures are specifically aimed at getting the property or money connected to the crime for which the individual was convicted. So, in a RICO situation, a convicted party could stand to lose the enterprise itself, as well as all profits from that activity.

Racketeer Influenced and Corrupt Organizations Act
(19 U.S.C. 1961). A broadly applied 1970 federal law that creates certain "racketeering offenses," which include participation in various criminal schemes and conspiracies, and that allows government seizure of property acquired in violation of the act.

forfeiture
A deprivation of money, property, or rights, without compensation, as a consequence of a default or the commission of a crime.

The *H.J.* case is a civil case. However, many aspects of civil RICO are identical to criminal RICO. One such aspect is the pattern requirement. Whether the case is civil or criminal, a pattern of racketeering must be proven. The United States Supreme Court addressed the pattern question because the various appellate courts of the United States were divided on how to define that phrase. This case is also a good illustration of how "legitimate businesses" are subject to RICO.

 C A S E

H.J. INC. V. NORTHWESTERN BELL TELEPHONE CO.

492 U.S. 229 (1989)

Petitioners, customers of respondent Northwestern Bell Telephone Co., filed this putative class action in 1986 in the District Court for the District of Minnesota. Petitioners alleged violations of 18 U.S.C. §§ 1962(a), (b), (c), and (d) by Northwestern Bell and other respondents—some of the telephone company's officers and employees, various members of the Minnesota Public Utilities Commission (MPUC), and other unnamed individuals and corporations—and sought an injunction and treble damages under RICO's civil liability provisions, §§ 1964(a) and (c).

The MPUC is the state body responsible for determining the rates that Northwestern Bell may charge. Petitioners' 5-count complaint alleged that between 1980 and 1986 Northwestern Bell sought to influence members of the MPUC in the performance of their duties—and in fact caused them to approve rates for the company in excess of a fair and reasonable amount—by making cash payments to commissioners, negotiating with them regarding future employment, and paying for meals, for tickets to sporting events and the like, and for airline tickets.

* * *

Our guides in the endeavor must be the text of the statute and its legislative history. We find no support in those sources for the proposition, espoused by the Court of Appeals for the Eighth Circuit in this case, that predicate acts of racketeering may form a pattern; only then they are part of separate illegal schemes. Nor can we agree with those courts that have suggested that a pattern is established merely by proving two predicate acts. . . .

The legislative history, which we discussed in [another case] shows that Congress indeed had a fairly flexible concept of a pattern in mind. A pattern is not formed by "sporadic activity," and a person cannot "be subjected to the sanctions of [RICO] simply by committing two widely separated and isolated criminal offenses. . . . " Instead, "[t]he term 'pattern' itself requires the showing of a relationship" between the predicates and of "the threat of continuing activity. . . . " It is this factor of *continuity plus relationship* which combines to produce a pattern. RICO's legislative history reveals Congress's intent that to prove a pattern of racketeering activity a plaintiff or prosecutor must show that the racketeering predicates are related, *and* that they amount to or pose a threat of continued criminal activity.

forgery

Making a fake document (or altering a real one) with intent to commit a fraud.

Forgery.   Another crime related to fraud is **forgery.** *Forgery* is the (1) making of (2) false documents (or the alteration of existing documents making them false) (3) and passing the document (4) to another (5) with an intent to defraud.

The purpose of forgery statutes is both to prevent fraud and to preserve the value of written instruments. This is important because if forgery were to become common, people would no longer trust commercial documents, such as checks and contracts. The effect that would have on commerce is obvious.

The actus reus of forgery is the making of the document. That involves the actual writing and drafting of the document, as well as passing the document *(uttering)* to a potential victim. The mens rea of forgery is knowledge of the falsity of the document and an intent to defraud.

In many jurisdictions, forgery and uttering are separate crimes. In those states one must only make the false instrument and possess an intent to defraud. The defendant need not present the document (utter) to the victim. That act, when accompanied with an intent to defraud, is the crime of *uttering*.

Receiving Stolen Property

Not only is it a crime to steal another's property, but it is also a crime to receive property that one knows is stolen, if the intent is to keep that property. In essence, one who buys or receives as a gift property that is known to be stolen is an accessory (after the fact) to the theft. Although the law applies to anyone who violates its prohibitions, the primary focus of law enforcement is *fences*, people who purchase stolen property with the intent of reselling the property for a profit. They act as the retailers of stolen property, with the thieves acting as suppliers.

The elements of **receiving stolen property** are (1) receiving property (2) that has been stolen (3) with knowledge of its stolen character (4) with an intent to deprive the owner of the property.

receiving stolen property
The criminal offense of getting or concealing property known to be stolen by another.

Receipt of the property may be shown either by showing actual possession or constructive possession of the property. Constructive possession occurs any time the defendant has control over the property, even though the defendant does not have actual possession. For example, if one makes arrangements for stolen property to be delivered to one's home, there is receipt once the property is in the house, even if the defendant was not present when the property was delivered. Receiving includes not only purchases of stolen property, but also other transfers, such as gifts.

The property in question must have been stolen. In this context, stolen property includes that property acquired from larcenies, robberies, embezzlement, extortion, false pretenses, and similar crimes.

The final two elements deal with the mens rea of the crime of receiving stolen property. It is necessary that the defendant knew of the property's stolen character at the time of acquiring the property. Actual knowledge that the property was stolen is required. However, if it can be proven that the defendant had a subjective belief that the goods were stolen, but lacked absolute proof of that fact, the crime has still been committed. The fact that a reasonable person would have known that the property was stolen is not enough to convict for receiving stolen property. If one receives property under a bona fide belief that he or she has claim to the property, he or she is not guilty of receiving stolen property, even though that belief was unfounded.

The last element requires that the receiver of the property intend to deprive the owner of the property. Of course, if a defendant intends to keep the property for himself or herself, then this requirement is met. The language of the crime is broader, however, and includes any intent to deprive the owner of the use, ownership, or possession of the property. Thus, if one receives the property intending to destroy it or to give it as a gift, this element has been satisfied.

Not only do the states prohibit receiving stolen property, but the federal government also makes it a crime to receive stolen property that has traveled in interstate commerce or to receive stolen property while on lands controlled by the United States.[13]

Robbery

robbery
The illegal taking of property from the person of another by using force or threat of force.

The material elements of **robbery** are (1) a trespassory taking (2) and carrying away (asportation) (3) of personal property (4) from another's person or presence (5) using either force or threat (6) with an intent to steal the property.

Robbery is actually a type of assault mixed with a type of larceny. Because of the immediate danger created by the crime of robbery, it is punished more severely than either larceny or simple assault. Robbery was a crime under the common law and is a statutory crime in all states today.

The elements of trespassory taking, asportation, intent to steal, and that the property belongs to another, are the same as for larceny. However, robbery also requires that the property be taken from the victim's person or presence. So property taken from another's hands, off another's body, or from another's clothing is taken from the person. Property that is taken from another's presence, but not from the person, also qualifies. For example, if a bank robber orders a teller to stand back while the thief empties the cash drawer, there has been a robbery. The states differ in their definitions of "from another's presence," but it is generally held that property is in a victim's presence any time the victim is in control of the property. This is true in the bank robbery example, as the teller was exercising control over the cash drawer at the time of the robbery.

It is also necessary that the crime be committed with the use of force or threat. This element is the feature that most distinguishes robbery from larceny. As far as force is concerned, if any force is used beyond what is necessary to simply take the property, there is robbery. For example, it is larceny, not robbery, if a pickpocket steals a wallet free of the owner's knowledge. Only the force necessary to take the wallet was used. It is robbery, however, if the victim catches the pickpocket, and an altercation ensues over possession of the wallet. The same result is true when dealing with purse snatchers. If the snatcher makes a clean grab and gets away without an altercation, it is larceny from the person. If the victim grabs the bag and fights to keep it, then it is robbery. A threat of force may also satisfy this requirement. So, if the robber states to the victim, "Give me your wallet or I'll blow your head off," there is a robbery, even though there was no physical contact.

In most jurisdictions, the threatened harm must be immediate; threats of future harm are not adequate. It is also possible that the threat will be to someone else, such as a family member. The thief who holds a man's wife and threatens to harm her if the man does not give up his money is not free from the charge of robbery because the person giving up the money is not the one threatened.

The mens rea of robbery is the specific intent to take the property and deprive the owner of it. As with the other theft crimes, a good faith, but incorrect, claim of right to the property is a defense. In *Richardson v. United States*, 403 F.2d 574 (D.C. Cir. 1968), a defendant's claim of right to money was a gambling debt. The trial court did not permit the illegal debt to be used as a defense, but the appellate court reversed. It stated in its opinion that:

> The government's position seems to be that no instruction on a claim of right is necessary unless the defendant had a legally enforceable right to the property he took. But specific intent depends upon a state of mind, not upon a legal fact. If the jury finds that the defendant believed himself entitled to the money, it cannot properly find that he had the requisite specific intent for robbery.

Not only is robbery a crime pursuant to state law, but the United States has also prohibited certain robberies. Robbery of a federally insured bank is an example.[14]

Robbery is usually, if not always, graded. Robbery is graded higher if it results in serious injury to the victim or is committed using a deadly weapon.

CRIME IN THE UNITED STATES   Robbery is defined as the "taking or attempting to take anything of value from the care, custody, or control of a person or persons by force or threat of force or violence and/or by putting the victim in fear." During 2000, there were a total of 407,842 reported robberies under this definition. This represents 145 robberies per 100,000 people. Robberies composed 3.5 percent of the crime in 2000.

Source: *Uniform Crime Reports*, U.S. Department of Justice, Federal Bureau of Investigation, 2001.

SIDEBAR

Extortion

extortion
To compel, force, or coerce; for example, to get a confession by depriving a person of food and water. To get something by illegal threats of harm to person, property, or reputation. The process is called *extortion*.

Extortion is more commonly known as *blackmail*. Extortion is similar to robbery because both involve stealing money under threat. However, the threat in a robbery must be of immediate harm. Extortion involves a threat of future harm. At common law, extortion applied only against public officers. Today, extortion is much broader. The elements of extortion are (1) the taking or acquisition of property (2) of another (3) using a threat (4) with an intent to steal the property. In a few jurisdictions, the extortionist must actually receive the property, whereas others require only that the threat be made.

A threat of future physical harm satisfies the threat element as do threats to injure another's reputation, business, financial status, or family relationship. As was the case with robbery, the threat may be directed at one person and the demand for property made on another. For example, if a thief states to John, "Give me $100,00 or I will kill your wife," he is an extortionist, even though he has not threatened John.

The threatened conduct itself need not be illegal to be extortion. For example, if Stacy tells Lisa that she is going to inform the authorities of Lisa's involvement in illegal drug trade unless Lisa pays her $10,000, she is an extortionist, even though informing the police of the activity is not only legal, but encouraged by society.

The federal government has made it a crime for federal officers to extort the public, to be involved in an extortion that interferes with interstate commerce, and to extort another by threatening to expose a violation of federal law.

The *Dioguardi* case deals with extortion in the labor relations area. In most situations it is proper for unions and employees to threaten to picket an employer. In this case the threats were not part of usual labor-management relations; they were made with the purpose of extorting corporate money. Accordingly, the threats were found to be extortion, not protected labor activity.

 CASE

PEOPLE V. DIOGUARDI

8 N.Y.2d 260, 203
N.Y.S.2d 870 (1960)

The Appellate Division has reversed defendants' convictions for extortion and conspiracy to commit extortion, dismissed the indictment, and discharged them from custody. In addition to the conspiracy count, the indictment charged defendants with extorting $4,700 from the officers of two corporations. Said corporations were nonunion, conducted a wholesale stationery and office supply business in Manhattan, did an annual business of several million dollars, and their stock was wholly owned by a family named Kerin. Anthony Kerin, Sr., president and "boss" of the Kerin companies, made all the important corporate decisions. The other two corporate officers were his son Kerin, Jr., and one Jack Shumann.

Defendant McNamara, the alleged "front man" in the extortive scheme, was an official of Teamster's Local 295 and 808, as well as a member of the Teamster's Joint Council. Defendant Dioguardi, the immediate beneficiary of the payments and the alleged power behind the scene, was sole officer of Equitable Research Associates, Inc.—a *publishing house,* according to its certificate of incorporation, a *public relations concern,* according

to its bank account and the Yellow Pages of the telephone directory, a *labor statistics concern,* according to its office secretary and sole employee, and a *firm of labor consultants,* according to its business card. . . .

[During late 1955 and early 1956 various unions were attempting to unionize Kerin's business. The two primary unions involved in this attempt were both locals of the Teamsters. Eventually, one union began picketing the business while the other was on the premises handing out literature.]

The appearance of the picket line—which truck drivers from two companies refused to cross—thoroughly alarmed the Kerin officers, since they were in an "extremely competitive business," and a cessation of incoming or outgoing truck deliveries for as short a period as two weeks would effectively force them out of business.

* * *

McNamara assured Kerin, Sr., that his troubles could be ended, and *would be,* if he did three things: (1) "joined up" with McNamara's local 295, (2) paid $3,500 to Equitable to defray the "out-of-pocket" expenses incurred by the various unions that had sought to organize the companies, and (3) retained Equitable as labor consultant at $100 per month for each company for the period of the collective bargaining contract. . . . McNamara repeatedly assured Kerin, Sr., that the picketing would stop immediately and the companies would be guaranteed labor peace if his program were accepted.

Kerin, Sr., stated that he was not adverse to having his employees organized by local 295, if it was a good honest union, and that he could "accept the idea of a hundred dollars a month as a retainer fee for labor counsel and advise." He protested against the proposed payment of $3,500, however, as an "extraordinary charge" that sounded "like a holdup," to which McNamara replied: "It may seem that way to you, Mr. Kerin, but that is the amount of money that these unions that have sought to organize you. . . have

expended, and *if we are going to avoid further trouble and further difficulties, it is my suggestion that you pay that to the Equitable Associates."*

* * *

Upon the proof in this record, a jury could properly conclude that defendants were guilty of extortion—cleverly conceived and subtly executed, but extortion nonetheless. The essence of the crime is obtaining property by a wrongful use of fear, induced by a threat to do an unlawful injury. It is well-settled law in this State that fear of economic loss or harm satisfies the ingredient of fear necessary to the crime.

Consolidated Theft Statutes

The distinctions among the three common-law crimes of theft, larceny, embezzlement, and false pretenses, are often hard to draw. This fact, matched with the belief that there is no substantive difference between stealing by fraud or by quick use of the hands, has led many jurisdictions to do away with the common-law crimes of larceny, false pretenses, and embezzlement, and replace them with a single crime named theft. Exactly what crimes are included in such statutes differs, but larceny, false pretenses, and embezzlement are always included. Many jurisdictions also add one or more of the following: fraudulent checks, receiving stolen property, and extortion.

These statutes often use the language of the common law in defining theft. For example, Florida's statute reads:

> A person is guilty of theft if he knowingly obtains or uses, or endeavors to obtain or to use, the property of another with intent to, either temporarily or permanently: (a) Deprive the other person of a right to the property or a benefit therefrom or Appropriate the property to his own use or to the use of any person not entitled thereto.[15]

This statute includes the three common-law theft crimes. The primary change of consolidated theft statutes is that prosecutors no longer need to charge which specific crime has occurred. At trial, if the jury decides that a defendant has committed a larceny and not an embezzlement, they can convict. At common law, if the defendant was charged with embezzlement, not larceny, the jury would be forced to acquit if they determined that the defendant committed larceny rather than embezzlement.

Robbery is usually not included in consolidated theft statutes because of its significant threat of harm. Consolidation usually includes only misappropriations of property that do not pose serious risks to life.

Of course, those crimes that are included in consolidation statutes are not always punished equally. Grading of such offenses based on the amount of property appropriated, the nature of the theft, and the type of property stolen is common.

Identity Theft

It is possible to steal a person's identity as well as a person's property. The advent of the computer has made identity theft more common. Identity theft occurs whenever an individual uses a victim's name, social security number, e-mail address, or other identifying items in an effort to represent him- or herself as the victim. The mens rea of most identity theft statutes is an intention to either gain something of value through the deceit or to commit any other crime. This is the text of the Washington identity theft statute:

RCW 9.35.020 Identity theft.
(1) No person may knowingly obtain, possess, use, or transfer a means of identification or financial information of another person, living or dead, with the intent to commit, or to aid or abet, any crime.
(2) (a) Violation of this section when the accused or an accomplice uses the victim's means of identification or financial information and obtains an aggregate total of credit, money, goods, services, or anything else of value in excess of one thousand five hundred dollars in value shall constitute identity theft in the first degree. Identity theft in the first degree is a class B felony.
   (b) Violation of this section when the accused or an accomplice uses the victim's means of identification or financial information and obtains an aggregate total of credit, money, goods, services, or anything else of value that is less than one thousand five hundred dollars in value, or when no credit, money, goods, services, or anything of value is obtained shall constitute identity theft in the second degree. Identity theft in the second degree is a class C felony.
(3) A person who violates this section is liable for civil damages of five hundred dollars or actual damages, whichever is greater, including costs to repair the victim's credit record, and reasonable attorneys' fees as determined by the court.
(4) In a proceeding under this section, the crime will be considered to have been committed in any locality where the person whose means of identification or financial information was appropriated resides, or in which any part of the offense took place, regardless of whether the defendant was ever actually in that locality.
(5) The provisions of this section do not apply to any person who obtains another person's driver's license or other form of identification for the sole purpose of misrepresenting his or her age.

(6) In a proceeding under this section in which a person's means of identification or financial information was used without that person's authorization, and where there has been a conviction, the sentencing court may issue such orders as are necessary to correct a public record that contains false information resulting from a violation of this section.

An offender may be charged and convicted of both identity theft and the underlying crime. The defendant in the following case was convicted under the Washington statute. On appeal she alleged that her conviction of both identity theft and forgery put her in double jeopardy.

 CASE

STATE V. BALDWIN

45 P.3d 1093
Wash.App. Div. 1,2002.

Jeanne Baldwin was found guilty of three counts of identity theft and two counts of forgery. The trial court imposed an exceptional sentence premised on the crimes being "major economic offenses" because Baldwin had utilized a complicated scheme to purchase a home and several automobiles with the stolen identities. Baldwin's central argument is that her convictions for both identity theft and forgery violate double jeopardy principles. We disagree, and affirm because the offenses involved different victims.

I

Baldwin, representing herself as "Kaytie Allshouse," purchased a house, forging Allshouse's name to two deeds of trust. The first deed of trust secured the interest of an institutional lender, Global Holdings; the second, subordinate, deed was in favor of the sellers, Diane Masin and David Swadberg. The deeds secured payment of $45,500, and $6,500, respectively.

Two months later, Baldwin rented a mailbox at the Mail Room, a mailbox-rental outlet in Everett. Baldwin presented herself as "Monica Schultz" and produced a Washington driver's license bearing that name. She signed Schultz's name to the mailbox application and began receiving mail in some fifteen other names. Baldwin later rented a mailbox from Jerald Landwehr at Cascade Storage, another mailbox-rental outlet. Baldwin again rented under a false name, this time as "Carol Hopey." She produced two pieces of identification, including a Washington driver's license. Baldwin told Landwehr the mailbox was for "Econo Accounting," and a number of her "employees" would be receiving mail. Letters and packages in a number of names were received at that mailbox.

Meanwhile, a U.S. postal inspector acting on a complaint placed a thirty-day mail cover on the Cascade Storage box address. Under a mail cover, all mail to a specific address is recorded by postmark, addressee, sender, and class of mail. The mail cover revealed mail in numerous names being sent to the rented box. The inspector then contacted a Detective who investigates financial crimes for the Snohomish County Sheriff's Office.

The detective traced the telephone number listed on the Cascade Storage rental paperwork to Baldwin. His suspicions that Baldwin had stolen Hopey's identity were confirmed when Cascade Storage manager Jerald Landwehr picked Baldwin's picture out of a photomontage.

As the detective and inspector proceeded to attempt to locate and call individuals whose names had been gleaned from the Cascade Storage mail cover, they learned the Everett Police Department had been independently investigating allegations of similar multiple name use at the Mail Room in Everett. The detective showed the same photomontage to the Mail Room's manager who immediately picked out Baldwin's picture. . . .

* * *

A search of the Granite Falls property yielded a wallet containing a Washington driver's license in the name of "Kaytie Allshouse" bearing Baldwin's picture, and two VISA cards, also in the name of "Kaytie Allshouse." The search also uncovered vehicle titles and registrations for four different vehicles in the names of "Kaytie Allshouse" and "Carol Hopey," and auto insurance policies or cards in the names of "Kaytie Allshouse," "Carol Hopey," and "Monica Schultz." Officers also found a social security card for "Kaytie Allshouse" as well as homeowner's insurance correspondence and a utility bill, all addressed to "Kaytie Allshouse" at the Granite Falls address.

Baldwin was charged with six counts: (1) theft of Kaytie Allshouse's identity; (2) theft of Monica Schultz's identity; (3) theft of Carol Hopey's identity; (4) forgery of a deed in Allshouse's name; (5) forgery of Allshouse's name on an adjustable rider; and (6) forgery of a junior deed in Allshouse's name.

At trial, Kaytie Allshouse testified that she did not sign her name to the two trust deeds on the Granite Falls property. When asked how she felt about finding that someone had used her name to buy a house, she stated, "I don't want this in my name. It's not mine. I do not own it. . . . I just can't afford it. I don't want it." Likewise, Hopey testified she did not know Baldwin, had never lived in Snohomish County, had never rented a private mailbox, and had given no one permission to use her name. The jury found Baldwin guilty on all counts except the alleged forgery of the adjustable rate rider. . . .

Baldwin next contends that separate convictions and punishments for counts 1, 4, and 6 twice expose her to jeopardy. Her contention fails because each offense, as charged, includes elements not included in the other and each offense includes different victims.

The double jeopardy clause is not violated if the Legislature specifically authorizes multiple punishments. Washington applies the "same evidence" test to determine legislative intent. By this test, a defendant cannot be convicted of offenses that are identical both in fact and in law. The convictions stand, however, if there is an element in each offense which is not included in the other, and if proof of one offense would not necessarily also prove the other. . . .

Proof of theft of identity does not ipso facto prove forgery. Forgery requires the making, completion, or alteration of a written instrument. Theft of identity, on the other hand, requires use of a means of identification with the *intent* to commit an unlawful act. Thus, a jury could find Baldwin guilty of theft of identity, but not forgery. Because the elements of the two crimes are not the same, there is a strong presumption that the Legislature authorized multiple punishments for the same crime.

In addition to the three crimes not being the same in law, they are not the same in fact. As noted in *State v. McJimpson,* two crimes may not be the same in fact even though they arose from the same transaction. The court in *McJimpson* held that because each offense harmed a different victim, they were not the same in fact. Thus, the two offenses were not the same offense under the "same evidence" test. The same reasoning applies to this case. Baldwin was not subjected to double jeopardy because counts 1, 4 and 6 each has different victims.

Nor are we persuaded by Baldwin's assertion that the convictions for theft of identity and forgery merge. The merger doctrine applies only when the Legislature has clearly indicated that to prove a particular degree of a crime, "the State must prove not only that a defendant committed that crime . . . but that the crime was accompanied by an act which is defined as a crime elsewhere in the criminal statutes. . . . " It is relevant only when a crime is "elevated to a higher degree by proof of another crime proscribed elsewhere in the criminal code."

Here, neither of these crimes are crimes of degree; thus, neither crime elevates the other. Baldwin counters that to be convicted of **identity theft,** the State had to prove forgery. She claims that forgery is therefore an element of and merely incidental to the central crime of theft of identity, thus merging the two offenses. This "lesser included" offense argument fails because the State was not required to prove forgery in order to convict of theft of identity. Accordingly, the two crimes do not merge. . . . [Conviction affirmed].

The federal government also has an identity theft statute, the Identity Theft and Assumption Deterrence Act of 1998 (Identity Theft Act). Specifically, the Act[16] makes it a federal crime when anyone:

> knowingly transfers or uses, without lawful authority, a means of identification of another person with the intent to commit, or to aid or abet, any unlawful activity that constitutes a violation of Federal law, or that constitutes a felony under any applicable State or local law.

The Model Penal Code Consolidation

The Model Penal Code contains a comprehensive consolidation of theft offenses.[17] Provided that a defendant is not prejudiced by doing so, the specification of one theft crime by the prosecution does not prohibit a conviction for another. So if the defendant is specifically charged with larceny, he or she may be convicted of false pretenses or embezzlement by a jury.

The Code recognizes the following forms of theft:

1. Theft by taking (includes common-law larceny and embezzlement).
2. Theft by deception (includes common-law false pretenses).
3. Theft by extortion.
4. Theft of property known to be mislaid, misdelivered, or lost, and no reasonable attempt to find the rightful owner is made.
5. Receiving stolen property.
6. Theft of professional services by deception or threat.
7. Conversion of entrusted funds.
8. Unauthorized use of another's automobile.

The Code declares that thefts are felonies of the third degree if the amount stolen exceeds $500 or if the property stolen is a firearm, automobile, airplane, motorcycle, motorboat, or other vehicle, and, in cases of receiving stolen property, if the receiver of the property is a fence, then it is a felony of the third degree regardless of the value of the property. The Code makes all unauthorized uses of automobiles misdemeanors.

Because the crime of robbery involves a danger to people, it is treated as a separate crime.[18] If during the commission of a theft the defendant - inflicts serious bodily injury upon another, threatens serious bodily injury, or threatens to commit a felony of the first or second degree, there is a robbery. It is a felony of the second degree unless the defendant attempts to kill or cause serious bodily injury, in which case it is a felony of the first degree.

Forgery is also treated as a separate offense.[19] Forgery is treated as a felony of the second degree if money, securities, postage stamps, stock, or other documents issued by the government are involved. It is a felony of the third degree if the forged document affects legal relationships, such as wills and contracts. All other forgeries are misdemeanors.

Destruction of Property

Every year a significant amount of financial loss is the result of destruction of property. Arson accounts for much of this total, but not all. Most, if not all, states have statutes making the destruction of another's property criminal. These laws may be part of the statute covering arson or may be a separate section of the criminal code.

malicious (criminal) mischief
The criminal offense of intentionally destroying another person's property.

Destruction of property, commonly called **criminal mischief,** is normally a specific-intent crime and includes all types of destruction that affect the value or dignity of the property. For example, defacing a Jewish tombstone by painting a swastika on it would be criminal mischief, even though the paint can be removed and the tombstone is left physically unharmed.

Mischief is often graded so that offenses against public property, which result in damage in excess of a stated dollar amount, or which involve a danger to human life, are penalized more heavily than others. The most serious mischiefs are usually low-grade felonies, and the remainder misdemeanors. For example, the Kentucky mischief statutes read:

> *Ky. Rev. Stat. § 512.020*
>   (1) A person is guilty of criminal mischief in the first degree when, having no right to do so or any reasonable ground to believe that he has such right, he intentionally or wantonly defaces, destroys, or damages any property causing pecuniary loss of $1,000 or more.
>   (2) Criminal mischief in the first degree is a Class D felony.

> *Ky. Rev. Stat. § 512.030*
>   (1) A person is guilty of criminal mischief in the second degree when, having no right to do so or any reasonable ground to believe that he has such a right, he intentionally or wantonly defaces, destroys, or damages any property causing pecuniary loss of $500 or more.
>   (2) Criminal mischief in the second degree is a Class A misdemeanor.

> *Ky. Rev. Stat. § 512.040*
>   (1) A person is guilty of criminal mischief in the third degree when:
>   (a) Having no right to do so or any reasonable ground to believe that he has such right, he intentionally or wantonly defaces, destroys, or damages any property; or
>   (b) He tampers with property so as knowingly to endanger the person or property of another.
>   (2) Criminal mischief in the third degree is a Class B misdemeanor.

At common law, hairline distinctions existed among the three crimes against property: larceny, embezzlement, and false pretenses. Today, statutes in most states have consolidated theft crimes so that the focus is now on whether a theft occurred, not whether the correct crime has been charged. These consolidation statutes include larceny, false pretenses, and embezzlement. Although it varies, often such statutes will also include receiving stolen property, various forms of fraud, and extortion. Robbery and forgery are treated as separate crimes.

Arson and burglary are separate crimes because they involve more than a threat to property. At common law, only residences were protected by arson and burglary laws. Because of the sanctity that our culture attaches to dwellings and because of the danger to human life created by arson and burglary, these crimes received special attention. Today, arson and burglary have been broadened to include more than just dwellings.

In addition to criminal remedies for these crimes, victims often have civil remedies available. As previously discussed, the victim is responsible for filing and proving such a civil case. However, a prior admission of guilt (or conviction) may prevent the defendant from relitigating his or her innocence in a civil trial.

Computer Crimes

Computer-related crimes are costly and are on the rise. According to a report jointly issued by the Federal Bureau of Investigation and the Computer Security Institute in 2002, 90 percent of the corporations and government agencies surveyed detected security breaches in the previous year, 80 percent suffered a financial loss due to computer breaches, 85 percent were infected with at least one computer virus, and 25 percent reported having proprietary information stolen. The total costs of these crimes is estimated to be $378 billion, the highest in history.[20]

Computer crimes take two general forms. First, computers can be the target of a crime. Theft of hardware and software is an example. Destruction and vandalism of computers is another crime where the computer is itself the target of an unlawful act. Viruses are also used to destroy computer programs.

A second form of computer crime involves using a computer as a tool in the commission of a crime. Violating privileges by improperly obtaining confidential information, threat and harassment through cyberspace, and the illegal distribution of obscenities fall into this category. Computers can also be used to steal. Obtaining illegal entry into a bank's computer records from a personal computer in order to steal money is an example, as is using another person's personal identification number and bank card to access an automatic teller machine.

Many computer-related crimes are punishable without special computer crimes laws. Existing penal laws such as theft, larceny, and criminal mischief may include computer activity. For example, stealing funds from a bank through a computer can usually be prosecuted under existing theft laws if a special computer theft statute has not been enacted. Similarly, criminal mischief statutes could be used to prosecute the intentional destruction of computer programs by viruses.

In addition to existing laws, the federal government and 49 states had enacted special legislation to deal with computers and crimes by 1998. The *Briggs* case provides an illustration of the application and complexity of computer crimes. The Federal Counterfeit Access Device and Computer Fraud and Abuse Act became law in 1984 and was amended in 1986 by the Computer Fraud and Abuse Act. That law prohibits:

1. A knowing, unauthorized access to information contained in a federal interest computer.
2. An intentional, unauthorized access to financial information held by a financial institution or credit agency.

CASE

BRIGGS V. MARYLAND

704 A.2d 904 (Md. Ct.
App. 1998)

RAKER, JUDGE.

Terry Dewain Briggs appeals his conviction for the crime of unauthorized access to computers, in violation of Maryland Code. . . . The primary issue raised in this case is the meaning of the statutory requirement of access "without authorization" as used in § 146. The question we must answer is whether an employee who is entitled to use an employer's computer system in connection with employment duties, but who exceeds the scope of that authorization, is acting in a manner proscribed by Article 27, § 146. Briggs contends that his conduct did not come within the prohibition of the statute. We agree, and accordingly, shall reverse.

I

In November, 1994, the Scarborough Group, Inc. (Scarborough), a medium-sized securities investment company, hired Terry Briggs as a computer programmer and system administrator. Briggs, a twenty-three-year-old computer specialist, was hired to program and design software to maintain the company computer system. As part of his job responsibilities, he entered data in the computer system and placed passwords on the files to secure the data. The management of the entire computer system was entrusted to Briggs. Following a dispute on July 24, 1995, about the terms of his employment contract, Briggs resigned as an employee of the company. Shortly after Briggs left the company, Scarborough realized that some of its computer files were secured with passwords known only to Briggs. Scarborough and Briggs were unable to resolve the situation. Scarborough filed a civil suit against Briggs, and also contacted the Anne Arundel County police.

The State charged Briggs in a two-count criminal information: count one, theft of computers, in violation of Article 27, § 342(a) (1) and, count two, unauthorized access to computers, in violation of Article 27, § 146(c) (2). At trial, Scarborough contended that Briggs changed the passwords two days before the meeting about Briggs's employment contract, and put them in a subdirectory named "ha-ha he-he," dated July 22, 1995 by the computer. Scarborough maintained that Briggs never had permission to place the company files in a directory and to protect the file with passwords, without anyone else in the company having access to the passwords. Although he denied any knowledge about "ha-ha he-he," Briggs admitted that he placed passwords on company files months earlier as part of his job in securing files, but that he had difficulty remembering the passwords because so much time had passed. Briggs suggested that Scarborough filed criminal charges against him in order to discredit him as a government witness in a Securities and Exchange Commission investigation that Briggs had initiated alleging that certain activities at Scarborough violated federal security regulations. Briggs maintained that the computer date on the password subdirectory had been changed to incriminate him.

The State alleged that Briggs intentionally and willfully and without authorization accessed a computer system to interrupt the operation of the computer system and computer services. In his motion for judgment of acquittal, Briggs argued that he was not guilty as a matter of law (that the statute did not apply to his activities) and as a matter of fact (that he was fulfilling his employment responsibilities). Briggs reasoned that Article 27, § 146 was not intended to apply to authorized computer users who, arguably, used their positions to cause harm to their employers by misusing the computer. The State argued that Briggs was guilty of unauthorized access, because although Briggs was authorized to access the computer system, he was not authorized to access the system in such a way as to interrupt the operation of the computer services of the system.

The trial court denied Briggs's motion for judgment of acquittal, and the jury found Briggs guilty of unauthorized access to computers in violation of Article 27, § 146(c)(2)(i). The court sentenced Briggs to one year incarceration, with all but two days suspended, two years supervised probation, 150 hours of community service, and a fine of $500. The court also ordered him to cooperate with Scarborough and required him to release any remaining password information and client files. Briggs noted a timely appeal to the Court of Special Appeals. We granted certiorari on our own motion before consideration by that court.

Appellant argues before this Court that Article 27, § 146 criminalizes the conduct of an individual who intentionally and willfully accesses a computer without authorization and is inapplicable to conduct that can be characterized as only exceeding authorized access. He concludes that the statute is inapplicable on its face because, as part of his employment, he was authorized to access the computer system. The purpose of the statute, Appellant continues, was to deter unauthorized users from breaking into computer systems, i.e., to prevent "hackers" from gaining unauthorized access. Briggs distinguishes operating a computer system without authorization from exceeding authorized access by using the computer in an improper manner. He concludes that application of this statute to his conduct is contrary to legislative intent.

The State contends that even though access for other activities may have been authorized, a person, whether he is an employee, "hacker," or otherwise, violates the statute when that person "intentionally, willfully, and without authorization" accesses a computer system or any part of a computer system to cause the malfunction or interrupt the operations of the computer system or any part of that system. The State maintains that there was sufficient evidence to support the verdict because Briggs did not have authority to place passwords on the files without anyone else in the company having those passwords, and that he did so with the intent of interrupting the operation of the computer system. . . .

We need not address Appellant's factual argument that he was authorized to place passwords on Scarborough's computer system, because we find the second element dispositive and hold that Appellant's access to the computer was not "without authorization" within the meaning of the statute. When faced with a question of statutory construction, we look first to the plain meaning of the words of the statute, with the goal to ascertain and effectuate legislative intent. *Whack v. State,* 338 Md. 665, 672, 659 A.2d 1347, 1350 (1995). We give the words of the statute their ordinary and natural meaning. *Gargliano v. State,* 334 Md. 428, 435, 639 A.2d 675, 678 (1994). If the language of the statute is plain and clear and expresses a meaning consistent with the statute's apparent purpose, no further analysis is ordinarily required. *Id.* at 435, 639 A.2d at 678. On the other hand, if the language of the statute is ambiguous or unclear, "we must consider 'not only the literal or usual meaning of the words but their meaning and effect in light of the setting, the objectives and purpose of the enactment,' in our attempt to discern the construction that will best further the legislative objectives or goals."

Id. at 436, 639 A.2d at 678 (quoting *Tucker v. Fireman's Fund Ins. Co.,* 308 Md. 69, 75, 517 A.2d 730, 732 (1986)). . . .

The statute prohibits unauthorized access of a computer, computer network, or computer systems. "Access" is defined in the statute "to instruct, communicate with, store data in, retrieve data from, or otherwise make use of equipment including. . . computers." § 146 (a) (9). "Without authorization" modifies the word "access." Therefore, the unlawful act is unauthorized access. "Authorization" is not defined in the statute. Turning to dictionary definitions of "authorize," we find that *Black's Law Dictionary* 133–34 (6th ed. 1990) defines "authorize" to mean "[t]o empower; to give a right or authority to act. To endow with authority or effective legal power, warrant, or right. To permit a thing to be done in the future." (Citation omitted.) Similarly, *Webster's New International Dictionary,* Unabridged 186 (2d ed.

1950) defines "authorize" to mean "to clothe with authority or legal power; to give right to act; to make legal; to legalize; to give authoritative permission to or for; to justify." The testimony at trial that Briggs had authority to enter data in the computer and to place passwords on the files to secure the data establishes that he was authorized, under the statute, to "instruct, communicate with, store data in, retrieve data from and to make use of computer data equipment and other data processing equipment." . . .

The plain language of the statute suggests that if an employee were initially permitted to "instruct," "communicate with," "store data in," or "retrieve data from" the computer system, then that employee's access would be authorized. The statute makes no reference to authorized users who exceed the scope of their authority. If the Legislature intended the statute to cover employees who exceeded the scope of their authority or who misused their authority, it could have done so explicitly. We conclude that the intent of the General Assembly was to criminalize the misuse of computers or computer networks by those whose initial access was unauthorized. [Judgment of conviction reversed.]

3. An intentional, unauthorized access of a computer of the United States that would affect the government's operation of the computer.
4. Thefts of property by use of computer as a result of a knowing and intentional scheme to defraud.
5. Knowingly altering, damaging, or destroying information within a federal interest computer or preventing the authorized use of such a computer.
6. Knowingly trafficking in any password without authorization if the trafficking affects interstate commerce or is used by or for the United States government.

Some of these crimes are misdemeanors and others are felonies. The federal government regulated computer crime further through the Computer Abuse Amendments Act of 1994.[21] This statute criminalizes the transmission of any data intended to cause damage to a computer used by the federal government or a financial institution. It also prohibits "trafficking in passwords" that provide access to government computers or that interfere with interstate or foreign commerce.

In addition, there is a federal electronic espionage statute. Statute 18 U.S.C. § 1831 protects corporate propriety information. It reads, in part:
In General–

Whoever, intending or knowing that the offense will benefit any foreign government, foreign instrumentality, or foreign agent, knowingly–

(1) steals, or without authorization appropriates, takes, carries away, or conceals, or by fraud, artifice, or deception obtains a trade secret;
(2) without authorization copies, duplicates, sketches, draws, photographs, downloads, uploads, alters, destroys, photocopies, replicates, transmits, delivers, sends, mails, communicates, or conveys a trade secret;

    (3) receives, buys, or possesses a trade secret, knowing the same to have been stolen or appropriated, obtained, or converted without authorization;

    (4) attempts to commit any offense described in any of paragraphs (1) through (3); or

    (5) conspires with one or more other persons to commit any offense described in any of paragraphs (1) through (3), and one or more of such persons do any act to effect the object of the conspiracy, shall, except as provided in subsection (b), be fined not more than $500,000 or imprisoned not more than 15 years, or both.

The private sector expends considerable resources in the prevention and detection of computer crimes. Law enforcement agencies have been forced to hire investigators and consultants with computer expertise to effectively investigate claims and educate the public in preventing computer crimes. As computer use and dependence increase, so will computer crimes.

On the other side, computer technology has advanced law enforcement in some respects. The **National Crime Information Center** (NCIC) is used by law enforcement agencies nationwide in the reporting and detection of wanted persons. Computers are used to organize and manage case files. Graphics programs are used to recreate crimes and to project a fugitive's appearance after donning a disguise or after having aged. These are but a few of the uses computers play in law enforcement.

National Crime Information Center
Computerized records of criminals, warrants, stolen vehicles, etc.

 WEB LINKS

Crime Data

Two excellent sites will provide a huge amount of data on crime. Reports on crime-related issues may also be found in these locations. The first is the National Institute of Justice and the second is the Bureau of Justice Statistics. Both are United States Department of Justice offices. *http://www.ojp.usdoj.gov/nij/ and http://www.ojp.usdoj.gov/bjs/*.

KEY TERMS

arson	forfeiture	Racketeer Influenced and
burglary	forgery	Corrupt Organizations Act
conversion	larceny	receiving stolen property
embezzlement	malicious (criminal) mischief	robbery
extortion	National Crime Information	
false pretenses	Center (NCIC)	

REVIEW QUESTIONS

1. What is "constructive breaking," when referring to the crime of burglary?
2. Define larceny.
3. What is criminal mischief?
4. Embezzlement is often punished more severely than simple larceny. Why?
5. What does the acronym RICO represent? What are the basic elements of RICO?
6. What are "fences"? At common law, what crime do fences commit?
7. How is destruction of a building by explosion treated by the Model Penal Code? At common law?
8. Brogan runs by a woman on the street and grabs her purse as he passes her. The purse is easily pulled from her arm, and Brogan's intent is to keep the contents. What crime has been committed?
9. Brogan runs by a woman on the street and grabs her purse as he passes her. The woman catches the strap and fights to keep the purse; however, the strap breaks, and Brogan is successful. He keeps the contents of the purse. What crime has been committed?
10. What is the difference between forgery and uttering?

REVIEW PROBLEMS

1. Arson is quite different today than it was at common law. What are the major differences?
2. Burglary is quite different today than it was at common law. What are the major differences?
3. Doug and Sherri are an elderly couple who are retired and residing in Florida. Both have suffered substantial physical deterioration, including vision loss and poor memory. Ned, who had coveted their 1962 Corvette for years, told the couple that they should trust him with their financial affairs, including giving him title to their vehicle. He told the two that he would drive them to the places they needed to go, but that state law required that his name appear on the title of the car, as he would be the sole driver. Doug and Sherri complied with his request, believing that his statement concerning Florida law was correct.

   Subsequently, the couple created a trust account and named Ned as trustee. The purpose of the account was to provide Ned with a general fund from which he was to pay the household bills. Ned withdrew all the money and placed it into his personal account. When this occurred, the couple contacted Ned, who claimed to know nothing of the account.

   Sherri contacted the local prosecutor, who conducted an investigation. Through that investigation, it was discovered that Ned held title to the Corvette.

   You work for the prosecutor. Your assignment is to determine what crimes have been committed, if any. Your state has no theft statute, but recognizes common-law theft crimes.

4. Gary and Paige were friends until they discovered that they shared an interest in Tracy. After Paige won her affection, Gary became enraged and took a key and ran it down the side of Paige's car. He then poured gasoline over the car and set it on fire. Gary has been arrested. What crimes should be charged?

5. Kevin was walking down the sidewalk that passed in front of Sean's home. As he passed Sean's house, he looked in a front window and noticed a carton of soft drinks sitting in the kitchen. As he was thirsty, Kevin broke the front window and crawled into Sean's house. Once inside, he poured himself a glass of cola and sat down at the dining room table. While seated at the table, he picked up a ring with

a value in excess of $1,000, and put it into his pocket. When he finished his drink, he placed the empty glass in the sink and left. He later sold the ring and bought a stereo with the proceeds. What crimes have been committed, using common-law theft crimes?

6. Brogan has an affair with Janice, who is married. After Janice ends the affair, Brogan threatens to tell Janice's husband about their sexual involvement unless Janice pays Brogan $5,000. Janice complies. What crime has been committed?

7. Penni is working the night shift at a local convenience store when Craig and Guido come in. Craig states to Penni, "Give us all the money in the register and we will not hurt you. Give us any trouble and we will knock the #?!@ out of you!" Penni complied. What crime has been committed? What if they had been brandishing weapons?

8. Discuss what crimes you think should be included in consolidated theft statutes and why. Explain why particular crimes should be left out of such a statute.

END NOTES

1. 5 Am. Jur. 2d *Arson* 2 (1962).
2. Model Penal Code § 220.1.
3. Model Penal Code § 220.1(1) and (2).
4. *People v. Richards,* 108 N.Y. 137, 15 N.E. 371 (1988).
5. LaFave & Scott, *Criminal Law* 797 (Hornbook Series, St. Paul: West, 1986).
6. A Loewy, *Criminal Law,* 2d ed. (Nutshell Series, St. Paul, West, 1987).
7. *Bazeley's Case,* 2 East P.C. 571 (Cr. Cas. Res. 1799); *see* LaFave & Scott, *Criminal Law* § 8.1 (Hornbook Series, St. Paul: West, 1986).
8. 18 U.S.C. § 641 *et seq.*
9. LaFave & Scott, *Criminal Law* § 8.9 (Hornbook Series, St. Paul: West, 1986).
10. 18 U.S.C. § 1341.
11. 18 U.S.C. § 1961 *et seq.*
12. *N.O.W. v. Scheidler,* 114 S. Ct. 798 (1994).
13. 18 U.S.C. § 2311 *et seq.*
14. 18 U.S.C. § 2113.
15. Fla. Stat. Ann. § 812.012 *et seq.*
16. 18 U.S.C. § 1028.
17. Model Penal Code § 223 *et seq.* deals with theft offenses.
18. *Id.* § 222.1.
19. *Id.* § 224.1.
20. Computer Security Issues and Trends (Computer Security Institute Spring 2002) (http://www.gocsi.com/).
21. 18 U.S.C. §§ 1029–1030.

CHAPTER 6

Crimes Against the Public

CHAPTER OUTLINE

Defining a "Crime Against the Public"

Crimes Against Public Morality

   Prostitution and Solicitation

   Deviate Sexual Conduct

   Indecent Exposure and Lewdness

   Obscenity

   Regulating the Internet

Crimes Against the Public Order

   Introduction

   Riot and Unlawful Assembly

   Disturbing the Peace

   Incitement/Advocacy of Unlawful Conduct

   Threats

   Vagrancy and Panhandling

   Crimes Involving Firearms

   Drug and Alcohol Crimes

Crimes Against the Administration of Government

   Perjury

   Bribery

   Tax Crimes

   Obstruction of Justice

   Contempt

Crimes Against Sovereignty and Security

   Treason

   Sedition and Espionage

   Terrorism

Crimes Against the Environment

   Clean Water Act

   Clean Air Act

   Comprehensive Environmental Response, Compensation and Liability Act

   Resource Conservation and Recovery Act

   Occupational Safety and Health Act

   Toxic Substances Control Act

   Federal Insecticide, Fungicide, and Rodenticide Act

   Emergency Planning and Community Right-to-Know Act

   Endangered Species Act

   Marine Mammal Protection Act

CHAPTER OBJECTIVES

In this chapter, you should:

- learn the elements of historic and contemporary crimes against the public, including crimes against the public order, against the administration of government, against public morality, and against the environment.

- learn and critically examine the laws of terrorism, especially those laws enacted in response to the September 11, 2001 attacks on the United States.

- begin thinking about the tension between national security and freedom.

- begin thinking about the role morality should play in penal law.

- continue to develop your case analysis and legal reasoning skills.

DEFINING A "CRIME AGAINST THE PUBLIC"

Chapters 4 and 5 were concerned with crimes that victimize individuals or entities, such as corporations and other business organizations. This chapter examines crimes that do not have individual victims. These are crimes involving the public welfare, social order, and society's morals. Many, if not most, of these crimes are malum prohibitum in nature, not malum in se.

Religion has played a role in the "criminalization" of "victimless" crimes. Of course, religious groups do not dictate such policy—this would violate the First Amendment's prohibition of mixing church and state. Religion does, however, influence the moral values of the members of a society. In the United States this influence is predominately Christian. This is the reason that some acts that directly harm no one are prohibited.

Some critics call for an end to "victimless crimes." In spite of this, many victimless crimes exist and are likely to continue to be prohibited. However, in a democracy such as the United States, it is important to examine such crimes carefully to avoid an unwarranted infringement of civil liberties. The more a law is premised upon a moral judgment, the greater the scrutiny should be.

Some of the crimes discussed here bear directly upon the administration of government and justice and less upon moral determinations. For example, contempt of court is a crime against the public, and the premise of its prohibition is the theory that if society punishes offenders, others will comply with court orders, and the administration of justice will be enhanced. Prostitution is an example of a crime that is prohibited more for moral reasons than any other.

The crimes included in this chapter have been divided into five subsections: crimes against public morality; crimes against the public order; crimes against the administration of government; crimes against sovereignty and security; and crimes against the environment.

CRIMES AGAINST PUBLIC MORALITY

Prostitution and Solicitation

Often said to be the oldest profession, **prostitution** is prohibited in every state except Nevada, where each county is given the authority to determine whether it should be permitted.

Prostitution is defined as (1) providing (2) sexual services (3) in exchange for compensation. In a few states, only intercourse is included in the definition of sexual services. In most states, however, sexual services include sodomy, fellatio, cunnilingus, and the touching of another's genitals. The Model Penal Code includes homosexual and other deviate sexual conduct in its definition of sexual activity.[1]

The service must be provided in exchange for compensation. The person who is sexually promiscuous, but unpaid, goes unpunished. Compensation normally means money, but it can come in any form. Thus, the prostitute who accepts legal services from a lawyer in exchange for sexual services has received compensation. Where prostitution is illegal, it is common for prostitutes to use businesses, such as massage parlors and escort services, as a front.

Solicitation is a related crime. Any person who engages in selling sex, buying sex, or attempting to buy sex is guilty of solicitation. Note that a prostitute may be guilty of both solicitation and prostitution, if the prostitute makes the first contact with the buyer. There need not be the actual sale of sex for solicitation—only an attempt to sell sexual services. The clients of prostitutes, when prosecuted, are charged with solicitation.

The Model Penal Code states that "A person commits a violation if he hires a prostitute to engage in sexual activity with him, or if he enters or remains in a house of prostitution for the purpose of engaging in sexual activity."[2]

Those who promote prostitution (*pimps*) are usually punished more severely than prostitutes and customers. The Model Penal Code makes knowingly promoting prostitution a felony of the third degree if a child under sixteen years of age is prostituted; the defendant's wife, child, or other ward is prostituted; the defendant forces or encourages another to engage in prostitution; or the defendant owns, controls, or manages a house of prostitution. In all other cases promotion is a misdemeanor.

Nearly all sex-for-hire cases fall under state jurisdiction. However, the federal government may be involved in prosecution when a prostitute is transported in interstate commerce, or any other person is transported in interstate commerce for an immoral purpose.[3]

Deviate Sexual Conduct

Rape and related crimes were discussed in Chapter 4. That chapter focused on sexual behavior that results in harm to a victim. This discussion is different, as there is usually no victim other than society as a whole. Deviate sexual conduct has many definitions, but most states include fellatio, cunnilingus, anal sex, and all homosexual activity within the grasp of their deviate sexual

prostitution
A person offering her (in most states, his or her) body for sexual purposes in exchange for money. A crime in most states.

statutes. Therefore, consenting adults, married or not, may be prosecuted for participating in such sexual activity.

The foundation of the prohibition of sodomy and related acts is morality. Adherents to many religions, including Christianity, believe that all sex other than vaginal intercourse between a man and woman is deviate. The reality is that many, if not most, people engage in sex that falls into the definition of deviate sex. For this reason, it is argued that such acts are normal and should not be prohibited. Others argue that it does not matter if the behavior is normal or deviate—that sex between two consenting adults is private and involves no victims and, as such, is of no concern of the government. However, such laws continue to exist. Further, they have survived constitutional challenges in most instances.

Despite continued prohibition of sodomy, and related acts, in many states, the laws are seldom enforced. One reason is that law enforcement officials have shown a reluctance to enforce such laws, often because crimes perceived as more serious are time-demanding and leave little manpower and resources to enforce victimless crimes. In addition, there simply is the problem of discovering violations. Most sexual conduct occurs privately, and thus the police rarely discover violations independently. Of course, those who participate in prohibited sexual conduct are not likely to report their sex partners' acts to law enforcement.

 CASE

BOWERS V. HARDWICK

478 U.S. 186 (1986)

MAJORITY OPINION BY JUSTICE WHITE:

In August 1982, respondent was charged with violating the Georgia statute criminalizing sodomy by committing that act with another adult male in the bedroom of respondent's home. After a preliminary hearing, the District Attorney decided not to present the matter to the grand jury unless further evidence developed.

Respondent then brought suit in the Federal District Court, challenging the constitutionality of the statute insofar as it criminalized sodomy. He asserted that he was a practicing homosexual, that the Georgia sodomy statute, as administered by the defendants, placed him in imminent danger of arrest, and that the statute for several reasons violates the Federal Constitution. . . .

This case does not require a judgment on whether laws against sodomy between consenting adults in general, or between homosexuals in particular, are wise or desirable. It raises no question about the right or propriety of state legislative decisions to repeal their laws that criminalize homosexual sodomy, or of state court decisions invalidating those laws on state constitutional grounds. The issue presented is whether the Federal Constitution confers a fundamental right upon homosexuals to engage in sodomy and hence invalidates the laws of the many States that still make such conduct illegal. . . .

Respondent, however, asserts that the result should be different where the homosexual conduct occurs in the privacy of the home. He relies on *Stanley v. Georgia*, 394 U.S. 557 (1969), where the Court held that the First Amendment prevents convicting for possessing and reading obscene material in the privacy of his home: "If the First

Amendment means anything, it means that a State has no business telling a man, sitting alone at his house, what books he may read or what films he may watch."

Stanley did protect conduct that would not have been protected outside the home, and it partially prevented the enforcement of state obscenity laws; but the decision was firmly grounded in the First Amendment. The right pressed upon us here has no similar support in the text of the Constitution, and it does not qualify for recognition under the prevailing principles for construing the Fourteenth Amendment. . . .

[The vote of the Court was 5–4. Justice White wrote the majority opinion. Chief Justice Burger and Justices Powell, O'Connor, and Rehnquist joined in that opinion. Burger and Powell also filed concurring opinions. Justice Stevens filed a dissenting opinion, which Justices Brennan and Marshall joined. Justice Blackmun also filed a dissent in which Justices Marshall, Brennan, and Stevens joined.]

DISSENTING OPINION BY
JUSTICE BLACKMUN:

This case is no more about a "fundamental right to engage in homosexual sodomy," than *Stanley v. Georgia* was about a fundamental right to watch obscene movies. . . . Rather, this case is about "the most comprehensive of rights and the most valued by civilized men," namely, "the right to be left alone." . . .

Like Justice Holmes, I believe that "[i]t is revolting to have no better reason for a rule of law than that so it was laid down in the time of Henry IV. It is still more revolting if the grounds upon which it was laid down have vanished long since, and the rule simply persists from blind imitation of the past." I believe we must analyze respondent's claim in light of the values that underlie the constitutional right to privacy. If that right means anything, it means that, before Georgia can prosecute its citizens for making choices about the most intimate aspects of their lives, it must do more than assert that the choice they have made is an "abominable crime not fit to be named among Christians." . . .

"Our cases long have recognized that the Constitution embodies a promise that a certain private sphere of individual liberty will be kept largely beyond the reach of government". . . . In construing the right to privacy, the Court has proceeded along two somewhat distinct, albeit complementary, lines. First, it has recognized a privacy interest with reference to certain decisions that are properly for the individual to make. . . . Second, it has recognized a privacy interest with reference to certain places without regard for the particular activities in which the individuals who occupy them are engaged. . . .

Only the most willful blindness could obscure the fact that sexual intimacy is a "sensitive, key relationship of human existence, central to family life, community welfare, and the development of human personality." The fact that individuals define themselves in a significant way through their intimate sexual relationships with others suggests, in a Nation as diverse as ours, that there may be many "right" ways of conducting those relationships, and that much of the richness of a relationship will come from the freedom an individual has to choose the form and nature of these intensely personal bonds. . . .

The behavior for which Hardwick faces prosecution occurred in his own home, a place to which the Fourth Amendment attaches special significance. . . . Just as the right to privacy is more than the mere aggregation of a number of entitlements to engage in specific behavior, so too, protecting the physical integrity of the home is more than merely a means of protecting specific activities that often take place there. . . .

I can only hope . . . the Court soon will reconsider its analysis and conclude that depriving individuals of the right to choose for themselves how to conduct their intimate relationships poses a far greater threat to the values most deeply rooted in our Nation's history than tolerance of nonconformity could ever do. Because I think the Court today betrays those values, I dissent.

Indecent Exposure and Lewdness

Indecent exposure, or the exposure of one's "private parts" in public, was a common-law misdemeanor. Today, the crime is usually criminalized by state statute or local ordinance.

Most indecent exposure laws require (1) an intentional exposure (2) of one's private parts (3) in a public place. In some jurisdictions, it is required that the exposure be done in an "offensive manner."

In 1991, the United States Supreme Court examined a public nudity statute in the context of nude barroom dancing. In *Barnes v. Glen Theater, Inc.*, 501 U.S. 560 (1991), the Court upheld an Indiana statute that required dancers to wear pasties and g-strings. Although the court found that nude dancing was expressive conduct, it determined that states may require the dancers to cover their genitals. The court did say that erotic performances were protected by the First Amendment, provided the dancers wear a scant amount of clothing. The Court upheld the law because it determined that the state's objective was not to regulate expression, but to regulate for order and morality. Further, the Court held that the interference with expression was minimal.

The Model Penal Code prohibits public indecency. The Code goes further with a provision proscribing all lewd acts that the defendant knows are likely to be observed by others who would be "affronted or alarmed" by the acts.[4]

Obscenity

Congress shall make no law respecting the establishment of religion, or prohibiting the free exercise thereof; *or abridging the freedom of speech*, or of the press; or the right of the people peaceably to assemble, and to petition the Government for a redress of grievances.

This is the First Amendment to the United States Constitution. Most, if not all, states have a similar provision in their constitutions. The italicized portion represents the only protection of speech in the Constitution. Because it is brief and broad, it is dependent upon a great amount of interpretation to give it meaning. Also, because of its brevity and broadness, courts often interpret it differently. Even the Supreme Court has changed its interpretation of the clause, in particular areas, on several occasions. Freedom of speech encompasses far more than will be examined in this chapter. What will be discussed here is the extent of governmental power to regulate conduct that it deems to be indecent. Specifically, this section addresses sexually explicit materials, including films, books, and erotic dancing. It is well-established that the term *speech*, as used in the First Amendment, means more than spoken utterances. It includes all forms of expression.

Both the federal and state governments regulate conduct, speech, books, movies, and other forms of expression that are believed to be "obscene." State governments are the most involved with regulating obscenity, due to general police power (the power to regulate for the health, welfare, and safety of citizens). However, the federal government is also involved; for example, it has criminalized sending obscene materials through the mail.[5]

Not all indecencies may be criminalized. Simply because something strikes one person as indecent does not mean that it should be prohibited. People have differing values, and to allow governments to prohibit all conduct (or other things) that is found offensive by some member of society would be to allow our government to criminalize all aspects of life. In addition, people perceive things differently. For example, in 1990 the Cincinnati Arts Center was charged with obscenity for displaying photographs taken by a respected artist, Robert Mapplethorpe. Included in the photos were depictions of nude children. The prosecutor contended that the pictures were obscene. A jury did not agree. The Arts Center and its director were acquitted, and many of the jurors commented that the testimony of art experts convinced them that the pictures had serious artistic value and were not obscene.[6]

It is important that the First Amendment be flexible and tolerant of new ideas and methods of expression. Simply because the majority of citizens would not see value in a form of expression does not mean it has no value. If the opposite were true, then expression aimed at particular minority groups could be censored. This is not to say that there is no limit on the freedom of expression. When considering sexually oriented expression, that line is drawn when the expression becomes obscene.[7]

Obscenity has proven to be an elusive concept for the Supreme Court. Through a series of decisions, from 1957 to the present, the Court has attempted to define *obscenity*. The famous quotation from Justice Potter Stewart ("I shall not today attempt further to define [obscenity]; and perhaps I could never succeed in intelligibly doing so. But I know it when I see it."—*Jacobellis v. Ohio*, 378 U.S. 184 [1964]) is a testament to the difficulty in defining such a concept. It also reflects what many people believe, that they may not be able to define obscenity, but they recognize it when they see it.

In *Roth v. United States*, 354 U.S. 476 (1957), it was held that obscenity is not protected by the First Amendment because it lacks redeeming social importance. The Court then established a test for determining whether something was obscene, and, as such, not protected by the First Amendment. That test was "whether to the average person, applying contemporary community standards, the dominant theme of the material taken as a whole appeals to prurient interest." In addition, the material had to be "utterly without redeeming social value." Simply because "literature is dismally unpleasant, uncouth, and tawdry is not enough to make it 'obscene.'"[8]

In 1973 the Supreme Court reexamined the *Roth* obscenity test in *Miller v. California*, 413 U.S. 15 (1973). In *Miller* the Court rejected the requirement that the material be "utterly without redeeming social value," and lowered the standard to lacking "serious literary, artistic, political, or scientific value." The test under *Miller* has three parts:

1. The average person, applying contemporary community standards, would find that the work, taken as a whole, appeals to the prurient interest and

2. the work must depict or describe, in a patently offensive manner, sexual conduct specifically defined by the applicable state law, and
3. the work, when taken as a whole, must lack serious literary, artistic, political, or scientific value.

The *Miller* test makes it easier for states to regulate sexual materials. An "average person" has been equated with a reasonable person, as used in tort law.[9] The material must appeal to "prurient interest." Materials that have a tendency to excite a lustful, "shameful or morbid interest in nudity, sex or excretion" meet the prurient interest element.[10] Material that provokes normal, healthy, sexual desires is not obscene because it does not appeal to prurient interest.[11]

The Court gave examples in *Miller* of "patently offensive" materials that included depictions or descriptions of "ultimate sex acts, normal or perverted, actual or simulated . . . of masturbation, excretory functions, and lewd exhibition of the genitals."

One area where the states have substantially more power to regulate obscenity is when minors are involved. The Court has held that all child pornography is unprotected because of the special need to protect children from exploitation.[12] Similarly, governments may prohibit the distribution and sale of erotic materials to minors, even if such materials are not obscene.[13] Also, in *Osborne v. Ohio*, 494 U.S. 103 (1990), the Supreme Court held that a person may be convicted for possession of child pornography in the home. This is an exception to the general rule that a person may possess obscene material in the home.

As mentioned in *Miller*, governments may control the time, place, and manner of expression. Accordingly, certain restrictions may be valid that deal with expression in certain places, such as establishments that sell alcohol. (Chapter 8 addresses constitutional defenses to criminal accusations and discusses other time, place, and manner issues.)

One place where the power of the government to regulate sexually explicit materials is lessened is in homes. In many respects, the law reflects the attitude that a "man's home is his castle," and deserves special protection. Thus, the United States Supreme Court struck down the conviction of a man for possession of obscene materials in his home.[14] However, as previously mentioned, a person is not privileged to possess child pornography in the home.

The Model Penal Code makes it a misdemeanor to knowingly or recklessly do any of the following:[15]

1. Sell, deliver, or provide (or offer to do one of the three) any obscene writing, picture, record, or other obscene representation.
2. Present or perform in an obscene play, dance, or other performance.
3. Publish or exhibit obscene materials.
4. Possess obscene materials for commercial purposes.
5. Sell or otherwise commercially distribute materials represented as obscene.

The Code presumes that anyone who distributes obscene materials in the course of business has done so knowingly or recklessly.

Material is considered obscene under the Code if "considered as a whole, its predominant appeal is to prurient interest, that is, a shameful or morbid interest, in nudity, sex, or excretion, and if in addition it goes substantially beyond customary limits of candor in describing or representing such matter." Note that the Code's definition is similar to the Supreme Court's definition. The Code does add the requirement that the material go beyond "customary limits of candor." The Code makes it an affirmative defense that the obscene material was possessed for governmental, scientific, educational, or other justified causes. It also is not a crime for a person to give such materials to personal associates in non-commercial situations. The Code focuses on punishing commercial dissemination of obscene material.

Obscenity is a complex area of law. Many different criminal prohibitions exist throughout the states and federal government that focus on the sale, distribution, and possession of sexually oriented materials, performance of erotic dance, and public nudity. So long as minors are not involved, the activity is protected unless it is obscene. To determine whether pornography is obscene (hardcore), one must apply the three-part *Miller* test. The states are free to regulate if children are involved, either as participants in the erotic materials (or performance) or as buyers of erotic materials, even if the material is not obscene.

Because of the plethora of cases in this area, it is strongly recommended that thorough research be conducted. There is a good chance that precedent with similar facts may be found. Beware, however, that this is an issue that often leaves courts split. Be sure that the opinions you find reflect the law of your jurisdiction.

Regulating the Internet

The ability of the World Wide Web to penetrate every home and community across the globe has both positive and negative implications—while it can be an invaluable source of information and means of communication, it can also override community values and standards, subjecting them to whatever more may or may not be found online. . . . [T]he Internet is a challenge to the sovereignty of civilized communities, States, and nations to decide what is appropriate and decent behavior.[16]

In 2001, Nielsen/NetRatings reported that 500 million computers were connected to the Internet. Unquestionably, the Internet is a powerful and driving force. Some commentators believe it is reshaping the political identity of people all over the world. Others believe it is a great social equalizer, tearing down class, education, and economic barriers. Still others are concerned about the negative social impact the Internet may present. Many of the barriers that are being destroyed were in place to protect those individuals who are not capable or mature enough to protect themselves. In order to protect these people, state legislatures and Congress have acted to regulate the Internet.

Obscene and harmful information is the primary source of regulation, although commercial transactions, gambling, and other subjects are also regulated. In 1998, 16 million children under the age of 18 were using the Internet. Over 6 million of the children using the Internet were under the age of 13. Simultaneous to the growth in child use of the Internet has been a growth in adult sites. In 1998, it was estimated that there were more than 30,000 adult sites on the Internet and that as much as 70 percent of all Web traffic was unsuitable for children.[17] The first major national attempt to protect children from adult-oriented information on the Internet was the Communications Decency Act of 1996.[18] This statute limited the transmission of "obscene" and "indecent" materials to children. However, this statute was held unconstitutional by the Supreme Court in *Reno v. ACLU* (1997).[19] "The Supreme Court held that the law was overbroad because it prohibited both protected speech (indecent materials) and unprotected speech (obscene materials)." Obscene material, as defined by *Miller* and other cases, may be regulated but indecent material may not. In addition, the Court found that the law was overbroad because it limited access, both adult and juvenile. While it is lawful to limit the access of children to indecent materials (even if not obscene), the law limited the access of everyone because under current technology there is not a way to create zones that children cannot enter. In real space, such zones exist. Adult bookstores, for example, are zones where children may not enter.

Congress attempted again to protect children from the dangers of the Internet in 1998 through the Child Online Protection Act.[20] This law limited regulation to material that is harmful to minors. The law specifically incorporates the *Miller* test into its definition of what is prohibited. In a narrowly drafted decision, the Supreme Court upheld this law in 2002.[21] The court made it clear, however, that there may be other constitutional issues that need to be examined in an attempt to correct the error of the Communications Decency Act. It remains to be seen if this law is constitutional.

In another piece of legislation from 1996, the Child Pornography Prevention Act, Congress prohibited not only images of actual children in pornography, but also "virtual" images created with the use of computers. As was true of the Communications Decency Act, the Supreme Court found the law to be contrary to First Amendment principles in *Ashcroft v. Free Speech Coalition*.

 CASE

ASHCROFT V. FREE SPEECH COALITION

122 S.Ct. 1389 (2002)

We consider in this case whether the Child Pornography Prevention Act of 1996 (CPPA), 18 U. S. C. §2251 *et seq.*, abridges the freedom of speech. The CPPA extends the federal prohibition against child pornography to sexually explicit images that appear to depict minors but were produced without using any real children. The statute prohibits, in specific circumstances, possessing or distributing these images, which may be created by using adults who look like minors or by using computer imaging. The new technology, according to Congress, makes it possible to create realistic images of children who do not exist. . . .

By prohibiting child pornography that does not depict an actual child, the statute goes beyond *New*

York v. Ferber, 458 U. S. 747 (1982), which distinguished child pornography from other sexually explicit speech because of the State's interest in protecting the children exploited by the production process. See *id.*, at 758. As a general rule, pornography can be banned only if obscene, but under *Ferber*, pornography showing minors can be proscribed whether or not the images are obscene under the definition set forth in *Miller v. California*, 413 U. S. 15 (1973). *Ferber* recognized that "[t]he *Miller* standard, like all general definitions of what may be banned as obscene, does not reflect the State's particular and more compelling interest in prosecuting those who promote the sexual exploitation of children." 458 U. S., at 761.

While we have not had occasion to consider the question, we may assume that the apparent age of persons engaged in sexual conduct is relevant to whether a depiction offends community standards. Pictures of young children engaged in certain acts might be obscene where similar depictions of adults, or perhaps even older adolescents, would not. The CPPA, however, is not directed at speech that is obscene; Congress has proscribed those materials through a separate statute. 18 U. S. C. §§1460–1466. Like the law in *Ferber*, the CPPA seeks to reach beyond obscenity, and it makes no attempt to conform to the *Miller* standard. For instance, the statute would reach visual depictions, such as movies, even if they have redeeming social value.

The principal question to be resolved, then, is whether the CPPA is constitutional where it proscribes a significant universe of speech that is neither obscene under *Miller* nor child pornography under *Ferber*.

I

Before 1996, Congress defined child pornography as the type of depictions at issue in *Ferber*, images made using actual minors. 18 U. S. C. §2252 (1994 ed.). The CPPA retains that prohibition at 18 U. S. C. §2256(8)(A) and adds three other prohibited categories of speech, of which the first, §2256(8)(B), and the third, §2256(8)(D), are at issue in this case. Section 2256(8)(B) prohibits "any visual depiction, including any photograph, film, video, picture, or computer or computer-generated image or picture" that "is, or appears to be, of a minor engaging in sexually explicit conduct." The prohibition on "any visual depiction" does not depend at all on how the image is produced. The section captures a range of depictions, sometimes called "virtual child pornography," which include computer-generated images, as well as images produced by more traditional means. For instance, the literal terms of the statute embrace a Renaissance painting depicting a scene from classical mythology, a "picture" that "appears to be, of a minor engaging in sexually explicit conduct." The statute also prohibits Hollywood movies, filmed without any child actors, if a jury believes an actor "appears to be" a minor engaging in "actual or simulated . . . sexual intercourse." §2256(2).

These images do not involve, let alone harm, any children in the production process; but Congress decided the materials threaten children in other, less direct, ways. Pedophiles might use the materials to encourage children to participate in sexual activity. "[A] child who is reluctant to engage in sexual activity with an adult, or to pose for sexually explicit photographs, can sometimes be convinced by viewing depictions of other children 'having fun' participating in such activity." Congressional Findings, note (3) following §2251. Furthermore, pedophiles might "whet their own sexual appetites" with the pornographic images, "thereby increasing the creation and distribution of child pornography and the sexual abuse and exploitation of actual children." *Id.*, notes (4), (10)(B). Under these rationales, harm flows from the content of the images, not from the means of their production. In addition, Congress identified another problem created by computer-generated images: Their existence can make it harder to prosecute pornographers who do use real minors. See *id.*, note (6)(A). As imaging technology improves, Congress found, it becomes more difficult to prove that a particular picture was produced using actual children. To ensure that defendants possessing child pornography using real minors cannot evade prosecution, Congress extended the ban to virtual child pornography.

Section 2256(8)(C) prohibits a more common and lower tech means of creating virtual images, known as computer morphing. Rather than creating original images, pornographers can alter innocent pictures of real children so that the children appear to be engaged in sexual activity. Although morphed images may fall within the definition of virtual child pornography, they implicate the interests of real children and are in that sense closer to the images in *Ferber*. Respondents do not challenge this provision, and we do not consider it.

Respondents do challenge §2256(8)(D). Like the text of the "appears to be" provision, the sweep of this provision is quite broad. Section 2256(8)(D) defines child pornography to include any sexually explicit image that was "advertised, promoted, presented, described, or distributed in such a manner that conveys the impression" it depicts "a minor engaging in sexually explicit conduct." One Committee Report identified the provision as directed at sexually explicit images pandered as child pornography. See S. Rep. No. 104-358, p. 22 (1996) ("This provision prevents child pornographers and pedophiles from exploiting prurient interests in child sexuality and sexual activity through the production or distribution of pornographic material which is intentionally pandered as child pornography"). The statute is not so limited in its reach, however, as it punishes even those possessors who took no part in pandering. Once a work has been described as child pornography, the taint remains on the speech in the hands of subsequent possessors, making possession unlawful even though the content otherwise would not be objectionable.

Fearing that the CPPA threatened the activities of its members, respondent Free Speech Coalition and others challenged the statute. . . .

The First Amendment commands, "Congress shall make no law . . . abridging the freedom of speech." The government may violate this mandate in many ways, *e.g., Rosenberger v. Rector and Visitors of Univ. of Va.*, 515 U. S. 819 (1995); *Keller v. State Bar of Cal.*, 496 U. S. 1 (1990), but a law imposing criminal penalties on protected speech is a stark example of speech suppression. The CPPA's

penalties are indeed severe. A first offender may be imprisoned for 15 years. §2252A(b)(1). A repeat offender faces a prison sentence of not less than 5 years and not more than 30 years in prison. *Ibid.* While even minor punishments can chill protected speech, see *Wooley v. Maynard*, 430 U. S. 705 (1977), this case provides a textbook example of why we permit facial challenges to statutes that burden expression. With these severe penalties in force, few legitimate movie producers or book publishers, or few other speakers in any capacity, would risk distributing images in or near the uncertain reach of this law. The Constitution gives significant protection from overbroad laws that chill speech within the First Amendment's vast and privileged sphere. Under this principle, the CPPA is unconstitutional on its face if it prohibits a substantial amount of protected expression. See *Broadrick v. Oklahoma*, 413 U. S. 601, 612 (1973).

The sexual abuse of a child is a most serious crime and an act repugnant to the moral instincts of a decent people. In its legislative findings, Congress recognized that there are subcultures of persons who harbor illicit desires for children and commit criminal acts to gratify the impulses. See Congressional Findings, notes following §2251; see also U. S. Dept. of Health and Human Services, Administration on Children, Youth and Families, Child Maltreatment 1999 (estimating that 93,000 children were victims of sexual abuse in 1999). Congress also found that surrounding the serious offenders are those who flirt with these impulses and trade pictures and written accounts of sexual activity with young children.

Congress may pass valid laws to protect children from abuse, and it has. *E.g.,* 18 U. S. C. §§2241, 2251. The prospect of crime, however, by itself does not justify laws suppressing protected speech. . . .

As a general principle, the First Amendment bars the government from dictating what we see or read or speak or hear. The freedom of speech has its limits; it does not embrace certain categories of speech, including defamation, incitement, obscenity, and pornography produced with real children. . . .

The CPPA prohibits speech despite its serious literary, artistic, political, or scientific value. The statute proscribes the visual depiction of an idea—that of teenagers engaging in sexual activity— that is a fact of modern society and has been a theme in art and literature throughout the ages. Under the CPPA, images are prohibited so long as the persons appear to be under 18 years of age. 18 U. S. C. §2256(1). This is higher than the legal age for marriage in many States, as well as the age at which persons may consent to sexual relations.

Both themes—teenage sexual activity and the sexual abuse of children—have inspired countless literary works. William Shakespeare created the most famous pair of teenage lovers, one of whom is just 13 years of age. See Romeo and Juliet, act I, sc. 2, l. 9 ("She hath not seen the change of fourteen years"). In the drama, Shakespeare portrays the relationship as something splendid and innocent, but not juvenile. The work has inspired no less than 40 motion pictures, some of which suggest that the teenagers consummated their relationship. *E.g.,* Romeo and Juliet (B. Luhrmann director, 1996). Shakespeare may not have written sexually explicit scenes for the Elizabethan audience, but were modern directors to adopt a less conventional approach, that fact alone would not compel the conclusion that the work was obscene.

Contemporary movies pursue similar themes. Last year's Academy Awards featured the movie, Traffic, which was nominated for Best Picture. See Predictable and Less So, the Academy Award Contenders, N. Y. Times, Feb. 14, 2001, p. E11. The film portrays a teenager, identified as a 16-year-old, who becomes addicted to drugs. The viewer sees the degradation of her addiction, which in the end leads her to a filthy room to trade sex for drugs. The year before, American Beauty won the Academy Award for Best Picture. See "American Beauty" Tops the Oscars, N. Y. Times, Mar. 27, 2000, p. E1. In the course of the movie, a teenage girl engages in sexual relations with her teenage boyfriend, and another yields herself to the gratification of a middle-aged man. The film also contains a scene where, although

the movie audience understands the act is not taking place, one character believes he is watching a teenage boy performing a sexual act on an older man.

Our society, like other cultures, has empathy and enduring fascination with the lives and destinies of the young. Art and literature express the vital interest we all have in the formative years we ourselves once knew, when wounds can be so grievous, disappointment so profound, and mistaken choices so tragic, but when moral acts and self-fulfillment are still in reach. Whether or not the films we mention violate the CPPA, they explore themes within the wide sweep of the statute's prohibitions. If these films, or hundreds of others of lesser note that explore those subjects, contain a single graphic depiction of sexual activity within the statutory definition, the possessor of the film would be subject to severe punishment without inquiry into the work's redeeming value. This is inconsistent with an essential First Amendment rule: The artistic merit of a work does not depend on the presence of a single explicit scene. See *Book Named "John Cleland's Memoirs of a Woman of Pleasure" v. Attorney General of Mass.,* 383 U. S. 413, 419 (1966) (plurality opinion) ("[T]he social value of the book can neither be weighed against nor canceled by its prurient appeal or patent offensiveness"). Under *Miller,* the First Amendment requires that redeeming value be judged by considering the work as a whole. Where the scene is part of the narrative, the work itself does not for this reason become obscene, even though the scene in isolation might be offensive. See *Kois v. Wisconsin,* 408 U. S. 229, 231 (1972) *(per curiam).* For this reason, and the others we have noted, the CPPA cannot be read to prohibit obscenity, because it lacks the required link between its prohibitions and the affront to community standards prohibited by the definition of obscenity.

[I]n *Osborne v. Ohio,* 495 U. S. 103 (1990), the Court ruled that these same interests justified a ban on the possession of pornography produced by using children. "Given the importance of the State's interest in protecting the victims of child pornography," the State was justified in "attempting to stamp out this vice at all levels in the distribution chain." *Id.*, at 110. *Osborne* also noted the State's interest in preventing child pornography from being used as an aid in the solicitation of minors. *Id.*, at 111. The Court, however, anchored its holding in the concern for the participants, those whom it called the "victims of child pornography." *Id.*, at 110. It did not suggest that, absent this concern, other governmental interests would suffice. See *infra*, at 13–15.

In contrast to the speech in *Ferber*, speech that itself is the record of sexual abuse, the CPPA prohibits speech that records no crime and creates no victims by its production. Virtual child pornography is not "intrinsically related" to the sexual abuse of children, as were the materials in *Ferber*. 458 U. S., at 759. While the Government asserts that the images can lead to actual instances of child abuse, see *infra*, at 13–16, the causal link is contingent and indirect. The harm does not necessarily follow from the speech, but depends upon some unquantified potential for subsequent criminal acts.

The CPPA, for reasons we have explored, is inconsistent with *Miller* and finds no support in *Ferber*. The Government seeks to justify its prohibitions in other ways. It argues that the CPPA is necessary because pedophiles may use virtual child pornography to seduce children. There are many things innocent in themselves, however, such as cartoons, video games, and candy, that might be used for immoral purposes, yet we would not expect those to be prohibited because they can be misused. The Government, of course, may punish adults who provide unsuitable materials to children, see *Ginsberg v. New York*, 390 U. S. 629 (1968), and it may

enforce criminal penalties for unlawful solicitation. The precedents establish, however, that speech within the rights of adults to hear may not be silenced completely in an attempt to shield children from it. . . .

The Government submits further that virtual child pornography whets the appetites of pedophiles and encourages them to engage in illegal conduct. This rationale cannot sustain the provision in question. The mere tendency of speech to encourage unlawful acts is not a sufficient reason for banning it. . . .

The Government next argues that its objective of eliminating the market for pornography produced using real children necessitates a prohibition on virtual images as well. Virtual images, the Government contends, are indistinguishable from real ones; they are part of the same market and are often exchanged. In this way, it is said, virtual images promote the trafficking in works produced through the exploitation of real children. The hypothesis is somewhat implausible. If virtual images were identical to illegal child pornography, the illegal images would be driven from the market by the indistinguishable substitutes. Few pornographers would risk prosecution by abusing real children if fictional, computerized images would suffice.

In sum, §2256(8)(B) covers materials beyond the categories recognized in *Ferber* and *Miller*, and the reasons the Government offers in support of limiting the freedom of speech have no justification in our precedents or in the law of the First Amendment. The provision abridges the freedom to engage in a substantial amount of lawful speech. For this reason, it is overbroad and unconstitutional.

States also have laws regulating the Internet. Of course, these laws must be crafted to avoid First Amendment and state-law free speech barriers. Additionally, the interstate character of the Internet can create jurisdictional problems for states. In *American Library Association v. Pataki* (S.D. N.Y. 1997),[22] a New York statute that regulated the Internet in much the same manner as the federal Communications Decency Act was invalidated not on First Amendment grounds, but on jurisdictional grounds. The federal court that heard the case ruled that New York was without the authority to regulate conduct outside its borders.

CRIMES AGAINST THE PUBLIC ORDER

Introduction

Crimes against the public order are crimes that involve **breaches of the peace.** The phrase *breaches of the peace* refers to all crimes that involve disturbing the tranquility or order of society. Making breaches of the peace criminal has its roots in early English common law. In England, breaches of the peace by individuals were criminal, as were breaches by groups.

Three groups of breaches were recognized; all were punished as misdemeanors. If three or more people met with an intention of causing a disturbance, they committed the common-law offense of unlawful assembly. If the group took some action in an attempt to breach the peace, they were guilty of rout; if they were successful, the crime was riot.

Today, all jurisdictions prohibit breaches of the peace in some form by statute. The names of statutory crimes include disorderly conduct, unlawful assembly, riot, inciting violence, unlawful threat, and vagrancy.

Riot and Unlawful Assembly

Most states now have legislation that prohibits groups of people from meeting with the purpose of committing an unlawful act or committing a lawful act in an unlawful manner. This crime may be named unlawful assembly or riot. A group, or "assembly," is a specified minimum number of people, often three or five. Some jurisdictions continue to recognize the distinctions between unlawful assembly, rout, and riot.

The Model Penal Code recognizes two related crimes: riot and failure to disperse. Both crimes require an assembly of two or more persons who are behaving in a disorderly manner. If the purpose of the assembly is to commit a crime (felony or misdemeanor), to coerce public officials to act or not act, or if a deadly weapon is used, then the crime is riot.[23]

Failure to disperse occurs when a law enforcement officer, or other official, orders the members of a group of three or more to disperse, and someone refuses. The disorderly conduct that the assembly is engaged in must be "likely to cause substantial harm or serious inconvenience, annoyance, or alarm," before an officer may order the group to disperse. This provision is included because the freedoms to associate and assemble are protected by the First Amendment to the United States Constitution, and such activity may be regulated only when it poses a threat to person, property, or society.

Most jurisdictions punish these crimes as misdemeanors. However, they may be elevated to felony if committed with a dangerous weapon, if someone

breach of the peace
A vague term for any illegal public disturbance; sometimes refers to the offense known as "disorderly conduct." It is defined and treated differently in different states.

is injured as a result of the activity, or if law enforcement officers are obstructed from performing their duties. The Model Penal Code makes rioting a felony of the third degree and failure to disperse a misdemeanor.

Disturbing the Peace

As mentioned, individuals may also commit crimes against the public order. Disturbing the peace is such a crime. This crime is also known as disorderly conduct, threat, excessive noise, and affray. In essence, any time the public order or tranquility is unreasonably interrupted by an individual, disturbance of the peace has occurred. States may have one law that encompasses all such acts or separate statutes for each.

Disturbances may occur in hundreds of forms. One may disturb the peace by making loud noises in a residential area at midnight, by attempting to cause fights with others, or by encouraging others to engage in similar conduct. Statutes often also prohibit indecent language and gestures.

These statutes are often broadly worded and are vague. As such, they are often attacked as being unconstitutional. The defenses of overbreadth and vagueness are discussed in Chapter 8 on defenses and are not covered here. One defense that will be examined is the First Amendment right to free speech and its relationship to offensive words and gestures.

As you have learned, the First Amendment protects all forms of expression. This protection prohibits government from making expression criminal. However, exceptions to the First Amendment have been created. Words that have a likelihood of causing a riot are such an exception. That is, even though the words are expression, they may be punished. The reason is obvious: riots lead to property damage, personal injuries, and sometimes death. As such, the interest of the government to control such behavior outweighs the First Amendment interest.

fighting words

Speech that is not protected by the First Amendment to the U.S. Constitution because it is likely to cause violence by the person to whom the words are spoken.

The **fighting words** doctrine is another exception. The Supreme Court has defined *fighting words* as those that inflict injury, tend to incite an immediate breach of the peace, or by their nature will cause a violent reaction by a person who hears them.[24] Laws that regulate speech that may be regulated, such as fighting words, must be drafted narrowly; that is, only the conduct intended must be prohibited. If a law is drawn so broadly that both fighting words and legitimate speech are criminalized, it is unconstitutional and void.

The defendant in the *Witucki* case was convicted of disorderly conduct. The court found that his speech was unprotected because he used fighting words.

Incitement/Advocacy of Unlawful Conduct

Whenever one person, acting independently, encourages another to commit an unlawful act or intends to cause a riot, the crimes of incitement of lawful behavior or incitement of riot may be charged. Unlike riot, which requires a group, one person may commit this crime. Unlike disturbing the peace, it may be committed in a peaceful manner.

CASE

CITY OF LITTLE FALLS V. EDWIN GEORGE WITUCKI

295 N.W.2d 243 (Minn. 1980)

On December 11, 1978, a Morrison County Court jury found defendant guilty of disorderly conduct in violation of Little Falls, Minnesota, Ordinances. . . .

At approximately 11:00 P.M. on September 19, 1978, defendant Edwin George Witucki and a few of his friends entered the West Side Bar in Little Falls, Minnesota. Just outside the building defendant found a cat which he carried into the building and placed on the bar. Pursuant to defendant's request, one bartender served the cat some beef jerky and a shotglass of cream and served defendant a drink.

About five minutes later, the other bartender, Paula Erwin, told defendant to take the cat outside. He refused. She told him he was cut off from being served until the cat was removed. He responded, "I let you slip once too many times, I'm not going to let you slip again." Erwin, for the third time, told defendant to remove the cat. He responded by saying, "Hey, Butch, I don't have to take any of your crap." She then turned to return to the other end of the bar, and Witucki called her a "black-haired witch," a "cocksucker," and a "son-of-a-bitch."

When asked at trial about her reaction to the words, Erwin testified, "I didn't care for them very well. It scared me. There was nothing I could do about it. There were no guys around so I thought the best thing for me to do, because I was really mad at the time, was just to walk away from him." She also testified that calling the police or any sort of violent action on her part would not be wise or safe because he might wait for her outside after hours and because he was much larger than she and there were no men around to help her.

* * *

The question is, did defendant's words in the circumstances in which they were uttered constitute "those personally abusive epithets which, when addressed to the ordinary citizen, are as a matter of common knowledge, inherently likely to provoke violent reaction.". . .

In *In re S.L.J.* the appellant was a fourteen-year-old girl who yelled "fuck you pigs" at two police officers. . . . The court noted that although "no ordered society would condone the vulgar language" and although "her words were intended to, and did, arouse resentment in the officers, the constitution requires more before a person can be convicted for mere speech." The court held that where the words were spoken in retreat by a small teenage girl who was between fifteen and thirty feet from the two police officers sitting in their squad car, "there was no reasonable likelihood that [the words] would tend to incite an immediate breach of the peace or to provoke violent reaction by an ordinary, reasonable person.

In *Cohen v. California*, 403 U.S. 15, 91 S.Ct. 1780, 29 L. Ed. 2d 284 (1971), the defendant wore a jacket on which the words "Fuck the Draft" were plainly visible. The words were not directed against the person of any possibly offended person; they were directed against the draft.

The instant case is readily distinguishable from both *In re S.L.J.* and *Cohen v. California.* Unlike the defendant's language in *Cohen*, Witucki's language was directed at and was intended to be about a person, namely Erwin. The abusive language hurled by defendant at Erwin could readily be found by a jury to be inherently likely to incite violence. Defendant was not, as in *Cohen*, merely expressing a controversial political opinion in a vulgar way; he was directly insulting and intimidating an innocent person.

* * *

The fact that the words used by appellant are vulgar, offensive, and insulting, and that their use is condemned by an overwhelming majority of citizens does not make them punishable under the criminal statutes of this state unless they fall outside the protection afforded to speech by the First Amendment.

* * *

Defendant's speech in this case is not a "trifling and annoying instance of individual distasteful abuse of a privilege." He addressed such abusive, vulgar, insulting and obscene language toward the bartender that his language was properly found to be within the fighting words category of unprotected speech. . . . [Conviction affirmed.]

clear and present danger
A test of whether or not speech may be restricted or punished. It may be if it will probably lead to violence soon or if it threatens a serious, immediate weakening of national safety and security.

However, because the First Amendment applies, such statutes must be narrowly drawn. In fact, only speech which creates a **clear and present danger** may be controlled. The United States Supreme Court has said that "incitement of imminent lawless action" may be regulated.[25] Anything less may not be regulated. Hence, merely advocating unlawful conduct in the abstract is protected. Advocating future unlawful conduct is also protected, as it poses no imminent threat.

Threats

Finally, in the speech arena, threats are addressed. Threat statutes may make threatening individuals, groups, or even property criminal. Threats to harm people are similar to assaults. However, threat is broader, as it often protects property and the people at large. The purpose of threat statutes is to preserve public order, and the purpose of assault statutes is to protect individuals.

For example, if a defendant were to call in a bomb threat to a public office, there would be no assault, but there is a threat. A person may be guilty of threat by making the prohibited statements, even if untrue. So, if a defendant makes a bomb threat, but has placed no bomb in the building, a crime has been committed. Threats are misdemeanors in most jurisdictions and are punished less severely than assaults. In the *Thomas* case, the defendant was convicted under the Kentucky threat statute.

Vagrancy and Panhandling

Vagrancy, as a criminal law issue, has received considerable attention. Most states and municipalities have statutes that forbid vagrancy. At common law, a *vagrant* was one who wandered from place to place with no means of support, except the charity of others. At one time, in early English law, vagrancy applied to disorderly persons, rogues (a dishonest wanderer), and vagabonds (a homeless person with no means of support).

Beginning in the 1880s, it was common in the United States for statutes to prohibit a wide range of behavior as vagrancy. These statutes were drafted broadly to allow law enforcement officers considerable discretion in their enforcement. This discretion was used to control the "undesirables" of society. Many statutes made the status of being homeless, a gambler, and a drug addict a crime.

CASE

**THOMAS V.
COMMONWEALTH
OF KENTUCKY**

574 S.W.2d 903 (Ky. Ct.
App. 1978)

The case for the Commonwealth was based solely on the testimony of Gladys Thomas. Mrs. Thomas on direct examination stated that on the Friday before she went to swear out the warrant that she was in her front yard cutting weeds with a butcher knife when appellant came out of the house, hit her across the back with his hand, laughed and ran into a barber shop next door. Appellant then came back laughing and hit her across the back with a belt and then ran into a liquor store about three doors down from the house. Appellant continued to aggravate Mrs. Thomas until she asked him to go and get her a coke. Mrs. Thomas then testified thusly:

> So, we went about an hour, an hour and a half after my mom left and he came in and said, "I told you to get ready to go," and I said, "I'm not going," and he grabbed me by the hair of the head and threw me against the refrigerator and said, "you are going or I will kill you and prove self-defense. This is one time everything is on my side. So, just get dressed and let's go somewhere and show everybody what a happy family we are."

Next, Mrs. Thomas gave testimony concerning the circumstances surrounding the threat which is the basis for the charge against appellant:

> So, on Wednesday, he came in and he said, "I will come home. I'm coming home." I said, "you can't. You absolutely cannot. I went and applied for welfare," and he said, "I have to tell the man, Mr. Clark, that I'm here or I'll be in trouble." One thing led to another and he jumped in the middle of the floor and said, "you and Brenda have got me against the wall. You're going to get me in trouble. I will cut both your heads off before I go back." Those are almost the exact words. And

I looked around and the little girl was standing right in the screen door.

On cross examination, Mrs. Thomas testified that this threat was made in the late afternoon and that on the next morning, on July 15, 1976, she sent and got a warrant.

[The applicable Kentucky statute] provides thusly:

A person is guilty of terroristic threatening when:

(a) He threatens to commit any crime likely to result in death or serious bodily injury to another person or likely to result in substantial property damage to another person; or
(b) He intentionally makes false statements for the purpose of causing evacuation of a building, place of assembly, or facility of public transportation.
(c) Terroristic threatening is a Class A misdemeanor.

This court believes that [this statute] is not unconstitutionally vague and overbroad since the conduct proscribed, "threaten[ing] to commit a crime likely to result in death or serious physical injury" is not protected under either the Kentucky or United States Constitutions. Further, the language of the statute is sufficiently explicit to put the average citizen on notice as to the nature of the conduct so proscribed.

This court is aware of the recent decision in *U.S. v. Sturgill*, 563 F.2d 307 (6th Cir. 1977), which invalidated [another Kentucky statute] on the basis that it was unconstitutionally overbroad. [The invalidated statute] provides: "A person is guilty of harassment when with intent to harass, annoy or alarm another person he: (b) In a public place, makes an offensively coarse utterance, gesture, or display, or addresses abusive language to any person present."

In *Sturgill*, the court held that in order for a statute, which punishes spoken words only, to withstand an attack on its constitutionality, it must be first authoritatively interpreted by the state courts as not interfering with speech protected by the First Amendment.

This case can be distinguished from *Sturgill*, in that the language is proscribed under [the terroristic threatening statute] is clearly without constitutional protection under the First Amendment. . . .

Certainly, [the terroristic threat statute] does not apply in the case of idle talk or jesting. The defendant's intent to commit the crime of "terroristic threatening" can be plainly inferred from the defendant's own words and the circumstances surrounding them. All the statute requires is that the defendant threaten "to commit any crime likely to result in death or serious physical injury to another person or likely to result in substantial property damage to another person."

[Conviction] Affirmed.

Today, states may not make personal status, such as drug addiction or alcoholism, a crime. The United States held that doing so violates the Eighth Amendment's prohibition of cruel and unusual punishment.[26] However, until 1972, people found undesirable by the police could be arrested under broadly worded vagrancy statutes for "wandering," or walking around a city, because this was an act, not a status. This ended in 1972 when the United States Supreme Court handed down *Papachristou v. City of Jacksonville*, 405 U.S. 156 (1972). The Court announced in that case that vagrancy statutes that prohibit walking around, frequenting liquor stores, being supported by one's wife, and similar behavior, to be "too precarious for a rule of law" and violative of the Due Process and Cruel and Unusual Clauses of the Constitution.

The result of *Papachristou* has been more narrowly drawn vagrancy statutes. Today such laws focus on more particularized behavior, and in many instances a mens rea element has been added. This prevents simple acts, such as walking at night, from being criminal. For example, a vagrancy law may prohibit "loitering or standing around with an intent to gamble," or "loitering or standing in a transportation facility [e.g., bus station] with the intent of soliciting charity."

In recent years panhandling (begging) has increasingly become a problem for most cities. Panhandlers often choose to congregate in and near public transportation egresses and ingresses, because of the large number of people who use such facilities. Because panhandlers are sometimes aggressive and intimidating to patrons of such facilities, some jurisdictions have chosen to prohibit begging at public transportation sites.

As the number of homeless persons grows in the United States, so will the problems associated with vagrancy and panhandling. Examine statutes and ordinances that prohibit such activities with an awareness that they must be drawn carefully to avoid a First Amendment speech problem. Also be aware that other constitutional provisions may be implicated, such as the First Amendment's freedom of association and the Due Process and Equal Protection Clauses of the Fifth and Fourteenth Amendments.

Crimes Involving Firearms

A discussion of the regulation of firearms properly begins with the Second Amendment to the United States Constitution, which reads:

> A well regulated Militia, being necessary to the security of a free State, the right of the people to keep and bear Arms, shall not be infringed.

In spite of the tireless efforts of firearms lobbyists to convince the Nation that the Second Amendment was intended to protect the individual's right to possess arms, the Supreme Court of the United States as well as nearly all lower courts that have heard this issue have concluded that the Amendment is intended to preserve a collective right, the right to have a well-regulated militia. The second half of the clause, to keep and bear arms, is interpreted as conjunctive with the first half of the clause, which provides for a well-regulated militia.

In a 1939 Supreme Court decision, *United States v. Miller*, [27] a defendant who had been charged under a federal law prohibiting possession of short-barreled shotguns and rifles challenged the law as violating his Second Amendment right to possess a firearm. The Court stated:

> The Constitution as originally adopted granted to the Congress power— 'To provide for calling forth the Militia to execute the Laws of the Union, suppress Insurrections and repel Invasions; To provide for organizing, arming, and disciplining, the Militia, and for governing such Part of them as may be employed in the Service of the United States, reserving to the States respectively, the Appointment of the Officers, and the Authority of training the Militia according to the discipline prescribed by Congress.' U.S.C.A. Const. art. § 8. With obvious purpose to assure the continuation and render possible the effectiveness of such forces the declaration and guarantee of the Second Amendment were made. It must be interpreted and applied with that end in view.
>
> The Militia which the States were expected to maintain and train is set in contrast with Troops which they were forbidden to keep without the consent of Congress. The sentiment of the time strongly disfavored standing armies; the common view was that adequate defense of country and laws could be secured through the Militia—civilians primarily, soldiers on occasion.
>
> The signification attributed to the term Militia appears from the debates in the Convention, the history and legislation of Colonies and States, and the writings of approved commentators. These show plainly enough that the Militia comprised all males physically capable of acting in concert for the common defense. 'A body of citizens enrolled for military discipline.' And further, that ordinarily when called for service these men were expected to appear bearing arms supplied by themselves and of the kind in common use at the time.

The Supreme Court affirmed this interpretation of the Second Amendment in the 1980 case *United States v. Lewis*.[28] The Court has not passed on this issue since Lewis, although it has allowed many lower court decisions enforcing *Miller* and *Lewis* stand without review.

Since the federal Constitution has been interpreted as not establishing an individual's right to bear arms, each State and the federal government are free to design its weapons law in nearly any manner. Some states have constitutional guarantees of the right to bear arms. Absent such a guarantee, a State is free to regulate guns in any manner. Today, many federal, state, and local gun laws exist.

Possession, Sale, and Transfer Laws.   One of the most common forms of weapons regulation is possession. Both federal and state laws prohibit a variety of possession-related offenses. These include improper possession of a weapon that is otherwise permitted, e.g., concealed possession; possession of altogether prohibited weapons, e.g., machine guns; and possession by certain classes of persons, e.g., possession by ex-felons, aliens, fugitives, mental incompetents, individuals who were dishonorably discharged from the military, those under stalking-related court orders, and individuals convicted of misdemeanor domestic violence. The possession of firearms is also prohibited in certain areas designated by statute. Near schools, in public buildings, in airports, in national and state parks, and on airplanes are examples.

One of the most significant federal firearms statutes is The National Firearms Act.[29] Enacted in reaction to the organized crime problem of the 1930s, this law prohibited the sale and possession of automatic weapons (machine guns). Another important federal law is The Gun Control Act of 1968. Among its many provisions are a prohibition of mail order guns and the prohibition of the possession, transfer, or receipt of firearms by felons, aliens, and certain other persons. The federal Brady Handgun Violence Prevention Act of 1993, which was named for President Ronald Reagan's White House Press Secretary James Brady who was shot during an attempted assassination of the President, requires all federally licensed gun dealers to conduct background checks of firearms purchasers to ensure that purchasers do not fall into one of the categories of ineligible buyers under the Gun Control Act of 1968. Records checks are now being implemented through the National Instant Background Check System (NICS). Another federal statute, the Violent Crime Control and Law Enforcement Act of 1994 prohibits the sale of semi-automatic weapons and large ammunition magazines.

Firearms Use Laws.   Many jurisdictions forbid the discharge of firearms in urban areas, absent good cause. Arizona's unlawful discharge statute (A.R.S. § 13-3107) reads:

A. A person who with criminal negligence discharges a firearm within or into the limits of any municipality is guilty of a class 6 felony. . . .

C. This section does not apply if the firearm is discharged:
   1. As allowed pursuant to the provisions of chapter 4 of this title.
   2. On a properly supervised range.

3. In an area recommended as a hunting area by the Arizona game and fish department, approved and posted as required by the chief of police, but any such area may be closed when deemed unsafe by the chief of police or the director of the game and fish department.
4. For the control of nuisance wildlife by permit from the Arizona game and fish department or the United States fish and wildlife service.
5. By special permit of the chief of police of the municipality.
6. As required by an animal control officer in the performance of duties as specified in section 9-499.04.
7. Using blanks.
8. More than one mile from any occupied structure as defined in section 13-3101.
9. In self-defense or defense of another person against an animal attack if a reasonable person would believe that deadly physical force against the animal is immediately necessary and reasonable under the circumstances to protect oneself or the other person.

Other law forbids the use of certain weapons for hunting and fishing. For example, shotguns may not be permitted in the hunting of certain game. Some statues prohibit "aiming," "pointing," and otherwise threatening people with firearms.

The use of a weapon in the commission of a crime is sometimes a separate crime from the underlying offense. Nearly all jurisdictions require or permit enhancement of sentences for crimes committed while in possession of a firearm.

Registration and Licensing. In addition to background checks, many states require guns to be registered. In some instances, licenses must be obtained to carry or use weapons.

The National Firearms Act[30] requires national registration of all firearms manufactured or transferred in the United States, and it prohibits the sale of automatic weapons (machine guns).

Drug and Alcohol Crimes

Introduction. Crimes that involve the use of narcotics and alcohol may be classified in many ways. In one sense, such activity offends many people in society and appears to be an offense against the public morality. Whenever a pimp uses a young woman's drug addiction to induce her to become involved in prostitution, it appears to be a crime against an individual.

Drug and alcohol crimes are included in this section because of their impact on the order of society. Alcohol-related driving accidents are the cause of many fatalities. Drug addiction often is the cause of other crimes, such as theft, assaults, and prostitution. Police report that a number of domestic problems are caused by alcohol and drugs and that much of the violence directed toward law-enforcement officers is drug-related. Large cities, such as Detroit and Washington, D.C., have experienced a virtual drug boom, which has led to increased assaults, batteries, and drug-related homicides. Many addicts, desperate for a "fix," steal for drug money.

Drug and alcohol use are also expensive. Corporate America has recently awakened to the expenses associated with employee drug use. Employees who use drugs have a high absenteeism and low productivity. Decreased performance caused by drug use can be costly, in both human and dollar terms. This is true especially in positions that require great concentration or pose risks to others, such as that of commercial pilots. In addition to business expenses, the high cost of rehabilitation can disable a family financially, and the price of drug-abuse detection and prosecution is high.

Alcohol Crimes.   Let it not be mistaken, alcohol is a drug. However, the law treats alcohol differently than it does other drugs. Alcohol may be legally possessed, consumed, and sold, subject only to a few restrictions. Narcotics, on the other hand, are significantly restricted. Their sale, possession, and consumption are limited to specific instances, such as for medical use. The federal government, as well as every state, has statutes that spell out what drugs are regulated.

There are many alcohol-related crimes. Public drunkenness laws make it criminal for a person to be intoxicated in a public place. This crime is a minor misdemeanor and rarely prosecuted, as many law enforcement agencies have a policy of allowing such persons to "sleep it off" and then releasing them.

All states have a minimum age requirement for the sale or consumption of alcohol. Those below the minimum age are minors. Any minor who purchases or consumes alcohol is violating the law. Additionally, any adult who knowingly provides alcohol to a minor is also guilty of a crime, commonly known as contributing to the delinquency of a minor.

Merchants holding liquor licenses may be subject to criminal penalties for not complying with liquor laws, such as selling alcohol on holidays, Sundays, or election day, as well as for selling alcohol to minors. A merchant who violates liquor laws may also suffer the civil penalty of revocation of liquor license.

Alcohol and automobiles have proven to be a deadly and expensive combination. All states have laws that criminalize driving while under the influence of alcohol or drugs. Driving while under the influence of alcohol or drugs, driving while intoxicated, and driving with an unlawful blood-alcohol level are the names of these crimes.

These statutes are generally of two genres. One type of law generally prohibits the operation of a motor vehicle while under the influence of any drug, including alcohol. To prove this charge, the quantity of the drug or alcohol in the defendant's system is not at issue; the defendant's ability to operate the vehicle safely is. In such cases, field sobriety tests are often required of the suspect. These are tests that the suspect usually performs at the location where the police made the stop. Coordination, spatial relations, and other driving-related skills are tested by field sobriety tests.

The second type of law prohibits driving a motor vehicle any time a person's blood-alcohol level is above a stated amount. The states vary in the quantity required, although 8 percent (.08) and 10 percent (.10) are common. The effect of these laws is that an irrebuttable presumption is created. The law presumes that anyone with the stated blood-alcohol level or above cannot safely operate a motor vehicle. Under such statutes, evidence that a person can safely operate a motor vehicle with a blood-alcohol level greater than the maximum allowed is not permitted.

In recent years drunk driving has received considerable public and legislative attention. The result has been stricter laws and greater punishment for offenders. The once-common police practice of driving drunk drivers home is virtually nonexistent today.

First offenses are usually misdemeanors. Second or third offenses are felonies. In many jurisdictions, there has been a move toward alcohol treatment rather than incarceration. This often involves house arrest, alcohol treatment, and defensive driving education. Also, while in these programs, convicted persons are commonly required to submit to periodic blood or urine screening.

For first-time offenders, these programs have many advantages over prison. First, the focus is on curing the alcohol problem. If successful, the possibility of repetition is eliminated. Second, convicted persons are often permitted to continue to work and maintain family relationships. Finally, the cost of administration of alcohol programs is lower than the cost of incarceration. The value of such programs for repeat offenders is questionable, and in many jurisdictions jail time is required as early as a second conviction.

Drug Crimes.   Unlike alcohol, possession of other drugs is a crime. Every state and the federal government have enacted some variation of the Uniform Controlled Substance Act, a model act (similar to the Model Penal Code) drafted by the Commissioners on Uniform Laws. These statutes establish schedules of drugs that categorize drugs based on their danger, potential for abuse, and medical benefits. These factors then determine a drug's allowed usage. For example, one schedule exists for drugs that may not be used under any condition, and another schedule permits use for medical and research purposes only. There are three basic drug crimes: possession, sales/distribution, and use.

Possession of prohibited drugs is a crime. Of course, actual possession is sufficient actus reus, but some jurisdictions also make constructive possession criminal. Constructive possession permits conviction of those people who exercise dominion and control over property where the illegal drug is located, even though the person has no "actual physical possession" of the prohibited narcotic. However, the Model Penal Code[31] and most jurisdictions require knowledge that the drug was present before culpability is imposed. As such, if a guest stays in Robert's home, Robert is not criminally liable for any drugs the guest has stowed away, unless Robert is aware of their presence. Once Robert becomes aware, he must see that the drugs are removed within a reasonable time or risk a possession charge.

First-time conviction of possession, if the quantity is small, is a misdemeanor and normally results in probation. In many states, if a person pleads guilty, submits to a term of probation, and successfully completes the probation, then no adjudication of guilt is entered; so, no record of conviction exists. Probation terms usually include drug counseling, periodic drug testing, and no other arrests during the period. This type of procedure is known as *deferred sentencing* or *suspended imposition of sentence*. See Chapter 11 for a discussion of sentencing.

The sale or distribution of prohibited drugs is the second primary drug offense. Generally, it is punished more severely than possession. Not only are sales prohibited, but any "delivery" or "distribution" of drugs is also illegal. "Possession with an intent to deliver or sell" is similar to simple possession, except a mens rea of intending to sell must be proven. Possession with an intent to sell or deliver is punished more severely than possession, often punished equally with actual sale or delivery.

The quantity of the drug involved affects the level of punishment for both possession and sale/distribution offenses. Other factors, such as selling to minors, may aggravate the sentence.

Unauthorized use of a controlled substance is also a crime. The Mens Rea is knowing use. So, if a person takes a pill containing a controlled substance that someone gives him or her, who represented it to be an aspirin, there is no crime. Of course, the taking must be voluntary. If a person is forced down and injected with an illegal drug, he or she has committed no crime.

Recall from the earlier discussion of actus reus that addiction to controlled substances may not be made criminal. The United States Supreme Court has held that criminalizing a person's status as an addict is cruel and unusual punishment, as prohibited by the Eighth Amendment to the United States Constitution.[32] It is permitted, however, to punish a person for the act of taking a controlled substance.

SIDEBAR

DRUG COURTS Drug cases began to clog court dockets in the 1980s. As a result, legislators, judges, and others searched for alternatives to deal with drug offenders. One alternative that has proven to be popular is the drug court. The first drug court opened in Miami, Florida, in 1989. By 1997, 161 programs were in existence in thirty-eight states, the District of Columbia, and Puerto Rico. Forty percent of those courts were in Florida and California. Additionally, nearly every state without a drug court was in the process of developing one.

As the name implies, the drug court hears only drug cases. In most drug courts, only nonviolent drug offenders are eligible for admission. The time of admission varies between programs. In some courts, the offender is deferred into the program. If the offender successfully completes the program, no conviction results. In others, offenders are channeled into the program after a plea of guilty or postconviction.

The drug court specializes in the treatment and monitoring of drug offenders. All programs have a treatment component, although the form of treatment varies significantly among programs. In addition, drug court programs are characterized by intensive monitoring. Participants are required to submit to daily or weekly drug screenings and they are required to frequently appear in court. Many programs also use a system of "graduated sanctions" to punish participants who fail to meet program requirements.

The data concerning the success of drug programs is not clear. Unfortunately, one study indicates that 48 percent of the participants do not successfully complete their programs. It is too early to know the degree to which recidivism is decreased as compared to processing individuals through other courts, but at least one researcher has found that graduated sanctions programs may be successful in this regard.

Sources: *Drug Courts: Overview of Growth, Characteristics, and Results*. Report of the General Accounting Office (GAO/GGD 97–106), July 31, 1997 and Adele Harrell, *Drug Courts and the Role of Graduated Sanctions*, U.S. Department of Justice, National Institute of Justice (1998).

RICO and CCE.   You have already learned that the Racketeer Influenced and Corrupt Organizations Act (RICO) was enacted to fight organized crime in all its forms. Another federal statute, Continuing Criminal Enterprise (CCE),[33] was enacted specifically to combat drug trafficking. The statute is aimed at prosecuting the people at the top of the drug dealing and smuggling pyramid, and, accordingly, it has become known as the "Drug Kingpin statute."

A person engages in a criminal enterprise if (1) he is an administrator, organizer, or other leader (2) of a group of five or more people (3) who are involved in a series of drug violations. A *series* of violations means three or more drug convictions.[34]

Conviction of CCE results in stern punishment. A general violation receives twenty years to life in prison. Second convictions carry thirty years to life. If a person is determined to be a "principal leader," the amount of drugs involved was enormous, or the enterprise made $10 million or more in one year from drugs, then life imprisonment is mandatory. Fines may also be imposed. Also, the statute provides for imprisonment or death when murder results from the enterprise.[35]

Finally, the Comprehensive Forfeiture Act of 1984[36] applies to both RICO and CCE violations. This statute permits the government to seize property and money that is used in the commission of the crimes and that is a product of the crimes. So, if a drug dealer uses a boat to smuggle drugs, the boat can be seized, even though it may have been purchased with "honest" money. Any items acquired with drug money may be seized, as can bank accounts and trusts.

RICO AND CCE IN ACTION   RICO and CCE are two potent tools that federal law enforcement officials have to combat businesses with a criminal mission (criminal enterprises). The penalties for violating these laws are higher than for other laws directed at the same criminal behavior.

Regardless of the publicity and attention RICO and related statutes have received, they are not commonly used by federal prosecutors. For example, in 1990, only 996 RICO and 128 CCE prosecutions were filed in the United States, although 17,135 people were prosecuted for drug trafficking under other laws.

SIDEBAR

In total, only 2 percent of all criminals in the federal system are convicted of racketeering or CCE crimes.

The most common predicate offenses upon which racketeering charges are based are gambling, drugs, and threats. RICO and CCE cases consume more time and effort than other crimes. On average, CCE cases take twice as long to complete as cases for other offenses and RICO cases take 50 percent longer.

Defendants are less likely to plead guilty in RICO and CCE cases, are just about as likely to be convicted, and are usually punished more severely than defendants convicted under similar laws. Most people prosecuted under these laws are white males.

Source: *Prosecuting Criminal Enterprises* (Bureau of Justice Statistics 1993).

Possession of Drug Paraphernalia.   Another tool in the government's arsenal against drug use are laws that prohibit the sale, use, and possession of drug paraphernalia. These laws are often aimed at retailers who sell the devices that are used to take drugs. Needles, roach clips, and specialized pipes are examples of the type of paraphernalia that are proscribed.

These laws have been challenged on many fronts. One challenge asserts that such laws are vague because they do not adequately describe what is proscribed. In addition, it has been asserted that these laws are overly broad because they include devices that may be used for both legitimate and illegal purposes.[37] These issues were considered by the United States Supreme Court in the 1994 case, *Posters 'N' Things, Ltd. v. United States*.[38] In this case, the Court held that a law proscribing items "primarily intended" or "designed for" drug use was neither too vague or overly broad and accordingly, found it constitutional.

CRIMES AGAINST THE ADMINISTRATION OF GOVERNMENT

Perjury

perjury
Lying while under oath, especially in a court proceeding. It is a crime.

Perjury was a crime at common law and continues to be prohibited by statute in all states.

The basic elements of perjury are (1) the making of a (2) false statement (3) with knowledge that it is false (4) while under oath. To gain a conviction, the prosecution has the tough burden of proving the mens rea: that the person who made the statement knew that it was false. As with other crimes, juries are permitted to infer a defendant's knowledge from surrounding facts.

In addition, the statement must be made while under oath. Be aware that this includes far more than testifying in court. Most laws cover all statements made before one authorized to administer oaths. Therefore, perjury laws apply to people who sign affidavits before notary publics and appear as witnesses before a court reporter (e.g., for deposition), a grand jury, and all others who have the authority to administer oaths. For those individuals who have a religious objection to "swearing," the law permits an affirmation. This is simply an acknowledgment by the witness that the testimony he or she renders is truthful. The law treats an affirmation in the same manner as it does an oath.

Some jurisdictions require that the false statement be "material," or important to the matter. This prevents prosecutions for trivial matters. Some jurisdictions have defined *materiality* as any matter that may affect the outcome of a case. If a statement is not material, even if untrue, then a perjury conviction is not permitted.

A related crime is **subornation of perjury.** This occurs when one convinces or procures another to commit perjury. One who commits subornation is treated as a perjurer for the purpose of sentencing.

subornation of perjury
The crime of asking or forcing another person to lie under oath.

In addition to being a crime in every state, the United States has also made perjury criminal by statute. 18 U.S.C. § 1621 reads:

Whoever (1) having taken an oath before a competent tribunal, officer, or person, in any case in which a law of the United States authorizes an oath to be administered, that he will testify, declare, depose, or certify truly . . . is true, willfully and contrary to such oath states or subscribes any material matter which he does not believe to be true. . . .

Of course, truth is a complete defense to a charge of perjury. What is truthful is not always easy to determine, and in most questionable cases prosecutors choose not to pursue the matter. This is in large part due to the mens rea element.

THE PROBLEMS OF PRESIDENT CLINTON: A CASE STUDY IN CRIMES AGAINST THE PUBLIC   One of the most public cases of crimes against the public occurred in the late 1990s. For several years independent Counsel Kenneth Starr investigated President William J. Clinton and many of his associates for activities that transpired before and after Clinton assumed the presidency. In December 1998 the House of Representatives of the United States impeached President Clinton after receiving a referral from Mr. Starr. The House issued a two-count impeachment alleging both perjury and obstruction of justice.

In the impeachment, the President was accused of committing perjury to a grand jury. The House alleged that Mr. Clinton lied about the nature of his relationship with a White House intern, Monica Lewinsky. He was also accused of lying about a prior perjury he committed in a deposition in a sexual harassment action filed by Paula Jones who had been an employee of the State of Arkansas when Mr. Clinton was Governor of that State. In addition, he was charged directly with perjury in the Paula Jones sexual harassment lawsuit, with suborning perjury in that case, and with obstructing justice in that case.

Perjury can be a tricky affair because language can be a tricky affair. Proving perjury requires actual knowledge of falsity, materiality, and an oath. The mens rea is the difficult part, as demonstrated in the Clinton case. In response to questions concerning whether he had sexual relations with Ms. Lewinsky, Mr. Clinton answered in the negative. Later, it was discovered that these answers were true using Mr. Clinton's definition of sex, which he narrowly defined as intercourse. He later admitted to having oral and other forms of sexual contact with Ms. Lewinsky. Mr. Clinton also used semantics to evade disclosing other facts. For example, he relied on distinctions in tense when responding to certain questions. Mr. Clinton responded to one question by stating "[I]t depends on what the meaning of the word is is. If the, if he, if is means is and never has been, that is not, that is one thing. If it means there is none, that was a completely true statement."

Another problem prosecutors faced in the Clinton case was his inability to recall facts. In response to many details, the President answered that he was unable to remember or he would provide a qualified answer (e.g., I believe, but I'm not sure). In such cases, a prosecutor must prove that the witness did know the answer in order to prove perjury, a very difficult task.

Concerning the obstruction of justice charges, Mr. Starr alleged that Mr. Clinton attempted to retrieve gifts he had given to Ms. Lewinsky in an attempt to prevent them from falling into the hands of investigators. In addition, Mr. Starr accused the President of attempting to coach witnesses into testifying in a certain manner. For example, his secretary testified that the President met with her, told her that there were several things she needed to know, and that he had been asked about Monica Lewinsky in deposition the day before. He then posed these questions and statements to the secretary: "You were always there when she was there, right? We were never really alone. Monica came on to me, and I never touched her, right? You can see and hear everything, right?"

On February 12, 1999 the Senate of the United States voted 45 to 55 in favor of conviction on the perjury count and 50–50 on the obstruction of justice count, both falling short of the 67 votes necessary to convict and remove the President. Because Kenneth Starr (as well as many constitutional scholars) was of the opinion that a president must be impeached and removed before a criminal action may be filed against the president, Mr. Starr did not file criminal charges against Mr. Clinton. Mr. Clinton may now be charged and tried for both the perjury and obstruction allegations. In 1999, the trial judge in the Paula Jones case held Mr. Clinton in contempt of court for "giving false, misleading and evasive answers that were designed to obstruct the judicial process. . . . Simply put, the President's deposition testimony regarding whether he had ever been alone with Ms. Lewinsky was intentionally false, and his statements regarding whether he had ever engaged in sexual relations with Ms. Lewinsky likewise were intentionally false, notwithstanding tortured definitions and interpretations of the term 'sexual relations.'" The court ordered Mr. Clinton to pay plaintiff's expenses resulting from efforts to disprove his statements, as well as related court costs.

Source for contempt information:
http://www.foxnews.com/news/packages/president/side0414a99.sml

Bribery

As is true of perjury, **bribery** was a crime at English common law. Actually, bribery was initially a violation of biblical law, because it was wrong to attempt to influence judges, who were considered to be God's earthly representatives. Eventually, the crime was recognized by the courts of England.

Today, bribery is a statutory crime in the states and in the United States. The essential elements of the crime are (1) soliciting or accepting (2) anything of value (3) with the purpose of (4) violating a duty or trust. Two primary forms of bribery are that of a public official and commercial bribery.

As mentioned, bribery began as a prohibition of influencing a judge. The crime was eventually extended to include bribery of all public officials and public servants. Statutes make it bribery to be the one accepting or giving the "thing of value." Hence, if a corporate official gives a public official money in exchange for awarding a contract to the company, both the corporate officer and the public official have committed bribery.

Most bribery statutes declare that unsuccessful offers are bribes. Thus, if the public official rejects the offer of the corporate officer, there is still a bribery violation. The offer need not be of money in exchange for a favor; anything of value is sufficient. Automobiles, tickets to a St. Louis Cardinals game, and a promise of sexual favors all satisfy this requirement.

The offer must be made to a *public official* or *servant*. Both terms are defined broadly. Further, the offeror must be seeking to influence the official in a matter over which the official has authority. Most courts have held that whether the officer actually had the authority to carry out the requested act is not dispositive; the issue is whether the offeror believes that the official possesses the authority. Awarding of government contracts, setting favorable tax assessments, and overlooking civil and criminal violations are examples of corrupt acts.

The offer alone makes the offeror guilty of bribery. For the public official to be convicted, there must be an acceptance. This usually means that the official does the requested act; however, it is widely held that an acceptance is all that is necessary to support a conviction.

Bribery has been extended beyond the public affairs realm to commercial life. Whenever a person who is engaged in business activities breaches a duty or trust owed to someone (or something, such as a business organization) in exchange for something of value, bribery has been committed.

The Model Penal Code declares that commercial bribery is a misdemeanor. The Code applies to people in specific positions, such as lawyers, accountants, trustees, and officers of corporations.[39] Anyone who makes an offer to someone in one of these positions to violate the trust or duty created by the position is guilty of bribery. Of course, any person holding such a position who accepts such an offer is also guilty of bribery. The Code specifically states that any person who holds himself or herself out to the public to be in the business of appraising the value of services or commodities is guilty of bribery if he or she accepts a benefit to influence the decision or appraisal. Knowing that one is violating the trust is the mens rea under the Code.

bribery
The offering, giving, receiving, or soliciting of anything of value in order to influence the actions of a public official.

If a seller for the Widgcom Company were to offer the purchasing agent of Retailers, Inc., money in exchange for receiving the contract to supply Retailers with Widgets for the next year, commercial bribery has occurred. A corporate officer who accepts free personal air travel in exchange for buying all corporate airline tickets from the same airline has committed bribery.

Finally, note that there are statutes that prohibit "throwing" athletic contests for pay. That is, any player, coach, owner, or official who accepts a benefit to cause one participant to win or lose commits bribery. These laws often apply to both professional and amateur sports.

Tax Crimes

You have likely heard the quip, "In life, only two things are certain, death and taxes." Tax revenues are the lifeblood of government. In the United States, people are taxed at the federal level, state level, and local level (county, municipal, and school district taxes). These taxes come in many forms, including income tax, gift and estate tax, sales tax, and excise taxes. Tax laws apply to individuals, estates, and business entities.

All taxing authorities have statutes that impose both civil and criminal penalties for violation of tax laws. Common violations of tax laws are tax evasion, failing to file a required tax return, filing a fraudulent return, and unlawful disclosure of tax information. These are not the only crimes related to taxes, however, as shown by the applicable federal statutes, which embody sixteen tax-related crimes.[40]

tax evasion
The deliberate nonpayment or underpayment of taxes that are legally due. Criminal tax evasion has higher fines than civil fraud and the possibility of a prison sentence upon the showing of "willfulness."

Tax evasion involves paying less tax than required or underreporting one's income with the intent of paying less tax. The federal statute covering tax evasion reads:

> *26 U.S.C. § 7201 Attempt to evade or defeat tax*
> Any person who willfully attempts in any manner to evade or defeat any tax imposed by this title or the payment thereof shall, in addition to other penalties provided by law, be guilty of a felony and, upon conviction thereof, shall be fined not more than $100,000 ($500,000 in the case of a corporation), or imprisoned not more than 5 years, or both, together with the costs of prosecution.

tax fraud
The deliberate nonpayment or underpayment of taxes that are legally due.

Tax fraud, a crime closely related to evasion, involves using fraud or false statements to avoid a tax obligation. This may occur in many ways, including falsifying statements that are provided to a revenue agency, such as fraudulent receipts used for deductions. Filing false tax returns is also a form of tax fraud.

Failure to file a required tax return is also criminal. The relevant federal statute reads:

> *26 U.S.C. § 7203 Willful failure to file return, supply information, or pay tax*
> Any person required under this title to pay any estimated tax or tax, or required by this title or by regulations made under authority thereof to make a return, keep any records, or supply any information, who willfully fails to

pay such estimated tax or tax, make such return, keep such records, or supply such information . . . [shall] be guilty of a misdemeanor and, upon conviction thereof, shall be fined not more than $25,000 ($100,000 in the case of a corporation), or imprisoned not more than 1 year, or both, together with the costs of prosecution.

Note that § 7203 applies to anyone who is required to file a tax return, pay a tax, or supply information. Therefore, this provision can be the basis of a prosecution of an employer who pays his or her employees in cash and makes no report to the Internal Revenue Service. Likewise, although some entities are not taxed, such as partnerships, they are required to file informational returns, and failure to do so violates this provision.

Tax evasion, filing fraudulent tax returns, and the unauthorized disclosure of information are crimes of commission. That is, an affirmative act is required to commit these crimes.

Failing to file a required return, or other information, is an act of omission. Proving such crimes requires not proof of an illegal act, but that a required act was not taken. The quoted statutes require willful violations. Negligence in preparing a tax return or in filing the return is not criminal. However, such errors may lead to civil penalties.

The willfulness requirement was considered by the Supreme Court in *Cheek v. United States*.

Tax laws require the disclosure of all income and profits. This includes income from illegal sources. Gamblers are required to report their winnings, prostitutes their income, and drug dealers the profits derived from their sales. Failure to report income from illegal acts is the same as failure to report legally earned income. Because requiring people to report income from illegal activities raises a self-incrimination problem, tax laws require that all information obtained be kept confidential. Tax officials are not permitted to disclose such information to law enforcement authorities, and to do so is *unlawful disclosure*. The privilege against self-incrimination is discussed more thoroughly in Chapter 8.

 CASE ◆

CHEEK V. UNITED STATES

498 U.S. 192 (1991)

Willfulness, as construed by our prior decisions in criminal tax cases, requires the Government to prove that the law imposed a duty on the defendant, that the defendant knew of this duty, and that he voluntarily and intentionally violated this duty. We deal first with the case where the issue is whether the defendant knew of the duty purportedly imposed by the provision of the statute or regulation he is accused of violating, a case in which there is no claim that the provision at issue is invalid. In such a case, if the Government proves actual knowledge of the pertinent legal duty, the prosecution, without more, has satisfied the knowledge component of the willfulness requirement. But carrying this burden requires negating a defendant's claim of ignorance of the law or a claim that because of a misunderstanding of the law, he had a good-faith belief that he was not violating any of the provisions of the tax laws. This is so because one cannot be aware that the law imposes a duty upon him and yet be ignorant of it, misunderstand the law, or believe that the duty does not exist. In the end, the issue is whether, based on all the evidence, the Government has proved that the defendant was aware of the duty at issue, which cannot be true if the jury credits a good-faith misunderstanding and belief submission, whether or not the claimed belief or misunderstanding is objectively reasonable.

In this case, if Cheek asserted that he truly believed that the Internal Revenue Code did not purport to treat wages as income, and the jury believed him, the Government would not have carried its burden to prove willfulness, however, unreasonable a court might deem such a belief. . . .

We thus disagree with the Court of Appeals' requirement that a claimed good-faith belief must be objectively reasonable if it is to be considered as possibly negating the Government's evidence purporting to show a defendant's awareness of the legal duty at issue. Knowledge and belief are characteristically questions for the fact-finder.

In the *Moon* case, the tax evasion and fraud conviction of Reverend Sun Myung Moon, father of the "Moonies," was upheld by the Second Circuit Court of Appeals.

Obstruction of Justice

Obstruction of justice refers to any number of unlawful acts. As a general proposition, any act that interferes with the performance of a public official's duties obstructs justice. However, the crime is most commonly associated with law enforcement and judicial officials.

The types of acts that fall under such statutes include tampering with witnesses or jurors, interfering with police officers, destroying evidence needed for a court proceeding, and intentionally giving false information to a prosecutor in an effort to hinder a prosecutorial effort. However, obstruction statutes are drafted broadly, thereby permitting creative prosecutions. For example, it is common for women who are physically abused by their husbands to contact the police during a violent episode and demand the husband's arrest, usually in an effort to get the man out of the house. Once the husband is arrested, many women lose interest in prosecuting and often refuse to testify against their husbands in court. In such a case, a prosecutor could charge the wife with obstruction of justice because of her refusal to testify.

Resisting arrest is a similar crime. At common law, one could resist an unlawful arrest. Although a few jurisdictions have retained this rule, this is not presently the law in most jurisdictions. Most states have followed the Model Penal Code approach, which prohibits even moderate resistance to any arrest.[41] It is a wise rule, considering the remedies that are available if a police officer makes an unlawful arrest. If the arrest is unlawful, but in good faith, the arrestee will be released either at the police station or after the first judicial hearing. If the arrest was unlawful and made maliciously, the arrestee not only will be released, but also has a civil cause of action for false imprisonment and violation of civil rights.

CASE

UNITED STATES V. SUN MYUNG MOON

718 F.2d 1210
(2d Cir. 1983)

Defendants argue that the evidence presented was insufficient to find them guilty beyond a reasonable doubt on the substantive tax offenses charged in Counts Two through Six. To find defendants guilty of fraud in the filing of Moon's income tax returns, the jury had to find that statements contained in the returns which were verified as true were in fact false, and that these false statements were willfully made. . . .

Under the government's theory of the case, Moon failed to report interest income earned on the Chase Manhattan Bank accounts that he purportedly owned and income recognized as a result of distribution of Tong Il stock to him at no cost. Appellants' principal contentions at trial were that the Chase accounts and Tong Il stock belonged to the Church, that Moon merely held these assets as the nominee, agent, and/or trustee of the Church, and that therefore he was not taxable on either the Chase interest or Tong Il stock distribution.

In concluding that the jury properly found the Chase accounts and Tong Il stock to be Moon's personal property, we start first with the fact that the Chase accounts and Tong Il securities were maintained in Moon's name and controlled by him. Second, some funds clearly destined for Church entities were put in existing Church bank accounts which were owned and controlled by Church operations. Third, from his handling of the Chase accounts and Tong Il stock Moon seemingly regarded them as his own, not belonging to the Church. Fourth, high-ranking members of the Church were told that the Chase funds belonged to "Father," not to the Church. . . .

We turn to the evidence that Moon willfully filed income tax returns for the 1973–75 tax years knowing that these returns contained false information. . . . Willfulness in tax fraud cases has become equated with bad faith, want of justification, or knowledge that the taxpayer should have reported more income than he did. . . .

The evidence presented on this issue, although circumstantial, was sufficient to sustain the jury's verdict. The salient points follow. Moon signed his 1974 and 1975 returns, acknowledging that he had read them and that they were accurate, and he signed an RSC-12 form giving similar assurances as to his 1973 return; Moon and Kamiyama both knew of Moon's interest income at Chase and income from the distribution of Tong Il stock; Moon actively supervised all of his personal financial matters and never signed anything until he understood it. . . . [Conviction affirmed.]

Contempt

Failure to comply with a court order is contemptuous, as is taking any act with the purpose of undermining a court's authority or intending to interfere with its administration and process. Although statutes provide for contempt, it is widely accepted that the contempt power is inherent.

Contempt is broken down into direct and indirect criminal contempt and direct and indirect civil contempt. *Direct contempt* refers to acts that occur in the presence of the judge. Although usually in the courtroom, the judges' chambers and office area are included. *Indirect contempt* refers to actions taken outside the presence of a court, but which are violative of a court order.

contempt
A willful disobeying of a judge's command or official court order. Contempt can be *direct* (within the judge's notice) or *indirect* (outside the court and punishable only after proved to the judge). It can also be *civil contempt* (disobeying a court order in favor of an opponent) or *criminal contempt*.

Criminal contempt is levied to punish a person for violating a court order. Civil contempt, in contrast, does not have punishment as its purpose. It is intended to coerce a person into complying with a court order. For example, if Mary refuses to testify at a trial despite an order to testify, the judge may order her confined until she complies. Once she testifies, she is free. It is often said that civil contemnors hold the keys to their jail cells, whereas criminal contemnors do not. In theory, one who has been held in civil contempt can be punished for criminal contempt after complying with the court order. In practice this seldom occurs, presumably because judges and prosecutors feel that the civil punishment imposed is adequate.

The contempt power is significant. Indirect criminal contemnors are entitled to all the protections of other criminal defendants, such as a right to a trial, assistance of counsel, and proof beyond a reasonable doubt. Direct criminal contemnors have no such rights, as the act took place in the presence of a judge. However, any sentence imposed may be appealed and reviewed for fairness.

Civil contemnors have few rights. They do not possess the rights of those accused of crimes, because civil contempt is not considered a criminal action. In most instances they enjoy no right to appeal. A civil contemnor holds his or her own key; he or she must comply with the court's order. Of course, if an appellate court determines that the underlying order is unlawful, the civil contemnor is released. However, they may be charged with criminal contempt for failure to comply with the order before it was held unlawful by an appellate court. The fact that a court order may be nullified at some future date does not justify noncompliance. Court orders must be obeyed to assure the orderly administration of justice.

SIDEBAR

TWO CASES OF CONTEMPT Contempt of court orders are common in domestic law cases. One case, which received considerable media attention, involved Dr. Elizabeth Morgan, who refused to obey a court order to disclose the location of her child, Heather, claiming that her ex-husband had molested the child. The judge ordered that she disclose the location of the child so her ex-husband could exercise his court-ordered visitation rights. She refused, and the judge ordered that she be incarcerated until she disclosed the child's whereabouts. Dr. Morgan spent a total of 759 days in jail and was released only after an act of Congress limited the amount of time a civil contemnor could spend in jail to one year.

A case from Houston, Texas, teaches that the contempt power of judges is powerful. Houston attorney John O'Quinn was found in criminal contempt by a federal district judge for sleeping in a jury room. The basis for the contempt citation was an order from the judge that O'Quinn (and others) "stay out of the facilities up here on this floor unless you get prior permission." The Fifth Circuit Court of Appeals reversed the conviction, finding that the judge's order was too vague. However, this is a good example of the breadth of the contempt power; had the judge's order been more specific, it would have been upheld.

Source: "A Hard Case of Contempt," *Time*, Sept. 18, 1989; "A Mother's 759 Days of Defiance," *U.S. News & World Report*, Oct. 9, 1989.

Legislatures also have the power to cite for contempt. Legislatures, usually through committees, conduct hearings and other proceedings when considering bills and amendments to statutes. The contempt power serves the same function for legislatures that it does for courts. It furthers the orderly performance of legislative duties. Refusal to testify before a legislative body (usually a committee), to produce documents or other items, and disrupting a proceeding are examples of legislative contempt. Persons charged with legislative contempt possess the same rights as defendants charged with other crimes. In most instances, legislative bodies refer contempt cases to prosecutors, rather than adjudicating such cases themselves.

CRIMES AGAINST SOVEREIGNTY AND SECURITY

In the last section you read about crimes that interfere with public administration. Those crimes may, but are not necessarily, intended to destroy the government or to make a political statement. This section examines the very serious crimes of treason, sedition, espionage, and terrorism.

Treason

The United States has had law dealing with treason since its earliest years. The only crime mentioned in the Constitution is treason. Article III, section 3 reads:

> Clause 1: Treason against the United States, shall consist only in levying War against them, or in adhering to their Enemies, giving them Aid and Comfort. No Person shall be convicted of Treason unless on the Testimony of two Witnesses to the same overt Act, or on Confession in open Court.

> Clause 2: The Congress shall have Power to declare the Punishment of Treason, but no Attainder of Treason shall work Corruption of Blood, or Forfeiture except during the Life of the Person attainted.

Congress implemented Clause 1[42] and the resulting elements of the offense are:

1. A person who owes an allegiance to the United States
2. *Levies* war or *Adheres* to an enemy of the United States and
3. commits an overt act and
4. possesses treasonable intent.

Interestingly, one does not have to be a citizen of the United States to commit treason. Persons living in the United States owe allegiance to the Nation and may be charged with treason. Generally, speech is not an overt act, except when state secrets are revealed to an enemy. To satisfy the mens rea requirement, one must intend to betray the United States. Clause two requires two witnesses to the treasonous act. The two witnesses may testify to separate acts, so long as they support the same act of treason.

ATTENTION ESTATE: The Social Security # is
~ing requested by this state agency in order to
~rue its statutory responsibility. Disclosure is
~luntary and there will be no penalty for refusal.

OFFICIAL COPY
VIGO COUNTY HEALTH DEPARTMENT
CERTIFICATE OF DEATH

ocal No. ...... 599 ......

THE RECORDS IN THIS SERIES ARE CONFIDENTIAL PER IC 16-37-1-10

YPE/PRINT IN ERMANENT 3LACK INK	1 DECEASED—NAME: Timothy James McVeigh · 2 SEX: Male · 3a TIME OF DEATH: 7:14 A. · 3b DATE OF DEATH: June 11, 2001

ECEDENT

4 SOCIAL SECURITY NUMBER: 129-58-4709 · 5a AGE—Last Birthday: 33 · 5b UNDER 1 YEAR · 5c UNDER 1 DAY · 6 DATE OF BIRTH: April 23, 1968 · 7 BIRTHPLACE: Lockport, NY

8a WAS DECEDENT A U.S. VETERAN? Yes · 8b YEAR LAST SERVED IN U.S. ARMED FORCES? 1991 · 8c PLACE OF DEATH: HOSPITAL ☐ · OTHER ☒ Other (Specify): U S Penitentiary

9a FACILITY NAME: U S Penitentiary, 4200 Bureau Road · 9b CITY, TOWN OR LOCATION OF DEATH: Terre Haute · 9c COUNTY OF DEATH: Vigo

10 MARITAL STATUS: Never Married · 11 SURVIVING SPOUSE: N/A · 12a DECEDENT'S USUAL OCCUPATION: Soldier · 12b KIND OF BUSINESS/INDUSTRY: US Army

13a RESIDENCE—STATE: New York · 13b COUNTY: Niagara · 13c CITY, TOWN, OR LOCATION: Lockport · 13d STREET AND NUMBER: 6289 Campbell Blvd

13e ZIP CODE: 14094 · 13f INSIDE CITY LIMITS: ☐ No ☒ Yes · 13g ON A FARM? ☒ No ☐ Yes · 14 CITIZEN OF WHAT COUNTRY? USA · 15 WAS DECEDENT OF HISPANIC ORIGIN? ☒ No ☐ Yes · 16 RACE: White · 17 DECEDENT'S EDUCATION: Elementary/Secondary (0-12): 12 · College (1-4 or 5+)

RENTS

18 FATHER'S NAME: William McVeigh · 19 MOTHER'S NAME: Mildred Noreen Hill

FORMANT

20a INFORMANT'S NAME: Robert Nigh · 20b MAILING ADDRESS: 2 West 6th St Tulsa, OK 74119 · 20c Relationship: Attorney

POSITION

21a METHOD OF DISPOSITION: ☐ Burial ☒ Cremation ☐ Removal from State ☐ Donation ☐ Other (Specify) · 21b DATE AND PLACE OF DISPOSITION: June 11, 2001 Terre Haute Crematory · 21c LOCATION—City or Town, State: Terre Haute, IN

22a EMBALMER'S NAME: No Embalming · 22b EMBALMER'S LICENSE NO.: N/A · 23 WAS DEATH REPORTED TO CORONER? ☐ No ☒ Yes

24a SIGNATURE OF FUNERAL DIRECTOR · 24b LICENSE NUMBER: FD09200035 · 25 NAME, ADDRESS, AND LICENSE NUMBER OF FUNERAL HOME: Mattox Ryan Funeral Home 602 S 7th Street Terre Haute, IN 4780 FH19900001

USE OF ATH

26 PART I. Enter the diseases, injuries, or complications that caused the death...

IMMEDIATE CAUSE (Final disease or condition resulting in death) a. *Lethal Injection*
DUE TO (OR AS A CONSEQUENCE OF):

Conditions, if any, which give rise to the immediate cause... b. DUE TO (OR AS A CONSEQUENCE OF):

c. DUE TO (OR AS A CONSEQUENCE OF):

d.

PART II. Other significant conditions

27 WAS DECEDENT PREGNANT OR 90 DAYS POSTPARTUM? NO · 28a WAS AN AUTOPSY PERFORMED? NO · 28b WERE AUTOPSY FINDINGS AVAILABLE PRIOR TO COMPLETION OF CAUSE OF DEATH? NO

TIFIER

29a CERTIFIER (Check only one): ☐ CERTIFYING PHYSICIAN · ☐ HEALTH OFFICER · ☒ CORONER

29b SIGNATURE AND TITLE OF CERTIFIER: ___ S. Amos MD VigoCounty Coroner · 29c MEDICAL LICENSE NO: 01 03111 7 · 29d DATE SIGNED: June 11, 2001

30 NAME AND ADDRESS OF PERSON WHO COMPLETED CAUSE OF DEATH ITEM 26: Susan Amos Coroner 501 Hospital Lane Terre Haute, IN 47802

LTH ICER

31 HEALTH OFFICER'S SIGNATURE · 32 DATE FILED: JUN 11 2001

33 MANNER OF DEATH: ☐ Natural ☐ Pending Investigation ☐ Accident ☐ Suicide ☐ Could not be Determined ☒ Homicide · 34a DATE OF INJURY: June 11, 2001 · 34b TIME OF INJURY: 7:14 A.M. · 34c INJURY AT WORK? No · 34d DESCRIBE HOW INJURY OCCURRED: Judicial Execution by Lethal injection

34e PLACE OF INJURY: U.S. Penitentiary · 34f LOCATION: 4200 Bureau Rd. Terre Haute, IN

34g DATE PRONOUNCED DEAD: June 11, 2001 · 34h MOTOR VEHICLE ACCIDENT? No

SDH06-004 State Form 10110 (R5/1-99)

Sedition and Espionage

Sedition has been recognized as a crime since the first days of the Constitution. The Alien and Seditions Acts of the late eighteenth century made it a crime to write false, scandalous, or malicious stories about the government; increased the residency period to become a citizen; and increased the President's authority to deport dangerous aliens.

The provisions of the sedition laws prohibiting free speech were controversial and many prominent Americans opposed them, including both Thomas Jefferson and James Madison. After the law expired by its own sunset provision, Congress reimbursed the paid fines for all those who had been convicted under its authority.[43]

Today, there are several sedition laws, including a prohibition of seditious conspiracies to overthrow the government[44] the Logan Act, which prohibits individuals from corresponding with foreign governments in relation to disputes such governments may have with the United States, and a prohibition of recruiting members of the United States armed forces to act against the United States.[45]

Many forms of espionage and subversive activities are made criminal in the federal statutes.[46] Most of these require either an intention or reason to believe the United States will be injured and an overt act in furtherance of the crime.

Terrorism

Recent acts of terrorism, however, have been the catalyst to new terrorism and sedition laws. The Foreign Intelligence Surveillance Act of 1978 (FISA) delegated substantial authority to federal law enforcement officials. FISA provided for secret court orders authorizing surveillance (without probable cause) of non-U.S. persons. The objective of such orders is not to build cases for criminal prosecution, but to gather foreign intelligence.

Following the bombing of the federal building in Oklahoma City, Oklahoma, the Antiterrorism and Effective Death Penalty Act of 1996 was enacted. Through this statute habeas corpus relief was limited, inter alia, by requiring petitions to be filed within one year and limiting the number of petitions that may be filed in any one case. The Act also requires victim compensation and requires courts to provide closed circuit television access to victims in instances where the venue of trial is changed from the location of the crime.

Following the attacks of September 11, 2001, the Uniting and Strengthening America by Providing Appropriate Tools Required to Intercept and Obstruct Terrorism Act of 2001 was enacted. This law is commonly known as the Patriot Act. The Patriot Act changed existing law (including the Omnibus Crime Control and Safe Streets Act of 1968) in many ways, including:

- Federal law enforcement authority to monitor e-mail and other forms of communication was expanded. Examples include treating stored voicemail messages like e-mail, not as telephone conversations. E-mail enjoy less protection than telephone conversations.

- Federal court authority to issue pen register and trap orders (devices used to determine the origin of electronic communications) was broadened to include the entire nation.
- Prior to the Patriot Act, law enforcement officers did not have to establish probable cause to obtain a court order to a telephone company to trace (using pen register/traps). Because the content of telephone conversations was not being intruded upon, law enforcement officers were only required to show that the data is "relevant to an ongoing investigation." The Patriot Act extended this procedure to obtaining a record of Web addresses a suspect visits, even though identification of a Web address also identifies content.
- The Patriot Act authorizes "roving wiretaps." A roving wiretap is authorization to move a wiretap from one telephone or form of communication to another in order to follow the communications of the person under surveillance.
- Several new crimes were created, including money laundering of cybercrime and terrorism, overseas use of fraudulent U.S. credit cards, terrorist attacks on mass transit, and harboring terrorists, and it increased the penalties for counterfeiting.
- The Attorney General of the United States was delegated greater authority to deport suspected alien terrorists.
- Law enforcement agencies were given the authority to share grand jury and wiretap information that constitutes "foreign intelligence" with intelligence agencies. Previously, this was not permitted.

Also in response to the September 11 attacks, President Bush issued Military Order 1. This order empowered the Secretary of Defense to detain members of al Qaeda who have participated in, or planned, terrorist activity. The order also provided for military tribunals for terrorists with a 2/3 majority of each commission required for conviction. The Secretary of Defense then issued Military Commission Order 1, which was an elaboration of the responsibilities and authorities issued by President Bush in Military Order 1. This order established the procedures for implementing President Bush's order. For example, it permits the imposition of the death sentence, mandates a secret vote of the military judges, and allows for forfeiture of the property of those convicted.

These new laws are not without their critics. The most common criticism is that civil liberties are being lost in the effort to increase national security. To these critics, two threats are posed by terrorism. The first is terrorism. The second is the possible overreaction to terrorism. Proponents of these new laws believe that terrorism is substantially different from other crime and that the loss of some freedoms is needed to maintain security.

Finally, remember that terrorists are subject to all the "traditional" penal laws of the states and nation. Terrorists that steal can be prosecuted for larceny and those that kill can be prosecuted for murder. Following the tragic attacks of September 11, 2001, Zacarias Moussaoui was charged as being the twentieth hijacker. Moussaoui could not board any of the hijacked flights on September 11, 2001, because he was in federal custody. What follows is an excerpt of his indictment.

*Indictment of the 20th
Hijacker in the September
11, 2001, Attacks on the
United States*

IN THE UNITED STATES DISTRICT COURT FOR THE EASTERN DISTRICT
OF VIRGINIA ALEXANDRIA DIVISION

UNITED STATES OF AMERICA) CRIMINAL NO:
)
         -v-   ) Conspiracy to Commit Acts of Terrorism
) Transcending National Boundaries
ZACARIAS MOUSSAOUI,   ) (18 U.S.C. §§ 2332b(a)(2) & (c))
   a/k/a "Shaqil,"   ) (Count One)
a/k/a "Abu Khalid al Sahrawi,")
) Conspiracy to Commit Aircraft Piracy
      Defendant.   ) (49 U.S.C. §§ 46502 (a)(1)(A) and (a)(2)(B))
) (Count Two)
)
) Conspiracy to Destroy Aircraft
) (18 U.S.C. §§ 32(a)(7) & 34)
) (Count Three)
)
) Conspiracy to Use Weapons of Mass
                             Destruction
) (18 U.S.C. § 2332a(a))
) (Count Four)
)
) Conspiracy to Murder United States Employees
) (18 U.S.C. §§ 1114 & 1117)
) (Count Five)
)
) Conspiracy to Destroy Property
) (18 U.S.C. §§ 844(f), (i), (n))
) (Count Six)

DECEMBER 2001 TERM - AT ALEXANDRIA INDICTMENT

THE GRAND JURY CHARGES THAT:

COUNT ONE

(Conspiracy to Commit Acts of Terrorism Transcending National Boundaries)

Background: al Qaeda

1. At all relevant times from in or about 1989 until the date of the filing of this Indictment, an international terrorist group existed which was dedicated to opposing non-Islamic governments with force and violence. This organization grew out of the "mekhtab al khidemat" (the "Services Office") organization which had maintained offices in various parts of the world, including Afghanistan, Pakistan (particularly in Peshawar), and the United States. The group was founded by Usama Bin Laden and Muhammad Atef, a/k/a "Abu Hafs al Masry," together with "Abu Ubaidah al Banshiri," and others. From in or about 1989 until the present, the group called itself "al Qaeda" ("the Base"). . . .

2. Bin Laden and al Qaeda violently opposed the United States for several reasons. First, the United States was regarded as an "infidel" because it was not governed in a manner consistent with the group's extremist interpretation of Islam. Second, the United States was viewed as providing essential support for other "infidel" governments and institutions, particularly the governments of Saudi Arabia and Egypt, the nation of Israel, and the United Nations organization, which were regarded as enemies of the group. Third, al Qaeda opposed the involvement of the United States armed forces in the Gulf War in 1991 and in Operation Restore Hope in Somalia in 1992 and 1993. In particular, al Qaeda opposed the continued presence of American military forces in Saudi Arabia (and elsewhere on the Saudi Arabian peninsula) following the Gulf War. Fourth, al Qaeda opposed the United States Government because of the arrest, conviction and imprisonment of persons belonging to al Qaeda or its affiliated terrorist groups or those with whom it worked. For these and other reasons, Bin Laden declared a jihad, or holy war, against the United States, which he has carried out through al Qaeda and its affiliated organizations.

3. One of the principal goals of al Qaeda was to drive the United States armed forces out of Saudi Arabia (and elsewhere on the Saudi Arabian peninsula) and Somalia by violence. Members of al Qaeda issued *fatwahs* (rulings on Islamic law) indicating that such attacks were both proper and necessary.

4. Al Qaeda functioned both on its own and through some of the terrorist organizations that operated under its umbrella, . . .

7. Since at least 1989, until the filing of this Indictment, Usama Bin Laden and the terrorist group al Qaeda sponsored, managed, and/or financially supported training camps in Afghanistan, which camps were used to instruct members and associates of al Qaeda and its affiliated terrorist groups in the use of firearms, explosives, chemical weapons, and other weapons of mass destruction. In addition to providing training in the use of various weapons, these camps were used to conduct operational planning against United States targets around the world and experiments in the use of chemical and biological weapons. . . .

The September 11 Hijackers

9. On September 11, 2001, co-conspirators Mohammed Atta, Abdul Alomari, Wail al-Shehri, Waleed al-Shehri, and Satam al-Suqami hijacked American Airlines Flight 11, bound from Boston to Los Angeles, and crashed it into the North Tower of the World Trade Center in New York. (In this Indictment, each hijacker will be identified with the flight number of the plane he hijacked.)

10. On September 11, 2001, co-conspirators Marwan al-Shehhi, Fayez Ahmed, a/k/a "Banihammad Fayez," Ahmed al-Ghamdi, Hamza al-Ghamdi, and Mohald al-Shehri hijacked United Airlines Flight 175, bound from Boston to Los Angeles, and crashed it into the South Tower of the World Trade Center in New York.

11. On September 11, 2001, co-conspirators Khalid al-Midhar, Nawaf al-Hazmi, Hani Hanjour, Salem al-Hamzi, and Majed Moqed hijacked American Airlines Flight 77, bound from Virginia to Los Angeles, and crashed it into the Pentagon.

12. On September 11, 2001, co-conspirators Ziad Jarrah, Ahmed al-Haznawi, Saaed al-Ghamdi, and Ahmed al-Nami hijacked United Airlines Flight 93, bound from Newark to San Franscisco, and crashed it in Pennsylvania.

The Defendant

13. ZACARIAS MOUSSAOUI, a/k/a "Shaqil," a/k/a "Abu Khalid al Sahrawi," was born in France of Moroccan descent on May 30, 1968. Before 2001 he was a resident of the United Kingdom. MOUSSAOUI held a masters degree from Southbank University in the United Kingdom and traveled widely.

The Charge

16. From in or about 1989 until the date of the filing of this Indictment, in the Eastern District of Virginia, the Southern District of New York, and elsewhere, the defendant, ZACARIAS MOUSSAOUI, a/k/a "Shaqil," a/k/a "Abu Khalid al Sahrawi," with other members and associates of al Qaeda and others known and unknown to the Grand Jury, unlawfully, wilfully and knowingly combined, conspired, confederated and agreed to kill and maim persons within the United States, and to create a substantial risk of serious bodily injury to other persons by destroying and damaging structures, conveyances, and other real and personal property within the United States, in violation of the laws of States and the United States, in circumstances involving conduct transcending national boundaries, and in which facilities of interstate and foreign commerce were used in furtherance of the offense, the offense obstructed, delayed, and affected interstate and foreign commerce, the victim was the United States Government, members of the uniformed services, and officials, officers, employees, and agents of the governmental branches, departments, and agencies of the United States, and the structures, conveyances, and other real and personal property were, in whole or in part, owned, possessed, and leased to the United States and its departments and agencies, resulting in the deaths of thousands of persons on September 11, 2001.

Overt Acts

In furtherance of the conspiracy, and to effect its objects, the defendant, and others known and unknown to the Grand Jury, committed the following overt acts:

MOUSSAOUI Trains at Al Qaeda Training Camp

14. In or about April 1998, ZACARIAS MOUSSAOUI was present at the al Qaeda-affiliated Khalden Camp in Afghanistan.

The German Cell

28. On or about May 17, 2000, in Germany, Ramzi Bin al-Shibh applied for a visa to travel to the United States, listing a German telephone number ("German Telephone #1"). This visa application was denied.

MOUSSAOUI Inquires About Flight Training

34. On or about September 29, 2000, ZACARIAS MOUSSAOUI contacted Airman Flight School in Norman, Oklahoma using an e-mail account he set up on September 6 with an internet service provider in Malaysia.

35. In or about October 2000, ZACARIAS MOUSSAOUI received letters from Infocus Tech, a Malaysian company, stating that MOUSSAOUI was appointed Infocus Tech's marketing consultant in the United States, the United Kingdom, and Europe, and that he would receive, among other things, an allowance of $2500 per month.

MOUSSAOUI Travels from London to Pakistan

38. On or about December 9, 2000, ZACARIAS MOUSSAOUI flew from London, England to Pakistan.

MOUSSAOUI Comes to the United States

43. On or about February 7, 2001, ZACARIAS MOUSSAOUI flew from Pakistan to London, England.

44. On or about February 23, 2001, ZACARIAS MOUSSAOUI flew from London, England to Chicago, Illinois, declaring at least $35,000 cash on his Customs declaration, and then from Chicago to Oklahoma City, Oklahoma.

45. On or about February 26, 2001 ZACARIAS MOUSSAOUI opened a bank account in Norman, Oklahoma, depositing approximately $32,000 cash.

46. Between on or about February 26, 2001, and on or about May 29, 2001, ZACARIAS MOUSSAOUI attended the Airman Flight School in Norman, Oklahoma, ending his classes early.

MOUSSAOUI Contacts a Commercial Flight School

51. On or about May 23, 2001, ZACARIAS MOUSSAOUI contacted an office of the Pan Am International Flight Academy in Miami, Florida via e-mail.

Hijackers Open Bank Accounts

52. In Summer 2001, Fayez Ahmed (#175), Saeed al-Ghamdi (#93), Hamza al-Ghamdi (#175), Waleed al-Shehri (#11), Ziad Jarrah (#93), Satam al-Suqami (#11), Mohald al-Shehri (#175), Ahmed al-Nami (#93), and Ahmed al-Haznawi (#93) each opened a Florida Sun Trust bank account with a cash deposit.

MOUSSAOUI Inquires About Aerial Application of Pesticides

53. In or about June 2001, in Norman, Oklahoma, ZACARIAS MOUSSAOUI made inquiries about starting a crop dusting company.

MOUSSAOUI Purchases Flight Training Equipment

56. On or about June 20, 2001, ZACARIAS MOUSSAOUI purchased flight deck videos for the Boeing 747 Model 400 and the Boeing 747 Model 200 from the Ohio Pilot Store.

MOUSSAOUI Pays for Flight Lessons

60. On or about July 10 and July 11, 2001, ZACARIAS MOUSSAOUI made credit card payments to the Pan Am International Flight Academy for a simulator course in commercial flight training.

Bin al-Shibh Moves Money to MOUSSAOUI from UAE

65. Between on or about July 29 and August 2, 2001, in Norman, Oklahoma, ZACARIAS MOUSSAOUI made several telephone calls from public telephones to a number in Duesseldorf, Germany ("German Telephone #2").

66. On or about July 30 and 31, 2001, in Hamburg, Germany, Ramzi Bin al-Shibh, using the name "Ahad Sabet," received two wire transfers, totaling approximately $15,000, from "Hashim Abdulrahman" in UAE.

67. On or about August 1 and 3, 2001, Ramzi Bin al-Shibh, using the name "Ahad Sabet," wired approximately $14,000 in money orders to ZACARIAS MOUSSAOUI in Oklahoma from train stations in Dusseldorf and Hamburg, Germany.

MOUSSAOUI Purchases Knives

68. On or about August 3, 2001, ZACARIAS MOUSSAOUI purchased two knives in Oklahoma City, Oklahoma.

MOUSSAOUI Travels from Oklahoma to Minnesota

70. On or about August 9 and August 10, 2001, ZACARIAS MOUSSAOUI was driven from Oklahoma to Minnesota.

MOUSSAOUI Takes Commercial Flying Lessons in Minnesota

71. On or about August 10, 2001, in Minneapolis, Minnesota, ZACARIAS MOUSSAOUI paid approximately $6,300 in cash to the Pan Am International Flight Academy.

72. Between August 13 and August 15, 2001, ZACARIAS MOUSSAOUI attended the Pan Am International Flight Academy in Minneapolis, Minnesota, for simulator training on the Boeing 747 Model 400.

MOUSSAOUI Possesses Knives and Other Items

73. On or about August 16, 2001, ZACARIAS MOUSSAOUI possessed, among other things:
- two knives;
- a pair of binoculars;
- flight manuals for the Boeing 747 Model 400;
- a flight simulator computer program;
- fighting gloves and shin guards;
- a piece of paper referring to a handheld Global Positioning System receiver and a camcorder;
- software that could be used to review pilot procedures for the Boeing 747 Model 400;
- a notebook listing German Telephone #1, German Telephone #2, and the name "Ahad Sabet;"
- letters indicating that MOUSSAOUI is a marketing consultant in the United States for Infocus Tech;
- a computer disk containing information related to the aerial application of pesticides; and
- a hand-held aviation radio.

MOUSSAOUI Lies to Federal Agents

74. On or about August 17, 2001, ZACARIAS MOUSSAOUI, while being interviewed by federal agents in Minneapolis, attempted to explain his presence in the United States by falsely stating that he was simply interested in learning to fly.

Final Preparations for the Coordinated Air Attack

76. On or about August 22, 2001, Fayez Ahmed (#175) used his VISA card in Florida to obtain approximately $4,900 cash, which had been deposited into his Standard Chartered Bank account in UAE the day before.

77. On or about August 22, 2001, in Miami, Florida, Ziad Jarrah (#93) purchased an antenna for a Global Positioning System ("GPS"), other GPS related equipment, and schematics for 757 cockpit instrument diagrams. (GPS allows an individual to navigate to a position using coordinates pre-programmed into the GPS unit.)

78. On or about August 25, 2001, Khalid al-Midhar and Majed Moqed purchased with cash tickets for American Airlines Flight 77, from Virginia to Los Angeles, California, scheduled for September 11, 2001.

79. On or about August 26, 2001, Waleed al-Shehri and Wail al-Shehri made reservations on American Airlines Flight 11, from Boston, Massachusetts, to Los Angeles, California, scheduled for September 11, 2001, listing a telephone number in Florida ("Florida Telephone #1") as a contact number.

80. On or about August 27, 2001, reservations for electronic, one-way tickets were made for Fayez Ahmed and Mohald al-Shehri, for United Airlines Flight 175, from Boston, Massachusetts, to Los Angeles, California, scheduled for September 11, 2001, listing Florida Telephone Number #1 as a contact number.

81. On or about August 27, 2001, Nawaf al-Hazmi and Salem al-Hazmi booked flights on American Airlines Flight 77.

82. On or about August 28, 2001, Satam al-Suqami purchased a ticket with cash for American Airlines Flight 11.

83. On or about August 28, 2001, Mohammed Atta and Abdulaziz Alomari reserved two seats on American Airlines Flight 11, listing Florida Telephone #1 as a contact number.

84. On or about August 29, 2001, Ahmed al-Ghamdi and Hamza al-Ghamdi reserved electronic, one-way tickets for United Airlines Flight 175.

85. On or about August 29, 2001, Ahmed al-Haznawi purchased a ticket on United Airlines Flight 93 from Newark, New Jersey, to San Francisco, California, scheduled for September 11, 2001.

86. On or about August 30, 2001, Mohammed Atta (#11) purchased a utility tool that contained a knife.

87. On or about September 3, 2001, in Hamburg, Germany, Ramzi Bin al-Shibh, using the name "Ahad Sabet," received approximately $1500 by wire transfer from "Hashim Ahmed" in UAE.

88. On or about September 4, 2001, Mohammed Atta (#11) sent a FedEx package from Florida to UAE.

89. On or about September 5, 2001, Ramzi Bin al-Shibh traveled from Dusseldorf, Germany, to Madrid, Spain, and did not return to Germany.

90. On or about September 6, 2001, Satam al-Suqami (#11) and Abdulaziz Alomari (#11) flew from Florida to Boston.

The September 11, 2001 Terrorist Attacks

100. On or about September 11, 2001, the hijackers possessed a handwritten set of final instructions for a martyrdom operation on an airplane using knives.

101. On or about September 11, 2001, Mohammed Atta (#11) and Abdulaziz Alomari (#11) flew from Portland, Maine to Boston, Massachusetts.

102. On or about September 11, 2001, Mohammed Atta (#11) possessed operating manuals for the Boeing 757 and 767, pepper spray, knives, and German travel visas.

103. On or about September 11, 2001, Ziad Jarrah (#93) possessed flight manuals for Boeing 757 and 767 aircraft.

104. On or about September 11, 2001, Mohammed Atta, Abdul Aziz Alomari, Satam al-Suqami, Waleed M. al-Shehri, and Waleed al-Shehri hijacked American Airlines Flight 11, a Boeing 767, which had departed Boston at approximately 7:55 a.m. They flew Flight 11 into the North Tower of the World Trade Center in Manhattan at approximately 8:45 a.m., causing the collapse of the tower and the deaths of thousands of persons.

105. On or about September 11, 2001, Hamza al-Ghamdi, Fayez Ahmed, Mohald al-Shehri, Ahmed al-Ghamdi, and Marwan al-Shehhi hijacked United Airlines Flight 175, a Boeing 767, which had departed from Boston at approximately 8:15 a.m. They flew Flight 175 into the South

Tower of the World Trade Center in Manhattan at approximately 9:05 a.m., causing the collapse of the tower and the deaths of thousands of persons.

106. On or about September 11, 2001, Khalid al-Midhar, Majed Moqed, Nawaf al-Hazmi, Salem al-Hazmi, and Hani Hanjour hijacked American Airlines Flight 77, a Boeing 757, which had departed from Virginia bound for Los Angeles, at approximately 8:10 a.m. The flew Flight 77 into the Pentagon in Virginia at approximately 9:40 a.m., causing the deaths of 189 persons.

107. On or about September 11, 2001, Saeed al-Ghamdi, Ahmed al-Nami, Ahmed al-Haznawi, and Ziad Jarrah hijacked United Airlines Flight 93, a Boeing 757, which had departed from Newark, New Jersey bound for San Francisco at approximately 8:00 a.m. After resistance by the passengers, Flight 93 crashed in Somerset County, Pennsylvania at approximately 10:10 a.m., killing all on board.

COUNT TWO

(Conspiracy to Commit Aircraft Piracy)

1. The allegations contained in Count One are repeated.

2. From in or about 1989 until the date of the filing of this Indictment, in the Eastern District of Virginia, the Southern District of New York, and elsewhere, the defendant, ZACARIAS MOUSSAOUI, a/k/a "Shaqil," a/k/a "Abu Khalid al Sahrawi," and other members and associates of al Qaeda and others known and unknown to the Grand Jury, unlawfully, wilfully and knowingly combined, conspired, confederated and agreed to commit aircraft piracy, by seizing and exercising control of aircraft in the special aircraft jurisdiction of the United States by force, violence, threat of force and violence, and intimidation, and with wrongful intent, with the result that thousands of people died on September 11, 2001.

Overt Acts

3. In furtherance of the conspiracy, and to effect its illegal objects, the defendant, and others known and unknown to the Grand Jury, committed the overt acts set forth in Count One of this Indictment, which are fully incorporated by reference.

(In violation of Title 49, United States Code, Sections 46502(a)(1)(A) and (a)(2)(B).)

COUNT THREE

(Conspiracy to Destroy Aircraft)

1. The allegations contained in Count One are repeated.

2. From in or about 1989 until the date of the filing of this Indictment, in the Eastern District of Virginia, the Southern District of New York, and elsewhere, the defendant, ZACARIAS MOUSSAOUI, a/k/a "Shaqil," a/k/a "Abu Khalid al Sahrawi," and other members and associates of al Qaeda and others known and unknown to the Grand Jury, unlawfully, wilfully and knowingly combined, conspired, confederated and agreed to willfully destroy and wreck aircraft in the special aircraft jurisdiction of the United States, and to willfully perform acts of violence against and incapacitate individuals on such aircraft, so as likely to endanger the safety of such aircraft, resulting in the deaths of thousands of persons on September 11, 2001.

Overt Acts

3. In furtherance of the conspiracy, and to effect its illegal objects, the defendant, and others known and unknown to the Grand Jury, committed the overt acts set forth in Count One of this Indictment, which are fully incorporated by reference.

(In violation of Title 18, United States Code, Sections 32(a)(7) and 34.)

COUNT FOUR

(Conspiracy to Use Weapons of Mass Destruction)

1. The allegations contained in Count One are repeated.

2. From in or about 1989 until the date of the filing of this Indictment, in the Eastern District of Virginia, the Southern District of New York, and elsewhere, the defendant, ZACARIAS MOUSSAOUI, a/k/a "Shaqil," a/k/a "Abu Khalid al Sahrawi," and other members and associates of al

Qaeda and others known and unknown to the Grand Jury, unlawfully, wilfully and knowingly combined, conspired, confederated and agreed to use weapons of mass destruction, namely, airplanes intended for use as missiles, bombs, and similar devices, without lawful authority against persons within the United States, with the results of such use affecting interstate and foreign commerce, and against property that was owned, leased and used by the United States and by departments and agencies of the United States, with the result that thousands of people died on September 11, 2001.

Overt Acts

3. In furtherance of the conspiracy, and to effect its illegal objects, the defendant, and others known and unknown to the Grand Jury, committed the overt acts set forth in Count One of this Indictment, which are fully incorporated by reference.

(In violation of Title 18, United States Code, Section 2332a(a).)

COUNT FIVE

(Conspiracy to Murder United States Employees)

1. The allegations contained in Count One are repeated.

2. From in or about 1989 until the date of the filing of this Indictment, in the Eastern District of Virginia, the Southern District of New York, and elsewhere, the defendant, ZACARIAS MOUSSAOUI, a/k/a "Shaqil," a/k/a "Abu Khalid al Sahrawi," and other members and associates of al Qaeda and others known and unknown to the Grand Jury, unlawfully, wilfully and knowingly combined, conspired, confederated and agreed to kill officers and employees of the United States and agencies and branches thereof, while such officers and employees were engaged in, and on account of, the performance of their official duties, and persons assisting such employees in the performance of their duties, in violation of Section 1114 of Title 18, United States Code, including members of the Department of Defense stationed at the Pentagon.

Overt Acts

3. In furtherance of the conspiracy, and to effect its illegal objects, the defendant, and others known and unknown to the Grand Jury, committed the overt acts set forth in Count One of this Indictment, which are fully incorporated by reference.

(In violation of Title 18, United States Code, Sections 1114 and 1117.)

COUNT SIX

(Conspiracy to Destroy Property of the United States)

1. The allegations contained in Count One are repeated.

2. From in or about 1989 until the date of the filing of this Indictment, in the Eastern District of Virginia, the Southern District of New York, and elsewhere, the defendant, ZACARIAS MOUSSAOUI, a/k/a "Shaqil," a/k/a "Abu Khalid al Sahrawi," and other members and associates of al Qaeda and others known and unknown to the Grand Jury, unlawfully, wilfully and knowingly combined, conspired, confederated and agreed to maliciously damage and destroy, by means of fire and explosives, buildings, vehicles, and other real and personal property used in interstate and foreign commerce and in activities affecting interstate and foreign commerce, and buildings, vehicles, and other personal and real property in whole and in part owned and possessed by, and leased to, the United States and its departments and agencies, and as a result of such conduct directly and proximately caused the deaths of thousands of persons on September 11, 2001, including hundreds of public safety officers performing duties as a direct and proximate result of the said damage and destruction.

Overt Acts

3. In furtherance of the conspiracy, and to effect its illegal objects, the defendant, and others known and unknown to the Grand Jury, committed the overt acts set forth in Count One of this Indictment, which are fully incorporated by reference.

(In violation of Title 18, United States Code, Sections 844(f), (i), and (n).)

FOREPERSON

MICHAEL CHERTOFF
ASSISTANT ATTORNEY GENERAL

PAUL J. McNULTY
UNITED STATES ATTORNEY EASTERN
DISTRICT OF VIRGINIA

MARY JO WHITE
UNITED STATES ATTORNEY SOUTHERN
DISTRICT OF NEW YORK

PUBLICATION DATE:
January 15, 2002
DATE:
20020115

CRIMES AGAINST THE ENVIRONMENT

With the modernization of the United States has come a threat to the environment. The air and water that people depend upon for sustenance have become polluted. Many species of flora and fauna have been lost and many more are threatened.

Modernization threatens the environment in several ways. By "developing" land, habitats are lost. Also, the use of dangerous chemicals and toxins has become commonplace. In many industries, toxic byproducts of manufacturing are common. Toxic wastes and substances pose use, transportation, and disposal problems. The release of dangerous substances into the air or into water endangers the health and safety of the public. It is estimated that air pollution kills 14,000 people annually and that 100,000 workers die annually from exposure to toxins.[47] The increased population aggravates the problem. Greater numbers of people place greater stress on natural systems. Resources are depleted faster and nature's cleansing process becomes strained and less effective.

Today, there is a large body of environmental law that, to some extent, addresses these problems. The federal government's policy is to create and maintain conditions in which man and nature can exist in productive harmony. Both the federal and state governments play a role in regulation of the environment, although the federal government has the larger part currently. The federal government's role in regulating the environment dates back to at least 1899, when Congress enacted a statute making it a crime to discharge pollutants into navigable waters.

Several federal administrative agencies are charged with overseeing the enforcement and administration of environmental laws, including the

Environmental Protection Agency, the Coast Guard, the Department of the Interior, the Occupational Health and Safety Commission, and the Department of Justice. Federal law provides for administrative, civil, and criminal sanctions on environmental law violators.

There are two classes of environmental laws. One class of laws is intended to further the public health and safety. The Clean Air Act, the Clean Water Act, and similar statutes are examples of this type of environmental regulation. A second class of laws is intended to protect the environment itself, for its aesthetic, recreational, and other values. The Endangered Species Act is an example of a conservation law. Of course, many laws serve both objectives.

Until recently, environmental offenses were not usually treated as criminal; rather, they were viewed as civil or administrative infractions. The federal government relied almost exclusively on administrative and civil processes to enforce environmental laws. Fines were the most common penalty sought by the government against offenders.

The belief that environmental violations are serious and should be prosecuted as criminal offenses is a recent development. For example, one of the most notorious environmental cases was Love Canal, where it was discovered in 1978 that the improper disposal of toxins was causing death and illness to local residents. An entire community was forced to relocate to escape the danger—yet not one person was prosecuted in the Love Canal case.

The fear of another Love Canal, or an accident like the one involving Union Carbide in Bhopal, India, where 2,000 people were killed and 200,000 people were injured, and the dangers posed by other environmental wrongs led Congress to strengthen environmental laws. The measures included added criminal sanctions. Relying on civil remedies alone had proved ineffective. Individuals were not being held accountable and corporations found it more cost-effective to violate the law and pay any fines than to comply with the law.

Therefore, although most violations continue to be handled through civil and administrative proceedings, the number of environmental criminal cases is increasing. Of the 500 largest corporations in the United States, one-fourth have been convicted of an environmental crime or have been subject to civil penalties for violating environmental laws.[48] Within the Department of Justice is a special division charged with prosecuting environmental law crimes.

Unlike at common law, today business entities, such as corporations, may be charged with crimes. Fines and dissolution of a corporation are examples of the penalties that may be imposed. Charging corporations for environmental violations is common. Of course, individuals may also be charged with violating environmental laws and corporate employees may be charged for actions taken on behalf of a corporation. It is not a defense for an employee to claim that he or she was following a supervisor's directive, nor may it be a defense for the supervisor to claim that he or she is innocent because he or she delegated performance of the act to an employee.

Some environmental crimes are strict liability. Others, and of course those that can be punished with jail time, require some mens rea, usually a knowing violation.

Several federal environmental laws contain criminal sanctions. The most significant of these laws are the Clean Water Act; the Clean Air Act; the Comprehensive Environmental Response, Compensation, and Liability Act; the Resource Conservation and Recovery Act; the Occupational Safety and Health Act; the Toxic Substances Control Act; the Federal Insecticide, Fungicide, and Rodenticide Act; the Emergency Planning and Community Right-to-Know Act; and the Endangered Species Act. The first eight statutes are examples of regulation for the public health, and the final statute is a conservation law. All these laws provide for administrative and civil remedies and procedures, in addition to criminal sanctions.

Clean Water Act

The Clean Water Act (CWA)[49] regulates the discharge of pollutants into the nation's navigable waters. The CWA establishes a scheme of permits and reporting. The contamination of water with a pollutant, without a permit or exceeding the limits of a permit, is criminal under the Clean Water Act.

Both negligent and knowing acts are criminalized and may be punished with fines and imprisonment. A knowing act is punished more severely than a negligent act. Offenders who have acted negligently may be sentenced to one year in prison, whereas knowing offenders may be sentenced to three years in prison.[50] Fines may also be imposed for both, in addition to any civil remedies.

Also, the CWA contains a "knowing endangerment" provision. If a person violates the CWA with knowledge that the violation "places another person in imminent danger of death or serious bodily injury," the offender may be sentenced to up to fifteen years in prison, and significant fines may be imposed.

Finally, false reporting under the Act is criminal and may be punished by up to two years in prison, in addition to a fine.

Clean Air Act

The goal of the Clean Air Act (CAA) is to preserve air quality. It does this by regulating emissions of dangerous substances into the air.

Similar to the CWA in its criminal aspects, the CAA criminalized negligent and knowing violations of its mandates, punishing the latter more severely.[51] Further, it contains knowing endangerment and false reporting provisions.

Comprehensive Environmental Response, Compensation and Liability Act

The Comprehensive Environmental Response, Compensation and Liability Act (CERCLA) is commonly known as *Superfund*. The purpose of CERCLA is to identify and clean up existing hazardous waste sites.

Any person who knowingly falsifies or destroys any required record or who fails to report a spill of hazardous materials may be punished with fines and imprisonment.[52]

Resource Conservation and Recovery Act

The Resource Conservation and Recovery Act (RCRA) is similar to CERCLA in that they regulate the same subject matter: hazardous materials. However, CERCLA is an after-the-fact regulation intended to clean up existing sites, whereas RCRA is intended to regulate the day-to-day use, storage, transportation, handling, and disposal of hazardous materials.

There are no negligent violations under RCRA; rather, the mens rea for conviction of its prohibitions is knowledge. For example, the knowing transportation of hazardous waste to an unlicensed facility; the knowing treatment, storage, or disposal of hazardous waste without a permit; and the knowing violation of a permit are criminal and may be punished with both imprisonment and fines. As with the CWA and the CAA, knowingly endangering another enhances the punishment for a violation of RCRA.[53]

Occupational Safety and Health Act

The Occupational Safety and Health Act (OSHA) regulates the work environment of the American worker. The objective of the law is to create safe working conditions. There is a plethora of regulations enforcing this mandate.

Any employer who causes the death of an employee as a result of noncompliance with OSHA may be prosecuted and sentenced to imprisonment and a fine. Of course, the employer may also be liable under other criminal laws, such as negligent manslaughter.

Additionally, OSHA requires employers to notify their employees of potential exposure to dangerous chemicals and to provide information and resources to protect the employees. Failure to notify employees of this risk is a criminal omission under OSHA. False reporting is also a crime under this statute.

Toxic Substances Control Act

The Toxic Substances Control Act (TSCA) is the most comprehensive federal law concerning dangerous substances. The Environmental Protection Agency (EPA) is delegated considerable authority under the TSCA to regulate the sale, manufacture, development, processing, distribution, and disposal of toxic substances. Under the TSCA, the EPA is empowered to ban, or otherwise control, the production and distribution of chemicals. Asbestos and radon are examples of chemicals that the EPA has heavily regulated under the TSCA.

Any person who knowingly or willfully violates the TSCA concerning the manufacture, testing, or distribution of a chemical may be punished with both a fine and imprisonment. Also, false reporting, failing to maintain records, and failing to submit records as required by law are criminal acts under the TSCA.[54]

Federal Insecticide, Fungicide, and Rodenticide Act

Chemicals that are lethal to pests may also be lethal or at least harmful to humans. In addition to being inhaled, pesticides find their way into human drinking water and food.

The Federal Insecticide, Fungicide, and Rodenticide Act (FIFRA) delegates to the EPA the task of regulating the manufacture, sale, distribution, and use of these chemicals. Some chemicals are forbidden; there are limits on the use of others. There are labelling and reporting requirements.

Knowing violations of any of FIFRA's requirements are criminal and may be punished with fines and imprisonment.[55]

Emergency Planning and Community Right-to-Know Act

Bhopal, India; Chernobyl; and closer to home, Three Mile Island—all three are reminders that accidents happen, or that the actions of one person, such as a terrorist, can cause a tragedy of enormous proportion. In both the Chernobyl and Bhopal incidents, there was no planning or preparation for an accident.

The purpose of the Emergency Planning and Community Right-to-Know Act is to better prepare the community in which a facility is sited for disaster and to inform the community about emissions of hazardous substances by the facility. The Act requires facilities that use or produce chemicals to report both accidental and routine releases of substances into the air or water. Further, facilities are required to provide local officials (e.g., hospitals) with information about the chemicals used.

Knowing or willful failure to give notice of a release may be punished by both imprisonment and a fine.

Endangered Species Act

The Endangered Species Act (ESA)[56] and the Marine Mammal Protection Act represent a different form of environmental law from those discussed so far. The purpose of these laws is not to protect the public health; rather, the intent is to preserve the integrity of the environment itself.

The ESA establishes a program of conservation of threatened and endangered species of plants and animals and the habitats where they are found. The law is co-administered by the Departments of Interior, Commerce, Agriculture, and Justice.

The ESA prohibits the sale, taking, possession, importation, and exportation of endangered species and the products of those species. Violations of the law are punishable by both fines and imprisonment.

Marine Mammal Protection Act

Similar to the ESA, the Marine Mammal Protection Act (MMPA)[57] is intended to protect and conserve marine mammals. The taking of such creatures without a permit by a U.S. flag vessel while on the high seas is a crime. The taking, possession, and trade of animals protected under the law is prohibited within the United States unless a permit has been obtained. Fines and imprisonment may be imposed on violators.

These are but a few of the federal environmental laws. Also, many states have similar laws. In some instances, the states have been delegated the authority to enforce federal law. Environmental laws affect every person, not just businesses that use or trade in hazardous materials.

Because of overpopulation, high-density urbanization, industrialization, resource exploitation, and technological advances, every person has a duty to be environmentally aware, and the laws of the nation impose environmental obligations on the individual. The proper disposal of trash, car batteries, and motor oil, and the regulation of hunting and fishing, are examples of environmental laws that affect the daily lives of members of the public.

 WEB LINKS

IRS

The Internal Revenue Service's site contains information on tax law, compliance and filing (including updated forms that may be downloaded), tax statistics, and other information. *http://www.irs.ustreas.gov*

KEY TERMS

breach of the peace	fighting words	subornation of perjury
bribery	perjury	tax evasion
clear and present danger	prostitution	tax fraud
contempt		

REVIEW QUESTIONS

1. Andy approaches Roberta, who is standing on a street corner, and offers her $50 for sex. Roberta, an undercover vice officer, arrests Andy. What crime should he be charged with?

2. Is there a constitutional right to engage in homosexual conduct between mature, consenting adults?

3. When may a state regulate material that is thought to be sexually repulsive? What constitutional provision hinders governments from regulating such expression?

4. What are fighting words? Are they protected by the First Amendment?

5. Is proof that a driver's blood-alcohol level exceeded the statutory maximum the only way to prove that a driver was under the influence? Is it a valid defense for a driver-defendant to claim that he or she could drive safely, even though his or her blood-alcohol level exceeded the amount allowed by statute?

6. What are the elements of Continuing Criminal Enterprise, and who is the statute aimed at?

7. What are the basic elements of bribery? The Model Penal Code recognizes two types of bribery. Name the two.

8. Distinguish criminal contempt from civil contempt. Do the same for direct contempt and indirect contempt.

9. Is this statement true? "Perjury is a law that applies only to judicial proceedings." Explain your answer.

10. What are the elements of indecent exposure?

11. What are the elements of treason?

12. Identify two ways that the Patriot Act of 2001 expanded the authority of federal officials to address terrorism.

REVIEW PROBLEMS

1. Are the following statutes constitutional? Explain, if not.

   Statute One: Loitering

   Any person who loiters in a place in an unusual manner for longer than fifteen minutes and reasonably causes a person to be concerned for their safety must identify himself to police when requested. Any person who refuses to identify himself under these circumstances or takes flight when approached by a police officer is guilty of loitering.

   Statute Two: Loitering

   Any person who continually loiters in public parks without apparent employment or who lives off the handouts of others is guilty of loitering.

2. State law prohibits "hardcore pornography." Among the many prohibitions of the law is a provision making it a felony to possess or sell materials that are known to depict bestiality (sex between a human and an animal). Sam, a local adult bookstore owner, sold a magazine to Herb entitled "Wild on the Farm." The magazine was sealed, and its contents were not visible. The magazine was delivered to Sam in error, part of a large shipment of magazines and books.

   During a raid on Sam's establishment the local police discovered the sales ticket reflecting Herb's purchase, his name, and his address. The police then obtained a search warrant for Herb's home and found the magazine during their search. Sam and Herb have both been charged with violating the state's obscenity law. Should they be convicted? Explain your answer.

3. Do you believe that acts that harm no one, but that most members of society find immoral, should be criminalized? Explain your position.

4. How has bribery been changed since it has become a statutory crime?

5–7. Classify each of the following as direct or indirect contempt and civil or criminal contempt.

5. During a personal injury trial, Noah told the judge to "kiss my ass" and then threw an apple, striking the judge in the head.

6. During a union dispute, a judge ordered striking employees back to work. They refused to comply with the order and the judge ordered that each employee pay $50 per day until he or she returned to work.

7. Jon received a court order to tear down a fence he had constructed. The order was served by a sheriff. Immediately after the sheriff handed the order to him, Jon screamed, "Forget that idiot judge, I'm not tearing down the fence!" Jon never removed the fence, and the judge had him arrested, and ordered him to remain in jail until he agreed to comply with the order.

8. Consider and discuss this statement: Possession and use of drugs or alcohol should not be a crime. The only dangers presented from these substances arise when a person works, drives, or conducts some activity that requires the full use of the senses, while under their influence. Criminal statutes should be narrow and proscribe

only the harm sought to be prevented. No harm is created by use in controlled environments, such as in the home. Accordingly, statutes should only proscribe engaging in certain undertakings while under the influence of alcohol or drugs.

9. Do you believe terrorists should be considered criminals (and handled by the criminal justice system) on combatants (and handled by the military)? Does it matter if the accused is a U.S. citizen?

END NOTES

1. Model Penal Code § 251.2(1).
2. Model Penal Code § 251.2(5).
3. 18 U.S.C. § 2421.
4. Model Penal Code § 251.1.
5. 18 U.S.C. § 1461.
6. Anderson, "Mapplethorpe Photos on Trial," *A.B.A. J.* 28 (Dec. 1990).
7. There are other limits on First Amendment freedoms. Some of these are discussed in Chapter 8, in the constitutional defenses section.
8. *Manual Enterprises, Inc. v. Day*, 370 U.S. 478 (1962) (opinion by Justice Harlan).
9. 50 Am. Jur. 2d *Lewdness, Indecency, etc.* 7 (1970).
10. *See Roth v. United States*, 354 U.S. 476, 487, n.20 (1957).
11. *United States v. Guglielmi*, 819 F.2d 451 (4th Cir. 1987).
12. *See New York v. Ferber*, 458 U.S. 747 (1982).
13. *See Capitol News Co. v. Metropolitan Government*, 562 S.W.2d 430 (Tenn. 1978).
14. *Stanley v. Georgia*, 394 U.S. 557 (1969).
15. Model Penal Code § 251.4.
16. 143 *Cong. Rec.* E1633 (Sept. 3, 1997).
17. Timothy Zick, "Congress, The Internet, and The Intractable Pornography Problem: The Child Online Protection Act of 1998," 32 *Creighton L. Rev.* 1147 (1999).
18. 110 Stat. 56.
19. 521 U.S. 844 (1997).
20. 47 U.S.C. § 231.
21. Ashcroft v. ACLU (2002).
22. 969 F.Supp. 160 (S.D. N.Y. 1997).
23. Model Penal Code § 250.1.
24. *Champlinsky v. New Hampshire*, 315 U.S. 568 (1942).
25. *Brandenburg v. Ohio*, 395 U.S. 444 (1969).
26. See Chapter 3 on personal status as an act.
27. 307 U.S. 174 (1939).
28. 445 U.S. 55 (1980).
29. 26 U.S.C. § 5801 *et seq.*
30. 26 U.S.C. § 5801 *et seq.*
31. Model Penal Code § 2.01(4).
32. *Robinson v. California*, 370 U.S. 660 (1962).
33. 21 U.S.C. § 848.
34. *United States v. Brantley*, 733 F.2d 1429 (11th Cir. 1984).
35. 21 U.S.C. § 848(e).
36. 21 U.S.C. § 853(a).
37. Kenneth Johnson, "The Constitutionality of Drug Paraphernalia Laws," 81 *Columbia L. Rev.* 581 (1981).
38. *Posters 'N' Things, Ltd. v. United States*, 511 U.S. 513 (1994).
39. Model Penal Code § 224.8.
40. 26 U.S.C. § 7201 *et seq.*
41. Model Penal Code § 3.04(2)(a)(i).
42. 18 U.S.C. § 2381.
43. See 70 Am. Jur. 2d 70.
44. 18 U.S.C. § 2384.
45. 18 U.S.C. § 2389.
46. 18 U.S.C. § 792, *et seq.* and 50 U.S.C. § 783.
47. Michael Norton, *Federal Environmental Criminal Law Enforcement in the 1990's* 1 (ALI-ABA, C868, 1993).
48. *Id.*
49. 33 U.S.C. § 1319(a).
50. 33 U.S.C. § 1319(c).
51. 42 U.S.C. § 7413.
52. 42 U.S.C. § 9603.
53. 42 U.S.C. § 6928.
54. 15 U.S.C. §§ 2614–2615.
55. 7 U.S.C. § 136i–1(d).
56. 16 U.S.C. §§ 1531–1543.
57. 16 U.S.C. §§ 1361–1384, 1401–1407.

Parties and Inchoate Offenses

CHAPTER OUTLINE

Parties to Crimes

Inchoate Crimes

  Attempt

Conspiracy

Solicitation

CHAPTER OBJECTIVES

In this chapter, you should:

- learn about the relative culpability of the participants to a crime.
- learn the law of culpability for unsuccessful attempts to commit a crime.

- continue to develop your case analysis and legal reasoning skills.

PARTIES TO CRIMES

Not all crimes are committed by only one person. Not all planned crimes are completed. This chapter examines the two topics of group criminal responsibility and uncompleted crimes. Those who participate in a crime are referred to as *parties*. Uncompleted crimes are referred to as *inchoate crimes*.

At common law, there were four parties to crimes: principals in the first degree; principals in the second degree; accessories before the fact; and accessories after the fact.

A **principal** in the first degree is the participant who actually committed the proscribed act. For example, three people (A, B, and C) agree to rob a grocery store. A enters the store and points a gun at a checker and demands that money be placed in a bag. A is a principal in the first degree.

A principal in the second degree is a party who aids, counsels, assists, or encourages the principal in the first degree during commission of the crime. A party must be present during a crime to be a principal in the second degree. However, constructive presence is sufficient. Whenever a party is physically absent from the location of the crime, but aids from a distance, that party is a principal in the second degree. So, if B, from our hypothetical case, waits in the getaway car outside the store, B is a principal in the second degree. First-degree and second-degree principals are punished equally. Principals in the second degree are also referred to as *accomplices*, as are accessories before the fact.

Anyone who aids, counsels, encourages, or assists in the preparation of a crime, but is not physically present during the crime, is an **accessory** before the fact. If C, an expert in bank security, assisted in planning the robbery, then C is an accessory before the fact. The primary distinction between a principal in the second degree and an accessory before the fact is the lack of presence during the crime of an accessory before the fact.

At common law, accessories could not be convicted until the principals were convicted. In addition, procedural rules made it more difficult to convict accessories than principals. These rules are no longer the law. Statutes commonly group principals in the first and second degree together with accessories before the fact and punish all equally.

The mens rea of an accomplice (before and during a crime) is usually intentional (specific) in common-law terms, or knowing or purposeful in Model Penal Code language. Negligent and reckless acts do not make a person a principal in the second degree or an accessory.

Accessories after the fact continue to be treated differently. A person is an accessory after the fact if (1) aid, comfort, or shelter is provided to a criminal (2) with the purpose of assisting the criminal in avoiding arrest or prosecution (3) after the crime is committed (4) and the accessory was not present during commission of the crime. D is an accessory after the fact, if A and B flee to D's house and D hides A and B from the police. It is possible to be an accessory both before and after the fact. Hence, if C were to hide A and B from the police, C would be both an accessory before and after the fact. Accessories after the fact are not punished as severely as the other three classifications of parties.

principal

A person directly involved with committing a crime, as opposed to an accessory.

accessory

A person who helps commit a crime without being present. An *accessory before the fact* is a person who, without being present, encourages, orders, or helps another to commit a crime. An *accessory after the fact* is a person who finds out that a crime has been committed and helps to conceal the crime or the criminal.

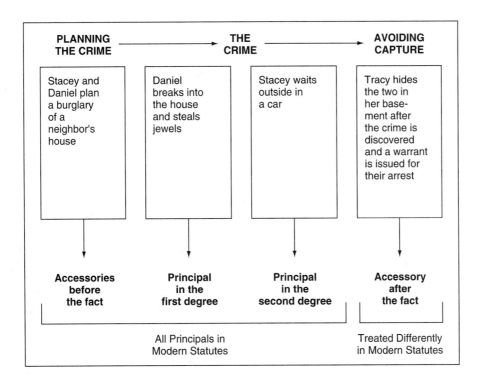

Parties to a Burglary

The mental state required to prove that a person was an accessory after the fact is twofold: first, it must be shown that the defendant was aware of the person's criminal status (scienter) and second, that the defendant intended to hinder attempts to arrest or prosecute the criminal.

INCHOATE CRIMES

Not all planned crimes are completed. Because of the danger posed by substantial planning, accompanied by an intent to carry out a plan, some uncompleted crimes may be punished.

By punishing inchoate acts, the deterrent purpose of the criminal justice system is furthered. If the rule were otherwise, law enforcement officials would have no incentive to intervene in a criminal enterprise before it is completed. By punishing attempt, conspiracy, and solicitation, an officer may prevent a planned criminal act from occurring without risking losing a criminal conviction.

Attempt

The reasons planned crimes are not always successful are numerous. In some instances, law enforcement intervention prevents completion of a crime. If a police officer stops Penny from shooting Tom moments before she commits the act, should she be free from criminal liability because she was not successful? The law answers that question in the negative, calling such uncompleted crimes *attempt*.

attempt

An effort to commit a crime that goes beyond preparation and that proceeds far enough to make the person who did it guilty of an "*attempt crime*." For example, if a person fires a shot at another in a failed effort at murder, the person is guilty of *attempted murder*.

Attempt was not a crime at early common law; however, attempt cases do appear later in English common law. The first cases began to appear in the late 1700s and early 1800s.[1] Many of the early cases have been traced to an English court that is no longer in existence, the Star Chamber. Today, attempt is recognized in the United States by all states.

The purpose of attempt laws is to deter people from planning to commit crimes; to punish those who intended to commit a crime, but were unsuccessful; and to encourage law enforcement officers to prevent unlawful activity. The last may appear obvious; however, if it were not for making attempts illegal, police would have an incentive to permit illegal acts, so as to be able to punish the wrongdoer.

There are essentially three element to all attempts. One, the defendant must intend to commit a crime. Two, the defendant must act in furtherance of that intent. Three, the crime is not completed.

First, the mens rea element: The defendant must intend to take some act that amounts to a crime; in common-law language, specific intent, and under the Model Penal Code, knowingly or purposefully. Some statutes specifically identify what crime must be intended, whereas others simply refer to an intent to commit any felony. In any event, the accused must intend to commit some specific crime, such as murder, rape, or theft.

The second element, the actus reus of attempt, can be problematic. The problem revolves around this question: how close to completion of the intended crime must a defendant come to be guilty of attempt? It is well established that thoughts alone do not establish a crime; mere preparation without anything further does not amount to the crime of attempt. The failing student who sits at home and contemplates how to "do in" his criminal law instructor commits no crime. It is not until the student goes further that he can be liable for attempt.

Various tests are used to determine if an act is close enough to completion to permit an attempt conviction. The four commonly used tests are proximity, res ipsa loquitur, probable desistance, and the Model Penal Code's "substantial steps" test.

The *proximity test* examines what acts have been taken and what acts are left to be taken to complete the crime. Justice Holmes said that there "must be a dangerous proximity to success."[2]

The *res ipsa loquitur test* (also called the *unequivocality test*) looks at crimes individually and finds an act, a certain point in time, which indicates that the defendant has "no other purpose than the commission of that specific crime."[3] For example, most courts have held that once a defendant hires another to commit a crime, attempt has been committed. The step of hiring the person who will complete the crime crosses the line between mere preparation and illegal act.

The third test, *probable desistance*, focuses on the likelihood that the defendant would have followed through with the crime had the opportunity existed. The foundation of the theory is that all people may plan illegal acts at some time in life, but that there is a point where most stop. Any person who passes this line of demarcation has exhibited that the crime would have been completed, had the situation permitted. Critics have attacked this test, claiming that the determination of such a line, if it exists, is arbitrary.

The Model Penal Code uses a *"substantial step"* to completion test.[4] That is, one is guilty of attempt if substantial steps have been taken toward commission of a crime. The Code specifically states that the conduct in question must "strongly corroborate" the actor's criminal purpose. The Code goes further and lists acts that may constitute attempts, provided that they "strongly corroborate" an intent to commit a crime. That list includes:

1. Lying in wait or searching for the intended victim.
2. Enticing or seeking to entice the intended victim to go to the place where the crime will be committed.
3. Investigating the location where the crime is to be committed.
4. Unlawfully entering a structure where the crime is to be committed.
5. Possession of materials necessary to complete the crime, provided that the tools are specially designed for the commission of the crime.
6. Possession, collection, or fabrication of materials to be used in the crime, near the scene of the crime, when the materials serve no lawful purpose.
7. Soliciting someone to commit a crime.

Keep in mind that different results are possible if these tests are applied to the same facts. In the *Murray* case, the line between preparation and attempt is examined. Do you agree with the court?

Regardless of which test is applied, if a defendant has a change of heart and does not complete the crime, even after crossing the line, then abandonment may be a valid defense.

Of course, the abandonment must be voluntary. Generally, any reason that causes a defendant to desist, other than the defendant's independent decision not to complete the crime, falls outside the defense. A criminal who chooses to not rob a store because a police officer arrives at the scene moments before the planned act was to occur is not entitled to the defense of abandonment.

Two other defenses that arise in the context of attempt are legal and factual impossibility. **Legal impossibility** refers to the situation when a defendant believes that his or her acts are illegal when they are not.

If a defendant commits an act believing it illegal, when it is actually lawful, he or she is not liable. The law of attempt does not punish one for attempting to do a lawful thing, even if the person had an evil mind.

Factual impossibility refers to situations when people attempt to commit a crime, but it is impossible to do so. For example, John breaks into his friend's school locker to steal property, but discovers that the locker is empty. Distraught by the situation, John decides to relax by smoking marijuana. Unknown to John, the cigarette contains no marijuana or other illegal drug. John has made two factual errors. In both instances John could be convicted because factual impossibility is not a defense. This rule is justified by the fact that the defendant possessed the required mens rea and took all the acts necessary to commit the offense. The only reason the crime was not fully completed was because of an extraneous fact unknown to the defendant.

legal impossibility
A person who is unable to commit a crime because of legal impossibility cannot be convicted of a crime he or she intends or attempts.

CASE

PEOPLE V. MURRAY

15 Cal. 160 (1859)

The evidence in this case entirely fails to sustain the charge against the defendant of an attempt to contract an incestuous marriage with his niece. It only discloses declarations of his determination to contract the marriage, his elopement with the niece for that avowed purpose, and his request to one of the witnesses to go for a magistrate to perform the ceremony. It shows very clearly the intention of the defendant, but something more than mere intention is necessary to constitute the offense charged. Between preparation for the attempt and the attempt itself, there is a wide difference. The preparation consists of devising or arranging the means or measures necessary for the commission of the offense; the attempt is the direct movement toward the commission after the preparation is made. To illustrate: a party may purchase and load a gun, with the declared intention to shoot his neighbor; but until some movement is made to use the weapon upon the person of his intended victim, there is only preparation and not attempt. For the preparation, he may be held to keep the peace; but he is not chargeable with any attempt to kill. So in the present case, the declarations, and elopement, and request for a magistrate, were preparatory to the marriage; but until the officer was engaged, and the parties stood before him, ready to take the vows appropriate to the contract of marriage, it cannot be said, in strictness, that the attempt was made. The attempt contemplated by the statute must be manifested by acts that would end in the consummation of the particular offence, but for the intervention of circumstances independent of the will of the party. [Conviction reversed.]

In the *Haines* case, a defendant appealed his conviction for attempted murder. He alleged that because of factual improbability, he did not take a "substantial step" toward completing a murder.

The Indiana Court of Appeals rejected factual impossibility (leaving open the issue of inherent factual impossibility) as a defense and rejected the factual assertion that AIDS cannot be transmitted through spitting and throwing blood on a person. Further, the court found that the acts of spitting and throwing blood on a person by a person with AIDS are substantial steps toward the commission of murder, thereby supporting an attempted murder conviction.

Conspiracy

conspiracy

A crime that may be committed when two or more persons agree to do something unlawful (or to do something lawful by unlawful means). The agreement can be inferred from the persons' actions.

Conspiracy is (1) an agreement (2) between two or more persons (3) to commit an unlawful act or a lawful act in an unlawful manner. The agreement is the actus reus of the crime, and the intent to commit an unlawful act or a lawful act in an unlawful manner is the mens rea.

In some jurisdictions, the agreement alone satisfies the actus reus. In others, some act must be taken in furtherance of the objective of the agreement. Although at least one jurisdiction requires the conspirators to take "substantial steps" to be liable for conspiracy, most require less; often proof of an "overt act" will sustain a conviction. Hence, although mere preparation is not sufficient to impose liability for attempt, it is sufficient in many jurisdictions to prove conspiracy.

CASE

STATE V. HAINES

545 N.E.2d 834 (Ind.
Ct. App. 1989)

On August 6, 1987, Lafayette, Indiana, police officers John R. Dennis (Dennis) and Brad Hayworth drove to Haines' apartment in response to a radio call of a possible suicide. Haines was unconscious when they arrived and was lying face down in a pool of blood. Dennis attempted to revive Haines and noticed that Haines' wrists were slashed and bleeding. When Haines heard the paramedics arriving, he stood up, ran toward Dennis, and screamed that he should be left to die because he had AIDS. Dennis told Haines they were there to help him, but he continued yelling and stated he wanted to [infect Dennis with the disease.] Haines told Dennis that he would "use his wounds" and began jerking his arms at Dennis, causing blood to spray into Dennis' mouth and eyes. Throughout the incident, as the officers attempted to subdue him, Haines repeatedly yelled that he had AIDS, that he could not deal with it, and that he was going to make Dennis deal with it.

Haines also struggled with emergency medical technicians Dan Garvey (Garvey) and Diane Robinson, threatening to infect them with AIDS, and began spitting at them. When Dennis grabbed Haines, Haines scratched, bit, and spit at him. At one point, Haines grabbed a bloodsoaked wig and struck Dennis in the face with it. This caused blood again to splatter onto Dennis' eyes, mouth, and skin. When Dennis finally handcuffed Haines, Dennis was covered with blood. He also had scrapes and scratches on his arms and a cut on his finger that was bleeding.

When Haines arrived at the hospital, he was still kicking, screaming, throwing blood, and spitting at Dennis, Garvey, and another paramedic. . . . Haines again announced that he had AIDS and that he was going to show everyone else what it was like to have the disease and die. At one point Haines bit Garvey on the upper arm, breaking the skin. . . .

Haines was charged with three counts of attempted murder. At trial, medical experts testified that the virus could be transmitted through blood, tears, and saliva. They also observed that policemen, firemen, and other emergency personnel are generally at risk when they are exposed to body products. One medical expert observed that Dennis was definitely exposed to the HIV virus and others acknowledged that exposure of infected blood to the eyes and the mouth is dangerous, and that it is easier for the virus to enter the bloodstream if there is a cut in the skin.

Following a trial by jury, Haines was convicted of three counts of attempted murder on January 14, 1988. On February 18, 1988, Haines moved for judgment on the evidence as to the three counts of attempted murder, which the trial court granted. The trial court did enter judgment of conviction on three counts of battery as a class D felony. Haines was ordered to serve a two-year sentence on each count to run consecutively.

The only issue before us is whether the trial court erred in granting Haines' motion for judgment on the evidence and vacating the three counts of attempted murder.

PARTIES' CONTENTIONS

The State maintains that the trial court erred in granting Haines' motion for judgment on the evidence because the trial judge misconstrued the requirements of proof necessary to constitute a substantial step in accordance with the law of attempt. Haines responds that his conduct did not constitute a substantial step toward murder as charged, because all evidence relating to the AIDS virus was introduced by the defense which led only to an inference in favor of Haines.

CONCLUSION

The trial court erred in granting Haines' motion for judgment on the evidence.

This appeal presents a novel question in Indiana.

* * *

Contrary to Haines' contention that the evidence did not support a reasonable inference that his conduct amounted to a substantial step toward murder, the record reflects otherwise. At trial, it was definitely established that Haines carried the AIDS virus, was aware of the infection, believed it to be fatal, and intended to inflict others with the disease by spitting, biting, scratching, and throwing blood. . . . His biological warfare with those attempting to help him is akin to a sinking ship firing on its rescuers.

Haines misconstrues the logic and effect of our attempt statute. . . .

"It is no defense that, because of a misapprehension of the circumstances, it would have been impossible for the accused person to commit the crime attempt." . . . [O]ur supreme court observed:

It is clear that section (b) of our statute rejects the defense of impossibility. It is not necessary that there be a present ability to complete the crime, nor is it necessary that the crime be factually possible. When the defendant has done all that he believes necessary to cause the particular result, regardless of what is actually possible under existing circumstances, he has committed an attempt. . . .

In accordance with [the statute], the State was not required to prove that Haines' conduct could actually have killed. It was only necessary for the State to show that Haines did all that he believed necessary to bring about an intended result, regardless of what was actually possible. . . . Haines repeatedly announced that he had AIDS and

desired to infect and kill others. At the hospital, Haines was expressly told by doctors that biting, spitting, and throwing blood was endangering others.

While [the statute] rejects the defense of impossibility, some jurisdictions provide for the dismissal of a charge or reduction in sentence on the basis of "inherent impossibility" if the defendant's conduct was so inherently unlikely to result or culminate in the commission of a crime. . . .

While we have found no Indiana case directly on point, the evidence presented at trial renders any defense of inherent impossibility inapplicable in this case. . . .

In addition to Haines' belief that he could infect others, there was testimony by physicians that the virus may be transmitted through the exchange of bodily fluids. . . .

From the evidence in the record before us we can only conclude that Haines had knowledge of his disease and that he unrelentingly and unequivocally sought to kill the persons helping him by infecting them with AIDS, and that he took a substantial step towards killing them by his conduct, believing that he could do so, all of which was more than a mere tenuous, theoretical, or speculative "chance" of transmitting the disease. From all of the evidence before the jury, it could have concluded beyond a reasonable doubt that Haines took a substantial step toward the commission of murder.

Thus, the trial court improperly granted Haines' motion for judgment on the evidence. . . . The trial court's judgment is reversed with instructions to reinstate the jury's verdict and resentence Haines accordingly.

---

concert of action rule
The rule that, unless a statute specifies otherwise, it is not a conspiracy for two persons to agree to commit a crime if the definition of the crime itself requires the participation of two or more persons. Also called *Wharton Rule* and *concerted action rule*.

At least two people must join in the agreement. One limitation on this rule is the **concert of action rule (Wharton's Rule).** Under this rule, two people cannot be charged with conspiracy when the underlying offense itself requires two people. For example, gambling is a crime that requires the acts of at least two people. Wharton's Rule prohibits convictions of both gambling and conspiracy. Adultery and incest are other examples. This is not true of murder, as murder can be committed by one person. Wharton's Rule is limited, however, to two people. So if three people agree to gamble, a conviction of gambling and conspiracy to commit gambling is permitted.

The mens rea of conspiracy has two aspects. First, conspirators must have an intent to enter into an agreement. Second, conspirators must possess a specific intent to commit some unlawful objective. That objective must be to commit an unlawful act or a lawful act in an unlawful manner. The language of conspiracy speaks of doing unlawful acts, not necessarily criminal. This is important because some acts, when taken by an individual, may lead to civil, but not criminal, liability. However, when the same acts are taken by a group, the law of conspiracy makes them criminal. This is common in the area of fraud.

The mens rea requirement of conspiracy is strict. Contrary to the general rule, mistake of law and fact are often accepted defenses. It is a defense for a party to have been under the mistaken belief that the group's actions and objectives were legal. This is because the conspiracy must be corrupt; the parties must have had an evil purpose for their union.

What if a party withdraws from the conspiracy while it is ongoing? As a general rule, withdrawal is not a defense, because the crime was complete when the parties entered into the agreement. However, if the jurisdiction requires an agreement plus an overt act or substantial steps, and the withdrawal is made before those acts occur, there is no criminal liability on behalf of the withdrawn party. To determine when withdrawal occurred, courts look to the defendant's actions. Withdrawal is effective at the time his or her acts would have conveyed to a reasonable person, standing in a co-conspirator's shoes, that he or she was abandoning the conspiracy. Additionally, the withdrawal must occur within a time that permits the other parties to abandon the objective. A last-second withdrawal, when it is too late to stop the wheels from turning, is not a defense. The Model Penal Code recognizes voluntary withdrawal as an affirmative defense.[5]

A few procedural issues are unique to conspiracy. As a whole, these rules favor prosecution. First, conspiracy is considered a crime, independent of any crime that is the objective of the conspiracy. If Amy and Ashley conspire to murder Elsa, they have committed two offenses: murder and conspiracy to murder. It is not a violation of the Fifth Amendment's double jeopardy prohibition to punish both crimes (cumulative punishment). Conspiracy to commit a crime and the commission of that crime do not merge into one. This is why conspiracy can be inchoate; it can be charged in cases where the objective is not met. If Amy and Ashley are not successful in their murderous plot, they are still liable for conspiracy to murder. One exception to the general rule of cumulative punishments is Wharton's Rule, discussed earlier.

Prosecutors must show an agreement between two or more parties to prove conspiracy. This creates some difficulties at trial. One difficulty concerns whether alleged co-conspirators should be tried together or separately. Because the United States Supreme Court has approved trial of all parties either at the location where the agreement was entered into or at any location where an act in furtherance of the conspiracy occurred, defendants are usually tried together.[6] It is possible for a defendant to be tried in a location where he or she has never been, and some argue that this is unconstitutional. In addition, critics argue that trying defendants together creates an increased likelihood of conviction because a form of "guilt by association" occurs in jurors' minds.

co-conspirator's rule

The principle that statements by a member of a proven conspiracy may be used as evidence against any of the members of the conspiracy.

hearsay

A statement about what someone else said (or wrote or otherwise communicated). *Hearsay evidence* is evidence, concerning what someone said outside of a court proceeding, that is offered in the proceeding to prove the truth of what was said. The *hearsay rule* bars the admission of hearsay as evidence *to prove the hearsay's truth* unless allowed by a hearsay exception.

Another procedural irregularity is the **co-conspirator hearsay rule. Hearsay** is an out-of-court statement. Although hearsay evidence is normally inadmissible at trial, the co-conspirator exception permits the statements of one party that are made out of court to be admitted. The rule is limited to statements made during planning and commission of the conspiracy; statements made after it is completed are inadmissible.

Because two people (or more) are required to have a conspiracy, if only two people are charged, and one is acquitted, then the other cannot be punished. For example, Edgar and Robert are charged and tried together for conspiring to rob a bank. If the jury acquits one, the other must also be acquitted. At least two people must be convicted. So, if a group of people are charged, and the jury acquits all but two, the convictions stand.

Finally, be aware that many statutes deal with conspiracies, even though they are not named so. You have already examined two federal conspiracy statutes, the Racketeer Influenced and Corrupt Organizations Act and Continuing Criminal Enterprise. In recent years there has been a rise in the number of conspiracy filings. This is largely the result of RICO and related statutes and because of the procedural advantages that prosecutors have, as discussed earlier.

Solicitation

solicitation

Asking for; enticing; strongly requesting. This may be a crime if the thing being urged is a crime.

You have already encountered **solicitation** in the discussion of prostitution. But solicitation is much broader than attempting to engage someone in prostitution. Solicitation is the (1) encouraging, requesting, or commanding (2) of another (3) to commit a crime.

Solicitation is a specific-intent crime: the person must intend to convince another to commit an offense. Although the crime may be prostitution, it can be any crime in most jurisdictions. A few states limit the pool to felonies. The actus reus of the crime is the solicitation.

The crime is different from attempt, because the solicitation itself is a crime, and no act to further the crime need be taken. Of course, if Gwen asks Tracy to kill Jeff, and the deed is completed, then Gwen is an accessory before the fact of murder, as well as a solicitor.

 WEB LINKS

GPO Gate

This University of California site provides access to many databases maintained by the Government Printing Office. This includes the United States Code, Federal Register, and Code of Federal Regulations, among others. Direct access the GPO site at *http://www. access.gpo.gov/su_docs*

KEY TERMS

accessory

attempt

co-conspirator's rule

concert of action rule

conspiracy

hearsay

legal impossibility

principal

solicitation

REVIEW QUESTIONS

1. Distinguish a principal in the first degree from a principal in the second degree. Which is punished more severely?
2. A person who helps principals prepare to commit a crime, but is not present during the commission, is called what?
3. Has Jan committed attempted murder if she decides to kill her sister and mentally works out the details of when, how, and where?
4. What are the elements of conspiracy?
5. What is hearsay? What is the co-conspirator hearsay rule?
6. What is meant by the phrase "inchoate crimes"?
7. What is the difference between solicitation and attempt?

REVIEW PROBLEMS

1–3. Use the following facts to answer questions one through three.

Abel and Baker were inmates sharing a cell in state prison. During their stay they planned a convenience store robbery for after their release. They decided which store to rob, when they would rob it, and what method they would use. Having frequented the store on many occasions, Abel knew that the store had a safe and that the employees did not have access to its contents. Neither Abel or Baker had any experience with breaking into safes and decided to seek help.

Accordingly, they sought out "Nitro," a fellow inmate who was a known explosives expert. They requested his assistance and promised to pay him one-third of the total recovery. He agreed. However, he would only be able to teach the two how to gain entry to the safe, because he was not scheduled for release until after the day they had planned for the robbery. He added that he owned a house in the area and that it would be available for them to use as a "hide-out until the heat was off."

The two were released as planned and drove to the town where the store was located. As instructed by Nitro, the two went to a store and purchased the materials necessary to construct an explosive, which was to be used to gain entry to the safe. That evening Abel and Baker went to the store with their homemade explosive. They left the car they were traveling in and went to the rear of the store to gain entry through a back door. However, as they entered the alley behind the store, they encountered a police officer. The officer, suspicious of them, examined their bag and discovered the bomb. Abel and Baker escaped from the officer and stayed in Nitro's house for three days before being discovered and arrested.

1. What crimes has Abel committed?
2. What crimes has Baker committed?
3. What crimes has Nitro committed?

4. John and Tyrone have a fight in a bar. Tyrone returns home, climbs into bed, and suffers a fatal heart attack. John, still angry from the earlier fight, climbs through a window into Tyrone's room and shoots Tyrone twice in the head. Has John committed a murder? Attempted murder? Explain your answer.

END NOTES

1. See *Rex v. Scofield*, Cald. 397 (1784) and *Rex v. Higgins*, 2 East 5 (1801).
2. *Hyde v. United States*, 225 U.S. 347 (1912).
3. Turner, "Attempts to Commit Crimes," 5 *Cambridge L.J.* 230, 236 (1934).
4. Model Penal Code § 5.01.
5. Model Penal Code § 5.03.
6. *Hyde v. United States*, 225 U.S. 347 (1912).

CHAPTER 8

Factual and Statutory Defenses

CHAPTER OUTLINE

"Defense" Defined

Affirmative Defenses

Insanity

  M'Naghten

  Irresistible Impulse

  Durham

  The Model Penal Code Test

  Guilty But Mentally Ill

  Procedures of the Insanity Defense

  Disposition of the Criminally Insane

  Insanity at the Time of Trial

Duress and Necessity

Use-of-Force Defenses

  Self-Defense

  Defense of Others

  Defense of Property and Habitation

  Imperfect Self-Defense

  Arrests

Infancy

Intoxication

Mistake

Entrapment

Alibi and Consent

Statutes of Limitation

CHAPTER OBJECTIVES

In this chapter, you should:

- learn common factual defenses to criminal accusations, such as alibi.
- learn common statutory defenses to criminal accusations, such as the insanity defense.
- be challenged to think critically about these defenses.
- continue to develop your case analysis and legal reasoning skills.

"DEFENSE" DEFINED

Criminal defendants usually claim that they are innocent of the charges against them. A defendant's reason for asserting that he is innocent is called a *defense*. Defenses can be factual: "I didn't do it!" They can also be legal: "I did it, but the case was filed after the statute of limitation had run." Many defenses have been developed under the common law; however, many others have been created by legislation. Finally, some defenses find their origin in the constitutions of the states and federal government. Some defenses are complete (perfect); that is, if successful, the defendant goes free. Other defenses are partial; the defendant avoids liability on one charge, but may be convicted of a lesser offense.

This chapter examines several factual and statutory defenses. Chapter 9 discusses constitutional defenses.

AFFIRMATIVE DEFENSES

affirmative defense

A defense that is more than a simple denial of the charges. It raises a new matter that may result in an acquittal or reduction of liability. It is a defense that must be affirmatively raised, often prior to trial or it is lost.

burden of proof

The requirement that to win a point or have an issue decided in your favor in a lawsuit you must show that the weight of evidence is on your side, rather than "in the balance" on that question.

burden of going forward (production)

The requirement that one side in a lawsuit produce evidence on a particular issue or risk losing on that issue.

burden of persuasion

The requirement that to win a point or have an issue decided in your favor in a lawsuit you must show that the weight of evidence is on your side, rather than "in the balance" on that question.

There is a special class of defenses known as **affirmative defenses.** Affirmative defenses go beyond a simple denial; they raise special or new issues, which, if proven, can result in an acquittal or lesser liability. Defenses that raise the question of a defendant's mental state to commit a crime (e.g., insanity and intoxication), whether justification or excuse existed to commit the crime (e.g., self-defense), and alibi fall into the affirmative defenses class.

As a general rule, criminal defendants may sit passively during trial, as the prosecution bears the burden of proving the government's allegations. In all instances, **burden of proof** refers to two burdens, the burden of production and the burden of persuasion. Because it is not practical to require prosecutors to prove that every defendant was sane, was not intoxicated, or did not have justification to use force, the burdens for affirmative defenses are different than for other defenses. First, defendants have the duty of raising all affirmative defenses. At trial this means that defendants must produce some evidence to support the defense. This is known as the **burden of production.**

After defendants have met the burden of production, the **burden of persuasion** then must be met. There is a split among the states; some require the defendant to carry this burden, whereas others require it of the prosecution. If the defendant has the burden, then he or she must convince the factfinder that the defense is true. Defendants must prove this by a preponderance of evidence. In jurisdictions that require prosecutors to disprove an affirmative defense, there is again a split as to the standard of proof required. Some require proof by a preponderance and others require proof beyond a reasonable doubt.

Some of the defenses covered in this chapter are affirmative defenses. It is necessary to research local law to determine which procedure is followed in a particular jurisdiction and what defenses are considered affirmative defenses.

INSANITY

Few aspects of criminal law have received as much public attention as the insanity defense. The defense has also been the subject of considerable scholastic research and discussion. Some critics charge that the defense should not be available. Others criticize not the availability of such a defense, but the particular tests employed to determine sanity. Despite its critics, insanity is recognized by nearly all jurisdictions as a defense. At least four states—Montana, Utah, Kansas, and Idaho—have abolished the insanity defense. In 1994, the United States Supreme Court denied certiorari in a case challenging the abolition of the defense as violative of due process.

In reality, insanity is a mens rea defense. If a defendant was insane at the time of the crime, it is unlikely that the requisite mens rea existed. It is generally held that one who is insane is incapable of forming a rational purpose or intent. In fact, in most jurisdictions defendants may put on evidence to establish that insanity prevented the requisite mens rea from being formed. This is the defense of **diminished capacity.** It is a direct attack on the mens rea element of the crime, separate from the defense of insanity. If successful, the result could be conviction of a lesser, general-intent crime. However, a few states have made defendants choose between the insanity defense and the assertion of lack of mens rea due to insanity.

The theory underlying the defense of insanity is that no purpose of criminal law is served by subjecting insane persons to the criminal justice system. Because they have no control over their behavior, they cannot be deterred from similar future behavior. Similarly, no general deterrence will occur, as others suffering from a mental or physical disease of the mind cannot alter their behavior. The one purpose that may be served, incapacitation, is inappropriate if the defendant no longer suffers from a mental disease, or if the disease is now controlled. If the defendant continues to be dangerous, there is no need to use the criminal justice system to remove him or her from society, because this can be accomplished using civil commitment.

Something that must be remembered is that criminal law has its own definition of insanity. Other areas of law (e.g., civil commitment) use different tests, as do other professions (e.g., psychiatry). Each jurisdiction is free to use whatever test it wishes to determine insanity. Three tests are used to determine sanity in the criminal law context: M'Naghten; irresistible impulse; and the Model Penal Code. A fourth test, the Durham, is no longer used in any jurisdiction, but is mentioned because of its historical significance.

diminished capacity
The principle that having a certain recognized form of *diminished mental capacity* while committing a crime should lead to the imposition of a lesser punishment or to lower the degree of the crime.

TWINKIES, WITCHCRAFT, PMS, AND MORE   A number of interesting insanity-related defenses have been raised by defendants. Although some are in the nature of full insanity defenses, most are asserted as diminished-capacity defenses.

One of the most famous is the so-called "Twinkie defense," raised by a defendant in California who was charged with murdering a mayor and another official. He claimed that his large consumption of white sugar, primarily through

SIDEBAR

snack foods, caused him to have a diminished capacity. The defense was successful in reducing the crime from murder to manslaughter. He was sentenced to a short prison term and committed suicide after his release. The California legislature responded to the decision by barring diminished-capacity defenses in future cases.

In addition to the Twinkie defense, all of the following have been pleaded by defendants in support of either an insanity or diminished-capacity defense: premenstrual syndrome, involuntary subliminal television intoxication, brainwashing syndrome, and posttraumatic stress disorder. One defendant even asserted a witchcraft defense, claiming that witchcraft made him do it.

Many states have followed California's lead and eliminated the diminished-capacity defense. Others require defendants to choose between asserting insanity or diminished capacity.

M'Naghten

In 1843 Daniel M'Naghten was tried for killing the British prime minister's secretary. M'Naghten was laboring under the paranoid delusion that the prime minister was planning to kill him, and he killed the minister's secretary, believing him to be the prime minister. The jury found M'Naghten not guilty by reason of insanity.[1] The decision created controversy, and the House of Lords asked the justice of the Queens Bench to state what the standards for acquittal on the grounds of insanity were.[2] Those standards were attached to the decision and set forth the following standard, known as the **M'Naghten** test.

M'Naghten rule
A test employed in a number of jurisdictions for determining whether a criminal defendant had the capacity to form criminal intent at the time he or she committed the crime of which he or she is accused. The M'Naghten rule is also referred to as the right-wrong test.

1. At the time that the act was committed
2. the defendant was suffering from a defect of reason, from a disease of the mind, which caused
3. the defendant to not know
   a. the nature and quality of the act taken or
   b. that the act was wrong.

This test has become known as the M'Naghten, or the right-wrong test. It is the test used by most jurisdictions today. First, the defendant must have suffered from a disease of the mind at the time the act occurred. *Disease of the mind* is not clearly defined, but it appears that any condition that causes one of the two events from the third part of the test is sufficient. That is, any disease of the mind that causes a defendant to not know the quality of an act or that an act is wrong is sufficient. In at least one case extremely low intelligence was found adequate.[3]

The phrase "the defendant must not know the nature and quality of the act" simply means that the defendant did not understand the consequences of his or her physical act. The drafters of the Model Penal Code gave the following illustration: a man who squeezes his wife's neck, believing it to be a lemon, does not know the nature and quality of his actions.[4]

What is meant by "wrong," as used in the M'Naghten test? Courts have defined it two ways. One asks whether the defendant knew that the act was legally wrong, and the other asks whether the defendant knew that the act was morally wrong.

Irresistible Impulse

Under the M'Naghten test, a defendant who knew that his or her actions were wrong, but could not control his or her behavior because of a disease of the mind, is not insane. This has led a few jurisdictions, which follow M'Naghten, to supplement the rule. These states continue to follow the basic rule, but add that a defendant is not guilty by reason of insanity if a disease of the mind caused the defendant to be unable to control his or her behavior. This is true even if the defendant understood the nature and quality of the act or knew that the behavior was wrong. This is known as **irresistible impulse.**

Irresistible impulse-type tests actually predate M'Naghten and can be found in American cases as far back as 1863.[5] Of course, the largest problem with implementing the irresistible impulse test is distinguishing acts that can be resisted from those that cannot.

irresistible impulse
The loss of control due to insanity that is so great that a person cannot stop from committing a crime.

Durham

In 1871 the New Hampshire Supreme Court rejected the M'Naghten test and held that a defendant was not guilty because of insanity if the crime was the "product of mental disease." No other jurisdictions followed New Hampshire's lead until 1954, when the District of Columbia Court of Appeals handed down *Durham v. United States*, 214 F.2d 862 (D.C. Cir. 1954). Generally, the **Durham rule** requires an acquittal if the defendant would not have committed the crime if he or she had not been suffering from a mental disease or mental defect.

Durham was overturned in 1972 by the District of Columbia Court of Appeals in favor of a modified version of the Model Penal Code test.[6] Today, Durham is not used by any jurisdiction.

Durham rule
The principle, used in *Durham v. U.S.* (214 F.2d. 862 (1954)), that a defendant is not guilty of a crime because of insanity if he or she was "suffering from a disease or defective mental condition at the time of the act and there was a causal connection between the condition and the act."

The Model Penal Code Test

The Model Penal Code contains a definition of insanity similar to, but broader than, the M'Naghten and irresistible impulse tests. This test is also referred to as the *substantial capacity test*. The relevant section of the Code reads:[7]

> A person is not responsible for criminal conduct if at the time of such conduct as a result of mental disease or defect he lacks substantial capacity either to appreciate the criminality [wrongfulness] of his conduct or to conform his conduct to the requirements of law.

The Code is similar to M'Naghten in that it requires that mental disease or defect impair a defendant's ability to appreciate the wrongfulness of his or her act. The final line, "conform his conduct to the requirements of law," incorporates the irresistible impulse concept.

The Code's approach differs from the M'Naghten and irresistible impulse test in two important regards: First, the Code requires only substantial impairment, whereas M'Naghten requires total impairment of the ability to know the nature or wrongfulness of the act. Second, the Code uses the term "appreciate,"

rather than "know." The drafters of the Code clearly intended more than
knowledge, and, as such, evidence concerning the defendant's personality and
emotional state are relevant.

The Model Penal Code test has been adopted by a few jurisdictions. The
federal courts used the test until Congress enacted a statute that established a
test similar to the M'Naghten test.[8] That statute places the burden of proving
insanity, by clear and convincing evidence, on the defendant.

Guilty But Mentally Ill

In 1981 John Hinckley attempted to assassinate President Ronald Reagan. The
President was seriously wounded and his press secretary, James Brady, suffered
permanent brain injury. It was later learned that Hinckley committed the act in
order to impress a movie actress he had never met. At trial, Hinckley was found
not guilty by reason of insanity. There was both a public and legislative back-
lash to the decision and to the insanity defense. As a result, legislators throughout the nation moved to abolish or limit the scope of the insanity defense.
Today, four states, Idaho, Montana, Utah, and Kansas, have abolished the
defense altogether.[9]

Rather than abolishing the defense, other states sought to limit or alter its
impact. One such measure was the establishment of the Guilty But Mentally Ill
(GBMI) verdict. Pennsylvania's GBMI statute reads, in part, that a "person who
timely offers a defense of insanity in accordance with the Rules of Criminal
Procedure may be found 'guilty but mentally ill' at trial if the trier of facts finds,
beyond a reasonable doubt, that the person is guilty of an offense, was mentally
ill at the time of the commission of the offense and was not legally insane at the
time of the commission of the offense."[10] As you can see, the GBMI verdict is a
finding of mental illness at the time of the crime, but not insanity as defined by
the applicable legal test. Unlike a defendant who is not guilty by reason of
insanity, a defendant who is GBMI is both punished and treated. The defendant
is sentenced as any other offender for the crime, but in addition, the state
provides mental health treatment.

Procedures of the Insanity Defense

Insanity is an affirmative defense. In the federal system and in many states,
defendants must provide notice to the court and government that insanity will
be used as a defense at trial. These statutes usually require that the notice be
filed a certain number of days prior to trial. This notice provides the prosecution with an opportunity to prepare to rebut the defense prior to trial.

In most instances, lay testimony is not adequate to prove insanity; psychiatric examination of defendants is necessary. The judge presiding over the case
will appoint a psychiatrist, who will conduct the exam and make the findings
available to the judge. Often defendants wish to have a psychiatrist of their own
choosing perform an examination. This is not a problem if the defendant can
afford to pay for the service. In the case of indigent defendants who desire an

independent mental examination, statutes often provide reimbursement from the government for independent mental examinations up to a stated maximum. In the federal system, trial courts may approve up to $1,000 in defense-related services. Defendants who seek reimbursement for greater expenses must receive approval from the chief judge of the circuit.[11]

As with all affirmative defenses, the defendant bears the burden of production at trial. Generally, the defendant must present enough evidence to create some doubt of sanity. The states are split on the issue of persuasion. Some require that the prosecution disprove the insanity claim, usually beyond a reasonable doubt. In other jurisdictions the defendant bears the burden of persuasion, usually by preponderance of the evidence. One exception is federal law, which requires the defendant to prove insanity by the higher standard—clear and convincing evidence.[12]

Disposition of the Criminally Insane

Contrary to popular belief, those adjudged insane by a criminal proceeding are not immediately and automatically released. In most jurisdictions, after a defendant has been determined "not guilty by reason of insanity," the court (the jury in a few states) must make a determination of whether the person continues to be dangerous. If so, commitment is to be ordered. If the defendant is determined not to be dangerous, then release follows. A few jurisdictions have followed the Model Penal Code approach,[13] which requires automatic commitment following a finding of not guilty by reason of insanity. This is the rule in the federal system.[14]

In theory, those committed have a right to be treated for their mental disease. In fact, because of lack of funds, security concerns, and overcrowding problems in facilities, adequate treatment is often not provided.

Once a committed person has been successfully treated and is no longer a danger, release is granted. The determination of dangerousness is left to the judge, not hospital administrators or mental health professionals—an often-criticized practice. Patients, doctors, government officials, and even the judge can begin the process of release. Some states provide for periodic reviews of the patient's status in order to determine the propriety of release. The relevant federal statute reads, in part:[15]

> When the director of the facility in which an acquitted person is hospitalized . . . determines that the person has recovered from his mental disease or defect to such an extent that his release, or his conditional release under a prescribed regimen of medical, psychiatric, or psychological care or treatment, would no longer create a substantial risk of bodily injury to another person or serious damage to property of another, he shall promptly file a certificate to that effect with the clerk of the court that ordered the commitment . . . The court shall order a discharge of the acquitted person or, on the motion of the attorney for the government or on its own motion, shall hold a hearing [to determine if the patient is dangerous].

Insanity and Criminal
Procedure

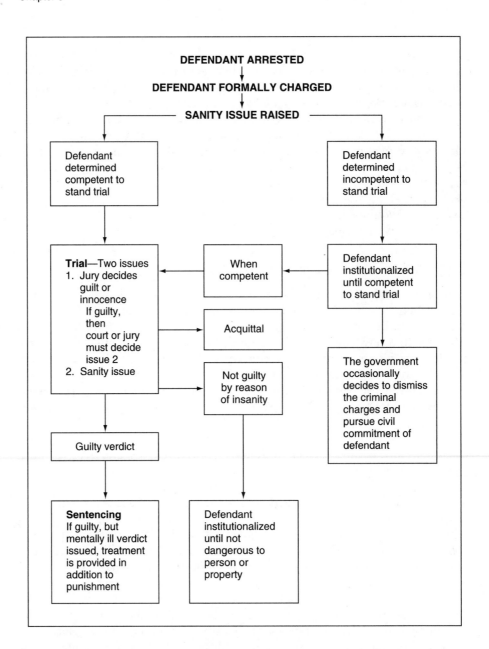

At that hearing, the defendant has the burden of proving by clear and convincing evidence that a risk to people or property is not created by release.

Finally, some states have a "guilty, but mentally ill" verdict. Juries may return such a verdict when the defendant's illness does not rise to the level of negating culpability, but when treatment should be provided in addition to incarceration.

IMPACT OF THE INSANITY DEFENSE   In spite of the attention it receives and strong feelings it engenders, the insanity defense is not a significant defense tool. The defense is raised in only 1 percent of felony cases in the United States and it succeeds in only about 25 percent of the cases in which it is asserted. This computes to about 300 insanity pleas per state per year.

Source: Angela Paulsen, "Limiting the Scope of State Power to Confine Insanity Acquittees: *Foucha v. Louisiana*," 28 *Tulsa L.J.* (1993).

Insanity at the Time of Trial

The United States Supreme Court has held that a defendant who is insane at the time of trial may not be tried.[16] The Court found that the Due Process Clauses of the Fifth and Fourteenth Amendments require that a defendant be able to assist in his or her defense and understand the proceeding against him or her.

The test for determining insanity in this context is different from that discussed earlier. Insanity exists when a defendant lacks the capacity to understand the proceedings or assist in his or her defense. This simply means that defendants must be rational, possess the ability to testify coherently, and be able to meaningfully discuss their cases with their lawyers. The burden of establishing incompetence is placed on the defendant in many jurisdictions. While this procedure comports with due process, requiring the defendant to establish incompetence by clear and convincing evidence does not. In *Cooper v. Oklahoma* (1996),[17] the Supreme Court held that the burden of proof can be placed on the defendant, but that the standard of proof cannot exceed preponderance of evidence.

If defendants are unable to stand trial because they are insane, they are usually committed until they are competent. Many statutes have mandatory commitment of defendants determined incompetent to stand trial. However, indefinite confinement is unconstitutional, based solely upon a finding of incompetence to stand trial. Generally, the Supreme Court has held that a lengthy (eighteen months or longer) detention (awaiting competence to stand trial) is tantamount to punishment and violative of the Due Process Clause.[18] In such cases, there must be a separate finding of dangerousness to continue to hold such persons.

A mistrial is to be declared in the event that a defendant becomes incompetent during a trial, and defendants who are sane at trial but become insane before sentencing should be sentenced to a psychiatric facility.

Last, the Supreme Court has held that a person who has become insane after being sentenced to death may not be executed until his or her sanity is regained.[19] The constitutional basis of the Court's decision was the Eighth Amendment's prohibition of cruel and unusual punishment. Justice Marshall has stated that "It is no less abhorrent today than it has been for centuries to exact in penance the life of one whose mental illness prevents him from comprehending the reasons for the penalty or its implications."[20] Similarly, the Court has held that mentally retarded individuals may not be executed.[21]

DURESS AND NECESSITY

Consider these facts: Terry Teller is ordered by bank robber, who is brandishing a gun, to place the money in her drawer in a bag and give it to bank robber or "she will be planted six feet under." Has Terry committed theft? Although the elements of theft may be satisfied, she has the defense of **duress.** To prove duress, one must show (1) that one was threatened (2) and that the threat caused a reasonable belief (3) that the only way of avoiding serious personal injury or death to oneself or others (4) was to commit the crime. Duress was recognized at common law and continues to be a statutory defense today.

First, it must be shown that a threat was made. Second, the threat must create a reasonable fear of immediate serious bodily harm or death. This fear must be reasonable; that is, even if the person making the threat had no intention of following through, the defense is still valid if a reasonable person would have thought the threat was real. Hence, even if bank robber never intended to kill Terry, she has the defense of duress. Terry need not be the one threatened for her to be able to claim duress. So if bank robber threatened to kill a customer unless Terry complied, Terry could claim duress. The fear must not only be reasonable, but it must also be of serious bodily injury or death. If bank robber exclaims, "Put the money in the bag or I'll smack you across the face," the threatened danger is not sufficient to support the defense of duress. In addition, the threat of harm must be imminent or immediate. Threats of future harms are not adequate duress.

One limitation that is recognized nearly everywhere is that murder is not justified by duress. This rule is criticized, rightfully so, because it does not account for those situations where taking one life may save many more.

It is no defense to a crime to claim that one was only carrying out the orders of a superior, such as an employer or military superior. This issue was addressed in *United States v. Calley*.

The court mentioned that the order's illegality was "apparent upon even cursory evaluation by a man of ordinary sense and understanding." What if an order appears to be legal and the person who follows it has a reasonable belief of its legality? In such cases, the defense of duress does apply.[22]

Necessity is similar to duress. However, whereas duress is created by human pressures, necessity comes about by natural forces. When a person is confronted with two choices, both causing harm, he or she is to choose the lesser harm. If he or she does, he or she may have the defense of necessity to the act taken. For example, a person may be justified in breaking into someone's cabin to avoid freezing to death. Or a captain of a ship may be justified in a trespassory use of another's dock, if setting ashore is necessary to save the ship and its passengers.

Necessity is a broad and amorphous concept. As a general proposition, it applies any time a person is confronted with the task of choosing between two or more evils. The harm avoided need not be bodily injury; it can also be harm to property. Of course, choosing property over life is never justified. Finally, if an alternative existed that involved less harm than the chosen act, the defense is invalid.

Duress and necessity are complete defenses. When valid, they result in acquittal of all related charges.

duress
Unlawful pressure on a person to do what he or she would not otherwise have done. It includes force, threats of violence, physical restraint, etc.

necessity
Necessity often refers to a situation that requires an action that would otherwise be illegal or expose a person to tort liability.

CASE

UNITED STATES V. CALLEY

46 C.M.R. 1131 (1975)

[D]uring midmorning on 16 March 1968 a large number of unresisting Vietnamese were placed in a ditch on the eastern side of My Lai and summarily executed by American soldiers.

[PFC] Meadlo gave the most graphic and damning evidence. He had wandered back into the village alone after the trial incident. Eventually, he met his fire team leader, Specialist Four Grzesik. They took seven or eight Vietnamese to what he labeled a "ravine," where Lieutenants Calley, Sledge, and Dursi and a few other Americans were located with what he estimated as seventy-five to a hundred Vietnamese. Meadlo remembered also that Lieutenant Calley told him, "We got another job to do, Meadlo," and that the appellant started shoving people into the ravine and shooting them. Meadlo, in contrast to Dursi, followed the directions of his leader and himself fired into the people at the bottom of the "ravine." Meadlo then drifted away from the area but he doesn't remember where.

Specialist Four Grzesik found PFC Meadlo, crying and distraught, sitting on a small dike on the eastern edge of the village. He and Meadlo moved through the village, and came to the ditch, in which Grzesik thought were thirty-five dead bodies. Lieutenant Calley walked past and ordered Grzesik to take his fire team back into the village and help the following platoon in their search. He also remembered that Calley asked him to "finish them off," but he refused.

Specialist Four Turner saw Lieutenant Calley for the first time that day as Turner walked out of the village near the ditch. Meadlo and a few other soldiers were also present. Turner passed within fifteen feet of the area, looked into the ditch and saw a pile of approximately twenty bodies covered with blood. He saw Lieutenant Calley and Meadlo firing from a distance of five feet into another group of people who were kneeling and squatting in the ditch. . . .

Of the several bases for his argument that he committed no murder at My Lai because he was void of mens rea, appellant emphasized most of all that he acted in obedience to orders. . . .

An order of the type appellant says he received is illegal. Its illegality is apparent upon even cursory evaluation by a man of ordinary sense and understanding. . . .

We find no impediment to the findings that appellant acted with murderous mens rea, including premeditation.

USE-OF-FORCE DEFENSES

In some situations, the law permits actors to use physical force against others. Self-defense, defense of others, defense of property, and use of force to make arrests fall into this area. Self-defense, defense of others, and defense of property, when successful, are complete defenses. Imperfect self-defense (including defense of another) does not lead to acquittal; however, it does reduce murder to manslaughter.

Self-Defense

To prove **self-defense,** it must be shown that the actor (1) was confronted with an unprovoked, (2) immediate threat of bodily harm, (3) that force was necessary to avoid the harm, (4) and that the amount of force used was reasonable.

self-defense

Physical force used against a person who is threatening the use of physical force or using physical force.

One who initiates an attack on another cannot claim self-defense, as a general proposition. There are two exceptions to this rule. First, if an attacker is met with excessive force in return, then he or she may defend himself or herself. For example, Mike attacks Norm with his fists, and in defense Norm uses a deadly weapon. In such a circumstance, Mike may also use deadly force to protect himself. Second, if an attacker withdraws from the attack and is pursued by the intended victim, then he or she may claim self-defense. Suppose Randy attacks Sue with an intent to sexually assault her. After he grabs her, she displays a gun, and he runs. If Sue follows after him, intending to cause him harm, then he would be privileged to use force to defend himself.

The threat of harm must be immediate in most jurisdictions. Threat of future harm does not justify using force against another. To satisfy this requirement, the harm must be one that will occur unless force is used, and no other means of avoiding the harm exists. However, this principle is occasionally stretched. For example, some jurisdictions have permitted a jury to be instructed on the **battered woman syndrome** defense. Under this defense a woman who is constantly abused by her husband may be justified in using force at a time when she is not strictly in "immediate danger." The theory is that women in such circumstances have two choices: either wait for their husbands to kill them or strike first in a form of offensive self-defense. Critics of this defense contend that because other remedies are available, such as leaving the husband and obtaining a court order restraining him from bothering her, there is no immediate danger.

Finally, the force used to defend oneself must be reasonable. It would be unreasonable to knife a person who is attempting to slap one's hand. Deadly force may be used to defend against an attack that threatens serious bodily injury or death. Deadly force may not be used to defend against other attacks.

All jurisdictions require that a person retreat from an attack, if possible, before using deadly force. This is known as the **retreat** doctrine. There are many exceptions to the doctrine. Some states, for example, do not require one to retreat from his home (the castle doctrine) or to retreat when it poses a danger to the victim of the attack. Police officers are not required to retreat when performing their lawful duties. The Model Penal Code has a retreat provision that recognizes these exceptions:

> The use of deadly force is not justifiable . . . [if] the actor knows that he can avoid the necessity of using such force without complete safety by retreating or by surrendering possession of a thing to a person asserting a claim of right thereto or by complying with a demand that he abstain from any action which he has no duty to take, except that (1) the actor is not obliged to retreat from his dwelling or place of work, unless he was the initial aggressor. . . .[23]

The Code provides that public officials need not retreat during the performance of their duties. There is no duty to retreat rather than using nondeadly force.

Also, notice that the Code requires not only retreat, but that "thing[s]" be surrendered and one comply with another's demands before deadly force is

---

battered woman syndrome

Continuing **abuse** of a woman by a spouse or lover, and the resulting physical or psychological harm.

retreat to the wall

The doctrine that before a person is entitled to use deadly force in self defense, he or she must attempt to withdraw from the encounter by giving as much ground as possible.

used. Of course, one can later use civil law to recover unlawfully taken items or to recover for complying with a demand that caused damage. The aggressor will be liable both civilly and criminally for such unlawful demands.

Defense of Others

It is also a justified use of force to defend another. The rules are similar to that of self-defense: there must be a threat of immediate danger to the other person; the perception of threat must be reasonable; the amount of force used must be reasonable; and deadly force may be used only to repel a deadly attack.

At common law, one was only privileged to defend those with whom a special relationship existed, such as parent and child. Today, most jurisdictions permit any person to use force to protect another.

What happens when a person uses force to defend another who is *not* privileged to use force? For example, Perry is an undercover police officer attempting to arrest Norm, who is resisting. Randa observes what is happening and comes to Norm's defense, believing that Norm was being unlawfully attacked. There is a split of authority concerning this problem. Some jurisdictions limit the authority of the defender to use force to the privilege held by the person being attacked. Because Norm was not privileged to use force against the police officer, Randa is guilty of assault. Other states, however, use an objective test. Under such a test, if a reasonable person standing in Randa's shoes would have believed that force was justified, then he or she would be acquitted.

Defense of Property and Habitation

At common law and by legislative enactment today, one may use force to defend property. As with defending oneself, only reasonable force may be used. Because property is not as valuable as life, deadly force may not be used to protect property. Thus, one must allow another to take or destroy property before killing to defend it. No force is reasonable if other methods of protecting the property were available. So, if one has ample time to seek assistance from the police or the courts, force would be unreasonable. In contrast, if an enemy appears at one's house and begins to destroy a car in the driveway, force would be permitted to protect the vehicle. The actor must have a reasonable belief that his or her property is in danger of trespass or destruction and that the force used was necessary to defend the property.

The basic rules concerning defense of property also apply to defense of habitation: one must have a reasonable belief that the property is threatened; only reasonable force may be used to protect the property; and other nonviolent remedies must be utilized before resorting to force. However, one difference between dwellings and other property is that deadly force may be used, under some circumstances, to protect one's home.

In early common law, the security of the home was as important as life itself. Therefore, people were permitted to use deadly force against any forcible intruder after warning the person not to enter. Today the rule has been narrowed, and statutes now commonly require that the occupant must believe that the intruder intends to commit a felony once inside before deadly force may be used.

The Model Penal Code allows the use of deadly force if either (1) the intruder is attempting to take the dwelling (with no legal claim to do so) or (2) the intruder is there to commit a crime (arson, burglary, theft) and has threatened deadly force or poses a substantial risk to those inside.[24]

This provision of the Code incorporates a self-defense concept. Remember, the rules of self-defense apply in the home also. So, any time a person's life (or another's) is threatened, deadly force may be used.

Some people choose to protect their property with manmade devices, such as electric fences and spring guns. Others have used natural protection, such as dogs and snakes. Whichever is used, the rules are the same. If the device employs nondeadly force, it is likely to be lawful. An electric fence that does not have sufficient electric current to kill is a justified use of force.

However, the result is often different when one uses deadly force. There are two perspectives on the use of deadly traps to protect property. One permits the use of deadly force so long as the person who set the trap would have been permitted to use such force himself or herself, if he or she had been present. So, if a murderer gains entry to a house and is killed by a spring gun, the occupant is not criminally liable because he or she would have been privileged to use deadly force against the murderer. The second perspective, adopted by the drafters of the Model Penal Code, rejects the use of deadly traps in all instances.[25] This position is sound, as deadly traps do not discriminate between the dangerous and the non-dangerous. The occupant who sets such a trap is simply lucky if the intruder is a criminal and not a firefighter responding to a blaze in the home.

Imperfect Self-Defense

The so-called "imperfect self-defense" is actually a mens rea defense. It applies to situations when a person cannot make a successful self-defense (or defense of another) claim, but because he or she lacked malice aforethought (or purpose), the crime should not be murder, but manslaughter. The defense applies only to homicides and is not recognized everywhere.

As stated, a person must have a reasonable belief that he or another is in danger of serious bodily injury or death before deadly force may be used. What if a person possesses a good faith, but unreasonable belief? Self-defense is unavailable, but because there is no malicious intent, purpose, or malice afore-thought (depending on the jurisdiction's definition of murder), the crime is reduced to manslaughter. The defense is available in a second situation: whenever a person who initiates an attack using nondeadly force later justifiably uses deadly force to defend herself.

Arrests

Sometimes it is necessary for law enforcement officers to use force to execute their duties and to defend themselves. When a police officer uses force in defense of another's attack, the rules of self-defense that you have already learned apply. In addition, because the use of force is an integral part of law enforcement, it is often justified. However, a person making an arrest does not have an unlimited right to use force against an arrestee. This section examines a person's right to resist an unlawful arrest, the so-called "citizen's arrest," and arrests by law enforcement officers.

Resisting Unlawful Arrests.   In some states, people may use force to resist an unlawful arrest. The amount of force is usually limited to nondeadly, although some jurisdictions permit one to use deadly force. Of course, if a person uses force against a lawful arrest, he or she is fully liable for whatever crime results (assault, battery, or murder), as well as for resisting a lawful arrest.

The rule permitting force to resist a lawful arrest evolved during a time when arrestees were detained for long periods before appearing before a court, jail conditions were extremely poor, and no civil remedies existed for unlawful arrests. In light of these harsh facts, public policy was best served by permitting people to resist unlawful arrests.

Today, many jurisdictions have adopted an approach closer to the Model Penal Code's, which prohibits any resistance to an arrest by a law enforcement officer. This is the sensible approach, as the reasons for permitting resistance no longer exist: arrestees must be promptly brought before judges and released if there is no probable cause. When available, bail is set immediately. Also, federal law now permits civil suits against law enforcement officers for violation of a person's civil rights. Prohibiting resistance advances two important public policy objectives: first, it fosters obedience to police and, second, it reduces violence.

Arrests by Law Enforcement Officers.   A law enforcement officer is privileged to use reasonable force to apprehend criminals and to prevent those incarcerated from escaping. At common law, police could use all but deadly force to arrest misdemeanants and deadly force to arrest felons. This latter rule was justified by the fact that all felons were put to death at early common law.

In 1974 a Memphis, Tennessee, police officer shot and killed a fifteen-year-old male who was fleeing a burglary. The boy had stolen forty dollars. The family of the deceased boy sued the police department in federal court for violating his constitutional rights. The case ended up before the United States Supreme Court.

In *Tennessee v. Garner*, 471 U.S. 1 (1985), the Court held that the use of deadly force by a police officer is a "seizure" under the Fourth Amendment. Accordingly, the test used to determine whether the use of deadly force is proper is the Fourth Amendment's test: reasonability. The Court then held that the use of deadly force is reasonable only when the person fleeing is a dangerous felon. The Court did not state what standard must be applied in cases of nondeadly force.

In 1989 the Court handed down *Graham v. Connor*, in which the standard was set for all preconviction arrests. In that opinion, the Court held that all seizures are to be evaluated under the Fourth Amendment reasonableness standard.

CASE

GRAHAM V. CONNOR

490 U.S. 386 (1989)

This case requires us to decide what constitutional standard governs a free citizen's claim that law-enforcement officials used excessive force in the course of making an arrest, investigatory stop, or other "seizure" of his person. We hold that such claims are properly analyzed under the Fourth Amendment's "objective reasonableness" standard. . . .

On November 12, 1984, Graham, a diabetic, felt the onset of an insulin reaction. He asked a friend, William Berry, to drive him to a nearby convenience store so he could purchase some orange juice to counteract the reaction. Berry agreed, but when Graham entered the store, he saw a number of people ahead of him in the checkout line. Concerned about the delay, he hurried out of the store and asked Berry to drive him to a friend's house instead.

Respondent Connor, an officer of the Charlotte, North Carolina, Police Department, saw Graham hastily enter and leave the store. The officer became suspicious that something was amiss and followed Berry's car. About one-half mile from the store, he made an investigatory stop. Although Berry told Connor that Graham was simply suffering from a "sugar reaction," the officer ordered Berry and Graham to wait while he found out what, if anything, had happened at the convenience store. When Officer Connor returned to his patrol car to call for backup assistance, Graham got out of the car, ran around it twice, and finally sat down on the curb, where he passed out briefly.

In the ensuing confusion, a number of other Charlotte police officers arrived on the scene in response to Officer Connor's request for backup. One of the officers rolled Graham over on the sidewalk and cuffed his hands tightly behind his back, ignoring Berry's pleas to get him some sugar. Another officer said: "I've seen a lot of people with sugar diabetes that never acted like this. Ain't nothing wrong with the M.F. but drunk. Lock the

S.B. up." Several officers then lifted Graham up from behind, carried him over to Berry's car, and placed him face down on the hood. Regaining consciousness, Graham asked the officers to check in his wallet for a diabetic decal that he carried. In response, one of the officers told him to "shut up" and shoved his face down against the hood of the car. Four officers grabbed Graham and threw him head-first into the police car. A friend of Graham's brought some orange juice to the car, but the officers refused to let him have it. Finally, Officer Connor received a report that Graham had done nothing wrong at the convenience store, and the officers drove him home and released him.

At some point during the encounter with the police, Graham sustained a broken foot, cuts on his wrists, a bruised forehead, and an injured shoulder; he also claims to have developed a loud ringing in his right ear that continues to this day. . . . [The Court then discussed previous cases which held that a due process standard should be applied in all cases of excessive force. To be successful using the due process standard, a plaintiff had to prove the actions of the police were "sadistic and malicious."]

We reject this notion that all excessive force claims brought under § 1983 [a federal statute permitting cases against government officials to be brought in federal court] are governed by a single generic standard. As we have said many times, § 1983 "is not itself a source of substantive rights," but merely provides "a method for vindication of federal rights elsewhere conferred. . . . In addressing an excessive force claim brought under § 1983, analysis begins by identifying the specific constitutional right allegedly infringed by the challenged application of force. . . . In most instances, that will be either the Fourth Amendment's prohibition against unreasonable seizures of the person, or the Eighth Amendment's ban on cruel and unusual punishments, which are the two primary sources of constitutional protection against physically abusive governmental conduct. . . .

Today we make explicit what is implicit in *Garner's* analysis, and hold that *all* claims that law-enforcement officers have used excessive force—deadly or not—in the course of an arrest, investigatory stop, or other "seizure" of a free citizen should be analyzed under the Fourth Amendment and its "reasonableness" standard. . . .

The "reasonableness" of a particular use of force must be judged from the perspective of a reasonable officer on the scene, rather than with the 20/20 vision of hindsight. . . . The calculus of reasonableness must embody allowance for the fact that police officers are often forced to make split-second judgments—in circumstances that are tense, uncertain, and rapidly evolving—about the amount of force that is necessary in a particular situation.

As in other Fourth Amendment contexts, however, the "reasonableness" inquiry in an excessive force case is an objective one: the question is whether the officer's actions are "objectively reasonable" in light of the facts and circumstances confronting them, without regard to their underlying intent or motivation.

Exactly how *Tennessee v. Garner* is affected by *Graham* remains to be seen. There are two theories. First, some contend that *Graham* emasculates *Tennessee v. Garner* by overruling the dangerousness standard. That is, in cases where deadly force is used, it need not be shown that the person posed a danger to the police or another—it only has to be proved that the use of the force was reasonable. The second theory, similar to the first, contends that all claims of excessive force are to be judged under the reasonableness standard, but that *Tennessee v. Garner* sets a threshold: that the use of deadly force on a non-dangerous fleeing suspect is *per se* unreasonable. Under the first theory, a jury would be permitted to determine whether the use of deadly force on a non-dangerous fleeing felon was reasonable. Using the second theory, if a jury decided that the victim of deadly force did not pose a danger, they would not be permitted to return a finding that the officer's actions were reasonable.

Finally, note that police officers are often put into positions where they must defend themselves, such as during an arrest. The same rules discussed earlier concerning self-defense apply in these situations, with one exception: police officers are not required to retreat. Thus, if a police officer is involved in an arrest that involves escalating violence, it is possible that the police officer may have to use deadly force to defend against the criminal's attack.

Arrests by Citizens. At common law, a private citizen was privileged to arrest those who committed a felony or misdemeanor (which amounted to a breach of the peace) in his presence. Some jurisdictions have retained this rule and others have changed it by statute.

In jurisdictions that have changed the rule, it is common to permit so-called *citizens' arrests* any time probable cause exists to believe that the person has committed a felony. In most jurisdictions a citizen may not arrest a misdemeanant unless the person making the arrest witnessed the crime. Even in such cases, only certain misdemeanors may lead to such an arrest.

The reason for these rules is to provide citizens who make such arrests with immunity from civil and criminal prosecution. However, the citizen must be privileged to make the arrest and, even when privileged, a reasonable amount of force must be used.

In some jurisdictions, a private person making an arrest may use deadly force only when the person is in fact a felon. The jurisdictions employing this rule are split: some permit the use of deadly force by private citizens to arrest for any felony and others only for specific felonies (e.g., murder and rape). These jurisdictions are similar in one important regard. The person against whom the deadly force is used must have *in fact* committed the crime. A reasonable, but incorrect, belief that the person has committed a crime is not a defense. So, if Pat kills Sam while attempting to arrest Sam for a crime he did not commit, Pat is liable for manslaughter, even though she had a reasonable belief that he committed the crime. Some states have followed the Model Penal Code approach, which prohibits the use of deadly force by private persons in all circumstances.[26]

The results are different if a private person is assisting a law enforcement officer. In fact, many states have statutes that require citizens to assist police officers upon order. In such cases, the private party is privileged to use whatever force is reasonable. In addition, a private person responding to a police officer's order to assist in an arrest is privileged, even if the police officer was exceeding his or her authority and had no cause to make the arrest. In such instances, the police officer may be liable for both his or her own actions and the actions of the private party summoned. Of course, there are limits to the rule. For example, a private person who obeys a police officer's order to strike an already apprehended and subdued criminal would not be privileged.

INFANCY

At common law, it was a complete defense to a charge that the accused was a child under the age of seven at the time the crime was committed. It was irrebuttably presumed that children under seven were incapable of forming the requisite mens rea to commit a crime. A rebuttable presumption of incapacity existed for those between seven and fourteen years of age. The presumption could be overcome for those between seven and fourteen if the prosecution could prove that the defendant understood that the criminal act was wrong.

Few minors are charged with crimes today. This is the result of the advent of the juvenile court systems in the United States. Currently each state has a juvenile court system that deals with juvenile delinquency and neglected children.

Statutes vary, but it is common for juvenile courts to be given exclusive jurisdiction over criminal behavior of juveniles. However, some states give concurrent jurisdiction to criminal courts and juvenile courts. If concurrent, the juvenile court usually must waive jurisdiction before the criminal court can hear the case. Determining who is a juvenile also differs, with some jurisdictions utilizing a method similar to the common law (irrebuttable and rebuttable presumptions) and others simply setting an age cutoff, such as fourteen or sixteen.

The purpose of the juvenile justice system differs from that of the criminal justice system. Whereas criminal law has punishment as one of its major purposes, the purpose of the juvenile system is not to punish, but to reform the delinquent child.

INTOXICATION

In this context, *intoxication* refers to all situations in which a person's mental or physical abilities are impaired by drugs or alcohol. It is generally said that voluntary intoxication is a defense if it has the effect of negating the required mens rea. In common-law language, this means that if intoxication prevents a defendant from being able to form a specific intent, then the crime is reduced to a similar general-intent crime. For the crime of murder, intoxication is a defense if it prevents the defendant from forming the premeditation, deliberation, or purposeful element. In such cases the charge is reduced from first-degree to second-degree murder. Not all states recognize voluntary intoxication as a defense.

In the rare case of involuntary intoxication, the defendant is relieved of liability entirely. To be successful with such a claim, the defendant is required to show that the intoxication had the same effect as insanity. In jurisdictions using the M'Naghten test for insanity, a defendant is required to prove that the intoxication prevented him or her from knowing right from wrong.

MISTAKE

People may be mistaken in two ways. First, one may believe that some act is legal when it is not. This is a mistake of law. Second, a person may not understand all the facts of a given situation. This is a mistake of fact. As a general proposition, mistake of fact is a defense, and mistake of law is not. However, many exceptions to each rule have been developed. A few of these exceptions are noted here.

Mistake of fact is a defense whenever it negates the mens rea aspect of a crime. For example, an intent to steal another's property is an element of theft. If an attorney picks up a briefcase believing it to be his when it is actually someone else's, it is not theft. The mistake negates the intent to steal. To be valid, mistakes must be made honestly and in good faith.

Although honest mistakes of fact usually constitute a defense, there are exceptions. One exception is obvious: strict liability crimes, as there is no requirement of mens rea to negate.

In some instances, an honest but unreasonable mistake of fact may not eliminate culpability entirely; however, it may reduce the crime. The imperfect self-defense previously discussed falls into this category.

We have all heard, if not quipped, "Ignorance of the law is no excuse." As a general rule, this statement is true. There are two situations in which a person can make a mistake of law. The first occurs when an individual is unaware that his or her actions are prohibited by statute: "I didn't know it was against the law not to file a tax return!" The second occurs when a person takes an act, under the color of a legal right and in good faith, only to find out later that the act was illegal. For example, a landlord may have a reasonable, but mistaken, belief that she has a right to take possessions from a tenant's house to satisfy a delinquent rent debt.

For the most part, unawareness that an act is illegal is not a defense. The law presumes that everyone knows what is legal and what is not. Mistakes that fall into the second group act to negate mens rea and are more likely to be successful. The landlord in the example would not be guilty of larceny because of the mistake. Another example of such a defense is when a person has a reasonable, but mistaken, belief that he or she has the authority to take a person into custody. Therefore, officers who arrest people in good faith, but without probable cause, are not guilty of kidnapping or criminal confinement.

Another exception to the rule that mistake of law is no defense exists when a person relies on statutes, judicial opinions, or certain administrative decisions that later turn out to be wrong. The rule is sound for two reasons. First, as a matter of public policy it is not wise to prosecute people for acting in conformity with the law. The result would be individual interpretation of all laws and disregard for those statutes, regulations, or judicial decisions believed incorrect. Second, as a matter of due process, it appears that no notice has been provided that compliance with the law will be punished.

Finally, one defense that is not accepted is reliance on the advice of counsel. If a lawyer advises a client that a particular act is legal when it is not, the client will be liable for the crime if the act is taken.

ENTRAPMENT

entrapment
The act of government officials (usually police) or agents inducing a person to commit a crime that the person would not have committed without the inducement.

To what extent should police officers be permitted to encourage someone to commit a crime? This question underlies the defense of **entrapment.** Entrapment occurs when law enforcement officers encourage another to commit a crime with the intent of arresting and prosecuting that person for the commission of that crime.

Perjury traps are another form of entrapment. Perjury traps are committed by prosecutors whenever they inquire of a witness as to matters that are tangential or peripheral to an investigation in order to catch the witness in perjury.[27]

Entrapment is a defense of recent development, although all states and the federal government recognize some form of the defense today. There is no constitutional basis for the entrapment defense, so each jurisdiction is free to structure the defense in any manner. Of course, a state may also do away with the defense, although none have done so. This is a sound policy decision, as most people would agree that there must be some limit on police conduct. However, where the line should be drawn is debated. Currently two tests are used to determine whether a defendant was entrapped: the subjective and objective tests.

The test used in the federal system and most widely used by the states is the subjective test. The test attempts to distinguish between those who are predisposed to commit crime from those who are not. The test is subjective; the defendant's mental state at the time of the encouragement is imperative. A defendant is predisposed if he or she is ready to commit the crime and is only awaiting the opportunity. The Supreme Court has said that the subjective test is designed to draw a line between the "unwary innocent and the unwary criminal."[28]

Under the subjective approach, evidence of the defendant's criminal record may be relevant to show predisposition. For example, recent drug convictions may evidence a predisposition to enter into future drug purchases or sales.

The second method of determining whether a person was entrapped is objective. The Model Penal Code[29] adopts this approach, as do a minority of states. The objective approach does not focus on the particular defendant's predisposition, but asks whether the police conduct creates a "substantial risk that an offense will be committed by persons other than those who are ready to commit it."[30]

The defendant's actual state of mind is not relevant to this inquiry, and, accordingly, evidence of a defendant's criminal history is irrelevant. Under this approach, a defendant may be acquitted even though he or she was predisposed to commit the crime. Suppose a police officer offers a prostitute $150,000 for sex. The prostitute would have agreed had the officer offered $50. Using the subjective approach, the prostitute would be convicted because she was predisposed to engage in prostitution. However, in jurisdictions using the objective test, she may have been entrapped, as women who do not normally sell sex might be encouraged to do so for $150,000.

In many states entrapment may not be used to defend against crimes involving violence to people, such as battery and murder. The Model Penal Code also takes this view.

ALIBI AND CONSENT

Alibi and consent are two factual defenses. An **alibi** is a claim by a defendant that he or she was not present at the scene of the crime at the time it was committed. Whenever a defendant asserts an alibi, he or she is simply refuting the government's factual claims. Alibi is an affirmative defense and defendants are usually required to give the government notice of the alibi claim prior to trial. Alibi notice laws have been approved by the Supreme Court.[31] Of course, the government must prove the elements of the crime (e.g., presence at the crime) beyond a reasonable doubt. This means that the defendant bears no burden in an alibi defense.

Victim **consent** is a defense to some crimes, such as rape or larceny. That is, if a person consents to sex or to give you his property, there is no crime. Consent is, however, not a defense to many crimes, such as statutory rape, incest, child molestation, battery, and murder.

STATUTES OF LIMITATION

Many crimes must be prosecuted within a specified time after being committed. A **statute of limitation** sets the time limit. If prosecution is initiated after the applicable statute has expired, the defendant is entitled to a dismissal.

alibi
(Latin) "Elsewhere"; the claim that at the time a crime was committed a person was somewhere else. [pronounce: *al*-eh-bi]

consent
Voluntary and active agreement.

statute of limitation
Federal and state statutes prescribing the maximum period of time during which various types of civil actions and criminal prosecutions can be brought after the occurrence of the injury or the offense.

Statutes vary in length, and serious crimes, such as murder, have no limitation. Generally, the higher the crime, the longer the statute. Statutes begin running when the crime occurs; however, statutes may be tolled in some situations. *Tolling* refers to stopping the clock. The time during which a defendant is a fugitive is commonly tolled. For example, assume that the limitation on felony assault is six years. The assault was committed on June 1, 2002. Normally, prosecution would have to be started by June 1, 2008. However, if the defendant was fugitive from June 1, 2003 to June 1, 2004, then the statute would be tolled, and the new date of limitation would be June 1, 2009.

At common law there were no limitations. Statutes of limitation are legislative creations. There is no constitutional basis for limiting the time in which to prosecute someone for criminal behavior. This being so, legislatures are free to alter or abolish statutes of limitation. If there is no limitation fixed, prosecution may occur any time after the crime.

Sometimes a prosecution for a serious crime may begin after the statute on a lesser included crime has expired. For example, battery is a lesser included crime of aggravated battery. Assume that aggravated battery has a six-year statute and battery three. In most jurisdictions, a prosecutor may not circumvent the three-year statute by charging aggravated battery and including the lesser battery offense in the information or indictment. After the time has run out on the lesser offense, but not on the more serious offense, the defendant is either convicted of the greater offense or acquitted, but can no longer be convicted on the lesser offense. However, at least one jurisdiction does not follow this rule.[32]

WEB LINKS

International and Comparative Law
Several sites contain government, law, and justice information from many nations and international organizations from around the globe.

At *http://www.lawresearch.com* you will find both United States and foreign government legal information. Hieros Gamos claims to have descriptions and laws from all the nations of the world. It is an excellent site full of text and graphics. The URL is *http://www.hg.org/hg.html*

Constitutions of nations can be found in the following locations:

http://confinder.richmond.edu/
http://www.findlaw.com/01topics/06constitutional/03forconst/index.html

KEY TERMS

affirmative defense	burden of proof	irresistible impulse
alibi	consent	M'Naghten rule
battered woman syndrome	diminished capacity	necessity
burden of going forward	duress	retreat to the wall
(production)	Durham rule	self-defense
burden of persuasion	entrapment	statute of limitations

REVIEW QUESTIONS

1. What are affirmative defenses? How do affirmative defenses differ from other defenses?
2. What are the elements of the M'Naghten test for insanity? Irresistible impulse? Model Penal Code?
3. What must be proven to support a claim of self-defense?
4. What is the retreat doctrine?
5. What is imperfect self-defense? When is it applicable?
6. When may a law enforcement officer use deadly force to stop a fleeing suspect?
7. What is entrapment? What are the two tests used to determine if a defendant was entrapped?
8. May an insane defendant be tried? If not, what standard is used to determine whether the defendant is insane?
9. What is a statute of limitations?
10. Distinguish legal from factual impossibility and state whether a person is criminally culpable in both circumstances.

REVIEW PROBLEMS

1. Should law enforcement be permitted to encourage children to engage in criminal activity with the purpose of arresting and prosecuting the child? Should law enforcement be permitted to use family and friend relationships to induce another to engage in criminal activity with the purpose of arresting and prosecuting the family member or friend? How about preying on another's drug or alcohol addiction?
2. Ira stabbed his good friend, inflicting a fatal wound. At trial, a psychiatrist testified that Ira could not control his behavior, as he has a brain tumor that causes him to act violently. The doctor also testified that the condition did not impair Ira's ability to know what he was doing or that it was wrong. Assume that the jury believes the psychiatrist's explanation. Would Ira be convicted in a jurisdiction that uses the M'Naghten test? The irresistible impulse test? The Model Penal Code?
3. Jane was attacked by an unknown man. She was able to free herself and ran to a nearby house, with the man chasing close behind. She screamed and knocked at the door of the house. The occupants of the house opened the door and she requested refuge. The occupant refused, but Jane forced her way into the house. To gain entry, Jane had to strike the occupant. Once inside, she used the telephone to contact the police, who responded within minutes. At the insistence of the occupants of the house, Jane has been charged with trespass and battery. Does she have a defense?
4. Gary and Gene were both drinking at a bar. Gary became angered after Gene asked Gary's

wife to dance. Gary walked up to Gene and struck him in the face. Gene fell to the floor, and as he was returning to his feet Gary hit him again. In response, Gene took a knife out of his pocket and attacked Gary with it. Gary then shot Gene with a gun he had hidden in his coat. The injury proved fatal. What crime has Gary committed?

END NOTES

1. *M'Naghten's Case*, 8 Eng. Rep. 718 (H.L. 1843).
2. LaFave & Scott, *Criminal Law* § 4.2A(a) (Hornbook Series, St. Paul: West, 1986).
3. *State v. Johnson*, 290 N.W. 159 (Wis. 1940).
4. Model Penal Code, Tent. Draft 4, at 156.
5. LaFave & Scott at § 4.2(d).
6. *United States v. Brawner*, 471 F.2d 969 (D.C. Cir. 1972).
7. Model Penal Code § 4.01(1).
8. 18 U.S.C. § 17.
9. Justine A. Dunlap, "What's Competence Got To Do With It: The Right Not To Be Acquitted by Reason of Insanity," 50 *Okla. L. Rev.* 495 (1997).
10. 18 Pa. C.S.A. § 314.
11. 18 U.S.C. § 3006A(e)(3).
12. 18 U.S.C. § 17.
13. Model Penal Code § 4.08.
14. 18 U.S.C. § 4243(a).
15. 18 U.S.C. § 4243(f).
16. *Dusky v. United States*, 362 U.S. 402 (1960).
17. 517 U.S. 348.
18. *Jackson v. Indiana*, 406 U.S. 715 (1972).
19. *Ford v. Wainwright*, 477 U.S. 399 (1986).
20. *Id.* at 417.
21. *Atkins v. Virginia* 122 S.Ct. 2242 (2002).
22. *See* LaFave & Scott at § 5.3(g).
23. Model Penal Code § 3.04(2)(b)(ii).
24. Model Penal Code § 3.06(d).
25. Model Penal Code § 3.06(5).
26. Model Penal Code § 3.07(2)(b)(ii).
27. *See Vermont v. Tonzola*, 621 A.2d 243 (Vt. 1993).
28. *Sherman v. United States*, 356 U.S. 369 (1958).
29. Model Penal Code § 2.13.
30. Model Penal Code § 2.13(2).
31. *Williams v. Florida*, 399 U.S. 78 (1970).
32. 21 Am. Jur. 2d 225 (1990); *State v. Borucki*, 505 A.2d 89 (Me. 1986).

CHAPTER 9

Constitutional Defenses

CHAPTER OUTLINE

Introduction

Double Jeopardy

Self-Incrimination and Immunity

Due Process and Equal Protection

Vagueness and Overbreadth

Ex Post Facto and Bills of Attainder

First Amendment and Religion

First Amendment and Speech

Privacy and Other Unenumerated Rights

CHAPTER OBJECTIVES

In this chapter, you should:

- learn several constitutional provisions and amendments that are commonly invoked in criminal cases.

- learn common constitutional defenses to criminal accusations.

- continue to develop your case analysis and legal reasoning skills.

INTRODUCTION

A variety of defenses arise from the United States Constitution. Most of these rights are found in the First nine amendments. You have already learned a few of these, such as the First Amendment's protection of expression. In addition, many rights that are procedural, such as the right to a speedy trial, are discussed later. A few critical defenses have been chosen for discussion here.

Be aware that each state has its own constitution, which may provide greater protection than the United States Constitution. During this discussion you may want to refer to the United States Constitution, which is reprinted as Appendix A of this text.

DOUBLE JEOPARDY

double jeopardy
A second prosecution by the same government against the same person for the same crime (or for a lesser included offense) once the first prosecution is totally finished and decided. This is prohibited by the U.S. Constitution.

The Fifth Amendment to the United States Constitution provides that "no person shall be subject for the same offense to be twice put in jeopardy of life or limb." The principle of not punishing someone twice for the same act can be found back as far as Blackstone's Commentaries.[1] The **Double Jeopardy** Clause applies only to criminal proceedings.

There are actually two prohibitions in the Double Jeopardy Clause. The clause prevents: (1) a second prosecution for the same offense and (2) a second punishment for the same offense.

Often the question is whether a prior "jeopardy" occurred. It is generally held that a person has been put in jeopardy once a plea of guilty has been entered and accepted by a court. An unapproved plea will not suffice, and a subsequent prosecution will not be prohibited by the Double Jeopardy Clause. In jury trials, jeopardy attaches once a jury has been selected and sworn. States treat bench trials differently, although the prevailing view is that jeopardy attaches once the first witness has been sworn.

Once jeopardy attaches, the defendant may not be tried again. However, there are a few exceptions. A defendant may be retried if the first trial was terminated by a properly declared mistrial. Mistrials may be declared for a variety of reasons. Death of the trial judge or one of the participating attorneys would likely result in a mistrial. If a witness blurts out an answer to a question before the judge has an opportunity to sustain an objection to the question, and the answer is extremely prejudicial, a mistrial may be declared. The causes of a mistrial are endless. Note that the mistrial must be proper. That is, if an appellate court later determines that a mistrial should not have been declared, the defendant has been put into jeopardy. It is always proper to retry a defendant whose prior trial was declared a mistrial upon the defendant's motion. If a defendant objects to a government motion for a mistrial, there must be a "manifest necessity" (darn good reason) for the mistrial.[2]

It is also not a violation of the Fifth Amendment to prosecute a defendant who was previously charged, but whose charges were dismissed prior to jeopardy attaching. Additionally, if a defendant appeals a conviction and prevails, the defendant may be retried, unless the appellate court finds that insufficient evidence exists to retry the defendant. However, if a defendant is acquitted on a serious charge and convicted on a lesser and then prevails on appeal, he or she may be retried only on the lesser. It is violative of the Fifth Amendment to retry the defendant on the more serious offense. Whether a defendant may be retried following government appeals has been an issue in many cases. Clearly, the government may not win a new trial following an acquittal. However, a conviction may be reinstated by an appellate court if a trial court's order setting aside the conviction is found invalid.[3] But an appellate court may not order a new trial where the trial judge entered a judgment of acquittal following a hung jury.[4] The outcomes in this area of law are dependent upon what judgment is first entered by the trial court. If it is a conviction, then an appellate court may tamper with trial judge reversals of convictions. If it is an acquittal, then double jeopardy bars acting further against the accused.

The Supreme Court has also held that double jeopardy does not bar correcting a sentence on appeal or rehearing because such a procedure is not retrial of an "offense." However, the outcome may be different if resentencing results in the application of the death penalty.[5]

The Fifth Amendment only forbids retrial for the same offense. Determining whether two acts constitute the same offense is not always an easy task. Two offenses are the same unless one requires proof of a fact that the other does not.[6] This is the "same evidence test."

The Double Jeopardy Clause is fully applicable to the states through the Fourteenth Amendment. However, the clause does not prevent second punishments for the same offense by different sovereigns. For example, a person who robs a federally insured bank may be prosecuted by both the state where the bank resides and the United States. This is true even though the offenses arise from the same acts. Although the Double Jeopardy Clause does not prohibit two sovereigns from prosecuting for the same offense, many states prohibit this by statute. In practice, and sometimes by policy, most prosecutors do not pursue a defendant who has been previously prosecuted in another jurisdiction for the same crime. The Model Penal Code incorporates this approach in certain circumstances.[7] Municipalities are not independent beings; they owe their existence not to the Constitution of the United States, but to a state. Accordingly, prosecutions by cities are treated as being brought by the state, and it is a violation of the Double Jeopardy Clause for a state and city to punish one for the same offense.

SELF-INCRIMINATION AND IMMUNITY

The Fifth Amendment also states that no person "shall be compelled in any criminal case to be a witness against himself." The following passage explains why the framers of the Constitution included a privilege against self-incrimination.

> Perhaps the best-known provision of the Fifth Amendment is the clause against forced "self-incrimination," whose origin goes back to England where persons accused of crimes before ecclesiastical courts were forced to take an ex officio

oath. That is, they had to swear to answer all questions even if the questions did not apply to the case at trial. This requirement was later adopted by the Court of Star Chamber. One of the victims of the Court was a printer and book distributor named John Lilburne, charged in 1637 with treason for importing books "that promoted Puritan dissent." Lilburne told his accusers, "I am not willing to answer to you any more of these questions because I see you go about by this examination to ensnare me. For seeing the things for which I am imprisoned cannot be proved against me, you will get other material out of my examination; and therefore if you will not ask me about the thing laid to my charge, I shall answer no more. . . . I think by the law of the land, that I may stand upon my just defense." Lilburne was convicted, fined, whipped, pilloried, and gagged, and imprisoned until he agreed to take the oath. . . .

One notorious instance of forced self-incrimination in the American colonies occurred in the Salem witch trials. In 1692, Giles Corey, an elderly Massachusetts farmer, was accused of witchcraft. He knew whether he pleaded guilty or not guilty he would be convicted and executed and his property confiscated. So to assure that his heirs inherited his property, he refused to plead and thus could not be convicted. The judges ordered him strapped to a table, and stones were loaded upon his chest to force the plea out of him. Corey's final words were "more weight." Then his chest caved in.[8]

John Bradshaw, John Lilburne's attorney, stated it best when he said that "It is contrary to the laws of God, nature and the kingdom for any man to be his own accuser."

Generally, the Amendment prohibits the government from compelling people to testify when incrimination is possible. Most people have heard of "pleading the Fifth." However, if immunity from prosecution is granted to a witness, he or she may be compelled to testify. If a witness refuses to testify because of the fear of self-incrimination, the government may offer the witness immunity from prosecution so that the testimony may be compelled. There are two types of immunity: transactional and derivative use.

transactional immunity
Freedom from prosecution for all crimes related to the compelled testimony, so long as the witness tells the truth.

Transactional immunity shields the witness from prosecution for all offenses related to his or her testimony. For example, if a witness testifies concerning a robbery, the government may not prosecute the witness for that robbery, even though the government may have evidence of guilt independent of the witness's testimony. Transactional immunity gives more protection to the witness than required by the Constitution, so when it is granted a witness may be ordered to testify.

use immunity
Freedom from prosecution based on the compelled testimony and on anything the government learns from following up on the testimony.

The minimum immunity that must be provided a witness to overcome a Fifth Amendment claim is derivative **use immunity.** This prohibits the government from using the witness's testimony or any evidence derived from that testimony to prosecute the witness. However, all evidence that is independently obtained may be used against the witness.

Use immunity only prohibits the government from using the witness's testimony against him or her. Statutes that provide only for use immunity are unconstitutional, as derivative use is the minimum protection required by the Fifth Amendment.

States vary in how immunity is granted. Some permit the prosecutor to give the immunity; others require both the request of the prosecutor and the approval of the trial judge.

A person may also waive the Fifth Amendment privilege against self-incrimination. Generally, once a person testifies freely, the privilege is waived as to the subject discussed during the same proceeding. A witness (or defendant) may not testify selectively concerning a subject. It is often said that testifying to a fact waives to the details. This prevents a witness from testifying only to the information beneficial to one party and then refusing to testify further, even though he or she may have omitted important facts. However, a witness may not be compelled to testify if there is a chance of incriminating himself or herself beyond the original testimony.

The fact that a witness may waive the Fifth Amendment privilege against self-incrimination on one occasion does not mean it is waived forever. First, a defendant (or witness) may speak to the police during the investigative stage and later refuse to testify at trial, provided such testimony may be incriminating. Second, it is generally held that a person who testifies before a grand jury without claiming the Fifth does not waive the right to raise the defense at trial. Third, even within the same proceeding a person may invoke the Fifth Amendment privilege against self-incrimination if the two hearings are separate and distinct. For example, a defendant may testify at a suppression hearing without waiving the privilege not to testify at trial.

Finally, the Fifth Amendment applies to all proceedings, whether civil, criminal, or administrative.[9] Therefore, a person called to testify in a civil proceeding may invoke the Fifth Amendment's privilege and refuse to testify.

DUE PROCESS AND EQUAL PROTECTION

The Fifth Amendment to the United States Constitution prohibits the government from depriving a person of life, liberty, or property without due process of law. This Amendment acts to constrain the power of the federal government. You have previously learned that the Fourteenth Amendment has similar language and constrains the power of state governments.

The Fourteenth Amendment expressly requires the states to extend equal protection of the laws to the people. There is no express equal protection clause in the Fifth Amendment, but the Supreme Court has found it to be implied in the Due Process Clause. Equal protection concerns classifications and discrimination.

Discrimination is not inherently evil. Students discriminate between professors, possibly due to grading policy or teaching skill, when deciding what courses to enroll in. Governments also discriminate and make classifications, most of which are sensible and acceptable. For example, those who commit homicides are divided into groups: murderers, manslaughterers, and those who are excused or justified in killing. When classifications are based upon meaningful criteria (e.g., mens rea), the law is valid. However, our society has decided that certain classifications are improper and violative of equal protection. A classification between those who exercise a constitutional right and those who do not, if it results in prosecution or increased punishment for the former, is unconstitutional. Classifications based on race, religion, gender, and other immutable conditions are suspect and possibly violative of equal protection.

These clauses are important to criminal law and particularly to criminal procedure. Due process requires the government to treat people fairly; therefore, whenever a law or other governmental action appears to be unfair, there is a due process issue. In a sense, due process is a safety net, protecting the individual when another specific constitutional provision does not.

Due process has two aspects, substantive and procedural. The protection of privacy discussed later in this chapter is an example of substantive due process. On the procedural side, due process is the constitutional source of the **principle of legality,** which requires that criminal laws (and punishments) be written and enacted before an act may be punished. This is a notice concept. It would be unfair to announce that an act is illegal, or increase its punishment, after that act has been committed. You will learn later in this chapter that overly broad or vague laws may be violative of due process.

Through the Fourteenth Amendment's Due Process Clause, most of the provisions of the Bill of Rights, which initially applied only against the federal government, have been extended to the states. Today, the Fourth Amendment's right to be free from unreasonable searches and seizures, the Fifth Amendment's right to be free from self-incrimination, the Sixth Amendment's right to counsel at critical stages of criminal adjudications, and the Eighth Amendment's prohibition of cruel and unusual punishment are among the many rights that are now available to defendants in state courts.

In some instances, due process or equal protection increases the scope of a right found in the Bill of Rights. For example, the Sixth Amendment's right to counsel is limited to the critical stages of criminal proceedings. Appeals are not critical stages, and therefore the Sixth Amendment does not mandate counsel. But the Supreme Court has held that if a state provides for felony appeals by right, then the Equal Protection Clause requires that indigent defendants receive appointed counsel. To hold otherwise would unfairly discriminate against the indigent.[10]

Although the Fourteenth Amendment is the source of the incorporation of most of the Bill of Rights, its importance extends beyond this. Any time an issue of fairness surfaces, due process should be examined. If the issue concerns one of improper classifications, equal protection law should be considered. The Supreme Court stated of substantive due process:

> The inescapable fact is that adjudication of substantive due process claims may call upon the Court in interpreting the Constitution to exercise that same capacity which by tradition courts always have exercised: reasoned judgment. Its boundaries are not susceptible of expression as a simple rule. That does not mean we are free to invalidate state policy choices with which we disagree: yet neither does it permit us to shrink from the duties of our office. As Justice Harlan observed: "Due process has not been reduced to any formula: its content cannot be determined by reference to any code. The best that can be said is that through the course of this Court's decisions it has represented the balance which

principle of legality
The procedural side of due process, which requires that criminal laws (and punishments) be written and enacted before an act may be punished.

our Nation, built upon postulates of respect for liberty of the individual, has struck between that liberty and the demands of organized society."

VAGUENESS AND OVERBREADTH

The Due Process Clauses of the Fifth and Fourteenth Amendments to the United States Constitution are the foundation of the void-for-vagueness and overbreadth doctrines.

A statute is void for **vagueness** whenever "men of common intelligence must necessarily guess at its meaning and differ as to its application."[11] As to the meaning of a statute, confusion among lower courts, resulting in varying interpretations, is evidence of vagueness.[12] The Supreme Court has held that uncertain statutes do not provide notice of what conduct is forbidden and are violative of due process. The Court has also found statutes that permit arbitrary or discriminatory enforcement void. That is, if the police or courts are given unlimited authority to decide who will be prosecuted, the statute is invalid.

It has been under the void-for-vagueness doctrine that many vagrancy laws have been attacked. If it were not for the doctrine, legislatures could draft statutes so that nearly everyone would be engaged in criminal activity at one time or another, and police and prosecutors would have the unfettered discretion to decide who to arrest and prosecute.

A closely related doctrine is **overbreadth.** A statute is overbroad if it includes within its grasp not only unprotected activity, but also activity protected by the Constitution. For example, in one case a city ordinance made it illegal for "one or more persons to assemble" on a sidewalk and conduct themselves in an annoying manner. The United States Supreme Court found that the law was unconstitutional not only because it made unprotected activity illegal (fighting words or riotous activity), but it also included activity that is protected by the First Amendment's free assembly and association provisions.[13] It is possible for a statute to be clear and precise (not vague), but overbroad.

EX POST FACTO AND BILLS OF ATTAINDER

Article I of the United States Constitution prohibits the state and federal governments from enacting both ex post facto laws and bills of attainder.

An **ex post facto law** is one that (1) makes an act illegal after the act was taken, (2) increases the punishment or severity of a crime after it occurred, (3) changes the procedural rules so as to increase the chances of conviction after the crime occurs. In short, a government may not make criminal law retroactive, if doing so is detrimental to the defendant. However, changes that benefit a defendant may be applied retroactively. So, if a legislature increases the prosecution's burden of proof after a defendant has committed a crime, but before trial, the legislature may make the change applicable to the defendant. The clause advances the notice theory (due process) and also prevents malicious legislative action from being taken against a particular person.

vagueness doctrine

The *vagueness doctrine* is the rule that a criminal law may be unconstitutional if it does not clearly say what is required or prohibited, what punishment may be imposed, or what persons may be affected. A law that violates due process of law in this way is *void for vagueness.*

overbreadth doctrine

A law will be declared void for *overbreadth* if it attempts to punish speech or conduct that is protected by the Constitution and if it is impossible to eliminate the unconstitutional part of the law without invalidating the whole law.

ex post facto law

(Latin) After the fact. An *ex post facto* law is one that retroactively attempts to make an action a crime that was not a crime at the time it was done, or a law that attempts to reduce a person's rights based on a past act that was not subject to the law when it was done.

bill of attainder
A legislative act pronouncing a person guilty (usually of treason) without a trial and sentencing the person to death and attainder. This is now prohibited by the U.S. Constitution.

A **bill of attainder** is a legislative act punishing a person without a judicial trial. This provision reinforces the concept of separation of powers. It is the duty of the legislative branch to make the laws, and it is the duty of the judicial branch to determine who has violated those laws.

In a few instances, however, Congress may act in a judicial role. Congress may punish those who disrupt its functions for contempt. In addition, Congress is authorized by the Constitution to conduct impeachment hearings of the president, federal judges, and other federal officers and to discipline its own members.

FIRST AMENDMENT AND RELIGION

The First Amendment contains a large number of protections, including freedom of the press; freedom to choose and practice a religion; freedom of speech; and freedom to peaceably assemble. Although the First Amendment is only directly applicable against the national government, the Fourteenth Amendment extends its prohibitions to the states.

Concerning freedom of religion, the First Amendment states that "Congress shall make no law respecting an establishment of religion, or prohibiting the free exercise thereof." The free exercise clause is of the most importance in criminal law. The freedom to believe is, of course, absolute. Any law prohibiting a certain religious belief is void. However, the Supreme Court has held that some religious practices may be regulated.

To determine whether a specific religious act may be criminalized, the governmental interest in regulating the behavior is balanced against the First Amendment infringement. If the governmental interest is greater than the infringement, then a state may regulate the conduct. For example, it has been held that the Mormon practice of polygamy may be regulated.[14] Also, a parent who depends upon prayer to save a dying child may be charged with manslaughter for failing to seek competent medical care. In this instance the state's interest in protecting the child's life outweighs the parent's interest in practicing his or her religion in such a manner.

On the other side, the California Supreme Court disallowed the conviction of a member of the Native American Church for possession of peyote, a drug made from cactus. The court found that peyote was an important part of worship in the Native American Church, and, as such, California's interest in regulating the use of the drug was outweighed by the drug's religious significance.[15] Note that the United States Supreme Court took the opposite view concerning the use of peyote in *Department of Human Resources v. Smith*, 494 U.S. 872 (1990), wherein the Court stated that

> [T]he right of free exercise does not relieve an individual of the obligation to comply with a valid and neutral law of general applicability on the ground that the law proscribes (or prescribes) conduct that his religion prescribes (or proscribes).

In the *Hialeah* case, the Supreme Court invalidated several ordinances that prohibited the adherents of Santeria from sacrificing animals as part of their religious rites.

 CASE

CHURCH OF LUKUMI BABALU AYE, INC. V. HIALEAH

113 S. Ct. 2217 (1993)

This case involves practices of the Santeria religion, which originated in the nineteenth century. When hundreds of thousands of members of the Yoruba people were brought as slaves from eastern Africa to Cuba, their traditional African religion absorbed significant elements of Roman Catholicism. The resulting syncretion, or fusion, is Santeria, "the way of the saints." The Cuban Yoruba express their devotion to spirits, called *orishas,* through the iconography of Catholic saints, Catholic symbols are often present at Santeria rites, and Santeria devotees attend the Catholic sacraments. . . .

The Santeria faith teaches that every individual has a destiny from God, a destiny fulfilled with the aid and energy of orishas. The basis of the Santeria religion is the nurture of a personal relation with the orishas, and one of the principal forms of devotion is an animal sacrifice. . . . The sacrifice of animals as part of religious rituals has ancient roots. . . . Animal sacrifice is mentioned throughout the Old Testament . . . and it played an important role in the practice of Judaism before destruction of the second Temple in Jerusalem. . . . In modern Islam, there is an annual sacrifice commemorating Abraham's sacrifice of a ram in the stead of his son. . . .

According to Santeria teaching, the orishas are powerful but not immortal. They depend for survival on the sacrifice.

Santeria adherents faced widespread persecution in Cuba, so the religion and its rituals were practiced in secret. The open practice of Santeria and its rites remains infrequent. . . . The religion was brought to this Nation most often by exiles from the Cuban revolution. The District Court estimated that there are at least 50,000 practitioners in South Florida today.

Petitioner Church of Lukumi Babalu Aye, Inc. (Church), is a not-for-profit corporation organized under Florida law in 1973. The Church and its congregants practice the Santeria religion. The president of the Church is petitioner Ernesto Pichardo, who is also the Church's priest and holds the religious title of Italero, the second highest in the Santeria faith. In April 1987, the Church leased land in the city of Hialeah, Florida, and announced plans to establish a house of worship as well as a school, cultural center, and museum. Pichardo indicated that the Church's goal was to bring the practice of the Santeria faith, including its ritual of animal sacrifice, into the open.

The Church began the process of obtaining utility service and receiving the necessary licensing, inspection, and zoning approvals. Although the Church's efforts at obtaining the necessary licenses and permits were far from smooth . . . it appears that it received all needed approvals by early August 1987.

The prospect of a Santeria church in their midst was distressing to many members of the Hialeah community, and the announcement of the plans to open a Santeria church in Hialeah prompted the city council to hold an emergency public session on June 9, 1987. [The city council enacted ordinance] 87–66, which noted the "concern" expressed by residents of the city "that certain religions may propose to engage in practices which are inconsistent with public morals, peace or safety," and declared that "[t]he City reiterates its commitment to a prohibition against any and all acts of any and all religious groups which are inconsistent with public morals, peace or safety."

Next, the council approved an emergency ordinance, Ordinance 87–40, that incorporated in full, except as to penalty, Florida's animal cruelty laws. . . . Among other things, the incorporated state law subjected to criminal punishment "[w]hoever . . . unnecessarily or cruelly . . . kills any animal."

[In September 1987, the city council adopted three additional ordinances prohibiting owning or possessing an animal for purpose of sacrifice and regulating the slaughtering of animals.] Violations of each of the four ordinances were punishable by fines not exceeding $500 or imprisonment not exceeding 60 days, or both.

Following enactment of these ordinances, the Church and Pichardo filed this action pursuant to 42 U.S.C. § 1983 in the United States District Court for the Southern District of Florida. Named as defendants were the city of Hialeah and its mayor and members of its city council in their individual capacities. [The defendants prevailed at the trial and appellate levels.]

. . . The city does not argue that Santeria is not a "religion" within the meaning of the First Amendment. Nor could it. Although the practice of animal sacrifice may seem abhorrent to some, "religious beliefs need not be acceptable, logical, consistent, or comprehensible to others in order to merit First Amendment protection. . . . Given the historical association between animal sacrifice and religious worship . . . petitioners' assertion that animal sacrifice is an integral part of their religion "cannot be deemed bizarre or incredible." . . . Neither the city nor the courts below, moreover, have questioned the sincerity of petitioners' professed desire to conduct animal sacrifices for religious reasons. We must consider petitioners' First Amendment claim.

In addressing the constitutional protection for free exercise of religion, our cases establish the general proposition that a law that is neutral and of general applicability need not be justified by a compelling governmental interest even if the law has the incidental effect of burdening a particular religious practice. . . . Neutrality and general applicability are interrelated, and, as

becomes apparent in this case, failure to satisfy one requirement is a likely indication that the other has not been satisfied. A law failing to satisfy these requirements must be justified by a compelling governmental interest and must be narrowly tailored to advance the interest. These ordinances fail to satisfy the [constitutional] requirements. . . .

There are, of course, many ways of demonstrating that the object or purpose of a law is the suppression of religion or religious conduct. To determine the object of a law, we must begin with its text, for the minimum requirement of neutrality is that a law not discriminate on its face. A law lacks facial neutrality if it refers to a religious practice without a secular meaning discernable from the language or context. Petitioners contend that three of the ordinances fail this test of facial neutrality because they use the words "sacrifice" and "ritual," words with strong religious connotations. . . . We agree that these words are consistent with the claim of facial discrimination, but the argument is not conclusive. The words "sacrifice" and "ritual" have a religious origin, but current use admits also of secular meanings. . . .

We reject the contention advanced by the city . . . that our inquiry must end with the text of the laws at issue. Facial neutrality is not determinative. The Free Exercise Clause, like the Establishment Clause, extends beyond facial discrimination. The Clause "forbids subtle departures from neutrality". . . . The Free Exercise Clause protects against governmental hostility which is masked, as well as overt. "The Court must survey meticulously the circumstances of governmental categories to eliminate, as it were, religious gerrymanders." . . .

The record in this case compels the conclusion that suppression of the central element of the Santeria worship service was the object of the ordinances. First, though the use of the words "sacrifice" and "ritual" does not compel a finding of improper targeting of the Santeria religion, the choice of these words is support for our conclusion. . . . [One of the ordinances] recited that "residents and citizens of the City of Hialeah have expressed their concern that certain religions may propose to engage in practices which are inconsistent with public morals, peace or safety," and "reiterate[d]" the city's commitment to prohibit "any and all [such] acts of any and all religious groups." No one suggests, and on this record it cannot be maintained, that city officials had in mind a religion other than Santeria.

It becomes evident that these ordinances target Santeria sacrifice when the ordinances' operation is considered. Apart from the text, the effect of a law in its real operation is strong evidence of its object. To be sure, adverse impact will not always lead to a finding of impermissible targeting. . . .

It is a necessary conclusion that almost the only conduct subject to [the ordinances] is the religious exercise of Santeria Church members. The texts show that they were drafted in tandem to achieve this purpose. . . . [One of the ordinances] prohibits the sacrifice of animals but defines sacrifice as "to unnecessarily kill . . . an animal in a public or private ritual or ceremony not for the primary purpose of food consumption." The definition excludes almost all killings of animals except for religious sacrifice, and the primary purpose requirement narrows the proscribed category even further, in particular by exempting Kosher slaughter. . . .

The net result of the gerrymander is that few if any killings of animals are prohibited other than Santeria sacrifice, which is proscribed because it occurs during a ritual or ceremony and its primary purpose is to make an offering to the orishas, not food consumption. Indeed, careful drafting ensured that, although Santeria sacrifice is prohibited, killings that are no more necessary or humane in almost all other circumstances are unpunished.

Operating in similar fashion [is another ordinance] which prohibits the "possess[ion], sacrifice, or slaughter" of an animal with the inten[t] to use such animal for food purposes." This prohibition, extending to the keeping of an animal as well as the killing itself, applies if the animal is killed in "any type of ritual". . . . The ordinance exempts, however, "any licensed [food]

establishment" with regard to "any animals which are specifically raised for food purposes," if this activity is permitted by zoning and other laws. This exception, too, seems intended to cover Kosher slaughter. Again, the burden of the ordinance, in practical terms, falls on Santeria adherents but almost no others. . . .

We also find significant evidence of the ordinances' improper targeting of Santeria sacrifice in the fact that they proscribe more religious conduct than is necessary to achieve their stated ends. . . .

The legitimate governmental interests in protecting the public health and preventing cruelty to animals could be addressed by restrictions stopping far short of a flat prohibition of all Santeria sacrificial practice. If improper disposal, not the sacrifice itself, is the harm to be prevented, the city could have imposed a general regulation on the disposal of organic garbage. It did not do so. Indeed, counsel for the city conceded at oral argument that, under the ordinances, Santeria sacrifices would be illegal even if they occurred in licensed, inspected, and zoned slaughterhouses. . . . Thus, these broad ordinances prohibit Santeria sacrifice even when it does not threaten the city's interest in the public health. . . .

Respondent claims that [the ordinances] advance two interests: protecting the public health and preventing cruelty to animals. The ordinances are underinclusive for those ends. They fail to prohibit nonreligious conduct that endangers these interests in a similar or greater degree than Santeria sacrifice does. The underinclusion is substantial, not inconsequential. Despite the city's proffered interest in preventing cruelty to animals, the ordinances are drafted with care to forbid few killings but those occasioned by religious sacrifice. Many types of animal deaths or kills for nonreligious reasons are either not prohibited or approved by express provision. For example, fishing . . . is legal. Extermination of mice and rats within a home is also permitted. Florida law incorporated by [the ordinances] sanctions euthanasia of "stray, neglected, abandoned, or unwanted animals . . . and the use of live animals "to pursue or take wildlife or to participate in any hunting". . . .

The ordinances are underinclusive as well with regard to the health risk posed by consumption of uninspected meat. Under the city's ordinances, hunters may eat their kill and fisherman may eat their catch without undergoing governmental inspection. . . .

A law burdening religious practice that is not neutral or not of general application must undergo the most rigorous of scrutiny. To satisfy the commands of the First Amendment, a law restrictive of religious practice must advance "interests of the highest order" and must be narrowly tailored in pursuit of those interests. . . . The compelling interest standard [applies].

. . . As we have discussed . . . all four ordinances are overbroad or underinclusive in substantial respects. . . .

Respondent has not demonstrated, moreover, that, in the context of these ordinances, its governmental interests are compelling. . . .

The Free Exercise Clause commits government itself to religious tolerance, and upon even slight suspicion that proposals for state intervention stem from animosity to religion or distrust of its practices, all officials must pause to remember their own high duty to the Constitution and to the rights it secures. Those in office must be resolute in resisting importunate demands and must ensure that the sole reasons for imposing the burdens of law and regulation are secular. Legislators may not devise mechanisms, overt or disguised, designed to persecute or oppress a religion or its practices. The laws here in question were enacted contrary to these constitutional principles and they are void. Reversed.

Smith can be distinguished from the Hialeah case because Smith involved a law of general applicability. That is, use of the drugs, including peyote, was generally prohibited to everyone. Clearly, the laws were not enacted solely to regulate religious worship. However, in the Hialeah case, the Court determined that the regulation was intended to target the Santeria's religious practices.

Determining whether an act is truly an exercise of religious beliefs is not always easy. The practices of one religion may appear unusual, or even bizarre, to another. But this is not determinative. The Hodges case both illustrates the sensitivity with which our society treats religion and stands as an example of an activity that is not a religion, although the opinion does not contain the latter finding, for reasons you will see.

How does a court distinguish between fraudulent and bona fide religious practices? First, it must be determined that the defendant is asserting a religious belief, not a personal or philosophical belief. Several factors are considered. How well established is the religion in the world? If a defendant is the only adherent, or one of only a few followers, of a religion, it is less likely to be deemed legitimate. How old is the religion? For how long has the defendant practiced the religion? What is the nature of the practice in question? How important is the practice to the religion? Once it is determined that a religious practice is being regulated by the state, then the state's interest in regulating the defendant's conduct must be weighed against the defendant's First Amendment interest. If the state's interest is compelling, then the conduct may be regulated.

CASE

STATE V. HODGES

695 S.W.2d 171
(Tenn. 1985)

In January, 1983, defendant was charged in a multiple count indictment with tampering with utility metering devices. His lawyer appeared before the trial judge on February 22, 1983, asking for a trial date for the misdemeanors with which defendant was charged. The trial judge informed defendant's counsel on that occasion that he would not "put up with [defendant's] foolishness" and if "he comes in here dressed like a chicken, I am going to order him out of here under guard."

On June 28, 1983, defendant appeared for trial, with the same counsel, and to say that he was dressed "like a chicken" as the trial judge had anticipated, is a mild description of the outrageous attire in which defendant barely covered himself. [In a footnote the court described his appearance. The defendant "appeared for trial dressed in a grossly shocking and bizarre attire, consisting of brown and white fur tied around his body at his ankles, loins and head, with a like vest made out of fur, and complete with eye goggles over his eyes. He had colored his face and chest with a very pale green paint for coloring. He had what appeared to be a human skull dangling from his waist and in his hand he carried a stuffed snake. . . . [T]he so-called vest consisted of two pieces of fur that covered each arm but did not meet in front and back, leaving defendant's chest and back naked to his waist. His legs were also naked from mid-way between his knee and waist to his ankles. He appeared to be carrying a military gas mask and other unidentifiable ornaments."]

The trial judge first addressed defendant's attorney and asked him to have his client appear in proper clothes. Defendant's attorney responded by informing the court that defendant wished to exercise his right of "freedom of expression." The trial judge then directed his remarks to defendant and ordered him to put on "regular clothes" for the trial scheduled that day. The trial judge sought a yes or no answer, but defendant responded with the following assertion:

> "This is a spiritual attire and it is my religious belief and I have never worn anything else in court but this when I am on trial."

Whereupon, the trial judge found him to be in contempt of court, revoked his bond, and ordered him committed to jail for ten days or until he agreed to appear for trial in proper clothes.

Defendant's counsel asked the court to allow him to "build a record for appeal" which was denied. Motions were filed the following day, June 29, 1983, on behalf of defendant for a new trial, for reconsideration of the finding of contempt, and for bail pending appeal. At the hearing held the same day, defense counsel again sought an evidentiary hearing on the issue of defendant's religious belief which was again denied. . . . The court of Criminal Appeals reversed the contempt adjudication, holding that the trial judge erred in failing to inquire into the "nature and sincerity of appellant's beliefs, the denomination of his religion, its origin, organization and the length of time which appellant has espoused it."

We agree that the trial judge erred in failing to inquire into the religious belief of defendant and in failing to allow a full record to be developed for appeal. However, we think the intermediate court's instructions on remand, quoted above, may be misleading and not entirely in conformity with United States Supreme Court opinions.

A Rhode Island litigant appeared in court wearing a white, knitted skull cap and the trial judge ordered him to remove it or leave the courtroom and refused to consider the litigant's claim that he was a Sunni Muslim, that he was wearing a prayer cap that was a religious symbol of that sect, that indicated that the wearer was in constant prayer. . . . On appeal, the Supreme Court of Rhode Island accurately summarized the first amendment principle enunciated by the United States Supreme Court applicable where a religious belief or practice collides with a state law or regulation, as follows:

> Despite the exalted status so rightly afforded to religious beliefs and activities that are motivated and embody those beliefs, the freedom of an individual to practice his religion does not enjoy absolute immunity from infringement by the state. Individuals have been subject to mandatory inoculations despite religious objections to such medical care. . . . Thus while the freedom to hold religious beliefs and opinions is absolute, the freedom to act in harmony with these religious beliefs and opinions is not beyond state regulation where such restriction serves the public interest by promoting public health and safety or preserving order. We must then accommodate the right to exercise the religious freedoms safeguarded by the first amendment with the right of the state to regulate those individual freedoms for the sake of societal interests. The problem is one of balance and degree—the courts are called upon to determine when the societal interest becomes so important as to justify an incursion by the state into religious activity that is otherwise protected by the free exercise clause of the first amendment. . . .

After discussion of the United States Supreme Court's application of the balancing test to the facts . . . the Supreme Court of Rhode Island continued as follows:

> We believe that because petitioner claimed that his act was protected by the free exercise clause, in order to justifiably curtail the exercise of the alleged right the trial justice should have first allowed petitioner to display the sincerity of his religious belief, and then should have . . . [balanced] petitioner's first amendment right with the interest of the court in maintaining decorum in its proceedings by regulating dress in the courtroom. . . .

Thus, the threshold inquiry is whether or not the religious belief or practice asserted qualifies for the protection of the free exercise clause of the first amendment. The record in this case, though meager, clearly indicates that that issue may be decisive, particularly if it proves to be true that defendant is the sole adherent to his asserted religious belief and practice. . . .

Although a determination of what is a "religious" belief or practice entitled to constitutional protection may present a most delicate question, the very concept of ordered liberty precludes allowing every person to make his own standards of matters of conduct in which society as a whole has important interests. . . .

Paraphrasing an additional observation of the Court that involved Thoreau's isolation at Walden Pond, the Court made it clear that a belief which is philosophical and personal rather than religious, does not rise to the demands of the free exercise clause of the first amendment. . . .

Only beliefs rooted in religion are protected by the Free Exercise Clause, which, by its terms, gives special protection to the exercise of religion. . . . The determination of what is a "religious" belief or practice is more often than not a difficult and delicate task. . . . However, the resolution of that question is not to turn upon a judicial perception of the particular belief or practice in question; religious beliefs need not be acceptable, logical, consistent, or comprehensible to others in order to merit First Amendment protection.

One can, of course, imagine an asserted claim so bizarre, so clearly nonreligious in motivation, as not to be entitled to protection under the First Amendment. . . .

This case is clearly illustrative of what Mr. Justice Jackson had in mind when he said, "The price of freedom of religion or of speech or of the press is that we must put up with, and even pay for, a good deal of rubbish." . . .

The judgment of the Court of Criminal Appeals is affirmed and this case is remanded to the trial court for further proceedings consistent with this opinion.

FIRST AMENDMENT AND SPEECH

The First Amendment also protects speech. Not all speech is protected. You have already learned that fighting words and those words that create a "clear and present danger" may be regulated. Slanderous and libelous statements also fall outside the protection of the First Amendment. Fighting words, dangerous words, slanderous and libelous words are all content-based doctrines; that is, the substance of what is being said is regulated.

In some instances, a state may regulate speech, not because of its content, but by its time, place, and manner of being expressed. Here, a balancing of interests is conducted: does the government's interest in enforcing the statute outweigh the First Amendment interest? For example, it is unlawful to stand in the middle of the street to make a speech. The interest in maintaining a safe, consistent flow of traffic outweighs the First Amendment interest. However, the result would be different if a state attempted to prohibit all speeches made in a public place. Such a statute would be overbroad, as it includes not only activity that the state may regulate (standing in traffic), but also lawful activity. Commercial speech is also protected by the First Amendment, but is subject to greater control than other speech.

Not only is the actual spoken word protected: expression of ideas through acts is also protected, although to a lesser degree than pure speech. Picketing is an example of protected expression, as is flag burning.

 CASE

TEXAS V. GREGORY LEE JOHNSON

491 U.S. 397 (1989)

After publicly burning the American flag as a means of political protest, Gregory Lee Johnson was convicted of desecrating a flag in violation of Texas law. This case presents the question whether his conviction is consistent with the First Amendment. We hold that it is not.

While the Republican National Convention was taking place in Dallas in 1984, respondent Johnson participated in a political demonstration dubbed the "Republican War Chest Tour." As explained in literature distributed by the demonstrators and in speeches made by them, the purpose of this event was to protest the policies of the Reagan administration and of certain Dallas-based corporations. The demonstrators marched through the Dallas streets, chanting political slogans and stopping at several corporate locations to stage "die-ins" intended to dramatize the consequences of nuclear war. On several occasions they spray-painted the walls of buildings and overturned potted plants, but Johnson himself took no part in such activities. He did, however, accept an American flag handed to him by a fellow protester who had taken it from a flag pole outside one of the targeted buildings.

The demonstration ended in front of Dallas City Hall, where Johnson unfurled the American flag, doused it with kerosene, and set it on fire. While the flag burned, the protesters chanted, "America, the red, white, and blue, we spit on you." After the demonstrators dispersed, a witness to the flag-burning collected the flag's remains and buried them in his backyard. No one was physically injured or threatened with injury, though several witnesses testified that they had been seriously offended by the flag-burning. . . .

Johnson was convicted of flag desecration for burning the flag rather than for uttering insulting words. That fact somewhat complicates our consideration of his conviction under the First Amendment. We must first determine whether Johnson's burning of the flag constituted expressive conduct, permitting him to invoke the First Amendment. . . . If his conduct was expressive, we next decide whether the State's regulation is related to the suppression of free expression. If the State's regulation is not related to expression, then the less stringent standard . . . for regulations of noncommunicative conduct controls. . . . If it is, then we are outside of the *O'Brien* test, and we must ask whether this interest justifies Johnson's conviction under a more demanding standard. . . .

The First Amendment literally forbids the abridgment only of "speech," but we have long recognized that its protection does not end at the spoken or written word. While we have rejected "the view that an apparently limitless variety of conduct can be labeled 'speech' whenever the person engaging in the conduct intends thereby to express an idea," . . . we have acknowledged that conduct may be "sufficiently imbued with elements of communication to fall within the scope of the First and Fourteenth Amendments." . . .

In deciding whether particular conduct possesses sufficient communicative elements to bring the First Amendment into play, we have asked whether "[a]n intent to convey a particularized message was present, and [whether] the likelihood was great that the message would be understood by those who viewed it." . . . Hence, we have recognized the expressive nature of students' wearing of black armbands to protest American military involvement in Vietnam . . . of a sit-in by blacks in a "whites only" area to protest segregation. . . .

The expressive, overtly political nature of this conduct was both intentional and overwhelmingly apparent. At his trial, Johnson explained his reasons for burning the flag as follows:

"The American Flag was burned as Ronald Reagan was being nominated as President. And a more powerful statement of symbolic speech, whether you agree with it or not, couldn't have been made at that time. It's quite a just position [juxtaposition]. We had new patriotism and no patriotism." In these circumstances, Johnson's burning of the flag was conduct "sufficiently imbued with elements of communication." . . .

In order to decide whether the *O'Brien* test applies here, therefore, we must decide whether Texas has asserted an interest in support of Johnson's conviction that is unrelated to the suppression of expression. If we find that an interest asserted by the State is simply not implicated on the facts before us, we need not ask whether *O'Brien* applies. . . . The State offers two separate interests to justify his conviction: preventing breaches of the peace, and preserving the flag as a symbol of nationhood and national unity. We hold that the first interest is not implicated on this record and that the second is related to the suppression of expression. . . .

The State's position, therefore, amounts to a claim that an audience that takes serious offense at particular expression is necessarily likely to disturb the peace and that the expression may be prohibited on this basis. Our precedents do not countenance such a presumption. On the contrary, they recognize that a principal "function of free speech under our system of government is to invite dispute. It may indeed best serve its high purpose when it induces a condition of unrest, creates dissatisfaction with conditions as they are, or even stirs people to anger." . . .

The State also asserts an interest in preserving the flag as a symbol of nationhood and national unity. . . .

Johnson was not, we add, prosecuted for the expression of just any idea; he was prosecuted for his expression of dissatisfaction with the policies of this country, expression situated at the core of our First Amendment values. . . .

Moreover, Johnson was prosecuted because he knew that his politically charged expression would cause "serious offense." If he had burned the flag as a means of disposing of it because it was dirty or torn, he would not have been convicted of flag desecration under the Texas law; federal law designates burning as the preferred means of disposing of a flag "when it is in such condition that it is no longer a fitting emblem for display." . . .

If there is a bedrock principle underlying the First Amendment, it is that the Government may not prohibit the expression of an idea simply because society finds the idea itself offensive or disagreeable. . . .

We are tempted to say, in fact, that the flag's deservedly cherished place in our community will be strengthened, not weakened, by our holding today. Our decision is a reaffirmation of the principles of freedom and inclusiveness that the flag best reflects, and of the conviction that our toleration of criticism such as Johnson's is a sign and source of our strength. . . .

The way to preserve the flag's special role is not to punish those who feel differently about these matters. It is to persuade them that they are wrong. . . . And, precisely because it is our flag that is involved, one's response to the flag-burner may exploit the uniquely persuasive power of the flag itself. We can imagine no more appropriate response to burning a flag than waving one's own, no better way to counter a flag-burner's message than by saluting the flag that burns, no surer means of preserving the dignity even of the flag that burned than by—as one witness here did—according its remains a respectful burial. We do not consecrate the flag by punishing its desecration, for in doing so we dilute the freedom that this cherished emblem represents. . . . Justice Kennedy, concurring.

I write not to qualify the words Justice Brennan chooses so well, for he says with power all that is necessary to explain our ruling. I join his opinion without reservation, but with a keen sense that his case, like others before us from time to time, exacts its personal toll. This prompts me to add to our pages these few remarks.

The case before us illustrates better than most that the judicial power is often difficult in its exercise. We cannot here ask another branch to share responsibility, as when the argument is made that a statute is flawed or incomplete. For we are presented with a clear and simple statute to be judged against a pure command of the Constitution. The outcome can be laid at no door but ours.

The hard fact is that sometimes we must make decisions we do not like. We make them because they are right, right in the sense that the law and the Constitution, as we see them, compel the result. And so great is our commitment to the process that, except in the rare case, we do not pause to express distaste for the result, perhaps for fear of undermining a valued principle that dictates decision. This is one of those rare cases.

Our colleagues in dissent advance powerful arguments why respondent may be convicted for his expression, reminding us that among those who will be dismayed by our holding will be some who have had the singular honor of carrying the flag into battle. And I agree that the flag holds a lonely place of honor in an age when absolutes are distrusted and simple truths are burdened by unneeded apologetics.

With respect to those views, I do not believe the Constitution gives us the right to rule as the dissenting members of the Court urge, however painful this judgment is to announce. . . . It is poignant but fundamental that the flag protects those who hold it in contempt . . .

First Amendment free exercise of speech claims also arise in the context of hate crime legislation. Such legislation either makes it illegal to express prejudicial opinions or enhances the penalty for a crime that is motivated by prejudice. The former is unconstitutional. As to the latter, most states enhance the penalties for crimes such as trespass, assault, battery, and harassment if the motive of the crime was the victim's race, religion, color, or other characteristic.

Two Supreme Court opinions, only one year apart, set the limits of hate crime laws. Both are excerpted here. In the first, the Court held an ordinance unconstitutional. In the second, the Court upheld the law.

R.A.V. and *Mitchell* establish that although bigoted expressions themselves may not be prohibited (legislation aimed at content), bigotry as a motive may be considered at sentencing to enhance a penalty (legislation aimed at the motive of content).[16]

 C A S E ——————————————————————————————————◆

R.A.V. V.
CITY OF ST. PAUL

505 U.S. 377 (1992)

In the predawn hours of June 21, 1990, petitioner and several other teenagers allegedly assembled a crudely-made cross by taping together broken chair legs. They then allegedly burned the cross inside the fenced yard of a black family that lived across the street from the house where petitioner was staying. Although this conduct could have been punished under any number of laws, one of the two provisions under which respondent city of St. Paul chose to charge petitioner (then a juvenile) was the St. Paul-Motivated Crime Ordinance, which provides:

> "Whoever placed on public property or private property a symbol, object, appellation, characterization or graffiti, including, but not limited to, a burning cross or Nazi swastika, which one knows or has reasonable grounds to know arouse anger, alarm or resentment in others on the basis of race, color, creed, religion or gender commits disorderly conduct and shall be guilty of a misdemeanor."

Petitioner moved to dismiss this count on the ground that the St. Paul ordinance was substantially overbroad and impermissibly content-based and therefore facially invalid under the First Amendment. The trial court granted this motion, but the Minnesota Supreme Court reversed. That court rejected petitioner's overbreadth claim because, as construed in prior Minnesota cases . . . the modifying phrase "arouses anger, alarm or resentment in others" limited the reach of the ordinance to conduct that amounts to "fighting words," . . . and therefore the ordinance reached only expression "that the first amendment does not protect." . . . The court also concluded that the ordinance was not impermissibly content-based because, in its view, "the ordinance is a narrowly tailored means toward accomplishing the compelling governmental interest in protecting the community against bias-motivated threats to public safety and order." . . .

Assuming, arguendo, that all of the expression reached by the ordinance is proscribable under the "fighting words" doctrine, we nonetheless conclude that the ordinance is facially unconstitutional in that it prohibits otherwise permitted speech solely on the basis of the subjects the speech addresses. . . .

The proposition that a particular instance of speech can be proscribable on the basis of one feature (e.g., obscenity) but not on the basis of another (e.g., opposition to the city government) is commonplace, and has found application in many contexts. We have long held, for example, that nonverbal expressive activity can be banned because of the action it entails, but not because of the ideas it expresses—so that burning the flag in violation of an ordinance against outdoor fires could be punishable, whereas burning a flag in violation of an ordinance against dishonoring the flag is not. . . .

Similarly, we have upheld reasonable "time, place, or manner" restrictions, but only if they are "justified without reference to the content of the regulated speech." . . . And just as the power to proscribe particular speech on the basis of a noncontent element (e.g., noise) does not entail the power to proscribe it on the basis of a content element; so also, the power to proscribe it on the basis of one content element (e.g., obscenity) does not entail the power to proscribe it on the basis of other content elements.

In other words, the exclusion of "fighting words" from the scope of the First Amendment simply means that, for purposes of that Amendment, the unprotected features of the words are, despite their verbal character, essentially a "nonspeech" element of communication. Fighting words are thus analogous to a noisy sound truck: Each is, as Justice Frankfurter recognized, a "mode of speech," . . . both can be used to convey an idea; but neither has, in and of itself, a claim upon the First Amendment. As with the sound truck, however, so also with fighting words: The government may not regulate use based on hostility—or favoritism—towards the underlying message expressed. . . .

Applying these principles to the St. Paul ordinance, we conclude that, even as narrowly construed by the Minnesota Supreme Court, the ordinance is facially unconstitutional. Although the phrase in the ordinance, "arouses anger, alarm or resentment in others," has been limited by the Minnesota Supreme Court's construction to reach only those symbols or displays that amount to "fighting words," the remaining, unmodified terms make clear that the ordinance applies only to "fighting words" that insult, or provoke violence, "on the basis of race, color, creed, religion or gender." Displays containing abusive invective,

no matter how vicious or severe, are permissible unless they are addressed to one of the specified disfavored topics. Those who wish to use "fighting words" in connection with other ideas—to express hostility, for example, on the basis of political affiliation, union membership, or homosexuality—are not covered. The First Amendment does not permit St. Paul to impose special prohibitions on those speakers who express views on disfavored subjects. . . .

In its practical operation, moreover, the ordinance goes even beyond mere content discrimination, to actual viewpoint discrimination. Displays containing some words—odious racial epithets, for example—aspersions upon a person's mother, for example—would seemingly be usable ad libitum in the placards of those arguing in favor of racial, color, etc. tolerance and equality, but could not be used by the speaker's opponents. One could hold up a sign saying, for example, that all "anti-catholic bigots" are misbegotten; but not that all "papists" are, for that would insult or provoke violence "on the basis of religion." St. Paul has no such authority to license one side of a debate to fight freestyle, while requiring the other to follow Marquis of Queensbury Rules. . . .

Let there be no mistake about our belief that burning a cross in someone's front yard is reprehensible. But St. Paul has sufficient means at its disposal to prevent such behavior without adding the First Amendment to the fire. . . .

 CASE

WISCONSIN V. MITCHELL

113 S. Ct. 2194 (1993)

Respondent Todd Mitchell's sentence for aggravated battery was enhanced because he intentionally selected his victim on account of

the victim's race. The question presented in this case is whether this penalty enhancement is prohibited by the First and Fourteenth Amendments. We hold that it is not.

On the evening of October 7, 1989, a group of young black men and boys, including Mitchell, gathered at an apartment complex in Kenosha,

Wisconsin. Several members of the group discussed a scene from the motion picture "Mississippi Burning," in which a white man beat a young black boy who was praying. The group moved outside and Mitchell asked them: "Do you all feel hyped up to move on some white people?" . . . Shortly thereafter, a young white boy approached the group on the opposite side of the street where they were standing. As the boy walked by, Mitchell said: "You all want to fuck somebody up? There goes a white boy: go get him." . . . Mitchell counted to three and pointed in the boy's direction. The group ran towards the boy, beat him severely, and stole his tennis shoes. The boy was rendered unconscious and remained in a coma for four days.

After a jury trial in the Circuit Court for Kenosha County, Mitchell was convicted of aggravated battery. . . . That offense ordinarily carries a maximum sentence of two years imprisonment. . . . But because the jury found that Mitchell had intentionally selected his victim because of the boy's race, the maximum sentence for Mitchell's offense was increased to seven years under a [Wisconsin statute]. That provision enhances the maximum penalty for an offense whenever the defendant "[i]ntentionally selects the person against whom the crime . . . is committed . . . because of race, religion, color, disability, sexual orientation, national origin or ancestry of that person." . . .

The Circuit Court sentenced Mitchell to four years' imprisonment for the aggravated battery. . . .

Mitchell unsuccessfully sought postconviction relief in the Circuit Court. Then he appealed his conviction and sentence, challenging the constitutionality of Wisconsin's penalty-enhancement provision on First Amendment grounds. The Wisconsin Court of Appeals rejected Mitchell's challenge, but the Wisconsin Supreme Court reversed. The Supreme Court held that the statute "violates the First Amendment directly by punishing what the legislature has deemed to be offensive thought." . . . It rejected the State's contention "that the statute punishes only the conduct of intentional selection of a victim." According to the court, "[t]he statute punishes the 'because of' aspect of the defendant's selection, the

reason the defendant selected the victim, the motive behind the selection." . . .

The Supreme Court also held that the penalty-enhancement statute was unconstitutionally overbroad. It reasoned that, in order to prove that a defendant intentionally selected his victim because of the victim's protected status, the State would often have to introduce evidence of the defendant's prior speech, such as racial epithets he may have uttered before the commission of the offense. . . .

We granted certiorari because of the importance of the question presented and the existence of a conflict of authority among the states' high courts on the constitutionality of statutes similar to Wisconsin's penalty-enhancement provision. . . . We reverse. . . .

Mitchell argues (and the Wisconsin Supreme Court held) that the statute violates the First Amendment by punishing offenders' bigoted beliefs.

Traditionally, sentencing judges have considered a wide variety of factors in addition to evidence bearing on guilt in determining what sentence to impose on a convicted defendant. . . . [T]he defendant's motive for committing the offense is one important factor. . . . Thus, in many states the commission of a murder, or other capital offense, for pecuniary gain is a separate aggravating circumstance under the capital-sentencing statute. . . .

But it is equally true that a defendant's abstract beliefs, however obnoxious to most people, may not be taken into consideration by a sentencing judge. . . . In [*Dawson v. Delaware,* 503 U.S. 159 (1992)] the State introduced evidence at a capital-sentencing hearing that the defendant was a member of a white supremacist prison gang. Because "the evidence proved nothing more than [the defendant's] abstract beliefs," we held that its admission violated the defendant's First Amendment rights. . . . In so holding, however, we emphasized that "the Constitution does not erect a per se barrier to the admission of evidence concerning one's beliefs and associations at sentencing simply because those beliefs and associations are protected by the First Amendment. . . . Thus, in *Barclay v. Florida,* 463 U.S.

939 (1983) . . . we allowed the sentencing judge to take into account the defendant's racial animus towards his victim. The evidence in that case showed that the defendant's membership in the Black Liberation Army and desire to provoke a "race war" were related to the murder of a white man for which he was convicted. . . . Because "the elements of racial hatred in [the] murder" were relevant to several aggravating factors, we held that the trial judge permissibly took his evidence into account in sentencing the defendant to death. . . .

Mitchell suggests that *Dawson* and *Barclay* are inapposite because they did not involve application of a penalty-enhancement provision. But in *Barclay* we held that it was permissible for the sentencing court to consider the defendant's racial animus in determining whether he should be sentenced to death, surely the most severe "enhancement" of all. And the fact that the Wisconsin Legislature has decided, as a general matter, that bias-motivated offenses warrant greater maximum penalties across the board does not alter the result here. For the primary responsibility for fixing criminal penalties lies with the legislature. . . .

Mitchell argues that the Wisconsin penalty-enhancement statute is invalid because it punishes the defendant's discriminatory motive, or reason, for acting. But motive plays the same role under the Wisconsin statute as it does under federal and state antidiscrimination laws, which we have previously upheld against constitutional challenge. . . . Title VII, for example, makes it unlawful for an employer to discriminate against an employee "because of such individual's race, color, religion, sex, or national origin." . . . In [another case] we rejected the argument that Title VII infringed employers' First Amendment rights. Nothing in our decision last Term in *R.A.V.* compels a different result here. That case involved a First Amendment challenge to a municipal ordinance prohibiting the use of " 'fighting words' that insult or provoke violence, on the basis of race, color, creed, religion or gender." . . .

Finally, there remains to be considered Mitchell's argument that the Wisconsin statute is unconstitutionally overbroad because of the "chilling effect" on free speech. Mitchell argues (and the Wisconsin Supreme Court agreed) that the statute is "overbroad" because evidence of the defendant's prior speech or associations may be used to prove that the defendant intentionally selected his victim on account of the victim's protected status. Consequently, the argument goes, the statute impermissibly chills free expression with respect to such matters by those concerned about the possibility of enhanced sentences if they should in the future commit a criminal offense covered by the statute. We find no merit in this contention.

The sort of chill envisioned here is far more attenuated and unlikely than that contemplated in traditional "overbreadth" cases. We must conjure up a vision of a Wisconsin citizen suppressing his unpopular bigoted opinions for fear that if he later commits an offense covered by the statute, these opinions will be offered at trial to establish that he selected his victim on account of the victim's protected status, thus qualifying him for penalty-enhancement. To stay within the realm of rationality, we must surely put to one side minor misdemeanor offenses covered by the statute, such as negligent operation of a motor vehicle . . . for it is difficult, if not impossible, to conceive of a situation where such offenses would be racially motivated. We are left, then, with the prospect of a citizen suppressing his bigoted beliefs for fear that evidence of such beliefs will be introduced against him at trial if he commits a more serious offense against person or property. This is simply too speculative a hypothesis to support Mitchell's overbreadth claim.

The First Amendment, moreover, does not prohibit the evidentiary use of speech to establish the elements of a crime or to prove motive or intent. Evidence of a defendant's previous declarations or statements is commonly admitted in criminal trials subject to evidentiary rules dealing with relevancy, reliability, and the like. Nearly half a century ago, . . . we rejected a contention similar to that advanced by Mitchell here. Haupt was tried for the offense of treason, which, as defined by the Constitution, may depend very much on proof of motive. To prove that the acts in question were committed out of "adherence to the enemy" rather than "parental solicitude," . . . the Government introduced evidence of conversations that had taken place long prior to the indictment, some of which consisted of statements showing Haupt's sympathy with Germany and Hitler and hostility towards the United States. We rejected Haupt's argument that this evidence was improperly admitted. While "[s]uch testimony is to be scrutinized with care to be certain the statements are not expressions of mere proper appreciation of the land of birth," we held that "these statements . . . clearly were admissible on the question of intent and adherence to the enemy." . . .

For the foregoing reasons, we hold that Mitchell's First Amendment rights were not violated by the application of the Wisconsin penalty-enhancement provision in sentencing him. The judgment of the Supreme Court of Wisconsin is therefore reversed, and the case is remanded for further proceedings not inconsistent with this opinion.

PRIVACY AND OTHER UNENUMERATED RIGHTS

Unlike some state constitutions, the United States Constitution does not expressly protect privacy. Many of the expressly stated rights in the Bill of Rights protect privacy, such as the Fourth Amendment, which has been interpreted as applying to searches that encroach upon a person's reasonable expectation to privacy.

The issue is whether the Constitution protects privacy to a greater extent than through its express provisions. Stated another way, is there an independent and inherent privacy right in the Constitution? If so, what is the textual source of that right?

The Supreme Court answered the former question affirmatively in 1965 in *Griswold v. Connecticut.*[17] In that case, a Connecticut statute that prohibited the use of contraceptives, even by married couples, was held unconstitutional as invasive of a right to privacy.

As to the second issue, the source of the right, the Court found that the right to privacy grows out of the First, Fourth, Fifth, Ninth, and Fourteenth Amendments. Justice Douglas, writing for the Court, found the right to privacy to be a "penumbra" of these expressly protected rights. The Court stressed that the First Amendment's right to association protected the marriage relationship and that the intimate subject sought to be regulated was especially protected. The Court stated that

> [Prior case law] suggests that specific guarantees in the Bill of Rights have penumbras, formed by emanations from those guarantees that help give them life and substance. . . . Various guarantees create zones of privacy. The right of association contained in the penumbra of the First Amendment is one, as we have seen. The Third Amendment in its prohibition against the quartering of soldiers "in any house" in time of peace without the consent of the owner is another facet of that privacy. The Fourth Amendment explicitly affirms the "right of the people to be secure in their persons, houses, papers, and effects, against unreasonable searches and seizures." The Fifth Amendment in its Self-Incrimination Clause enables the citizens to create a zone of privacy which

government may not force him to surrender to his detriment. The Ninth Amendment provides: "The enumeration in the Constitution, of certain rights, shall not be construed to deny or disparage others retained by the people." . . .

The present case, then, concerns a relationship lying within the zone of privacy created by several fundamental constitutional guarantees. . . .

We deal with a right to privacy older than the Bill of Rights—older than our political parties, older than our school system. Marriage is a coming together for better or worse, hopefully enduring, and intimate to the degree of being sacred. It is an association that promotes a way of life, not causes; a harmony in living, not political faiths; a bilateral loyalty, not commercial or social projects. Yet it is an association for as noble a purpose as any involved in our prior decisions.

Note that Justice Douglas found that the right to privacy was a penumbra of other fundamental, express rights. He did not find the right to privacy to be an independent constitutional right. This is because he believed that the Fourteenth Amendment was intended to extend the rights found in the Bill of Rights to the states, but that it was not intended to create independent rights. This is known as *total incorporation.*

Privacy has also been an issue in abortion cases. Abortion cases are complicated by a competing interest that did not exist in *Griswold,* that is, the interest of the state in protecting the fetus. In 1973 the Supreme Court handed down the landmark decision of *Roe v. Wade,*[18] in which the Court declared that the right to privacy protects a woman's right to elect to abort a fetus in some situations.

Specifically, the Court adopted a trimester analysis wherein the state's authority to regulate abortion increases as the pregnancy lengthens. During the first trimester, states could not regulate abortion procedures. During the second trimester, states could regulate abortions insofar as necessary to protect the health and life of the woman. Finally, states could protect the fetus during the third trimester, including proscribing abortion, except in cases in which abortion was necessary to protect the life or health of the mother. The Court decided that governmental interest in protecting fetuses during the third trimester was compelling because fetuses are viable at that time.

The trial court found Roe's right to privacy in the Ninth Amendment, but the Supreme Court refused to rely on the Ninth Amendment alone. Rather, the Court found the right to privacy to stem from the Fourteenth, Ninth, and other amendments.

The *Roe v. Wade* decision was the subject of intense political and legal controversy during the 1980s and 1990s. *Certiorari* was sought in several abortion-related cases during this period; so-called "right to life" groups believed that, with a more conservative Court than had existed since the *Roe v. Wade* decision issued, the chances of reversing the decision were good. The Court granted *certiorari* in several abortion-related cases, but the cardinal principle announced in *Roe v. Wade* was reaffirmed again and again: the decision whether to abort a fetus is, in some circumstances, so private and intimate that it is protected by the Constitution from governmental intrusion. This occurred in *Casey v. Planned Parenthood,* wherein the Court also rejected the trimester analysis.[19]

CASE

CASEY V. PLANNED PARENTHOOD OF SOUTHEASTERN PENNSYLVANIA

112 S. Ct. 2791 (1992)

Liberty finds no refuge in a jurisprudence of doubt. Yet 19 years after our holding that the Constitution protects a woman's right to terminate her pregnancy in its early stages, the respondents as amicus curiae, the United States, as it has done in five other cases in the last decade, again asks us to overrule *Roe*. . . .

At issue in these cases are five provisions of the Pennsylvania Abortion Control Act of 1982 as amended in 1988 and 1989. . . . The Act requires that a woman seeking an abortion give her informed consent prior to the abortion procedure, and specifies that she be provided with certain information at least 24 hours before the abortion is performed. For a minor to obtain an abortion, the Act requires the informed consent of one of her parents, but provided for [a] judicial bypass option if the minor does not wish to or cannot obtain a parent's consent. Another provision of the Act requires that, unless certain exceptions apply, a married woman seeking an abortion must sign a statement indicating that she has notified her husband of her intended abortion. . . .

Before any of these provisions took effect, the petitioners, who are five abortion clinics and one physician representing himself as well as a class of physicians who provide abortion services, brought this suit seeking declaratory and injunctive relief. Each provision was challenged as unconstitutional on its face. . . .

After considering the fundamental constitutional questions resolved by *Roe*, principles of institutional integrity, and the rule of stare decisis, we are led to conclude this: the essential holding of *Roe v. Wade* should be retained and once again reaffirmed.

It must be stated at the outset and with clarity that *Roe's* essential holding, the holding we reaffirm, has three parts. First is a recognition of the right of the woman to choose to have an abortion before viability and to obtain it without undue interference from the State. Before viability, the State's interests are not strong enough to support a prohibition of abortion or the imposition of a substantial obstacle to the woman's effective right to elect the procedure. Second is a confirmation of the State's power to restrict abortions after fetal viability, if the law contains exceptions for pregnancies which endanger a woman's life or health. And third is the principle that the State has legitimate interests from the outset of the pregnancy in protecting the health of the woman and the life of the fetus that may become a child. These principles do not contradict one another; and we adhere to each.

Constitutional protection of the woman's decision to terminate her pregnancy derives from the Due Process Clause of the Fourteenth Amendment. It declares that no State shall "deprive any person of life, liberty, or property, without due process of law." The controlling word in the case before us is "liberty." . . . We have held that the Due Process Clause of the Fourteenth Amendment incorporates most of the Bill of Rights against the States. . . . It is tempting, as a means of curbing the discretion of federal judges, to suppose that liberty encompasses no more than those rights already guaranteed to the individual against federal interference by the express provisions of the first eight amendments to the Constitution. . . . But of course this Court has never accepted that view. It is also tempting, for the same reason, to suppose that the Due Process Clause protects against government interference by other rules of law when the Fourteenth Amendment was ratified. . . . But such a view would be inconsistent with our law. It is a promise of the Constitution that there is a realm of personal liberty which the government may not enter. We have vindicated this principle before. Marriage is mentioned nowhere in the Bill of Rights and interracial marriage was illegal in most States in the 19th century, but the Court was no doubt correct in finding it to be an aspect of liberty protected against state interference by the substantive component of the Due Process Clause. . . . Neither the Bill of Rights nor the specific practices of States at the time of the adoption of the Fourteenth Amendment marks the outer limits of the substantive sphere of liberty which the Fourteenth Amendment protects. . . .

Our law affords constitutional protection to personal decisions relating to marriage, procreation, contraception, family relationships, child rearing, and education. . . . These matters, involving the most intimate and personal choices a person may make in a lifetime, choices central to personal dignity and autonomy, are central to the liberty protected by the Fourteenth Amendment. At the heart of liberty is the right to define one's own concept of existence, of meaning, of the universe, and of the mystery of human life. Beliefs about these matters could not define the attributes of personhood were they formed under compulsion of the State.

The consideration begins our analysis of the woman's interest in terminating her pregnancy but cannot end it, for this reason: though the abortion decision may originate within the zone of conscience and belief, it is more than a philosophic exercise. Abortion is a unique act. It is an act fraught with consequences for others: for the woman who must live with the implications of her decision; for the persons who perform and assist in the procedure; for the spouse, family and society which must confront the knowledge that these procedures exist, procedures some deem nothing short of an act of violence against innocent human life; and depending on one's beliefs, for the life or potential life that is aborted: Though abortion is conduct, it does not follow that the State is entitled to proscribe it in all instances. That is because the liberty of the woman is at stake in a sense unique to the human condition and so unique to the law. The mother who carries a child to full term is subject to anxieties, to physical constraints, to pain that only she must bear. . . .

No evolution of legal principle has left *Roe's* doctrinal footings weaker than they were in 1973. No development of constitutional law since the case was decided has implicitly or explicitly left *Roe* behind as a mere survivor of obsolete constitutional thinking. . . .

We have seen how time has overtaken some of *Roe's* factual assumptions: advances in maternal health care allow for abortions safe to the mother later in pregnancy than was true in 1973 . . . and advances in neonatal care have advanced viability to a point somewhat earlier. . . . But these facts go only to the scheme of the limits on the realization of competing interests, and the divergences from the factual premises of 1973 have no bearing on the validity of *Roe's* central holding, that viability marks the earliest point at which the State's interest in fetal life is constitutionally adequate to justify a legislative ban on nontherapeutic abortions. The soundness or unsoundness of that constitutional judgment in no sense turns on whether viability occurs at 23 to 24 weeks. . . . Whenever it may occur, the attainment of viability may continue to serve as the critical fact, just as it has done since *Roe* was decided; which is to say that no change in *Roe's* factual underpinnings has left its central holding obsolete, and none supports an argument for overruling it. . . .

Only where a state regulation imposes an undue burden on a woman's ability to make this decision does the power of the State reach into the heart of the liberty protected by the Due Process Clause. . . .

The very notion that the State has a substantial interest in potential life leads to the conclusion that not all regulations must be deemed unwarranted. Not all burdens on the right to decide whether to terminate a pregnancy will be undue. . . .

A finding of undue burden is a shorthand for the conclusion that a state regulation has the purpose or effect of placing a substantial obstacle in the path of a woman seeking an abortion of a nonviable fetus. A statute with this purpose is invalid. . . .

Although the Court reaffirmed the right to privacy in the abortion context, it also rejected the trimester analysis in favor of an "undue interference" test. That is, a regulation is invalid if it unduly interferes with a woman's choice. Also, the Court reaffirmed the *Roe* holding that until a fetus is viable outside of the mother's womb, a state may not prohibit its abortion. Further, even after viability, abortion is permitted to save the life or health of the mother.

The Court examined the Pennsylvania statute and concluded that:

1. Requiring information concerning abortions and abortion procedures to be distributed to patients before the procedure is performed is not unduly burdensome.
2. Mandating twenty-four-hour waiting periods between receipt of the information and performance of the procedure is not unduly burdensome.
3. Requiring parental consent (with a judicial bypass) by minor girls is not unduly burdensome.
4. Requiring spousal notification by married women is unduly burdensome, and therefore, invalid.

The right to privacy applies outside the abortion context as well. For example, as the Court stated in *Casey*, the right to engage in an interracial marriage is also protected by the Fourteenth Amendment.[20] In *Eisenstadt v. Baird*,[21] the Supreme Court invalidated a statute that prohibited the sale and distribution of contraceptives to unmarried persons. The Court stated in that opinion, "If the right of privacy means anything, it is the right of the individual, married or single, to be free from unwarranted governmental intrusion into matter so fundamentally affecting a person as the decision whether to bear or beget a child."

These are a few examples of how the power of the state to regulate conduct is limited by the right to privacy. Today, courts are likely to rely on the Fourteenth Amendment as the source of the right to privacy. Arguably, the privacy right has its roots in other amendments as well, such as the Ninth Amendment, which declares that the enumeration in the Constitution of certain rights shall not be construed as denying or disparaging others retained by the people. Although this amendment appears to be an independent source of rights, probably with natural rights origins, it has received little attention by the courts, and standing alone has never been relied upon by the Supreme Court to establish an unenumerated right.

The Supreme Court refused to extend the right to privacy to include a right for consenting adults to engage in "deviate sexual" behavior. In *Bowers v. Hardwick*,[22] the Court upheld a Georgia statute that criminalized sodomy.

Finally, be aware that the Court has recognized other unenumerated rights. A right to travel within the United States and abroad is not expressed in the Constitution, but is recognized by the Court. Of course, all rights may be regulated if the government has cause. Most rights may be regulated if the government has a legitimate and compelling interest. The right to travel abroad is subject to reasonable restrictions and regulations,[23] because of national security and foreign affairs concerns.

Any time a statute conflicts with a constitutionally protected activity, the statute will fail unless the government has a compelling interest. The defenses discussed in this chapter are only a few of the many constitutional defenses. Not all, but most criminal constitutional defenses appear in the Bill of Rights.

Nor does this chapter exhaust all the nonconstitutional defenses that may be asserted. Do not forget that each state is free to design its criminal law in any manner it wishes, so long as it is constitutional. The most common factual, legislative, and constitutional substantive law defenses have been discussed. Many procedural defenses are examined in later chapters of this text.

 WEB LINKS

Comparative Criminal Justice
At the World Factbook of Criminal Justice Systems you will find descriptions of the legal and criminal justice systems of many nations of the world. *http://www.ojp.usdoj.gov/bjs/abstract/wfcj.htm*

The United States Department of Justice's National Institute of Justice and Bureau of Justice Statistics both offer some comparative justice information. *http://www.ojp.usdoj.gov/nij/* and *http://www.ojp.usdoj.gov/bjs/*

KEY TERMS

bill of attainder
double jeopardy
ex post facto law

overbreadth doctrine
principle of legality
transactional immunity

use immunity
vagueness doctrine

REVIEW QUESTIONS

1. Differentiate overbreadth from vagueness. Give an example of each.
2. Differentiate a bill of attainder from an ex post facto law.
3. May racially derogatory statements be made criminal? May racial motives be used to enhance the punishment for crimes such as assault and battery?
4. Is a right to privacy specifically expressed in the United States Constitution?
5. Through what amendment are rights incorporated and applied against the states?

6. May religious beliefs be regulated by the state? May religious practices be regulated by the state?
7. Which of the following is protected by the First Amendment's free speech clause?
   a. A public flag burning in protest of a recently enacted law.
   b. An advertisement for potato chips found on a billboard.
   c. The placing of a hand over one's heart while the national anthem is played.

REVIEW PROBLEMS

1. Senator Bob Kerry of Nebraska was initially outraged by the *Texas v. Johnson* flag-burning decision. However, he later stated, "I was surprised to discover . . . [that the decision was] reasonable, understandable and consistent with those values which I believe have made America wonderful." Do you agree with Senator Kerry? Explain your position.

2. State law requires that all children between five years and sixteen years attend an approved school. Defendants have been charged with violating the statute, as they do not permit their children to attend school. The defendants are Mennonites and claim that it would violate their First Amendment right to freely exercise their religion. The defendants teach their children consistent with their religious teachings. Should they be convicted?

3. Do you believe that a person should be subjected to two prosecutions, by different sovereigns, for the same offense? Consider specifically the prosecution of the Los Angeles police officers who arrested and beat Rodney King. They were acquitted of assault and battery in state court. Federal civil rights charges were brought in apparent reaction to the acquittal. In your opinion, is this proper? Support your answer.

4. Do you believe that the federal Constitution implicitly protects privacy? Support your conclusion. If so, name one right not mentioned in this text that you believe should be protected.

END NOTES

1. 21 Am. Jur. *Criminal Law* 243 (1978).
2. *Arizona v. Washington*, 434 U.S. 497 (1978).
3. *United States v. Dreitzler*, 577 F.2d 539 (9th Cir. 1978).
4. *United States v. Martin Linen Supply Co.*, 430 U.S. 564 (1977).
5. *See Monge v. California*, 524 U.S. 721 (1998).
6. *Blockburger v. United States*, 284 U.S. 299 (1932).
7. Model Penal Code § 1.10.
8. Passage taken from a 1991 calendar prepared by the Commission on the Bicentennial of the United States Constitution, Washington, D.C.
9. *Pillsbury v. Conboy*, 459 U.S. 248 (1983).
10. *Douglas v. California*, 372 U.S. 353 (1963).
11. *Connally v. General Construction Co.*, 269 U.S. 385 (1926).
12. *United States v. Cardiff*, 344 U.S. 174 (1952).
13. *Coates v. Cincinnati*, 402 U.S. 611 (1971).
14. *Reynolds v. United States*, 98 U.S. 145 (1878).
15. *People v. Woody*, 61 Cal. 2d 716, 394 P.2d 813 (1965).
16. The Supreme Court issued a decision in *Virginia v. Black* (2003) as this book went to press. In *Black* the Supreme Court upheld a Virginia statute that criminalized cross burning. The Supreme Court did not overrule *R.A.V.* Rather, it distinguished the Virginia statute from the challenged law in *R.A.V.* The distinguishing characteristic was Virginia's requirement that the burning occur with an intent to intimidate. There was no such element in the challenged law in *R.A.V.* The Court analogized intimidating cross burning to threatening speech, which it had previously determined could be regulated.
17. 381 U.S. 479 (1965). The Supreme Court noted in *Roe v. Wade*, 410 U.S. 113 (1973) that the right to privacy may have been recognized by the Court as early as 1891, in *Union Pacific Railroad v. Botsford*, 141 U.S. 250 (1891), in which it held that a plaintiff in a tort action could not be compelled to submit to a medical examination because it would have been an invasion of privacy.
18. 410 U.S. 113 (1973).
19. *See also Webster v. Reproductive Health Services*, 492 U.S. 490 (1989).
20. *Loving v. Virginia*, 388 U.S. 1 (1967).
21. 405 U.S. 438 (1972).
22. 478 U.S. 186 (1986).
23. *Zemel v. Rusk*, 381 U.S. 1 (1965).

P A R T

II

Criminal Procedure

CHAPTER 10 Introduction and Participants

CHAPTER 11 The Constitutional Aspects of Criminal Procedure

CHAPTER 12 Searches, Seizures, and Arrests

CHAPTER 13 Interrogation and Other Law Enforcement
                Practices

CHAPTER 14 The Pretrial Process

CHAPTER 15 Trial

CHAPTER 16 Sentencing and Appeal

Introduction and Participants

CHAPTER OUTLINE

Criminal Procedure Defined

A Common-Law, Adversarial,
  and Accusatorial System

The Due Process Model

The Participants

  Law Enforcement Officers

Prosecutors

Judges

Defense Attorneys

Victims

Liability of Governments
  and Their Officials

CHAPTER OBJECTIVES

In this chapter, you should:

- learn about the Common Law, adversarial nature of the United States criminal justice systems.
- be challenged to think critically about the due process and crime control models of criminal justice.
- learn about the role and the ethics considerations of major players in the

criminal justice system, law enforcement officers, defense attorneys, prosecutors and judges.

- be introduced to the liability that government officials can incur when performing their duties.
- continue to develop your case analysis and legal reasoning skills.

CRIMINAL PROCEDURE DEFINED

The second section of this text addresses criminal procedure. *Criminal procedure,* as a field of law, describes the methods used in bringing an alleged criminal to justice. To state it another way, criminal procedure puts substantive criminal law into action.

Each state and the federal government has its own procedural rules. In some instances, the variation is significant. For the purpose of this text, most references will be to federal procedure. Many federal procedural rules can be found in the United States Code. A good number of procedures are judicially created (and approved by Congress) and are found in the Federal Rules of Criminal Procedure (Fed. R. Crim. P.). Finally, the constitutions of the national government and the states play a major role in defining procedures of criminal adjudications.

What follows is a discussion of the constitutional aspects of criminal procedure; the process, from investigation to appeal; searches and seizures; arrests; confessions and admissions; and the right to counsel.

A COMMON-LAW, ADVERSARIAL, AND ACCUSATORIAL SYSTEM

The colonists brought with them the common law of England. Today, all states, except Louisiana, which is of the civil law family, are common law.

In addition to being common law in nature, the legal system is **adversarial.** Adversarial adjudications resemble sporting events. There are two opposing parties and a neutral umpire. In criminal adjudications, these roles are played by the defendant, prosecutor, and judge. The judge in criminal adjudications is a passive participant, usually becoming involved only as needed by the parties or as required by law. Of course, the approach of judges varies and some are more proactive than others. A pure adversarial system is not employed in the United States and judges are expected to supervise the proceedings to assure fairness. The adversary system is built upon the foundation theory that the truth is more likely to be discovered when there are two competing parties, each conducting its own investigation of the facts, asserting differing theories of law, and presenting its own case to the court. From this adversarial stance, it is expected that all theories and facts will be discovered and developed.

adversary system
The system of law in the U.S. The judge acts as the decision maker between opposite sides (between two individuals, between the state and an individual, etc.) rather than acting as the person who also makes the state's case or independently seeks out evidence.

SIDEBAR

WHY LOUISIANA IS DIFFERENT   As you learn the law, you will learn that the law of Louisiana is often different from the rest of the states because, unlike the rest of the colonies, which were founded by the English (who imported the common law), Louisiana was founded by the French. In 1712 French Emperor Louis XIV issued a Charter for the development of Louisiana with an order requiring the application of French law, also known as Civil Law. But for the period between 1762 and 1800, when the territory was under the control of the Spanish, French law applied. In 1803 the United States took possession of the territory. The first territorial legislature of Louisiana chose to retain the Civil Law.

So, how is Civil Law different from common law? As you have learned, the common law developed through judicial pronouncements, in response to specific disputes. The civil law, which was born in France, is more "legislative" and less "judicial." The legislative code is the primary source of law, not judicial decisions. Even more, judges have less authority to interpret and expand the meaning of the law in civil law nations. The procedures of the two families of law are also different. Many historians cite 529 as the birth of the civil law. In that year, Roman Emperor Justinian issued his famous Corpus Juris Civilis. Later, in 1804, Napoleon issued his code, which has been the foundation for many codes still in existence, including Louisiana's Code. There are four major legal families recognized by contemporary comparativists: Common, Civil, Islamic, and Socialist. This author includes a fifth, traditional and transitional law.

Even though it is a member of the Civil Law family, Louisiana is equally bound by the United States Constitution and, accordingly, has much in common with the other states.

Also, the role of the judge as impartial, neutral, and detached is believed to increase the fairness of the proceedings, unlike in an inquisitorial system, where the judges sometimes develop an opinion or theory and then work toward proving that theory to be true. In the adversarial system, the parties are largely responsible for development of the case, that is, discovery of the evidence and, accordingly, the issues of law as well.

The adversarial system has its critics. Opponents contend that the truth is not found because the system encourages the opposing parties to present a distorted, misleading, and sometimes untruthful account of the facts. The factfinder, who is not part of the investigative process, is often left to choose between polarized versions of the same event. The adversarial system is also challenged as being unfair because it rests upon the theory that there will be two equally competent competing parties. However, because of differences in the ability of counsel and the respective powers of the parties, this premise is questionable.

In addition to being adversarial, the criminal justice system is accusatorial. This means that the government, as the accuser, bears the burden of proving a defendant's guilt. If the government fails in its burden, then a defendant is entitled to a directed verdict or a judgment of acquittal. The accusatorial nature of the system extends beyond placing the burden of proof on the government at trial. The entire process is designed to minimize the risk of convicting an innocent person. The belief that it is better to free several guilty persons than to convict one innocent person is a major theme of the criminal justice system. Accordingly, the system is designed so that the accused enjoys several advantages, the most critical one being the presumption of innocence; the freedom from self-incrimination, the right to a jury trial, and the right to counsel are others.

The fact that a defendant enjoys a few advantages does not mean that the defendant has the advantage on whole. The government, whether it be state or federal, can commit substantial resources to a prosecution.

THE DUE PROCESS MODEL

Criminal justice systems are commonly characterized as adhering to either a *crime control model* or a *due process model.* The repression, detection, and efficient prosecution of crime is central to the crime control model. Failure to detect and successfully prosecute criminals is perceived as a failure of government. This failure leads to a loss of individual liberties because citizens live in constant fear of, and are actually subject to, criminal conduct. A secondary consequence is a loss of confidence in government by the public, thereby further hindering its ability to detect and prevent crime. Prosecution in such systems tends to be bureaucratic, that is, a form of "assembly-line" justice. Some civil law and socialist law nations tend toward the crime control model.

The due process model focuses on the integrity of individual rights, not the rights of the community to be free from crime. Because of the importance afforded individual rights, legal guilt is at issue, as opposed to factual guilt in the crime control model. *Factual guilt* refers to whether a defendant has in fact committed a crime. *Legal guilt* is concerned not only with factual guilt, but also with whether the defendant's rights have been observed and respected by the government in the processes of investigation and prosecution. It is possible, under the due process model, there may be sufficient evidence to prove a defendant factually guilty, but because of a civil rights violation the defendant must be declared legally not guilty. The due process model has little tolerance for conviction of the innocent; the crime control model equally abhors crimes going unsolved and defendants unpunished. The investigation and adjudication of defendants is less efficient and more costly under the due process model than under the crime control model.

This is a simplification of the two models.[1] No system falls squarely into one of the two models, although most systems can be generally characterized as adhering to the principles of one more than the other. The United States follows the due process model. Individual rights and fair procedures are the hallmark of the United States system of criminal justice. All individuals are innocent until proven guilty. The process itself presumes innocence, and deprivations of liberties are sharply limited and regulated before guilt is found.

Also, as the severity of the government's intrusions or deprivations increases, so must the evidence of guilt. For example, less evidence is required to establish probable cause to support a search of an automobile than to bind a defendant over to trial. This is because binding a defendant over to trial entails greater losses of liberty (possible pretrial detention and the cost and humiliation of being publicly tried) than does the search. You will learn many procedures that support the conclusion that the United States adheres to the due process model. Attempt to identify these characteristics as you read the following chapters. Chapters 11 through 16 examine the basic procedures and constitutional aspects of bringing criminals to justice. First, however, you must become familiar with the participants in this process.

THE PARTICIPANTS

Besides the accused and witnesses, there are five primary participants in criminal adjudications: law enforcement officers, prosecutors, judges, defense attorneys, victims, and jurors. What follows is a discussion of all these participants except jurors. Jurors are discussed later.

Law Enforcement Officers

The front line of law enforcement in the United States is what the public commonly refers to as the *police*. Law enforcement officers exist at the national, state, and local levels.

Federal law enforcement agencies include the Federal Bureau of Investigation, the Drug Enforcement Administration, Customs, the Coast Guard, U.S. Marshals, the Secret Service, and the Bureau of Alcohol, Tobacco, and Firearms, to name only a few.

Each state has a police department and many have a counterpart to the FBI, such as the Kansas Bureau of Investigation (KBI). In addition, within each state, county sheriffs and municipal police departments enforce the laws of the state, as well as the laws of their locality. There are more than 20,000 local law enforcement agencies in the United States. This includes 12,502 local police departments; 3,086 sheriffs' offices; 49 state police departments; and more than 700,000 sworn police officers and 300,000-plus civilian personnel. The federal government employed an additional 88,000 sworn officers.[2]

Discretion. Law enforcement personnel are expected to keep the peace, investigate possible wrongdoing, enforce the laws, and further crime prevention. Although it is generally held that the police must enforce the laws, it is also recognized that not all the laws can be or should be enforced. Consequently, officers exercise much discretion when performing their daily duties. Deciding whether to conduct an investigation, whether to arrest an offender, or whether a search is necessary, all usually fall within the individual officer's discretion. However, the conduct of police officers must comply with constitutional, statutory, and departmental policy standards.

Ethics. As is true of prosecutors and defense attorneys, the police officer's paramount ethical code is the Constitution. Police officers have a legal and ethical obligation to keep themselves within constitutional limits when performing their duties.

More specifically, the International Association of Chiefs of Police (IACP) has formulated a set of ethical principles intended to guide the law enforcement officer in the performance of his or her duties. The IACP has issued two ethics documents, the "Law Enforcement Code of Ethics" and the "Police Code of Conduct." The Code of Ethics is a general statement of ethical responsibility that may be used as an oath of office. The first paragraph of that Code reads:

> As a law enforcement officer, my fundamental duty is to serve the
> community; to safeguard lives and property; to protect the innocent against
> deception, the weak against oppression or intimidation and the peaceful

against violence or disorder, and to respect the constitutional rights of all to liberty, equality and justice.

The Code of Ethics continues by recognizing that police officers hold a special public trust and that they have an obligation not to violate that trust.

Although substantially the same, the Police Code of Conduct is more specific than the Code of Ethics. The Code of Conduct prohibits discriminatory treatment of individuals based upon status, sex, religion, political belief, or aspiration; the unnecessary use of force; the infliction of cruel, degrading, or inhuman treatment; violation of confidences, except when necessary in the performance of duties or as required by law; bribery; the acceptance of gifts; refusals to cooperate with other law enforcement officials; and other unreasonable and inappropriate behavior. The Code of Conduct further qualifies the necessary force requirement by stating that force should be used "only with the greatest restraint and only after discussion, negotiation and persuasion have been found to be inappropriate or ineffective."

Officers are expected to behave in a manner that inspires confidence and respect for law enforcement officials. Further, police officers are to attempt to obtain maximum public cooperation and to enforce all laws with courtesy, consideration, and dignity. Although the IACP has no enforcement authority, the Codes do provide an excellent standard for adoption by law enforcement agencies, as well as by individual officers.

For the remainder of this book, references to police or law enforcement officers are to any one of the previously mentioned agencies.

Prosecutors

Prosecutors are also central to the administration of justice. *Prosecutors* are government attorneys responsible for prosecuting violators. This role includes preparing and filing documents; engaging in pretrial activity, such as discovery; and appearing in court. Prosecutors often also act as legal counsel to law enforcement officers, rendering advice on the law of searches, seizures, arrests, surveillance techniques, and similar matters. Prosecutors appear at grand jury hearings, where they present evidence and assist the jury in other ways. Finally, in some jurisdictions, prosecutors act in a supervisory capacity as the head of a law enforcement agency, such as the Attorney General of the United States, who is the head of the Department of Justice.

At the federal level, the highest law enforcement official and prosecutor is the Attorney General, who undergoes the presidential nomination and senatorial confirmation process. The Attorney General is a cabinet member who heads the Department of Justice.

Within each judicial district is one United States Attorney, a subordinate of the Attorney General, who also is selected through the nomination and confirmation process. United States Attorneys, with the aid of several Assistant United States Attorneys (AUSAs), are responsible for most federal prosecutions. In rare cases, however, another attorney from the Department of Justice may travel to a district to handle a case. Federal law also provides for the appointment of an independent counsel (special prosecutor) when government officials are suspected of violating the law.

Similar to the federal government, each state has an attorney general. The states vary in the structure of their prosecutorial agencies, but most have locally elected prosecutors, who may be titled *prosecutor, district attorney,* or *state attorney.* The degree to which these individuals answer to the state attorney general differs greatly. Additionally, local forms of government have attorneys. In some localities, these attorneys prosecute ordinance violations.

Prosecutorial Discretion.   Prosecutors enjoy considerable discretion in the performance of their duties. The decision whether to prosecute an individual is one aspect of prosecutorial **discretion.** This decision must be made by a prosecutor in most cases. In a small number of cases, however, the prosecutor may not be in a position to make this decision, such as when a traffic ticket acts as the charging instrument and the case proceeds directly to court without the prosecutor's involvement. However, most cases are initiated directly by a prosecutor, grand jury, or, as is usually the case, the police (through the arrest and complaint procedure). A case may not proceed under a complaint; rather, the prosecutor must file an information (or an indictment issued by a grand jury), which replaces the complaint. If a prosecutor refuses, or files a ***nolle prosequi,*** the case proceeds no further.

There are two general reasons that discretion must be exercised. First, the prosecutor's ethical obligation requires that he or she seek justice, not convictions. Prosecutors are not to maintain a prosecution simply because there is a probability of prevailing. Rather, the totality of the facts must be examined and it must be determined that a prosecution will further justice. The justice obligation continues through the entire adjudicative process.

Economics is the second reason prosecutors cannot pursue every case. The resources of the prosecutor and law enforcement agencies are limited. Not every case can be prosecuted because there are inadequate investigators, police officers, prosecutors, and other resources. Prosecutors must prioritize cases for prosecution. The decision whether to prosecute is influenced by many factors. The facts of the case; the accused's criminal, social, and economic history; the likelihood of success; the cost of prosecution, including the probable time investment; public opinion; the seriousness of the crime; the desires of the victims; police expectations and desires; political concerns; and whether the prosecution will further the administration of justice are all considered.

Although prosecutorial discretion is broad, it is not absolute. First, the authority to file a *nolle prosequi* or dismissal may be limited. The further along a case is in the process, the more involved the court becomes in the decision. Generally, the decision not to prosecute before the formal charge (information or indictment) is filed is left to the prosecutor without judicial intervention. However, a small number of states require judicial approval of *nolle prosequi* decisions.

Once the formal charge has been filed, judicial approval of dismissal is the rule rather than the exception. This is true in the federal system, which also requires leave of court to dismiss complaints.[3]

discretion
The power to act within general guidelines, rules, or laws, but without either specific rules to follow or the need to completely explain or justify each decision or action.

nolle prosequi
(Latin) The ending of a criminal case because the prosecutor decides or agrees to stop prosecuting. When this happens, the case is "*nolled,*" "*nollied,*" or "*nol. prossed.*"

Second, decisions to prosecute that are motivated by improper criteria may violate equal protection. The Fourteenth Amendment prohibits each state from taking actions that "deny to any person within its jurisdiction the equal protection of the laws." Although the Fifth Amendment does not contain this language, the Supreme Court has interpreted the Fifth Amendment's Due Process Clause as requiring equal protection of the laws. A claim that it is unfair to prosecute a person because other known violators are not prosecuted will not be successful, unless it can be shown that the accused has been singled out for an improper reason.

Generally, three elements must be shown to establish improper, discriminatory prosecution: first, that other people similarly situated were not prosecuted; second, that the prosecutor intentionally singled out the defendant; third, that the selection was based upon an arbitrary classification. As the Supreme Court stated in *Oyler v. Boles*,[4] for there to be an equal protection violation it must be shown that "the selection was *deliberately* based upon an unjustified standard." What is an unjustified standard? Prosecutions based upon race, religion, and gender are examples. A prosecution intended to punish an individual for exercising a constitutional right is also improper. The Supreme Court discusses selective prosecution in *United States v. Armstrong* (1996).

To determine whether a classification is proper, equal protection analysis must be employed. Most decisions are tested under the rational relationship test. That is, if the decision to prosecute is rationally related to a legitimate governmental objective, it is valid. If a decision is based upon race or religion, or in

 CASE

UNITED STATES V. ARMSTRONG

517 U.S. 456 (1996)

OPINION

Chief Justice Rehnquist delivered the opinion of the Court.

In this case, we consider the showing necessary for a defendant to be entitled to discovery on a claim that the prosecuting attorney singled him out for prosecution on the basis of his race. We conclude that respondents failed to satisfy the threshold showing: They failed to show that the Government declined to prosecute similarly situated suspects of other races.

In April 1992, respondents were indicted in the United States District Court for the Central District of California on charges of conspiring to possess with intent to distribute more than 50 grams of cocaine base (crack) and conspiring to distribute the same, in violation of 21 U.S.C. §§ 841 and 846 (1988 ed. and Supp. IV), and federal firearms offenses. For three months prior to the indictment, agents of the Federal Bureau of Alcohol, Tobacco, and Firearms and the Narcotics Division of the Inglewood, California, Police Department had infiltrated a suspected crack distribution ring by using three confidential informants. On seven separate occasions during this period, the informants had bought a total of 124.3 grams of crack from respondents and witnessed respondents carrying firearms during the sales. The agents searched the hotel room in which the sales were transacted, arrested respondents Armstrong and Hampton in the room, and found more crack and a loaded gun. The agents later arrested the other respondents as part of the ring.

In response to the indictment, respondents filed a motion for discovery or for dismissal of the indictment, alleging that they were selected for federal prosecution because they are black. In support of their motion, they offered only an affidavit by a "Paralegal Specialist," employed by the Office of the Federal Public Defender representing one of the respondents. The only allegation in the affidavit was that, in every one of the 24 § 841 or § 846 cases closed by the office during 1991, the defendant was black. Accompanying the affidavit was a "study" listing the 24 defendants, their race, whether they were prosecuted for dealing cocaine as well as crack, and the status of each case.

The Government opposed the discovery motion, arguing, among other things, that there was no evidence or allegation "that the Government has acted unfairly or has prosecuted nonblack defendants or failed to prosecute them." App. 150. The District Court granted the motion. It ordered the Government (1) to provide a list of all cases from the last three years in which the Government charged both cocaine and firearms offenses, (2) to identify the race of the defendants in those cases, (3) to identify what levels of law enforcement were involved in the investigations of those cases, and (4) to explain its criteria for deciding to prosecute those defendants for federal cocaine offenses. *Id.,* at 161–162.

The Government moved for reconsideration of the District Court's discovery order. With this motion it submitted affidavits and other evidence to explain why it had chosen to prosecute respondents and why respondents' study did not support the inference that the Government was singling out blacks for cocaine prosecution. The federal and local agents participating in the case alleged in affidavits that race played no role in their investigation. An Assistant United States Attorney explained in an affidavit that the decision to prosecute met the general criteria for prosecution, because

> "there was over 100 grams of cocaine base involved, over twice the threshold necessary for a ten year mandatory minimum sentence; there were multiple sales involving multiple defendants, thereby indicating a fairly substantial crack cocaine ring; . . . there were multiple federal firearms violations intertwined with the narcotics trafficking; the overall evidence in the case was extremely strong, including audio and videotapes of defendants;. . . and several of the defendants had criminal histories including narcotics and firearms violations." *Id.,* at 81.

The Government also submitted sections of a published 1989 Drug Enforcement Administration report which concluded that "large-scale, interstate trafficking networks controlled by Jamaicans, Haitians and Black street gangs dominate the manufacture and distribution of crack." J. Featherly & E. Hill, *Crack Cocaine Overview* 1989; App. 103.

In response, one of respondents' attorneys submitted an affidavit alleging that an intake coordinator at a drug treatment center had told her that there are "an equal number of caucasian users and dealers to minority users and dealers." *Id.,* at 138. Respondents also submitted an affidavit from a criminal defense attorney alleging that in his experience many nonblacks are prosecuted in state court for crack offenses, *id.,* at 141, and a newspaper article reporting that federal "crack criminals . . . are being punished far more severely than if they had been caught with powder cocaine, and almost every single one of them is black." Newton, "Harsher Crack Sentences Criticized as Racial Inequity," *Los Angeles Times,* Nov. 23, 1992, p. 1; App. 208–210.

The District Court denied the motion for reconsideration. When the Government indicated it would not comply with the court's discovery order, the court dismissed the case.

A divided three-judge panel of the Court of Appeals for the Ninth Circuit reversed, . . .

A selective-prosecution claim is not a defense on the merits to the criminal charge itself, but an independent assertion that the prosecutor has brought the charge for reasons forbidden by the Constitution. Our cases delineating the necessary elements to prove a claim of selective prosecution have taken great pains to explain that the standard is a demanding one. These cases afford a "background presumption," cf. *United States v. Mezzanatto,* 513 U.S. 196, 203, 130 L. Ed. 2d 697, 115 S. Ct. 797 (1995), that the showing necessary to obtain discovery should itself be a significant barrier to the litigation of insubstantial claims.

A selective-prosecution claim asks a court to exercise judicial power over a "special province" of the Executive. *Heckler v. Chaney,* 470 U.S. 821, 832, 84 L. Ed. 2d 714, 105 S. Ct. 1649 (1985). The Attorney General and United States Attorneys retain "broad discretion" to enforce the Nation's criminal laws. *Wayte v. United States,* 470 U.S. 598, 607, 84 L. Ed. 2d 547, 105 S. Ct. 1524 (1985) (quoting *United States v. Goodwin,* 457 U.S. 368, 380, n. 11, 73 L. Ed. 2d 74, 102 S. Ct. 2485 (1982)). They have this latitude because they are designated by statute as the President's delegates to help him discharge his constitutional responsibility to "take *Care that the Laws be* faithfully executed." U.S. Const., Art. II, § 3; see 28 U.S.C. §§ 516, 547. As a result, "the presumption of regularity supports" their prosecutorial decisions and, "in the absence of clear evidence to the contrary, courts presume that they have properly discharged their official duties." *United States v. Chemical Foundation, Inc.,* 272 U.S. 1, 14–15, 71 L. Ed. 131, 47 S. Ct. 1 (1926). In the ordinary case, "so long as the prosecutor has probable cause to believe that the accused committed an offense defined by statute, the decision whether or not to prosecute, and what charge to file or bring before a grand jury, generally rests entirely in his discretion." *Bordenkircher v. Hayes,* 434 U.S. 357, 364, 54 L. Ed. 2d 604, 98 S. Ct. 663 (1978).

Of course, a prosecutor's discretion is "subject to constitutional constraints." *United States v. Batchelder,* 442 U.S. 114, 125, 60 L. Ed. 2d 755, 99 S. Ct. 2198 (1979). One of these constraints, imposed by the equal protection component of the Due Process Clause of the Fifth Amendment, *Bolling v. Sharpe,* 347 U.S. 497, 500, 98 L. Ed. 884, 74 S. Ct. 693 (1954), is that the decision whether to prosecute may not be based on "an unjustifiable standard such as race, religion, or other arbitrary classification," *Oyler v. Boles,* 368 U.S. 448, 456, 7 L. Ed. 2d 446, 82 S. Ct. 501 (1962). A defendant may demonstrate that the administration of a criminal law is "directed so exclusively against a particular class of persons . . . with a mind so unequal and oppressive" that the system of prosecution amounts to "a practical denial" of equal protection of the law. *Yick Wo v. Hopkins,* 118 U.S. 356, 373, 30 L. Ed. 220, 6 S. Ct. 1064 (1886).

In order to dispel the presumption that a prosecutor has not violated equal protection, a criminal defendant must present "clear evidence to the contrary." *Chemical Foundation, supra,* at 14–15. We explained in *Wayte* why courts are "properly hesitant to examine the decision whether to prosecute." 470 U.S. at 608. Judicial deference to the decisions of these executive officers rests in part on an assessment of the relative competence of prosecutors and courts. "Such factors as the strength of the case, the prosecution's general deterrence value, the Government's enforcement priorities, and the case's relationship to the Government's overall enforcement plan are not readily susceptible to the kind of analysis the courts are competent to undertake." *Id.,* at 607. It also stems from a concern not to unnecessarily impair the performance of a core executive constitutional function. "Examining the basis of a prosecution delays the criminal proceeding, threatens to chill law enforcement by subjecting the prosecutor's motives and decision making to outside inquiry, and may undermine prosecutorial effectiveness by revealing the Government's enforcement policy." *Ibid.* The requirements for a selective-prosecution claim draw on "ordinary equal protection standards." *Id.,* at 608. The claimant must demonstrate that the federal prosecutorial policy "had a discriminatory effect and that it was motivated by a discriminatory purpose." *Ibid.;* accord, *Oyler, supra,* at 456. To establish a discriminatory effect in a race case, the claimant must show that similarly situated individuals of a different race were not prosecuted. This requirement has been established in our case law since *Ah Sin v. Wittman,* 198 U.S. 500, 49 L. Ed. 1142, 25 S. Ct. 756 (1905). Ah Sin, a subject of China, petitioned a California state court for a writ of habeas corpus, seeking discharge from imprisonment under a San Francisco County ordinance prohibiting persons from setting up gambling tables in rooms barricaded to stop police from entering. *Id.,* at 503. He alleged in his habeas petition "that the ordinance is enforced 'solely and exclusively against persons of the Chinese race and not otherwise.'" *Id.,* at 507. We rejected his contention that this averment made out a claim under the Equal Protection Clause, because it did not allege "that the conditions and practices to which the ordinance was directed did not exist exclusively among the Chinese, or that there were other offenders against the ordinance than the Chinese as to whom it was not enforced." *Id.,* at 507–508.

The similarly situated requirement does not make a selective-prosecution claim impossible to prove. Twenty years before *Ah Sin,* we invalidated an ordinance, also adopted by San Francisco, that prohibited the operation of laundries in wooden buildings. *Yick Wo,* 118 U.S. at 374. The plaintiff in error successfully demonstrated that the ordinance was applied against Chinese nationals but not against other laundry-shop operators. The authorities had denied the applications of 200 Chinese subjects for permits to operate shops in wooden buildings, but granted the applications of 80 individuals who were not Chinese subjects to operate laundries in wooden buildings "under similar conditions." *Ibid.* We explained in *Ah Sin* why the similarly situated requirement is necessary:

"No latitude of intention should be indulged in a case like this. There should be certainty to every intent. Plaintiff in error seeks to set aside a criminal law of the State, not on the ground that it is unconstitutional on its face, not that it is discriminatory in

tendency and ultimate actual operation as the ordinance was which was passed on in the *Yick Wo* case, but that it was made so by the manner of its administration. This is a matter of proof, and *no fact should be omitted to make it out completely,* when the power of a Federal court is invoked to interfere with the course of criminal justice of a State." 198 U.S. at 508 (emphasis added).

Although *Ah Sin* involved federal review of a state conviction, we think a similar rule applies where the power of a federal court is invoked to challenge an exercise of one of the core powers of the Executive Branch of the Federal Government, the power to prosecute. . . .

Having reviewed the requirements to prove a selective-prosecution claim, we turn to the showing necessary to obtain discovery in support of such a claim. If discovery is ordered, the Government must assemble from its own files documents which might corroborate or refute the defendant's claim. Discovery thus imposes many of the costs present when the Government must respond to a prima facie case of selective prosecution. It will divert prosecutors' resources and may disclose the Government's prosecutorial strategy. The justifications for a rigorous standard for the elements of a selective-prosecution claim thus require a correspondingly rigorous standard for discovery in aid of such a claim.

The parties, and the Courts of Appeals which have considered the requisite showing to establish entitlement to discovery, describe this showing with a variety of phrases, like "colorable basis," "substantial threshold showing," Tr. of Oral Arg. 5, "substantial and concrete basis," or "reasonable likelihood," Brief for Respondents Martin et al. 30. However, the many labels for this showing conceal the degree of consensus about the evidence necessary to meet it. The Courts of Appeals "require some evidence tending to show the existence of the essential elements of the defense," discriminatory effect and discriminatory intent. *United States v. Berrios,* 501 F.2d 1207, 1211 (CA2 1974).

In this case we consider what evidence constitutes "some evidence tending to show the existence" of the discriminatory effect element. The Court of Appeals held that a defendant may establish a colorable basis for discriminatory effect without evidence that the Government has failed to prosecute others who are similarly situated to the defendant. 48 F.3d at 1516. We think it was mistaken in this view. The vast majority of the Courts of Appeals require the defendant to produce some evidence that similarly situated defendants of other races could have been prosecuted, but were not, and this requirement is consistent with our equal protection case law. *United States v. Parham,* 16 F.3d 844, 846–847 (CA8 1994); *United States v. Fares,* 978 F.2d 52, 59–60 (CA2 1992); *United States v. Peete,* 919 F.2d 1168, 1176 (CA6 1990); *C. E. Carlson, Inc. v. SEC,* 859 F.2d 1429, 1437–1438 (CA10 1988); *United States v. Greenwood,* 796 F.2d 49, 52–53 (CA4 1986); *United States v. Mitchell,* 778 F.2d 1271, 1277 (CA7 1985). As the three-judge panel explained, " 'selective prosecution' implies that a selection has taken place." 21 F.3d at 1436.

The Court of Appeals reached its decision in part because it started "with the presumption that people of *all* races commit *all* types of crimes— not with the premise that any type of crime is the exclusive province of any particular racial or ethnic group." 48 F.3d at 1516–1517. It cited no authority for this proposition, which seems contradicted by the most recent statistics of the United States Sentencing Commission. Those statistics show: More than 90 percent of the persons sentenced in 1994 for crack cocaine trafficking were black, United States Sentencing Comm'n, 1994 Annual Report 107 (Table 45); 93.4 percent of convicted LSD dealers were white, *ibid.;* and 91 percent of those convicted for pornography or prostitution were white, *id.,* at 41 (Table 13). Presumptions at war with presumably reliable statistics have no proper place in the analysis of this issue.

The Court of Appeals also expressed concern about the "evidentiary obstacles defendants face."

48 F.3d at 1514. But all of its sister Circuits that have confronted the issue have required that defendants produce some evidence of differential treatment of similarly situated members of other races or protected classes. In the present case, if the claim of selective prosecution were well founded, it should not have been an insuperable task to prove that persons of other races were being treated differently than respondents. For instance, respondents could have investigated whether similarly situated persons of other races were prosecuted by the State of California and were known to federal law enforcement officers, but were not prosecuted in federal court. We think the required threshold—a credible showing of different treatment of similarly situated persons—adequately balances the Government's interest in vigorous prosecution and the defendant's interest in avoiding selective prosecution.

In the case before us, respondents' "study" did not constitute "some evidence tending to show the existence of the essential elements of" a selective-prosecution claim. *Berrios, supra,* at 1211. The study failed to identify individuals who were not black and could have been prosecuted for the offenses for which respondents were charged, but were not so prosecuted. This omission was not remedied by respondents' evidence in opposition to the Government's motion for reconsideration. The newspaper article, which discussed the discriminatory effect of federal drug sentencing laws, was not relevant to an allegation of discrimination in decisions to prosecute. Respondents' affidavits, which recounted one attorney's conversation with a drug treatment center employee and the experience of another attorney defending drug prosecutions in state court, recounted hearsay and reported personal conclusions based on anecdotal evidence. The judgment of the Court of Appeals is therefore reversed, and the case is remanded for proceedings consistent with this opinion.

It is so ordered.

retaliation for a person's exercise of a right, the decision is tested under the strict scrutiny test and is invalid unless it can be shown to further a compelling governmental interest. Finally, a few classifications, such as those based upon gender, are tested under a standard less demanding than strict scrutiny but more demanding than the rational relationship test. Such laws must bear a substantial relationship to a legitimate governmental interest. In reality, claims of selective enforcement are rarely successful.

Ethics.   All attorneys are bound by ethical rules. Two sets of rules are used in the United States: the Model Code of Professional Responsibility and the Model Rules of Professional Conduct. The two are similar and every state has adopted some form of these rules. Ethical violations may result in discipline by the bar, an offended court, or both. Common sanctions include private and public reprimands, suspension, and disbarment. Under court rules and rules of procedure, other sanctions, such as monetary penalties, may be assessed. Also, all courts possess the authority to punish for contempt.

Prosecutors have special ethical responsibilities. You have already learned that the mission of the prosecutor is to achieve justice. The Model Code of Professional Responsibility states that the "responsibility of a public prosecutor differs from that of the usual advocate; his duty is to seek justice, not merely to convict."[5]

Prosecutors have an ethical obligation to be sure that a prosecution is warranted and to seek dismissal immediately upon discovering that one is not. Prosecutors are not to trump up charges to increase their power during plea negotiations. Prosecutors are only to request a fair sentence from a court. Of course, prosecutors may not use perjured or falsified evidence to obtain a conviction. In addition, you will learn later in this text that prosecutors have a constitutional duty to disclose exculpatory evidence.[6] Evidence that mitigates the degree of an offense or reduces a sentence must also be disclosed.[7] Further, prosecutors are not to avoid pursuing evidence because it may damage the government's case or assist the defendant.[8] Through discovery rules, prosecutors have a duty to disclose other evidence prior to or during trial. In short, prosecutors have an obligation to deal with defendants fairly.

On the other side, prosecutors have an obligation to pursue a prosecution when the facts of the case demand it. At trial, unless a prosecutor becomes convinced that the accused is innocent, the prosecutor is to zealously pursue a conviction.

Judges

Judges are not executive branch officials, as are prosecutors and law enforcement officers. Judges are part of the judiciary, a separate and independent branch of government. Generally, the judiciary is responsible for the resolution of disputes and the administration of justice. In regard to criminal law, judges are responsible for issuing warrants, supervising pretrial activity, presiding over hearings and trial, deciding guilt or innocence in some cases, and passing sentence on those convicted.

Having a fair and impartial party make these determinations is an important feature of the United States criminal justice system, and is mandated by the Constitution in many instances, as you will learn in the following chapters. A judge has the obligation to remain unbiased, fair, and impartial in all cases before the bar.

Ethics.   Like attorneys, judges are subject to a code of ethics. Most states have enacted the Code of Judicial Conduct. Judges are to be fair and impartial.[9] In criminal cases, judges must be sensitive to defendants' rights and be careful not to imply to a jury that a defendant is guilty.

Defense Attorneys

Because of the complexity of the legal system and the advantage of having an advocate, competent legal counsel has become an important feature of the American system of criminal justice. The Sixth Amendment to the Constitution provides that all persons have a right to be represented by counsel in criminal cases. Today, indigent defendants have a right to counsel in all cases that may result in incarceration.

Ethics.   Defense attorneys have high, and sometimes morally challenging, ethical responsibilities. Unlike the prosecutor, whose duty is to see that justice is achieved, the defense attorney must zealously represent the accused, within the bounds of the law,[10] regardless of innocence or guilt.

This obligation is the cause of some public disrespect for the legal profession. Attorneys are perceived as hired guns, not as advocates of civil liberties. Defense lawyers are frequently asked how they can defend people they know are guilty. There are two responses to this inquiry. First, defense attorneys often do not know whether their clients are in fact guilty, as this question is rarely asked. Second, defense attorneys are not defending the actions that the defendant is accused of committing; rather, defense attorneys are defending the rights of the accused, specifically, the right to have the government prove its case beyond a reasonable doubt using lawfully obtained evidence. By defending the rights of one person against governmental oppression, the rights of all the people are defended.

This approach, which is a vital part of the United States criminal justice system, is often misunderstood by the public. The defense attorney who fulfills this constitutional and ethical mission is often the source of public animosity and ridicule.

Communications between attorneys and clients are confidential and privileged. Attorneys are generally prohibited from disclosing those communications.[11] In the *Belge* case, an attorney was indicted for not revealing a client's privileged communication and was the subject of considerable public disdain. The indictment was dismissed in the interests of justice, namely, preservation of the attorney-client privilege. However, nothing could be done by the court to restore the attorney's good reputation and standing in his community.

Belge turned on the fact that the crimes had already occurred and the defendant posed no threat. An attorney is allowed, but not required, to report a client's intention to commit a crime.[12] Therefore, if a client informs his counsel that he intends to kill a witness if he is released on bond, the attorney may disclose this information without breaching any ethical obligations.

 CASE

PEOPLE V. BELGE

372 N.Y.S.2d 798
(1975)

In the summer of 1973 Robert F. Garrow, Jr. stood charged in Hamilton County with the crime of murder. The defendant was assigned two attorneys, Frank H. Armani and Francis R. Belge. A defense of insanity had been interposed by counsel for Mr. Garrow. During the course of the discussions between Garrow and his two counsel, three other murders were admitted by Garrow, one being in Onondaga County. On or about September of 1973 Mr. Belge conducted his own investigation based upon what his client had told him and with the assistance of a friend the location of the body of Alicia Hauck was found in Oakwood Cemetery in Syracuse. Mr. Belge personally inspected the body and was satisfied, presumably, that this was Alicia Hauck that his client had told him he murdered.

This discovery was not disclosed to the authorities, but became public during the trial of Mr. Garrow in June of 1974, when, to affirmatively establish the defense of insanity, these three other murders were brought before the jury by the defense in the Hamilton County trial. Public indignation reached the fever pitch; statements were made by the District Attorney of Onondaga County relative to the situation and he caused the Grand Jury of Onondaga County, then sitting, to conduct a thorough investigation. As a result of this investigation Frank Armani was No Billed by the Grand Jury, but [an i]ndictment . . . was returned against Francis R. Belge, Esq., accusing him of having violated [the public health law], which, in essence, requires that a decent burial be accorded the dead, and . . . requires anyone knowing of the

death of a person without medical attendance, to report the same to the proper authorities. Defense counsel moved for dismissal of the Indictment on the grounds that a confidential, privileged communication existed between him and Mr. Garrow, which should excuse the attorney from making full disclosure to the authorities. The National Association of Criminal Defense Lawyers, as Amicus Curiae . . . succinctly stated the issue in the following language:

> "If this indictment stands, the attorney-client privilege will be effectively destroyed. No defendant will be able to freely discuss the facts of his case with his attorney. No attorney will be able to listen to those facts without being faced with the Hobson's choice of violating the law or violating his professional code of Ethics."

Initially in England the practice of law was not recognized as a profession and certainly some people are skeptics today. However, the practice of learned and capable men appearing before the Court on behalf of a friend or an acquaintance became more and more demanding. Consequently, the King granted a privilege to certain of these men to engage in such practice. There had to be rules governing their duties. These came to be known as "Canons." The King has, in this country, been substituted by a democracy, but the "Canons" are with us today, having been honed and refined over the years to meet the changes of time. Most are constantly being studied and revamped by the American Bar Association and by the bar associations of the various states. While they are, for the most part, general by definition, they can be brought to bear in a particular situation. Among those is the [rule that] confidential communications between an attorney and his client are privileged from disclosure . . . as a rule of necessity in the administration of justice. . . .

The effectiveness of counsel is only as great as the confidentiality of its client-attorney relationship. If the lawyer cannot get all the facts about the case, he can only give his client half of a defense. . . .

When the facts of the other homicides became public, as a result of the defendant's testimony to substantiate his claim of insanity, "Members of the public were shocked at the apparent callousness of these lawyers with the public interest and with simple decency." A hue and cry went up from the press and other news media suggesting that the attorneys should be found guilty of such crimes as obstruction of justice or becoming an accomplice after the fact. From a layman's standpoint, this certainly was a logical conclusion. However, the constitution of the United States of America attempts to preserve the dignity of the individual and to do that guarantees him the services of an attorney who will bring to the bar and to the bench every conceivable protection from the inroads of the state against such rights as are vested in the constitution for one accused of a crime. Among those substantial constitutional rights is that a defendant does not have to incriminate himself. His attorneys were bound

to uphold that concept and maintain what has been called a sacred trust of confidentiality.

The following language of the brief of the Amicus Curiae further points up the statements just made: "The client's Fifth Amendment rights cannot be violated by his attorney. . . . Because the discovery of the body of Alicia Hauck would have presented 'a significant link in the chain of evidence tending to establish his guilt'. . . Garrow was constitutionally exempt from any statutory requirement to disclose the location of the body. And Attorney Belge, as Garrow's attorney, was not only equally exempt, but under a positive stricture precluding such disclosure. Garrow, although constitutionally privileged against a requirement to compulsory disclosure, was free to make such a revelation if he chose to do so. Attorney Belge was affirmatively required to withhold disclosure. The criminal defendant's self-incrimination rights become completely nugatory if compulsory disclosure can be exacted through his attorney." . . .

It is the decision of this Court that Francis R. Belge conducted himself as an officer of the Court with all the zeal at his command to protect the constitutional rights of his client. Both on the grounds of a privileged communication and the interests of justice the Indictment is dismissed.[13]

Attorneys are generally obligated to represent criminal defendants when appointed by a court or upon request by a bar association. However, an attorney may be excused for compelling reasons. In no event is belief in a defendant's guilt or disgust with the alleged acts compelling.[14]

An interesting ethical dilemma is presented when a defense attorney knows (or has a strong belief) that either the client or one of the defense witnesses has given or intends to give false testimony. On the one hand, the attorney is an officer of the court and thus prohibited from defrauding the court. On the other hand, the defense attorney has an obligation to the client. There is a split in the jurisdictions concerning how this situation is to be handled. There are three possibilities. First, the most preferable, the defense attorney dissuades the client from committing perjury. Second, the attorney moves to withdraw from the case, keeping the reason secret. Third, the attorney discloses the client's intention to commit perjury to the court. The law in each jurisdiction must be examined to determine which of these options is permitted or preferred.

Defense attorneys are sometimes asked to represent co-defendants. This can create a conflict of interest for a defense attorney if the defendants have conflicting or antagonistic defenses. Because of the inherent dangers of representing co-defendants, many defense attorneys refuse joint representation. It is a violation of a defendant's Sixth Amendment right to the assistance of effective counsel to have a lawyer with divided loyalties.

Finally, trial counsel for criminal defendants have an obligation to continue on appeal unless new counsel is retained or the court has authorized withdrawal. This is different from civil cases, where there is no general obligation to continue after trial.

Legal Assistants. Legal assistants are employed by both prosecutors and defense attorneys, with the latter being more common.[15] In the defense context, legal assistants may be asked to perform several tasks, including conducting initial interviews, conducting legal research, preparing drafts of motions and other documents, maintaining and organizing files, acting as a contact with incarcerated clients, assisting in preparing the defendant and other witnesses for trial, and preparing the defendant for the presentence investigation interview. Some paralegals are called upon to conduct investigations.

As employees of attorneys, legal assistants must also follow ethical guidelines and responsibilities. Although no state has yet established mandatory certification of legal assistants, and therefore there is no enforceable set of ethics rules, the National Federation of Paralegal Organizations and the National Association of Legal Assistants (NALA) have promulgated Codes of Ethics.

The NALA Code states that first, legal assistants may not engage in the practice of law.[16] This includes rendering legal advice, establishing an attorney-client relationship, setting fees, and appearing in court on behalf of a client. Although some administrative agencies permit legal assistants to represent clients at hearings, this is never so in criminal law. The unauthorized practice of law is both criminal and unethical. Further, legal assistants are to act prudently in determining the extent to which a client may be assisted without the presence of a lawyer.[17] Finally, it is imperative that the attorney directly supervise the legal assistant's work in criminal law.[18]

Second, all employees of an attorney are bound by the confidentiality rule.[19] All communications made by a client to a legal assistant fall within the scope of the attorney-client privilege and may not be disclosed by the legal assistant.

Third, legal assistants must be careful not to suborn perjury when preparing the client and witnesses for trial. Instructing a witness in effective techniques, including dress and personal appearance, and methods of responding to inquiries (e.g., answer directly, honestly, and as succinctly as possible; look at the jury during your response) is proper. Suggesting, urging, encouraging, or directing a witness to lie or mislead a court is suborning perjury.

Fourth, legal assistants are bound through their attorney-supervisors by the American Bar Association's Model Rules of Professional Conduct and Model Code of Professional Responsibility.[20]

Victims

Recall that the legal victim of crimes is the government. That is why criminal prosecutions are brought in the name of the government. However, most crimes have another victim, the victim-in-fact. This is the person assaulted, battered, raped, or robbed. Victims affect criminal adjudications in a number of ways.

First, law enforcement officers may decline to make an arrest or conduct an investigation if the victim is disinterested in having the matter pursued. Second, the prosecutor may file a *nolle prosequi,* if there has been an arrest, or otherwise refuse to proceed with a prosecution if that is the victim's desire. Third, if the matter proceeds to trial, the victim may be required to testify at both pretrial hearings and trial. A victim may choose to attend even if his or her testimony is not required. Fourth, the victim may participate in the sentencing portion of the trial. As you will learn, statements concerning how a victim and a victim's family have been affected may be considered by judge and jury when passing sentence. Restitution is also made a condition of some sentences.

Victims' rights have received considerable attention since the mid-1980s. Victims' rights organizations have strenuously—and successfully—lobbied to introduce both state constitutional amendments and legislation concerning victims' rights. For example, the Arizona Constitution was amended to include a "Victims' Bill of Rights." Through that amendment and its enabling legislation, crime victims are allowed to participate in the initial appearance, be heard on conditions of release, be present at all court proceedings, confer with the prosecutor concerning disposition of the case, refuse a defense interview or other discovery request, provide an impact statement for sentencing, receive restitution and other damages, receive notice of probation modifications of the perpetrator, and receive notice of parole or death of the perpetrator.[21]

Rape shield legislation is another form of victims' rights laws. Rape shield laws exclude from trial evidence of a rape victim's sexual history (except evidence of sexual history with the accused) and reputation in the community. These laws were enacted to protect the rape victim from embarrassing, harassing, and intimidating inquiries.

In most jurisdictions, victims' rights are a matter of statutory, not constitutional, law. Change came quickly in this area. In 1982, only four states had victims' bills of rights. That number increased to forty-four by 1987. In 1982, only eight states allowed the use of **victim impact statements** at sentencing. By 1987, the number of states permitting victim impact evidence to be considered by sentencing judges and juries increased to thirty-nine. Only one state provided that a crime victim had a right to confer with the prosecutor concerning important prosecutorial decisions in 1982. That number increased to twenty-eight by 1987. Restitution was mandated by the law of eight states in 1982; twenty-nine states required the imposition of restitution in 1987.[22]

In addition to laws providing for victim participation in court proceedings, laws have been enacted for the protection of both victims and witnesses. These laws provide for the relocation of a witness or victim whose cooperation with an investigation or prosecution endangers his or her life. The federal law is well

victim impact statement
At the time of sentencing, a statement made to the court concerning the effect the crime has had on the victim or on the victim's family.

known. It provides for relocation of the victim or witness and his or her immediate family at taxpayer expense. Further, the United States provides the family with a new identity.[23]

Victims are likely to have civil remedies against perpetrators under traditional civil law theories. Intentional tort actions for assault, battery, invasion of privacy, and conversion are examples.

Finally, *victim assistance organizations* are available in many jurisdictions. Some are independent, not-for-profit corporations and others are governmental entities. These organizations provide information, counseling, and other assistance to victims. Also, most states have enacted *victim compensation programs*. In many instances restitution proves inadequate, such as when the perpetrator is indigent. In these instances, a victim can request compensation from a state victim compensation fund. These programs reimburse victims for medical expenses and, sometimes, loss of income. Generally, they do not compensate victims for property losses.

LIABILITY OF GOVERNMENTS AND THEIR OFFICIALS

Government officials, including law enforcement officers, prosecutors, and judges, are not above the law. Violation of an individual's rights by an official, even if during the performance of official duties, may lead to civil and criminal liability.[24] It is not in society's best interest, however, to create an environment where officials are threatened with civil or criminal liability for every incorrect decision and action, especially when they act in good faith and after thoughtful consideration of alternatives and repercussions. In such a world, civil authorities would be afraid to act and government would be paralyzed. Therefore, the laws governing liability of government officials are designed to provide remedies only for acts that are outrageous, malicious, shocking, or in clear violation of established rights.

States have laws that may provide remedies to the victims of improper governmental conduct. A police officer who commits an unjustified assault, battery, or false imprisonment may be liable under traditional tort and criminal law theories. These and other actions may lead to civil and criminal liability under state civil rights laws. In addition, violations of federally secured rights by state or federal officers can result in both civil and criminal prosecutions under federal civil rights statutes.[25] It was under these laws that several Los Angeles, California, police officers were prosecuted for violating the civil rights of Rodney King in 1993. Similarly, a prosecutor who violates a person's civil rights may be liable under federal law,[26] or a similar state law, or under a state tort theory. In fewer instances, judges may also be liable for their actions.

The civil liability of officials is limited by immunity doctrines. Immunities developed at common law, and the United States Supreme Court has determined that Congress did not intend to abolish these immunities when it enacted the civil rights acts.[27] Therefore, governmental officials may assert immunity as a defense if sued under the federal civil rights statutes.

There is a judicial immunity. Any action that is judicial in nature is shielded by *absolute immunity.* Because it is absolute, a government official is free from both suit and liability when performing judicial functions. Issuing orders (including warrants) and presiding over hearings are examples of judicial acts.

Most judicial acts are performed by judges, but not all. Prosecutors perform quasi-judicial acts and are shielded with absolute immunity for the performance of these acts. Appearing in court (including ex parte warrant application hearings) and complying with court orders are considered quasi-judicial acts. Similarly, police officers are shielded with absolute immunity when enforcing court orders (including warrants) and when testifying in court.

In other situations, another form of immunity may apply. A person entitled to *qualified immunity* is free from liability, but not necessarily free from suit. That means that the process of establishing nonliability may involve a greater commitment of time, energy, and money by a defendant. Under absolute immunity, issues of malice, intent, or the nature of the right alleged to be violated are immaterial, because the defendant is immune regardless. In contrast, whether an official acted with malice or whether the alleged right violated was clearly established at law are material in the qualified immunity case. Under some laws, an official is liable only if malice is shown, or, as required by federal law, a plaintiff can prove that a clearly established right was violated.

So, under federal law, although prosecutors are absolutely immune from civil liability for quasi-judicial acts, such as appearing in court and filing charges, they enjoy only a qualified immunity when performing other acts, such as rendering legal advice to law enforcement officers.[28] Similarly, judges are protected by qualified immunity when performing nonjudicial, but work-related, functions, such as making personnel decisions.[29] Police officers are shielded by qualified immunity when conducting investigations, making warrantless searches or seizures, and engaging in administrative and personnel matters.

Finally, the government itself may be sued in some circumstances. A serious obstacle, which must be overcome to establish governmental liability, is **sovereign immunity.** The doctrine of sovereign immunity holds that the government is immune from lawsuits. Therefore, governments must consent to be sued. This is true of both state and federal governments. Most states have abolished sovereign immunity to some degree, some by statute, and a few by judicial decision.

The federal government has consented to be sued under several laws. One is the Federal Tort Claims Act (FTCA).[30] Through this statute the United States has waived immunity from suit for a number of torts. In 1974, the statute was amended to permit suits based upon assault, battery, false imprisonment, false arrest, abuse of process, or malicious prosecution committed by federal law enforcement officers.

States may not be sued directly under federal civil rights statutes, nor may the federal government. However, local forms of government may be sued under federal civil rights laws if the acts alleged to have violated the plaintiff's civil rights were committed pursuant to an ordinance, regulation, policy, or decision of the locality.[31]

sovereign immunity

The government's freedom from being sued. In many cases, the U.S. government has waived immunity by a statute such as the Federal Tort Claims Act states have similar laws.

WEB LINKS

United States and International Law
Professor Cecil Greek maintains a comprehensive criminal justice site with hundreds of useful links. *http://www.criminology.fsu.edu/CJLinks/*

KEY TERMS

adversary system   *nolle prosequi*   victim impact statement
discretion   sovereign immunity

REVIEW QUESTIONS

1. What is the constitutional mission of a prosecutor?
2. What is the policy behind requiring defense attorneys to zealously represent guilty persons?
3. What is the attorney-client privilege?
4. Legal assistants and other nonlawyers are prohibited from practicing law. What acts constitute the practice of law?
5. Are legal assistants who are employed in law offices obligated to maintain client confidences?
6. What are victims' bills of rights? Name three rights typically included in such a law.
7. According to the Police Code of Conduct promulgated by the International Association of Chiefs of Police, when may force be used?
8. What do "U.S.C." and "Fed. R. Crim. P." represent?

REVIEW PROBLEMS

1. Create a set of facts under which co-defendants could not be represented by the same attorney. Explain why separate counsel is necessary under your scenario.
2. Do you believe that a defense attorney should be required to zealously represent a client who has admitted guilt to the lawyer? What if the result is the release of a violent criminal (i.e., acquittal or dismissal of charges)? Can you suggest an alternative method?
3. Do you believe that police officers should arrest every violator they encounter, discover, or are made aware of? Support your answer. What factors should an officer consider when making the decision whether to arrest or otherwise pursue a prosecution?
4. In some nations, prosecutors are required to file a criminal charge if sufficient evidence exists. What are the advantages of such a system? What are the disadvantages of such a system? Should this form of compulsory prosecution replace the United States model of prosecutorial discretion? Explain your answer.
5. In some nations, individual victims are permitted to file a criminal charge against the person(s) who committed the alleged act(s). In these nations, the victim may prosecute the case or a public prosecutor may prosecute on the victim's behalf. Should such a method be employed in the United States? Explain your answer.

END NOTES

1. For more information concerning the due process and crime control models, *see* N. Gary Holten & Lawson Lamar, *The Criminal Courts* ch. 1 (McGraw-Hill 1991).

2. Bureau of Justice Statistics 2001.

3. Fed. R. Crim. P. 48.

4. 368 U.S. 448 (1962).

5. Ethical Consideration (EC) 7-13.

6. *Id. See also Brady v. Maryland,* 373 U.S. 83 (1963).

7. Model Code of Professional Responsibility, Disciplinary Rule (DR) 7-103 reads: "[a] public prosecutor or other government lawyer in criminal litigation shall make timely disclosure to counsel for the defendant, or to the defendant if he has no counsel, of the existence of evidence, known to the prosecutor or other government lawyer, that tends to negate the guilt of the accused, mitigate the degree of the offense, or reduce the punishment."

8. EC 7-13.

9. Code of Judicial Conduct, Canon 3.

10. EC 7-1; DR 7-101.

11. DR 4-101.

12. Model Code of Professional Responsibility, DR 4-101(c)(3); Model Rules of Professional Conduct 1.6(b)(1).

13. The decision was affirmed on appeal. *See* 376 N.Y.S.2d 771 (1975) and 390 N.Y.S.2d 867 (1976).

14. EC 2-29.

15. Approximately 13 percent of all paralegals in the United States work in criminal law. *See* Angela Schneeman, *Paralegals in American Law* (Lawyers Cooperative/ Delmar Publishers 1994).

16. NALA Code of Ethics, Canons 1, 3, 4, and 6.

17. *Id.,* Canon 5.

18. *Id.,* Canon 2.

19. *Id.,* Canon 7.

20. *Id.,* Canon 12.

21. Christopher Johns, "Criminal Justice in America—Part One, The Costs of Victims' Rights," 29 *Arizona Attorney* 27 (Oct. 1992).

22. Don Siegelman & Courtney Tarver, "National Association of Attorneys General," 1 EISCL 163 (WL 1988).

23. Victim and Witness Protection Act, 18 U.S.C. § 224.

24. For a more thorough discussion of governmental liability, including the liability of government officials, *see* Daniel Hall, *Administrative Law* (Lawyers Cooperative/ Delmar Publishers 1994).

25. *See* 42 U.S.C. § 1983; 18 U.S.C. § 241 *et seq.*

26. *See* 42 U.S.C. § 1983.

27. *See Burns v. Reed,* 111 S. Ct. 1934 (1991); *Pierson v. Ray,* 386 U.S. 547 (1967).

28. *See* Daniel Hall, *Administrative Law* § 10.4 (West Legal Studies 1994) for a discussion of prosecutorial immunity.

29. *Id.*

30. 28 U.S.C. §§ 1291, 1346, 1402, 1504, 2110, 2401–2402, 2411–2412, 2671–2678, and 2680.

31. *Monell v. Department of Social Services,* 436 U.S. 658 (1978). *See also* Daniel Hall, *Administrative Law* § 10.4 (Lawyers Cooperative/Delmar Publishers 1994).

CHAPTER 11

The Constitutional Aspects of Criminal Procedure

CHAPTER OUTLINE

Introduction

Incorporation

Expansion of Rights

Exclusionary Rule

  Exclusionary Rule and Exceptions

Fruit of the Poisonous Tree

Standing

State Constitutions and the
  "New Federalism"

CHAPTER OBJECTIVES

In this chapter, you should:

- be introduced to the major provisions in the Constitution of the United States and its amendments that apply in the criminal context.
- learn why the U.S. Constitution's prominence in criminal justice has increased in recent decades.
- learn the Exclusionary Rule and related doctrines.

- learn about the authority of the States to increase individual liberties through their constitutions.
- continue to develop your case analysis and legal reasoning skills.

INTRODUCTION

Criminal justice is a policy subject that belongs largely to the states. Nearly 95 percent of all criminal prosecutions occur in state courts. Not only do the states conduct most of the prosecutions, but each state is free, with few limitations, to design its criminal justice system in any manner it chooses. This was especially true in the early years of the United States. For the most part, the national government did not involve itself in state criminal law for 150 years.

This began to change in the 1950s, and today the United States plays a major role in defining the rights of criminal defendants in state prosecutions, as well as federal. The source of federal involvement is the United States Constitution, and two developments account for its increased role in state criminal law. First, the reach of the Constitution has been extended to the states through what is known as *incorporation*. Second, the rights found in the Bill of Rights have been significantly expanded.

INCORPORATION

Prior to the adoption of the Fourteenth Amendment, the Bill of Rights guarantees were interpreted by the Supreme Court as only restricting the authority of the national government. That meant that fundamental rights, such as the right to counsel and the right to be free from unreasonable searches and seizures, were only guaranteed to a defendant when prosecuted in federal court. If a state did not have a constitutional or statutory provision granting the right, the defendant was not entitled to its protection when prosecuted in state court.

In 1868 the Fourteenth Amendment to the United States Constitution was adopted. One objective of the Fourteenth Amendment is to protect certain civil liberties from state action. Section One of that amendment reads:

> All persons born or naturalized in the United States, and subject to the jurisdiction thereof, are citizens of the United States and of the State wherein they reside. No State shall make or enforce any law which shall abridge the privileges or immunities of citizens of the United States; nor shall any State deprive any person of life, liberty, or property, without due process of law; nor deny to any person within its jurisdiction the equal protection of the laws.

The language of the Fourteenth Amendment is similar to that found in the Fifth Amendment, insofar as they both contain a Due Process Clause. It is through the Due Process and Equal Protection Clauses that the powers of the states are limited. However, what is meant by *due process* has been the subject of great debate among jurists.

Note that the language of the Fourteenth Amendment does not include any of the specific guarantees found in the Bill of Rights, except that it requires the states to afford due process whenever depriving a person of life, liberty, or property. Thus, one of the most important issues raised in the context of the

Fourteenth Amendment is whether it includes the rights found in the Bill of Rights, such as the rights to counsel, to freedom of the press, to freedom of speech, to be free from self-incrimination, to be free of unreasonable searches and seizures, and to be free from cruel and unusual punishments. Several theories have developed in answer to this question.

At one extreme is the *independent content approach*. Under this theory, the Fourteenth Amendment's Due Process Clause does not include any right found in the Bill of Rights, that is, due process does not overlap with the Bill of Rights. Rather, due process has an independent content and none of the rights secured in the Bill of Rights apply against the states. The Supreme Court has never adopted this position.

At the other extreme is *total incorporation*. Proponents of total incorporation, who included Supreme Court Associate Justice Black, argue that the entire Bill of Rights is incorporated by the Fourteenth Amendment and that all the rights contained therein may be asserted by defendants in both state and federal courts. The incorporation occurs automatically, as the proponents of this position believe that the drafters of the Fourteenth Amendment intended to incorporate the entire Bill of Rights. Under this approach, however, the Due Process Clause was limited to recognizing rights contained in the Bill of Rights. Another group of jurists have been labeled *"total incorporation plus,"* because they contend that the Due Process Clause not only incorporates the Bill of Rights, but also secures additional independent rights. Neither of these positions has been adopted by the Supreme Court.

Another position, which was held by the Supreme Court until the 1960s, is known as *fundamental fairness*. Those rights that are "fundamental" and "essential to an ordered liberty" are incorporated through this approach. The fundamental fairness doctrine held that no relationship existed between the Bill of Rights and those deemed fundamental, although the rights recognized under the fundamental fairness doctrine may parallel rights recognized by the Bill of Rights.

The Supreme Court rejected the fundamental fairness doctrine in the 1960s and replaced it with the *selective incorporation doctrine*. Similar to the fundamental fairness doctrine, a right is incorporated under this doctrine if it is both fundamental and essential to the concept of ordered liberty. Like the fundamental fairness approach, independent rights are also recognized under selective incorporation analysis.

However, the two approaches differ in two major respects. First, under the fundamental fairness approach, cases were analyzed case-by-case. That is, it was possible to have essentially the same facts with different outcomes under the fundamental fairness doctrine. Critics charged that the approach was too subjective. Under the selective incorporation method, blanket rules are established to act as precedent for all similar cases in the future. In addition, the entire body of precedent interpreting a federal amendment becomes applicable to the states as a result of an amendment's incorporation.

Second, selective incorporation gives special attention to the rights contained in the Bill of Rights. A right secured by the Bill of Rights is more likely to be protected by the Fourteenth Amendment's Due Process Clause than others. Selective incorporation continues to be the approach of the Supreme Court today.

Nearly the entire Bill of Rights has been incorporated under the selective incorporation doctrine. The right to grand jury indictment has not been incorporated,[1] nor has the right to a jury trial in civil cases. Once incorporated, a right applies against the states to the extent and in the same manner as it does against the United States. Also, several independent due process rights have been declared. You will learn many of these in the following chapters.

EXPANSION OF RIGHTS

Another major development in the area of constitutional criminal procedure has been the expansion of many rights. The language of the Constitution is concise. It refers to "unreasonable searches and seizures," "due process," "equal protection," "speedy and public trial," and so on. No further definition or explanation of the meaning of these provisions is provided. The process of determining the meaning of such phrases is known as *constitutional interpretation*. It is possible to make each right ineffective by reading it narrowly. The opposite is also true.

During the 1960s, many rights found in the Bill of Rights were expanded by court decisions. *Expansion* refers to extending a right beyond its most narrow reading. The effect of expansive interpretation is to increase defendants' rights. An example of an expansive interpretation is the *Miranda v. Arizona* decision, 384 U.S. 436 (1966). Although the language of the Fifth Amendment does not explicitly state that a defendant must be advised of the right to remain silent, to have the assistance of counsel, and so forth, the Court now requires that such admonishments be given because of an expanded interpretation of the Fifth Amendment.

Another example of expanded individual rights is the right to privacy. No explicit constitutional language provides for a right to privacy. However, the Supreme Court has found a right to privacy to be implicit in the Constitution. The Court has held that the right to privacy protects a woman's right to abortion, in some circumstances,[2] and a couple's right to use contraceptives,[3] amongst many others. Many more expansions will be discussed later.

EXCLUSIONARY RULE

exclusionary rule
"*The exclusionary rule*" often means the rule that illegally gathered evidence may not be used in a criminal trial. The rule has several exceptions, such as when the evidence is used to impeach a defendant's testimony and when the evidence was gathered in a good faith belief that the process was legal.

Another important constitutional development was the creation of the **exclusionary rule.** The rule is simple: Evidence that is obtained by an unconstitutional search or seizure is inadmissible at trial.

The rule was first announced by the Supreme Court in 1914.[4] However, at that time the rule had not been incorporated, and therefore the exclusionary rule did not apply to state court proceedings. This changed in 1961 when the Supreme Court declared that evidence obtained in violation of the Constitution could not be used in state or federal criminal proceedings. The case was *Mapp v. Ohio.*

The exclusionary rule has been the subject of intense debate. There is no explicit textual language establishing the rule in the Constitution. For that reason, many contend that the Supreme Court exceeded its authority by creating it; that it is the responsibility of the legislative branch to make such laws.

On the other side is the argument that without the exclusionary rule, the Bill of Rights is ineffective. Why have constitutional standards if there is no method to enforce them? For example, why require that the officers in the *Mapp* case have a search warrant, yet permit them to conduct a warrantless search and use the evidence obtained against the defendant? These questions go to the purpose of the exclusionary rule: it discourages law enforcement personnel from engaging in unconstitutional conduct.

The exclusionary rule works to prevent the admission into evidence of any item, confession, or other thing that was obtained by law enforcement officers in an unconstitutional manner.

The evidence must be obtained by the police in an unlawful manner. However, if a private citizen working on his or her own obtains evidence illegally and then turns it over to the police, it may be admitted.[5] People hired or authorized to assist the police are considered agents of the government, and therefore the exclusionary rule applies to their actions.

The exclusionary rule does not apply to pretrial matters. A defendant may not challenge a grand jury indictment because the grand jury considered illegally obtained evidence. The defendant's remedy is at trial. In addition, a defendant may not refuse to answer questions before a grand jury concerning illegally obtained evidence. In most cases, but not all, evidence obtained illegally may be used at sentencing.

Another important exception to the exclusionary rule allows the government to use illegally seized evidence to rebut statements made by a defendant.[6] The government may not use the evidence if the defendant does not "open the door." That is, the government may use the evidence if the defense refers to it in its case.

Most exclusionary rule issues are resolved prior to trial by way of a motion to suppress. In some instances the motion may be made at the moment the prosecutor attempts to introduce such evidence at trial. This is known as a *contemporaneous objection*.

THE EXCLUSIONARY RULE IN PRACTICE   Few topics in criminal procedure are as controversial and divisive as the exclusionary rule. Clearly the public perception of the rule is that it is a device that frees the guilty, allowing murderers, rapists, and other miscreants to continue their carnage because of technicalities. Whether constraining the government to constitutional procedures should be characterized as "technical" is for each individual to decide.

In spite of its reputation, the exclusionary rule is not responsible for opening the door for countless criminals. In fact, less than 0.02 percent of all felony arrests in the United States are not prosecuted because of exclusionary rule

SIDEBAR

problems. Davies, "A Hard Look At What We Know (And Still Need To Learn) About The 'Costs' of The Exclusionary Rule," 1983 *A.B.F. Research J.* 611, 635, cited in *Commonwealth v. Edmunds,* 526 Pa. 374 (1991). The total number of cases not prosecuted and unsuccessfully prosecuted that are attributable to the exclusionary rule is estimated at between 0.6 percent and 2.35 percent. *Id.*

In another study of federal cases, searches and seizures were conducted in 30 percent of the prosecutions, and 11 percent of all defendants filed motions to suppress on Fourth Amendment grounds. Motions to suppress were only granted in 1.3 percent of the total number of cases, and half of the defendants who were successful in having evidence suppressed were convicted. In cases not prosecuted, exclusionary rule problems were the cause in only 0.4 percent. Report of the Comptroller General, *Impact of the Exclusionary Rule on Federal Criminal Prosecutions* (1979).

 CASE

MAPP V. OHIO

367 U.S. 643 (1961)

Appellant stands convicted of knowingly having had in her possession and under her control certain lewd and lascivious books, pictures, and photographs in violation [of Ohio law]. . . .

On May 23, 1957, three Cleveland police officers arrived at appellant's residence in that city pursuant to information that "a person [was] hiding out in the home, who was wanted for questioning in connection with a recent bombing.". . .

Upon their arrival at that house, the officers knocked on the door and demanded entrance but appellant, after telephoning her attorney, refused to admit them without a search warrant. They advised their headquarters of the situation and undertook a surveillance of the house.

The officers again sought entrance some three hours later when four or more additional officers arrived on the scene. When Miss Mapp did not come to the door immediately, at least one of the several doors to the house was forcibly opened and the policemen gained admittance. Meanwhile Miss Mapp's attorney arrived, but the officers, having secured their own entry, and continuing in their defiance of the law, would permit him neither to see Miss Mapp nor to enter the house.

It appears that Miss Mapp was halfway down the stairs from the upper floor to the front door when the officers, in this highhanded manner, broke into the hall. She demanded to see the search warrant. A paper, claimed to be a warrant, was held up by one of the officers. She grabbed the "warrant" and placed it in her bosom. A struggle ensued in which the officers recovered the piece of paper and as a result of which they handcuffed appellant because she had been "belligerent" in resisting their official rescue of the "warrant" from her person. Running roughshod over appellant, a policeman "grabbed" her, "twisted [her] hand," and she "yelled [and] pleaded with him" because "it was hurting." Appellant, in handcuffs, was then forcibly taken upstairs to her bedroom where the officers searched a dresser, a chest of drawers, a closet and some suitcases. They also looked into a photo album and through personal papers belonging to the appellant. The search spread. . . . The obscene materials for possession of which she was ultimately convicted were discovered in the course of that widespread search.

At the trial no search warrant was produced by the prosecution, nor was the failure to produce one explained or accounted for. At best, "There is, in the record, considerable doubt as to whether there ever was any warrant for the search.". . .

We hold that all evidence obtained by searches and seizures in violation of the Constitution is, by that same authority, inadmissible in a state court.

Since the Fourth Amendment's right of privacy has been declared enforceable against the States through the Due Process Clause of the Fourteenth, it is enforceable against them by the same sanction of exclusion as it used against the Federal Government. . . .

Moreover, our holding that the exclusionary rule is an essential part of both the Fourth and Fourteenth Amendments is not only the logical dictate of prior cases, but it also makes very good sense. There is no war between the Constitution and common sense. Presently, a federal prosecutor may make no use of evidence illegally seized, but a State's attorney across the street may, although he supposedly is operating under the enforceable prohibitions of the same Amendment. Thus the State, by admitting evidence unlawfully seized, serves to encourage disobedience to the Federal Constitution which it is bound to uphold.

Exclusionary Rule and Exceptions

The rule. Evidence obtained by the government in an unconstitutional or otherwise illegal manner is inadmissible at criminal trial, unless one of the exceptions applies. The rule is not specifically expressed in the Constitution, but has been held to be implicitly part of the Fourth, Fifth, Sixth, and Fourteenth Amendments.

Exceptions and limitations.

1. Pretrial hearings, including grand jury review
2. Sentencing
3. Independent source
4. Inevitable discovery
5. Rebuttal evidence
6. Evidence obtained by private source
7. Standing

FRUIT OF THE POISONOUS TREE

The exclusionary rule applies to *primary evidence,* that is, evidence that is the direct result of an illegal search or seizure. It is possible that such primary evidence may lead the police to other evidence. Suppose that police officers beat a confession out of a bank robber. In that confession the defendant tells the police where he has hidden the stolen money. The confession is the primary evidence and is inadmissible under the exclusionary rule. The money (after it is retrieved by the police) is secondary, or "derivative," evidence. Such evidence is known as **fruit of the poisonous tree** and is also inadmissible. Generally, evidence that is "tainted" by the prior illegal conduct is inadmissible. The rule does not make all evidence later obtained by law enforcement inadmissible. In some instances, evidence may be admissible

fruit of the poisonous tree doctrine

The rule that evidence gathered as a *result* of evidence gained in an illegal search or questioning cannot be used against the person searched or questioned even if the later evidence was gathered lawfully.

because the connection between the illegally seized evidence and the subsequently obtained evidence is marginal, or as the Supreme Court has stated it, "the causal connection . . . may have become so attenuated as to dissipate the taint."[7]

Another situation in which such evidence may be admitted is when an independent source exists. An **independent source** must be an unconnected and legal method of obtaining evidence. Consider the preceding bank robbery example. If a co-conspirator in the robbery also told the police where the money is, it is admissible regardless of the illegal confession, so long as the co-conspirator's admission was lawfully obtained.

Finally, evidence that would be inevitably discovered by law enforcement may be admitted. This doctrine is similar to the independent source doctrine. However, police must actually obtain evidence from an untainted, lawful source to invoke the independent source doctrine. The **inevitable discovery doctrine** holds that evidence that is the fruit of an illegal search, seizure, or arrest may be admitted if it is probable that the evidence would have been obtained lawfully at a later date.

STANDING

A defendant must have **standing** before he or she may successfully have evidence suppressed. There are two aspects to standing. First, the person challenging the evidence must have an adversarial interest in the proceeding. Basically, only defendants in criminal cases may challenge evidence as seized in violation of the Fourth Amendment. A defendant's mother may not intervene in the criminal case and attempt to have evidence suppressed because her Fourth Amendment rights were violated by an illegal search and seizure—even if the claim is true. A mother lacks standing to make the claim.

The second aspect concerns the defendant's interest in the area searched or thing seized. A defendant must have a reasonable expectation of privacy to a place or thing before he or she can have it excluded at trial. To say it another way, the defendant's constitutional rights must have been violated before evidence will be suppressed. Therefore, the defendant may not assert his mother's right to be free from illegal searches and seizures.

Note that in *Simmons v. United States*, 390 U.S. 377 (1968), the Supreme Court held that a defendant may testify at a suppression hearing without waiving the right not to testify at trial and that any testimony given at a suppression hearing by a defendant may not be used against him or her at trial.

Simmons eliminated the quandary many defendants had: should they give incriminating evidence during a suppression hearing in hopes of having the evidence excluded? Of course, if the suppression claim was unsuccessful, then a defendant faced the incriminating testimony at trial. This put many defendants in a position of having to choose one right or another: the right to be free from self-incrimination versus the right to have illegally seized evidence

---

independent source

The general rule that if new evidence can be traced to a source completely apart from the illegally gathered evidence that first led to the new evidence, it may be used by the government in a criminal trial.

inevitable discovery rule

The principle that even if criminal evidence is gathered by unconstitutional methods, the evidence may be admissible if it definitely would have come to light anyway.

standing

A person's right to bring (start) or join a lawsuit because he or she is directly affected by the issues raised. This is called "standing to sue."

excluded from trial. The Supreme Court held that defendants should be free from such dilemmas.

During the 1960s and early 1970s, many jurists predicted that the Supreme Court would become so involved with criminal procedure that it would, in effect, write its own "constitutional criminal procedure code." This has not proven to be true; however, many areas of criminal procedure are greatly influenced by Supreme Court decisions. It is common to refer to the expansion of individual rights and the extension of those rights to the states as the *constitutionalization* of criminal procedure.

In recent years, though, there appears to be a trend away from expansive interpretation. This is in large part because the composition of the Supreme Court is more conservative than it was during the 1960s. Some believe that the trend of increasing individual rights was hindering law enforcement and welcome regression. Those who believe strongly in the rights of the individual proclaim that it is better to free ten guilty persons than to imprison one innocent person. In any event, it is probable that the Supreme Court's policy of favoring expansive interpretation of individual rights is likely to cease.

STATE CONSTITUTIONS AND THE "NEW FEDERALISM"

Each state has its own constitution. Most states bills of rights are identical in language to the national Constitution's Bill of Rights. There are exceptions, however. For example, Florida's Bill of Rights protects "expression," whereas the national Constitution protects "speech." As you will learn later, however, the term *speech* has been interpreted as meaning "expression." Also, the Florida Constitution expressly protects the right to privacy and the national Constitution does not. Rather, a national right to privacy has only recently been declared by the Supreme Court and is somewhat controversial because of the absence of express language establishing the right in the Constitution.

Until recently, state constitutions have not played an important role in defining civil liberties. This is because both state and federal courts have looked almost exclusively to the national Constitution to answer questions concerning civil liberties. It is also due to the tendency of state courts to interpret state constitutional rights as identical to those secured by the national Constitution.

Increasingly, this is not the case. During the past two decades, commentators, judges, and attorneys have exhibited a renewed interest in state constitutional law. The resurgence in state constitutional law is known as the "New Federalism." State constitutions can be an independent source of civil liberties. Of course, a state constitution cannot be used to limit or encroach on a federally secured right, but it can be used to extend the scope of a right.

In several instances, state courts have determined that their state constitutions protect criminal defendants to a greater extent than does the national

Constitution. The Supreme Court of Pennsylvania strongly asserted that its state's constitution has its own meaning separate and independent from the federal Constitution. In a 1991 case, that Court stated:

> [T]he decisions of the [U.S. Supreme] Court are not, and should not be, dispositive of questions regarding rights guaranteed by counterpart provisions of State Law. Accordingly, such decisions are not mechanically applicable to state law issues, and state court judges and members of the bar seriously err if they so treat them. Rather, state court judges, and also practitioners, do well to scrutinize constitutional decisions by federal courts, for only if they are found to be logically persuasive and well-reasoned, paying due regard to precedent and the policies underlying specific constitutional guarantees, may they properly claim persuasive weight as guide posts when interpreting counter-part state guarantees.[8]

The California courts have taken a similar approach. Even if a provision's interpretation parallels national law, the courts favor citing state law over federal law.

Whether a state court depends on state or federal law in defining a right determines what court has the final word on the subject. If a right is founded upon federal law, the Supreme Court of the United States is the final arbiter. If a right is founded upon state law, the highest court of the state is the final arbiter, again assuming that no federal right is encroached upon by the state decision. This problem normally arises when one person's exercise of a right affects another person's rights. For example, if a state court were to find that a fetus has a right to life in every instance, the decision would be void as violative of the federally secured right to privacy held by the mothers to elect abortions in some circumstances.

If a state court relies upon federal law when defining a right, the possibility of reversal by a federal court, usually the Supreme Court, exists. This is what occurred in California concerning the use of peyote, a drug made from cactus, by Native Americans. The Supreme Court of California decided in 1965 that the use of peyote by Native Americans during religious ceremonies was protected by the U.S. Constitution's First Amendment free exercise of religion clause.[9] That decision was not disturbed until 1990, when the Supreme Court of the United States decided that the regulation of peyote as a drug was a reasonable burden upon the First Amendment[10] and therefore overruled the 1965 California decision. Although the defendant asserted both the federal and state free exercise guarantees, the California Supreme Court relied entirely upon federal law in making its decision. Whether that court will later find the activity protected by the California constitution remains to be seen.

Today, state courts are looking to state law with increasing frequency to define civil rights. Even when state courts rely on federal law, it is common to cite state law as well, thereby providing an alternative basis for upholding a decision.

The *Leon* case, issued by the Supreme Court of the United States, recognized a good-faith exception to the exclusionary rule; the *Edmunds* decision, by the Supreme Court of Pennsylvania, expressly rejects the good-faith exception in state prosecutions.

As another example, several states have not followed the Supreme Court's lead in allowing statements made in violation of *Miranda* to be used by the prosecution in impeachment of a defendant.[11] These are but a few of the many instances in which a right has received greater protection under state law than under federal law.[12]

 CASE

UNITED STATES V. LEON

468 U.S. 897 (1984)

[Facially valid warrants were issued by a state judge. The searches conducted under the warrants produced narcotics and other evidence of narcotics violations.]

The respondents . . . filed motions to suppress the evidence seized pursuant to the warrant. The District Court held an evidentiary hearing and, while recognizing that the case was a close one, . . . granted the motions to suppress in part. It concluded that the affidavit was insufficient to establish probable cause. . . . In response to a request from the Government, the court made clear that Officer Rombach had acted in good faith. . . . [This decision was affirmed on appeal before the court of appeals.]

The Government's petition for certiorari expressly declined to seek review of the lower courts' determinations that the search warrant was unsupported by probable cause and presented only the question "[w]hether the Fourth Amendment exclusionary rule should be modified so as not to bar the admission of evidence seized in reasonable, good-faith reliance on a search warrant that is subsequently held to be defective." . . .

[T]he exclusionary rule is designed to deter police misconduct rather than to punish the errors of judges and magistrates. . . .

If exclusion of evidence obtained pursuant to a subsequently invalidated warrant is to have any deterrent effect, therefore, it must alter the behavior of the individual law enforcement officers or the policies of their departments. One could argue that applying the exclusionary rule in cases where the police failed to demonstrate probable cause in the warrant application deters future inadequate presentations or "magistrate shopping" and thus promotes the ends of the Fourth Amendment. Suppressing evidence obtained pursuant to a technically defective warrant supported by probable cause also might encourage officers to scrutinize more closely the form of the warrant and to point out suspected judicial errors. We find such arguments speculative and conclude that suppression of evidence obtained pursuant to a warrant should be ordered only on a case-by-case basis and only in those unusual cases in which exclusion will further the purposes of the exclusionary rule.

We conclude that the marginal or nonexistent benefits produced by suppressing evidence obtained in objectively reasonable reliance on a subsequently invalidated search warrant cannot justify the substantial costs of exclusion. We do not suggest, however, that exclusion is always inappropriate in cases where an officer has obtained a warrant and abided by its terms. . . . [A]n officer's reliance on the magistrate's probable-cause determination and on the technical sufficiency of the warrant he issues must be objectively reasonable . . . and it is clear that in some circumstances the officer will have no reasonable grounds for believing that the warrant was properly issued.

CASE ———◆

COMMONWEALTH V. EDMUNDS

526 Pa. 374 (1991)

[Defendant who was convicted in the Court of Common Pleas, Criminal Division, of possession of marijuana and related offenses, appealed. The Superior Court affirmed the conviction.]

The issue presented to this court is whether Pennsylvania should adopt the "good faith" exception to the exclusionary rule as articulated by the United States Supreme Court in the case of *United States v. Leon,* 468 U.S. 897, 104 S. Ct. 3405, 82 L. Ed. 2d 677 (1984). We conclude that a "good faith" exception to the exclusionary rule would frustrate the guarantees embodied in Article I, Section 8, of the Pennsylvania Constitution. Accordingly, the decision of the Supreme Court is reversed. . . .

The trial court held that the search warrant failed to establish probable cause that the marijuana would be at the location to be searched on the date it was issued. The trial court found that the warrant failed to set forth with specificity the date upon which the anonymous informants observed the marijuana. . . . However, the trial court went on to deny the defendant's motion to suppress the marijuana. Applying the rationale of *Leon,* the trial court looked beyond the four corners of the affidavit, in order to establish that the officers executing the warrant acted in "good faith" in relying upon the warrant to conduct the search. . . .

We must now determine whether the good-faith exception to the exclusionary rule is properly part of the jurisprudence of this Commonwealth, by virtue of Article 1, Section 8 of the Pennsylvania Constitution. In concluding that it is not, we set forth a methodology to be followed in analyzing future state constitutional issues which arise under our own Constitution. . . .

This Court has long emphasized that, in interpreting a provision of the Pennsylvania Constitution, we are not bound by the decisions of the United States Supreme Court which interpret similar (yet distinct) federal constitutional provisions. . . . [T]he federal constitution establishes certain minimum levels which are "equally applicable to the [analogous] state constitutional provision." . . . However, each state has the power to provide broader standards, and go beyond the minimum floor which is established by the federal Constitution. . . .

Here in Pennsylvania, we have stated with increasing frequency that it is both important and necessary that we undertake an independent analysis of the Pennsylvania Constitution, each time a provision of that fundamental document is implicated. . . .

The recent focus on the "New Federalism" has emphasized the importance of state constitutions with respect to individual rights and criminal procedure. As such, we find it important to set forth certain factors to be briefed and analyzed by litigants in each case hereafter implicating a provision of the Pennsylvania constitution. The decision of the United States Supreme Court in *Michigan v. Long,* 463 U.S. 1032, 103 S. Ct. 3469, 77 L. Ed. 2d 1201 (1983), now requires us to make a "plain statement" of the adequate and independent state grounds upon which we rely, in order to avoid any doubt that we have rested our decision squarely on Pennsylvania jurisprudence. Accordingly, as a general rule it is important that litigants brief and analyze at least the following four factors:

1. text of the Pennsylvania constitutional provision;
2. history of the provision, including Pennsylvania case-law;
3. related case-law from other states;
4. policy considerations, including unique issues of state and local concern, and applicability within modern Pennsylvania jurisprudence.

Depending on the particular issue presented, an examination of related federal precedent may be useful as part of the state constitutional analysis, not as binding authority, but as one form of guidance. . . . Utilizing the above four factors, and having reviewed *Leon,* we conclude that a "good faith" exception to the exclusionary rule would frustrate the guarantees embodied in Article I, Section 8 of our Commonwealth's Constitution. . . .

The United States Supreme Court in *Leon* made clear that, in its view, the sole purpose for the exclusionary rule under the 4th Amendment [to the Constitution of the United States] was to deter police misconduct. . . . The *Leon* majority also made clear that, under the Federal Constitution, the exclusionary rule operated as "a judicially created remedy designed to safeguard Fourth Amendment rights generally through its deterrent effect, rather than a personal constitutional right of the party aggrieved.". . .

[T]he exclusionary rule in Pennsylvania has consistently served to bolster the twin aims of Article I, Section 8, to wit, the safeguarding of privacy and the fundamental requirement that warrants shall only be issued upon probable cause. . . .

The linch-pin that has been developed to determine whether it is appropriate to issue a search warrant is the test of probable cause. . . .

It is designed to protect us from unwarranted and even vindictive incursions upon our privacy. It insulates from dictatorial and tyrannical rule by the state, and preserves the concept of democracy that assures the freedom of citizens. This concept is second to none in its importance in deliniating the dignity of the individual living in a free society. . . .

Whether the United States Supreme Court has determined that the exclusionary rule does not advance the 4th Amendment purpose of deterring police conduct is irrelevant. Indeed, we disagree with the Court's suggestion in *Leon* that we in Pennsylvania have been employing the exclusionary rule all these years to deter police corruption. We flatly reject this notion. . . . What is significant, however, is that our Constitution has historically been interpreted to incorporate a strong right to privacy, and an equally strong adherence to the requirement of probable cause under Article I, Section 8. Citizens in this Commonwealth possess such rights, even where a police officer in "good faith" carrying out his or her duties inadvertently invades the privacy or circumvents the strictures of probable cause. To adopt a "good faith" exception to the exclusionary rule, we believe, would virtually emasculate those clear safeguards which have been carefully developed under the Pennsylvania Constitution over the past 200 years.

 WEB LINKS

Metasearching the World Wide Web
Savvy Search, found at *http://www.search.com/* is a multiengine search tool. Savvy Search claims that your search terms are run through twelve search engines at one time increasing total hits between 200 percent and 800 percent and relevant hits by 60 percent.

KEY TERMS

exclusionary rule
fruit of the poisonous tree
   doctrine

independent source
inevitable discovery rule

standing

REVIEW QUESTIONS

1. What is selective incorporation? Total incorporation? Which reflects current law?
2. Name three rights that have been incorporated and one that has not.
3. What is the exclusionary rule?

4. Give an example of when evidence would be fruit of the poisonous tree.
5. Name three exceptions to the fruit of the poisonous tree doctrine.
6. What is the "New Federalism" in the context of constitutional law?

REVIEW PROBLEMS

1. The Constitution of the United States significantly affects all criminal law. Why is that so when more than 95 percent of all prosecutions occur in state courts?
2. Do you believe that evidence that has been obtained by law enforcement in an unconstitutional manner should be inadmissible at trial? Explain your position.

3. England does not employ the exclusionary rule. Rather, police officers are subject to civil liability for illegal searches. Is this a satisfactory remedy that should be employed in the United States? Can you think of alternative remedies?

END NOTES

1. *Hurtado v. California,* 110 U.S. 516 (1884).
2. *Roe v. Wade,* 410 U.S. 113 (1973).
3. *Griswold v. Connecticut,* 381 U.S. 479 (1965).
4. The rule, as it applied in federal courts, was announced in *Weeks v. United States,* 232 U.S. 383 (1914). However, it appears that the rule was applied in at least one case prior to that date. *See* LaFave & Israel, *Criminal Procedure* 78 (Hornbook Series, St. Paul: West, 1985).
5. *Burdeau v. McDowell,* 256 U.S. 465 (1921).
6. *Walder v. United States,* 347 U.S. 62 (1954); *United States v. Havens,* 446 U.S. 620 (1980).
7. *Nardone v. United States,* 308 U.S. 338 (1939).

8. *Commonwealth v. Ludwig,* 527 Pa. 472, 478 (1991).
9. *People v. Woody,* 61 Cal. 2d 716, 394 P.2d 813 (1965).
10. *Department of Human Resources v. Smith,* 494 U.S. 872 (1990).
11. *See People v. Disbrow,* 16 Cal. 3d 101, 545 P.2d 272 (1976) (California law); *State v. Santiago,* 53 Haw. 254, 492 P.2d 657 (1971) (Hawaii law); *Commonwealth v. Triplett,* 462 Pa. 244, 341 A.2d 62 (1975) (Pennsylvania law).
12. *See* Joseph Cook, *Constitutional Rights of the Accused* 2d ed., § 1:8, n.16 (Lawyers Cooperative, 1989) for a more thorough list.

CHAPTER 12

Searches, Seizures, and Arrests

CHAPTER OUTLINE

The Fourth Amendment

  Privacy

  Probable Cause

Searches and Seizures

  The Warrant Requirement

  Exceptions to the Search Warrant Requirement

Arrest

  Defining Arrest

The Warrant Preference

Arrests in Protected Areas

Misdemeanor Arrests

Search Incident to Arrest and the Protective Sweep

Executing Arrest Warrants

Illegal Arrests

Analyzing Fourth Amendment Problems

CHAPTER OBJECTIVES

In this chapter, you should:

- examine in depth the law of searches and seizures.
- learn how privacy is an underlying principle in the law of searches and seizures.
- learn the requirements for the issuance of search and arrest warrants.
- learn the many exceptions to the probable cause and warrant requirements.

- learn search and seizure law as it is applied to homes, automobiles, and other locations.
- critically examine recent developments intended to curb drugs and terrorism.
- continue to develop your case analysis and legal reasoning skills.

THE FOURTH AMENDMENT

Searches, seizures, and arrests are vital aspects of law enforcement. Because they involve significant invasions of individual liberties, limits on their use can be found in the constitutions, statutes, and other laws of the states and federal government.

The most important limitation is the Fourth Amendment of the United States Constitution, which reads:

> The right of the people to be secure in their persons, papers and effects, against unreasonable searches and seizures, shall not be violated, and no warrants shall issue but upon probable cause, supported by oath or affirmation, and particularly describing the place to be searched and the persons or things to be seized.

All searches and seizures must satisfy the Fourth Amendment's reasonableness requirement. Some searches and seizures must be supported by probable cause, but can be warrantless; other searches and seizures can occur only if supported by probable cause and upon a warrant. In still other instances, of lesser intrusions, the Fourth Amendment applies, but reasonable suspicion will support an intrusion. In this chapter you will learn when each of these standards applies.

Two remedies are available to the defendant whose Fourth Amendment rights have been violated by the government. First, in a criminal prosecution he or she may invoke the exclusionary rule. Second, he or she may have a civil action against the offending officer under a civil rights statute, under constitutional tort theory,[1] or under traditional tort theory.

Note that the protections in the Bill of Rights apply only against the government. Evidence obtained by a private citizen, acting on his or her own, is not subject to the exclusionary rule. So, if Ira's neighbor illegally enters and searches his house, discovers evidence of a crime, and turns that evidence over to law enforcement, it may be used at trial. Of course, the result would be different if the neighbor was working under the direction of a government official.

The concepts of "reasonable expectation of privacy" and "probable cause" are important throughout the law of searches, seizures, and arrests. Accordingly, they are examined first.

Privacy

Until 1967 the Fourth Amendment had been interpreted to protect "areas." For a violation of the Fourth Amendment to occur, law enforcement officers had to physically trespass upon the property of the defendant. This standard was changed in *Katz v. United States*.

In *Katz*, the Supreme Court held that the Fourth Amendment protects people, not places. The Court established a two-part test to determine if the Fourth Amendment is implicated. First, an individual must have a subjective expectation to privacy. Second, that expectation must be objectively reasonable. The *Katz* "reasonable expectation of privacy" test continues to be the method of determining whether a search or seizure has occurred. Consistent with *Katz*, the Supreme Court has defined a search as "when an expectation of privacy that society is prepared to consider reasonable is infringed." In the same opinion the court defined a *seizure* as a "meaningful interference with an individual's possessory interest" in property.[2]

If there is no invasion of a reasonable expectation of privacy, there is no search. For example, a police officer's observations made from a public place, such as a sidewalk, are not searches, even if they are of the inside of a house through a window. Observing the exterior of an automobile, including a license plate, is not a search, nor is a dog sniff of an item or person.[3]

 CASE

KATZ V. UNITED STATES

389 U.S. 347 (1967)

The petitioner was convicted in the District Court for the Southern District of California under an eight-count indictment charging him with transmitting wagering information by telephone from Los Angeles to Miami and Boston, in violation of a federal statute. At trial the Government was permitted, over the petitioner's objection, to introduce evidence of the petitioner's end of telephone conversations, overheard by FBI agents who had attached an electronic listening and recording device to the outside of the public telephone booth from which he had placed his calls. In affirming his conviction, the Court of Appeals rejected the contention that the recordings had been obtained in violation of the Fourth Amendment, because "[t]here was no physical entrance into the area occupied by [the petitioner]." We granted certiorari in order to consider the constitutional questions thus presented.

The petitioner has phrased those questions as follows:

A. Whether a public telephone booth is a constitutionally protected area so that evidence obtained by attaching an electronic listening and recording device to the top of such booth is obtained in violation of the right to privacy of the user of the booth.

B. Whether physical penetration of a constitutionally protected area is necessary before a search and seizure can be said to be violative of the Fourth Amendment to the United States Constitution.

We decline to adopt this formulation of the issues. In the first place, the correct solution of Fourth Amendment problems is not necessarily promoted by incantation of the phrase "constitutionally protected area." Secondly, the Fourth Amendment cannot be translated into a general constitutional "right to privacy." That Amendment protects individual privacy against certain kinds of governmental intrusion, but its protections go further, and often have nothing to do with privacy at all. Other provisions of the Constitution protect personal privacy from other forms of governmental invasion. But the protection of a person's *general* right to privacy—his right to be left alone by other people—is, like the protection of property and of his very life, left largely to the law of the individual States.

Because of the misleading way the issues have been formulated, the parties have attached great significance to the characterization of the telephone booth from which the petitioner placed his calls. The petitioner has strenuously argued that the booth was a "constitutionally protected area." The Government has maintained with equal vigor that it was not. But this effort to decide whether or not a given "area," viewed in the abstract, is "constitutionally protected" deflects attention from the problem presented by this case. For the Fourth Amendment protects people, not places. What a person knowingly exposes to the public, even in his own home or office, is not a subject of Fourth Amendment protection. . . . But what he seeks to preserve as private, even in an area accessible to the public, may be constitutionally protected. . . .

The Government stresses the fact that the telephone booth from which the petitioner made his calls was constructed partly of glass, so that he was as visible after he entered it as he would have been if he had remained outside. But what he sought to exclude when he entered the booth was not the intruding eye—it was the uninvited ear. He did not shed his right to do so simply because he made his calls from a place where he might be seen. No less than an individual in a business office, in a friend's apartment, or in a taxicab, a person in a telephone booth may rely upon the protection of the Fourth Amendment. One who occupies it, shuts the door behind him, and pays the toll that permits him to place a call is surely entitled to assume that the words he utters into the mouthpiece will not be broadcast to the world. To read the Constitution more narrowly is to ignore the vital role that the public telephone has come to play in private communication.

The Government contends, however, that the activities of its agents in this case should not be tested by Fourth Amendment requirements, for the surveillance technique they employed involved no physical penetration of the telephone booth from which the petitioner placed his calls. It is true that the absence of such penetration was at one time thought to foreclose further Fourth Amendment inquiry. . .for that Amendment was thought to limit only searches and seizures of tangible property . . . we have since departed from the narrow view on which that decision rested. Indeed, we have expressly held that the Fourth Amendment governs not only the seizure of tangible items, but extends as well to the recording of oral statements, overheard without any "technical trespass under . . . local property law." *Silverman v. United States,* 365 U.S. 505, 511. Once this much is acknowledged, and once it is recognized that the Fourth Amendment protects people—and not simply "areas"—against unreasonable searches and seizures, it becomes clear that the reach of that Amendment cannot turn upon the presence or absence of a physical intrusion into any given enclosure.

We conclude that the underpinnings of [prior decisions] have been so eroded by our subsequent decisions that the "trespass" doctrine there enunciated can no longer be regarded as controlling. . . .

[The Court then held that the warrantless search was conducted in violation of the Fourth Amendment.]

The use of simple technology to enhance the senses has been held not to be searches. For example, a police officer may use a flashlight to look into a stopped car. However, the area where the enhancement is used, the sophistication of the technology, and the threat to privacy must all be considered. This was the issue in *Kyllo,* where the Supreme Court invalidated warrantless use of thermo-imaging on a home.

Every case presents different (and often unique) facts. Accordingly, the determination of whether a defendant's expectation to privacy is reasonable is fact sensitive. However, there are Supreme Court cases holding, as a matter of law, whether an expectation to privacy is reasonable in a given context. As an illustration, let us consider whether a person has a reasonable expectation to privacy in another person's property.

It should first be mentioned that the law distinguishes between commercial property and other private property. Generally, there is less legal right to privacy in commercial premises than in dwellings.[4]

CASE

KYLLO V. UNITED STATES

533 U.S. 27 (2001)

This case presents the question whether the use of a thermal-imaging device aimed at a private home from a public street to detect relative amounts of heat within the home constitutes a "search" within the meaning of the Fourth Amendment.

I

In 1991 Agent William Elliott of the United States Department of the Interior came to suspect that marijuana was being grown in the home belonging to petitioner Danny Kyllo, part of a triplex on Rhododendron Drive in Florence, Oregon. Indoor marijuana growth typically requires high-intensity lamps. In order to determine whether an amount of heat was emanating from petitioner's home consistent with the use of such lamps, at 3:20 a.m. on January 16, 1992, Agent Elliott and Dan Haas used an Agema Thermovision 210 thermal imager to scan the triplex. Thermal imagers detect infrared radiation, which virtually all objects emit but which is not visible to the naked eye. The imager converts radiation into images based on relative warmth—black is cool, white is hot, shades of gray connote relative differences; in that respect, it operates somewhat like a video camera showing heat images. The scan of Kyllo's home took only a few minutes and was performed from the passenger seat of Agent Elliott's vehicle across the street from the front of the house and also from the street in back of the house. The scan showed that the roof over the garage and a side wall of petitioner's home were relatively hot compared to the rest of the home and substantially warmer than neighboring homes in the triplex. Agent Elliott concluded that petitioner was using halide lights to grow marijuana in his house, which indeed he was. Based on tips from informants, utility bills, and the thermal imaging, a Federal Magistrate Judge issued a warrant authorizing a search of petitioner's home, and the agents found an indoor growing operation involving more than 100 plants. Petitioner was indicted on one count of manufacturing marijuana. . . .

The Fourth Amendment provides that "[t]he right of the people to be secure in their persons, houses, papers, and effects, against unreasonable searches and seizures, shall not be violated." "At the very core" of the Fourth Amendment "stands the right of a man to retreat into his own home and there be free from unreasonable governmental intrusion.". . .

In assessing when a search is not a search, we have applied somewhat in reverse the principle first enunciated in *Katz v. United States,* 389 U.S. 347, 88 S.Ct. 507, 19 L.Ed.2d 576 (1967). *Katz* involved eavesdropping by means of an electronic listening device placed on the outside of a telephone booth—a location not within the catalog ("persons, houses, papers, and effects") that the Fourth Amendment protects against unreasonable searches. We held that the Fourth Amendment nonetheless protected Katz from the warrantless eavesdropping because he "justifiably relied" upon the privacy of the telephone booth. *Id.,* at 353, 88 S.Ct. 507. As Justice Harlan's oft-quoted concurrence described it, a Fourth Amendment search occurs when the government violates a subjective expectation of privacy that society recognizes as reasonable. . . .

The present case involves officers on a public street engaged in more than naked-eye surveillance of a home. We have previously reserved judgment as to how much technological enhancement of ordinary perception from such a vantage point, if any, is too much. While we upheld enhanced aerial photography of an industrial complex in *Dow Chemical,* we noted that we found "it important that this is *not* an area immediately adjacent to a private home, where privacy expectations are most heightened. . . .

The Government maintains, however, that the thermal imaging must be upheld because it detected "only heat radiating from the external surface of the house," Brief for United States 26. The dissent makes this its leading point, contending that there is a fundamental difference between what it calls "off-the-wall" observations and "through-the-wall surveillance." But just as a thermal imager captures only heat emanating from a house, so also a powerful directional microphone picks up only sound emanating from a house—and a satellite capable of scanning from many miles away would pick up only visible light emanating from a house. We rejected such a mechanical interpretation of the Fourth Amendment in *Katz,* where the eavesdropping device picked up only sound waves that reached the exterior of the phone booth. Reversing that approach would leave the homeowner at the mercy of advancing technology—including imaging technology that could discern all human activity in the home. While the technology used in the present case was relatively crude, the rule we adopt must take account of more sophisticated systems that are already in use or in development.

Where, as here, the Government uses a device that is not in general public use, to explore details of the home that would previously have been unknowable without physical intrusion, the surveillance is a "search" and is presumptively unreasonable without a warrant.

Since we hold the Thermovision imaging to have been an unlawful search, it will remain for the District Court to determine whether, without the evidence it provided, the search warrant issued in this case was supported by probable cause—and if not, whether there is any other basis for supporting admission of the evidence that the search pursuant to the warrant produced.

So, what about homes? In *Minnesota v. Olson* (1990) the Supreme Court held that an overnight guest may possess a reasonable expectation to privacy in the host's home.[5] Expanding on the reasoning in *Olson,* the defendant in *Minnesota v. Carter* (1998) asserted that a short-term guest in another's home should also be protected by the Fourth Amendment.

 CASE

MINNESOTA V. CARTER

119 S. Ct. 469 (1998)

Chief Justice Rehnquist delivered the opinion of the Court.

Respondents and the lessee of an apartment were sitting in one of its rooms, bagging cocaine. While so engaged they were observed by a police officer, who looked through a drawn window blind. The Supreme Court of Minnesota held that the officer's viewing was a search which violated respondents' Fourth Amendment rights. We hold that no such violation occurred.

James Thielen, a police officer in the Twin Cities' suburb of Eagan, Minnesota, went to an apartment building to investigate a tip from a confidential informant. The informant said that he had walked by the window of a ground-floor apartment and had seen people putting a white powder into bags. The officer looked in the same window through a gap in the closed blind and observed the bagging operation for several minutes. He then notified headquarters, which began preparing affidavits for a search warrant

while he returned to the apartment building. When two men left the building in a previously identified Cadillac, the police stopped the car. Inside were respondents Carter and Johns. As the police opened the door of the car to let Johns out, they observed a black zippered pouch and a handgun, later determined to be loaded, on the vehicle's floor. Carter and Johns were arrested, and a later police search of the vehicle the next day discovered pagers, a scale, and 47 grams of cocaine in plastic sandwich bags.

After seizing the car, the police returned to Apartment 103 and arrested the occupant, Kimberly Thompson, who is not a party to this appeal. A search of the apartment pursuant to a warrant revealed cocaine residue on the kitchen table and plastic baggies similar to those found in the Cadillac. Thielen identified Carter, Johns, and Thompson as the three people he had observed placing the powder into baggies. The police later learned that while Thompson was the lessee of the apartment, Carter and Johns lived in Chicago and had come to the apartment for the sole purpose of packaging the cocaine. Carter and Johns had never been to the apartment before and were only in the apartment for approximately 2½ hours. In return for the use of the apartment, Carter and Johns had given Thompson one-eighth of an ounce of the cocaine.

Carter and Johns were charged with conspiracy to commit controlled substance crime in the first degree and aiding and abetting in a controlled substance crime in the first degree, in violation of Minn. Stat. § 152.021, subd. 1(1), subd. 3(a) (1996); § 609.05. They moved to suppress all evidence obtained from the apartment and the Cadillac, as well as to suppress several postarrest incriminating statements they had made. They argued that Thielen's initial observation of their drug packaging activities was an unreasonable search in violation of the Fourth Amendment and that all evidence obtained as a result of this unreasonable search was inadmissible as fruit of the poisonous tree. The Minnesota trial court held that since, unlike the defendant in *Minnesota v. Olson,* 495 U.S. 91, 109 L. Ed. 2d 85, 110 S. Ct. 1684 (1990), Carter and Johns were not overnight social guests but temporary out-of-state visitors, they were not entitled to claim the protection of the Fourth Amendment against the government intrusion into the apartment. The trial court also concluded that Thielen's observation was not a search within the meaning of the Fourth Amendment. After a trial, Carter and Johns were each convicted of both offenses. The Minnesota Court of Appeals held that the respondent Carter did not have "standing" to object to Thielen's actions because his claim that he was predominantly a social guest was "inconsistent with the only evidence concerning his stay in the apartment, which indicates that he used it for a business purpose—to package drugs." *Minnesota v. Carter,* 545 N.W.2d 695, 698 (1996). In a separate appeal, the Court of Appeals also affirmed Johns' conviction, without addressing what it termed the "standing" issue. *Minnesota v. Johns,* 1996 Minn. App. LEXIS 685 (Minn. Ct. App. 1996), App. D-1, D-3 (unpublished).

A divided Minnesota Supreme Court reversed, holding that respondents had "standing" to claim the protection of the Fourth Amendment because they had "'a legitimate expectation of privacy in the invaded place.'" . . .

The Minnesota courts analyzed whether respondents had a legitimate expectation of privacy under the rubric of "standing" doctrine, an analysis which this Court expressly rejected 20 years ago in *Rakas* 439 U.S. at 139–140. In that case, we held that automobile passengers could not assert the protection of the Fourth Amendment against the seizure of incriminating evidence from a vehicle where they owned neither the vehicle nor the evidence. *Ibid.* Central to our analysis was the idea that in determining whether a defendant is able to show the violation of his (and not someone else's) Fourth Amendment rights, the "definition of those rights is more properly placed within the purview of substantive Fourth Amendment law than within that of standing." 439 U.S. at 140. Thus, we held that in order to claim the protection of the Fourth Amendment, a defendant must demonstrate that he personally has an expectation of privacy in the place searched, and that his expectation is reasonable; i.e., one which has "a source outside of the Fourth Amendment, either by reference to concepts of real or personal property law or to understandings that are recognized and permitted by society." *Id.* at 143–144, and n. 12. See also *Smith v. Maryland,* 442 U.S. 735, 740–741, 61 L. Ed. 2d 220, 99 S. Ct. 2577 (1979).

The Fourth Amendment guarantees: "The right of the people to be secure in their persons, houses, papers, and effects, against unreasonable searches and seizures, shall not be violated, and no Warrants shall issue, but upon probable cause, supported by Oath or affirmation, and particularly describing the place to be searched, and the persons or things to be seized." The Amendment protects persons against unreasonable searches of "their persons [and] houses" and thus indicates that the Fourth Amendment is a personal right that must be invoked by an individual. See *Katz v. United States,* 389 U.S. 347, 351, 19 L. Ed. 2d 576, 88 S. Ct. 507 (1967) ("The Fourth Amendment protects people, not places"). But the extent to which the Fourth Amendment protects people may depend upon where those people are. We have held that "capacity to claim the protection of the Fourth Amendment depends . . . upon whether the person who claims the protection of the Amendment has a legitimate expectation of privacy in the invaded place." *Rakas, supra,* at 143. See also

Rawlings v. Kentucky, 448 U.S. 98, 106, 65 L. Ed. 2d 633, 100 S. Ct. 2556 (1980).

The text of the Amendment suggests that its protections extend only to people in "their" houses. But we have held that in some circumstances a person may have a legitimate expectation of privacy in the house of someone else. In *Minnesota v. Olson,* 495 U.S. 91, 109 L. Ed. 2d 85, 110 S. Ct. 1684 (1990), for example, we decided that an overnight guest in a house had the sort of expectation of privacy that the Fourth Amendment protects. We said:

> "To hold that an overnight guest has a legitimate expectation of privacy in his host's home merely recognizes the everyday expectations of privacy that we all share. Staying overnight in another's home is a long-standing social custom that serves functions recognized as valuable by society. We stay in others' homes when we travel to a strange city for business or pleasure, we visit our parents, children, or more distant relatives out of town, when we are in between jobs, or homes, or when we house-sit for a friend. . . .
>
> "From the overnight guest's perspective, he seeks shelter in another's home precisely because it provides him with privacy, a place where he and his possessions will not be disturbed by anyone but his host and those his host allows inside. We are at our most vulnerable when we are asleep because we cannot monitor our own safety or the security of our belongings. It is for this reason that, although we may spend all day in public places, when we cannot sleep in our own home we seek out another private place to sleep, whether it be a hotel room, or the home of a friend." 495 U.S. at 98–99.

In *Jones v. United States,* 362 U.S. 257, 259, 4 L. Ed. 2d 697, 80 S. Ct. 725 (1960), the defendant seeking to exclude evidence resulting from a search of an apartment had been given the use of the apartment by a friend. He had clothing in the apartment, had slept there "'maybe a night,'" and at the time was the sole occupant of the apartment. But while the holding of *Jones*—that a search of the apartment violated the defendant's Fourth Amendment rights—is still valid, its statement that "anyone legitimately on the premises where a

search occurs may challenge its legality," *id.* at 267, was expressly repudiated in *Rakas v. Illinois,* 439 U.S. 128, 58 L. Ed. 2d 387, 99 S. Ct. 421 (1978). Thus an overnight guest in a home may claim the protection of the Fourth Amendment, but one who is merely present with the consent of the householder may not.

Respondents here were obviously not overnight guests, but were essentially present for a business transaction and were only in the home a matter of hours. There is no suggestion that they had a previous relationship with Thompson, or that there was any other purpose to their visit. Nor was there anything similar to the overnight guest relationship in *Olson* to suggest a degree of acceptance into the household. While the apartment was a dwelling place for Thompson, it was for these respondents simply a place to do business.

Property used for commercial purposes is treated differently for Fourth Amendment purposes than residential property. "An expectation of privacy in commercial premises, however, is different from, and indeed less than, a similar expectation in an individual's home." *New York v. Burger,* 482 U.S. 691, 700, 96 L. Ed. 2d 601, 107 S. Ct. 2636 (1987). And while it was a "home" in which respondents were present, it was not their home. Similarly, the Court has held that in some circumstances a worker can claim Fourth Amendment protection over his own workplace. See, e.g., *O'Connor v. Ortega,* 480 U.S. 709, 94 L. Ed. 2d 714, 107 S. Ct. 1492 (1987). But there is no indication that respondents in this case had nearly as significant a connection to Thompson's apartment as the worker in *O'Connor* had to his own private office. See *id.* at 716–717.

If we regard the overnight guest in *Minnesota v. Olson* as typifying those who may claim the protection of the Fourth Amendment in the home of another, and one merely "legitimately on the premises" as typifying those who may not do so, the present case is obviously somewhere in between. But the purely commercial nature of the transaction engaged in here, the relatively short period of time on the premises, and the lack of any previous connection between respondents and the householder, all lead us to conclude that respondents' situation is closer to that of one simply permitted on the premises. We therefore hold that any search which may have occurred did not violate their Fourth Amendment rights.

Because we conclude that respondents had no legitimate expectation of privacy in the apartment, we need not decide whether the police officer's observation constituted a "search." The judgment of the Supreme Court of Minnesota is accordingly reversed, and the cause is remanded for proceedings not inconsistent with this opinion.

It is so ordered. . . .

Dissent

Justice Ginsburg, with whom Justice Stevens and Justice Souter join, dissenting.

The Court's decision undermines not only the security of short-term guests, but also the security of the home resident herself. In my view, when a homeowner or lessor personally invites a guest into her home to share in a common endeavor, whether it be for conversation, to engage in leisure activities, or for business purposes licit or illicit, that guest should share his host's shelter against unreasonable searches and seizures. . . .

Do people enjoy the right to privacy in hotels? The purpose of the premises and the nature of the use of the premises must be considered in Fourth Amendment analysis. Because hotels are intended to provide individuals with safety and comfort when away from home, hotel guests may have a reasonable expectation to privacy. Several factors are considered when determining whether an individual possesses a reasonable expectation to privacy in a hotel room, including whether the defendant is a registered guest and if not, what his or her relationship to the registered guest is, whether the defendant paid any of the hotel charges, and the total time the defendant spent in the room. The Tenth Circuit Court of Appeals discussed this issue in the 1999 case *United States v. Gordon*.

Just as not all expectations to privacy are recognized at law, not all touchings of property by police amount to a search because they do not represent a "meaningful interference" with a property interest.

As to when physical contact of an "effect" by a law enforcement officer becomes a search, the Supreme Court has drawn a strict line in favor of preserving privacy. In *Bond v. United States*,[6] for example, a border patrol officer's quick squeeze of a bus passenger's soft luggage was determined to be a search, even though there was considerable evidence that passengers commonly touched each other's luggage in a manner no less intrusive than that of the border patrol officer's.

Probable Cause

Probable Cause Defined. The Fourth Amendment requires the existence of **probable cause** before warrants are to be issued. When a warrant is first obtained, the probable cause determination is made by a judge. In cases where a police officer acts without a warrant, the officer makes that determination. In both cases, as you will see, probable cause is required.

Probable cause is the minimum amount of evidence necessary for a search, seizure, or arrest to be proper under the Fourth Amendment. There is no one universal definition of probable cause. In fact, the definition of probable cause differs depending on the context. In all situations, it is more than mere suspicion and less than the standard required to prove a defendant guilty at trial

probable cause
The U.S. constitutional requirement that law enforcement officers present sufficient facts to convince a judge to issue a search warrant or an arrest *warrant*, and the requirement that no warrant should be issued unless it is more likely than not that the objects sought will be found in the place to be searched or that a crime has been committed by the person to be arrested.

C A S E

UNITED STATES

V.

GORDON

168 F. 3d 1222
(10th Cir. 1999)

I. BACKGROUND

On January 11, 1997, at approximately 9:00 P.M., the Wichita, Kansas, police department received an anonymous tip that two individuals, Tiffany Myers and Preston Espinoza, were engaged in drug activity in the Motel 6 on West Kellogg and had drawn a gun on the caller from a black Saturn. Officers Arnaldo Martinez and Bret Benjamin were dispatched in response to the tip.

Officers Martinez and Benjamin arrived at the Motel 6 and located a black Saturn in the motel parking lot. The vehicle was registered to Tiffany Myers. Upon further investigation, the motel clerk confirmed that a Tiffany Myers had rented room 209. Officer Martinez also learned through a check of police records that Preston Espinoza had an outstanding felony arrest warrant. Officer Martinez asked the motel clerk to call room 209 to determine if anyone was present. She did so and a male voice answered. The officers, believing Espinoza was in the room, called for backup. As the two officers were approaching room 209, they noticed an individual who fit Espinoza's description walking toward the black Saturn. When asked, Espinoza identified himself, and the officers arrested him on the outstanding warrant. After a pat-down search revealed that Espinoza was unarmed, Officer Benjamin escorted him to his police car.

Having found no gun on Espinoza, Officer Martinez became concerned that Myers, the remaining occupant of the room, might be armed. Therefore, Officer Martinez waited for backup to arrive before approaching room 209. After two additional officers arrived, they approached room 209 with their guns drawn. Martinez knocked on the door and said "police officers." A male voice responded "who?" and Martinez repeated "police officers, open the door." Defendant opened the door

about six inches. Defendant's hands were in his pocket, so Officer Martinez told him to remove them so he could see them. Defendant removed his hands and turned to his left, making a throwing motion toward the bed. As he did so, Defendant moved away from the door. Because Officer Martinez had placed his hand on the door to keep Defendant from shutting it, the door swung open as Defendant spun around, allowing Officer Martinez to see into the motel room. Officer Martinez observed several other people, a set of scales and sandwich bags. At that point, he noticed one of the individuals in the room, Connie Ramsey, moving toward the bathroom. Concerned that she was attempting to destroy evidence or reaching for a weapon, Officer Martinez entered the room and stopped her. After securing the room and its occupants, the officers obtained a search warrant for room 209. Officers executed the warrant early the next morning and seized cocaine, scales, sandwich bags, ammunition, film, a cellular phone, and various documents.

After Defendant was taken to the police station, Detective Beverly Brimer advised Defendant of his *Miranda* rights using a standard form. Defendant said he wanted to waive his rights and signed the form. When Detective Brimer asked Defendant about the room key found on his person, he said he was only using it so he could get back into the room quickly after he went to the parking lot to talk with someone. He did not tell Detective Brimer that the room key was his or that room 209 was his room. Detective Brimer also asked Defendant how long he had been in the room and he told her three minutes. Defendant explained that he was there to conduct some business with Preston Espinoza. When asked what kind of business, he stated: "Well, that's pretty obvious, isn't it." From this statement, Detective Brimer believed Defendant was referring to the narcotics business.

A few weeks prior to Defendant's arrest, Lieutenant M. Keith Barnes, chief investigator at the Kansas El Dorado Correctional Facility, received from the prison mail room a letter and photographs sent to an inmate by Defendant. Two of the photographs contained large sums of currency. Upon inspection, Barnes determined that the photographs were indicative of drug or gang activity. Therefore, he read the accompanying letter. Concerned that the photographs depicted illegal activity, he copied the letter and photographs and sent the originals to the inmate. Barnes then sent copies to Agent Rick Husselman with the Department of Corrections in Wichita, because the letter indicated that the writer was a parolee. Barnes handled a second letter and set of photographs sent by Defendant to another inmate in the same manner. After Defendant's arrest, Agent Husselman took the letters and photographs to the Wichita Police Department and was present when Detective Brimer questioned Defendant about them. Detective Brimer advised Defendant that the letters would be used as evidence against him.

Defendant filed a motion to suppress the evidence seized from the motel room and the photocopies of the letters and photographs. On September 12 and 15, 1997, the district court conducted an evidentiary hearing and denied the motion. On October 10, 1997, Defendant filed a motion to reconsider. The district court conducted another evidentiary hearing on October 17 and 27, 1997, and denied the motion to reconsider. Defendant subsequently entered a conditional guilty plea to possession with intent to distribute cocaine base, in violation of 21 U.S.C. § 841 (a) (1), and the district court sentenced him to 84 months' imprisonment. Defendant reserved the right to appeal the denial of his motion to suppress evidence. See Fed. R. Crim. P. 11 (a) (2).

II. ANALYSIS

A. REASONABLE EXPECTATION OF PRIVACY

Initially, we must determine whether Defendant can claim that his Fourth Amendment rights were violated when officers entered the motel room in Wichita, Kansas. To do so, we must decide whether Defendant had an "expectation of privacy in the place searched, and that his expectation is reasonable." *Minnesota v. Carter,* — U.S. —, —, 119

S. Ct. 469, 472, 142 L. Ed. 2d 373, — (1998). An expectation of privacy is reasonable if it arises from a source "outside the Fourth Amendment, either by reference to concepts of real or personal property law or to understandings that are recognized and permitted by society." *Rakas v. Illinois,* 439 U.S. 128, 143–144, 99 S. Ct. 421, 58 L. Ed. 2d 387 (1978). The Fourth Amendment protects people from unreasonable searches of their "persons, houses, papers, and effects." U.S. Const. amend. IV. Fourth Amendment protection is "a personal right that must be invoked by an individual."

Carter, — U.S. at —, 119 S. Ct. at 473. The extent of this protection sometimes depends upon the location of the person claiming the protection. See *id.* Thus, we must determine whether Defendant had a reasonable expectation of privacy in the motel room. The burden is on Defendant to show that he had such an expectation. . . .

We have recognized that an individual may have a reasonable expectation of privacy in a motel room. See *United States v. Carr,* 939 F. 2d 1442, 1446 (10th Cir. 1991). In making this determination, we have traditionally considered whether the individual had lawful ownership or control of the premises searched. See *id.* Of importance is the status of the defendant as an overnight guest. See *Carter,* — U.S. at —, 119 S. Ct. at 473 ("an overnight guest in a home may claim the protection of the Fourth Amendment, but one who is merely present with the consent of the householder may not"). Thus, we have required a defendant to demonstrate that he was the registered occupant of the room or that he was sharing it with the person to whom the room was registered. See *Carr,* 939 F. 2d at 1446; see also *Conway,* 73 F. 3d at 979 ("defendant must at least demonstrate that, in the case of a motel room, that he was the invited guest of the renter of the premises").

In a recent opinion, the Supreme Court effectively heightened the burden for a defendant claiming a reasonable expectation of privacy in a dwelling other than his own home, when the defendant's presence in the dwelling is for a commercial or business purpose. See *Minnesota v. Carter,* — U.S. —, 119 S. Ct. 469, 142 L. Ed. 2d 373 (1998). In *Carter,* the Supreme

Court held that two individuals, who were in an apartment leased to another person, had no reasonable expectation of privacy where they were "essentially present for a business transaction and were only in the home a matter of hours." 119 S. Ct. at 473. The two defendants were present in the apartment for the sole purpose of packaging cocaine and were there for $2\frac{1}{2}$ hours when an officer discovered the illegal activity. *Id.* at 471. The Supreme Court held that the defendants did not have a reasonable expectation of privacy in the apartment, emphasizing the commercial nature of defendants' conduct. The Court explained that an individual's expectation of privacy in commercial premises is "'less than, a similar expectation in an individual's home.'" *Id.* at 474 (quoting *New York v. Burger,* 482 U.S. 691, 700, 107 S. Ct. 2636, 96 L. Ed. 2d 601 (1987)). As the Court put it, although the apartment was a dwelling place, for the defendants it was "simply a place to do business."

Id.

In the present case, Defendant claims that because he had a key to the motel room, paid for the room, and men's clothing and toiletries were found in the room, he has proven that he had a reasonable expectation of privacy in the motel room. We disagree. The motel room was registered, not to Defendant, but to Tiffany Myers at a single occupant rate. Although Defendant had a room key in his pocket when he was arrested, he never claimed that it was his room key. In fact, Defendant told Detective Beverly Brimer after his arrest that he had only taken the key from the room so that he could enter the motel room after meeting with someone in the parking lot. The mere fact that the key was in his possession is not enough to establish a reasonable expectation of privacy in the motel room. See *Conway,* 73 F. 3d at 979–980 ("mere physical possession or control of property" insufficient to establish reasonable expectation of privacy). Furthermore, although Defendant testified that he gave Myers the money to pay for the room, he presented no testimony confirming his asserted status as co-occupant. See *id.* In addition, the fact that Defendant gave Myers $30.00 to pay for the room does not establish that he was the occupant of the room or that he was

staying there as Myers's guest. He may have merely owed or loaned Myers some money.

Finally, Defendant argues that because the police found men's clothing and toiletries in the motel room, it demonstrates that he was an occupant of the room. While the presence of Defendant's belongings in the motel room would be relevant to our determination of Defendant's reasonable expectation of privacy in the motel room, see *Carter,* — U.S. at —, 119 S. Ct. at 473, nothing in the record establishes that these items were Defendant's. Significantly, Defendant did not testify that the items belonged to him, and the clothing and toiletries could have belonged to Preston Espinoza, who was also present in the room on January 11, 1997. The confidential informant's claim that Espinoza and Myers, not Defendant and Myers, were dealing drugs from a room in the Motel 6 further supports the conclusion that the items belonged to Espinoza.

Under our traditional analysis, Defendant has failed to provide sufficient evidence to establish that he had a reasonable expectation of privacy in the motel room. Furthermore, in light of *Carter,* the evidence is even less persuasive. As in *Carter,* Defendant was present at the motel for a business purpose, i.e., distributing illegal drugs. Detective Brimer testified that Defendant told her the morning after his arrest that he was at the motel to see Preston Espinoza about "business." Defendant's testimony confirmed that he was at the motel that evening to talk to Preston about business. Detective Brimer also testified that when asked what kind of business, Defendant responded with: "Well, it's pretty obvious, isn't it."

Defendant was only present briefly in the motel room. He told Detective Brimer that a friend dropped him off at the motel approximately three minutes before Officer Martinez arrived. Although defense counsel argues that Defendant was present for seven or eight hours before Officer Martinez arrived, Defendant testified that the room had been rented for "seven or eight hours" before Officer Martinez arrived, but did not testify that he was present in the room for that period. He testified that after he arrived at the motel around 1 or 2 P.M., he left the room in a white Cadillac to get "beer and gas" and returned at "about 8 P.M." Thus, Defendant was present only a short time before

Officer Martinez knocked on the motel room door at approximately 9:30 P.M. At most, he was present in the room for a couple of hours. Similarly, the defendants in *Carter* were in the apartment for only $2\frac{1}{2}$ hours before officers arrived.

Thus, we are presented with a case very similar to *Carter*. Defendant was present in a motel room leased to another person, for a short time, and for the purpose of conducting business. As in *Carter*, Defendant's status was more like one "simply

permitted on the premises" instead of that of an "overnight guest." *Carter*, — U.S. at —, 119 S. Ct. at 474. The Supreme Court found no reasonable expectation of privacy in *Carter*; and likewise, we find none here. Because we conclude that Defendant had no reasonable expectation of privacy in the motel room, we need not decide whether Officer Martinez's conduct constituted an unconstitutional search. See *Carter*, — U.S. at —, 119 S. Ct. at 474. . . .

(beyond a reasonable doubt). As the Supreme Court has expressed, probable cause is present when the trustworthy facts within the officer's knowledge are sufficient in themselves to justify a "person of reasonable caution" in the belief that seizable property would be found or that the person to be arrested committed the crime in question.[7]

Sources Used to Establish Probable Cause.   When making the probable cause determination, an officer may rely on his or her own observations, hearsay evidence, and statements of witnesses, victims, and other law enforcement officers. The fact that evidence will be inadmissible at trial does not exclude it from the probable cause determination.

However, innuendo or conjecture that is not supported by facts may not be considered. Although the evidence does not have to rise to the level of being admissible at trial, it must have some credibility.

It is common for the police to depend on information from informants to obtain a search warrant. An *informant* is a person who has knowledge concerning a crime because of his or her involvement in crime. The reliability of such information (and whether it should be the basis of a warrant) is hotly debated.

In *Aguilar v. Texas*, 378 U.S. 108 (1964), the Supreme Court established a two-prong test for the use of such information (usually hearsay) when making a warrant determination. First, the affidavit had to contain information about the basis for the informant's information. This permitted the issuing judge to determine whether the informant's allegations were well founded.

Second, the officer had to provide the judge with reasons for believing that the informant was reliable. This could be done, for example, by showing that the informant had been truthful in the past.

In *Illinois v. Gates*, 462 U.S. 213 (1983), the Court reversed position and adopted a "totality of the circumstances" test, thereby overruling *Aguilar*. However, the Court did not abandon the two prongs of *Aguilar*. Although the two prongs are no longer determinative, they continue to be important factors when examining the totality of the circumstances. The Court stated that:

The task of the issuing magistrate is simply to make a practical, commonsense decision whether, given all the circumstances set forth in the affidavit before him, including the "veracity" and the "basis of knowledge" of persons supplying hearsay information, there is a fair probability that contraband or evidence of a crime will be found in a particular place.

Gates at 233. This test does not require that the officer name the informant in the application for the warrant. All that is required is that the magistrate be given enough information to make his or her own determination concerning the credibility and reliability of the informant. The law of this area was discussed fully in the Supreme Court's opinion in *Florida v. J. L.* (2000).

Probable cause may be established by an animal as well as a human. Dogs can be trained to discover bombs, drugs, and people. At the borders, dogs are used to sniff vehicles for the presence of illegal aliens. At airports, dogs are used to detect explosives. Many police departments depend upon dogs to detect drugs and track fugitives.

The Supreme Court has stated that the act of having a dog sniff a person or thing is not a search.[8] The question then becomes whether a dog's indication (a dog alert) that contraband is present is probable cause to issue a warrant or to pursue a warrantless search or seizure. That is the issue the Tenth Circuit Court of Appeals addressed in the *Ludwig* case.

 CASE

FLORIDA V. J.L.

529 U.S. 266 (2000)

The question presented in this case is whether an anonymous tip that a person is carrying a gun is, without more, sufficient to justify a police officer's stop and frisk of that person. We hold that it is not.

I

On October 13, 1995, an anonymous caller reported to the Miami-Dade Police that a young black male standing at a particular bus stop and wearing a plaid shirt was carrying a gun. . . . So far as the record reveals, there is no audio recording of the tip, and nothing is known about the informant. Sometime after the police received the tip—the record does not say how long—two officers were instructed to respond. They arrived at the bus stop about six minutes later and saw three black males "just hanging out [there]." One of the three, respondent J.L., was wearing a plaid shirt. Apart from the tip, the officers had no reason to suspect

any of the three of illegal conduct. The officers did not see a firearm, and J.L. made no threatening or otherwise unusual movements. One of the officers approached J.L., told him to put his hands up on the bus stop, frisked him, and seized a gun from J.L.'s pocket. The second officer frisked the other two individuals, against whom no allegations had been made, and found nothing.

J.L., who was at the time of the frisk "10 days shy of his 16th birth [day]," was charged under state law with carrying a concealed firearm without a license and possessing a firearm while under the age of 18. He moved to suppress the gun as the fruit of an unlawful search, and the trial court granted his motion. The intermediate appellate court reversed, but the Supreme Court of Florida quashed that decision and held the search invalid under the Fourth Amendment. Anonymous tips, the Florida Supreme Court stated, are generally less reliable than tips from known informants and can form the basis for reasonable suspicion only if accompanied by specific indicia of reliability, for example, the correct forecast of a subject's "'not easily predicted'" movements. The tip leading to the frisk of J.L., the court observed, provided no such predictions, nor did it contain any other qualifying indicia of reliability. Two justices dissented. The safety of the police and the public, they maintained, justifies a "firearm exception" to the general rule barring investigatory stops and frisks on the basis of bare-boned anonymous tips.

Seeking review in this Court, the State of Florida noted that the decision of the State's Supreme Court conflicts with decisions of other courts declaring similar searches compatible with the Fourth Amendment. See, *e.g., United States v. DeBerry,* 76 F.3d 884, 886–887 (C.A.7 1996); *United States v. Clipper,* 973 F.2d 944, 951 (C.A.D.C.1992). We granted certiorari, 528 U.S. 963, 120 S.Ct. 395, 145 L.Ed.2d 308 (1999), and now affirm the judgment of the Florida Supreme Court.

II

Our "stop and frisk" decisions begin with *Terry v. Ohio,* 392 U.S. 1, 88 S.Ct. 1868, 20 L.Ed.2d 889 (1968). This Court held in *Terry:*

"[W]here a police officer observes unusual conduct which leads him reasonably to conclude in light of his experience that criminal activity may be afoot and that the persons with whom he is dealing may be armed and presently dangerous, where in the course of investigating this behavior he identifies himself as a policeman and makes reasonable inquiries, and where nothing in the initial stages of the encounter serves to dispel his reasonable fear for his own or others' safety, he is entitled for the protection of himself and others in the area to conduct a carefully limited search of the outer clothing of such persons in an attempt to discover weapons which might be used to assault him."

In the instant case, the officers' suspicion that J.L. was carrying a weapon arose not from any observations of their own but solely from a call made from an unknown location by an unknown caller. Unlike a tip from a known informant whose reputation can be assessed and who can be held responsible if her allegations turn out to be fabricated. As we have recognized, however, there

are situations in which an anonymous tip, suitably corroborated, exhibits "sufficient indicia of reliability to provide reasonable suspicion to make the investigatory stop." *Id.,* at 327, 110 S.Ct. 2412. The question we here confront is whether the tip pointing to J.L. had those indicia of reliability.

In *White,* the police received an anonymous tip asserting that a woman was carrying cocaine and predicting that she would leave an apartment building at a specified time, get into a car matching a particular description, and drive to a named motel. *Ibid.* Standing alone, the tip would not have justified a *Terry* stop. Only after police observation showed that the informant had accurately predicted the woman's movements, we explained, did it become reasonable to think the tipster had inside knowledge about the suspect and therefore to credit his assertion about the cocaine. Although the Court held that the suspicion in *White* became reasonable after police surveillance, we regarded the case as borderline. Knowledge about a person's future movements indicates some familiarity with that person's affairs, but having such knowledge does not necessarily imply that the informant knows, in particular, whether that person is carrying hidden contraband. We accordingly classified *White* as a "close case."

The tip in the instant case lacked the moderate indicia of reliability present in *White* and essential to the Court's decision in that case. The anonymous call concerning J.L. provided no predictive information and therefore left the police without means to test the informant's knowledge or credibility. That the allegation about the gun turned out to be correct does not suggest that the officers, prior to the frisks, had a reasonable basis for suspecting J.L. of engaging in unlawful conduct: The reasonableness of official suspicion must be measured by what the officers knew before they conducted their search. All the police had to go on in this case was the bare report of an unknown, unaccountable informant who neither explained how he knew about the gun nor supplied any basis for believing he had inside information about J.L. If *White* was a close case on the reliability of anonymous tips, this one surely falls on the other side of the line.

Florida contends that the tip was reliable because its description of the suspect's visible attributes proved accurate: There really was a young black male wearing a plaid shirt at the bus stop. The United States as *amicus curiae* makes a similar argument, proposing that a stop and frisk should be permitted "when (1) an anonymous tip provides a description of a particular person at a particular location illegally carrying a concealed firearm, (2) police promptly verify the pertinent details of the tip except the existence of the firearm, and (3) there are no factors that cast doubt on the reliability of the tip. . . . " These contentions misapprehend the reliability needed for a tip to justify a *Terry* stop.

An accurate description of a subject's readily observable location and appearance is of course reliable in this limited sense: It will help the police correctly identify the person whom the tipster means to accuse. Such a tip, however, does not show that the tipster has knowledge of concealed criminal activity. The reasonable suspicion here at issue requires that a tip be reliable in its assertion of illegality, not just in its tendency to identify a determinate person. . . .

A second major argument advanced by Florida and the United States as *amicus* is, in essence, that the standard *Terry* analysis should be modified to license a "firearm exception." Under such an exception, a tip alleging an illegal gun would justify a stop and frisk even if the accusation would fail standard pre-search reliability testing. We decline to adopt this position.

Firearms are dangerous, and extraordinary dangers sometimes justify unusual precautions. Our decisions recognize the serious threat that armed criminals pose to public safety; *Terry's* rule, which permits protective police searches on the basis of reasonable suspicion rather than demanding that officers meet the higher standard of probable cause, responds to this very concern. But an automatic firearm exception to our established reliability analysis would rove too far. Such an exception would enable any person seeking to harass another to set in motion an intrusive, embarrassing police search of the targeted person simply by placing an anonymous call falsely reporting the target's unlawful carriage of a gun. Nor could one securely confine such an exception to allegations involving firearms. . . .

Finally, the requirement that an anonymous tip bear standard indicia of reliability in order to justify a stop in no way diminishes a police officer's prerogative, in accord with *Terry*, to conduct a protective search of a person who has already been legitimately stopped. We speak in today's decision only of cases in which the officer's authority to make the initial stop is at issue. In that context, we hold that an anonymous tip lacking indicia of reliability of the kind contemplated in *Adams* and *White* does not justify a stop and frisk whenever and however it alleges the illegal possession of a firearm.

The judgement of the Florida Supreme Court is affirmed.

 CASE

UNITED STATES V. LUDWIG

10 F. 3d 1523
(10th Cir. 1993)

[The trial court granted a motion to suppress evidence, finding that a warrantless search of a car trunk, based upon probable cause established by a dog alert indicating that drugs were present in the vehicle, was violative of the Fourth Amendment.]

The United States appeals the denial of its motion to reconsider the district court's suppression order. The government argues that the challenged dog sniff of Keith Ludwig's car was not a search under the Fourth Amendment, and that no warrant was required to search the car after the dog alerted. We agree and reverse.

At about 11:15 P.M. on December 12, 1992, Joel Nickles, a Border Patrol agent at the permanent checkpoint near Truth or Consequences, New

Mexico, walked a trained narcotics dog through the parking lot of the nearby Super 8 Motel to see if the dog would find any contraband. . . . Less than a week earlier the motel manager had given the Border Patrol permission to walk dogs through the motel parking lot for this purpose. . . .

As Nickles and the dog were walking through the lot, the dog pulled Nickles over to Keith Ludwig's Chevrolet Impala and alerted to the trunk, indicating that illegal drugs were in the trunk. . . . Around half an hour later Border Patrol agents began surveillance of the car, which continued through the night until Ludwig first approached his car the next morning at 10:00 A.M.

Agent Phillip Sanchez, who had been surveilling the car, approached Ludwig five minutes later and identified himself. Ludwig acknowledged that the car was his, but denied the agent's request to inspect the car and look in the trunk. Sanchez then directed Nickles to have the dog sniff the car again, and the dog again alerted to the trunk. When Ludwig refused to open the trunk, Sanchez took the keys from the ignition, opened the trunk, and found several large bags of marijuana. Ludwig was indicted for possession with intent to distribute less than fifty kilograms of marijuana. . . .

Ludwig also suggests that the dog sniffs of his car were unreasonable searches because the agents had no reason to suspect that there were drugs in his car. . . .

Regardless of whether Ludwig subjectively expected that the drugs in his trunk would be smelled, society does not recognize that expectation as legitimate. . . .

Ludwig suggests that dog sniffs are not as reliable as courts often assume, and therefore, the dog alert does not give the agents probable cause to open and search Ludwig's trunk. . . .

Probable cause means that "there is a fair probability that contraband or evidence of a crime will be found in a particular place.". . . Although Ludwig cites several cases of mistaken dog alerts, a dog alert usually is at least as reliable as many other sources of probable cause and is certainly reliable enough to create a "fair probability" that there is contraband.

The Tenth Circuit's ruling is the generally accepted rule. An alert by a properly trained dog furnishes probable cause. However, if the police are aware that a particular dog commonly errs, its alerts may not establish probable cause.

Good Faith Reliance on a Warrant. Judges can differ in opinion. Judges can make mistakes. What happens if a judge finds that probable cause exists and accordingly issues a warrant, only to have the probable cause finding reversed later? Should the evidence discovered during the search be excluded?

The Supreme Court has answered this question in the negative. The Court found, in *United States v. Leon*, 468 U.S. 897 (1984), that the exclusionary rule does not apply to evidence seized by a police officer, acting in good faith reliance on the warrant, while executing a facially valid warrant. The Court stated:

We conclude that the marginal or nonexistent benefits produced by suppressing evidence obtained in objectively reasonable reliance on a subsequently invalidated search warrant cannot justify the substantial costs of exclusion. We do not suggest, however, that exclusion is always inappropriate in cases where an officer has obtained a warrant and abided by its terms. . . . [A]n officer's reliance on the magistrate's probable-cause determination and on the technical sufficiency of the warrant he issues must be objectively reasonable . . . and it is clear that in some circumstances the officer will have no reasonable grounds for believing that the warrant was properly issued.

The Court found that exclusion of evidence when an officer is relying on a judicially issued warrant would not advance the objective of the exclusionary rule; it would not deter future police misconduct.

For *Leon* to apply, an officer's reliance must be in good faith. An officer who misleads a judge in order to obtain a warrant is not acting in good faith. Further, the warrant must be facially valid. If a reasonable officer should know that a warrant is facially defective, then any evidence obtained under it must be excluded. Examples of facially invalid warrants include: unsigned warrants, warrants that contain an inadequate description of the place or thing to be searched or seized, failure of the magistrate to require the supporting affidavit to be under oath, and such a lack of evidence that an officer could not in reasonable, good faith believe that probable cause exists. An officer may, however, rely on a warrant that contains mere technical and typographical errors, unless the errors are so fundamental that they render some element of the warrant (e.g., description) defective.

Leon is only applicable to searches and seizures that occur pursuant to warrants. An officer's good faith, but mistaken, belief that probable cause exists to conduct a warrantless search or to make a warrantless seizure does not justify the admission of evidence obtained as a result thereof. As discussed previously in this text, several state courts have refused to follow the *Leon* holding when interpreting their state constitutions.

The *Leon* reasoning has been extended to situations in which police officers act in good faith reliance upon a statute.[9] The same standards apply as in *Leon*, that is, the statute relied upon must be facially valid.

SEARCHES AND SEIZURES

The Warrant Requirement

Depending upon the circumstances, a search may be conducted with or without a warrant. The Supreme Court has expressed that there is a strong preference for the use of warrants, when possible, over warrantless actions.[10] The warrant preference serves an important purpose: it protects citizens from overzealous law enforcement practices.

> The presence of a search warrant serves a high function. Absent some grave emergency, the Fourth Amendment has interposed a magistrate between the citizen and police. This was done not to shield criminals nor to make the home a safe haven for illegal activities. It was done so that an objective mind might weigh the need to invade the privacy in order to enforce the law. The right of privacy was deemed too precious to entrust to the discretion of those whose job is the detection of crime and the arrest of criminals.[11]

Accordingly, a search conducted pursuant to a valid search warrant is per se reasonable. Warrantless searches are permitted only in special circumstances, and it is the responsibility of the government to prove that the facts of the case fit into one of the exceptions to the warrant requirement.

To give this preference some "teeth," the Supreme Court, in *Aguilar v. Texas,* 378 U.S. 108, 111 (1964), announced that "when a search is based upon a magistrate's, rather than a police officer's determination of probable cause," reviewing courts are to accept lesser competent evidence than if the officer made the determination personally, so long as there was a "substantial basis" for the magistrate's decision. To say it another way, less evidence is required to sustain a search if a warrant was obtained prior to the search.

"Reviewing courts" are referred to because the determination that probable cause exists by a magistrate when issuing a warrant is not final. A defendant may later attack any evidence seized pursuant to a warrant through a motion to suppress. As stated, determinations by a magistrate are less likely to be overturned than those made by police officers.

The Supreme Court created an exception to the rule that evidence must be suppressed if seized pursuant to an invalid warrant in *United States v. Leon,* 468 U.S. 897 (1984), wherein it held that evidence seized by an officer who executed a search warrant with a good faith belief that the warrant was valid will not be excluded, even though the warrant is later determined invalid. If a warrant is facially invalid, then any fruits of a search thereof must be excluded, because an officer cannot in good faith believe that such a warrant is valid. Of course, if an officer uses false information to convince the magistrate that probable cause exists, the good faith exception does not apply. The same is true if an officer knows that the magistrate issuing the warrant is not neutral and detached.

Requirements for Obtaining a Warrant.   The Fourth Amendment enumerates the requirements that must be met before a warrant can be issued. It is the responsibility of the law enforcement officer requesting the warrant to establish these elements to the judge making the warrant determination. The form application for search warrant used in the federal courts appears in Exhibit 12.1.

First, the evidence presented must establish probable cause to believe that within the area to be searched the items sought will be found. Second, there must be probable cause to believe that the items sought are connected to criminal activity.

Third, the area to be searched and any item to be seized must be described with particularity. The amount of specificity required varies from case to case. A warrant that authorizes a police officer to search a particular home for "unauthorized contraband" clearly violates the Fourth Amendment, whereas a warrant authorizing a search of the same home for a "nine-inch knife with an ivory handle" is valid, provided the warrant is valid in all other respects (probable cause, etc.).

Warrants for the seizure of items that are illegal in themselves do not have to be as particular as others. For example, a warrant to search for a book must be more specific than one for drugs. The description "book" is clearly insufficient, whereas a warrant to search for "cocaine" probably is sufficient.

EXHIBIT 12.1

Application and Affidavit
for Search Warrant

AO 106 (Rev. 5/85) Affidavit for Search Warrant _____

UNITED STATES DISTRICT COURT

_____ DISTRICT OF _____

In the Matter of the Search of
(Name, address or brief description of person or property to be searched)

**APPLICATION AND AFFIDAVIT
FOR SEARCH WARRANT**

CASE NUMBER:

I _____ being duly sworn depose and say:

I am a(n) _____ and have reason to believe
(Official Title)
that □ on the person of or □ on the premises known as (name, description and/or location)

in the _____ District of _____
there is now concealed a certain person or property, namely (describe the person or property)

which is (give alleged grounds for search and seizure under Rule 41(b) of the Federal Rules of
Criminal Procedure)

in violation of Title _____ United States Code, Section(s) _____ The facts
to support the issuance of a Search Warrant are as follows:

Continued on the attached sheet and made   □Yes   □No
a part hereof.

_____
Signature of Affiant

Sworn to before me, and subscribed in my
presence

_____ _____ at   _____
Date   City and State

_____   _____
Name and Title of Judicial Officer   Signature of Judicial Officer

Search Warrant upon
Oral Testimony

AO 93A (Rev. 5/85) Search Warrant Upon Oral Testimony _____

UNITED STATES DISTRICT COURT

_____ DISTRICT OF _____

In the Matter of the Search of
(Name, address or brief description of person or
property to be searched)

**SEARCH WARRANT UPON ORAL
TESTIMONY**

CASE NUMBER:

To _____ and any Authorized Officer of the United States

Sworn oral testimony has been communicated to me by _____
Affiant

that ☐ on the person of or ☐ on the premises known as (name, description and/or location)

in the _____ District of _____ there is now
concealed a certain person or property, namely (describe the person or property)

I am satisfied that the circumstances are such as to make it reasonable to dispense with a written affidavit and that there is probable cause to believe that the property or person so described is concealed on the person or premises above described and that grounds for application for issuance of the search warrant exist as communicated orally to me in a sworn statement which has been recorded electronically, stenographically, or in longhand and upon the return of the warrant, will be transcribed, certified as accurate and attached hereto.

YOU ARE HEREBY COMMANDED to search on or before _____
Date

the person or place named above for the person or property specified, serving this warrant and making the search (in the daytime — 6:00 AM to 10:00 PM) (at anytime in the day or night as I find reasonable cause has been established) and if the person or property be found there to seize same, leaving a copy of this warrant and receipt for the person or property taken, and prepare a written inventory of the person or property seized and promptly return this warrant to _____
as required by law. U.S. Judge or Magistrate

_____ at _____ _____
Date and Time Issued   City and State

_____ _____
Name and Title of Judicial Officer   Signature of Judicial Officer

I certify that on _____ at _____
Date   Time

_____ orally authorized the
U.S. Judge or Magistrate
issuance and execution of a search warrant conforming to all the foregoing terms.

_____ _____ _____
Name of affiant   Signature of affiant   Exact time warrant executed

Search Warrant upon
Oral Testimony
(continued)

AO 93A (Rev. 5/85) Search Warrant Upon Oral Testimony

RETURN

DATE WARRANT RECEIVED	DATE AND TIME WARRANT EXECUTED	COPY OF WARRANT AND RECEIPT FOR ITEMS LEFT WITH

INVENTORY MADE IN THE PRESENCE OF

INVENTORY OF PERSON OR PROPERTY TAKEN PURSUANT TO THE WARRANT

CERTIFICATION

I swear that this inventory is a true and detailed account of the person or property taken by me on the warrant.

_____

Subscribed, sworn to, and returned before me this date.

_____   _____
U.S. Judge or Magistrate   Date

As to location, a street address is normally sufficient. If there is no street address, the warrant should describe the location, owner, color, and architectural style of the property. Of course, any additional information that aids in describing property should be included. If the building to be searched is an apartment building or similar multiunit structure, the specific subunit to be searched must be stated in the warrant.

Fourth, the facts that are alleged to establish probable cause must be "supported by Oath or affirmation." In the typical case, this means that the government will produce one or more affidavits to prove that a warrant is justified. Note that the sample application for a search warrant (Exhibit 12.1) provides space for a supporting affidavit.

Finally, the warrant must be issued by a neutral and detached magistrate. Although judges are most commonly given the authority to issue warrants, a state may grant this authority to others. However, the Supreme Court has stated that the person authorized must be neutral and detached and be capable of determining whether probable cause exists.

Thus, a state law permitting a state's attorney general, who had investigated the crime and would later be responsible for its prosecution, to issue a warrant, was invalid.[12] In another case, a court clerk was found sufficiently detached, neutral, and capable to issue a warrant, because the clerk worked for a court and was under the supervision of a judge.[13]

Scope of Warrants. Warrants may be issued to search and seize any item that constitutes evidence of a crime, is the fruit of a crime, is contraband, or is used to commit a crime.[14] A warrant may be issued to search or seize any place or property, whether belonging to a suspected criminal or an innocent third party.

The particularity requirement acts to limit the breadth of a search. If an officer searches beyond the scope of a warrant, the exclusionary rule will make the fruits from the forbidden area inadmissible at trial.

In some circumstances the particularity requirement is heightened. For example, because of the importance of protecting the press from government intrusion, warrants to search newsrooms or similar areas must be drafted with "particular exactitude."[15] The same is true if a search will probe into confidential information, such as client records of attorneys and physicians.

As a general proposition, a warrant to search premises does not authorize the police to search the occupants of the premises.[16] Of course, a search may be conducted if an independent basis exists justifying the action. Generally, the occupants of an area to be searched may be detained until the search is complete. However, occupants cannot be detained for an "unduly prolonged" period of time.[17] Once the evidence sought is found or the threat of loss or destruction of evidence by an occupant has passed, he or she should be released.

Executing the Warrant. The warrant may direct a particular officer or an entire unit of police officers to conduct the search. The language of the warrant itself contains the duties of the officers executing the warrant, as well as their limitations.

As a general proposition, warrants are to be executed during the day. This is because a nighttime search is considered to be more intrusive than a daytime search[18] and because the probability of resistance is greater at night.

To conduct a nighttime search, a specific request for a warrant authorizing such must be made. To receive a warrant permitting a nighttime search, an officer must present the magistrate with facts evidencing the necessity for a nighttime search, usually including proof that a daytime search will not be successful. An anticipated nighttime delivery of illegal goods justifies a nighttime warrant, as does a concern that evidence of a crime will be destroyed in the night.

Most states have statutes requiring that warrants be executed within a specific amount of time after issuance. Warrants issued under federal law must be executed within ten days of issuance.[19]

In all cases, the search must be conducted when there is probable cause. If an officer fails to execute a warrant before probable cause has dissipated, then any resulting search is violative of the Fourth Amendment, and the fruits thereof are subject to the exclusionary rule. This is true even if the search is conducted within the period of time set by law.

At the premises of a search, the police must knock and announce their purpose before entering the premises. This is true whether entry is gained through the use of force or not. However, to prevent the destruction of evidence or injury to the officers, judges may issue "no-knock" warrants if the facts indicate that one or the other is likely to occur. The decision to issue a no-knock warrant must be based on the evidence. The Supreme Court has ruled that blanket exceptions to the knock-and-announce rule are violative of the Fourth Amendment. Instead, judges and police must make no-knock decisions based on the facts of each case.

After a search is completed, the officers are required to inventory items seized. Federal rules require that the owner of the property be given a receipt for the goods taken.[20] Property unlawfully taken must be returned to the owner, unless it is unlawful in itself, such as drugs.

Exceptions to the Search Warrant Requirement

Although the general rule is that a warrant must be obtained before a search may be undertaken, there are many exceptions. The exceptions to the warrant requirement are sometimes referred to as *exigent circumstances*.

consent
Voluntary and active agreement.

Consent Searches. A voluntary **consent** to a search obviates the warrant requirement. A person may consent to a search of his or her person or property. The scope of the search is limited by the person consenting. Absent special circumstances, a consent to search may be terminated at any time by the person giving consent.

A person's consent must be voluntary. All of the circumstances surrounding the consent are examined to determine whether the consent was voluntary. There is no requirement that police officers inform a person that he or she may refuse to consent.[21]

CASE

RICHARDS V. WISCONSIN

SUPREME COURT OF THE UNITED STATES (1997)

117 S. Ct. 1416 (1997)

Justice Stevens delivered the opinion of the Court.

In *Wilson v. Arkansas,* 514 U.S. 927, 115 S. Ct. 1914, 131 L. Ed. 2d 976 (1995), we held that the Fourth Amendment incorporates the common-law requirement that police officers entering a dwelling must knock on the door and announce their identity and purpose before attempting forcible entry. At the same time, we recognized that the "flexible requirement of reasonableness should not be read to mandate a rigid rule of announcement that ignores countervailing law enforcement interests," *id.,* at 934, 115 S. Ct., at 1918, and left "to the lower courts the task of determining the circumstances under which an unannounced entry is reasonable under the Fourth Amendment." *Id.,* 936, 115 S. Ct., at 1919.

In this case, the Wisconsin Supreme Court concluded that police officers are never required to knock and announce their presence when executing a search warrant in a felony drug investigation. In so doing, it reaffirmed a pre-*Wilson* holding and concluded that *Wilson* did not preclude this *per se* rule. We disagree with the court's conclusion that the Fourth Amendment permits a blanket exception to the knock-and-announce requirement for this entire category of criminal activity. But because the evidence presented to support the officers' actions in this case establishes that the decision not to knock and announce was a reasonable one under the circumstances, we affirm the judgment of the Wisconsin court.

I

On December 31, 1991, police officers in Madison, Wisconsin, obtained a warrant to search Steiney Richards's hotel room for drugs and related paraphernalia. The search warrant was the culmination of an investigation that had uncovered substantial evidence that Richards was one of several individuals dealing drugs out of hotel rooms in Madison. The police requested a warrant that would have given advance authorization for a "no-knock" entry into the hotel room, but the magistrate explicitly deleted those portions of the warrant. App. 7, 9.

The officers arrived at the hotel room at 3:40 A.M. Officer Pharo, dressed as a maintenance man, led the team. With him were several plainclothes officers and at least one man in uniform. Officer Pharo knocked on Richards's door and, responding to the query from inside the room, stated that he was a maintenance man. With the chain still on the door, Richards cracked it open. Although there is some dispute as to what occurred next, Richards acknowledges that when he opened the door he saw the man in uniform standing behind Officer Pharo. Brief for Petitioner 6. He quickly slammed the door closed and, after waiting two or three seconds, the officers began kicking and ramming the door to gain entry to the locked room. At trial, the officers testified that they identified themselves as police while they were kicking the door in. App. 40. When they finally did break into the room, the officers caught Richards trying to escape through the window. They also found cash and cocaine hidden in plastic bags above the bathroom ceiling tiles.

Richards sought to have the evidence from his hotel room suppressed on the ground that the officers had failed to knock and announce their presence prior to forcing entry into the room. The trial court denied the motion, concluding that the officers could gather from Richards's strange behavior when they first sought entry that he knew they were police officers and that he might try to destroy evidence or to escape. *Id.,* at 54. The judge emphasized that the easily disposable nature of the drugs the police were searching for further justified their decision to identify themselves as they crossed the threshold instead of announcing their presence before seeking entry. *Id.,* at 55. Richards appealed the decision to the Wisconsin Supreme Court and that court affirmed. . . .

In reaching this conclusion, the Wisconsin court found it reasonable—after considering criminal conduct surveys, newspaper articles, and other judicial opinions—to assume that all felony drug crimes will involve "an extremely high risk of serious if not deadly injury to the police as well as the potential for the disposal of drugs by the occupants prior to entry by the police."

II

We recognized in *Wilson* that the knock-and-announce requirement could give way "under circumstances presenting a threat of physical violence," or "where police officers have reason to believe that evidence would likely be destroyed if advance notice were given." 514 U.S., at 936, 115 S. Ct., at 1919. It is indisputable that felony drug investigations may frequently involve both of these circumstances. The question we must resolve is whether this fact justifies dispensing with case-by-case evaluation of the manner in which a search was executed.

The Wisconsin court explained its blanket exception as necessitated by the special circumstances of today's drug culture, 201 Wis. 2d, at 863–866, 549 N.W. 2d, at 226–227, and the State asserted at oral argument that the blanket exception was reasonable in "felony drug cases because of the convergence in a violent and dangerous form of commerce of weapons and the destruction of drugs." Tr. of Oral Arg. 26. But creating exceptions to the knock-and-announce rule based on the "culture" surrounding a general category of criminal behavior presents at least two serious concerns.

First, the exception contains considerable overgeneralization. For example, while drug investigation frequently does pose special risks to officer safety and the preservation of evidence, not every drug investigation will pose these risks to a substantial degree. . . .

A second difficulty with permitting a criminal-category exception to the knock-and-announce requirement is that the reasons for creating an exception in one category can, relatively easily,

be applied to others. Armed bank robbers, for example, are, by definition, likely to have weapons, and the fruits of their crime may be destroyed without too much difficulty. If a *per se* exception were allowed for each category of criminal investigation that included a considerable—albeit hypothetical—risk of danger to officers or destruction of evidence, the knock-and-announce element of the Fourth Amendment's reasonableness requirement would be meaningless.

Thus, the fact that felony drug investigations may frequently present circumstances warranting a no-knock entry cannot remove from the neutral scrutiny of a reviewing court the reasonableness of the police decision not to knock and announce in a particular case. Instead, in each case, it is the duty of a court confronted with the question to determine whether the facts and circumstances of the particular entry justified dispensing with the knock-and-announce requirement.

In order to justify a "no-knock" entry, the police must have a reasonable suspicion that knocking and announcing their presence, under the particular circumstances, would be dangerous or futile, or that it would inhibit the effective investigation of the crime by, for example, allowing the destruction of evidence. This standard—as opposed to a probable cause requirement—strikes the appropriate balance between the legitimate law enforcement concerns at issue in the execution of search warrants and the individual privacy interests affected by no-knock entries. . . .

III

Although we reject the Wisconsin court's blanket exception to the knock-and-announce requirement, we conclude that the officers' no-knock entry into Richards's hotel room did not violate the Fourth Amendment. We agree with the trial court, and with Justice Abrahamson, that the circumstances in this case show that the officers had a reasonable suspicion that Richards might destroy evidence if given further opportunity to do so.

The judge who heard testimony at Richards's suppression hearing concluded that it was reasonable for the officers executing the warrant to believe that Richards knew, after opening the door to his hotel room the first time, that the men seeking entry to his room were the police. App. 54. Once the officers reasonably believed that Richards knew who they were, the court concluded, it was reasonable for them to force entry immediately given the disposable nature of the drugs. *Id.*, at 55.

In arguing that the officers' entry was unreasonable, Richards places great emphasis on the fact that the magistrate who signed the search warrant for his hotel room deleted the portions of the proposed warrant that would have given the officers permission to execute a no-knock entry.

But this fact does not alter the reasonableness of the officers' decision, which must be evaluated as of the time they entered the hotel room. At the time the officers obtained the warrant, they did not have evidence sufficient, in the judgment of the magistrate, to justify a no-knock warrant. Of course, the magistrate could not have anticipated in every particular the circumstances that would confront the officers when they arrived at Richards's hotel room. These actual circumstances— petitioner's apparent recognition of the officers combined with the easily disposable nature of the drugs—justified the officers' ultimate decision to enter without first announcing their presence and authority.

Courts examine the totality of the circumstances when determining whether a consent was voluntary. The following factors are considered, but none are dispositive:

1. The suspect's knowledge of the right to refuse.
2. The age, intelligence, and language skills of the suspect.
3. The degree of cooperation exhibited by the suspect.
4. The suspect's attitude about the likelihood of discovering contraband during the search.
5. The length of detention.
6. The nature of the detention, including the nature of the questions and whether police intimidated the suspect or coerced the statements.[22]

Police must respect any limitations placed on a suspect's consent. So, if a suspect indicates that police may search the family room of a house, but no more, any evidence discovered in another room of the house would be excluded. Also, consent may be revoked anytime before the search is completed. Prosecutors bear the burden of establishing that consents are voluntary by a preponderance of the evidence.

Of course, a defendant who is threatened or coerced into consenting has not voluntarily consented. It is not coercion for persons to be told that if they do not consent, a warrant will be obtained authorizing the desired search. It is coercion for officers to tell persons that if they do not consent to a search, a warrant will be obtained and the officers will ransack their home.[23]

Consent is invalid if it is obtained by a mistaken belief that the officer had a legal right to conduct the search. For example, if Officer Frisk tells Patty Patdown that he has a warrant, or that the law does not require that he have one, and she acquiesces, the search is invalid if he had no warrant or legal right to conduct the search.

The same is true when officers use fraud or deceit to obtain consent. For example, in one case a defendant was arrested and interrogated. He gave no incriminating information during the questioning. The following day the officers went to the home of the defendant and told his wife that he had confessed to the crime and had sent the police to seize the contraband. Based upon these statements, the defendant's wife consented to a search by the officers. The state court found that this tactic led to an involuntary consent and that the evidence seized was inadmissible at trial.[24]

The facts of that case raise another issue: third-party consent. This arises often in cases where many people share a single dwelling or room, such as families, fraternities, and dormitories. In *United States v. Matlock,* 415 U.S. 164 (1974), the Supreme Court found that a third party may consent as long as the parties share access, control, and use of the property. If co-inhabitants section off a dwelling, with each tenant having exclusive control over a specific area, then only the tenant using an area may consent. If closets, desks, or similar areas are reserved for one person's private use, only that person may consent.

Having a property interest in property does not give one a right to consent to a search of the property. The Supreme Court has said that neither landlords nor hotel managers may consent to the search of their tenants' rooms.[25] They may have a property interest, but the privacy interest rests with the tenants.

plain view doctrine

The rule that if police officers see or come across something while acting lawfully, that item may be used as evidence in a criminal trial even if the police did not have a search warrant.

Plain View. Another exception to the warrant requirement is the **plain view doctrine.** Under this rule, a warrantless seizure of evidence by an officer who is lawfully in a position to see the evidence is valid.

A large body of cases discusses the plain view doctrine. From those cases it can be gleaned that for a seizure to be lawful under the doctrine, the following must be shown: (1) The officer must lawfully be in an area (2) from which the object to be seized is in plain view (3) and the officer does in fact see the item (4) there is probable cause to believe the object is connected to a crime, and (5) the officer has a right to access the object itself.

First, the officer must be in a place where he or she has a right to be. An officer, as is true of anyone, has a right to be in public places. Thus, evidence seen in a public park, on the street, or in a business open to the public may be seized without a warrant.

Evidence located on private property is different. As a general rule, the police have no right to enter private property to seize evidence that was in plain view from a public area. In such cases the officer is expected to obtain a warrant; the officer's observation provides the requisite probable cause. However, if an exception applies, such as preventing the destruction of the evidence, the officer may immediately seize the evidence.

If an officer is on private property for a lawful reason, then the officer may seize evidence in plain view without first obtaining a warrant. There are many reasons why an officer may be in a position to see evidence. Many of these were discussed in *Coolidge.* An officer who has to enter a home to execute an arrest warrant is not expected to overlook illegal objects in plain sight. The same is true if the officer is executing a search warrant, is in hot pursuit, is responding to an emergency, or is conducting a stop and frisk.

An officer who sees evidence because he or she has gone beyond the scope of the law enforcement right violates the Fourth Amendment, and the plain view doctrine will not support a seizure. For example, if an officer has a warrant to search a defendant's garage, any evidence obtained, even if in plain view, from the defendant's home may not be used at trial.

Second, the evidence seized must be in plain sight or plain view. Only the senses of sight and touch may be used to establish plain view. Use of the sense of touch is discussed later. Of course, whether an item is in plain sight depends on the scope of the officer's authority. An officer who has a search warrant authorizing the search of a closet for a gun may seize cocaine lying on the floor of the closet. The same is not true if the warrant did not authorize a search of the closet. In any case, the item must be plainly visible from a place where the officer has a right to be.

If an officer moves something with the intent of gaining a better vantage of the item, it is not in plain view. In one case, the movement of a stereo to record its serial number was considered an illegal search, because the officers were on the premises for another reason. The Court noted in that case that merely observing the stereo, which was in plain view, was legal. If the serial number

 CASE

COOLIDGE V. NEW HAMPSHIRE

403 U.S. 443 (1971)

It is well established that under certain circumstances the police may seize evidence in plain view without a warrant. But it is important to keep in mind that, in the vast majority of cases, *any* evidence seized by the police will be in plain view, at least at the moment of seizure. The problem with the "plain view" doctrine has been to identify the circumstances in which plain view has legal significance rather than being simply the normal concomitant of any search, legal or illegal.

An example of the applicability of the "plain view" doctrine is the situation in which the police have a warrant to search a given area for specified objects, and in the course of the search come across some other article of incriminating character. . . . Where the initial intrusion that brings the police within plain view of such an article is supported, not by a warrant, but by one

of the recognized exceptions to the warrant requirement, the seizure is also legitimate. Thus, the police may inadvertently come across evidence while in "hot pursuit" of a fleeing suspect. . . . And an object that comes into view during a search incident to arrest that is appropriately limited in scope under existing law may be seized without a warrant. . . . Finally, the "plain view" doctrine has been applied where a police officer is not searching for evidence against the accused, but nonetheless inadvertently comes across incriminating evidence. . . .

What the "plain view" cases have in common is that the police officer in each of them had a prior justification for an intrusion in the course of which he came inadvertently across a piece of evidence incriminating the accused. . . . Of course, the extension of the original justification is legitimate only where it is immediately apparent to the police that they have evidence before them; the "plain view" doctrine may not be used to extend a general exploratory search from one object to another until something incriminating at last emerges.

had been visible without moving the stereo, then recording its number would not have been violative of the Fourth Amendment. But moving the stereo constituted a "new invasion" of the defendant's rights.[26]

Officers may use mechanical or electrical aids in seeing evidence, so long as they are in a place they have a right to be and they are not conducting a search (encroaching on someone's right to privacy). Flashlights and binoculars are examples of such aids.

Third, the officer must see the item. In *Coolidge*, the Court stated that:

> [T]he discovery of evidence in plain view must be inadvertent. The rationale of the exception to the warrant requirement, as just stated, is that a plain-view seizure will not turn an initially valid (and therefore limited) search into a "general" one, while the inconvenience of procuring a warrant to cover an inadvertent discovery is great. But where the discovery is anticipated, where the police know in advance that location of the evidence and intend to seize it, the situation is altogether different. The requirement of a warrant imposes no inconvenience whatever.[27]

In most cases, the discovery will be inadvertent. However, in *Horton v. California*, 496 U.S. 128 (1990), the Supreme Court rejected inadvertence as a requirement of plain view, although it recognized that, in most instances, a discovery will be inadvertent. In *Horton*, an officer sought a search warrant for both the proceeds of a robbery and the weapons used during the robbery. The warrant was issued, but only for the proceeds. During the search, the officer discovered the weapon, as expected, in plain view. The Court held that even though expected, the gun was properly seized.

Fourth, the officer must have probable cause to believe that the object is subject to seizure, or, as the Court stated in *Horton*, the incriminating character of the object must be immediately apparent. *Contraband* (an item which is illegal itself, such as drugs) can be seized, as can property used to commit crimes, which has been used in a crime, or which has been stolen.

Fifth, the officer must be located such that he or she had a legal right to access the object. If not, the officer must obtain a warrant.

Stop and Frisk. On October 31, 1963, a Cleveland, Ohio, police detective observed three men standing on a street corner. Suspicious of the men, the detective positioned himself to watch their behavior. After some time the officer concluded that the men were "casing a job, a stick-up."

The officer approached the men, identified himself, and asked them to identify themselves. After the men "mumbled something," the officer grabbed one of the men and conducted a frisk, or a pat-down, of the man's clothing. The officer felt a pistol in the man's coat pocket. He removed the gun from his coat and then "patted down" the other two men. Another gun was discovered during those frisks.

The officer testified that he conducted the frisks because he believed the men were carrying weapons. The first man frisked was defendant Terry. At trial he was convicted of carrying a concealed weapon and was subsequently sentenced to one to three years in prison. His appeal made it to the United States Supreme Court.

In *Terry v. Ohio*, 392 U.S. 1 (1968), the Supreme Court was confronted with these issues: Did the officer's behavior amount to a search or seizure under the Fourth Amendment? If so, was the search or seizure by the officer reasonable?

The Court decided that defendant Terry had been seized under the Fourth Amendment. "It must be recognized that whenever a police officer accosts an individual and restrains his freedom to walk away, he has 'seized' that person." As to the frisk, the Court stated that "it is nothing less than sheer torture of the English language to suggest that a careful exploration of the outer surfaces of a person's clothing all over his or her body in an attempt to find weapons is not a search."

With these statements, the Court made it clear that the police practice of stopping and frisking people is one governed by the Fourth Amendment. However, the Court then concluded that an exception to the probable cause requirement was justified because the intrusion upon a person's privacy is limited in a stop and frisk, as opposed to an arrest and full search.

Officers are not given carte blanche to stop and frisk. Although probable cause is not required, officers must have a "reasonable suspicion" that the person to be stopped has committed, is committing, or is about to commit a crime. The officer's suspicion must be supported by "specific and articulable facts which, taken together with rational inferences from those facts, reasonably warrant that intrusion."[28] An officer's intuition alone is not enough suspicion to support a *Terry* seizure. When reviewing an officer's reasonable suspicion decision, a court is to examine the "totality of the circumstances" as known to the officer. Facts that may not be admissible at trial may be considered.[29]

In *Terry*, the facts that the Court found established reasonable cause included the officer's personal observation of the defendant and another man pacing near a business, repeatedly looking into the business's window, and briefly encountering and conferring with a third man. In addition, the Court noted that the detective who stopped Terry had thirty-nine years experience in policing and the officer testified that in his experience the men appeared to be "casing" the business. While the Court stressed that an officer's intuition alone is insufficient to establish reasonable cause, it can be relied upon in conjunction with specific facts to support a temporary detention. Another example of how much evidence is required to establish reasonable suspicion can be found in the 2000 Supreme Court case *Illinois v. Wardlow*. In *Wardlow* a defendant, who was in a high crime area, took flight immediately upon seeing police officers. The Court stated that even though a person's presence in a high crime area is not enough to establish reasonable suspicion, that fact combined with the defendant's unprovoked flight is enough[30]

Not all contacts between an officer and a citizen amount to a seizure. A seizure occurs anytime a reasonable person believes that he or she is not free to leave. There need not be an attempt to leave. A person may feel restrained by physical contact from a police officer, tone of voice, threatening language, or the threatening presence of many officers.[31]

Mere questioning of a citizen by a police officer does not rise to the level of a detention. However, if the interrogation becomes accusatory or its duration lengthy, the Fourth Amendment may come into play. A Texas statute that required an individual to comply with a police officer's order to identify himself, even though there was no basis to believe criminal activity was afoot, was held unconstitutional by the Supreme Court in 1979.[32] The Court held that the Fourth Amendment prohibits the police from temporarily detaining a person and demanding identification without at least a reasonable suspicion to believe the individual has committed, or is engaged in committing, a crime.

A motorist may be temporarily detained under *Terry*. Also, the Supreme Court has said that once a person is lawfully pulled over, he or she may be ordered out of the vehicle, even though there is no reason to believe that the driver is a threat. See later in this chapter for a more thorough discussion of automobiles and the Fourth Amendment.

In addition to requiring reasonable suspicion, the *Terry* Court also stated that stops are to "last no longer than is necessary," and the investigative methods employed during the stop should be the "least intrusive means reasonably available to verify or dispell the officer's suspicion in a short period of time." If an officer detains a person longer than necessary, the investigatory detention turns into a full seizure (arrest), and the probable cause requirement of the Fourth Amendment commences.

Florida v. Royer, 460 U.S. 491 (1983) provides an example of the distinction between an investigatory detention and an arrest. The defendant, a suspected drug dealer, was questioned in a public area of an airport. After a few minutes he was taken forty feet to a small police office, where he consented to a search of his luggage. The Court concluded that the search was the product of an illegal arrest, as less-intrusive methods of investigation were available. As alternatives, the Court mentioned that the officers could have used narcotics dogs to inspect the luggage or could have immediately requested consent to search the defendant's luggage. The act of requiring the defendant to accompany the officers to a small room forty feet away transformed the detention from a *Terry* stop to an arrest, which was violative of the Fourth Amendment because it was not supported by probable cause.

The fact that there has been a lawful stop does not itself justify a frisk. The purpose behind permitting investigatory stops is the advancement of crime detection and prevention. Frisks, on the other hand, are permitted to protect officers and others from the person stopped.

To conduct a frisk, an officer must have a reasonable belief that the person is armed and dangerous. Again, the officer must be able to point to facts to support this conclusion. An officer may draw on his or her experience as a police officer in making the decision. Again, however, intuition (suspicion not supported by any facts) alone is not adequate.

Full searches require probable cause. A *Terry* frisk requires less, and, accordingly, the permitted intrusion is less. The search must be limited to the outer clothing. A search of interior clothing or pockets is improper.

If the defendant is in an automobile, the officer may search those areas within the person's immediate control.[33] Once any lawful stop of a vehicle is made, the driver may be ordered out of the vehicle. However, to frisk an occupant of a vehicle, the *Terry* standard must be met.

If during a pat-down an officer feels an item that may be a weapon, then the officer may reach into the clothing of the citizen to seize the item. Any item seized, whether a weapon, contraband, or other item associated with a crime, may be used as evidence.

If the officer does not feel an item that may be a weapon, the search can go no further. If the officer feels evidence of another crime, the intrusion may continue under the "plain feel" doctrine.

Plain Feel. You have learned both the plain view doctrine and the *Terry* exception to the warrant and probable cause requirements of the Fourth Amendment. The plain feel doctrine is the product of their joining. That is, what happens when an officer who is conducting a *Terry* pat-down discovers, through the sense of touch, not a weapon, but contraband? May this information be used to establish probable cause allowing a more intrusive search? This question was answered in the *Dickerson* case.

 CASE ———————————————————————————————◆

MINNESOTA V. DICKERSON

113 S. Ct. 2130 (1993)

On the evening of November 9, 1989, two Minneapolis police officers were patrolling an area on the city's north side in a marked squad car. At about 8:15 P.M., one of the officers observed respondent leaving a 12-unit apartment building on Morgan Avenue North. The officer, having previously responded to complaints of drug sales in the building's hallways and having executed several search warrants on the premises, considered the building to be a notorious "crack house." According to testimony credited by the trial court, respondent began walking toward the police but, upon spotting the squad car and making eye contact with one of the officers, abruptly halted and began walking in the opposite direction. His suspicion aroused, this officer watched as respondent turned and entered an alley on the other side of the apartment building. Based upon respondent's seemingly evasive actions and the fact that he had just left a building known for cocaine traffic, the officers decided to stop respondent and investigate further.

The officers pulled their squad car into the alley and ordered respondent to stop and submit to a patdown search. The search revealed no weapons, but the officer conducting the search did take an interest in a small lump in respondent's nylon jacket. The officer later testified: "As I pat-searched the front of his body, I felt a lump, a small lump, in the front pocket. I examined it with my fingers and it slid and it felt to be a lump of crack cocaine in cellophane." The officer then reached into respondent's pocket and retrieved a small plastic bag containing one fifth of one gram of crack cocaine. Respondent was arrested and charged in Hennepin County District Court with possession of a controlled substance.

Before trial, respondent moved to suppress the cocaine. The trial court first concluded that the officers were justified under *Terry v. Ohio* . . . in stopping respondent. . . . The court further found that the officers were justified in frisking respondent to ensure that he was not carrying a weapon. Finally, analogizing to the "plain-view" doctrine . . . the trial court ruled that the officers' seizure of the cocaine did not violate the Fourth Amendment. . . . [The Minnesota Court of Appeals and Supreme Court reversed, rejecting the trial court's "plain feel" theory. In addition, the Supreme Court held that the search itself went beyond the frisk authorized by *Terry*.]

Most state and federal courts have recognized a so-called "plain feel" or "plain touch" corollary to the plain-view doctrine. . . . Some state courts, however, like the Minnesota court in this case, have rejected such a corollary. . . .

We have already held that police officers, at least under certain circumstances, may seize contraband detected during the lawful execution of a *Terry* search. In *Michigan v. Long,* for example, police approached a man who had driven his car into a ditch and who appeared to be under the influence of some intoxicant. As the man moved to reenter the car from the roadside, police spotted a knife on the floorboard. The officers stopped the man, subjected him to a patdown search, and then inspected the interior of the vehicle for other weapons. During the search of the passenger compartment, the police discovered an open pouch containing marijuana and seized it. This Court upheld the validity of the search and seizure under *Terry.* The Court held first that, in the context of a roadside encounter, where police have reasonable suspicion based on specific and articulable facts to believe that a driver may be armed and dangerous, they may conduct a protective search for weapons not only of the driver's person but also of the passenger compartment of the automobile. . . . "If, while conducting a legitimate *Terry* search of the interior of the automobile, the officer should, as here, discover contraband other than weapons, he clearly cannot be required to ignore the contraband, and the Fourth Amendment does not require its suppression in such circumstances." . . .

We think this doctrine has an obvious application by analogy to cases in which an officer discovers contraband through sense of touch during an otherwise lawful search. The rationale of the plain view doctrine is that if contraband is left in open view and is observed by a police officer from a lawful vantage point, there has been no invasion of a legitimate expectation of privacy and thus no "search" within the meaning of the Fourth Amendment—or at least no search independent of

the initial intrusion that gave the officers their vantage point. . . . The warrantless seizure of contraband that presents itself in this manner is deemed justified by the realization that resort to a neutral magistrate under such circumstances would often be impracticable and would do little to promote the objectives of the Fourth Amendment. . . . The same can be said of tactile discoveries of contraband. If a police officer lawfully pats down a suspect's outer clothing and feels an object whose contour or mass makes its identity immediately apparent, there has been no invasion of the suspect's privacy beyond that already authorized by the officer's search for weapons; if the object is contraband, its warrantless seizure would be justified by the same practical considerations that inhere in the plain view context. . . .

The Minnesota Supreme Court rejected an analogy to the plain view doctrine on two grounds: first, its belief that "the sense of touch is inherently less immediate and less reliable than the sense of sight," and second, that "the sense of touch is far more intrusive into the personal privacy that is at the core of the Fourth Amendment." We have a somewhat different view. First, *Terry* itself demonstrates that the sense of touch is capable of revealing the nature of an object with sufficient reliability to support a seizure. The very premise of *Terry*, after all, is that officers will be able to detect the presence of weapons through the sense of touch. . . . The court's second concern—that touch is more intrusive into privacy than is sight—is inapposite in light of the fact that the intrusion the court fears has already been authorized by the lawful search for weapons. . . .

It remains to apply these principles to the facts of this case. . . . Thus, the dispositive question before this Court is whether the officer who conducted the search was acting within the lawful bounds marked by *Terry* at the time he gained probable cause to believe the lump in respondent's jacket was contraband. . . .

Under the State Supreme Court's interpretation of the record before it, it is clear that the court was correct in holding that the police officer in this case overstepped the bounds of the "strictly circumscribed" search for weapons allowed under

Terry. [In *Terry*], as here, "an officer who is executing a valid search for one item seizes a different item," [and] this Court rightly "has been sensitive to the danger . . . that officers will enlarge a specific authorization, furnished by a warrant or an exigency, into the equivalent of a general warrant to rummage and seize at will.". . .

Although the officer was lawfully in a position to feel the lump in respondent's jacket, because *Terry* entitled him to place his hands upon respondent's jacket, the court below determined that the incriminating character of the object was not immediately apparent to him. Rather, the officer determined that the item was contraband only after conducting a further search, one not authorized by *Terry* or by another exception to the warrant requirement. Because this further search of respondent's pocket was constitutionally invalid, the seizure of the cocaine that followed is likewise unconstitutional.

For these reasons, the judgment of the Minnesota Supreme Court is affirmed.

If an officer discovers contraband through the sense of touch, during a *Terry* frisk, probable cause exists to search further. If contraband is recovered, it is admissible at trial. The rules set out in *Terry* apply. First, stops must be supported by reasonable suspicion. Second, pat-downs may be conducted only when an officer possesses a reasonable suspicion based on specific and articulable facts that the suspect may be armed and dangerous. Third, the pat-down must be limited. Exploration of the clothing beyond what is necessary to determine dangerousness is not permitted, unless probable cause to believe that there is contraband is created through the officer's sense of touch.

Search Incident to Arrest. Two search issues arise during and immediately following an arrest. First, may officers search the arrestee's person without first obtaining a warrant? Second, may officers search the arrestee's home, apartment, or other structure where the defendant is arrested?

The issue of searching the defendant's person was addressed in *United States v. Robinson*, 414 U.S. 260 (1973), in which the Court held that, after a lawful arrest, the defendant's person may be fully searched without first obtaining a warrant. The Court held that to require officers to obtain a warrant would needlessly endanger their lives and would increase the possibility of evidence being destroyed by the defendant. Search incident to arrest includes a search of the defendant's clothing. There is no probable cause requirement for a search incident to arrest.

The second issue concerns searching the area where the defendant is arrested. The premier case in this area is *Chimel v. California*.

Chimel significantly changed the law, as before *Chimel* was decided officers had the authority to search a much greater area as incident to arrest. The "within the defendant's immediate control" test continues to be the governing law. As with any other lawful search and seizure, any evidence obtained may be used to prosecute the defendant.

A related concept, the protective sweep, was given constitutional recognition in *Maryland v. Buie*, 494 U.S. 325 (1990). A *protective sweep* is a brief and limited warrantless search of an arrestee's home, which is permitted if the defendant is arrested therein. The purpose of the protective sweep is to check the house for other persons who may pose a danger to the arresting officers. See later in this chapter for an extended discussion of searches incident to arrest and protective sweeps.

Finally, "when a policeman has made a lawful custodial arrest of the occupant of an automobile, he may, as a contemporaneous incident of that arrest, search the passenger compartment of that automobile," including the contents of any containers found in that area.[34]

Preservation of Evidence.   In some instances evidence may be destroyed before a warrant can be obtained. In such cases an officer may make a warrantless search and seizure.

Although the typical case involves the destruction of evidence, the preservation-of-evidence theory also has been applied to evanescent evidence (evidence that may vanish on its own). For example, in one case a defendant, who was arrested for drunk driving, was subjected to a warrantless blood alcohol test. The Court concluded that the warrantless test was reasonable under the Fourth Amendment.

> The officer in the present case, however, might reasonably have believed that he was confronted with an emergency, in which the delay necessary to obtain a warrant, under the circumstances, threatened "the destruction of evidence." . . . We are told that the percentage of alcohol in the blood begins to diminish shortly after drinking stops, as the body functions to eliminate it from the system. Particularly in a case such as this, where time had to be taken to bring the accused to the hospital and to investigate the scene of the accident, there was no time to seek out a magistrate and secure a warrant. Given these special facts, we conclude that the attempt to secure evidence of blood-alcohol content in this case was an appropriate incident to petitioner's arrest.[35]

 CASE

CHIMEL V. CALIFORNIA

395 U.S. 752 (1969)

This case raises basic questions concerning the permissible scope under the Fourth Amendment of a search incident to a lawful arrest.

The relevant facts are essentially undisputed. Late in the afternoon of September 13, 1965, three police officers arrived at the Santa Ana, California, home of the petitioner with a warrant authorizing his arrest for the burglary of a coin shop. The officers knocked on the door, identified themselves to the petitioner's wife, and asked if they might come inside. She ushered them into the house, where they waited 10 to 15 minutes until the petitioner returned home from work. When the petitioner entered the house, one of the officers handed him the arrest warrant and asked for permission to "look around." The petitioner objected, but was advised that "on the basis of the lawful arrest," the officers would nonetheless conduct the search. No search warrant had been issued.

Accompanied by the petitioner's wife, the officers then looked through the entire three-bedroom house, including the attic, the garage, and a small workshop. In some rooms the search was relatively cursory. In the master bedroom and sewing room, however, the officers directed the petitioner's wife to open drawers and "to physically remove contents of the drawers from side to side so that [they] might view items that would have come from [the] burglary." After completing the search, they seized numerous items—primarily coins, but also several medals, tokens, and a few other objects. The entire search took between 45 minutes and an hour. . . .

When an arrest is made, it is reasonable for the arresting officer to search the person arrested in order to remove any weapons that the latter might seek to use in order to resist arrest or effect his escape. Otherwise, the officer's safety might well be endangered, and the arrest itself frustrated. In addition, it is entirely reasonable for the arresting officer to search for and seize any evidence on the arrestee's person in order to prevent its concealment or destruction. And the area into which an arrestee might reach in order to grab a weapon or evidentiary items must, of course,

be governed by a like rule. A gun on a table or in a drawer in front of one who is arrested can be as dangerous to the arresting officer as one concealed in the clothing of the person arrested. There is ample justification, therefore, for a search of the arrestee's person and the area "within his immediate control"—construing that phrase to mean the area from within which he might gain possession of a weapon or destructible evidence.

There is no comparable justification, however, for routinely searching any room other than that in which an arrest occurs—or, for that matter, for searching through all the desk drawers or other closed or concealed areas in the room itself. Such searches, in the absense of well-recognized exceptions, may be made only under the authority of a search warrant. . . .

Application of sound Fourth Amendment principles to the facts of this case produces a clear result. . . . The scope of the search was . . . "unreasonable" under the Fourth and Fourteenth Amendments, and the petitioner's conviction cannot stand.

Reversed.

So, any evidence that may be destroyed, intentionally or not, before a warrant can be obtained, can be the foundation of a warrantless search and seizure under the preservation-of-evidence exception to the Fourth Amendment's warrant requirement.

Emergency Responses and Hot Pursuit.   One of the many responsibilities of being a police officer is to respond to emergencies and to assist those in danger. Police officers are permitted to enter areas protected by the Fourth Amendment without a warrant if there is an emergency. For example, an officer may respond to cries for help from within a home or may enter a building that is on fire to assist firefighters. The possibilities are endless. Provided the officer has a genuine and reasonable belief that there is an emergency, the entry does not violate the Fourth Amendment. Of course, once inside, any evidence in plain view may be seized. Also, officers may remedy any immediate problems, secure the premises, and then obtain a warrant before proceeding further, provided that no exigent circumstances justify a continued presence and search.

It has been argued that the government has such a great interest, especially in murder cases, in having immediate access to crime scenes that the Fourth Amendment warrant requirement should be dispensed with. The Supreme Court rejected that position in *Mincey v. Arizona*, 437 U.S. 385 (1978), in which a warrantless four-day search of an apartment where a police officer was murdered was held violative of the Fourth Amendment.

Similar to the emergency exception is the hot pursuit exception. An officer who is chasing a suspect does not have to end the pursuit at the door of a home or business. The normally unlawful entry into the structure is permitted to catch the defendant. Again, once inside, the plain view exception applies.

Open Fields. The open fields doctrine is not, technically, an exception to the search warrant requirement. That is because, to be an exception to the Fourth Amendment warrant requirement, the Fourth Amendment must apply to the conduct of the officers. The Supreme Court has held that the "open fields" around one's home are not protected by the Fourth Amendment, so officers are free to intrude upon such areas without first obtaining a warrant. In addition, officers will not be liable for trespass if they make such an intrusion while performing a lawful duty.[36]

The reason that open fields are not protected is because of the language of the Fourth Amendment itself: "The right of the people to be secure in their persons, houses, papers, and effects. . . . " The Supreme Court has found that this extends the Fourth Amendment's protection only to a person's home and the curtilage of that home.

Curtilage is the area directly around one's home. It is treated as part of the home, as the Court has recognized that a person's privacy interest does not end at the front door of the home. Determining whether an area is curtilage, and protected, or an open field, and unprotected, can be troublesome. In *United States v. Dunn*, 480 U.S. 294 (1987), the high Court held that a barn located sixty yards from a house was not within the curtilage, even though a fence enclosed the barn. In that opinion, the Court stated four factors that should be considered when making an open fields determination. Those are:

1. The proximity of the area claimed to be curtilage from the home.
2. Whether the area enclosed is enclosed with the home.
3. The nature of the use of the area.
4. The attempts of the residents to keep the area private.

The proximity of the area in question to the home, the fact that it is enclosed by fencing, that it is commonly used by the residents, and that the residents have taken measures to assure privacy in the area, all increase the probability that the area will be determined to be curtilage. The issue is whether the residents have a reasonable expectation of privacy in the area.

The advent of aerial surveillance has made it possible for law enforcement officers to see what were once remote areas. The question in the Fourth Amendment context is: Do people have a reasonable expectation of privacy in areas observable from aircraft?

One federal district court outlined five factors to be considered when examining the validity of aerial surveillance:

1. The height of the aircraft.
2. The size of the objects viewed.
3. The nature of the use of the area.

4. The number of flights over the area.

5. The frequency and duration of the aerial surveillance.[37]

Structures, even though in an open field, may be protected if it appears that one took measures to assure privacy.[38] However, the fact that an area is curtilage does not mean that a warrantless aerial observation is unreasonable. In a 1986 case, the Supreme Court upheld an aerial observation of a backyard that was surrounded by a fence and not visible from the street.[39]

Finally, although the Fourth Amendment speaks of "houses," its protection extends to businesses and other structures as well. However, it is likely that the expectation of privacy will be less in a business than in a dwelling.

Border Searches and Profiles.   Unlike ordinary searches, searches at the borders of the United States do not require probable cause. In fact, no suspicion is required whatsoever. This rule applies to searches of both luggage and persons.[40] However, these searches must comply with the reasonableness requirement of the Fourth Amendment.[41]

For a strip search to be conducted, a customs official must have a "real suspicion" that illegality is afoot. As for more invasive searches, such as cavity searches, more suspicion is required. A customs official must be aware of a "clear indication" of illegality before such searches are conducted. Further, these searches must be conducted in a private and medically safe environment. A *clear indication* is less than probable cause, but more than either the *Terry* reasonable suspicion or the border strip-search "real suspicion" standards.

The border search exception to the Fourth Amendment actually extends beyond the border. For example, first arrival ports in the United States of international flights are treated as borders for purposes of the Fourth Amendment. Roadblock-style checkpoints miles from a border intended to discover illegal aliens have been approved,[42] but the authority to search is more limited than at the border. Officers may not search the occupants of the vehicles stopped at these checkpoints without probable cause.[43] Random stops of vehicles away from the border must be supported by reasonable suspicion, because they are treated as *Terry* detentions.

Customs officials commonly use profiles to determine who to detain and search. A *profile* is an established set of criteria that are believed to indicate a probability that a person is involved in illegal activity. For example, a person who makes frequent trips between the United States and Colombia (a nation noted for its drug production and exportation), who carries little or no luggage, who has paid for airline tickets with cash, whose visits to Colombia are for short periods of time (e.g., 48 hours), and who behaves nervously at the customs desk, would meet a drug courier profile. Similar profiles have been used to stop motorists in Florida suspected of transporting and trafficking drugs.

Two issues are raised by profiles: first, whether a profile may be used to establish a reasonable suspicion, thereby permitting a *Terry* stop; and second, whether profiles justify searches.

As to the first question, the answer is yes. However, a profile must be reasonable. Courts examine the totality of the circumstances when examining the validity of a profile. Although no one factor in a profile may justify a temporary detention, the whole picture may. Although race may be a factor in the decision, the Supreme Court held in *United States v. Brignoni-Ponce*, 422 U.S. 873 (1975), that race alone does not establish reasonable suspicion, even if the detention occurs near the Mexican border and the occupants appear to be of Mexican ancestry. The Court enumerated factors that may be taken into account:

1. The characteristics of the area, including the proximity to the border, the usual patterns of traffic on the road, and experience with alien traffic.
2. Information concerning recent illegal border crossings in the area.
3. The driver's behavior, such as erratic driving and obvious attempts to evade officers.
4. The type of vehicle, such as a station wagon with large compartments, which are frequently used for transporting concealed aliens.
5. Whether the vehicle appears heavily loaded or has an extraordinary number of occupants.
6. Whether passengers are attempting to hide.
7. The characteristics of persons living in Mexico, including mode of dress and hair styles.
8. Other meaningful factors in light of the officers' experiences in detecting illegal aliens.

This list is not exclusive, and profiles vary depending upon the situation. Nevertheless, the *Brignoni-Ponce* decision provided a basis upon which law enforcement agencies can create profiles and courts can adjudge the validity of those profiles.

This leads to the second question: May profiles be used to justify searches? Recall that at borders, no suspicion is necessary to conduct general searches of persons and things. However, to conduct body searches a "real suspicion" must exist, and to conduct more invasive searches there must be a "clear indication" of some illegality. Although a profile may satisfy the real suspicion test, it does not, acting alone, justify more invasive searches.

Outside the border areas, profiles may be used to conduct *Terry* stops, but no more. To conduct a frisk of the persons detained, a reasonable belief as to dangerousness must exist. Probable cause is required if a full search of a person, vehicle, or other things is conducted.

Finally, although profiles may be used to support detentions, they may not be used at trial to establish guilt.[44]

SIDEBAR   **THE RACIAL PROFILING CONTROVERSY**   In recent years the use of race as a factor in law enforcement and corrections officer's decision-making has been the subject of considerable controversy. Many scholars and commentators have asserted that it is common for police officers to stop black motorists simply because of their skin color. This phenomenon has become known as "driving while black." *In addition to traffic stops, race is often used as a factor to determine whose bags or person should be searched in airports and at borders.

Racial profiling was already the subject of considerable debate when the United States was attacked on September 11, 2001, by nineteen Muslim terrorists. Several hijackings in the 1970s and1980s, the 1993 World Trade Center bombing, the 1996 bombing of a U.S. military site in Saudi Arabia, the bombings of two U.S. embassies in 1996, the attack on the U.S.S. Cole in 2000, and other attacks on U.S. citizens and interests were all committed by Muslim extremists. In the wake of these events, many people called for increased scrutiny of people who appeared to be of Arab descent or who appeared to be Muslim. Others contended that such profiling was inherently wrong.

In an effort not to engage in "racial profiling," the United States Secretary of Transportation, Norman Mineta, ordered that race not be used as a factor by airport security officers when making decisions to search baggage or persons. This policy had many critics, who contended that ethnicity and dress were legitimate characteristics given the nature of threat to the United States.

The Supreme Court of the United States has found a middle ground. The Court has held that race, ethnicity, religion, skin color, and similar characteristics may not be the sole basis upon which a person is searched or seized. However, the Court held in *United States v. Brignoni-Ponce* (1975) that race may be one of many factors law enforcement officers may consider when stopping motorists or conducting border searches, provided that race can be connected with criminality in the particular circumstances in which the officers are operating.

*Source: David A. Harris, The Stories, The Statistics, and the Law: Why Driving While Black Matters, 84 Minnesota Law Review 265 (1999)

Motor Vehicles and Roadblocks. Privacy in automobiles is protected by the Fourth Amendment. However, the Supreme Court has not extended full Fourth Amendment protection to the occupants of automobiles. The Court's rationale for decreased protection is twofold. First, because of the mobile nature of automobiles, evidence can disappear quickly. Second, automobiles are used on the public roads where they and their occupants are visible to the public; thus, an occupant of an automobile has a lesser expectation of privacy than does the occupant of a home.

Stops. Of course, a motorist may be stopped if an officer has probable cause. In addition, a *Terry* stop may be made if there is reasonable suspicion that an occupant has committed a crime or that contraband will be found. As discussed earlier, *Terry* stops must be limited in duration and reasonable in method, and a frisk of the occupant is permissible only if the officer possesses a reasonable belief that the individual may have a weapon.

Fourth Amendment issues also arise in the context of roadblocks, which are used by law enforcement officers in two situations. First, they assist in the apprehension of a particular suspect. Second, serving the regulatory function of protecting the public from unsafe drivers, officers may stop vehicles to determine if the car satisfies the state's safety requirements, whether the driver is properly licensed, and whether the vehicle is properly registered. In regard to the former, reasonable suspicion is required before a stop can be made. As to the latter, temporary regulatory detentions are permitted so long as they are both objectively random and reasonable. That is, the police must use an objective system in deciding what automobiles will be stopped. Every car, or every tenth car, or some similar method is permissible.

The Supreme Court has also upheld roadblocks intended to discover drunk drivers. *Michigan State Police v. Sitz*, 496 U.S. 444 (1990), upheld a highway sobriety checkpoint program where 126 vehicles passed through the checkpoint, the average delay for each vehicle was 25 seconds, and 2 intoxicated drivers were arrested. The Court found that the stops were seizures under the Fourth Amendment, but that they were reasonable. In support of this conclusion, the Court stressed that the stops were of limited duration; that drunk drivers are a serious problem in the nation, and accordingly Michigan had a compelling interest in performing the sobriety checks; that all stops were governed by objective guidelines; that the guidelines required all vehicles to be stopped, thereby preventing arbitrary decisions by individual officers; that all officers were fully uniformed, thereby lessening motorists' concerns; and finally, that data support the conclusion that sobriety checkpoints are effective in apprehending drunk drivers. In the 2000 Supreme Court decision, *City of Indianapolis v. Edmonds*, the Court invalidated systematic stops of cars intended to intercept illegal drugs.

 CASE

CITY OF INDIANAPOLIS V. EDMOND

531 U.S. 32 (2000)

In *Michigan Dept. of State Police v. Sitz*, 496 U. S. 444 (1990), and *United States* v. *Martinez-Fuerte*, 428 U. S. 543 (1976), we held that brief, suspicionless seizures at highway checkpoints for the purposes of combating drunk driving and intercepting illegal immigrants were constitutional. We now consider the constitutionality of a highway checkpoint program whose primary purpose is the discovery and interdiction of illegal narcotics.

In August 1998, the city of Indianapolis began to operate vehicle checkpoints on Indianapolis roads in an effort to interdict unlawful drugs. The city conducted six such roadblocks between August and

November that year, stopping 1,161 vehicles and arresting 104 motorists. Fifty-five arrests were for drug-related crimes, while 49 were for offenses unrelated to drugs. *Edmond v. Goldsmith*, 183 F. 3d 659, 661 (CA7 1999). The overall "hit rate" of the program was thus approximately nine percent.

The parties stipulated to the facts concerning the operation of the checkpoints by the Indianapolis Police Department (IPD) for purposes of the preliminary injunction proceedings instituted below. At each checkpoint location, the police stop a predetermined number of vehicles. Approximately 30 officers are stationed at the checkpoint. Pursuant to written directives issued by the chief of police, at least one officer approaches the vehicle, advises the driver that he or she is being stopped briefly at a drug checkpoint, and asks the driver to produce a license and registration. The officer also looks for signs of impairment and conducts an open-view examination of the vehicle from the outside. A narcotics-detection dog walks around the outside of each stopped vehicle.

The directives instruct the officers that they may conduct a search only by consent or based on the appropriate quantum of particularized suspicion. The officers must conduct each stop in the same manner until particularized suspicion develops, and the officers have no discretion to stop any vehicle out of sequence. The city agreed in the stipulation to operate the checkpoints in such a way as to ensure that the total duration of each stop, absent reasonable suspicion or probable cause, would be five minutes or less.

The affidavit of Indianapolis Police Sergeant Marshall DePew, although it is technically outside the parties' stipulation, provides further insight concerning the operation of the checkpoints. According to Sergeant DePew, checkpoint locations are selected weeks in advance based on such considerations as area crime statistics and traffic flow. The checkpoints are generally operated during daylight hours and are identified with lighted signs reading, "NARCOTICS CHECKPOINT _____ MILE AHEAD, NARCOTICS K-9 IN USE, BE PREPARED TO STOP." App. to Pet. for Cert. 57a. Once a group of cars has been stopped, other traffic proceeds without interruption until all the stopped cars have been processed or diverted for further processing. Sergeant DePew also stated that the average stop for a vehicle not subject to further processing lasts two to three minutes or less.

Respondents James Edmond and Joell Palmer were each stopped at a narcotics checkpoint in late September 1998. Respondents then filed a lawsuit on behalf of themselves and the class of all motorists who had been stopped or were subject to being stopped in the future at the Indianapolis drug checkpoints. . . .

The Fourth Amendment requires that searches and seizures be reasonable. A search or seizure is ordinarily unreasonable in the absence of individualized suspicion of wrongdoing. *Chandler v. Miller,* 520 U. S. 305, 308 (1997). While such suspicion is not an "irreducible" component of

reasonableness, *Martinez-Fuerte,* 428 U. S., at 561, we have recognized only limited circumstances in which the usual rule does not apply. For example, we have upheld certain regimes of suspicionless searches where the program was designed to serve "special needs, beyond the normal need for law enforcement." See, *e.g., Vernonia School Dist. 47J v. Acton,* 515 U. S. 646 (1995) (random drug testing of student-athletes); *Treasury Employees v. Von Raab,* 489 U. S. 656 (1989) (drug tests for United States Customs Service employees seeking transfer or promotion to certain positions); *Skinner v. Railway Labor Executives' Assn.,* 489 U. S. 602 (1989) (drug and alcohol tests for railway employees involved in train accidents or found to be in violation of particular safety regulations). We have also allowed searches for certain administrative purposes without particularized suspicion of misconduct, provided that those searches are appropriately limited. See, *e.g., New York v. Burger,* 482 U. S. 691, 702–704 (1987) (warrantless administrative inspection of premises of "closely regulated" business); *Michigan v. Tyler,* 436 U. S. 499, 507–509, 511–512 (1978) (administrative inspection of fire-damaged premises to determine cause of blaze); *Camara v. Municipal Court of City and County of San Francisco,* 387 U. S. 523, 534–539 (1967) (administrative inspection to ensure compliance with city housing code).

We have also upheld brief, suspicionless seizures of motorists at a fixed Border Patrol checkpoint designed to intercept illegal aliens, *Martinez-Fuerte, supra,* and at a sobriety checkpoint aimed at removing drunk drivers from the road, *Michigan Dept. of State Police v. Sitz,* 496 U. S. 444 (1990). In addition, in *Delaware v. Prouse,* 440 U. S. 648, 663 (1979), we suggested that a similar type of roadblock with the purpose of verifying drivers' licenses and vehicle registrations would be permissible. In none of these cases, however, did we indicate approval of a checkpoint program whose primary purpose was to detect evidence of ordinary criminal wrongdoing.

In *Martinez-Fuerte,* we entertained Fourth Amendment challenges to stops at two permanent immigration checkpoints located on major United States highways less than 100 miles from the Mexican border. We noted at the outset the particular context in which the constitutional question arose, describing in some detail the "formidable law enforcement problems" posed by the northbound tide of illegal entrants into the United States. . . . In *Martinez-Fuerte,* we found that the balance tipped in favor of the Government's interests in policing the Nation's borders. . . .

In *Sitz,* we evaluated the constitutionality of a Michigan highway sobriety checkpoint program. The *Sitz* checkpoint involved brief suspicionless stops of motorists so that police officers could detect signs of intoxication and remove impaired drivers from the road. 496 U. S., at 447–448. Motorists who exhibited signs of intoxication were diverted for a license and registration check and, if warranted, further sobriety tests. *Id.,* at 447. This checkpoint program was clearly aimed at reducing the immediate hazard posed by the presence of drunk drivers on the highways, and there was an obvious connection between the imperative of highway safety and the law enforcement practice at issue. The gravity of the drunk driving problem and the magnitude of the State's interest in getting drunk drivers off the road weighed heavily in our determination that the program was constitutional. See *id.,* at 451.

In *Prouse,* we invalidated a discretionary, suspicionless stop for a spot check of a motorist's driver's license and vehicle registration. The officer's conduct in that case was unconstitutional primarily on account of his exercise of "standardless and unconstrained discretion." 440 U. S., at 661. We nonetheless acknowledged the States' "vital interest in ensuring that only those qualified to do so are permitted to operate motor vehicles, that these vehicles are fit for safe operation, and hence that licensing, registration, and vehicle inspection requirements are being observed." *Id.,* at 658. Accordingly, we suggested that "[q]uestioning of all oncoming traffic at roadblock-type stops" would be a lawful means of serving this interest in highway safety. *Id.,* at 663.

We further indicated in *Prouse* that we considered the purposes of such a hypothetical roadblock to be distinct from a general purpose of investigating crime. . . . Not only does the common

thread of highway safety thus run through *Sitz* and *Prouse,* but *Prouse* itself reveals a difference in the Fourth Amendment significance of highway safety interests and the general interest in crime control. . . .

It is well established that a vehicle stop at a highway checkpoint effectuates a seizure within the meaning of the Fourth Amendment. See, *e.g., Sitz, supra,* at 450. The fact that officers walk a narcotics-detection dog around the exterior of each car at the Indianapolis checkpoints does not transform the seizure into a search. See *United States v. Place,* 462 U. S. 696, 707 (1983). Just as in *Place,* an exterior sniff of an automobile does not require entry into the car and is not designed to disclose any information other than the presence or absence of narcotics. See *ibid.* Like the dog sniff in *Place,* a sniff by a dog that simply walks around a car is "much less intrusive than a typical search." *Ibid.* Cf. *United States v. Turpin,* 920 F. 2d 1377, 1385 (CA8 1990). Rather, what principally distinguishes these checkpoints from those we have previously approved is their primary purpose.

As petitioners concede, the Indianapolis checkpoint program unquestionably has the primary purpose of interdicting illegal narcotics. . . .

We have never approved a checkpoint program whose primary purpose was to detect evidence of ordinary criminal wrongdoing. Rather, our checkpoint cases have recognized only limited exceptions to the general rule that a seizure must be accompanied by some measure of individualized suspicion. We suggested in *Prouse* that we would not credit the "general interest in crime control" as justification for a regime of suspicionless stops. 440 U. S., at 659, n. 18. Consistent with this suggestion, each of the checkpoint programs that we have approved was designed primarily to serve purposes closely related to the problems of policing the border or the necessity of ensuring roadway safety. Because the primary purpose of the Indianapolis narcotics checkpoint program is to uncover evidence of ordinary criminal wrongdoing, the program contravenes the Fourth Amendment.

Petitioners propose several ways in which the narcotics-detection purpose of the instant checkpoint program may instead resemble the primary purposes of the checkpoints in *Sitz* and *Martinez-Fuerte*. Petitioners state that the checkpoints in those cases had the same ultimate purpose of arresting those suspected of committing crimes. Securing the border and apprehending drunk drivers are, of course, law enforcement activities, and law enforcement officers employ arrests and criminal prosecutions in pursuit of these goals. If we were to rest the case at this high level of generality, there would be little check on the ability of the authorities to construct roadblocks for almost any conceivable law enforcement purpose. Without drawing the line at roadblocks designed primarily to serve the general interest in crime control, the Fourth Amendment would do little to prevent such intrusions from becoming a routine part of American life.

Petitioners also emphasize the severe and intractable nature of the drug problem as justification for the checkpoint program. Brief for Petitioners 14–17, 31. There is no doubt that traffic in illegal narcotics creates social harms of the first magnitude. Cf. *Von Raab,* 489 U. S., at 668. The law enforcement problems that the drug trade creates likewise remain daunting and complex, particularly in light of the myriad forms of spin-off crime that it spawns. Cf. *Montoya de Hernandez,* 473 U. S., at 538. The same can be said of various other illegal activities, if only to a lesser degree. But the gravity of the threat alone cannot be dispositive of questions concerning what means law enforcement officers may employ to pursue a given purpose. Rather, in determining whether individualized suspicion is required, we must consider the nature of the interests threatened and their connection to the particular law enforcement practices at issue. We are particularly reluctant to recognize exceptions to the general rule of individualized suspicion where governmental authorities primarily pursue their general crime control ends.

Nor can the narcotics-interdiction purpose of the checkpoints be rationalized in terms of a highway safety concern similar to that present in *Sitz*. The detection and punishment of almost any criminal offense serves broadly the safety of the community, and our streets would no doubt be safer but for the scourge of illegal drugs. Only with respect to a smaller class of offenses, however, is society confronted with the type of immediate, vehicle-bound threat to life and limb that the sobriety checkpoint in *Sitz* was designed to eliminate.

Petitioners also liken the anticontraband agenda of the Indianapolis checkpoints to the antismuggling purpose of the checkpoints in *Martinez-Fuerte*. . . .

The primary purpose of the Indianapolis narcotics checkpoints is in the end to advance "the general interest in crime control," *Prouse,* 440 U. S., at 659, n. 18. We decline to suspend the usual requirement of individualized suspicion where the police seek to employ a checkpoint primarily for the ordinary enterprise of investigating crimes. We cannot sanction stops justified only by the generalized and ever-present possibility that interrogation and inspection may reveal that any given motorist has committed some crime.

Of course, there are circumstances that may justify a law enforcement checkpoint where the primary purpose would otherwise, but for some emergency, relate to ordinary crime control. For example, as the Court of Appeals noted, the Fourth Amendment would almost certainly permit an appropriately tailored roadblock set up to thwart an imminent terrorist attack or to catch a dangerous criminal who is likely to flee by way of a particular route. . . .

Petitioners argue that our prior cases preclude an inquiry into the purposes of the checkpoint program. For example, they cite *Whren v. United States,* 517 U. S. 806 (1996), and *Bond v. United States,* 529 U. S. 334 (2000), to support the proposition that "where the government articulates and pursues a legitimate interest for a suspicionless stop, courts should not look behind that interest to determine whether the government's 'primary purpose' is valid." Brief for Petitioners 34; see also *id.,* at 9. These cases, however, do not control the instant situation.

In *Whren,* we held that an individual officer's subjective intentions are irrelevant to the Fourth Amendment validity of a traffic stop that is justified objectively by probable cause to believe that a traffic violation has occurred. 517 U. S., at 810–813. We observed that our prior cases "foreclose any argument that the constitutional reasonableness of traffic stops depends on the actual motivations of the individual officers involved." *Id.,* at 813. In so holding, we expressly distinguished cases where we had addressed the validity of searches conducted in the absence of probable cause. See *id.,* at 811–812 (distinguishing *Florida v. Wells,* 495 U. S. 1, 4 (1990) (stating that "an inventory search must not be a ruse for a general rummaging in order to discover incriminating evidence"), *Colorado v. Bertine,* 479 U. S. 367, 372 (1987) (suggesting that the absence of bad faith and the lack of a purely investigative purpose were relevant to the validity of an inventory search), and *Burger,* 482 U. S., at 716–717, n. 27 (observing that a valid administrative inspection conducted with neither a warrant nor probable cause did not appear to be a pretext for gathering evidence of violations of the penal laws)).

Whren therefore reinforces the principle that, while "[s]ubjective intentions play no role in ordinary, probable-cause Fourth Amendment analysis," . . . It likewise does not preclude an inquiry into programmatic purpose here.

Last Term in *Bond,* we addressed the question whether a law enforcement officer violated a reasonable expectation of privacy in conducting a tactile examination of carry-on luggage in the overhead compartment of a bus. In doing so, we simply noted that the principle of *Whren* rendered the subjective intent of an officer irrelevant to this analysis.

Petitioners argue that the Indianapolis checkpoint program is justified by its lawful secondary purposes of keeping impaired motorists off the road and verifying licenses and registrations. Brief for Petitioners 31–34. If this were the case, however, law enforcement authorities would be able to establish checkpoints for virtually any purpose so long as they also included a license or sobriety check. For this reason, we examine the available evidence to determine the primary purpose of the checkpoint program. While we recognize the challenges inherent in a purpose inquiry, courts routinely engage in this enterprise in many areas of constitutional jurisprudence as a means of sifting abusive governmental conduct from that which is lawful. Cf. 183 F. 3d, at 665. As a result, a program driven by an impermissible purpose may be proscribed while a program impelled by licit purposes is permitted, even though the challenged conduct may be outwardly similar. While reasonableness under the Fourth Amendment is predominantly an objective inquiry, our special needs and administrative search cases demonstrate that purpose is often relevant when suspicionless intrusions pursuant to a general scheme are at issue.

It goes without saying that our holding today does nothing to alter the constitutional status of the sobriety and border checkpoints that we approved in *Sitz* and *Martinez-Fuerte,* or of the type of traffic checkpoint that we suggested would be lawful in *Prouse.* The constitutionality of such checkpoint programs still depends on a balancing of the competing interests at stake and the effectiveness of the program. See *Sitz,* 496 U. S., at 450–455; *Martinez-Fuerte,* 428 U. S., at 556–564. When law enforcement authorities pursue primarily general crime control purposes at checkpoints such as here, however, stops can only be justified by some quantum of individualized suspicion.

Our holding also does not affect the validity of border searches or searches at places like airports and government buildings, where the need for such measures to ensure public safety can be particularly acute. Nor does our opinion speak to other intrusions aimed primarily at purposes beyond the general interest in crime control. Our holding also does not impair the ability of police officers to act appropriately upon information that they properly learn during a checkpoint stop justified by a lawful primary purpose, even where such action may result in the arrest of a motorist for an offense unrelated to that purpose. Finally, we caution that the purpose inquiry in this context is to be conducted only at the programmatic level and is not an invitation to probe the minds of individual officers acting at the scene.

Because the primary purpose of the Indianapolis checkpoint program is ultimately indistinguishable from the general interest in crime control, the checkpoints violate the Fourth Amendment. The judgment of the Court of Appeals is accordingly affirmed.

Although systematic roadblocks are proper, discretionary spot checks are not. In the *Prouse* case, the Supreme Court held that arbitrary stops of automobiles by law enforcement officers violate the Fourth Amendment.

Finally, note that profiles are used by some law enforcement agencies to establish a reasonable suspicion to stop motorists. For example, drug courier profiles are used in Florida and illegal alien profiles are used by the Border Patrol. See earlier in this chapter for a more thorough discussion of the use of profiles. The Supreme Court has also held that the validity of a stop is determined by whether probable cause *exists* to believe a traffic violation has occurred, not the motives of the police. In *Whren v. United States* (1996)[45] the Court rejected a defendant's claim that a police officer who stops an individual who has violated a traffic law with the genuine purpose of investigating another crime (e.g. drug possession) has violated the Fourth Amendment, so long as the officer had probable cause to believe the driver has committed a traffic offense.

Searches.   Where the Fourth Amendment's mandates have been reduced is in the context of the warrant requirement. In *Carroll v. United States*, 267 U.S. 132 (1925), it was announced that a warrantless search of a vehicle stopped on a public road is reasonable, provided the officer has probable cause to believe that an object subject to seizure will be found in the vehicle. The existence of probable cause is the key to the search and no exigency has to exist for a police officer to conduct such a warrantless search.[46] This authority has been extended to permit the search to continue after the vehicle is impounded.[47] The Supreme Court has also validated warrantless seizures of vehicles when probable cause exists to believe the vehicle itself is forfeitable because the automobile had been used to traffic drugs.[48]

The sticky question in this area is the scope of the search. Generally, an officer is given the scope that a magistrate would have if a warrant were sought. Thus, if an officer has probable cause to believe that a shotgun used in a crime will be found in a car, a search of the glove box is improper. The opposite would be true if the item sought was a piece of jewelry, such as a ring.

Officers may also search closed items found in the vehicle, provided probable cause exists to believe an item sought may be contained therein.[49] The same rules apply as previously discussed. Rifling through a suitcase found in a car in search of a stolen painting that is larger than the suitcase is unreasonable and violative of the Fourth Amendment. Once the sought-after item is found, the search must cease.

An automobile may be searched incident to the arrest of its driver. However, a warrantless search of an automobile after issuing a traffic ticket to the driver is violative of the Fourth Amendment—even though the officer could have arrested the driver and then searched the car incident to the arrest.[50]

May the occupants of a vehicle be searched incident to a proper search of the vehicle? The answer is no[51]—but if an officer has probable cause to believe that one of the occupants has hidden the item sought on his or her person, a search of that occupant is permissible.

SUMMARY OF FOURTH AMENDMENT ISSUES AND AUTOMOBILES

SUBJECT	CASE
Stops and Arrests	
Stops may not be arbitrary.	*Delaware v. Prouse* (1979)
Stops may occur without suspicion if systematic.	*Michigan v. Sitz* (1990)
The motives of police are not relevant when determining if a stop is lawful. The issue is whether probable cause to believe a traffic violation exists.	*Whren v. United States* (1996)
States may delegate the discretion to arrest for misdemeanors, including traffic violations, to police.	*Atwater v. City of Lago Vista* (2001)
Systematic stops to intercept illegal drugs violate Fourth Amendment.	*Indianapolis v. Edmonds* (2000)
Occupants	
Drivers of lawfully stopped automobiles may be ordered out without specific cause.	*Pennsylvania v. Mimms* (1977)
Occupants of lawfully stopped automobiles may be ordered out without specific cause.	*Maryland v. Wilson* (1997)
Occupants of automobiles may not be searched as incident to lawful search of automobiles—probable cause to believe sought item will be found on person required.	*United States v. DiRe*, 332 U.S. 581 (1948)
Searches	
Warrantless search of automobile valid if probable cause exists to believe item sought will be found in automobile. No exigency required if probable cause exists.	*Carroll v. United States* (1925) *Maryland v. Dyson* (1999)
Warrantless searches of closed container in automobile valid if probable cause to believe item sought will be found in container.	*California v. Acevedo* (1991)

Warrantless search of personal item in automobile (e.g., purse) valid if probable cause to search for an item that may be concealed there exists.	*Wyoming v. Houghton* (1999)
Warrantless search of automobile invalid if probable cause exists to search container in automobile only.	*California v. Acevedo* (1991)
Warrantless search of automobile by officer who issued ticket but chose not to arrest driver is violative of the Fourth Amendment.	*Knowles v. Iowa* (1998)
Inventory searches of automobiles—including containers—are valid if systematic.	*Colorado v. Bertine*, 479 U.S. 367 (1986)
Properly framed profile may be used to stop an automobile, but searches and arrests require more.	*United States v. Brignoni-Ponce* (1975)
Automobile may be seized without a warrant if probable cause exists to believe it is contraband.	*Florida v. White* (1999)

Occupants. Concerning the occupants of lawfully stopped cars, the Supreme Court has held that both driver and passengers may be ordered to exit the car without cause to believe they hold contraband, a threat to the officer, or act out of fear of flight. The Court held that it may be done routinely to protect the safety of police officers.[52]

 CASE

DELAWARE V. PROUSE

440 U.S. 648 (1979)

At 7:20 P.M. on November 30, 1976, a New Castle County . . . patrolman in a police cruiser stopped the automobile occupied by respondent. The patrolman smelled marihuana smoke as he was walking toward the stopped vehicle, and he seized marihuana in plain view on the car floor. Respondent was subsequently indicted for illegal possession of a controlled substance. At a hearing on respondent's motion to suppress the marihuana seized as a result of the stop, the patrolman testified that prior to stopping the vehicle he had observed neither traffic or equipment violations nor any suspicious activity, and that he made the stop only in order to check the driver's license and registration. The patrolman was not acting pursuant to any standards, guidelines, or procedures pertaining to document spot checks, promulgated by either his department or the State Attorney General. Characterizing the stop as "routine," the patrolman explained, "I saw the car in the area and wasn't answering any complaints, so I decided to pull them off." The trial court granted the motion to suppress, finding the stop and detention to have been wholly capricious and therefore violative of the Fourth Amendment. . . .

The Delaware Supreme Court affirmed. . . .

But the State of Delaware urges . . . these stops are reasonable under the Fourth Amendment because the State's interest in the practice as a means of promoting public safety upon its roads more than outweighs the intrusion entailed. Although the record discloses no statistics concerning the extent of the problem of highway safety, in Delaware or in the Nation as a whole, we are aware of danger to life and property posed by vehicular traffic and the difficulties that even a cautious and experienced driver may encounter. We agree that the States have a vital interest in ensuring that only those qualified to do so are permitted to operate motor vehicles, that these vehicles are fit for safe operation, and hence that licensing, registration, and vehicle inspection requirements are being observed. . . .

The question remains, however, whether in the service of these important ends the discretionary spot check is a sufficiently productive mechanism to justify the intrusion upon Fourth Amendment interests which stops entail. On the record before us, that question must be answered in the negative. Given the alternative mechanisms available, both those in use and those that might be adopted, we are unconvinced that the incremental contribution to highway safety of the random spot check justifies the practice under the Fourth Amendment.

The foremost method of enforcing traffic and vehicle safety regulations, it must be recalled, is acting upon observed violations. Vehicle stops for traffic violations occur countless times each day; and on these occasions, licenses and registration papers are subject to inspection and drivers without them will be ascertained. Furthermore, drivers without licenses are presumably the less safe drivers whose propensities may well exhibit themselves. . . .

Much the same can be said about the safety aspects of automobiles as distinguished from drivers. Many violations of minimum vehicle-safety requirements are observable, and something can be done about them by the observing officer, directly and immediately. Furthermore, in Delaware, as elsewhere, vehicles must carry and display current license plates, which themselves evidence that the vehicle is properly registered; and, under Delaware law, to qualify for annual registration a vehicle must pass the annual safety inspection and be properly insured. . . .

The marginal contribution to roadway safety possibly resulting from a system of spot checks cannot justify subjecting every occupant of every vehicle on the roads to a seizure—limited in magnitude compared to other intrusions but nonetheless constitutionally cognizable—at the unbridled discretion of law enforcement officials. To insist neither upon an appropriate factual basis for suspicion directed at a particular automobile nor upon some other substantial and objective standard or rule to govern the exercise of discretion "would invite intrusions upon constitutionally guaranteed rights based on nothing more substantial than inarticulable hunches. . . . " This kind of standardless and unconstrained discretion is the evil the Court has discerned when in previous cases it has insisted that the discretion of the official in the field be circumscribed, at least to some extent. . . . "

Accordingly, we hold that except in those situations in which there is at least articulable and reasonable suspicion that a motorist is unlicensed or that an automobile is not registered, or that either the vehicle or an occupant is otherwise subject to seizure for violation of law, stopping an automobile and detaining the driver in order to check his driver's license and the registration of the automobile are unreasonable under the Fourth Amendment. This holding does not preclude the State of Delaware or other States from developing methods for spot checks that involve less intrusions or that do not involve unconstrained exercise of discretion. Questioning of all oncoming traffic at roadblock-type stops is one possible alternative. We hold only that persons in automobiles on public roadways may not for that reason alone have their travel and privacy interfered with at the unbridled discretion of police officers. The judgment below is affirmed.

Inventory Searches.   Police officers may impound vehicles whenever the driver or owner is arrested. *Impoundment* means towing the vehicle to a garage or parking lot for storage.

Although the decision to impound a vehicle is generally left to the discretion of the police officer, an officer may not refuse a less intrusive manner of caring for the vehicle. For example, if a husband and wife are riding together, and the husband is arrested for drunk driving, the wife is to be permitted to drive the vehicle home, provided she is capable.

Once impounded, an inventory search may be conducted. The purpose of an inventory search is to protect the owner of the vehicle from vandalism, protect the safety of the officers and others, and protect the police department from claims of theft.

Because inventory searches are not conducted with an intent to discover evidence, there is no requirement of probable cause. If the facts of a case show that the police impounded a vehicle for the purpose of searching it, the search is improper.

Inventory searches are limited in scope. Although it is reasonable to search unlocked glove compartments and trunks, it is unreasonable under the Fourth Amendment if they are locked. A search of a vehicle's seats, floor area, and dashboard are routine. The Supreme Court has also stated that closed items found in impounded vehicles are subject to inventory searches.[53]

To avoid arbitrary inventory searches, police departments are expected, if not required, to establish an inventory search policy and procedure. All items discovered during an inventory search are to be recorded.

Prisoners.   The Fourth Amendment is not fully applicable in prisons, for three reasons. First, security concerns outweigh privacy concerns. Second, loss of privacy is considered by our society to be an attribute of confinement and punishment. Third, inmates generally do not have reasonable expectations of privacy.

Hence, the Fourth Amendment is not implicated in the search of an inmate's cell, as there is no reasonable expectation of privacy in that area. The Supreme Court stated:

> A prison "shares none of the attributes of privacy of a home, an automobile, an office, or a hotel room." . . . We strike the balance in favor of institutional security, which we have noted is "central to all other correctional goals." . . . A right of privacy in traditional Fourth Amendment terms is fundamentally incompatible with the close and continual surveillance of inmates and their cells required to ensure institutional security and internal order. We are satisfied that society would insist that the prisoner's expectation of privacy always yield to what must be considered the paramount interest in institutional security. We believe that it is accepted by our society that "[l]oss of freedom of choice and privacy are inherent incidents of confinement."[54]

Although the Fourth Amendment does not apply to searches of inmates' cells, it does apply to searches of their persons. However, the probable cause and warrant requirements are dispensed with in the prison context. Rather, they are tested by the Fourth Amendment's reasonableness provision. Prisoners may be searched without any particular suspicion if the search is part of a routine system. Analogous to roadblocks, if the custodians search every prisoner, or every other prisoner, or use some other system, no suspicion is required. Prisoners may also be searched without suspicion if they have recently come into contact with visitors. In *Bell v. Wolfish,* 441 U.S. 520 (1979), the Supreme Court held that strip searches of prisoners, conducted after they have contact with visitors or upon their return to the institution from outside, are permissible even without individualized suspicion. Otherwise, individual searches of inmates are allowed only when an officer has a reasonable suspicion that the inmate possesses contraband.

Although searches of inmates' cells are not included within the grasp of the Fourth Amendment, repeated searches intended to harass an inmate may be violative of the Eighth Amendment's prohibition of cruel and unusual punishment, as may searches of an inmate's person.

ARREST

One of the most serious interferences with a person's liberty is to be physically seized by a government. Equally, arrest plays an important role in effective law enforcement.

Because of the significant impact arrest has on a person's life, the right to arrest is limited by the Fourth Amendment.

Defining Arrest

Generally, an *arrest* is a deprivation of freedom by a legal authority. As you have already learned, seizures by the police take two primary forms. First, at the lower end of the spectrum is the *Terry v. Ohio* seizure. Such seizures occur whenever a person reasonably believes that he or she is not free to leave. In addition, the seizure must be as brief as possible and be of limited intrusion to the person detained.

Any seizure that goes beyond the *Terry* standard is an arrest. A *Terry* investigatory detention may be transformed into an arrest if the person is detained for an unreasonable length of time or the police use intrusive investigatory tactics. Whether an officer intends to arrest is not dispositive, nor is an announcement to the citizen that he or she is or is not under arrest. The totality of the facts will determine whether the intrusion amounts to an arrest under the Fourth Amendment.

The requirements for a *Terry* stop were discussed previously in this chapter. The following is a discussion of the Fourth Amendment requirements for arrest.

The Warrant Preference

Searches must be conducted pursuant to a valid warrant, unless an exception to the warrant requirement can be shown. Arrests are quite different. Rather than a requirement for a warrant, in most instances, there is simply a preference for one. The "informed and deliberate determinations of magistrates empowered to issue warrants . . . are to be preferred over the hurried action of officers."[55] As is the case with warrantless searches, probable cause determinations by magistrates will be supported on appeal with less evidence than those made by police officers.

Notwithstanding the preference, most arrests are made without first obtaining a warrant. The authority to make warrantless arrests has a long history. Under the common law, a law officer could arrest whenever he had reasonable grounds to believe that a defendant committed a felony. Misdemeanants who breached the peace could be arrested without warrant if the crime was committed in the presence of an officer.

United States v. Watson, 423 U.S. 411 (1976), was the case in which the Supreme Court recognized that warrantless arrests in public places, based upon probable cause, did not violate the Fourth Amendment. There is no constitutional requirement that an officer obtain a warrant to effect an arrest in a public place—even if the officer has adequate time to get the warrant prior to making the arrest. However, the Fourth Amendment does require that probable cause exist before an arrest can be made.

For a warrantless arrest in a public place to be upheld it must be shown that the officer who made the arrest (1) had probable cause to believe that a crime was committed and (2) that the person arrested committed that crime. As with searches and seizures, probable cause can be established in a number of ways: statements from victims and witnesses; personal knowledge and observations of the officer; reliable hearsay; and informant tips.

Most, if not all, states permit officers to arrest without a warrant if there is probable cause to believe that the suspect committed a felony. States vary in their treatment of misdemeanors, but most only permit warrantless arrest for a misdemeanor committed in an officer's presence. Some states have a broader rule which permits the arrest of a misdemeanant, even if the crime was not committed in the presence of an officer, provided there is both probable cause and an exigent circumstance.

An officer's determination of probable cause may later be attacked by the defendant. If the officer was wrong, then the defendant may be successful in obtaining his or her freedom or suppressing any evidence that is the fruit of the illegal arrest.

When an officer does seek an arrest warrant, the requirements previously discussed concerning search warrants apply. That is, the warrant must be issued by a neutral and detached magistrate upon a finding of probable cause, supported by oath or affirmation.

Warrant for Arrest

AO 442 (Rev. 5/85) Warrant for Arrest _____

UNITED STATES DISTRICT COURT

_____ DISTRICT OF _____

UNITED STATES OF AMERICA

V.

WARRANT FOR ARREST

CASE NUMBER:

To: The United States Marshal
     and any Authorized United States Officer

YOU ARE HEREBY COMMANDED to arrest _____
                                                                    Name

and bring him or her forthwith to the nearest magistrate to answer a(n)

☐ Indictment   ☐ Information   ☐ Complaint   ☐ Order of Court   ☐ Violation Notice

☐ Probation Violation Petition

charging him or her with (brief description of offense)

in violation of Title _____ United States Code, Section(s) _____

_____   _____
Name of Issuing Officer   Title of Issuing Officer

_____   _____
Signature of Issuing Officer   Date and Location

_____
(By) Deputy Clark

Bail fixed at $ _____   by _____
                                                                 Name of Judicial Officer

RETURN
This warrant was received and executed with the arrest of the above-named defendant at _____

DATE RECEIVED	NAME AND TITLE OF ARRESTING OFFICER	SIGNATURE OF ARRESTING OFFICER
DATE OF ARREST		

Warrant for Arrest
(continued)

```
AO 442 (Rev. 5/85) Warrant for Arrest


                THE FOLLOWING IS FURNISHED FOR INFORMATION ONLY:


DEFENDANT'S NAME: _____

ALIAS:_____

LAST KNOWN RESIDENCE:_____

LAST KNOWN EMPLOYMENT: _____

PLACE OF BIRTH: _____

DATE OF BIRTH:_____

SOCIAL SECURITY NUMBER: _____

HEIGHT: _____      WEIGHT: _____

SEX: _____      RACE:_____

HAIR: _____      EYES: _____

SCARS, TATTOOS, OTHER DISTINGUISHING MARKS: _____

_____

_____

FBI NUMBER:_____

COMPLETE DESCRIPTION OF AUTO: _____

_____

INVESTIGATIVE AGENCY AND ADDRESS: _____

_____

_____
```

Arrests in Protected Areas

So far the discussion of arrests has been confined to arrests made in public. If the arrest is to be made in an area protected by the Fourth Amendment, such as a person's home, a warrant must be obtained, unless an exception exists.

In *Payton v. New York,* 445 U.S. 573 (1980), it was held that a valid arrest warrant implicitly carries with it a limited right to enter the suspect's home to effect the arrest, provided there is reason to believe the suspect is within. Under *Payton,* the search must be limited to areas where the suspect may be hiding. Because the entry is lawful, any evidence discovered in plain view may be seized.

Arrest warrants do not authorize entry into the private property of third persons. In the absence of consent or exigent circumstances, a search warrant must be obtained before a search of a third person's home or property may be conducted.[56]

The warrant requirement is obviated if the occupant gives consent to the search. Exigent circumstances, such as hot pursuit, also justify warrantless entries into homes to effect an arrest.

Misdemeanor Arrests   The authority of law enforcement officers to arrest in cases where probable cause exists to believe an individual has committed a felony is clear. Similarly, the authority to arrest misdemeanants who breach the peace has been clear since the early common law. However, whether the arrest authority extends to minor misdemeanors was not addressed by the Supreme Court until 2001.

 CASE ───◆

**ATWATER V.
CITY OF LAGO VISTA, ET AL.**

532 U.S. 318 (2001)

In Texas, if a car is equipped with safety belts, a front-seat passenger must wear one, Tex. Tran. Code Ann. § 545.413(a) (1999), and the driver must secure any small child riding in front, § 545.413(b). Violation of either provision is "a misdemeanor punishable by a fine not less than $ 25 or more than $ 50." § 545.413(d). Texas law expressly authorizes "any peace officer [to] arrest without warrant a person found committing a violation" of these seatbelt laws, § 543.001, although it permits police to issue citations in lieu of arrest, §§ 543.003–543.005.

In March 1997, Petitioner Gail Atwater was driving her pickup truck in Lago Vista, Texas, with her 3-year-old son and 5-year-old daughter in the front seat. None of them was wearing a seatbelt. Respondent Bart Turek, a Lago Vista police officer at the time, observed the seatbelt violations and pulled Atwater over. According to Atwater's complaint (the allegations of which we assume to be true for present purposes), Turek approached the truck and "yelled" something to the effect of "we've met before" and "you're going to jail." App. 20. He then called for backup and asked to see Atwater's driver's license and insurance documentation, which state law required her to carry. Tex. Tran. Code Ann. §§ 521.025, 601.053 (1999). When Atwater told Turek that she did not have the papers because her purse had been stolen the day before, Turek said that he had "heard that story two-hundred times."

Atwater asked to take her "frightened, upset, and crying" children to a friend's house nearby, but Turek told her, "you're not going anywhere." *Ibid.*

As it turned out, Atwater's friend learned what was going on and soon arrived to take charge of the children. Turek then handcuffed Atwater, placed her in his squad car, and drove her to the local police station, where booking officers had her remove her shoes, jewelry, and eyeglasses, and empty her pockets. Officers took Atwater's "mug shot" and placed her, alone, in a jail cell for about one hour, after which she was taken before a magistrate and released on $ 310 bond.

Atwater was charged with driving without her seatbelt fastened, failing to secure her children in seatbelts, driving without a license, and failing to provide proof of insurance. She ultimately pleaded no contest to the misdemeanor seatbelt offenses and paid a $50 fine; the other charges were dismissed.

B

Atwater and her husband, petitioner Michael Haas, filed suit in a Texas state court under 42 U.S.C. § 1983 against Turek and respondents City of Lago Vista and Chief of Police Frank Miller. So far as concerns us, petitioners (whom we will simply call Atwater) alleged that respondents (for simplicity, the City) had violated Atwater's Fourth Amendment "right to be free from unreasonable seizure," . . . [the plaintiffs lost in the trial court, prevailed before a three-judge penal in the appellate court, and subsequently, the full appellate court sitting en banc reversed the three-judge panel.]

We granted certiorari to consider whether the Fourth Amendment, either by incorporating common-law restrictions on misdemeanor arrests or otherwise, limits police officers' authority to arrest without warrant for minor criminal offenses. We now affirm.

The Fourth Amendment safeguards "the right of the people to be secure in their persons, houses, papers, and effects, against unreasonable searches and seizures." In reading the Amendment, we are guided by "the traditional protections against unreasonable searches and seizures afforded by the common

law at the time of the framing," *Wilson v. Arkansas*, 514 U.S. 927, 931, 131 L. Ed. 2d 976, 115 S. Ct. 1914 (1995), since "an examination of the common-law understanding of an officer's authority to arrest sheds light on the obviously relevant, if not entirely dispositive, consideration of what the Framers of the Amendment might have thought to be reasonable," *Payton v. New York*, 445 U.S. 573, 591, 63 L. Ed. 2d 639, 100 S. Ct. 1371 (1980) (footnote omitted). Thus, the first step here is to assess Atwater's claim that peace officers' authority to make warrantless arrests for misdemeanors was restricted at common law (whether "common law" is understood strictly as law judicially derived or, instead, as the whole body of law extant at the time of the framing). Atwater's specific contention is that "founding-era common-law rules" forbade peace officers to make warrantless misdemeanor arrests except in cases of "breach of the peace," a category she claims was then understood narrowly as covering only those nonfelony offenses "involving or tending toward violence." . . .

We begin with the state of pre-founding English common law and find that, even after making some allowance for variations in the common-law usage of the term "breach of the peace," the "founding-era common-law rules" were not nearly as clear as Atwater claims; on the contrary, the common-law commentators (as well as the sparsely reported cases) reached divergent conclusions with respect to officers' warrantless misdemeanor arrest power. Moreover, in the years leading up to American independence, Parliament repeatedly extended express warrantless arrest authority to cover misdemeanor-level offenses not amounting to or involving any violent breach of the peace. . . .

On one side of the divide there are certainly eminent authorities supporting Atwater's position. In addition to Lord Halsbury, quoted in *Carroll*, James Fitzjames Stephen and Glanville Williams both seemed to indicate that the common law confined warrantless misdemeanor arrests to actual breaches of the peace.

Sir William Blackstone and Sir Edward East might also be counted on Atwater's side, although they spoke only to the sufficiency of breach of the peace as a condition to warrantless misdemeanor arrest, not to its necessity. Blackstone recognized that at common law "the constable . . . hath great original and inherent authority with regard to arrests," but with respect to nonfelony offenses said only that "he may, without warrant, arrest any one for breach of the peace, and carry him before a justice of the peace." 4 Blackstone 289. Not long after the framing of the Fourth Amendment, East characterized peace officers' common-law arrest power in much the same way: "A constable or other known conservator of the peace may lawfully interpose upon his own view to prevent a breach of the peace, or to quiet an affray. . . . " 1 E. East, Pleas of the Crown § 71, p. 303 (1803). . . .

The great commentators were not unanimous, however, and there is also considerable evidence of a broader conception of common-law misdemeanor arrest authority unlimited by any breach-of-the-peace condition. Sir Matthew Hale, Chief Justice of King's Bench from 1671 to 1676, n3 wrote in his History of the Pleas of the Crown that, by his "original and inherent power," a constable could arrest without a warrant "for breach of the peace and some misdemeanors, less than felony." 2 M. Hale, The History of the Pleas of the Crown 88 (1736). Hale's view, posthumously published in 1736, reflected an understanding dating back at least 60 years before the appearance of his Pleas yet sufficiently authoritative to sustain a momentum extending well beyond the framing era in this country. See The Compleat Parish-Officer 11 (1744) ("The Constable . . . may for Breach of the Peace, and some Misdemeanors less than Felony, imprison a Man"); R. Burn, The Justice of the Peace 271 (1837) ("A *constable* . . . may at common law, for treason, felony, breach of the peace, and some misdemeanors less than felony, *committed in his view,* apprehend the supposed offender without any warrant") (italics in original); 1 J. Chitty, A Practical Treatise on the Criminal Law 20 (5th ed. 1847) ("[A constable] may for treason, felony, breach of the peace, and

some misdemeanors less than felony, committed in his view, apprehend the supposed offender *virtiute officii,* without any warrant"); 1 W. Russell, Crimes and Misdemeanors 725 (7th ed. 1909) (officer "may arrest any person who in his presence commits a misdemeanor or breach of the peace").

We thus find disagreement, not unanimity, among both the common-law jurists and the text-writers who sought to pull the cases together and summarize accepted practice. Having reviewed the relevant English decisions, as well as English and colonial American legal treatises, legal dictionaries, and procedure manuals, we simply are not convinced that Atwater's is the correct, or even necessarily the better, reading of the common-law history. . . .

A second, and equally serious, problem for Atwater's historical argument is posed by the "divers Statutes," M. Dalton, Country Justice ch. 170, § 4, p. 582 (1727), enacted by Parliament well before this Republic's founding that authorized warrantless misdemeanor arrests without reference to violence or turmoil. Quite apart from Hale and Blackstone, the legal background of any conception of reasonableness the Fourth Amendment's Framers might have entertained would have included English statutes, some centuries old, authorizing peace officers (and even private persons) to make warrantless arrests for all sorts of relatively minor offenses unaccompanied by violence. The so-called "nightwalker" statutes are perhaps the most notable examples. From the enactment of the Statute of Winchester in 1285, through its various readoptions and until its repeal in 1827, night watchmen were authorized and charged "as . . . in Times past" to "watch the Town continually all Night, from the Sun-setting unto the Sun-rising" and were directed that "if any Stranger do pass by them, he shall be arrested until Morning. . . .

Nor were the nightwalker statutes the only legislative sources of warrantless arrest authority absent real or threatened violence, as the parties and their *amici* here seem to have assumed. On the contrary, following the Edwardian legislation and throughout the period leading up to the framing,

Parliament repeatedly extended warrantless arrest power to cover misdemeanor-level offenses not involving any breach of the peace. . . .

An examination of specifically American evidence is to the same effect. Neither the history of the framing era nor subsequent legal development indicates that the Fourth Amendment was originally understood, or has traditionally been read, to embrace Atwater's position.

Nor does Atwater's argument from tradition pick up any steam from the historical record as it has unfolded since the framing, there being no indication that her claimed rule has ever become "woven . . . into the fabric" of American law. *Wilson, supra,* at 933; see also *Payton v. New York,* 445 U.S. at 590 (emphasizing "a clear consensus among the States adhering to [a] well-settled common-law rule"). The story, on the contrary, is of two centuries of uninterrupted (and largely unchallenged) state and federal practice permitting warrantless arrests for misdemeanors not amounting to or involving breach of the peace. . . .

Finally, both the legislative tradition of granting warrantless misdemeanor arrest authority and the judicial tradition of sustaining such statutes against constitutional attack are buttressed by legal commentary that, for more than a century now, has almost uniformly recognized the constitutionality of extending warrantless arrest power to misdemeanors without limitation to breaches of the peace. . . .

Small wonder, then, that today statutes in all 50 States and the District of Columbia permit warrantless misdemeanor arrests by at least some (if not all) peace officers without requiring any breach of the peace, as do a host of congressional enactments. . . .

Accordingly, we confirm today what our prior cases have intimated: the standard of probable cause "applies to all arrests, without the need to 'balance' the interests and circumstances involved in particular situations." *Dunaway v. New York,* 442 U.S. 200, 208, 60 L. Ed. 2d 824, 99 S. Ct. 2248 (1979). If an officer has probable cause to believe that an individual has committed even a very minor criminal offense in his presence, he may, without violating the Fourth Amendment, arrest the offender. . . .

The Court of Appeals's en banc judgment is affirmed.

Search Incident to Arrest and the Protective Sweep

As you learned earlier in this chapter, an officer may fully search an arrestee as incident to arrest. In addition, the area within the arrestee's immediate control may also be searched. The scope of a search incident to arrest, however, is limited to areas where a weapon might be obtained by the person arrested. Clearly, a search of any room other than the one where a defendant is being held is not supported by the doctrine of search incident to arrest.

The search-incident-to-arrest doctrine does not consider the possibility that other potentially dangerous persons may be present, but out of sight, when an arrest is made. Must police take the risk that no other dangerous persons are on the premises when making a lawful arrest? This question was answered by the Supreme Court in *Maryland v. Buie.*

It is important to note that the protective sweep may not be automatically conducted by the police, unlike a search incident to arrest. An officer must have a reasonable belief, supported by specific and articulable facts, that a dangerous person may be hiding in the home, before a protective sweep may be conducted. There need not be a belief of dangerousness to conduct a search incident to arrest.

A protective sweep must be limited to searching those areas where a person might be hiding. How far this will be permitted to go remains to be seen. Justice Brennan, dissenting in *Buie,* made this statement:

 CASE ——————————————————————————————————◆

MARYLAND V. BUIE

494 U.S. 325 (1990)

A "protective sweep" is a quick and limited search of a premises, incident to an arrest and conducted to protect the safety of police officers or others. It is narrowly confined to a cursory visual inspection of those places in which a person might be hiding. In this case we must decide what level of justification is required by the Fourth and Fourteenth Amendments before police officers, while effecting the arrest of a suspect in his home pursuant to an arrest warrant, may conduct a warrantless protective sweep of all or part of the premises. . . .

On February 3, 1986, two men committed an armed robbery of a Godfather's Pizza restaurant in Prince George's County, Maryland. One of the robbers was wearing a red running suit. The same day, Prince George's County police obtained arrest warrants for respondent Jerome Edward Buie and his suspected accomplice in the robbery, Lloyd Allen. Buie's house was placed under police surveillance.

On February 5, the police executed the arrest warrant for Buie. They first had a police department secretary telephone Buie's house to verify that he was home. The secretary spoke to a female first, then to Buie himself. Six or seven officers proceeded to Buie's house. Once inside, the officers fanned out through the first and second floors. Corporal James Rozar announced that he would "freeze" the basement so that no one could come up and surprise the officers. With his service revolver drawn, Rozar twice shouted into the basement, ordering anyone down there to come out. When a voice asked who was calling, Rozar announced three times: "this is the police, show me your hands." Eventually, a pair of hands appeared around the bottom of the stairwell and

Buie emerged from the basement. He was arrested, searched, and handcuffed by Rozar. Thereafter, Detective Joseph Frolich entered the basement "in case there was someone else" down there. . . . He noticed a red running suit lying in plain view on a stack of clothing and seized it.

The trial court denied Buie's motion to suppress the running suit, stating in part: "The man comes out from a basement, the police don't know how many other people are down there." . . .

It goes without saying that the Fourth Amendment bars only unreasonable searches and seizures. . . . Our cases show that in determining reasonableness, we have balanced the intrusion on the individual's Fourth Amendment interests against its promotion of legitimate governmental interests. . . . Under this test, a search of the house or office is generally not reasonable without a warrant issued on probable cause. There are other contexts, however, where the public interest is such that neither a warrant nor probable cause is required. . . .

The *Terry* case is most instructive for present purposes. There we held that an on-the-street "frisk" for weapons must be tested by the Fourth Amendment's general proscription against unreasonable searches because such a frisk involves "an entire rubric of police conduct— necessarily swift action predicated upon the on-the-spot observations of the officer on the beat—which historically has not been, and as a practical matter could not be, subjected to the warrant procedure." . . .

The ingredients to apply the balance struck in *Terry* and *Long* are present in this case. Possessing an arrest warrant and probable cause to believe Buie was in his home, the officers were entitled to enter and to search anywhere in the house in which Buie might be found. Once he was found, however, the search for him was over, and there was no longer that particular justification for entering any rooms that had not yet been searched.

That Buie had an expectation of privacy in those remaining areas of his house, however, does not mean such rooms were immune from entry. In *Terry* and *Long* we were concerned with the immediate interest of the police officers in taking steps to assure themselves that the persons with whom they were dealing were not armed with or able to gain immediate control of a weapon that could unexpectedly and fatally be used against them. In the instant case, there is an analogous interest of the officers in taking steps to assure themselves that the house in which the suspect is being or has just been arrested is not harboring other persons who are dangerous and who could unexpectedly launch an attack. The risk of danger in the context of an arrest in the home is as great as, if not greater than, it is in the on-the-street or roadside investigatory encounter. . . .

We should emphasize that such a protective sweep, aimed at protecting the arresting officers, if justified by the circumstances, is nevertheless not a full search of the premises, but may extend only to a cursory inspection of those spaces where a person may be found. The sweep lasts no longer than is necessary to dispel the reasonable suspicion of danger and in any event no longer than it takes to complete the arrest and depart from the premises.

. . . The Fourth Amendment permits a properly limited protective sweep in conjunction with an inhome arrest when the searching officer possesses a reasonable belief based on specific and articulable facts that the area to be swept harbors an individual posing a danger to those on the arrest scene.

Police officers searching for potential ambushers might enter every room including basements and attics, open up closets, lockers, chests, wardrobes, and cars; and peer under beds and behind furniture. The officers will view letters, documents and personal effects that are on tables or desks or are visible inside open drawers; books, records, tapes, and pictures on shelves; and clothing, medicines, toiletries and other paraphernalia not carefully stored in dresser drawers or bathroom cupboards. While perhaps not a "full-blown" or "top-to-bottom" search . . . a protective sweep is much closer to it than to a "limited patdown for weapons" or a "frisk" [as authorized by *Terry v. Ohio*].

Executing Arrest Warrants

Arrest warrants may be executed at the officer's discretion, whether day or night. However, common sense dictates that warrants be served at a reasonable hour, unless an exigency exists.

In *Ker v. California*, 374 U.S. 23 (1963), an unannounced entry into a person's home was found to be violative of the Fourth Amendment. Therefore, the general rule is that officers must knock and announce their reason for being there. A number of exceptions to this rule have been recognized, including:

1. When the safety of the police or others will be endangered by the announcement.
2. When the announcement will allow those inside to destroy evidence or escape.
3. When the occupants know the purpose of the officers.

The Court has said that the knock-and-announcement requirement applies whether the police gain entry by force or not. It is not important whether the police gain entry through using a key, opening an unlocked door, smashing a window, or breaking a door down. Police may obtain no-knock warrants in exceptional circumstances.

Illegal Arrests

Does the exclusionary rule apply to people as it does to things? That is, should a defendant be excluded from trial because he or she has been arrested unlawfully? Generally, the Supreme Court has answered no.[57] Therefore, the fact that a defendant is kidnapped has no bearing on whether the criminal proceeding will continue.

There may be an exception to this rule. If the conduct of the government is outrageous, shocking, and a gross invasion of a defendant's constitutional rights, he or she may be set free. This is known as a *Toscanino* claim, named after the defendant in that case.

Later, the Second Circuit Court of Appeals reiterated that the *Toscanino* reasoning only applies to situations in which the government's conduct is both shocking and outrageous, as was true of the allegations in *Toscanino*.[58] Be aware that not all courts have followed the Second Circuit's lead. Rather than deal with the thorny legal issue, most courts factually distinguish their cases from *Toscanino*. The Supreme Court has not yet addressed the issue.

Even though a defendant's person may not be excluded because of an illegal arrest, the evidence obtained pursuant to that arrest may be. For example, if there is a causal connection between an illegal arrest and a subsequent confession, then the statement must be excluded.[59] Or, if evidence is obtained through a search incident to an illegal arrest, it must also be suppressed. In short, any evidence obtained as a result of an illegal arrest must be excluded, unless an independent basis for its discovery can be shown by the government.

Analyzing Fourth Amendment Problems

Search and seizure problems can be complex. This area of the law is highly fact-sensitive. It is also an area where one must be careful and precise in analysis. Often search and seizure issues will be numerous in a single case, with all of the issues interrelated and interdependent.

Fourth Amendment analysis is ordered and sequential. See the illustration on page 373. In many instances, the validity of a search or seizure will depend on the validity of an earlier search or seizure. Therefore, if the government fails at an earlier stage, it is probable it may fail again later. For example, the police arrest Barry Burglar and conduct a search incident to arrest. During that search they discover burglar tools and other evidence of the alleged burglary. If it is determined that the arrest was invalid, then the fruits of the search incident to arrest must be suppressed. If the evidence discovered from the search led to other evidence, it may also be excluded.

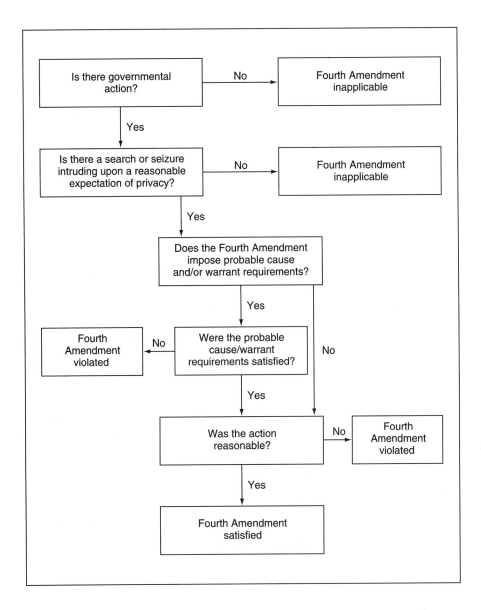

Fourth Amendment
Analysis

Often officers obtain evidence in stages—each stage increasing the governmental interest in crime prevention, and concurrently increasing the officer's suspicion—thereby permitting a greater invasion of a person's privacy.

Even though search and seizure laws can be complex, do not forget to use common sense when analyzing Fourth Amendment issues. The exceptions to the search warrant requirement are not surprising; common sense tells a person that an officer may continue to pursue a fleeing murderer into the suspect's home without first obtaining a warrant. Similarly, it is not shocking that illegally obtained evidence may not be used to convict a defendant.

Summary of Warrant
Rules and Exceptions

SUMMARY OF WARRANT RULES AND EXCEPTIONS

SEARCHES

RULE: Pursuant to the Fourth and Fourteenth Amendments, in both federal and state cases, a warrant to search must be obtained, unless one of the following exceptions is established.

EXCEPTIONS and LIMITATIONS:

1. Consent
2. *Terry* frisks
3. Plain view
4. Plain feel
5. Incident to arrest
6. Preservation of evidence
7. Emergencies and hot pursuit
8. Borders
9. Motor vehicles
10. Vehicle inventories
11. Prisoners
12. Protective sweeps
13. Open fields

ARRESTS

RULE: The Fourth and Fourteenth Amendments govern arrests by both federal and state officials. Arrests in public areas may be warrantless. Arrests made in the home or other property of the defendant must be supported by either an arrest warrant or a search warrant for the defendant's person. Arrests in the homes or other property of third parties must be supported by a search warrant authorizing the search for the defendant at the particular property.

Two very strong policies battle in Fourth Amendment issues: crime detection and prevention versus the citizen's right to be free from intrusive governmental behavior. Consider these concerns when contemplating Fourth Amendment problems.

 CASE ◆

UNITED STATES V. TOSCANINO

500 F.2d 267
(2d Cir. 1974)

Francisco Toscanino appeals from a narcotics conviction entered against him in the Eastern District of New York. . . .

Toscanino does not question the sufficiency of the evidence or claim any error with respect to the conduct of the trial itself. His principal argument . . . is that the entire proceedings in the district court against him were void because his presence within the territorial jurisdiction of the court had been illegally obtained. . . . He offered to prove the following:

"On or about January 6, 1973 Francisco Toscanino was lured from his home in Montevideo, Uruguay by a telephone call. This call has been placed by or at the direction of Hugo Campos Hermedia. Hermedia was at that time and still is a member of the police in Montevideo, Uruguay. . . .

"The telephone call ruse succeeded in bringing Toscanino and his wife, seven months pregnant at the time, to an area near a deserted bowling alley in the City of Montevideo. Upon their arrival there Hermedia together with six associates abducted Toscanino. This was accomplished in full view of Toscanino's terrified wife by knocking him unconscious with a gun. . . .

"At no time had there been any formal or informal request on the part of the United States or the government of Uruguay for the extradition of Francisco Toscanino nor was there any legal basis to justify this rank criminal enterprise. . . .

"Later that same day Toscanino was brought to Brasilia. . . . For seventeen days Toscanino was incessantly tortured and interrogated. Throughout this entire period the United States government and the United States Attorney for the Eastern District of New York . . . did in fact receive reports as to its progress. . . . [Toscanino's] captors denied him sleep and all forms of nourishment for days at a time. Nourishment was provided intravenously in a manner precisely equal to an amount necessary to keep him alive. Reminiscent of the horror stories told by our military men who returned from Korea and China, Toscanino was forced to walk up and down a hallway for seven or eight hours at a time. When he could no longer stand he was kicked and beaten but all in a manner contrived to punish without scarring. When he could not answer, his fingers were pinched with metal pliers. Alcohol was flushed into his eyes and nose and other fluids . . . were forced up his anal passage. Incredibly, these agents of the United States government attached electrodes to Toscanino's earlobes, toes, and genitals. Jarring jolts of electricity were shot throughout his body, rendering him unconscious for indeterminate periods of time but again leaving no physical scars. . . .

[Toscanino was eventually drugged and brought to the United States to stand trial.]

Since *Frisbie*, the Supreme Court in what one distinguished legal luminary describes as a "constitutional revolution," . . . has expanded the interpretation of "due process." No longer is it limited to the guarantee of "fair" procedure at trial. In an effort to deter police misconduct, the term has been extended to bar the government from realizing directly the fruits of its own deliberate and unnecessary lawlessness in bringing the accused to trial. . . .

Accordingly, we view due process as now requiring a court to divest itself of jurisdiction over the person of a defendant where it has been acquired as the result of the government's deliberate, unnecessary and unreasonable invasion of the accused's constitutional rights.

WEB LINKS

News
http://www.newspapers.com provides links to many newspapers in the United States and abroad.

KEY TERMS

consent   plain view doctrine   probable cause

REVIEW QUESTIONS

1. In what way did *Katz v. United States* change Fourth Amendment law?
2. What are the basic requirements for obtaining a search warrant?
3. Stacey is a suspect in an embezzlement investigation. The police believe that she has hidden evidence in her neighbor's house, without the neighbor's consent. The neighbor will not consent to a search. Can the police obtain a search warrant for the nonsuspect's home?
4. What is the plain view doctrine?
5. What is curtilage? Open fields? Why are the concepts important in criminal law?
6. Distinguish a stop from an arrest; a frisk from a search.
7. A police officer is approached by a man on the street who tells the officer that he was just robbed. The man points out the robber, who is standing in a park just across the street. Must the officer obtain a warrant to make the arrest?
8. A police officer is approached by a man on the street who tells the officer that he was just robbed. Although he did not see where the robber fled, he knew the assailant's name and address, as the two men "grew up together." The officer and the victim went to the police station and completed an incident report. After a telephone call to one of suspect's neighbors they learned that he was at home. Must the officer obtain a warrant to make the arrest?
9. Same facts as in question number seven, except the victim points to a fleeing suspect. The officer chases the suspect to a house, where the officer sees the suspect enter with the use of a key. Must the officer end the chase and obtain a warrant?
10. What is a protective sweep?

REVIEW PROBLEMS

1. Tommy Transmitter planned to burglarize a local audio/video dealer. On the night he intended to commit the burglary, Tommy was observed standing in an alley behind the shop by a police officer. It was 11:50 P.M., June, and Tommy was wearing a pair of jeans, tennis shoes, and a shirt.

   After five minutes, the officer approached Tommy and asked him "what he was doing in the alley at such a late hour." Tommy responded that he lived only a few blocks away, was suffering from insomnia, and had decided to take a walk. He produced identification that confirmed that he lived a short distance from the store. The officer then grabbed Tommy, swung him around, pushed him against the wall of the store, and "frisked him." After feeling a hard object in his back pocket, the officer reached in and discovered a small 3″ × 3″ container full of locksmith tools. He then arrested Tommy for possession of burglary tools and conducted a search incident to arrest. During that search he discovered a diagram of the audio/video store hidden in Tommy's pants.

   Tommy was subsequently charged with attempted burglary and possession of burglary tools. He has filed a motion to suppress the tools and diagram, as well as a motion to dismiss. Should the motions be granted? Discuss.

2–5. Assume that officers have a valid search warrant for the defendant's apartment. The warrant specifies that the officers may search for stolen stereos. May the officers do the following?

2. Search the defendant's desk drawers in his study?
3. Search the defendant's closets in his bedroom?
4. Search the defendant's body?
5. Seize a transparent bag of cocaine found lying on the defendant's dining room table?
6. Do you agree with Justice Brennan that the protective sweep goes beyond the *Terry v. Ohio* decision? Explain your position.

7. In *United States v. Leon,* the Supreme Court created a "good faith" exception to the probable cause requirement of the Fourth Amendment. Under *Leon,* evidence seized in good faith pursuant to a search warrant is admissible at trial, even though it is later determined that probable cause was lacking. Should this exception be extended to warrantless searches when an officer has a good faith belief that probable cause exists?
8. Do you believe that the exclusionary rule is required under the Fourth Amendment? Can you think of any alternatives to the rule?

END NOTES

1. *Bivens v. Six Unknown Named Agents,* 403 U.S. 388 (1971).
2. *United States v. Jacobsen,* 466 U.S. 109, 113 (1984).
3. *See,* for example, *United States v. Place,* 462 U.S. 696 (1983).
4. *New York v. Burger,* 482 U.S. 691 (1987).
5. *Minnesota v. Olson,* 495 U.S. 91 (1990).
6. 529 U.S. 334 (2000).
7. *Carroll v. United States,* 267 U.S. 132 (1934).
8. *United States v. Place,* 462 U.S. 696 (1983). A dog sniff of a person or thing, assuming no more intrusion, is not a search under the Fourth Amendment because no reasonable expectation of privacy has been violated.
9. *See Michigan v. DeFillippo,* 443 U.S. 31 (1979); *Illinois v. Krull,* 480 U.S. 340 (1987).
10. *Beck v. Ohio,* 379 U.S. 89 (1964).
11. *McDonald v. United States,* 335 U.S. 451, 455–56 (1948).
12. *Coolidge v. New Hampshire,* 403 U.S. 443 (1971).
13. *Shadwick v. Tampa,* 407 U.S. 345 (1972).
14. Fed. R. Crim. P. 41(b).
15. *Zurcher v. Stanford Daily,* 436 U.S. 547 (1978).
16. *Ybarra v. Illinois,* 444 U.S. 85 (1979).
17. *Michigan v. Summers,* 452 U.S. 692 (1981).
18. *Jones v. United States,* 357 U.S. 493 (1958).
19. Fed. R. Crim. P. 41(c)(1).
20. Fed. R. Crim. P. 41(d).
21. *Schneckloth v. Bustamonte,* 412 U.S. 218 (1973).
22. *See* Jeremy Calsyn et al., "Investigation and Police Practices: Warrantless Searches and Seizures," 86 *Georgetown L.J.* 1214, 1249–1251 (1998).
23. *United States v. Kampbell,* 574 F.2d 962 (8th Cir. 1978).
24. *Commonwealth v. Wright,* 190 A.2d 709 (Pa. 1963).
25. For a discussion of landlord-tenant situations, *see Stoner v. California,* 376 U.S. 483 (1964).
26. *Arizona v. Hicks,* 480 U.S. 321 (1987).
27. 403 U.S. at 470–71.
28. *Terry,* 392 U.S. at 21.
29. *United States v. Arvizu,* 122 S. Ct. 744 (2002).
30. *Illinois v. Wardlow,* 528 U.S. 119 (2000).
31. *United States v. Mendenhall,* 466 U.S. 544 (1980). and *United States V. Drayton,* 122 S. Ct. 405 (2002).
32. *Brown v. Texas,* 443 U.S. 47 (1979).
33. *Michigan v. Long,* 463 U.S. 1032 (1983).
34. *New York v. Belton,* 453 U.S. 454 (1981).
35. *Schmerber v. California,* 384 U.S. 757, 770–71 (1966).
36. *Oliver v. United States,* 466 U.S. 170 (1984).
37. *United States v. Bassford,* 601 F. Supp. 1324, 1330 (D. Mass. 1985).
38. *United States v. Broadhurst,* 612 F. Supp. 777 (C.D. Cal. 1985).
39. *California v. Ciraolo,* 476 U.S. 207 (1986).
40. *United States v. Ramsey,* 431 U.S. 606 (1977).

41. *See* Torcia, *Wharton's Criminal Evidence* § 733 (13th ed., New York: Lawyers Co-operative, 1986 Supp.).

42. *United States v. Martinez-Fuerte,* 428 U.S. 543 (1976).

43. *United States v. Ortiz,* 422 U.S. 891 (1975).

44. *See United States v. Hernandez-Cuartas,* 717 F.2d 552 (11th Cir. 1983).

45. 517 U.S. 806 (1996).

46. *Maryland v. Dyson,* 527 U.S. 465 (1999).

47. *Florida v. White,* 526 U.S. 559 (1999).

48. *Chambers v. Mahoney,* 399 U.S. 42 (1970).

49. *United States v. Ross,* 456 U.S. 798 (1982).

50. *Knowles v. Iowa,* (1998).

51. *United States v. DiRe,* 332 U.S. 581 (1948).

52. *Pennsylvania v. Mimms,* 434 U.S. 106 (1977) and *Maryland v. Wilson,* 117 S. Ct. 882 (1997).

53. *Colorado v. Bertine,* 479 U.S. 367 (1986).

54. *Hudson v. Palmer,* 468 U.S. 517 (1984).

55. *Aguilar v. Texas,* 378 U.S. 108, 110–11 (1964).

56. *Stealgald v. United States,* 451 U.S. 204 (1981).

57. *Frisbie v. Collins,* 342 U.S. 519 (1952).

58. *United States ex rel. Lujan v. Gengler,* 510 F.2d 62 (2d Cir.), *cert. denied,* 421 U.S. 1001 (1975).

59. *Taylor v. Alabama,* 457 U.S. 687 (1982).

CHAPTER 13

Interrogation and Other Law Enforcement Practices

CHAPTER OUTLINE

Interrogations, Confessions, and
   Admissions

   Miranda

   Sixth Amendment

   Voluntariness Requirement

Electronic Surveillance

   Title III of the Omnibus Crime
     Control Act

Pretrial Identification Procedures

   Lineups and One-Man Showups

   The Fairness Right

   Photographs

   Scientific Identification Procedures

   Exclusion of Improper Identifications

CHAPTER OBJECTIVES

In this chapter, you should:

- learn the law of interrogations, confessions, and admissions, including the important constitutional limitations upon governmental authority to extract confessions and admissions.
- learn the law of electronic surveillance.
- learn the law of lineups.

- learn the law of scientific identification procedures.
- be challenged to think critically about recent developments and controversies concerning the use of certain procedures.
- continue to develop your case analysis and legal reasoning skills.

INTERROGATIONS, CONFESSIONS, AND ADMISSIONS

interrogation

Questioning by police, especially of a person suspected or accused of a crime. A *custodial interrogation* involves a restraint of freedom, so it requires a Miranda warning. A routine *investigatory interrogation* involves no restraint and no accusation of a crime.

confession

A voluntary statement by a person that he or she is guilty of a crime.

admission

An "*admission*" is a voluntary statement that a fact or a state of events is true.

Questioning by police officers is a commonly used law enforcement tool. An **interrogation** occurs whenever officers question a person they suspect has committed a crime. A **confession** is a statement made by a person claiming that he or she has committed a crime. If a person asserts certain facts to be true, which are inculpatory, but do not amount to a confession, he or she has made an **admission.**

As a matter of evidence law, admissions or confessions are admissible, even though hearsay, as statements against interest.[1] However, the use of interrogations, confessions, and admissions to prove guilt is controversial. The United States Supreme Court has recognized that admissions are highly suspect when relied upon alone to obtain a confession. The Court stated, in *Escobedo v. Illinois*, 378 U.S. 478 (1964), that a "system of criminal law enforcement which comes to depend on the 'confession' will, in the long run, be less reliable and more subject to abuses than a system which depends on extrinsic evidence independently" obtained through other law enforcement practices.

At common law, confessions and admissions could be used freely, as long as they were made voluntarily. The early basis for excluding involuntary confessions was the Due Process Clauses of the Fifth and Fourteenth Amendments.[2] Eventually, federal defendants could seek to have confessions suppressed if they were not taken before a magistrate promptly after arrest. This was known as the McNabb-Mallory rule.

Today, interrogations, confessions, and admissions are governed by these rules, as well as two broader rights: the Fifth Amendment right to be free from self-incrimination and the Sixth Amendment right to counsel.

Miranda

Contrary to popular belief, the famous *Miranda v. Arizona* case is not a Sixth Amendment right to counsel case; rather, the right to counsel theory is founded upon the Fifth Amendment right to be free from self-incrimination.

Custodial Interrogation. Not all questioning by law enforcement officers must be preceded by the *Miranda* warnings. A defendant must be "in custody" and "interrogated" by police before *Miranda* has effect. This is known as the "custodial interrogation" requirement.

The Court used the phrase "taken into custody or otherwise deprived of his freedom of action in any significant way" to define the custody element of *Miranda*. An objective test is used to determine if a suspect is in custody so that a suspect's subjective beliefs or the beliefs of the interrogating police officer are not dispositive. The question is whether a reasonable person would have believed that he or she was not free to leave. Although a statement by a police officer to a suspect that he is not under arrest is not dispositive, it may be considered. Of course, a person is in custody if an officer announces that an arrest is being made or that the person is not free to leave. The Court made it clear that the in-custody element may be satisfied anywhere—it is not required that the defendant be at the police station to be in custody.

C A S E

MIRANDA V. ARIZONA

384 U.S. 436 (1966)

The cases before us raise questions that go to the roots of our concepts of American criminal jurisprudence: the restraints society must observe consistent with the Federal Constitution in prosecuting individuals for crime. More specifically, we deal with the admissibility of statements obtained from an individual who is subjected to custodial police interrogation and the necessity for procedures which assure that the individual is accorded his privilege under the Fifth Amendment to the Constitution not to be compelled to incriminate himself. . . .

Our holding will be spelled out with some specificity in the pages which follow but briefly stated it is this: the prosecution may not use statements, whether exculpatory or inculpatory, stemming from custodial interrogation of the defendant unless it demonstrates the use of procedural safeguards effective to secure the privilege against self-incrimination. By custodial interrogation, we mean questioning initiated by law-enforcement officers after a person has been taken into custody or otherwise deprived of his freedom of action in any significant way. As for the procedural safeguards to be employed, unless other fully effective means are devised to inform accused persons of their right of silence and to assure a continuous opportunity to exercise it, the following measures are required. Prior to any questioning, the person must be warned that he has a right to remain silent, that any statement he does make may be used as evidence against him, and that he has a right to the presence of an attorney, either retained or appointed. The defendant may waive effectuation of these rights, provided the waiver is made voluntarily, knowingly, and intelligently. If, however, he indicates in any manner and at any stage of the process that he wishes to consult with an attorney before speaking there can be no questioning. Likewise, if the individual is alone and indicates in any manner that he does not wish to be interrogated, the police may not question him.

The mere fact that he may have answered some questions or volunteered some statements on his own does not deprive him of the right to refrain from answering any further inquiries until he has consulted with an attorney and thereafter consents to be questioned.

The constitutional issue we decide in each of these cases is the admissibility of statements obtained from a defendant questioned while in custody or otherwise deprived of his freedom of action in any significant way. In each, the defendant was questioned by police officers, detectives, or a prosecuting attorney in a room in which he was cut off from the outside world. In none of these cases was the defendant given a full and effective warning of his rights at the outset of the interrogation process. In all of the cases, the questioning elicited oral admissions, and in three of them, signed statements as well which were admitted at their trials. They all thus share salient features—incommunicado interrogation of individuals in a police-dominated atmosphere, resulting in self-incriminating statements without full warnings of constitutional rights.

An understanding of the nature and setting of this in-custody interrogation is essential to our decisions today. The difficulty in depicting what transpires at such interrogations stems from the fact that in this country they have largely taken place incommunicado. From extensive factual studies undertaken in the early 1930s . . . it is clear that police violence and the "third degree" flourished at that time. In a series of cases decided by the Court long after those studies, the police resulted to physical brutality—beating, hanging, whipping—and to sustained and protracted questioning incommunicado in order to extort confessions. . . .

Again we stress that the modern practice of in-custody interrogation is psychologically rather than physically oriented. As we have stated before" . . . this court has recognized that coercion can be mental as well as physical, and that the blood of the accused is not the only hallmark of an unconstitutional inquisition.". . .

The circumstances surrounding in-custody interrogation can operate very quickly to overbear the will of one merely made aware of his privilege [against self-incrimination] by his interrogators. Therefore, the right to have counsel present at the interrogation is indispensable to the protection of the Fifth Amendment privilege under the system we delineate today. Our aim is to assure that the individual's right to choose between silence and speech remains unfettered throughout the interrogation process. A once-stated warning, delivered by those who will conduct the interrogation, cannot itself suffice to that end among those who most require knowledge of their rights. A mere warning given by the interrogators is not alone sufficient to accomplish that end. Prosecutors themselves claim that the admonishment of the right to remain silent without more "will benefit only the recidivist and the professional." Even preliminary advice given to the accused by his own attorney can be swiftly overcome by the secret interrogation process. . . . Thus, the need for counsel to protect the Fifth Amendment privilege comprehends not merely a right to consult with counsel prior to questioning, but also to have counsel present during any questioning if the defendant so desires.

The presence of counsel at the interrogation may serve several significant subsidiary functions as well. If the accused decides to talk to his interrogators, the assistance of counsel can mitigate the dangers of trustworthiness. With a lawyer present the likelihood that the police will practice coercion is reduced, and if coercion is nevertheless exercised the lawyer can testify to it in court. The presence of a lawyer can also help to guarantee that the accused gives a fully accurate statement to the police and that the statement is rightly reported to the prosecution.

 CASE

STANSBURY V. CALIFORNIA

511 U.S. 318 (1994)

OPINION: PER CURIAM

This case concerns the rules for determining whether a person being questioned by law enforcement officers is held in custody, and thus entitled to the warnings required by *Miranda v. Arizona,* 384 U.S. 436, 16 L. Ed. 2d 694, 86 S. Ct. 1602 (1966). We hold, not for the first time, that an officer's subjective and undisclosed view concerning whether the person being interrogated is a suspect is irrelevant to the assessment whether the person is in custody.

I

Ten-year-old Robyn Jackson disappeared from a playground in Baldwin Park, California, at around 6:30 p.m. on September 28, 1982. Early the next morning, about 10 miles away in Pasadena, Andrew Zimmerman observed a large man emerge from a turquoise American sedan and throw something into a nearby flood control channel. Zimmerman called the police, who arrived at the scene and discovered the girl's body in the channel. There was evidence that she had been raped, and the cause of death was determined to be asphyxia complicated by blunt force trauma to the head.

Lieutenant Thomas Johnston, a detective with the Los Angeles County Sheriff's Department, investigated the homicide. From witnesses interviewed on the day the body was discovered, he learned that Robyn had talked to two ice cream truck drivers, one being petitioner Robert Edward Stansbury, in the hours before her disappearance. Given these contacts, Johnston thought Stansbury and the other driver might have some connection with the homicide or knowledge thereof, but for reasons unimportant here Johnston considered only the other driver to be a leading suspect. After the suspect driver was brought in for interrogation, Johnston asked Officer Lee of the Baldwin Park Police Department to contact Stansbury to see if he would come in for questioning as a potential witness.

Lee and three other plainclothes officers arrived at Stansbury's trailer home at about 11:00 that evening. The officers surrounded the door and Lee knocked. When Stansbury answered, Lee told him the officers were investigating a homicide to which Stansbury was a possible witness and asked if he would accompany them to the police station to answer some questions. Stansbury agreed to the interview and accepted a ride to the station in the front seat of Lee's police car.

At the station, Lieutenant Johnston, in the presence of another officer, questioned Stansbury about his whereabouts and activities during the afternoon and evening of September 28. Neither Johnston nor the other officer issued *Miranda* warnings. Stansbury told the officers (among other things) that on the evening of the 28th he spoke with the victim at about 6:00, returned to his trailer home after work at 9:00, and left the trailer at about midnight in his housemate's turquoise, American-made car. This last detail aroused Johnston's suspicions, as the turquoise car matched the description of the one Andrew Zimmerman had observed in Pasadena. When Stansbury, in response to a further question, admitted to prior convictions for rape, kidnaping, and child molestation, Johnston terminated the interview and another officer advised Stansbury of his *Miranda* rights. Stansbury declined to make further statements, requested an attorney, and was arrested. Respondent State of California charged Stansbury with first-degree murder and other crimes.

Stansbury filed a pretrial motion to suppress all statements made at the station, and the evidence discovered as a result of those statements. The trial court denied the motion in relevant part, ruling that Stansbury was not "in custody"—and thus not entitled to *Miranda* warnings—until he mentioned that he had taken his housemate's turquoise car for a midnight drive. Before that stage of the interview, the trial court reasoned, "the focus in [Lieutenant

Johnston's] mind certainly was on the other ice cream [truck] driver," Tr. 2368; only "after Mr. Stansbury made the comment . . . describing the . . . turquoise-colored automobile" did Johnston's suspicions "shift to Mr. Stansbury," *ibid.* Based upon its conclusion that Stansbury was not in custody until Johnston's suspicions had focused on him, the trial court permitted the prosecution to introduce in its case in chief the statements Stansbury made before that time. At trial, the jury convicted Stansbury of first-degree murder, rape, kidnaping, and lewd act on a child under the age of 14, and fixed the penalty for the first-degree murder at death.

The California Supreme Court affirmed. . . .

We granted certiorari. 510 U.S. 943 (1993). . . . We held in *Miranda* that a person questioned by law enforcement officers after being "taken into custody or otherwise deprived of his freedom of action in any significant way" must first "be warned that he has a right to remain silent, that any statement he does make may be used as evidence against him, and that he has a right to the presence of an attorney, either retained or appointed." 384 U.S. at 444. Statements elicited in noncompliance with this rule may not be admitted for certain purposes in a criminal trial. . . .

Our decisions make clear that the initial determination of custody depends on the objective circumstances of the interrogation, not on the subjective views harbored by either the interrogating officers or the person being questioned. In *Beckwith v. United States,* 425 U.S. 341, 48 L. Ed. 2d 1, 96 S. Ct. 1612 (1976), for example, the defendant, without being advised of his *Miranda* rights, made incriminating statements to Government agents during an interview in a private home. He later asked that *Miranda* "be extended to cover interrogation in non-custodial circumstances after a police investigation has focused on the suspect." 425 U.S. at 345 (internal quotation marks omitted). We found his argument unpersuasive, explaining that it "was the compulsive aspect of custodial interrogation, and not the strength or content of the government's suspicions at the time the questioning was conducted, which led the Court to impose the

Miranda requirements with regard to custodial questioning." *Id.,* at 346–347 (internal quotation marks omitted). As a result, we concluded that the defendant was not entitled to *Miranda* warnings: "Although the 'focus' of an investigation may indeed have been on Beckwith at the time of the interview . . . , he hardly found himself in the custodial situation described by the *Miranda* Court as the basis for its holding." 425 U.S. at 347.

Berkemer v. McCarty, 468 U.S. 420, 82 L. Ed. 2d 317, 104 S. Ct. 3138 (1984), reaffirmed the conclusions reached in *Beckwith. Berkemer* concerned the roadside questioning of a motorist detained in a traffic stop. We decided that the motorist was not in custody for purposes of *Miranda* even though the traffic officer "apparently decided as soon as [the motorist] stepped out of his car that [the motorist] would be taken into custody and charged with a traffic offense." 468 U.S. at 442. The reason, we explained, was that the officer "never communicated his intention to" the motorist during the relevant questioning. *Ibid.* The lack of communication was crucial, for under *Miranda* "[a] policeman's unarticulated plan has no bearing on the question whether a suspect was 'in custody' at a particular time"; rather, "the only relevant inquiry is how a reasonable man in the suspect's position would have understood his situation." 468 U.S. at 442. Other cases of ours have been consistent in adhering to this understanding of the custody element of *Miranda.* See, e.g., *Mathiason, supra,* 429 U.S. 492 at 495 ("Nor is the requirement of warnings to be imposed simply because . . . the questioned person is one whom the police suspect. *Miranda* warnings are required only where there has been such a restriction on a person's freedom as to render him 'in custody'"); *Beheler, supra,* at 1124, n. 2 ("Our holding in *Mathiason* reflected our earlier decision in *[Beckwith],* in which we rejected the notion that the 'in custody' requirement was satisfied merely because the police interviewed a person who was the 'focus' of a criminal investigation"); *Minnesota v. Murphy,* 465 U.S. 420, 431, 79 L. Ed. 2d 409, 104 S. Ct. 1136 (1984) ("The mere fact that an investigation has focused on a suspect does not trigger the need for *Miranda* warnings in noncustodial settings, and the

probation officer's knowledge and intent have no bearing on the outcome of this case") (citation omitted); cf. *Pennsylvania v. Bruder,* 488 U.S. 9, 11, n. 2, 102 L. Ed. 2d 172, 109 S. Ct. 205 (1988).

It is well settled, then, that a police officer's subjective view that the individual under questioning is a suspect, if undisclosed, does not bear upon the question whether the individual is in custody for purposes of *Miranda.* See F. Inbau, J. Reid, &J. Buckley, *Criminal Interrogation and Confessions* 232, 236, 297–298 (3d ed. 1986). The same principle obtains if an officer's undisclosed assessment is that the person being questioned is not a suspect. In either instance, one cannot expect the person under interrogation to probe the officer's innermost thoughts. . . .

An officer's knowledge or beliefs may bear upon the custody issue if they are conveyed, by word or deed, to the individual being questioned. Cf. *Michigan v. Chesternut,* 486 U.S. 567, 575, n. 7, 100 L. Ed. 2d 565, 108 S. Ct. 1975 (1988) (citing *United States v. Mendenhall,* 446 U.S. 544, 554, n. 6, 64 L. Ed. 2d 497, 100 S. Ct. 1870 (1980) (opinion of Stewart, J.)). Those beliefs are relevant only to the extent they would affect how a reasonable person in the position of the individual being questioned would gauge the breadth of his or her "'freedom of action.'" *Berkemer, supra,* at 440. Even a clear statement from an officer that the person under interrogation is a prime suspect is not, in itself, dispositive of the custody issue, for some suspects are free to come and go until the police decide to make an arrest. The weight and pertinence of any communications regarding the officer's degree of suspicion will depend upon the facts and circumstances of the particular case. In sum, an officer's views concerning the nature of an interrogation, or beliefs concerning the potential culpability of the individual being questioned, may be one among many factors that bear upon the assessment whether that individual was in custody, but only if the officer's views or beliefs were somehow manifested to the individual under interrogation and would have affected how a reasonable person in that position would perceive his or her freedom to leave.

We decide on this state of the record that the California Supreme Court's analysis of whether

Stansbury was in custody is not consistent in all respects with the foregoing principles. Numerous statements in the court's opinion are open to the interpretation that the court regarded the officers' subjective beliefs regarding Stansbury's status as a suspect (or nonsuspect) as significant in and of themselves, rather than as relevant only to the extent they influenced the objective conditions surrounding his interrogation. See 4 Cal. 4th at 1050, 846 P.2d at 775 ("whether the investigation had focused on the" person being questioned is among the "most important considerations" in assessing whether the person was in custody). So understood, the court's analysis conflicts with our precedents. The court's apparent conclusion that Stansbury's *Miranda* rights were triggered by virtue of the fact that he had become the focus of the officers' suspicions, see 4 Cal. 4th at 1052, 1054, 846 P.2d at 776, 777–778; cf., e.g., *State v. Blanding*, 69 Haw. 583, 586–587, 752 P.2d 99, 101 (1988); *State v. Hartman*, 703 S.W.2d 106, 120 (Tenn. 1985), cert. denied, 478 U.S. 1010, 92 L. Ed. 2d 721, 106 S. Ct. 3308 (1986); *People v. Herdan*, 42 Cal. App. 3d 300, 307, n. 10, 116 Cal. Rptr. 641, 645, n. 10 (1974), is incorrect as well. Our cases make clear, in no uncertain terms, that any inquiry into whether the interrogating officers have focused their suspicions upon the individual being questioned (assuming those suspicions remain undisclosed) is not relevant for purposes of *Miranda*. See generally 1 W. LaFave & J. Israel,

Criminal Procedure § 6.6(a), pp. 489–490 (1984). The State acknowledges that Lieutenant Johnston's and the other officers' subjective and undisclosed suspicions (or lack thereof) do not bear upon the question whether Stansbury was in custody, for purposes of *Miranda*, during the station house interview. It maintains, however, that the objective facts in the record support a finding that Stansbury was not in custody until his arrest. Stansbury, by contrast, asserts that the objective circumstances show that he was in custody during the entire interrogation. We think it appropriate for the California Supreme Court to consider this question in the first instance. We therefore reverse its judgment and remand the case for further proceedings not inconsistent with this opinion.

It is so ordered.

CONCURBY: BLACKMUN.

CONCUR: JUSTICE BLACKMUN, CONCURRING.

I join the Court's *per curiam* opinion and merely add that, even if I were not persuaded that the judgment must be reversed for the reasons stated in that opinion, I would adhere to my view that the death penalty cannot be imposed fairly within the constraints of our Constitution. See my dissent in *Callins v. Collins*, 510 U.S. 1141, 1143, 127 L. Ed. 2d 435, 114 S. Ct. 1127 (1994). I therefore would vacate the death sentence on that ground, too.

All of the surrounding facts must be considered in making the custody determination. The location of the interrogation is very important. There is a greater chance of finding a person in custody if the questioning took place in a police station or prosecutor's office rather than the suspect's home or in public. The presence of other persons during the interrogation decreases the odds of the suspect being in custody. The Court found the fact that the suspects in *Miranda* were "cut off from the outside world" troubling. The length and intensity of the questioning are also relevant. A brief encounter between a citizen and a police officer is generally not a custodial situation.

In addition to being in custody, a defendant must be subjected to an interrogation before *Miranda* applies. Clearly, interrogation includes questioning by law enforcement officers, but this is not all. In *Rhode Island v. Innis*, 446 U.S. 291 (1980), the Supreme Court held that any "functional equivalent" to express questioning is also interrogation. That is, all actions or words by police officers that can reasonably be expected to elicit an incriminating response are interrogation.

The nature of the information elicited is not relevant; the *Miranda* court stated that the decision applies to both inculpatory and exculpatory statements. Accordingly, *Miranda* is effective whether a defendant confesses or simply makes an admission.

Exceptions to *Miranda.* Not every communication between a police officer and a suspect amounts to an interrogation under *Miranda*. First, volunteered statements are not the product of interrogation. The *Miranda* decision explicitly states that officers are under no duty to interrupt a volunteered confession in order to read a confessor his or her *Miranda* rights.

Second, routine questions that are purely informational and normally do not lead to incriminating responses, need not be preceded by a reading of the *Miranda* warnings. Questions about one's name, age, address, and employment, for example, are not treated as interrogation.

Third, questions made by officers in the interest of public safety need not be preceded by a *Miranda* warning. In one case, a woman told two police officers that she had just been raped by a man carrying a gun and that the rapist had gone into a nearby grocery. The officers went to the store and arrested the man. However, he did not have the gun on his person. One of the police officers asked the arrestee where the gun was, and the arrestee responded by indicating the location where the gun was hidden in the store. The Supreme Court decided that, despite the fact that the question was interrogation and the defendant had not been mirandized, the evidence could be used at trial. The Court recognized that in such situations, when there is a danger to the officers or the public, officers must be permitted to extinguish the public threat. Thus, the relatively rigid *Miranda* rules are relaxed when there is a public safety exigency that was the impetus of a brief and limited interrogation designed to meet that exigency.[3]

Fourth, related to the public safety exception is spontaneous questioning by police. If a question is asked spontaneously, such as in response to an emergency, there is no interrogation. For example, if an officer were to return to a room where he has placed two arrestees to find one dead, it would not be an interrogation if the officer were to excitedly utter, "Who killed this man?"

Fifth, the *Miranda* warnings do not have to be given by undercover officers because there is no custody, no "police-dominated atmosphere."[4] However, once criminal charges have been filed, undercover officers may not be used to extract information from a defendant.[5]

Sixth, the Supreme Court has determined that *Miranda* warnings do not have to be recited during routine traffic stops, even though an interrogation occurs. The Court concluded that although traffic stops are seizures for Fourth Amendment purposes, they are not custodial for Fifth Amendment purposes. The "noncoercive aspect of ordinary traffic stops prompts us to hold that persons temporarily detained pursuant to such stops are not 'in custody' for the purposes of *Miranda*."[6]

Multiple Interrogations and Reinterrogation. *Miranda* clearly states that once a defendant invokes the right to remain silent, whether before or during questioning, the interrogation must stop. The same is true once a defendant states that he or she wants counsel present; the interrogation must cease until the defendant's attorney is available. If the defendant's attorney is not available, the police are to respect the defendant's right to remain silent and not question him or her until the attorney arrives. However, ambiguous references to an attorney do not invoke a suspect's right to be free of questioning. A suspect's request must be clear enough that a reasonable officer would believe that the suspect wanted to see counsel.[7]

Under very limited circumstances, police officers may reattempt to interrogate a defendant who has invoked the right to remain silent. Although multiple attempts to interrogate an arrestee about the same crime are not permitted, it has been determined that a second interrogation about a separate and unrelated crime may be valid.[8]

Miranda clearly stated that once an accused has invoked the right to counsel, the police are prohibited from interrogating him or her until he or she has conferred with counsel. *Miranda* did not answer this question: may police reinterrogate a defendant without counsel present once the defendant has consulted with a lawyer? The answer is found in *Minnick v. Mississippi*. *Minnick* makes it clear that once an accused has asserted a right to counsel, all police-initiated interrogations must occur with defense counsel present.

 CASE

MINNICK V. MISSISSIPPI

498 U.S. 146 (1990)

To protect the privilege against self-incrimination guaranteed by the Fifth Amendment, we have held that the police must terminate interrogation of an accused in custody if the accused requests the assistance of counsel. *Miranda v. Arizona*, 384 U.S. 436, 474 (1966). We reinforced the protections of *Miranda* in *Edwards v. Arizona*, 451 U.S. 477, 484–485 (1981), which held that once the accused requests counsel, officials may not reinitiate questioning "until counsel has been made available" to him. The issue in the case before us is whether *Edwards* protection ceases once the suspect has consulted with an attorney.

Petitioner Robert Minnick and fellow prisoner James Dyess escaped from a county jail in Mississippi and, a day later, broke into a mobile home in search of weapons. In the course of the burglary they were interrupted by the arrival of the trailer's owner, Ellis Thomas, accompanied by Lamar Lafferty and Lafferty's infant son. Dyess and

Minnick used the stolen weapons to kill Thomas and the senior Lafferty. Minnick's story is that Dyess murdered one victim and then forced Minnick to shoot the other. Before the escapees could get away, two young women arrived at the mobile home. They were held at gunpoint, then bound by hand and foot. Dyess and Minnick fled in Thomas' truck, abandoning the vehicle in New Orleans. The fugitives continued to Mexico, where they fought, and Minnick then proceeded alone to California. Minnick was arrested in Lemon Grove, California, on a Mississippi warrant, some four months after the murders.

The confession at issue here resulted from the last interrogation of Minnick while he was held in the San Diego jail, but we first recount the events which preceded it. Minnick was arrested on Friday, August 22, 1986. Petitioner testified that he was mistreated by local police during and after the arrest. The day following the arrest, Saturday, two FBI agents came to the jail to interview him. Petitioner testified that he refused to go to the interview, but was told he would "have to go down or else." . . . The FBI report indicates that the agents read petitioner his *Miranda* warnings, and that he acknowledged he understood his rights. He refused to sign a rights waiver form, however, and said he would not answer "very many" questions. Minnick told the agents about the jail break and the flight, and described how Dyess threatened and beat him. Early in the interview, he sobbed "[i]t was my life or theirs," but otherwise he hesitated to tell what happened at the trailer. The agents reminded him he did not have to answer questions without a lawyer present. According to the report, "Minnick stated 'Come back Monday when I have a lawyer,' and stated that he would make a more complete statement then with his lawyer present." . . .

After the FBI interview, an appointed attorney met with petitioner. Petitioner spoke with the lawyer on two or three occasions, though it is not clear from the record whether all of these conferences were in person.

On Monday, August 25, Deputy Sheriff J.C. Denham of Clarke County, Mississippi, came to the San Diego jail to question Minnick. Minnick testified that his jailers again told him he would "have to talk" to Denham and that he "could not refuse." . . . Denham advised petitioner of his rights, and petitioner again declined to sign a rights waiver form. Petitioner told Denham about the escape and then proceeded to describe the events at the mobile home. . . .

Minnick was tried for murder in Mississippi. He moved to suppress all statements given to the FBI or other police officers, including Denham. The trial court denied the motion with respect to petitioner's statements to Denham, but suppressed his other statements. Petitioner was convicted on two counts of capital murder and sentenced to death.

On appeal, petitioner argued that the confession to Denham was taken in violation of his rights to counsel under the Fifth and Sixth Amendments. The Mississippi Supreme Court rejected the claims. . . .

The Mississippi Supreme Court relied on our statement in *Edwards* that an accused who invokes his right to counsel "is not subject to further interrogation by the authorities until counsel has been made available to him. . . ." 451 U.S., at 484–485. We do not interpret this language to mean, as the Mississippi court thought, that the protection of *Edwards* terminates once counsel has consulted with the suspect. In context, the requirement that counsel be "made available" to the accused refers to more than an opportunity to consult with an attorney outside the interrogation room.

In *Edwards*, we focused on *Miranda's* instruction that when the accused invokes his right to counsel, the "interrogation must cease until an attorney is *present* during custodial interrogation." 451 U.S., at 482 (emphasis added). In the sentence preceding the language quoted by the Mississippi Supreme Court, we referred to the "right to have counsel *present* during custodial interrogation." . . .

In our view, a fair reading of *Edwards* and subsequent cases demonstrates that we have interpreted the rule to bar police-initiated interrogation unless the accused has counsel with him at the time of questioning. Whatever the ambiguities of our earlier cases on this point, we now hold that when counsel is requested, interrogation must cease, and officials may not reinitiate interrogation without counsel present, whether or not the accused has consulted with his attorney.

The Warnings. Before a person in custody may be interrogated, the required warning must be recited to the arrestee. Specific language need not be used, as long as the defendant is fully and effectively apprised of each right.

The Supreme Court stated, in *Miranda*, that the following rights must be conveyed to the defendant:

1. The right to remain silent.
2. Any statements made may be used against the defendant to gain a conviction.
3. The right to consult with a lawyer and to have a lawyer present during questioning.
4. For the indigent, a lawyer will be provided without cost.

The warnings are to be read to all persons in custody who are to be interrogated. The law does not presume that any person, including an attorney, knows these rights. The warnings should be presented in a timely manner and read at such a speed that the arrestee can gain a full understanding of their import.

Many law enforcement agencies have made it a policy to record (video/audio or audio only) the giving of the warnings and any waiver of rights to eliminate any question concerning whether the warnings were given and whether coercion was used to gain a waiver.

Waiver. A defendant may waive the right to have the assistance of counsel and/or to remain silent. The waiver must be made voluntarily and knowingly. In *Miranda*, the Supreme Court said that the "heavy burden" of proving that a defendant made a knowing and voluntary waiver rests with the prosecution; courts are to presume no waiver.

In determining whether there has been a waiver, the totality of the circumstances is considered. The actions of the police, as well as the defendant's age, intelligence, and experience, are all relevant to this inquiry.

An express waiver, preferably written, is best for the prosecution. However, a defendant's waiver does not have to be express to be valid. In *North Carolina v. Butler*, 441 U.S. 369 (1962), the Court held that "in at least some cases waiver can be clearly inferred from the actions and words of the person interrogated." However, silence on the part of a defendant never amounts to a waiver. So, if a defendant refuses to state, or otherwise indicate, that he or she understands a right and wishes to waive it, the police should not conduct an interrogation.

Violating *Miranda*. Any statement obtained in violation of *Miranda* is inadmissible at trial to prove guilt. Further, any other evidence that is the fruit of such a statement must also be excluded from trial. The defendant ordinarily raises the issue prior to trial through a motion to suppress.

Although statements that are illegally obtained may not be admitted to prove a defendant's guilt, the Supreme Court has said that statements that violate *Miranda* may be admitted, under certain circumstances, to impeach the defendant.[9] So, if a defendant's testimony at trial is different from an earlier confession that was suppressed as violative of *Miranda*, the confession may be admitted to rebut the defendant's in-court testimony.

Sixth Amendment

Miranda has effect as soon as a person is in custody and is subject to interrogation. This can occur long before or directly prior to the filing of a formal charge. Once the adversary judicial proceeding has begun, the source of protection changes from the Fifth Amendment (*Miranda*) to the Sixth Amendment.

In *Michigan v. Jackson*, 475 U.S. 625 (1986), the Supreme Court held that the Sixth Amendment provides the same protections as *Miranda*, *Edwards*, and similar cases. The Court reasoned that interrogations by the government of a defendant after criminal charges have been filed are a critical stage at which counsel is necessary to protect the defendant's rights.

Voluntariness Requirement

As was true at common law, all confessions must be made voluntarily. This is required by the Due Process Clauses of the Fifth and Fourteenth Amendments. The totality of the circumstances must be examined when making the voluntariness determination.

Police officers do not have to physically coerce a confession for it to be involuntary. Mental or emotional coercion by law enforcement also violates a defendant's due process rights.

Involuntary confessions are to be excluded at trial. For years, the admission of a coerced confession resulted in an automatic reversal of conviction. This was changed in *Arizona v. Fulminante*, 499 U.S. 279 (1991), in which the United States Supreme Court decided that a conviction is not to be automatically reversed because a coerced confession was admitted at trial. Rather, the Court held that if the prosecution can show beyond a reasonable doubt that the trial court error was harmless, the conviction is to be affirmed. That is, if there was sufficient other evidence to sustain the conviction, then it stands.

ELECTRONIC SURVEILLANCE

Many forms of electronic surveillance are used by law enforcement agencies. Wiretaps and highly sensitive microphones are examples. When the Supreme Court first addressed the issue of wiretapping, it concluded that there was no Fourth Amendment protection because there was no trespass into a constitutionally protected area. This changed when the Court issued the *Katz* decision, which advanced the idea that the Fourth Amendment protects people, not places. Now, if a person has a justifiable expectation of privacy, the Fourth Amendment applies.

Despite the constitutional aspect of using such devices, this area of law is highly regulated by a federal statute: Title III of the Omnibus Crime Control Act and Safe Streets Act of 1968.

Title III of the Omnibus Crime Control Act

Title III of the Omnibus Crime Control Act and Safe Streets Act of 1968[10] is a federal statute that regulates the use of electronic surveillance. It is also known as the Federal Wiretap Act.

The act prohibits wiretapping, bugging, or other electronic surveillance of a conversation when the parties to that conversation possess a reasonable expectation of privacy. Violation of the act may result in civil and criminal penalties. Evidence obtained in violation of the act is excluded at trial.

The statute permits states to enact their own electronic surveillance laws; however, those laws cannot provide less protection of individual rights than the federal statute. A state may, however, provide greater protection of individual rights through its surveillance law than does the federal statute.

Court-Ordered Surveillance.   Law enforcement officers may not intercept telephone conversations or other electronic messages without first obtaining court approval. The act permits court approval only for certain crimes. Espionage, treason, murder, kidnapping, robbery, extortion, drug crimes, and bribery of public officials are included in that list.

To obtain a court order for the interception of electronic communications, an officer must present an application supported by oath or affirmation to a court. The requirements for obtaining such a court order are similar to those for obtaining a warrant. The application must contain the following:[11]

1. The identity of the official applying for the order and the official authorizing the application.
2. Evidence establishing probable cause to believe that the person whose communication is to be intercepted has committed, is committing, or is about to commit one of the named crimes.
3. Evidence establishing probable cause to believe that the communication to be intercepted concerns the crime.
4. A statement that other normal investigative procedures have been tried and failed, or that no other procedure is available.
5. The time period during which the interception will occur.
6. A full description of the location where the interception will take place.
7. A statement reflecting all prior attempts to obtain a similar order for any of the same places or persons.

If the judge grants the application, the order must specify the person whose communication is to be intercepted, the location of the interception, the nature of the communication to be intercepted, the crime involved, and the duration of the interception. In all cases, the surveillance is to cease once the desired information has been seized (recorded). After the interception has ended, the recording is to be given to the judge who issued the order, for safekeeping.

Execution of Title III Orders.   The statute provides that all communications intercepted shall, if possible, be recorded. The method of recording is to protect against editing and other alterations. The purpose of this requirement is obvious: to preserve the integrity of the evidence.

The statute also requires that all interceptions of irrelevant information be minimized. Said another way, if an officer intercepting a conversation knows that it is unrelated to the investigation, the interception is to cease. The minimization requirement is no more than a codification of the Fourth Amendment's reasonableness requirement.

Of course, determining whether an interception is related to the offense under investigation is not always easy, and courts tend to defer to the judgment of the intercepting officer in close cases. The following factors are considered by a reviewing court when a claim is made that interceptions were not properly minimized:

1. The percentage of calls that were related to the investigation. The lower the percentage, the greater the likelihood that the government did not properly minimize its interceptions.
2. The number of calls that were one-time only.

3. The length of the calls intercepted. The shorter the calls, the less opportunity the government had to determine whether the interception was proper.
4. The nature of the calls. The more ambiguous the call, the greater the government's interest in prolonging its interception.[12]

Other factors may also be important to the inquiry. For example, if a known co-conspirator makes frequent calls, interception of all the calls is probably valid, even though the majority of conversations does not concern the conspiracy. Each case must be examined on its own facts to determine whether Title III or the Fourth Amendment has been violated.

Implicit in court orders under this statute is the authority to enter premises to install listening devices. Courts have held that it would be nonsensical to give an officer the authority to conduct surveillance, but not to enter the premises of the defendant to install the necessary device. The court order does not have to specifically give this authority; it is implicit in the order itself. Of course, where an officer may go depends on the facts of each case.

The statute authorizes judges to order third parties, such as telephone company personnel, to assist law enforcement officers in executing an electronic surveillance order. Third parties must be compensated for their assistance.

Exceptions to Title III. In a number of situations, a court order is not required to intercept an electronic communication. Five exceptions are discussed here.

First, be aware that the act tracks the privacy aspect of the *Katz* decision; that is, only communications for which a person has a reasonable expectation of privacy are protected. Because Title III does not expand the privacy protection aspect of the Fourth Amendment, decisions concerning whether a person has a reasonable expectation of privacy under the Fourth Amendment are applicable to Title III.

One party to a communication has no reasonable expectation that the other party will not record the conversation or permit others to listen. Therefore, no court order has to be obtained for a law enforcement officer to listen in on an extension (or later listen to a recording), as long as one party to the conversation consents. The Federal Wiretap Act has a provision reflecting this position.

It has also been held that a person has no reasonable expectation of privacy when using a cordless telephone. Because cordless phones use radio waves, which are broadcast in all directions and are subject to being received by countless people, courts have reasoned that a person cannot have a reasonable expectation of privacy when using one.[13] However, whenever one party is using a cordless phone and the other a traditional line phone, it is likely, unless the second party knows that the other is using a cordless phone, that the second party has a reasonable expectation of privacy.

Critics of this position charge that whenever a person places a call to a particular person, whether on a cordless phone or a traditional phone, it is reasonable to expect the conversation to be private. Another view contends that such hair-splitting is confusing to the average person. As Professor Lawrence Tribe of Harvard University School of Law noted, it may be true that the professional criminal knows that he has no reasonable expectation of privacy on a cordless phone, but the average citizen does not.

Second, any employee of a communications company who intercepts an incriminating communication while engaged in ordinary duties (i.e., maintenance) may disclose such information to the authorities, and it may be used at trial.

Third, officers need not obtain a court order when engaged in certain national security investigations.

Fourth, in emergency situations, when an officer does not have time to obtain a court order, the interception may begin immediately, but an application must be made within forty-eight hours. If the judge determines that there was no emergency justifying a warrantless tap, then any evidence obtained must be suppressed.

Finally, electronic beepers and transmitters used to track a person or thing are governed by normal search and seizure law. Additionally, the Supreme Court has held that pen registers and similar devices that make a record of telephone numbers called do not implicate the Fourth Amendment because there is no search when they are used.[14]

PRETRIAL IDENTIFICATION PROCEDURES

Law enforcement officers use a variety of techniques to identify a person as a criminal, such as eyewitness identifications, fingerprinting, blood tests, and, recently, deoxyribonucleic acid (DNA) tests. The use of any of these procedures raises certain constitutional issues, such as the right to be free from self-incrimination and the right to counsel.

There is also another concern: reliability. Eyewitness identification, though powerful, has a few inherent problems. First, each person will testify to his or her perception of an event, and people often perceive the same event differently. Second, not every person will use the same language to describe what was witnessed. Third, a witness may simply have a faulty memory and unintentionally testify to an untruth. Fourth, for a variety of reasons, a witness may intentionally lie.

Scientific testing may also prove to be invalid or unreliable. How accurate is the test when performed properly? Was the test performed properly in this case? Is the evidence tested actually the defendant's? These types of questions are asked of expert witnesses who testify to the results of scientific testing. This discussion begins with eyewitness identification procedures.

LINEUPS AND ONE-MAN SHOWUPS

A **lineup** is where the police exhibit a group of people, among whom is the suspect, to a witness or victim for identification as the criminal. A one-man **showup** is an exhibition of one person to a witness or victim for identification as the criminal.

In practice, police first conduct a lineup and, then if the suspect is identified, the witness is asked at trial to testify that he or she identified the perpetrator of the crime at the lineup. Therefore, if the initial identification is faulty, the subsequent in-court identification is also faulty. Even if the witness is asked

lineup

A group of persons, placed side-by-side in a line, shown to a witness of a crime to see if the witness will identify the person suspected of committing the crime. A *lineup* should not be staged so that it is suggestive of one person.

showup

A pretrial Identification procedure in which only one suspect and a witness are brought together.

to identify anew the perpetrator of the crime, such an identification is tainted by the witness's earlier identification. In the landmark case of *United States v. Wade*, the Supreme Court addressed the problems inherent in pretrial identification procedures.

The Right to Counsel.   What *Wade* mandates is that counsel be provided at pretrial lineups and showups. For years it was unknown whether this meant all pretrial lineups and showups or just those after the Sixth Amendment attaches. *Kirby v. Illinois*, 406 U.S. 682 (1972), resolved this dispute by requiring counsel only after initiation of "adversary judicial proceedings—whether by way of formal charge, preliminary hearing, indictment, information, or arraignment."

The Fairness Right

In addition to having a right to counsel at postindictment lineups, an accused is entitled to a fair lineup, one that is not unnecessarily suggestive of guilt. In *Stoval v. Denno*, 388 U.S. 293 (1967), the Supreme Court found that the Due

 C A S E

UNITED STATES V. WADE

338 U.S. 218 (1967)

The question here is whether courtroom identifications of an accused at trial are to be excluded from evidence because the accused was exhibited to the witness before trial at a post-indictment lineup conducted for identification purposes without notice to and in the absence of the accused's appointed counsel.

The federally insured bank in Eustace, Texas, was robbed on September 21, 1964. A man with a small strip of tape on each side of his face entered the bank, pointed a pistol at the female cashier and the vice president, the only persons in the bank at the time, and forced them to fill a pillowcase with the bank's money. The man then drove away with an accomplice who had been waiting in a stolen car outside the bank. On March 23, 1965, an indictment was returned against respondent, Wade, and two others for conspiring to rob the bank, and against Wade and accomplice for the robbery itself. Wade was

arrested on April 2, and counsel was appointed to represent him on April 26. Fifteen days later an FBI agent, without notice to Wade's lawyer, arranged to have the two bank employees observe a lineup made up of Wade and five or six other prisoners and conducted in a courtroom of the local county courthouse. Each person in the line wore strips of tape such as allegedly worn by the robber and upon direction each said something like "put the money in the bag," the words allegedly uttered by the robber. Both bank employees identified Wade in the lineup as the bank robber.

At trial, the two employees, when asked on direct examination if the robber was in the courtroom, pointed to Wade. The prior lineup identification was then elicited from both employees on cross examination. . . . But the confrontation compelled by the State between the accused and the victim or witnesses to a crime to elicit identification evidence is peculiarly riddled with innumerable dangers and variable factors which might seriously, even crucially, derogate from a fair trial. The vagaries of eyewitness identification are well-known; the annals of criminal law are rife with instances of mistaken identification. . . . The identification of strangers is proverbially untrustworthy. . . . A major factor contributing to the high incidence of miscarriage of justice from mistaken identification has been the degree of suggestion inherent in the manner in which the prosecution presents the suspect to witness for pretrial identification. A commentator has observed that "[t]he influence of improper suggestion upon identifying witnesses probably accounts for more miscarriages of justice than any other single factor—perhaps it is responsible for more such errors than all other factors combined." . . . Suggestion can be created intentionally or unintentionally in many subtle ways. And the dangers for the suspect are particularly grave when the witness' opportunity for observation was insubstantial, and thus his susceptibility to suggestion the greatest.

> Moreover, "[i]t is a matter of common experience that, once a witness has picked out the accused at the line-up, he is not likely to go back on his word later on, so that in practice the issue of identity may (in the absence of other relevant evidence) for all practical purposes be determined there and then, before the trial." . . .

What facts have been disclosed in specific cases about the conduct of pretrial confrontations for identification illustrate both the potential for substantial prejudice to the accused at that stage and the need for its revelation at trial. A commentator provides some striking examples:

In a Canadian case . . . the defendant had been picked out of a line-up of six men, of which he was the only Oriental. In other cases, a black-haired suspect was placed among a group of light-haired persons, tall suspects have been made to stand with short non-suspects, and, in a case where the perpetrator of the crime was known to be a youth, a suspect under twenty was placed in a line-up with five other persons, all of whom were forty or over.

Similarly, state reports, in the course of describing prior identifications admitted as evidence of guilt, reveal numerous instances of suggestive procedures, for example, that all in the lineup but the suspect were known to the identifying witness, that the other participants in a lineup were grossly dissimilar in appearance to the suspect, that only the suspect was required to wear distinctive clothing which the culprit allegedly wore. . . .

Since it appears that there is grave potential for prejudice, intentional or not, in the pretrial lineup, which may not be capable of reconstruction at trial, and since presence of counsel can often avert prejudice and assure a meaningful confrontation at trial, there can be little doubt that for Wade the post-indictment lineup was a critical stage of the prosecution at which [he] was [entitled to counsel]. . . .

[The Court then concluded that in-court identifications must be excluded if they follow a lineup at which a defendant is not permitted counsel, unless the in-court identification has an independent origin.]

Process Clauses of the Fifth and Fourteenth Amendments prohibit identifications that are so unnecessarily suggestive that there is a real chance of misidentification. In addition to being impermissibly suggestive, an identification must be unreliable to be excluded.[15] When making the determination of whether an identification violates due process, a court is to examine the "totality of the circumstances" surrounding the identification. Examples of impermissibly suggestive were mentioned in the *Wade* opinion. For example, if a witness states that a white male committed a crime, it would be improper to exhibit four black men and one white man in a lineup.

One-man showups, obviously, are more suggestive of guilt than lineups. As such, they should be used with caution. Generally, a one-man showup should occur within a short period of time after the crime (minutes or hours). If there is time to organize a lineup, this is the preferable method of identification procedure.

Self-Incrimination.   It is not violative of the Fifth Amendment's privilege against self-incrimination for a defendant to be compelled to appear in a lineup. The privilege against self-incrimination applies to "testimony" and not to physical acts, such as walking, gesturing, measuring, or speaking certain words for identification purposes.[16] If a defendant has changed in appearance, he or she may be made to shave, to don a wig or hairpiece, or wear a certain article of clothing.

The question under the Fifth Amendment is whether the act requested is "communicative." If so, then the defendant may not be compelled to engage in the act. If not, the opposite is true.

Photographs

Police may show a witness photographs to obtain an identification. The due process test discussed earlier applies to the use of photos; that is, the event must not be impermissibly suggestive and unreliable. The showing of one picture is likely to be determined improper, absent an emergency. As is true of lineups, the people in the photos should be similar in appearance. Also, a "mug shot" (a picture taken by law enforcement agencies after arrest) of the accused should not be mixed with ordinary photos of nonsuspects. Nor should the photos be presented in such a manner that the defendant's picture stands out.

The Supreme Court has determined that there is no right to counsel at a photo identification session, either before initiation of the adversary judicial proceeding or thereafter.

Scientific Identification Procedures

Law enforcement officials may use scientific methods of identification to prove that a defendant committed a crime. Fingerprinting, blood tests, genetic tests (deoxyribonucleic acid, or DNA, testing), voice tests, and handwriting samples are examples of such techniques.

Such tests are not critical stages of the criminal proceedings, and, accordingly, there is no right to counsel. There is also no right to refuse to cooperate with such testing on Fifth Amendment grounds, because the defendant is not being required to give testimony. However, if a test involves an invasion of privacy, then the Fourth Amendment requires probable cause before the procedure may be forced on an unwilling defendant.

Validity and Reliability.   Scientific evidence must be reliable before it may be introduced at trial. In a landmark case, *Frye v. United States*, 293 F. 1013 (D.C. Cir. 1923), it was held that scientific techniques must be generally accepted as valid and reliable by the scientific community to be admissible. *Frye* was the law from 1923 until the Supreme Court issued *Daubert v. Merrell Dow Pharmaceuticals*, 113 S. Ct. 2786 (1993). *Daubert* changed the standard of admissibility from acceptance in the scientific community to scientific validity. Under this new standard, the trial judge is required to make a preliminary determination that the proffered evidence is valid before it may be presented to a jury. In making this decision, the trial judge is to consider the following factors:

1. Whether the evidence or theory has, or can be, tested.
2. Whether it has been reviewed and tested by other scientists.
3. Whether the method has been published and the quality of the publication(s) in which it is found.
4. Whether its error rate and other potential defects are known.
5. Whether standards and protocols for its use have been established.
6. Whether its use is widely accepted in the relevant scientific community.

Techniques that are experimental and not highly reliable are not admissible. A few common scientific techniques are discussed here. Note that the results of a specific test may be denied admission, even if the scientific basis of the testing is valid, if the test is administered incorrectly. Further, scientific testing also raises Fourth, Fifth, Sixth, and Fourteenth Amendment issues, some of which are discussed later.

Fingerprinting. A fingerprint consists of several identifiable characteristics, such as loops, arches, whorls, islands, and bifurcations. The arrangement, frequency, and design of these features are among the many characteristics used to distinguish prints from one another. Although it is common to state that every person has a unique set of prints, there is a possibility of duplication. However, the odds of that occurring has been estimated to be as low as one in 64 billion.[17]

Fingerprint identification is a highly accurate science and is universally accepted by federal and state courts.[18] Federal and state law enforcement agencies, as well as international agencies, possess libraries of fingerprints. Through the use of computers, fingerprints lifted from crime scenes, weapons, and other objects can be matched to a particular individual's fingerprints in a matter of minutes. Lifted prints may be matched to a print already on file or to a print taken from a suspect.

The taking of fingerprints does not implicate the Fifth Amendment because the accused is not compelled to give testimony. Further, it is not a search to take a suspect's fingerprints. This being so, neither probable cause nor a warrant is required to take the suspect's prints. Courts have analogized fingerprints to physical characteristics such as hair and eye color. Because it is not an invasion of a reasonable expectation to privacy (search) for an officer to visually observe a defendant, courts have reasoned that it is not an invasion of privacy to observe and record a suspect's fingerprints.

Blood Testing. Blood testing is commonly employed and universally accepted by courts in the United States. Although the science of blood testing is generally beyond scrutiny, individual blood tests are not. Laboratories make mistakes, and both the defense and the prosecution may challenge a particular test.

Securing a suspect's blood is different from rolling a fingerprint. The process of withdrawing blood involves a bodily invasion and the possibility of pain and infection. Therefore, a person's expectation of privacy is higher when the government seeks blood rather than fingerprints. Whether the government possesses the authority to compel a suspect to undergo a blood test was the subject of *Schmerber v. California.*

Schmerber stands for the principle that the withdrawal of blood, as well as other bodily-intrusive procedures, constitutes a search under the Fourth Amendment. Probable cause is required, as is a warrant, unless exigent circumstances, such as those in *Schmerber*, justify bypassing the warrant requirement. In addition, such procedures must be conducted in a safe, discrete, medical environment.

 CASE

SCHMERBER V. CALIFORNIA

384 U.S. 757 (1966)

Petitioner was convicted in Los Angeles Municipal Court of the criminal offense of driving an automobile while under the influence of intoxicating liquor. He had been arrested at a hospital while receiving treatment for injuries suffered in an accident involving the automobile that he was apparently driving. At the direction of a police officer, a blood sample was then withdrawn from petitioner's body by a physician at the hospital. The chemical analysis of this sample revealed a percent by weight of alcohol in his blood at the time of the offense which indicated intoxication, and the report of this analysis was admitted in evidence at trial. . . .

II. THE PRIVILEGE AGAINST SELF-INCRIMINATION CLAIM

. . . We . . . must now decide whether the withdrawal of the blood and admission in evidence of the analysis involved in this case violated petitioner's privilege. We hold that the privilege protects an accused only from being compelled to testify against himself, or otherwise provide the State with evidence of a testimonial or communicative nature, and that the withdrawal of blood and use of the analysis in question in this case did not involve compulsion to these ends. . . .

IV. THE SEARCH AND SEIZURE CLAIM

The overriding function of the Fourth Amendment is to protect personal privacy and dignity against unwarranted intrusion by the State. . . .

The values protected by the Fourth Amendment thus substantially overlap those the Fifth Amendment helps to protect. . . .

Because we are dealing with intrusions into the human body rather than with state interferences with property relationships or private papers—"house, papers, and effect"—we write on a clean slate. . . .

In this case, as will often be true when charges of driving under the influence of alcohol are pressed, these questions arise in the context of an arrest made by an officer without a warrant. Here, there was plainly probable cause for the officer to arrest petitioner and charge him with driving an automobile while under the influence of intoxicating liquor. The police officer who arrived at the scene shortly after the accident smelled liquor on petitioner's breath, and testified that petitioner's eyes were "bloodshot, watery, sort of a glassy appearance." The officer saw petitioner again at the hospital, within two hours of the accident. There he noticed similar symptoms of drunkenness. He thereupon informed petitioner "that he was under arrest and that he was entitled to the services of an attorney, and that he could remain silent, and that anything he told me would be used against him in evidence." . . .

Although the facts which established probable cause to arrest in this case also suggested the required relevance and likely success of a test of petitioner's blood for alcohol, the question remains whether the arresting officer was permitted to draw these inferences himself, or was required instead to procure a warrant before proceeding with the test. Search warrants are ordinarily required for searches of dwellings, and, absent an emergency, no less could be required where intrusions of the human body are concerned. . . . The importance of informed, detached and deliberate determinations of the issue whether or not to invade another's body in search of evidence of guilt is indisputable and great.

The officer in the present case, however, might reasonably have believed that he was confronted with an emergency, in which the delay necessary to obtain a warrant, under the circumstances, threatened "the destruction of evidence". . . . We are told that the percentage of alcohol in the blood begins to diminish shortly after drinking stops, as the body functions to eliminate it from the system. Particularly in a case such as this, where time had to be taken to bring the accused to a hospital and to investigate the scene of the accident, there was no time to seek out a magistrate and secure a warrant. . . .

Finally, the records show that the test was performed in a reasonable manner. Petitioner's blood was taken by physician in a hospital environment according to accepted medical practices. We are thus not presented with the serious questions which would arise if a search involving use of a medical technique, even of the most rudimentary sort, were made by other than medical personnel or in other than a medical environment—for example, if it were administered by police in the privacy of the stationhouse. To tolerate searches under these conditions might be to invite an unjustified element of personal risk of infection and pain.

There is a limit to the government's authority to intrude into the defendant's body. For example, in *Winston v. Lee*, 470 U.S. 753 (1985), the Supreme Court employed the analysis outlined in *Schmerber* and concluded that a defendant accused of armed robbery could not be compelled to undergo surgery to remove a bullet from his chest. The Court held that the suspect's interest in his health and bodily privacy outweighed the government's interest in obtaining the evidence. Also important to the Court was the fact that the government had other evidence to prove the defendant's guilt. This lowered the government's interest in having the bullet removed. If the bullet had been critical to the government's case, the result might have been different.

DNA Testing.   *Deoxyribonucleic acid (DNA)* is a complex compound with two strands that spiral around one another, forming a double helix. Within the helix are molecules, called *nucleotide bases*, that connect the strands. There are four bases, identified by the letters A, T, G, and C. The A base of one strand attaches to the T base of its counterpart strand. In the same manner, the G base of one strand connects to the C base of the opposing strand. There are more than three billion base pairs in human DNA. However, only three million of these differ from person to person. The precise vertical ordering of these pairs determines a person's genetic code.

DNA printing

Comparing body tissue samples (such as blood, skin, hair, or semen) to see if the genetic materials match. It is used to identify criminals by comparing their DNA with that found at a crime scene and used to identify a child's parent. Most states allow its use as evidence.

Through biological specimens, such as hair, blood, tissue, and semen, evidence from crime scenes can be compared with specimens from suspects. This testing is known as **DNA printing** or *genetic fingerprinting*. DNA printing compares the codes and determines if they are from the same individual. DNA testing is sophisticated, and if properly performed, nearly conclusively establishes identity. The possibility of a chance match, assuming perfect testing, has been estimated to be one in three trillion.[19]

DNA has proven to be an effective weapon for both prosecutors and defendants. In recent years, several convicted felons have used DNA testing to prove their innocence and secure their release. This has occurred, for example, in rape cases where blood and semen were used as prosecution evidence, but DNA testing was unavailable. After conviction, and from prison, these men used DNA testing to establish their innocence and set aside their verdicts.

DNA testing is not perfect. The testing method is sophisticated and errors can be made. For instance, methodology was hotly contested in the O.J. Simpson murder trial of 1995. Further, interpretations of test results differ. It is, therefore, imperative that a reliable laboratory be selected. Further, in some cases, the defense and prosecution may have independent DNA testing conducted. In spite of the possibility of error (false positive and false negative findings), courts have generally held that DNA evidence is sufficiently reliable for admission into evidence. The parties may, of course, challenge the accuracy of a particular DNA test.

Voice Tests. Compelling a suspect to speak for the purposes of audio identification is not violative of the Fifth Amendment's prohibition against compelled self-incrimination. This is because the purpose in compelling the statements is identification, not to secure testimony. Again, the voice is considered a physical characteristic that is readily observable to the ordinary person; accordingly, it is not a search under the Fourth Amendment to compel a suspect to speak.

Voice is also at issue whenever a party intends to introduce audio records that purport to be a particular individual's, such as the defendant. For example, assume John is charged with murdering Henry. The police have in their possession a tape from John's telephone answering machine. The tape contains a threat to Henry's life that the government claims was made by John. To prove that John made the threat, the prosecutor plans to introduce voice spectrographic identification evidence.

This test involves a comparison of the recording and a voice sample provided by the defendant. It compares the complex sound waves of the two for similarity. The accuracy of voice spectrographics is questionable, and therefore this type of evidence is not universally accepted by courts. In some jurisdictions, admissibility is prohibited, whereas in others the decision is left to the trial judge.

Polygraph Tests. Polygraph testing, also known as lie detection testing, measures a subject's physical responses, such as heartbeat, blood pressure, and perspiration, during questioning. This is not a new concept. The Chinese monitored the heartbeat of suspects as long as 4,000 years ago. If a suspect's heartbeat increased during a response, he was presumed to have lied.[20]

Until recently, courts have held that the results of polygraph evidence are too unreliable to be admitted at trial, unless the parties have stipulated to admission. Today, however, a few jurisdictions permit the introduction of polygraph evidence if it is determined reliable. That is, polygraph evidence is not automatically excluded, but may be if found to be unreliable in a specific case. In *United States v. Scheffer* (1998),[21] the Supreme Court held that defendants do not have a right to introduce the results of a polygraph examination over the objection of the prosecution and where evidentiary rules preclude polygraph results. The Court found that the right of defendants to present evidence has been limited historically to that which is reliable. The Court found that the scientific community is divided on the reliability of polygraph exams and asserts; the results of such exams may be excluded at trial.

In addition to the issue of reliability, a Fifth Amendment self-incrimination issue surfaces when a prosecutor seeks an order requiring a defendant to undergo a polygraph examination. The Supreme Court has stated in dictum,[22] and the lower courts have similarly ruled directly, that lie detector tests involve communications and, accordingly, that the Fifth Amendment applies. Defendants may refuse to respond to questions when the answers may be incriminating, and *Miranda*-type warnings should be given before the test begins, assuming that custody exists. Further, a prosecutor may not refer to a defendant's refusal to submit to polygraph testing at trial.

Chain of Custody. To assure that physical evidence discovered during an investigation remains unchanged and is not confused with evidence from other investigations, police must maintain the **chain of custody.** The officer who discovered the evidence must mark it, and all subsequent contacts with the evidence, such as by forensics officers, must be recorded. This creates a record known as the chain of custody. Chain-of-custody records must be kept from the time the evidence is seized until it is introduced at trial. Breaks in the chain of custody may result in exclusion of the evidence at trial.

In some instances, evidence may be admitted even though the chain of custody has been broken. If evidence is easily identified by a witness, such as its owner, then proving the chain of custody may not be necessary. This may also be true if an item is unique and can be precisely identified by its characteristics (e.g., serial and model numbers). Even in these cases, chain of custody is sometimes required, and the best practice is for the police to maintain a chain in every instance.

The burden of establishing the chain of custody rests with the party seeking admission. The standard of proof is characterized differently among the states, but usually amounts to a preponderance of the evidence. In some jurisdictions, proof of police policy, custom, and practice may be used to prove chain of custody.

chain of custody

The chronological list of those in continuous possession of a specific physical object. A person who presents physical evidence (such as a gun used in a crime) at a trial must account for its possession from time of receipt to time of trial in order for the evidence to be "admitted" by the judge. It must thus be shown that the *chain of custody* was unbroken.

Exclusion of Improper Identifications

The consequences of not providing counsel during an identification procedure after the adversary judicial proceeding has begun were discussed in *Wade*. First, testimony about an illegal identification must be excluded at trial. Second, in-court identifications may be excluded if tainted by the pretrial identification. However, if the government can show, by clear and convincing evidence, that an in-court identification has a source independent of the illegal pretrial identification, then it is to be allowed. The *Wade* Court said the following factors are to be considered when making the taint or no taint determination:

1. The prior opportunity to observe the criminal act.
2. The difference between a witness's pre-lineup description and actual description of an accused.
3. Whether the witness identified another person as the criminal before the lineup.
4. Whether the witness identified the accused by photograph prior to the lineup.
5. Whether the witness was unable to identify the accused on a previous occasion.
6. The lapse of time between the crime and the identification.

In most cases, a court will find an independent source for an in-court identification and will allow a witness to identify the defendant during trial, while prohibiting mention of the pretrial identification.

The same rules apply to identifications that are impermissibly suggestive and unreliable. They must be excluded, as must the fruits thereof, unless an independent basis for an in-court identification can be shown.

 WEB LINKS

Audio of Supreme Court
FindLaw has the oral arguments before the Supreme Court of the United States available in its site. You need audio software to listen to the arguments. Access the arguments through FindLaw's Supreme Court site. *http://www.findlaw.com/10fedgov/Judicial/supreme_court.html*

KEY TERMS

admission	DNA printing	lineup
chain of custody	interrogation	showup
confession		

REVIEW QUESTIONS

1. List the rights included in the *Miranda* warnings. When must they be read to a defendant?

2. What happens if an officer fails to read a defendant his or her rights prior to obtaining a confession?

3. Is it a violation of the Federal Wiretap Law (Title III of the Omnibus Crime Control and Safe Streets Act) for Gary to allow law enforcement officers to listen to a telephone conversation between himself and Terry without Terry's knowledge? If so, what happens if Terry makes incriminating statements?

4. Does a defendant have a right to counsel at a lineup? If so, what is the source of that right?

5. Does a defendant have a right to counsel at a photograph identification session? If so, what is the source of that right?

6. Why must law enforcement officers obtain a court order to intercept a telephone conversation using traditional line phones and not a conversation using a cordless phone?

7. What is chain of custody?

8. Assume that a prosecutor wants a defendant to submit to genetic testing to compare the defendant's DNA with that of hair found on a victim. Does the defendant have a Fourth Amendment challenge? A Fifth?

REVIEW PROBLEMS

1. While on patrol, Officer Norman heard a scream from the backyard of a house. The officer proceeded to the back of the house where he observed two people, a badly beaten victim and a young man (Tom) standing over her. Shocked by the sight of the victim, the officer exclaimed, "What happened here?" Tom responded, "I killed her and threw the baseball bat over the fence." Officer Norman restrained the young man, called for an ambulance, and retrieved the bat. While waiting for the ambulance to arrive, Officer Norman asked the young man what his motive was for injuring the woman. Tom explained his motive to the officer. The officer never mirandized Tom. A motion to suppress the statement, "I killed her and threw the baseball bat over the fence," as well as the statement explaining his motive, has been filed. Additionally, Tom claims that the bat should be excluded because it is a fruit of an illegal interrogation. What should be the outcome? Explain your answer.

2. An officer has made application for a court order approving electronic surveillance of Defendant. The order is granted, stating: "From June 1 to June 7, Officer X, having established probable cause, is granted the authority to intercept the wire communications of Defendant." The officer proceeded to enter Defendant's house, without a warrant, to install the listening device. Eventually, a recording is made of Defendant discussing his illegal activities with a friend. Defendant is arrested, charged, and has filed a motion to suppress the interception. Defendant asserts that the entry into his house was illegal. Discuss.

3. Why are the rules concerning the admissibility of confessions more stringent than for other forms of evidence?

4. Do you believe that it is self-incrimination to give blood, hair, and other such items that might prove one's guilt?

5. Describe a pretrial identification which you believe is unduly suggestive. Explain why it is too suggestive of guilt.

END NOTES

1. Fed. R. Evid. 804(b)(5).
2. *Brown v. Mississippi*, 295 U.S. 278 (1936).
3. *New York v. Quarles*, 467 U.S. 649 (1984).
4. *Illinois v. Perkins*, 496 U.S. 292 (1990).
5. *Massiah v. United States*, 377 U.S. 201 (1964).
6. *Pennsylvania v. Bruder*, 488 U.S. 9 (1988).
7. *Davis v. United States*, 512 U.S. 452 (1994).
8. *Michigan v. Mosley*, 423 U.S. 96 (1975).

9. *Oregon v. Haas*, 420 U.S. 714 (1975).
10. 18 U.S.C. § 2510 *et seq.*
11. 18 U.S.C. § 2518.
12. *Scott v. United States*, 436 U.S. 128 (1978).
13. *Tyler v. Berodt*, 877 F.2d 705 (8th Cir. 1989).
14. *Smith v. Maryland*, 442 U.S. 735 (1979).
15. *Manson v. Braithwaite*, 432 U.S. 98 (1977).
16. *Schmerber v. California*, 384 U.S. 757 (1966).
17. Braun, "Quantitative Analysis and the Law: Probability Theory as a Tool of Evidence in Criminal Trials," 1982 *Utah L. Rev.* 41, 57 n.82.
18. For a recent case where a U.S. district judge questioned whether the science of fingerprinting was adequately developed to satisfy the *Daubert* test, see *U.S. v. Llerla Plaza*, 179 F.Supp.2d 492 (E.D. Pa. 2002).
19. Dodd, "DNA Fingerprinting in Matters of Family and Crime," 26 *Med. Sci. L.* 5 (1986).
20. Morland, *An Outline of Scientific Criminology* 59–60 (2d ed. 1971).
21. 523 U.S. 303.
22. *Schmerber v. California*, 384 U.S. 757, 764 (1966).

CHAPTER 14

The Pretrial Process

CHAPTER OUTLINE

Introduction

Discovery and Investigation of Criminal
   Activity

Arrest

The Complaint

Initial Appearance

Pretrial Release and Detention

   Types of Release

   Eighth Amendment

   Detention

Preliminary Hearing

The Formal Charge

   Indictment and Grand Jury

   Information

Arraignment

Pretrial Activity

   Discovery

   Motion Practice

   Pretrial Conference

Extradition and Detainers

Removal

CHAPTER OBJECTIVES

In this chapter, you should:

- examine the processing of a criminal case from discovery of the criminal act to preparation for trial.
- learn how people are formally charged with crimes.
- learn the history, purpose, and procedures of grand juries.

- learn the law of pretrial release of defendants.
- continue to develop your case analysis and legal reasoning skills.

INTRODUCTION

What follows is an outline of the basic process a case goes through, from before arrest to after trial. As previously mentioned, the federal process is used for illustration; individual state procedures vary somewhat.

DISCOVERY AND INVESTIGATION OF CRIMINAL ACTIVITY

The process begins when law enforcement officials learn of a crime that has been committed (or is to be committed). Police learn of criminal activity in two ways. They may discover it themselves, or a citizen may report such activity.

Once police are aware of criminal activity, the pre-arrest investigation begins. There are two objectives to this stage. First, police must determine whether a crime has been committed. Second, if a crime has been committed, police attempt to gather sufficient evidence to charge and convict the person believed to have committed the crime.

ARREST

arrest
The official taking of a person to answer criminal charges. This involves at least temporarily depriving the person of liberty and may involve the use of force. An arrest is usually made by a police officer with a warrant or for a crime committed in the officer's presence.

Once adequate evidence exists, an **arrest** is made in most cases. However, in some misdemeanor cases a defendant is asked to come to the police station, and an arrest is not made unless the defendant refuses. The arrest may be made without an arrest warrant in some situations. In others, an *ex parte* hearing may be held to determine if probable cause exists to believe that the person under investigation committed the crime. If so, the judge may issue an arrest warrant.

At the time of arrest, police ordinarily search the defendant. Once at the police station, the defendant is "booked." *Booking* consists of obtaining biographical information about the defendant (name, address, etc.), fingerprinting the defendant, and taking the defendant's photograph, commonly known as a "mug shot." The defendant is usually permitted to make a telephone call at this stage.

The defendant is then searched (sometimes deloused and showered) and held in jail until further arrangements are made. For minor offenses, the defendant may be able to post bail prior to appearing before a judge. In such cases, defendants are out of jail within hours. All others have to wait for a judge to set a bail amount at an initial appearance. During and after this stage, law enforcement investigation and gathering of evidence may continue.

THE COMPLAINT

complaint
A *criminal complaint* is a formal document that charges a person with a crime.

At this stage, a police officer, or in some instances a prosecutor, files a **complaint,** which acts as the charging instrument. Fed. R. Crim. P. 3 states: "The complaint is a written statement of the essential facts constituting an offense charged. It shall be made upon oath before a magistrate." The complaint need not be written upon personal knowledge. That is, an officer may use hearsay and circumstantial evidence in a complaint. Affidavits from those who have personal knowledge, such as witnesses and victims, are often attached to the complaint.

When a warrant is sought to arrest a defendant, the complaint is often produced in support of the request for a warrant. This occurs at the *ex parte* hearing mentioned earlier. Federal law requires that a warrant be issued if probable cause is established by the complaint and its accompanying affidavits. Upon the request of the government, a summons (an order to appear) may be issued rather than an arrest warrant.[1]

If the defendant was arrested without a warrant, the complaint serves as the charging document at the initial appearance or preliminary hearing.

For traffic violations and some lesser misdemeanors, the complaint acts as both a summons to appear in court and the charging document. In such cases, the defendant appears in court on only one occasion and the ticket is used in place of an information or indictment.

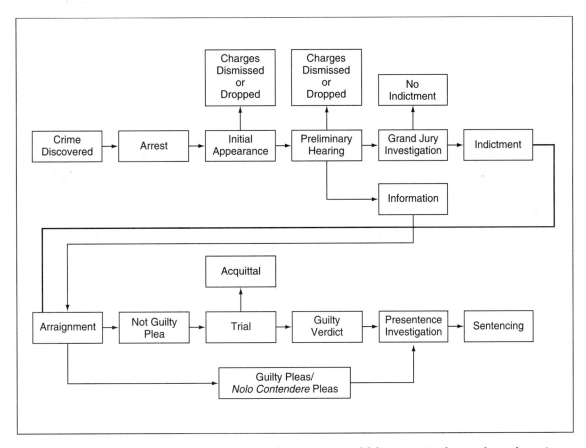

The Basic Criminal Process This charts the basic process of felony criminal cases from detection to sentencing. Misdemeanor cases normally progress through the system faster, as many stages are omitted. For example, misdemeanors are commonly prosecuted by information rather than indictment, and presentence reports are often not prepared in misdemeanor cases.

Criminal Complaint

AO 91 (Rev. 5/85) Criminal Complaint

United States District Court

_____ DISTRICT OF _____

UNITED STATES OF AMERICA
V.

CRIMINAL COMPLAINT

CASE NUMBER:

(Name and Address of Defendant)

I, the undersigned complainant being duly sworn state the following is true and correct to

the best of my knowledge and belief. On or about _____ in _____ county,

in the _____ District of _____ defendant(s) did, (Track Statutory Language of Offense)

in violation of Title _____ United States Code, Section(s) _____ .

I further state that I am a(n) _____ and that this complaint is based on

the following facts:

Continued on the attached sheet and made a part hereof: ☐ Yes   ☐ No

_____
Signature of Complainant

Sworn to before me and subscribed in my presence,

_____   at   _____
Date   City and State

_____   _____
Name & Title of Judicial Officer   Signature of Judicial Officer

AO 83 (Rev. 5/85) Summons in a Criminal Case

United States District Court

_____ DISTRICT OF _____

UNITED STATES OF AMERICA

SUMMONS IN A CRIMINAL CASE

CASE NUMBER:

(Name and Address of Defendant)

YOU ARE HEREBY SUMMONED to appear before the United States District Court at the place, date and time set forth below.

Place	Room
	Date and Time
Before:	

To answer a(n)

☐ Indictment ☐ Information ☐ Complaint ☐ Violation Notice ☐ Probation Violation Petition

Charging you with a violation of Title _____ United States Code, Section _____.

Brief description of offense:

_____   _____
Signature of Issuing Officer   Date

_____
Name and Title of Issuing Officer

Summons in a Criminal
Case (*continued*)

AO 83 (Rev. 5/85) Summons in a Criminal Case

RETURN OF SERVICE

Service was made by me on:[1]   Date

Check one box below to indicate appropriate method of service

☐ Served personally upon the defendant at: _____

_____

☐ Left summons at the defendant's dwelling house or usual place of abode with a person of suitable age and discretion then residing therein and mailed a copy of the summons to the defendant's last known address. Name of person with whom the summons was left: _____

_____

☐ Returned unexecuted: _____

_____

_____

_____

    I declare under penalty of perjury under the laws of the United States of America that the foregoing information contained in the Return of Service is true and correct.

Returned on _____   _____
          Date   Name of United States Marshal

                                   _____
                                   (by) Deputy United States Marshal

1) As to who may serve a summons see Rule 4 of the Federal Rules of Criminal Procedure

INITIAL APPEARANCE

After arrest, the defendant is taken "without unnecessary delay" before the nearest available federal magistrate.[2] In most cases this means that a defendant will be brought before the judge within twenty-four hours. However, if a defendant is arrested on a weekend, it may be the following Monday before the defendant has the initial appearance, unless a weekend session of court is held.

The first appearance is brief. If the arrest was executed under an arrest warrant, it is the duty of the presiding judge to make sure that the person arrested is the person named in the warrant. The defendant is also informed of various rights, such as the rights to remain silent and to have the assistance of counsel. If the defendant is indigent, the court will appoint counsel. The right to counsel is discussed more fully later. If the arrest was warrantless, an initial probable cause determination must occur.

In 1991, the United States Supreme Court examined the need for prompt probable cause determinations in warrantless arrest situations. In *County of Riverside v. McLaughlin*,[3] the Court held that persons arrested without a warrant must have a probable cause determination within forty-eight hours after arrest or quicker if reasonable. A defendant who asserts unreasonable delay, but was held less than forty-eight hours before a probable cause hearing was conducted, bears the burden of proving that the delay was unreasonable under the Fourth Amendment. If a defendant is held longer than forty-eight hours without a probable cause hearing, the burden of showing a bona fide emergency or other extraordinary circumstance falls on the government.

Time to gather additional evidence, ill will, or the fact that the defendant was arrested on a weekend are not sufficient to delay the probable cause determination longer than forty-eight hours.

Finally, a preliminary hearing date is set, and if the defendant is in jail, the court determines whether he or she should be released prior to trial.

PRETRIAL RELEASE AND DETENTION

In many cases, defendants are released prior to trial. A court may order many types of release, but the predominantly used methods are cash bail, surety bond, property bond, and personal recognizance.

Types of Release

The most obvious method of gaining release is to post **bail.** A defendant who has the resources may simply pay into the court the amount of the bail.

Whenever a third party, usually a professional bondsman, agrees to pay the bond for a defendant, a surety bond is created. The common practice is for the defendant to pay the surety 10 percent or more of the bond amount in exchange for the bondsman making the defendant's bail. The 10 percent is not refunded to the defendant after the case is concluded.

bail
The money or property given as security for a defendant's appearance in court. The money, often in the form of a bail bond, may be lost if the defendant released does not appear in court.

Some sureties require security (collateral) before a bond will be issued. Defendants may pledge cars, houses, or other property to obtain release. This is a property bond.

For many misdemeanors and a few felonies, a defendant may be released on personal recognizance. To gain such a release, a defendant need only promise to appear.

Regardless of the type of release, courts frequently impose conditions upon the defendant. Defendants who are arrested or caught intimidating witnesses or interfering with the judicial process may be jailed until trial.

Eighth Amendment

The Eighth Amendment proscribes the imposition of "excessive bail." This provision may be applicable to the states through the Fourteenth Amendment. The purpose of imposing money bail is to assure the defendant's appearance at trial, not to inflict punishment. Bail set higher than necessary to accomplish this purpose is deemed excessive.[4] In practice, courts have significant discretion in setting bail and are rarely reversed.

The Supreme Court has held that the mere fact that a defendant cannot pay the amount set by a court does not make it excessive. Additionally, the Court has stated that not all defendants have a right to bail. Defendants who are a danger to the community or are unlikely to appear for trial may be held without bail.

The exact meaning of the Eighth Amendment has not been spelled out by the Supreme Court. Whether pretrial detention laws, especially those that create a presumption of detention, are constitutional remains to be seen.

Detention

The federal government (and presumably most states, if not all) provides for detention of some defendants prior to trial.

Pretrial detention may not be used to punish a person. To do so violates a person's due process right to be free from punishment without a fair trial. However, a defendant may be detained if there is reason to believe that he or she will not appear for trial or if he or she poses a threat to others.

In the federal system, the defendant is entitled to an adversary hearing concerning pretrial detention, and the government must prove by clear and convincing evidence that the defendant is either dangerous or unlikely to appear for trial.[5] The adversary hearing must be held at the initial appearance, or upon the motion of the defendant or the government, it may be continued.

Although the general rule is that the government bears the burden of proving that a defendant must be detained, there are exceptions. There are two classes of presumptions in the federal statute. One presumes that certain defendants will not appear for trial, and another presumes that certain defendants are a danger to the community. For example, defendants charged with crimes of violence who have a prior conviction for a crime of violence, which was committed while the defendant was released pending trial, are presumed to be dangerous to the community. It is also presumed that defendants charged with drug crimes that carry ten years or more imprisonment will flee. These presumptions also apply to many other defendants.[6] The presumption is rebuttable, and the defendant has the burden of disproving it. Some question the constitutionality of such presumptions, and it remains to be seen whether such statutes will be reversed or upheld.

Many states have statutes that require detention of persons charged with crimes punishable by life imprisonment or death, provided that the proof of guilt is great.

PRELIMINARY HEARING

The defendant's second appearance before a judge is the **preliminary hearing.** How this stage is handled by the states varies significantly. At the preliminary hearing, the court determines if probable cause to believe the accused committed the crime exists. If probable cause is found, the defendant is "bound over" to the next stage of the process. The next stage is either trial or review by grand jury. If probable cause is not established, the defendant is released.

If indictment by grand jury is required, the case is bound over to the grand jury. The grand jury is not bound by the judge's decision that probable cause exists; it makes an independent decision whether to charge the defendant. If grand jury review is not required, the defendant is bound over for trial.

The purpose of the preliminary hearing is to have an impartial third party review the facts to be sure that probable cause exists. There is no constitutional requirement for a preliminary hearing.[7] However, many states do provide for preliminary hearings.

It is common to permit prosecutors to bypass the preliminary hearing either by submitting the case to a grand jury or by directly filing an information. Defendants often waive the preliminary hearing. In some states, prosecutors may demand a preliminary hearing over the objection of the defendant.

The preliminary hearing can be quite lengthy compared to a defendant's initial appearance. The hearing is adversarial. Witnesses are called and the attorneys are allowed to make arguments. Rules of evidence are applied in modified form, so hearsay and illegally obtained evidence are often considered. Defendants have a right to counsel, and may also be allowed to cross-examine the prosecution witnesses and to present defense witnesses. The right to counsel is a matter of federal constitutional law. The other two rights are granted by state laws. The preliminary hearing can be an important asset to both prosecution and defense, as it can serve as a source of discovery.

The preliminary hearing is different from the initial probable cause determination required by *County of Riverside v. McLaughlin*. The initial determination is constitutionally required, whereas the preliminary hearing is not. Further, although the same terminology is used (i.e., probable cause), less evidence is needed to satisfy the government's obligation at the initial determination than at the preliminary hearing. Probable cause at the initial hearing equates with the probable cause required to obtain a warrant, which is generally recognized

preliminary hearing
The first court proceeding on a criminal charge, in federal courts and many state courts, by a magistrate or a judge to decide whether there is enough evidence for the government to continue with the case and to require the defendant to post bail or be held for trial.

Subpoena to Testify
Before Grand Jury

AO 106 (Rev. 5/85) Subpoena to Testify Before Grand Jury

United States District Court

_____ DISTRICT OF _____

To

**SUBPOENA TO TESTIFY
BEFORE GRAND JURY**

SUBPOENA FOR:
☐ PERSON   ☐ DOCUMENT(S) OR OBJECT(S)

YOU ARE HEREBY COMMANDED to appear and testify before the Grand Jury of the United States District Court at the place, date, and time specified below.

PLACE	COURTROOM
	DATE AND TIME

YOU ARE ALSO COMMANDED to bring with you the following document(s) or object(s):*

☐ *Please see additional information on reverse*

This subpoena shall remain in effect until you are granted leave to depart by the court or by an officer acting on behalf of the court.

CLERK	DATE
(BY) DEPUTY CLERK	

This subpoena is issued on application of the United States of America	NAME, ADDRESS AND PHONE NUMBER OF ASSISTANT U.S. ATTORNEY

*If not applicable, enter "none"

AO 110 (Rev. 5/85) Subpoena to Testify Before Grand Jury

RETURN OF SERVICE[1]

	DATE	PLACE
RECEIVED BY SERVER		
SERVED	DATE	PLACE

SERVED ON (NAME)

SERVED BY	TITLE

STATEMENT OF SERVICE FEES

TRAVEL	SERVICES	TOTAL

DECLARATION OF SERVER[2]

    I declare under penalty of perjury under the laws of the United States of America that the foregoing information contained in the Return of Service and Statement of Service Fees is true and correct.

Executed on _____   _____
                    Date   *Signature of Server*

                                        _____
                                                    Address of Server

ADDITIONAL INFORMATION

(1) As to who may serve a subpoena and the manner of its service see Rule 17(d), Federal Rules of Criminal Procedure, or Rule 45(c), Federal Rules of Civil Procedure.

(2) "Fees and mileage need not be tendered to the witness upon service of a subpoena issued on behalf of the United States or an officer or agency thereof (Rule 45(c), Federal Rules of Civil Procedure Rule 17(d), Federal Rules of Criminal Procedure) or on behalf of certain indigent parties and criminal defendants who are unable to pay such costs (28 USC 1825, Rule 17(b) Federal Rules of Criminal Procedure)."

as requiring less proof than probable cause at the later preliminary hearing. Also in contrast is the fact that the probable cause hearing required by *County of Riverside* will likely be one-sided. That is, only the government will present evidence. Some states, however, such as California, permit defendants to present evidence at preliminary hearings.

Fed. R. Crim. P. 5 requires that the date for "preliminary examination" be scheduled at the defendant's initial appearance. It shall be held within ten days of the initial appearance if the defendant is in custody and within twenty if the defendant has been released.

In federal courts and in many states, probable cause may be founded upon hearsay evidence.[8] Motions to suppress illegally seized evidence are made after the preliminary hearing, so such evidence may be considered at the preliminary examination stage. If a grand jury has issued an indictment, the preliminary hearing may be dispensed within the federal system.[9] Many states have a similar rule.

THE FORMAL CHARGE

information

A formal accusation of a crime made by a proper public official such as a prosecuting attorney.

There are two formal charges: the **information** and the **indictment.** Informations are charges filed by prosecutors. Indictments are charges issued by grand juries. Once filed, an information or indictment replaces the complaint and becomes the formal charging instrument.

indictment

A sworn written accusation of a crime, made against a person by a prosecutor to a *grand* jury.

Indictment and Grand Jury

grand jury

Persons who receive complaints and accusations of crime, hear preliminary evidence on the complaining side, and make formal accusations or indictments.

Purpose of the Grand Jury.   In early American history, **grand juries** were used to guard against unfair and arbitrary government prosecutions. The framers of the United States Constitution believed grand jury review so important that they stated in the Fifth Amendment: "[N]o person shall be held to answer for a capital, or otherwise infamous, crime, unless on a presentment or indictment of a Grand Jury."

Grand juries consist of twelve to twenty-three persons who are usually selected in the same method as petit juries (juries that determine guilt or innocence). Grand juries sit for longer periods of time and are called to hear cases as needed.

The primary objective of grand jury review is the same as the preliminary hearing: to determine whether there is probable cause to believe that a target of the investigation committed the alleged crime. The grand jury, therefore, was intended to protect individuals from unwarranted prosecutions. Because the grand jury proceedings are closed, individuals investigated but not charged are not subjected to the public humiliation and damage to reputation that often results from a more public investigation. The secondary objective of the grand jury has become its primary purpose, as defined by prosecutors: to facilitate investigation.

Procedures of the Grand Jury.   First, grand juries are closed. The public, including the defendant, is not entitled to attend. Second, the prosecutor runs the show before the grand jury, and the defendant has no right to present evidence or to make a statement. Third, the actions of grand juries are secret. Those who attend are not permitted to disclose what transpires. Defendants have no right to know what evidence is presented to a grand jury, unless it is exculpatory (tends to prove the defendant's innocence). Fourth, those who testify before the grand jury are not entitled to have counsel in the jury room.[10] In most states witnesses are permitted to leave the proceeding to confer with counsel waiting directly outside. Because statements made to a grand jury can be used later, the Fifth Amendment right to be free from self-incrimination is available to witnesses. Grand juries can overcome Fifth Amendment claims (refusals to testify) by granting witnesses immunity from prosecution. Also, witnesses may not refuse to testify because the inquiry is the result of illegally seized evidence. To permit refusal or exclusion would not further the objective of the exclusionary rule (to deter police misconduct) and would substantially interfere with the grand jury process.[11]

Grand juries possess the power to order people to appear, to subpoena documents, to hold people in contempt, and to grant immunity in order to procure testimony.

As a general proposition, prosecutors control grand juries. For the most part, grand juries convene only when called by the prosecutor. The prosecutor decides what witnesses need to be called and who should be given immunity. Nearly all people targeted (the person the prosecutor believes guilty) by prosecutors are indicted. Many criticize the grand jury system for this reason: the government has too much control over the grand juries. The argument is reasonable when one considers the historical purpose of grand jury review.

The proponents of abolishing the grand jury system argue that not only have grand juries lost their independence, but they also now act to the benefit of prosecutors by allowing discovery of information that may have otherwise been unavailable.

The Indictment.   After a grand jury has completed its investigation, a vote on whether to charge is taken. In the federal system, grand juries consist of sixteen to twenty-three people. At least twelve must vote for indictment.[12] In many cases indictments are sealed until the indicted defendant is arrested.

The Constitution requires that all federal prosecutions for capital and infamous crimes be by indictment. However, if a defendant waives the right to grand jury review, he or she may be charged by information. The waiver of indictment form used in federal court is shown in Exhibit 14.1. Crimes punishable by one year or longer in prison are "infamous."[13] A defendant may not waive indictment in federal capital cases. It is always proper to charge corporations by information, as imprisonment is not possible.

The United States Supreme Court has ruled that grand jury review is not a fundamental right; therefore, the Fifth Amendment requirement for indictment is not applicable against the states. However, many states have grand juries and require that serious charges be brought by indictment.

Indictments must be written and state in "plain and concise" terms the essential facts constituting the offense charged.[14] Indictments are liberally read, and technical errors do not make them invalid. However, an indictment must

EXHIBIT 14.1

Waiver of Indictment

AO 455 (Rev. 5/85) Waiver of Indictment

United States District Court

_____ DISTRICT OF _____

UNITED STATES OF AMERICA
V.

WAIVER OF INDICTMENT

CASE NUMBER:

I, _____, the above named defendant, who is accused of

being advised of the nature of the charge(s), the proposed information, and of my rights,

hereby waive in open court on _____ prosecution by indictment and
                                                      Date

consent that the proceeding may be by information rather than by indictment.

_____
Defendant

_____
Counsel for Defendant

Before _____
              Judicial Officer

contain all the essential elements of the crime charged. If an indictment charges more than one crime, each crime must be made a separate count.[15] Jurisdiction must be noted, and the law upon which the charge is made must be cited. The indictment filed against Ted Bundy is shown in Exhibit 14.2. It was upon this indictment that Ted Bundy was prosecuted, convicted, and executed.

If a defendant believes that an indictment is fatally deficient it may be attacked by a **motion** to **quash.** Indictments are not quashed because of technical errors. An example of a valid reason to quash is failure to allege an essential element of the crime charged. It is not violative of the Fifth Amendment's Double Jeopardy Clause for a grand jury to issue a second indictment after the first has been quashed or dismissed.

In some jurisdictions, a prosecutor may refuse to prosecute, even though an indictment has been issued. In that situation, the prosecutor must assist the jury in preparing the document and must usually explain why a prosecution will not be maintained. In other instances, the prosecutor *must* pursue the case. The former situation represents federal law, that is, the decision on whether to prosecute falls within the purview of the federal prosecutor, who may properly refuse to sign an indictment and prosecute the case.[16]

motion

A request that a judge make a ruling or take some other action.

quash

Overthrow; annul; completely do away with. *Quash* usually refers to a court stopping a subpoena, an order, or an indictment.

SIDEBAR

PLEA BARGAINING   Statistics vary, but it is widely accepted that approximately 90 percent of all felony cases are disposed of by pleas of guilty. The number is probably higher for misdemeanors. There is no question that plea bargaining greatly reduces the amount of time expended on trials. Warren Burger, past Chief Justice of the United States Supreme Court, estimated that judicial resources in the United States would have to be doubled if only 20 percent of all criminal cases went to trial. This conclusion was in large part a matter of simple math and has been criticized. In any event, plea bargaining is an important part of the criminal justice system. It is so important that the Supreme Court has stated that it "is not only an essential part of the process but a highly desirable part." *Santobello v. New York,* 404 U.S. 257, 261 (1971).

In *Boykin v. Alabama,* 395 U.S. 238 (1969), it was announced that all defendants who plead guilty do so voluntarily and knowingly, the latter meaning that the defendant understands the rights that are waived by entering a plea of guilty.

The plea negotiation involves the defendant and the prosecutor. Judges do not participate in plea negotiations. After a bargain is reached, it is presented to the trial court. The court may then accept the agreement and sentence the defendant accordingly. With good cause, the court may also reject the agreement. Some states permit defendants to withdraw their guilty pleas if the judge rejects the bargain. In others the judge has the discretion of allowing the defendant to withdraw the guilty plea or sentencing the defendant contrary to the bargain.

Sources: Burger, *The State of the Judiciary,* 56 A.B.A. J. 929 (1970) and Note, *Is Plea Bargaining Inevitable?,* 97 Harv. L. Rev. 1037 (1984).

EXHIBIT 14.2

Ted Bundy Indictment

IN THE CIRCUIT COURT OF THE
SECOND JUDICIAL CIRCUIT, IN AND
FOR LEON COUNTY, FLORIDA.

CASE NO. 78–670

) INDICTMENT FOR:

THE STATE OF FLORIDA,

-vs-

THEODORE ROBERT BUNDY,

Defendant,

) BURGLARY OF DWELLING
) MURDER IN THE FIRST DEGREE
) MURDER IN THE FIRST DEGREE
) ATTEMPTED MURDER IN THE
)   FIRST DEGREE
) ATTEMPTED MURDER IN THE
)   FIRST DEGREE
) BURGLARY OF DWELLING
) ATTEMPTED MURDER IN THE
)   FIRST DEGREE

IN THE NAME OF AND BY THE AUTHORITY OF THE
STATE OF FLORIDA:

The Grand Jurors of the State of Florida, empaneled and sworn to inquire and true presentment made in and for the County of Leon, upon their oaths, do present that

THEODORE ROBERT BUNDY

on the 15th day of January, 1978, in Leon County, Florida, did then and there unlawfully enter or remain in a structure located at 661 West Jefferson Street, the dwelling of Karen Chandler and/or Kathy Kleiner, with the intent to commit the offense of Battery therein, and in the course of committing such burglary the said THEODORE ROBERT BUNDY did make an assault upon Karen Chandler and/or Kathy Kleiner, contrary to Section 810.02, Florida Statutes;

And Your Grand jurors being present in said Court further gives the Court to be informed and understand that THEODORE ROBERT BUNDY on the 15th day of January, 1978, in Leon County, Florida, did then and there unlawfully kill a human being, to-wit: Margaret Bowman, by strangling and/or beating her, and said killing was perpetuated by said THEODORE ROBERT BUNDY from, or with a premeditated design or intent to effect the death of said Margaret Bowman, contrary to Section 782.04, Florida Statutes;

And Your Grand Jurors being present in said Court further gives the Court to be informed and understand that THEODORE ROBERT BUNDY on the 15th day of January, 1978, in Leon County, Florida, did then and there . . .

Contrary to the form of the Statute in such case made and provided and against the peace and dignity of the State of Florida.

Harry Morrison

AS STATE ATTORNEY, SECOND JUDICIAL
CIRCUIT OF FLORIDA, IN AND FOR LEON
COUNTY; PROSECUTING FOR SAID STATE.

Information

The second formal method of charging someone with a crime is by information. Informations are filed by prosecutors without grand jury review. The trend is away from indictments and toward charging by information.

If a defendant has been initially charged by complaint, the prosecutor must independently review the evidence and determine whether a prosecution is warranted. If not, a prosecutor may file a *nolle prosequi*. If so, the information is filed.

Informations serve the same function as indictments. Under the federal rules, informations must take the same form as indictments. They must be plain, concise, and in writing. All essential elements, as well as the statute relied upon by the government, must be included.[17] (See the sample criminal information in Chapter 4, page 94) As is true of indictments, informations must be filed with the appropriate court.

Defendants may seek to have defective informations quashed or dismissed. The rules regarding defectiveness are the same for informations as for indictments. Technical errors are not fatal.

ARRAIGNMENT

After the formal charge has been filed, the defendant is brought to the trial court for **arraignment.** This is the hearing at which the defendant is read the formal charge and is asked to enter a **plea.**

Defendants may plead guilty, not guilty, or *nolo contendere*. By pleading guilty a defendant admits all the charges contained in the charging document, unless a plea agreement has been reached with the government. A **plea agreement**, also known as a *plea bargain*, is the product of negotiations between the prosecutor and the defendant. It is common for the prosecution to dismiss one or more charges of a multicount charge or to reduce a charge in exchange for a defendant's plea of guilty.

Plea bargaining is an important aspect of criminal procedure. More than 90 percent of all felony cases are disposed of by pleas of guilty. Most guilty pleas are the result of plea bargaining.

By pleading guilty defendants waive a host of rights. The right to a jury trial and to be proven guilty beyond a reasonable doubt are two of the rights waived by a guilty plea. Because of the significance of such waivers, courts must be sure that guilty pleas are given knowingly and voluntarily. To be knowing, a defendant must understand his or her rights and that he or she is waiving them by making the plea. The plea must be free of coercion or duress to be voluntary. Of course, the inducement of a plea bargain is not coercion.

The court must also find that a factual basis exists before a plea of guilty can be accepted. This means that there must be sufficient facts in the record to support the conclusion that the defendant committed the crime. A defendant has no right to plead guilty to a crime he or she did not commit. The factual basis may be established by the testimony of the investigating officer or by the

arraignment
The hearing at which a defendant is brought before a judge to hear the charges and to enter a plea (guilty, not guilty, etc.)

plea
The **defendant's** formal answer to a criminal charge. The defendant says: "guilty," "not guilty" or "nolo contendere" (no contest).

plea bargain (plea agreement)
Negotiations between a prosecutor and a criminal defendant's lawyer, attempting to resolve a criminal case without trial.

defendant recounting what transpired. Once the plea is taken, the court will either impose sentence or set a future date for sentencing.

If a defendant enters a not guilty plea, the court will set a trial date. In some instances, courts will set a pretrial schedule, which will include a pretrial conference date and a deadline for filing pretrial motions.

Finally, a plea of *nolo contendere* may be entered. *Nolo contendere* is a Latin phrase that translates to "I do not contest it." The defendant who pleads *nolo contendere* neither admits nor denies the charges and has no intent of defending himself or herself.

Nolo contendere is treated as a plea of guilty. That is, the government must establish that a factual basis exists to believe the defendant committed the offense, and the court accepting the plea must be sure that the plea is made voluntarily and knowingly. In most jurisdictions a defendant may plead *nolo contendere* only with the approval of the court. This is true in the courts of the United States.[18]

The advantage of a no contest plea over a guilty plea is that the no contest plea cannot be used in a later civil proceeding against the defendant, whereas a guilty plea may be used. If the case is not disposed of by a plea of guilty or *nolo contendere*, the parties begin preparing for trial.

PRETRIAL ACTIVITY

Discovery

discovery

The formal and informal exchange of information between the prosecution and the defense.

Discovery refers to a process of exchanging information between the prosecution and defense. Discovery is not as broad in criminal cases as in civil.

The amount of discovery that should be allowed is heavily debated. Those favoring broad discovery contend that limited discovery leads to "trial by ambush," which is not in the best interests of justice. The purpose of a trial is to discover the truth and achieve justice, not to award the better game-player. Proponents of this position claim that unexpected evidence at trial is inefficient, costly, and unfair. It is inefficient because trials often have to be delayed to give one party time to prepare a response to the unexpected evidence. Such tactics lead to time problems for the parties as well as the trial court. They may also be unfair. It is possible that evidence that was once available may not be so at trial. If the party surprised at trial had known about the unexpected evidence, other contrary evidence could have been secured and a proper defense or response could have been prepared.

Finally, it appears unfair to subject defendants to the possibility of surprise when the government is insulated from certain surprises. For example, affirmative defenses must be specially pled. Intent to rely on alibi and insanity defenses must be provided to the government in most jurisdictions, often with strict enforcement of time requirements. The purpose of these rules is to prevent surprises to the government at trial. Those who support expanded discovery feel that it is unfair to place such requirements upon defendants, but not upon the government.

Those opposed contend that expansive discovery increases the likelihood that defendants will manipulate the system. In particular, defendants might intimidate government witnesses. Additionally, opponents contend that it is easier for a defendant to skillfully plan his or her testimony, even if false, if a defendant knows the government's entire case. For example, if a defendant originally planned to assert an alibi but finds out through discovery that the government has a witness placing him at the location of the crime, he has been provided an opportunity to change his defense. Today, discovery in criminal proceedings is quite limited in many jurisdictions, including federal courts. A few states have enlarged what information may be obtained prior to trial.

What follows is an examination of the federal rules, as well as constitutional requirements for discovery.

Bill of Particulars. One method that defendants have to obtain information about the government's case is through a **bill of particulars.** The purpose of bills of particulars is to make general indictments and informations more specific. Fed. R. Crim. P. 7(f) allows district courts to order prosecutors to file a bill of particulars.

Bills of particulars are not true discovery devices. If the charging instrument is sufficiently clear and detailed, the court will not grant a defense motion for particularization of the charge. A bill of particulars is intended to provide a defendant with details about the charges that are necessary for the preparation of a defense and to avoid prejudicial surprise at trial.[19] The test is not whether the indictment is sufficiently drawn; the question is whether the information is necessary to avoid prejudice to the defendant.

bill of particulars
A detailed, formal, written statement of charges or claims by a plaintiff or the prosecutor (given upon the defendant's formal request to the court for more detailed information).

Statements of the Defendant. Fed. R. Crim. P. 16(a) (1) (A) states that upon request the government must allow the defendant to inspect, copy, or photograph all prior relevant written and recorded statements made by the defendant. This includes testimony that defendants give before grand juries—an exception to the rule of secrecy of grand jury proceedings.

Prosecutors are required to allow inspection of all statements made by the defendant that are in the possession of the prosecution or that may be discovered through due diligence. Hence, if a defendant makes a statement to an arresting officer, which is recorded or reduced to writing, the prosecutor must allow defense inspection even though the statement may be in the possession of the officer and not the prosecutor.

In addition to recorded statements and writings, the government is required to inform the defendant of "the substance of any oral statement that the government intends to offer in evidence." This means that statements made by a defendant that are summarized by the police (or other government agent), but not verbatim or signed by the defendant, are also discoverable. However, such evidence is discoverable only if the prosecution intends to use it at trial. This is not true of written and recorded statements of a defendant.

Criminal Record of the Defendant. Fed. R. Crim. P. 16 also requires prosecutors to furnish a copy of the defendant's criminal record to the defendant. This includes not only the records known to the prosecutor, but also those that can be discovered through due diligence.

Documents and Tangible Objects.   Under Rule 16, defendants are also entitled to inspect and copy photographs, books, tangible objects, papers, buildings, and places that are in the possession of the government if:

1. The item is material to preparation of the defendant's defense, or
2. The item is going to be used by the government at trial, or
3. The item was obtained from, or belongs to, the defendant.

The situations in which this might apply are countless. For example, if the police take pictures of the scene of a crime, this provision allows the defendant to view and copy those pictures prior to trial. Or, if the police seize a building that was used to manufacture drugs, the defendant can invoke this rule to gain access to the premises.

This section of Rule 16 has a reciprocal provision. That is, defendants must allow the government to inspect and copy defense items. However, the rule is not as broad for government discovery. Defendants only have to permit inspection and copy of those items intended to be used at trial.

Scientific Reports and Tests.   All scientific reports and tests in the possession of the government (or that can be discovered through due diligence) must be turned over to the defendant, if requested.

This provision includes reports and conclusions of mental examinations of the defendant, autopsy reports, drug tests, fingerprint analysis, blood tests, DNA (genetic) tests, ballistic tests, and other related tests and examinations.

The defendant must accord the government reciprocity, if requested. For example, if a defendant undergoes an independent mental examination, the government is entitled to review the report of the evaluator prior to trial.

Statements of Witnesses/Jencks Act.   In the federal system, defendants are not entitled to inspect or copy statements of prosecution witnesses prior to trial.

However, a federal statute, commonly known as the Jencks Act,[20] permits a defendant to review a prior written or recorded statement after the witness has testified for the government. Reviewing such statements may prove important to show that a witness is inconsistent, biased, or has a bad memory.

This procedure often causes trial delay, as defendants usually request time between direct examination and cross-examination to review such statements. For this reason, some federal prosecutors provide such information prior to trial. The Jencks Act is a matter of federal statutory law and does not apply in state criminal prosecutions.

deposition
The process of taking a witness's sworn out-of-court testimony. The questioning is usually done by a lawyer, with the lawyer from the other side given a chance to attend and participate.

Depositions.   A **deposition** is oral testimony given under oath, not in a court. In civil procedure, depositions are freely conducted. Upon notice to a party or subpoena to a witness, an attorney can call a person to testify prior to trial. This is not so in criminal practice.

Fed. R. Crim. P. 15 allows depositions only when "exceptional circumstances" exist. Expected absence of a witness at trial is an example of an exceptional circumstance. If such a circumstance is shown, the deposition may be ordered by the trial court, and the deposition may be used at trial. Of course, both the defendant and government have the opportunity to question the witness at the deposition.

Brady Doctrine. Although most discovery occurs under the authority of statutes and court rules, the Constitution also requires disclosure of information by the government in some situations. In *Brady v. Maryland*, the Supreme Court announced what is now referred to as the Brady doctrine.

Obviously, *Brady* applies to both state and federal prosecutions. Note that only exculpatory evidence must be provided. Evidence that tends to prove a defendant's innocence is exculpatory. *Brady* does not stand for the proposition that prosecutors must reveal incriminating evidence to defendants.

 CASE

BRADY V. MARYLAND

373 U.S. 83 (1962)

Petitioner and companion, Boblit, were found guilty of murder in the first degree and were sentenced to death. . . . Their trials were separate, petitioner being tried first. At his trial Brady took the stand and admitted his participation in the crime, but he claimed that Boblit did the actual killing. And, in his summation to the jury, Brady's counsel conceded that Brady was guilty of murder in the first degree, asking only that the jury return that verdict "without capital punishment." Prior to the trial petitioner's counsel had requested the prosecution to allow him to examine Boblit's extrajudicial statements. Several of those statements were shown to him; but one dated July 9, 1958, in which Boblit admitted the actual homicide, was withheld by the prosecution and did not come to petitioner's notice until after he had been tried, convicted, and sentenced, and after his conviction had been affirmed.

Petitioner moved the trial court for a new trial based on the newly discovered evidence that had been suppressed by the prosecution. Petitioner's appeal from a denial of that motion was dismissed by the Court of Appeals without prejudice to relief under the Maryland Post Conviction Procedures Act. . . . The petition for post-conviction relief was dismissed by the trial court; and on appeal the Court of Appeals held that suppression of the evidence by the prosecution denied petitioner due process of law and remanded the case for a retrial of the question of punishment, not the question of guilt. . . .

We now hold that the suppression by the prosecution of evidence favorable to an accused upon request violates due process where the evidence is material either to guilt or to punishment, irrespective of the good faith or bad faith of the prosecution.

[This principle] is not punishment of society for misdeeds of a prosecutor but avoidance of an unfair trial to the accused. Society wins not only when the guilty are convicted but when criminal trials are fair; our system of the administration of justice suffers when any accused is treated unfairly. An inscription on the walls of the Department of Justice states the proposition candidly for the federal domain: "The United States wins its point whenever justice is done its citizens in the courts." A prosecution that withholds evidence on demand of an accused which, if made available, would tend to exculpate him or reduce the penalty helps shape a trial that bears heavily on the defendant. That casts the prosecutor in the role of an architect of a proceeding that does not comport with standards of justice.

In most situations, disclosure at trial will satisfy *Brady*. However, if disclosure at trial would prejudice a defendant, pretrial disclosure may be constitutionally required. As is sometimes the case with Jencks Act materials, prosecutors may provide such information prior to trial as a courtesy.

In a case related to *Brady*, the Supreme Court found that it is violative of due process for prosecutors to use perjured testimony or to deceive juries. This is true even if the perjury was unsolicited by the prosecuting attorney. As such, a prosecutor has a duty to correct any testimony of a witness that he or she knows is false.[21]

Although *Brady* and related cases are law in both state and federal prosecutions, the other discovery rules differ. Be sure to check local law to determine what your client has a right to discover.

Freedom of Information Laws.   The federal government and most, if not all, states have statutes requiring the public disclosure of files, documents, and other information in the possession of the government.[22] The federal statute is known as the Freedom of Information Act (FOIA).[23]

There are nine exemptions to the federal FOIA. If a request for information falls into one of the nine exemptions, the government may withhold disclosure. Otherwise, disclosure is mandated.

One of the exemptions provides that law enforcement records may be withheld if disclosure will:

1. Interfere with enforcement proceedings.
2. Deprive a person of a fair trial or an impartial adjudication.
3. Constitute an unwarranted invasion of personal privacy.
4. Disclose the identity of a confidential source.
5. Disclose investigative techniques and procedures.
6. Endanger the life or physical safety of law enforcement personnel.

The FOIA is not a discovery device. It is a statute of general applicability and any person may request inspection or production of documents under its authority. The purpose of the FOIA, which is unrelated to litigation, is the promotion of democracy by having an informed citizenry; it keeps the governors accountable to the governed.

The fact that the FOIA was not specifically intended to be used for discovery in litigation does not foreclose that use. However, although the FOIA may be used to obtain information, it is not intended to displace or supplement the recognized forms of discovery.[24] Nor shall the process of obtaining information through the FOIA be cause for delaying a criminal proceeding. Therefore, requests for information under the FOIA are separate from a defendant's discovery requests in a criminal case.[25]

Hence, defendants may seek information under the FOIA, but such requests are not part of the criminal discovery process, and criminal proceedings will not be delayed to wait for such requests to be answered or disputes over disclosure to be adjudicated.

The same principles apply to other disclosure laws. For example, the federal Privacy Act[26] provides that individuals have a right to discover the contents of files containing information about them. Again, requests for information under this law are aside from, not in addition to, criminal discovery rules.

Motion Practice

In both civil and criminal practice, a motion is a request made to a court for it to do something. In most cases a party who files a motion is seeking an order from the court. Generally, when a person desires something from a court, a formal motion must be filed and copies sent to opposing counsel. On occasion, oral motions are made. This is most common during trials and hearings. Some of the most common motions are discussed here.

Motion to Dismiss/Quash. If a defendant believes that the indictment or information is fatally flawed, the appropriate remedy is a motion to dismiss. In some jurisdictions, this would be called a motion to quash. Examples of fatal flaws in the charging instrument are: the court lacks jurisdiction; the facts alleged do not amount to a crime; an essential element is not charged; or the defendant has a legal defense, such as double jeopardy.

If the form of the charging instrument is attacked, courts often permit prosecutors to amend the charge rather than dismissing it entirely. Dismissal of an indictment or information does not mean that the defendant cannot be recharged. A person is not in "jeopardy" under the Fifth Amendment until later in the proceeding.

Motion to Suppress. You have already learned that evidence obtained in an unconstitutional manner may not be used at trial. Objection at trial to the admission of such evidence is one method of excluding such evidence. Another is by way of a motion to suppress prior to trial.

A separate hearing is conducted prior to trial to determine whether the motion to suppress should be granted. Defendants may testify at suppression hearings, and their testimony may not be used against them at trial.[27] To allow a defendant's testimony from a suppression hearing to be used at trial would place the defendant in a position of choosing between the right to suppress evidence and the right to be free from self-incrimination. The best alternative is to allow the defendant to testify and to prohibit that testimony from being used later.

Who has the burden of proof in suppression hearings varies by jurisdiction and what it is the defendant wishes to be suppressed. For example, most jurisdictions place the burden of proving that a search pursuant to a warrant was unconstitutional on the defendant. The opposite is true if there was no warrant; the government bears the burden of proving the propriety of the search. Most jurisdictions also place the burden of proving that a confession was voluntary upon the prosecution.

Motion for Change of Venue. *Venue* means place for trial. In state criminal proceedings, venue usually lies in the county where the crime occurred. In federal proceedings, venue lies in the district where the crime occurred. Many federal crimes are interstate in character, and the charges may be filed in any district where the crime took place.

Fed. R. Crim. P. 21 permits transfer of a case from one district to another if "the defendant cannot obtain a fair and impartial trial" at the location where the case is pending. In addition, a district judge may transfer a case if it is most convenient for the defendant and witnesses.

Pretrial publicity of criminal matters may be cause to transfer a case (change venue in state proceedings). If a defendant receives considerable negative media coverage, it may be necessary to try the defendant in another location.

Because of the First Amendment free press issue, judges are generally prohibited from excluding the press or public from hearings.[28] In some instances judges may order the attorneys involved in a case not to provide information to anyone not involved in the proceeding.

Motion for Severance.   Fed. R. Crim. P. 8 permits two or more defendants to be charged in the same information or indictment if they were involved in the same crime. That rule also permits joinder of two offenses by the same person in one charging instrument, provided they are similar in character or arise out of the same set of facts.

In some situations, severance of the two defendants may be necessary to assure fair trials. For example, if two defendants have antagonistic defenses, severance must be granted. Defenses are *antagonistic* if the jury must disbelieve one by believing the other. For example, if Defendant A denies being at the scene of a crime, and Defendant B claims that they were both there, but also claims that A forced him to commit the crime, their defenses are antagonistic.

If a defendant is charged with two or more offenses, it may be necessary to sever them to have a fair trial. For example, if a defendant plans to testify concerning one charge and not the other, severance is necessary.

Motion In Limine.   Prior to trial, both the defendant and the prosecution may file motions in limine. This is a request that the court order the other party not to mention or attempt to question a witness about some matter. A motion in limine is similar to a motion to suppress, except that it encompasses more than admission of illegally seized evidence.

For example, if one anticipates that the opposing counsel will attempt to question a witness about evidence that is inadmissible under the rules of evidence (e.g., hearsay), a motion in limine may be filed to avoid having to object at trial. This is important, as often a witness may blurt out the answer before an attorney has had an opportunity to object. In addition, knowing whether the judge will permit the admission of evidence prior to trial helps an attorney to plan the case.

Other Motions.   A variety of other motions may be filed. If the prosecution fears that revealing information required under a discovery rule will endanger the case or a person's life, a motion for a protective order may be filed. In such cases the trial court reviews the evidence *in camera* and decides if it is necessary to keep it from the defendant. If so, the judge will enter a protective order so stating.

Motions for continuance of hearings and trial dates are common. In criminal cases, courts must be careful not to violate speedy trial requirements.

If two defendants have been charged jointly, one or both may file a motion for severance of trial. If defense counsel believes that the defendant is not competent to stand trial, a motion for mental examination may be filed.

Pretrial Conference

Sometime prior to trial, the court will hold a pretrial conference. This may be weeks or only days before trial.

At this conference the court will address any remaining motions and discuss any problems the parties have. In addition, the judge will explain his or her method of trying a case, such as how the jury will be selected. The next stage is trial.

EXTRADITION AND DETAINERS

If wanted persons are located outside the jurisdiction where they are, or will be, charged, **extradition** is one method of securing their presence in the charging jurisdiction. *Extradition* is the surrender of a person from one jurisdiction to another where the person has been charged or convicted of a crime.

Extradition usually occurs under the provisions of a treaty. Extradition includes transfers between states, as well as between nations. Extradition, especially international, is as much a political decision as a legal one.

Pursuant to the Uniform Interstate Criminal Extradition Act, which has been adopted by forty-seven states,[29] the request for extradition is made between governors. If a governor determines that the person sought should be delivered, an arrest warrant is issued by that governor.

Once seized, the arrestee is brought before a judge and may file a petition for writ of habeas corpus. During the proceedings, release on bail is permitted, unless the crime charged is one punishable by death or life imprisonment in the state where the crime was committed. If the person sought is under charge in the sending state, the governor may order his or her surrender immediately or may wait until the prosecution and punishment is completed in the first state.

Generally, the guilt or innocence of the accused may not be considered by the governor or courts during the proceedings; that issue is left to the requesting jurisdiction. It is the obligation of the governor and courts of the sending state to be sure that the correct person is seized and that proper procedures are followed.

Defendants may waive extradition. This waiver must be made in court, and defendants must be informed of their rights, including habeas corpus, for waivers to be valid.

extradition
One country (or state) giving up a person to a second country (or state) when the second requests the person for a trial on a criminal charge or for punishment after a trial.

The law permits arrests by police officers from outside a state in hot pursuit situations. If an arrest is made in hot pursuit, the officer is to bring the accused before a local court, which is to order the defendant held, or released on bail, until an extradition warrant is issued by the governor.

The Supreme Court has held that the exclusionary rule does not exclude persons who have been illegally seized from trial. In *Frisbie v. Collins*, 342 U.S. 519 (1952), the fact that Michigan police officers kidnapped a defendant from Illinois and returned him to Michigan, disregarding extradition laws, did not affect the court's jurisdiction to try the defendant. The same result was reached in a case in which international extradition laws were not followed.[30] Today, if the government's conduct in seizing a defendant were outrageous or shocking, there is a possibility that a court would bar prosecution.[31]

A **detainer** is a request (or order) for the continued custody of a prisoner. For example, suppose federal charges are pending against a Utah prisoner. The United States would issue a detainer requesting that Utah hold the prisoner after his or her sentence is completed so that the United States may take custody. This situation does not raise jurisdictional issues, as federal authorities have nationwide jurisdiction. As to interstate detention, the detainer is used in conjunction with extradition.

Pursuant to the Interstate Agreement on Detainers, a state may request the temporary custody of a prisoner of another state in order to try the person. Once the trial is completed, the prisoner is returned, regardless of the outcome. If convicted, a detainer is issued for the prisoner and he or she is again returned after the sentence is completed in the sending state.

The Agreement also provides that prisoners are to be notified of any detainers against them. Further, if a state issues a detainer for a prisoner, that prisoner may request to be temporarily transferred to that state for final disposition of that case. A request for final disposition by a prisoner is deemed a waiver of extradition to and from the sending state. Also, it is deemed a waiver of extradition to the receiving state to serve any resulting sentence after the sentence in the sending state is completed.

It is a common practice for jail and prison officials to conduct warrant checks before releasing or transferring prisoners. The importance of this practice was highlighted by the tragic events leading to the death of six-year-old Jake Robel. On February 20, 2000 a local jail in Missouri released Kim Davis. Within hours of his release, Davis carjacked an automobile owned by Christy Robel. Christy's son, Jake Robel, was in the automobile at the time Kim Davis stole the car. Ms. Robel attempted to remove her son from the car, but he became entangled in the seatbelt and her pleas to Kim Davis to stop were ignored. She was dragged for a short distance before she lost her grip of the car. Tangled in the seatbelt and hanging out of the car, Jake Robel was dragged five miles by Kim Davis while driving at speeds reaching eighty miles per hour. Jake was dead by the time Kim Davis was forced to stop the vehicle. It was discovered that there was an outstanding warrant for the arrest of Kim Davis when he was released and that a warrants check had not been conducted by jail officials. Kim Davis was subsequently convicted of second

detainer

A warrant or court order to keep a person in custody when that person might otherwise be released. This is often used to make sure a person will serve a sentence or attend a trial in one state at the end of a prison term in another state or in a federal prison.

degree murder and sentenced to life imprisonment. In response to the records check oversight, Missouri enacted "Jake's Law," a statute requiring records checks of individuals scheduled for release from jails and prison in Missouri.

REMOVAL

Congress has provided that, in certain circumstances, criminal cases may be removed from state courts to federal courts. Removal is premised upon the principle that certain cases are more properly adjudicated in a federal, rather than state, court. The purpose of removal is to preserve the sovereignty of the federal government by assuring a fair trial to particular criminal defendants. Otherwise, the states could interfere with the functioning of the federal government by harassing federal officials through criminal proceedings.

28 U.S.C. § 1442 provides that a federal official sued in state court, whether the action is civil or criminal, may remove the case to the federal district court where the action is pending, if the suit concerns the performance of his or her official duties. Similarly, 28 U.S.C. § 1442(a) provides for removal of cases, civil or criminal, filed against members of the United States armed forces for actions taken in the course of their duties. 28 U.S.C. § 1443 provides for removal of certain civil rights cases.

Removal of criminal cases is the same as for civil: the defendant must file a notice of, and petition for, removal.[32] Improperly removed actions are remanded to the state court from which they came.[33]

 WEB LINKS

Famous Trials
Professor Linder of the University of Missouri at Kansas City has an interesting and fun Web site. Information on famous trials can be found there, as can legal jeopardy and golf! *http://www.law.umkc.edu/faculty/projects/ftrials/ftrials.htm*

KEY TERMS

arraignment
arrest
bail
bill of particulars
complaint
deposition

detainer
discovery
extradition
grand jury
indictment
information

motion
plea
plea bargain (plea agreement)
preliminary hearing
quash

REVIEW QUESTIONS

1. For what two reasons may a defendant be detained prior to trial?
2. What is the difference between an indictment and an information?
3. What are the purposes of indictments and informations?
4. If a defendant needs more information than appears in the indictment to prepare a defense, what should be done?
5. What advantage does a plea of *nolo contendere* have over a guilty plea?
6. Kevin has been charged with murder. He believes a weapon that the prosecutor plans on using at trial was unconstitutionally seized from his home. How can he raise this issue prior to trial?
7. Place the following in the proper order of occurrence: preliminary hearing; formal charge; initial appearance; arraignment; trial; and complaint.
8. What is the Brady doctrine?
9. When is removal from state to federal court allowed?
10. What is extradition?

REVIEW PROBLEMS

1. What is the historical purpose of the grand jury? Many feel that grand juries should be abolished. Why?
2. Discovery in civil cases is very broad. Fed. R. Civ. P. 26 permits discovery of anything "reasonably calculated to lead to the discovery of admissible evidence." Should discovery in criminal cases be broader? Explain your position.
3. Do you believe that indictment by grand jury should be incorporated? Explain your position.

END NOTES

1. Fed. R. Crim. P. 4.
2. Fed. R. Crim. P. 5.
3. 500 U.S. 44 (1991).
4. *Stack v. Boyle*, 342 U.S. 1 (1951).
5. 18 U.S.C. § 3142(f).
6. 18 U.S.C. § 3142(e), (f).
7. *Gerstein v. Pugh*, 420 U.S. 103 (1975).
8. Fed. R. Crim. P. 5.1; 18 U.S.C. § 3060.
9. 18 U.S.C. § 3060(e).
10. *United States v. Mandujano*, 425 U.S. 564 (1976).
11. *United States v. Calandra*, 414 U.S. 338 (1974).
12. Fed. R. Crim. P. 6.
13. *Ex parte Wilson*, 114 U.S. 417 (1884). *See also* Fed. R. Crim. P. 7.
14. Fed. R. Crim. P. 7(c).
15. Fed. R. Crim. P. 8(a).
16. *See United States v. Cox*, 342 F.2d 167 (5th Cir.), *cert. denied*, 381 U.S. 935 (1965).
17. Fed. R. Crim. P. 7(c).
18. Fed. R. Crim. P. 11.
19. *United States v. Diecidue*, 603 F.2d 535 (5th Cir.), *cert. denied*, 445 U.S. 946 (1979).
20. 18 U.S.C. § 3500.
21. *Mooney v. Holohan*, 294 U.S. 103 (1935).
22. *See* Daniel Hall, *Administrative Law* ch. 9 (West Legal Studies, 1994), for a more thorough discussion of the Freedom of Information Act.
23. 5 U.S.C. § 552.

24. *John Doe Corp. v. John Doe Agency*, 493 U.S. 146 (1989).
25. *North v. Walsh*, 881 F.2d 1088 (D.C. Cir. 1989).
26. 5 U.S.C. § 552(a).
27. *Simmons v. United States*, 390 U.S. 377 (1968).
28. *Richmond Newspapers, Inc. v. Virginia*, 448 U.S. 555 (1980).
29. Rhonda Wasserman, "The Subpoena Power: *Pennoyer's* Last Vestige," 74 *Minn. L. Rev.* 37 (1989).
30. *Ker v. Illinois*, 119 U.S. 436 (1886).
31. *See United States v. Toscanino*, 500 F.2d 267 (2d Cir. 1974).
32. 28 U.S.C. § 1446.
33. 28 U.S.C. § 1447.

CHAPTER 15

Trial

CHAPTER OUTLINE

Trial Rights of Defendants

    The Right to a Jury Trial

    The Right to a Public Trial

    The Right to Confrontation
    and Cross-Examination

    The Presumption of Innocence/Burden
    of Proof

    The Right to Speedy Trial

    The Right to Counsel

Trial Procedure

    Voir Dire

Preliminary Instructions

Opening Statements

The Prosecution's Case in Chief

The Defense Case

Rebuttal

Closing Arguments

Final Instructions

Jury Deliberations and Verdict

JNOV/New Trial

CHAPTER OBJECTIVES

In this chapter, you should:

- learn the procedures of trial.
- learn the constitutional rights possessed by defendants at trial, such as the right to counsel, to remain silent, and to confront the accusers.

- continue to develop your case analysis and legal reasoning skills.

TRIAL RIGHTS OF DEFENDANTS

The Right to a Jury Trial

A trial is a method of determining guilt or innocence. In medieval England, trials by ordeal, combat, and compurgation were used.

To demonstrate how trials have changed, consider trial by ordeal. Trial by ordeal was considered trial by God; that is, God determined the person's guilt or innocence. There were two ordeals: by water and fire. Two water ordeals were used. In the first the accused was thrown into a body of water. If he sank he was adjudged innocent, and if he floated he was guilty. In the second water ordeal, the accused's arm was submerged in boiling water. The defendant had to survive this unhurt to be proven innocent. The fire ordeal was similar, the accused having to walk over fire or grasp hot irons.

Trial as we know it today finds its roots in the Magna Carta (1215), which guaranteed freemen trial by their peers. Unlike today, those juries comprised people who knew the facts of the case. The concept of trial by a jury of one's peers was of great importance to the colonists of the United States and made its way into the Constitution of the United States.

The Sixth Amendment to the United States Constitution reads, in part, "[i]n all criminal prosecutions, the accused shall enjoy the right to a speedy and public trial, by an impartial jury of the State and district wherein the crime shall have been committed." The Sixth Amendment is fully applicable against the states via the Fourteenth Amendment.

The Sixth Amendment has been interpreted to mean that defendants have a right to a jury trial for all offenses that may be punished with more than six months' imprisonment. Most crimes that have as their maximum punishment less than six months are "petty offenses," and there is no right to trial by jury.[1]

Note that the term "most" is used. Some argue that when fines become large enough, one is entitled to a jury trial, regardless of the amount of time one could be sentenced to spend in jail. In addition, it is argued that crimes that are moral in nature and subject the defendant to ridicule and embarrassment justify trial by jury, even when the punishment is less than six months' imprisonment. The same question is raised concerning crimes that were indictable at common law. The Supreme Court has not answered these questions, and the lower courts that have addressed these issues are split.

The maximum penalty allowed determines if a crime is petty, not the actual sentence. For example, if a crime is punishable by from three months to one year in jail, the defendant is entitled to a jury, even if the trial judge routinely sentences those convicted to three months for the offense. Some crimes do not have a legislatively established punishment, such as contempt. In such cases the issue is whether the defendant is sentenced to more than six months in jail. If so, the defendant is entitled to a jury.

Although the right to a jury trial for nonpetty offenses nearly always attaches, there are a few exceptions. There is no right to a jury in military trials. In addition, those appearing in juvenile court (delinquency proceedings) are not entitled to a jury trial.[2] Of course, juveniles who are tried as adults are entitled to the same rights as adults, including the right to have a jury trial.

Juries sit as factfinders. A defendant may be entitled to have a jury decide guilt or innocence, but there is no right to have a jury decide other matters, such as the proper sentence or what law to apply. Some jurisdictions have juries impose sentence, or make a sentence recommendation to the trial court; however, this is not usually the practice and there is no federal constitutional reason for it.

The Supreme Court has held that there is no constitutional requirement for twelve jurors.[3] Nor does the Constitution require juror unanimity. There is a limit to how small a jury may be and how few jurors must concur in a verdict. In one case, the Supreme Court found a law unconstitutional that required trial by six jurors and permitted conviction with a vote of five to one.[4]

It is common for six-person juries to be used for misdemeanors. However, a unanimous verdict is constitutionally required for conviction. If a twelve-member jury is used, it is constitutional to permit conviction upon a concurrence of nine or more jurors.

Finally, a defendant cannot be penalized for choosing to proceed to trial rather than pleading guilty. In *United States v. Jackson*, 390 U.S. 570 (1968), the Supreme Court found a statute that made the death penalty available for those who were tried and not for those who pled guilty violative of the Sixth Amendment.

The Right to a Public Trial

The Sixth Amendment also guarantees the right to a public trial. This applies throughout the trial, from openings to return of the verdict, and also applies to many pretrial hearings, such as suppression hearings. The presence of the public is intended to keep prosecutions "honest." As the Supreme Court stated in *Estes v. Texas*, 381 U.S. 532 (1965): "History has proven that secret tribunals were effective instruments of oppression."

The right to a public hearing does not mean that everyone who wishes to attend has to be permitted in. The trial judge is responsible for maintaining order in the courtroom and may require the doors to be shut once all seats have been filled. Also, a disruptive citizen may be removed.

The defendant's right to a public trial is not absolute. Trial judges, acting with extreme caution, may order that a hearing be conducted in private. Facts that support excluding the public are rare. An example of when exclusion of the public may be justified is when an undercover law enforcement agent testifies, and public exposure would put the officer's life in jeopardy.

If a court closes a hearing (or trial) without justification, the defendant is entitled to a new hearing, regardless of whether the defendant was actually harmed. The 1998 First Circuit Court of Appeals case, *United States v. DeLuca*, addressed both the presumption of innocence and the right to a public trial in what are rather unusual circumstances.

Generally members of the press have no greater right to attend a hearing than do other members of the public. However, many judges provide special seating for reporters.

CASE

UNITED STATES V. DELUCA

137 F.3d 24
(1st Cir. 1998)

[Defendants were tried and convicted of extortion. Because of fears of juror tampering and intimidation, the trial judge ordered that the identity of the jurors be kept anonymous. The judge also permitted the U.S. Marshal to screen trial spectators. The defendants appealed several issues, including whether an anonymous jury violates the presumption of innocence and whether the screening violated the Sixth Amendment right to a public trial.]

A. THE ANONYMOUS JURY EMPANELMENT

Appellants first contend that the decision to empanel an anonymous jury constituted an abuse of discretion. . . . We disagree.

Although the empanelment of an anonymous jury should be recognized as an extraordinary protective device, especially if it tends to suggest that the jurors may have something to fear from the accused, thereby conceivably encroaching upon the presumption of innocence, see *United States v. Krout*, 66 F.3d 1420, 1427 (5th Cir. 1995), it is a permissible precaution where (1) there are strong grounds for concluding that it is necessary to enable the jury to perform its factfinding function, or to ensure juror protection; and (2) reasonable safeguards are adopted by the trial court to minimize any risk of infringement upon the fundamental rights of the accused. See *United States v. Paccione*, 949 F.2d 1183, 1192 (2d Cir. 1991).

Our review takes into account not only the evidence available at the time the anonymous empanelment occurred, but all relevant evidence introduced at trial. See *Krout*, 66 F.3d at 1427. We conclude that the record as a whole affords sufficient foundation for empaneling an anonymous jury both as a prudent safety precaution and a means of ensuring unfettered performance of the factfinding function.

First, the record links appellants to organized crime, a factor which strongly indicated that clandestine "outside" assistance might be brought to bear in any effort to intimidate or punish jurors. See *United States v. Ross*, 33 F.3d 1507, 1520 (11th Cir. 1994); cf. *United States v. Doe*, 63 F.3d 121, 130 (2d Cir. 1995) ("The problem of retaliation against those producing adverse testimony is especially acute in the context of criminal organizations. . . . Hence, a district court in such a case might attribute the lack of a direct threat to the very confidentiality that the defendant or witness seeks to preserve."). Moreover, Ouimette's capacity and readiness to enlist criminal confederates in jury tampering plans was supported by actual precedent. See *Ross*, 33 F.3d at 1520 (court may consider "defendant's past attempts to interfere with the judicial process"); *United States v. Tutino*, 883 F.2d 1125, 1132–1133 (2d Cir. 1989).

Second, both Ouimette and DeLuca Sr. have long been involved in violent crimes, including robbery, assault with a dangerous weapon, larceny in a dwelling, and conspiracy to commit murder, not to mention their violent extortions in the instant case. See *United States v. Riggio*, 70 F.3d 336, 339–340 (5th Cir. 1995).

Third, appellants also attempted to tamper with witnesses and to suborn perjury in the instant case. DeLuca Sr. and Ouimette, through intermediaries, pressured prospective prosecution witnesses, Paula Coppola and Robert Buehne, to perjure themselves, and offered $5,000 to another prospective government witness, David Duxbury, to abscond prior to trial. Thereafter, when Duxbury nevertheless showed up at a pretrial hearing, Ouimette told an associate: "If we can't get [Duxbury], we'll get one of his kids." See *United States v. Edmond*, 311 U.S. App. D.C. 235, 52 F.3d 1080, 1091–1092 (D.C. Cir. 1995) (noting that a general preparedness to obstruct the judicial process may serve as indirect evidence of readiness to engage in jury tampering as well); *United States v. Aulicino*, 44 F.3d 1102, 1116 (2d Cir. 1995) (same).

Fourth, both Ouimette and DeLuca were confronting mandatory lifetime sentences upon conviction, which surely provided a strong inducement to resort to extreme measures in any effort to influence the outcome of their trial. See *Ross*, 33 F.3d at 1520. Moreover, their trial was prominently and extensively covered by local print and electronic media (e.g., several lengthy front-page stories in the *Providence Journal*), to the degree that any public disclosure of the jurors' identities would have enhanced the practicability, hence the likelihood, of efforts to harass, intimidate, or harm the jurors.

Finally, the district court adopted prudent measures designed to safeguard defendants' constitutional rights by informing the members of the jury that their identities would not be disclosed, so as to ensure that no extrajudicial information could be communicated to them during trial, either by the public or by media representatives. Thus, the court explained, the constitutional right of each defendant to a jury trial, based exclusively on the evidence, would be preserved.

In our view, the district court thereby satisfactorily averted any unacceptable risk of intrusion upon the constitutional rights of the individual defendants by diverting juror attention from the possible perception that anonymous empanelment was a safeguard against defendants' dangerousness. See *United States v. Darden*, 70 F.3d 1507, 1532 (8th Cir. 1995); *Ross*, 33 F.3d at 1520; *Paccione*, 949 F.2d at 1192. Accordingly, given the demonstrated need, coupled with the cautionary instruction fashioned by the district court, the anonymous jury empanelment did not constitute an abuse of discretion.

B. THE PROCEDURAL IMPEDIMENTS TO COURTROOM ACCESS BY SPECTATORS

The United States Marshal, acting sua sponte on the first day of trial, established a screening and identification procedure whereby each would-be spectator was required to present written identification before being allowed to enter the courtroom. Deputy marshals examined whatever written identification was presented, then recorded the type of identification and the bearer's name, address and birth date. The recorded information was retained by the United States Marshal for use in determining whether the bearer had a criminal background or any connection with a defendant on trial, such as might indicate a courtroom security risk. On the second day of trial the district court ratified the spectator screening procedure over appellants' objections.

Appellants contend on appeal that the screening procedure violated their Sixth Amendment right to a public trial. . . .

The Sixth Amendment right to a public trial enures to the benefit of the criminal justice system itself as well as the defendant, by enhancing due process, encouraging witnesses to come forward, and enabling the public at large to confirm that the accused are dealt with fairly and that the trial participants properly perform their respective functions. See *Waller*, 467 U.S. at 46; see also *Woods v. Kuhlmann*, 977 F.2d 74, 76 (2d Cir. 1992). Due to the important individual rights and public interests at stake, an alleged violation of the Sixth Amendment right to a public trial resulting from a "total" closure is not subject to "harmless error" analysis. *Waller*, 467 U.S. at 49 n.9 (stating that a requirement that prejudice be shown "would in most cases deprive [the defendant] of the [public-trial] guarantee, for it would be difficult to envisage a case in which he would have evidence available of specific injury") (citations and internal quotation marks omitted). Nevertheless, the Sixth Amendment right to a public trial is not absolute and must on occasion yield to competing interests in the fair and efficient administration of justice. *Id*. at 45.

The government initially urges, as a matter of law, that the Sixth Amendment right to a public trial was never implicated in the present case because the challenged screening procedure effected neither a total nor a partial closure. According to the government, a "closure" occurs only if the trial court unconditionally excludes persons from the courtroom, but not if it simply imposes universal preconditions on courtroom access which have the incidental effect of barring only those persons who elect not to comply. To cite an obvious example, magnetometer screenings are designed to prevent armed spectators from entering the courtroom, yet no one would suggest that conditioning spectator access on submission to reasonable security screening procedures for dangerous weapons violates the Sixth Amendment right to a public trial. Furthermore, the government correctly notes, no authority squarely holds that such "universal" preconditions to courtroom access constitute a Sixth Amendment "closure." Cf. *Brazel*, 102 F.3d at 1155 (assuming, arguendo, that similar identification procedure amounted to "partial" closure). We need not opt for the broad rule urged by the government, however, since the security screening procedure utilized below amounted at most to a permissible "partial" closure.

Although we have yet to rule on the matter, cf. *Martin v. Bissonette*, 118 F.3d 871, 874 (1st Cir. 1997), several other courts of appeals have held that the Sixth Amendment test laid down in *Waller*, 467 U.S. at 48, need be less stringent in the "partial" closure context; that is to say, a "substantial reason," rather than an "overriding interest," see *id.*, may warrant a closure which ensures at least some public access. See *Osborne*, 68 F.3d at 98–99; *United States v. Farmer*, 32 F.3d 369, 371–372 (8th Cir. 1994); *Woods*, 977 F.2d at 76; *United States v. Sherlock*, 962 F.2d 1349, 1357 (9th Cir. 1989); *Nieto v. Sullivan*, 879 F.2d 743, 753 (10th Cir. 1989); *Douglas v. Wainwright*, 739 F.2d 531, 533 (11th Cir. 1984) (per curiam). These courts essentially conclude that a less stringent standard is warranted in the "partial" closure context provided the essential purposes of the "public trial" guarantee are served and the constitutional rights of defendants are adequately protected. See, *e.g.*, *Osborne*, 68 F.3d at 99; *Woods*, 977 F.2d at 76. As yet, no court of appeals has held otherwise.

Unlike the "total" closure in *Waller*, 467 U.S. at 42, which excluded all persons (other than court personnel, witnesses, parties and trial counsel) throughout the entire suppression hearing, the screening and identification procedure employed below effected at most a "partial" closure, as it

(1) barred only those would-be spectators who opted not to submit written identification, and (2) presumably may have "chilled" attendance by some potential spectators who opted not to present themselves at the courthouse. Cf. *Woods*, 977 F.2d at 74 (finding "partial" closure where members of defendant's family were excluded while particular witness testified). Moreover, the district court supportably found that members of the general public, as well as members of the defendants' families, attended throughout the seven-day trial, cf. *id.* at 76, as did credentialed representatives of the print and electronic media, see *Douglas v. Wainwright*, 714 F.2d 1532, 1541 (11th Cir. 1983) (noting that media presence and coverage renders court order one for "partial" closure rather than total, by increasing the likelihood that witnesses with material evidence who are unknown to the parties may learn of perjured testimony through media reports even though they themselves do not attend the trial), vacated and remanded, 468 U.S. 1206, 82 L. Ed. 2d 874, 104 S. Ct. 3575 (1984), reinstated, 739 F.2d 531 (11th Cir. 1985).

Relying on the requirement that a closure be "no broader than necessary" to promote the asserted justification, *Waller*, 467 U.S. at 48, appellants suggest, alternatively, that (1) the anonymous empanelment and partial sequestration adequately addressed any legitimate security concerns, see *supra* Section II.A, or (2) the court could have resorted to less restrictive security measures, such as installing magnetometers immediately outside the courtroom. In addressing these contentions, we note at the outset that since the spectator-screening procedure resulted at most in a "partial" closure, the government was not required to establish that it furthered a "compelling" interest but simply a "substantial" one. See, *e.g.*, *Osborne*, 68 F.3d at 98–99.

Although anonymous empanelment and partial sequestration may afford jurors significant protections beyond the confines of the courtroom, prophylactic procedures of an entirely different nature may be required to safeguard against attempts to intimidate jurors and witnesses in the performance of their courtroom responsibilities.

These difficult judgments are matters of courtroom governance which require "a sensitive appraisal of the climate surrounding a trial and a prediction as to the potential security or publicity problems that may arise during the proceedings[.]" *Childress*, 58 F.3d at 702. Thus, in our view an appellate court should be hesitant to displace a trial court's judgment call in such circumstances. See *id.* at 705 ("The trial court's choice of courtroom security procedures requires a subtle reading of the immediate atmosphere and a prediction of potential risks–judgments nearly impossible for appellate courts to second-guess after the fact."); see also *United States v. Brooks*, 125 F.3d 484, 502 (7th Cir. 1997) ("The decisions of a district court concerning security in the courtroom are reviewed deferentially."); *Elledge v. Dugger*, 823 F.2d 1439, 1456 (11th Cir. 1987) ("We generally defer to a trial court's discretion in courtroom-security decisions."); cf. In re *San Juan Star Co.*, 662 F.2d 108, 117 (1st Cir. 1981) (noting that appellate court "must defer to the [district] court's . . . close familiarity with the nature of the [trial] publicity involved").

As the Eleventh Circuit acknowledged recently in relation to another spectator-screening procedure, given their many coincident duties trial judges cannot be expected to scan their courtrooms efficiently on a continuous basis for spectators whose very demeanor might represent an attempt to intimidate a witness or juror. See *Brazel*, 102 F.3d at 1155 (addressing "fixed stares" directed at witnesses by courtroom spectators). Similarly, in the circumstances presented here we cannot agree that prudent identification procedures suitably focused at deterring would-be trial spectators who may pose unacceptable risks—either to the security of the courtroom or the integrity of the factfinding process—need be held in abeyance pending evidence of an actual attempt to influence or harm a witness or juror in the case on trial. Therefore, though we cannot endorse the unilateral action by the United States Marshal, we hold that it did not strip away the substantial deference due the district court's subsequent assessment that the screening procedures were warranted.

These appellants either were directly associated with prior efforts to obstruct fair factfinding through untruthful trial testimony, or were found to possess the present means as well as ample inducement (viz., avoidance of potential life sentences) to sponsor similar efforts in the case at bar, see *supra* Section II.A. Moreover, the challenged spectator-screening procedure was reasonably designed to respond to these concerns, as it plainly alerted would-be spectators that their courtroom conduct would be closely monitored, thereby efficiently focusing the desired deterrent effect principally upon those most likely to impede a fair and orderly trial—particularly appellants' criminal associates. Thus, the challenged screening procedure represented a permissible response to defendants' demonstrated capacity and motivation to undermine the administration of justice at their trial.

Finally, as the district court supportably found, their extensive criminal histories (not to mention the violent criminal activity alleged in the pending indictment) generated realistic concerns that appellants might circumvent normal courtroom security procedures, as by attempting to coerce or bribe authorized personnel to facilitate the introduction of weapons into the courtroom or elsewhere in the courthouse.

In our view, therefore, the district court order ratifying these screening procedures adequately addressed and significantly minimized the demonstrated potential for harassment and intimidation of jurors and witnesses by would-be trial spectators, for many of the same reasons that warranted the anonymous empanelment and partial jury sequestration. See *supra* Section II.A. Although any courtroom closure represents a serious undertaking which ought never be initiated without prior judicial authorization, we conclude that the partial closure in this case did not contravene the Sixth Amendment, given the strong circumstantial and historical evidence that precautionary security measures were well warranted and the essential constitutional guarantees of a public trial were preserved.

The Right to Confrontation and Cross-Examination

The Sixth Amendment also contains a right to confront one's accusers. This means that a defendant has the right to cross-examine the witnesses of the prosecution. Each state drafts its own rules of evidence; however, it may not enact a rule of evidence that conflicts with a defendant's right to confrontation.

For example, a state procedure permitting government witnesses to refuse to identify themselves was found violative of the Sixth Amendment.[5] The Supreme Court reasoned that the procedure was invalid because it did not permit the defendant to conduct his or her own investigation into the credibility of government witnesses.

Statutes allowing victims to testify remotely, such as by closed-circuit television, also raise confrontation issues. However, the Supreme Court has stated that the Confrontation Clause does not per se prohibit child witnesses in child abuse cases from testifying outside the defendant's physical presence by one-way closed-circuit television. Before such a procedure is used, however, the court must examine the facts of the case and determine that remote testimony is necessary.[6] Failure to make such a finding (e.g., the child fears the defendant) can lead to reversal.[7]

The Confrontation Clause does not give defendants carte blanche to probe any area on cross-examination. If a state can show a compelling reason, it may prohibit cross-examination of a subject. For example, rape shield laws prohibit defendants from inquiring into a rape victim's sexual background in most cases. Courts have affirmed such laws, finding that the protection of the rape victims from unwarranted personal attacks is a legitimate reason to limit defense cross-examination.

The Confrontation Clause also restricts the government's use of hearsay evidence. *Hearsay* is a statement made by a person out of court. The Federal Rules of Evidence prohibit hearsay, unless it falls into a recognized exception. For the prosecution to use hearsay, it must be shown that (1) the witness is unavailable at trial through no fault of the government and (2) the statement was made in a situation wherein it appears reliable.

The Confrontation Clause implicitly includes a right of a defendant to be at the trial. This right includes the entire trial, from selection of the jury to return of the verdict. It also includes many pretrial matters, such as suppression hearings. Of course, defendants have a right to be present at both sentencing and probation revocation hearings. Although the right to be present during one's trial is fundamental, it may be lost by disruptive behavior.

The Presumption of Innocence/Burden of Proof

One of the most basic rights underlying the right to a fair trial is the presumption of innocence. All those accused must be proven guilty by the government. Criminal defendants have no duty to defend themselves and may remain silent throughout the trial. In fact, the government is prohibited from calling defendants to testify, and defendants cannot be made to decide whether they will testify at the start of the trial.[8] The fact that a defendant chooses not to testify may not be mentioned by the prosecutor to the jury. Defendants may testify in their own behalf. If so, they are subject to full cross-examination by the prosecutor. The Fifth Amendment right to be free from self-incrimination is discussed more fully in Chapter 9.

The standard imposed upon the government in criminal cases is to prove guilt **beyond a reasonable doubt.** A doubt that would cause a reasonable or prudent person to question the guilt of the accused is a reasonable doubt. Although not precisely quantified, beyond a reasonable doubt is greater than the civil preponderance (51 percent likely) and less than absolute (100 percent confidence of guilt). The prosecution must prove every element of the charged crime beyond a reasonable doubt. The reasonable doubt standard is an important feature of the accusatorial system of the United States and is required by due process.[9] A juror must vote for acquittal if he or she harbors a reasonable doubt.

To further the presumption of innocence, judges must be careful not to behave in a manner that implies to a jury that a defendant is guilty.

The Supreme Court has stated that the presence of a defendant at a jury trial in prison clothing is prejudicial.[10] In the *Young* case, a federal appellate court reviewed the use of "prisoner docks" for a Sixth Amendment violation. A criminal defendant also has a right to be free from appearing before the jury in handcuffs or shackles.

This right to be free of restraint is not absolute. Judges have the authority to take whatever measures are necessary to assure safety in the courtroom and to advance the administration of justice. Accordingly, a defendant who is disorderly may be expelled from the trial. However, before exclusion is ordered the court should consider other alternatives. Defendants who are threatening may be restrained, and those who verbally interfere with the proceeding may be gagged.[11]

beyond a reasonable doubt

The level of proof required to convict a person of a crime. For a jury to be convinced *"beyond a reasonable doubt,"* it must be fully satisfied that the person is guilty. This is the highest level of proof required in any type of trial.

The Right to Speedy Trial

All criminal defendants have a right to a speedy trial. It is the Sixth Amendment, as extended by the Fourteenth Amendment to the states, that guarantees speedy trial. This right has a history dating back to at least the Magna Carta.

To date, the United States Supreme Court has not set a specific number of days within which trial must be conducted. Rather, the Court said in *Barker v. Wingo* that four factors must be considered when determining if a defendant has enjoyed a speedy trial. First, the length of the delay; second, the reason for the delay; third, whether the defendant has asserted the right to a speedy trial; fourth, how seriously the defendant was prejudiced.[12]

Time for speedy trial begins once the defendant is arrested or formally charged.[13] If a defendant is charged by sealed indictment, speedy trial does not start until the indictment has been opened.

Dismissal with prejudice is the remedy for violation of speedy trial. That is, the charge is dismissed and may not be refiled by the prosecutor.

All the states and the national government have enacted speedy trial acts. The Speedy Trial Act of 1974[14] is the federal statute. That act requires that individuals be formally charged within thirty days from the date of arrest and

C A S E

**YOUNG V.
CALLAHAN**

700 F.2d 32
(1st Cir. 1983)

[The Court included a footnote which stated that a *prisoner dock* is "a box approximately four feet square and four feet high. It is open at the top so that the defendant's head and shoulders can be seen when he or she is seated. The dock is placed typically at the center of the bar enclosure which separates the spectator's section from that portion of the courtroom reserved for trial principals. The dock is usually fifteen to twenty feet behind counsel table, and is sometimes on a raised platform."]

In January of 1979 appellant was tried in Massachusetts Superior Court on one count of assault and battery with a dangerous weapon and two counts of murder. The jury returned a guilty verdict on the assault and battery but was unable to reach a verdict on the two murder indictments. In a new trial in February of 1979, appellant was found guilty of second-degree murder on both counts. These convictions were affirmed by the Massachusetts Supreme Judicial Court. . . .

Prior to appellant's second trial, counsel moved that he be allowed to sit at counsel table rather than in the prisoner's dock on the grounds that "forcing him to sit in the prisoner's dock would deprive him of his constitutional rights to a fair

trial, to the presumption of innocence, to access to counsel, non-suggestive eyewitness identifications, and due process of law." That motion was accompanied by an affidavit from appellant's trial counsel averring, based on his own observations and those of corrections officers during appellant's two years of incarceration and on appellant's conduct at the first trial, that "allowing [appellant] to sit at counsel table will not present any hazards to the orderly judicial process or to the security of its personnel," and that the trial of the case would involve a substantial amount of testimony concerning acts and conduct of the appellant over a several-day period and would thus "require consultation with the defendant.". . .

In once again evaluating for constitutional error the confinement of an accused to the prisoner's box, we reiterate . . . that such confinement, like appearance in prison attire, is a "constant reminder of the accused's condition" which "may affect a juror's judgment," eroding the presumption of innocence which the accused is due. . . .

The prisoner's dock, like other physical restraints, should thus be employed only when "the trial judge has found such restraint reasonably necessary to maintain order" and when cured by an instruction to the "jurors that such restraint is not to be considered in assessing the proof and determining guilty."

tried within seventy days of the date of the filing of the information or indictment or from the date the defendant had the initial appearance before the court that will try the case, whichever is later.

To avoid prejudice by having a trial before a defendant has had an opportunity to prepare a defense, the statute provides that trial shall not occur for thirty days, unless the defendant consents to an earlier date.

The statute specifies certain delays that are excluded from computing time for purpose of speedy trial. A few of the periods excluded by the Speedy Trial Act of 1974 are when the defendant is a fugitive; when trial is delayed because an issue is on appeal; when delays are caused by motions of the parties; and when delays result from mental examinations of the defendant.

The Speedy Trial Act of 1974 gives the trial court the discretion to decide whether violation of its provisions justifies a dismissal with or without prejudice. Factors that must be considered are the seriousness of the offense, the reason for delay, other facts of the case, and the impact of reprosecution on the administration of justice.[15]

Because the United States Supreme Court has not established specific time requirements for speedy trial, each state has its own time requirements. Of course, states must comply with the requirements of *Barker v. Wingo*. Most states have speedy trial provisions in their constitutions, which are similar, if not identical, to the Sixth Amendment. Other states set their speedy trial requirements out in statute or court rules. Time requirements differ, but trial within six months is common.

The Right to Counsel

The Sixth Amendment to the United States Constitution provides that "in all criminal prosecutions, the accused shall enjoy the right . . . to have the Assistance of Counsel for his defense." The right to counsel is one of the most fundamental rights guaranteed to criminal defendants and is fully applicable to the states.

The right to the assistance of counsel is found not only in the Sixth Amendment, but also in the Fifth and Fourteenth Amendments. These alternative sources are discussed later in the particular contexts within which they apply.

Indigency.   It has always been clear that criminal defendants are entitled to retain the attorney of their choice. It was not until 1923 that the United States Supreme Court recognized a constitutional right to appointed counsel for indigent defendants in *Powell v. Alabama*, 287 U.S. 45 (1923).

In the *Powell* case (commonly known as the Scottsboro case), nine young black males were charged with the rape of two white girls. Within one week of arrest, the defendants were tried. Eight of the "Scottsboro boys" were convicted and sentenced to death. The defendants appealed, claiming that they should have been provided counsel. The Supreme Court agreed.

However, the right to appointed counsel in *Powell* was not founded upon the Sixth Amendment, but upon the Fourteenth. The Court reasoned that the absence of counsel deprived the defendants of a fair trial, and, accordingly, violated the defendants' due process rights. This decision was narrow: it applied only to capital cases where the defendant was incapable of preparing an adequate defense and did not have the resources to hire an attorney.

The due process right to counsel was subsequently extended to all situations in which a defendant would not have a fair trial in the absence of defense counsel. Whether counsel was required depended on each particular case's "totality of facts." If denial of counsel was "shocking to the universal sense of justice," then the defendant's right to a fair trial, as guaranteed by the Fourteenth Amendment, was violated.[16] The Court refused to extend the right to counsel to all state criminal proceedings. Cases that involve complex legal issues or a defendant of low intelligence are the types of situation that required the appointment of counsel under the *Betts* due process standard.

In 1938 the Court decided *Johnson v. Zerbst*, 304 U.S. 458 (1938), which held that the Sixth Amendment guarantees a right to counsel. The Sixth Amendment right to counsel was found to be broader than the right to counsel announced in *Powell*, as it applied to all criminal prosecutions. However, *Zerbst* did not apply to state proceedings. Eventually, the Sixth Amendment right to counsel was extended to all state felony proceedings, in *Gideon v. Wainwright*.

Subsequently, the right to counsel was again extended to encompass all criminal cases punished with a jail term. Whether the crime is labeled a misdemeanor or felony is not dispositve of the right to counsel issue.[17] In the 2002 case, *Alabama v. Shelton*, the Supreme Court extended the right again. In *Shelton*, the right to counsel was found for convictees who are sentenced to imprisonment, but the entire sentence is suspended to probation.

In some cases, it may be to the prosecution's advantage for a defendant to have counsel, even though a sentence of imprisonment is not available for a first conviction, but is for subsequent convictions. This is because a sentence may not be enhanced to include jail time based on a prior conviction where the defendant possessed a right to, but was denied, counsel.[18] For example, the penalty for first-offense drunk driving is not punished by a term in jail; however, subsequent violations are. If Jack is arrested and convicted without counsel for his first offense, he may not be sentenced to jail time for his second drunk driving conviction because he did not have counsel during his first trial.

To qualify for appointed counsel, the defendant does not have to be financially destitute. It need only be shown that the defendant's financial situation will prevent him or her from being able to retain an attorney. An indigent defendant does not have a right to choose the appointed attorney; this decision falls within the discretion of the trial court.

 CASE

ALABAMA V. SHELTON

122 S.Ct. 1764 (2002)

This case concerns the Sixth Amendment right of an indigent defendant charged with a misdemeanor punishable by imprisonment, fine, or both, to the assistance of court-appointed counsel. Two prior decisions control the Court's judgment. First, in *Argersinger v. Hamlin*, 407 U.S. 25, 92 S.Ct. 2006, 32 L.Ed.2d 530 (1972), this Court held that defense counsel must be appointed in any criminal prosecution, "whether classified as petty, misdemeanor, or felony,". . ."that actually leads to imprisonment even for a brief period,". . . Later, in *Scott v. Illinois*, 440 U.S. 367, 373–374, 99 S.Ct. 1158, 59 L.Ed.2d 383 (1979), the Court drew the line at "actual imprisonment," holding that counsel need not be appointed when the defendant is fined for the charged crime, but is not sentenced to a term of imprisonment.

Defendant-respondent LeReed Shelton, convicted of third-degree assault, was sentenced to a jail term of 30 days, which the trial court immediately suspended, placing Shelton on probation for two years. The question presented is whether the Sixth Amendment right to appointed counsel, as delineated in *Argersinger* and *Scott*, applies to a defendant in Shelton's situation. We hold that a suspended sentence that may "end up in the actual deprivation of a person's liberty" may not be imposed unless the defendant was accorded "the guiding hand of counsel" in the prosecution for the crime charged.

After representing himself at a bench trial in the District Court of Etowah County, Alabama, Shelton was convicted of third-degree assault, a class A misdemeanor carrying a maximum punishment of one year imprisonment and a $2000 fine . . . He invoked his right to a new trial before a jury in Circuit Court. . . . where he again appeared without a lawyer and was again convicted. The court repeatedly warned Shelton about the problems self-representation entailed, see App. 9, but at no time offered him assistance of counsel at state expense.

The Circuit Court sentenced Shelton to serve 30 days in the county prison. As authorized by Alabama law, however, . . . the court suspended that sentence and placed Shelton on two years' unsupervised probation, conditioned on his payment of court costs, a $500 fine, reparations of $25, and restitution in the amount of $516.69.

Shelton appealed his conviction and sentence on Sixth Amendment grounds. . . .

. . . A suspended sentence is a prison term imposed for the offense of conviction. Once the prison term is triggered, the defendant is incarcerated not for the probation violation, but for the underlying offense. The uncounseled conviction at that point "result[s] in imprisonment. . . . This is precisely what the Sixth Amendment, as interpreted in *Argersinger* and *Scott*, does not allow. . . .

Satisfied that Shelton is entitled to appointed counsel at the critical stage when his guilt or innocence of the charged crime is decided and his vulnerability to imprisonment is determined, we affirm the judgment of the Supreme Court of Alabama. *It is so ordered.*

Effective Assistance of Counsel.   Defendants are entitled not only to have an attorney, but also to the "effective assistance of counsel." On appeal, defendants may challenge their convictions claiming that at a lower level (trial or appellate) they did not have effective counsel.

To be successful with such a claim, two facts must be shown. First, the representation must be extremely inadequate. Second, the defendant must show that he or she was actually harmed by the lack of adequate counsel. So, if an appellate court determines that a defendant would have been convicted with the best of attorneys, the defendant's claim of inadequate counsel fails.

A Sixth Amendment claim of ineffective assistance of counsel can take many forms. Incompetence of counsel is often claimed, but rarely successful. Attorneys are expected to make the legal and tactical decisions of the defense. The fact that defense counsel rendered incorrect legal advice is not determinative. The issue is whether the defendant's representation was shockingly substandard.

A defendant has a right to the "undivided loyalty" of defense counsel. Hence, it is common to have ineffective assistance of counsel claims where one attorney is representing co-defendants. In *Cuyler v. Sullivan*, 446 U.S. 335 (1980), it was held that an ineffective assistance of counsel claim based upon an alleged conflict of interest will be successful only if the defendant can show that the conflict "adversely affected" his or her rights.

CASE

GIDEON V. WAINWRIGHT

372 U.S. 335 (1963)

Petitioner was charged in Florida state court with having broken and entered a poolroom with intent to commit a misdemeanor. This offense is a felony under Florida law. Appearing in court without funds and without a lawyer, petitioner asked the court to appoint counsel for him, whereupon the following colloquy took place:

THE COURT: Mr. Gideon, I am sorry, but I cannot appoint Counsel to represent you in this case. Under the laws of the State of Florida, the only time the Court can appoint Counsel to represent a defendant is when that person is charged with a capital offense. I am sorry, but I will have to deny your request to appoint Counsel to defend you in this case.

THE DEFENDANT: The United States Supreme Court says I am entitled to be represented by Counsel.

Put to trial before a jury, Gideon conducted his defense about as well as could be expected from a layman. He made an opening statement to the jury, cross-examined the State's witnesses, presented witnesses in his own defense, declined to testify himself, and made a short argument "emphasizing his innocence to the charge contained in the Information filed in this case." The jury returned a verdict of guilty, and petitioner was sentenced to five years in the state prison. Since 1942, when *Betts v. Brady*, 316 U.S. 455, was decided by a divided Court, the problem of a defendant's federal constitutional right to counsel in a state court has been a continuing source of controversy and litigation in both state and federal courts. . . . Since

Gideon was proceeding in forma pauperis, we appointed counsel to represent him and requested both sides to discuss in their briefs and oral arguments the following: "Should this Court's holding in *Betts v. Brady* . . . be reconsidered?. . .

Governments, both state and federal, quite properly spend vast sums of money to establish machinery to try defendants accused of crime. Lawyers to prosecute are everywhere deemed essential to protect the public's interest in an orderly society. Similarly, there are few defendants charged with crime, few indeed, who fail to hire the best lawyers they can get to prepare and present their defenses. That government hires lawyers to prosecute and defendants who have the money to hire lawyers to defend are the strongest indications of the widespread belief that lawyers in criminal courts are necessities, not luxuries. The right of one charged with crime to counsel may not be deemed fundamental and essential to fair trials in some countries, but it is in ours. From the very beginning, our state and national constitutions and laws have laid great emphasis on procedural and substantive safeguards designed to assure fair trials before impartial tribunals in which every defendant stands equal before the law. This noble idea cannot be realized if the poor man charged with crime has to face his accusers without a lawyer to represent him. . . . The Court in *Betts v. Brady* departed from sound wisdom upon which the Court's holding in *Powell v. Alabama* rested. Florida, supported by two other States, has asked that *Betts v. Brady* be left intact. Twenty-two states, as friends of the Court, argue that *Betts* was "an anachronism when handed down" and that it should now be overruled. We agree. . . . Reversed.

Also, the accused has a right to confer with counsel to prepare a defense. If a court denies a defendant access to his or her counsel, a Sixth Amendment claim may be made.

Governmental eavesdropping on a defendant's conversation with his or her counsel is also improper and violative of the Sixth Amendment.

The Right to Self-Representation. In *Faretta v. California*, 422 U.S. 806 (1975), the right to self-representation was established. The Supreme Court recognized that the assistance of trained legal counsel is essential to preparing and presenting a defense. However, in balance, the Court found that a defendant's right of choice is of greater importance. Therefore, defendants may choose to act as their own counsel (pro se), even though the decision increases the probability of a conviction.

The record must clearly show that a defendant who has chosen to proceed pro se has done so voluntarily and knowingly. The defendant "must be made aware of the dangers and disadvantages of self-representation." Whether the defendant possesses any legal training or education is not relevant.

Trial judges are permitted to appoint "standby counsel" for trial. This attorney attends the trial and is available to counsel the defendant or take over the defense, if necessary. The Court later approved the practice of appointing standby counsel over the objection of the defendant. This is routinely done in felony cases in which the defendant has opted to proceed pro se.

The right to self-representation is not absolute. A defendant who engages in disruptive behavior during the proceeding may be relieved of pro se status. Standby counsel, if appointed, may be ordered to complete the trial.

The Scope of the Right. Through *Gideon*, the right to counsel in criminal prosecutions was extended to the states. *Argersinger* made it clear that counsel must be provided in all cases in which the defendant is sentenced to actual imprisonment. But when does the right begin?

The United States Supreme Court has stated that the Sixth Amendment right to counsel applies to all critical stages of a criminal prosecution. This definition requires that a "prosecution" be initiated before the right to counsel, under the Sixth Amendment, attaches. Accordingly, the Sixth Amendment does not apply to juvenile proceedings, nor to administrative hearings such as parole determination and revocation.

The right starts whenever the "adversary judicial proceeding" is initiated. Police contacts prior to the initiation of an adversary judicial proceeding are not covered by the Sixth Amendment.

In determining what constitutes a critical stage, courts focus on "whether substantial rights of the defendant may be affected." The greater the contact between the prosecutor and the defendant, the more likely the event is at a critical stage.

The first critical stage is normally the initial appearance or the arraignment. Courts have also determined that a defendant may be entitled to counsel at a police lineup, sentencing, preliminary hearing, and during a probation revocation hearing. Once charges are filed, all interrogations of the defendant by the government are critical stages.

The Sixth Amendment is not the only constitutional provision assuring counsel. The Fifth Amendment's right to be free from self-incrimination also guarantees counsel in some instances, as does the Fourteenth Amendment's Equal Protection and Due Process Clauses.

TRIAL PROCEDURE

Voir Dire

voir dire examination

(French) "To see, to say"; "to state the truth." The preliminary in-court questioning of a prospective witness (or juror) to determine competency to testify (or suitability to decide a case). [pronounce: vwahr deer]

challenge for cause

A formal objection to the qualifications of a prospective juror or jurors.

peremptory challenge

The automatic elimination of a potential juror by one side before trial without needing to state the reason for the elimination.

The first stage of trial is the **voir dire.** This is a French phrase that translates "look speak" (to speak the truth). Voir dire is also known as *jury selection.*

The process of selecting a jury differs among the jurisdictions. In all jurisdictions, prospective jurors are asked questions bearing upon their individual ability to serve fairly and impartially. Each state differs in how this information is obtained. In many, the judge is responsible for asking most of the questions. In others, the judge only makes a few brief inquiries, and the lawyers do most of the questioning.

There are two ways of eliminating a juror. First, if one of the attorneys believes that a juror could not be fair and impartial, the juror can be **challenged for cause.** If the judge agrees, the juror is released. An unlimited number of jurors may be eliminated for cause.

In addition to challenges for cause, a juror may be eliminated by a party using a **peremptory challenge.** Each party is given a specific number of peremptory challenges at the start of the trial and may strike jurors until that number is exhausted. A party is free to eliminate, without stating a reason, any potential juror. However, a juror may not be eliminated because of race.[19]

In the federal system, both defendant and prosecutor have twenty peremptory strikes in death cases and three in misdemeanors; in non-capital felony cases the defendant gets ten and the government six.[20] States have similar rules.

In addition to challenging individual jurors, entire jury panels may be challenged. For example, a defendant may challenge the method used to select prospective jurors if the method does not select individuals who represent a fair cross section of the community. In many instances, these challenges concern race or ethnicity.

Preliminary Instructions

The next stage in the trial proceeding is for the judge to give preliminary instructions to the jury. The trial judge explains to the jury what its obligation is and gives a brief introduction to the law and facts of the case. The judge may read the formal charge verbatim to the jury or may summarize its contents.

The presumption of innocence is explained, and the judge admonishes the jury not to discuss the case prior to deliberating. Jurors are told not to read newspaper articles or watch television reports concerning the trial. In rare cases, it may be necessary to keep the jurors' identities secret and to conduct the voir dire in private. Threat to the safety of the jurors is an example of such an instance. This method is to be used cautiously, as it encroaches upon First Amendment rights of media and of the defendant to a public trial. Moreover, when used, the trial judge should be careful not to prejudice the jury. If the reason for secrecy is a perceived threat, the judge should instruct the jury as to another reason, such as concern over pretrial publicity.[21]

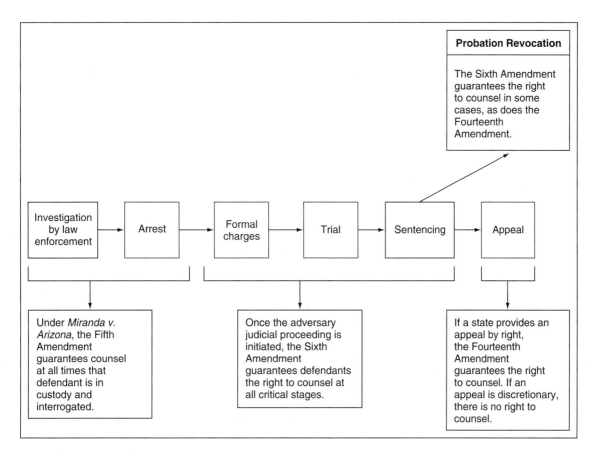

The Right to Counsel

Opening Statements

After the judge has given the preliminary instructions, the parties address the jury. These statements are commonly known as *opening statements*. The purpose of opening statements is to acquaint the jury with the basic facts of the case. Opening statement is not the time for counsel to argue the law; only the facts expected to be presented should be mentioned.

   In some cases the defense attorney may be permitted to wait until after the prosecution has put on its case before giving an opening. Because the purpose of opening statements is to present the facts surrounding the charge to the jury, opening statements are often waived in bench trials.

The Prosecution's Case in Chief

Because the government has brought the charges, it puts its case on first. This consists of calling witnesses to testify and producing exhibits.

All jurisdictions have rules of evidence that govern procedure and the admissibility of evidence. The Federal Rules of Evidence are used in the federal courts, and many states have modeled their rules after the federal ones.

Many evidentiary questions can be resolved prior to trial through a motion **in limine.** Those arising during trial are handled through **objections.** Any time an attorney believes that a question, statement, or action of the opposing lawyer is improper, he or she may object. The court will then rule on the objection, and the trial will continue. In some instances the attorneys will want to argue the objection outside the hearing of the jury. In such cases a **sidebar** may be held, or the judge may order that the jury be removed until the matter is resolved.

The Confrontation Clause assures the defendant the right to cross-examine the prosecution's witnesses. Normally, cross-examination is limited to matters raised during the prosecution's direct examination. The defense also has the right to review an exhibit before it is shown to the jury.

Directed Verdict and Judgment of Acquittal. After the government has rested (finished its case), the defendant may move for a directed verdict or, as it is also known, a judgment of acquittal. Upon such motion the trial judge reviews the evidence presented by the government. If the evidence to support a conviction is insufficient, the judge will enter a directed verdict favoring the defendant. A directed verdict may never be entered favoring the government.

The prosecution's evidence is insufficient if reasonable persons could not conclude that the defendant is guilty. If the trial court grants a motion for directed verdict, the jury never deliberates and is discharged. Directed verdicts are rarely granted, as most judges prefer to have the jury return a verdict.

The Defense Case

If the motion for directed verdict is denied, the defense may put on its case. The defendant is not required to put on a defense, and juries are instructed to not infer guilt by the absence of a defense.

If a defendant chooses to present a defense, the rules are the same as for the prosecution. The defendant may call witnesses and introduce exhibits, as limited by the rules of evidence. Defense witnesses are subject to cross-examination by the prosecutor. Defendants do not have to testify, but may choose to do so. If a defendant does testify, he or she is subject to cross-examination by the prosecutor.

Rebuttal

After the defense has concluded, the prosecution may call rebuttal witnesses in an effort to disprove the evidence of the defense. No new issues may be raised during rebuttal. The defense is then permitted to rebut the prosecution's rebuttal evidence.

---

in limine

(Latin) "At the beginning"; preliminary. A motion *in limine* is a (usually pretrial) request that prejudicial information be excluded as trial evidence.

objection

A claim that an action by your adversary in a lawsuit (such as the use of a particular piece of evidence) is improper, unfair, or illegal, and asking the judge for a ruling on the point.

sidebar

An in-court discussion among lawyers and the judge that is out of the hearing of witnesses and the jury. Sidebar conferences are usually *on the* record.

Closing Arguments

After the evidentiary stage of the trial has concluded, the parties present their closing arguments. The length of closing arguments is left to the discretion of the trial judge.

Attorneys may argue both the facts and the law during closing arguments. However, an attorney may not argue law different from what the judge will express to the jury as controlling in the case. Closing arguments give the parties an opportunity to summarize the evidence and explain their positions to the jury.

Attorneys must not make incorrect factual or legal statements to the jury. Objections to such statements may be made. If sustained, the jury will be instructed by the judge to disregard the statement. Prosecutors must be especially careful not to make inflammatory remarks about the defendant or defense counsel. Such remarks, if extreme, can lead to mistrial.

Final Instructions

After closing arguments are completed, the judge will instruct the jury. Through these instructions the judge explains the law to the jury. The information contained in the judge's instructions includes the prosecutorial burden, the standard of proof, the elements of the charged crime, how to weigh and value evidence, and rules for reaching a verdict.

Jury Deliberations and Verdict

After receiving its instructions, the jury goes into deliberations. Jury deliberations are secret in all cases.

Generally, no person has contact with the jury when it is deliberating. If the jury has a question for the judge, it is escorted into the courtroom where all the parties may hear the question. Some judges, but not all, permit juries to take the exhibits and instructions with them into the jury room.

On occasion, a jury may communicate to the judge that a verdict cannot be reached. Some courts will then give the jury an "Allen charge," an instruction encouraging jurors in the minority to re-examine their position. The charge gets its name from *Allen v. United States*, 164 U.S. 492 (1896), wherein the Supreme Court approved its use. Courts must be careful with such charges, but they are not violative of the United States Constitution. However, some states have banned the Allen charge.

In the event of a **hung jury,** the court will declare a mistrial and set a new trial date. Because of the expense and inconvenience of trying cases a second time, plea bargains are often reached.

If a verdict is reached, the parties are summoned to the courtroom and the jury verdict is read. The parties may request that the jury be polled. **Polling the jury** involves asking each juror how he or she voted. If there has been an error, the judge may order the jury to return to deliberations or may declare a mistrial.

hung jury
A **jury** that cannot reach a verdict (decision) because of disagreement among jurors.
polling the jury
Individually asking each member of a jury what his or her decision is. This is done by the judge, at the defendant's request, immediately after the verdict.

KEY TERMS

beyond a reasonable doubt	*in limine*	polling the jury
challenge for cause	objection	sidebar
hung jury	peremptory challenge	voir dire examination

REVIEW QUESTIONS

1. What rights are encompassed by the Confrontation Clause?
2. What is the standard of proof in criminal cases? Define that standard.
3. How soon after arrest must a defendant be tried to comply with the Sixth Amendment's speedy trial clause?
4. What is jury nullification? May a prosecutor ask a jury to nullify? May defense counsel?
5. Distinguish challenging a prospective juror for cause from using a peremptory challenge.
6. Does a defendant have a right to self-representation?
7. What must a defendant show on appeal to be successful with a claim of ineffective assistance of counsel at trial?

REVIEW PROBLEMS

1–4. Does each of the following defendants have a right to a jury trial? Explain your answer.

1. A juvenile delinquency proceeding has been initiated against John because of his involvement with drugs. For more than a year he has been dealing drugs, a crime punishable by as much as five years in prison in his state.
2. Jane is charged with simple assault. In her state that crime is punishable by a maximum fine of $2,500 and twelve months imprisonment. However, the judge assigned to her case has never sentenced a person to more than four months and customarily suspends that sentence to probation.
3. Nick is sixteen years old. He is charged with murder in state trial court. Murder in his state is punished with life imprisonment or death.
4. Norm, an officer in the military, has been charged with raping a female officer. Rape is punished with ten years to life imprisonment in the military.

END NOTES

1. *Baldwin v. New York*, 399 U.S. 66 (1970).
2. *McKeiver v. Pennsylvania*, 403 U.S. 528 (1971).
3. *Williams v. Florida*, 399 U.S. 78 (1970).
4. *Burch v. Louisiana*, 441 U.S. 130 (1979).
5. *Smith v. Illinois*, 390 U.S. 129 (1968).
6. *Maryland v. Craig*, 497 U.S. 836 (1990).
7. *Cumbie v. Singletary*, 991 F.2d 715 (11th Cir. 1993).
8. *Brooks v. Tennessee*, 406 U.S. 605 (1972).
9. *Johnson v. Louisiana*, 406 U.S. 356 (1972).
10. *Estelle v. Williams*, 425 U.S. 501 (1976).
11. *Stewart v. Corbin*, 850 F.2d 492 (9th Cir. 1988).
12. *Barker v. Wingo*, 407 U.S. 514 (1972).
13. *United States v. Marion*, 404 U.S. 307 (1971).
14. 18 U.S.C. § 3161.
15. 18 U.S.C. § 3162.
16. *Betts v. Brady*, 316 U.S. 455 (1942).
17. *Argersinger v. Hamlin*, 407 U.S. 25 (1972).

18. *Burgett v. Texas*, 389 U.S. 109 (1962).
19. *Batson v. Kentucky*, 476 U.S. 79 (1986).
20. Fed. R. Crim. P. 24(b).
21. *United States v. Locascio*, 6 F.3d 924 (2d Cir. 1993).
22. *See United States v. Avery*, 717 F.2d 1020 (6th Cir. 1983).
23. *United States v. Newman*, 743 F. Supp. 533 (M.D. Tenn. 1990).
24. *See Sparf v. United States*, 156 U.S. 51 (1895); *United States v. Martin Linen Supply Co.*, 430 U.S. 564 (1977).

Sentencing and Appeal

CHAPTER OUTLINE

Sentencing

    Sentencing Procedure

    Forms of Punishment

    Habitual Offender Statutes

Postconviction Remedies

    Appeal

    Habeas Corpus

CHAPTER OBJECTIVES

In this chapter, you should:

- learn the laws of punishment, including the constitutional limitations of punishment and the procedures of sentencing.
- be challenged to think about the relationship of the various forms of punishment to the objectives of criminal justice.
- learn the law of appeals and postconviction relief.
- continue to develop your case analysis and legal reasoning skills.

SENTENCING

After conviction, sentence must be imposed. For many misdemeanors and nearly all infractions, sentence is imposed immediately. For felonies and some misdemeanors, a future sentencing date is set.

In most cases sentence is imposed by the trial judge. A few jurisdictions provide for a jury sentence recommendation, and an even fewer number actually permit the jury to impose sentence. Although not constitutionally required, the jury always plays a role in deciding whether death should be imposed.

The legislature determines how a crime should be punished. Legislatures normally set ranges within which judges may punish violators. In recent years there has been a substantial movement to limit the discretion of judges. This has been done in the federal system and many states.

The right of the legislative branch in this area is curbed by the Eighth Amendment, which prohibits "cruel and unusual punishment." The protection of the Eighth Amendment has been extended to state proceedings through the Fourteenth Amendment. However, legislatures enjoy wide discretion in deciding how to punish criminals.

Sentencing Procedure

The Presentence Investigation/No Right to Counsel.   After a defendant is determined guilty, a sentencing date is set. For most felonies and misdemeanors the date will be set far enough in the future to permit the probation officer to complete a presentence investigation.

The investigation typically begins with an interview of the defendant. Information concerning the defendant's drug habits, criminal history, family, employment history, education, medical and psychological problems, and personal finances is obtained. The defendant is also permitted to give his or her version of the facts surrounding the offense. There appears to be no right to counsel during this interview,[1] although most courts and probation officers permit attorneys to attend. The Seventh Circuit Court of Appeals held that the Sixth Amendment right to counsel does not apply at presentence interviews by probation officers. The court reasoned that because probation officers are neutral judicial employees, and not law enforcement officers, interviews conducted by them are not critical stages of an *adversarial* proceeding.[2] The Seventh Circuit, like other courts that have considered the issue, thus determined that the presentence interview is a neutral, nonadversarial meeting between the probation officer and the defendant. This is so even though the defendant may be in custody and admissions could lead to greater punishment.

Three facts support the conclusion that there is no right to counsel during a presentence investigation interview. First, the objective of the interview is to gather information to assist the sentencing court, not to establish that the defendant committed a crime. Second (and related to the first), a probation officer is not, strictly speaking, a law enforcement officer. Third, the questions asked at the interview are routine and defense counsel can properly advise the client of his or her rights before the interview occurs.

In addition to conducting an interview of the defendant, the probation officer will obtain copies of vital documents, such as the defendant's "rap sheet" and relevant medical records. The probation officer will attempt to verify the information provided by the defendant through these documents and other investigatory processes.

When the probation officer has completed the investigation, a presentence report is prepared. This report reflects the information discovered during the investigation and is used by the court in determining what sentence should be imposed. Often, the prosecutor and law enforcement officers involved in prosecuting the defendant, family members of the defendant, and the victim of the crime are permitted to make statements that are incorporated into the report.

There is no constitutional right to the preparation of a presentence report; however, most jurisdictions have followed the lead of the federal government, which requires a presentence report unless there is in the record information sufficient to enable the meaningful exercise of sentencing discretion.[3]

In the federal system, the defendant is entitled to review the presentence report prior to sentencing. This is true in most states as well, but right is not absolute. For example, the recommendation of the probation officer may be kept confidential.[4]

At the sentencing hearing, the defendant may disprove factual statements contained in the report. To this end witnesses may be called and exhibits introduced.

The Sentencing Hearing.   The next stage in the process is the sentencing hearing. Sentencing hearings are adversarial. Witnesses may be called, other evidence introduced, and arguments made. In most instances the hearing is before a judge, not a jury, and accordingly the rules of evidence are relaxed. When before a jury, such as in capital cases, the rules of evidence are fully effective. This is a critical stage under the Sixth Amendment, and therefore there is a right to counsel.

In most instances, sentencing facts are established by preponderance of the evidence and are found by the sentencing judge. In rare instances, however, clear and convincing evidence or proof beyond a reasonable doubt is required. Death cases are an example. This issue has also arisen in the context of sentence enhancements. For example, due process requires that any fact that increases the penalty for a crime beyond the prescribed statutory maximum, other than the fact of a prior conviction, must be submitted to a jury and proved beyond a reasonable doubt. So, a sentencing scheme that increases the punishment for racially motivated second degree murder beyond the limits set by the second degree murder statute is invalid unless the racial motive is proved to the jury beyond a reasonable doubt.[5]

One issue that has received considerable attention, and contradictory treatment, from the Supreme Court in recent years is the use of **victim impact statements** at sentencing. A *victim impact statement* is an oral or written statement to the sentencing judge explaining how the crime has affected the victim and, possibly, the victim's family. In 1987 the Supreme Court handed down *Booth v. Maryland*, 482 U.S. 496 (1987), wherein it invalidated a state statute

victim impact statement
At the time of sentencing, a statement made to the court concerning the effect the crime has had on the victim or on the victim's family.

requiring sentencing judges to consider victim impact statements in capital cases. The Court determined that the use of victim impact statements could prejudice the proceeding by injecting irrelevant, but inflammatory, evidence into the sentencing determination.

Only four years later, though, the Supreme Court overruled *Booth* in *Payne v. Tennessee*. Thus, victim impact evidence may be admitted, even if it is not related to the facts surrounding the crime. The decision concerning admissibility must be made on a case-by-case basis, and it is a violation of due process to admit evidence that is so prejudicial that the sentencing becomes fundamentally unfair.

On the other side of the coin, defendants are generally allowed to present nearly any evidence at sentencing. This is constitutionally mandated in capital cases; the Supreme Court has said that a state cannot preclude a defendant from proffering evidence in support of a sentence less than death.[6]

Punishing Acquitted Crimes.   Historically, judges have held considerable discretion in sentencing. The rules of evidence are relaxed and judges may hear evidence that is otherwise inadmissible. Victim impact evidence, family history, medical history, mental health history, employment history, and criminal history are examples of the type of evidence that is considered at sentencing.

Additionally, the nature of the crime committed and the particular manner in which it was committed are considered as well. In some cases, evidence concerning the nature and manner of the offense may include evidence of other crimes that were committed in conjunction with the offense under sentence. An interesting question concerns whether a defendant may have a sentence increased for acquitted crimes. This issue was before the Supreme Court in *United States v. Watts* (1997).[7] Police discovered both cocaine and guns in a search of Watts's property and he was subsequently charged and tried for possession of cocaine and possession of a gun in relation to a drug offense. The jury convicted him of the former charge and acquitted him of the latter charge. At sentencing, however, the trial judge found that Watts did use the gun in relation to a drug offense and accordingly, increased his sentence for the cocaine possession conviction.

On appeal, the Supreme Court affirmed the sentence enhancement. The Court stressed that judges have historically had significant discretion in sentencing and that the enhancement was not punishment for an acquitted offense, but instead was an enhanced punishment for the manner in which the defendant committed the crime of conviction. Also important are the differing standards of proof between conviction and sentencing. Conviction requires a finding beyond a reasonable doubt while sentencing requires proof by preponderance of the evidence. The high standard of proof for conviction, according to the Court, means that an acquittal cannot be interpreted as a finding of fact. An acquittal means that the government has not proved its case, not that the defendant did not commit the act in question.

Forms of Punishment

The legislature determines what type of sentence may be imposed; judges impose sentences.

Capital Punishment.   Clearly the most controversial punishment is the death penalty. In early American history, capital punishment was commonly used. During the nineteenth century, use of the death penalty greatly declined. Today, more than half the states provide for the death penalty, and its use has regained popular support. Although the number of inmates actually executed every year is small, the number is increasing.

The contention that the death penalty is inherently cruel and unusual and therefore violative of the Eighth Amendment has been rejected. However, the Court has struggled, as have state courts and legislatures, with establishing standards for its use.

In *Furman v. Georgia*, 408 U.S. 238 (1972), the Court held that the death penalty cannot be imposed under a sentencing procedure that creates a substantial risk of being implemented in an arbitrary manner. It found that Georgia's law permitted arbitrary decisions and so declared it void. *Furman* required that the sentencer's discretion be limited by objective standards to eliminate unfairness— specifically, to eliminate racial and other bias from death sentence decisions.

States responded to *Furman* in a variety of ways. Some chose to eliminate discretion entirely by mandating capital punishment for certain crimes. The Supreme Court invalidated mandatory capital punishment laws in *Locket v. Ohio*, 438 U.S. 586 (1978). In *Locket* the Court held that individualized sentencing was constitutionally required. The Court stated that any law prohibiting a sentencer from considering "as a mitigating factor, any aspect of a defendant's character or record and any circumstances of the offense that the defendant proffers as a basis for a sentence less than death" creates an unconstitutional risk that the "death penalty will be imposed in spite of factors which may call for a less severe penalty."[8]

 CASE ━━━◆

PAYNE V.

TENNESSEE

501 U.S. 808 (1991)

In this case we reconsider our holdings in *Booth v. Maryland* . . . that the Eighth Amendment bars the admission of victim impact statement evidence during the penalty phase of a capital trial.

The petitioner, Pervis Tyrone Payne, was convicted by a jury on two counts of first-degree murder and one count of assault with intent to commit murder in the first degree. He was sentenced to death for each of the murders, and to 30 years in prison for assault.

The victims of Payne's offenses were 28-year-old Charisse Christopher, her 2-year-old daughter Lacie, and her 3-year-old son Nicholas. The three lived together . . . across the hall from Payne's girlfriend, Bobbie Thomas. On Saturday, June 27, 1987, Payne visited Thomas's apartment several times in expectation of her return from her mother's house in Arkansas, but found no one at home. One visit, he left his overnight bag, containing clothes and other items for his weekend stay, in the hallway outside Thomas's apartment. With the bag were three cans of malt liquor.

Payne passed the morning and early afternoon injecting cocaine and drinking beer. Later, he drove around the town with a friend in the friend's car, each of them taking turns reading a pornographic magazine. Sometime around 3 p.m., Payne returned to the apartment complex, entered the

Christophers' apartment, and began making sexual advances toward Charisse. Charisse resisted and Payne became violent. A neighbor who resided in the apartment directly beneath the Christophers heard Charisse screaming, " 'Get out, get out,' as if she were telling the children to leave." The noise briefly subsided and then began "horribly loud." The neighbor called the police after she heard a "bloodcurdling scream" from the Christopher apartment. . . .

When the first police officer arrived at the scene, he immediately encountered Payne, who was leaving the apartment building, so covered with blood that he appeared to be "sweating blood." The officer confronted Payne, who responded, "I'm the complainant.". . . When the officer asked, "What is going on up there?" Payne struck the officer with the overnight bag, dropped his tennis shoes, and fled.

Inside the apartment, the police encountered a horrifying scene. Blood covered the walls and floor throughout the unit. Charisse and her children were lying on the floor in the kitchen. Nicholas, despite several wounds inflicted by a butcher knife that completely penetrated through his body from front to back, was still breathing. Miraculously, he survived. . . . Charisse and Lacie were dead.

Charisse's body was found on the kitchen floor on her back, her legs fully extended. . . . None of the 84 wounds inflicted by Payne were individually fatal; rather, the cause of death was most likely bleeding from all of the wounds. She had suffered stab wounds to the chest, abdomen, back, and head. The murder weapon, a butcher knife, was found at her feet. Payne's baseball cap was snapped on her arm near her elbow. Three cans of malt liquor bearing Payne's fingerprints were found near her body, and a fourth empty was on a landing outside the apartment door.

Payne was apprehended later that day. . . .

[T]he jury returned guilty verdicts against Payne on all counts.

During the sentencing phase of the trial, Payne presented the testimony of four witnesses, his mother and father, Bobbie Thomas, and Dr. John T.

Huston, a clinical psychologist specializing in criminal court evaluation work. Bobbie Thomas testified that she met Payne at church, during a time when she was being abused by her husband. She stated that Payne was a very caring person, and that he devoted much time and attention to her three children, who were being affected by her marital difficulties. She said that the children had come to love him very much and would miss him, and that he "behaved just like a father that loved his kids." She asserted that he did not drink, nor did he use drugs, and that it was generally inconsistent with Payne's character to have committed these crimes. . . .

The State presented the testimony of Charisse's mother, Mary Zvolanek. When asked how Nicholas had been affected by the murder of his mother and sister, she responded:

He cries for his mom. He doesn't seem to understand why she doesn't come home. And he cries for his sister Lacie. He comes to me many times during the week and asks me, Grandma, do you miss Lacie. And I tell him yes. He says, I'm worried about my Lacie.

In arguing for the death penalty during closing argument, the prosecutor commented on the continuing effects of Nicholas's experience, stating:

But we do know that Nicholas was alive. And Nicholas was in the same room. Nicholas was still conscious. His eyes were open. He responded to the paramedics. He was able to follow their directions. He was able to hold his intestines in as he was carried to the ambulance. So he knew what happened to his mother and baby sister. . . .

Somewhere down the road Nicholas is going to grow up, hopefully. He's going to want to know what happened. And he is going to know what happened to his baby sister and mother. He is going to want to know what type of justice was done. He is going to want to know what happened. With your verdict, you will provide the answer. . . .

In the rebuttal to Payne's closing argument, the prosecutor stated:

You saw the videotape this morning. You saw what Nicholas Christopher will carry in his mind forever. When you talk about cruel, when you talk about atrocious, and when you talk about heinous, that picture will always come into your mind, probably throughout the rest of your lives.

* * *

No one will ever know about Lacie Jo because she never had a chance to grow up. Her life was taken from her at the age of two years old. . . . His mother will never kiss [Nicholas] good night or pat him as he goes off to bed, or hold him and sing him a lullaby. [Petitioner's attorney] wants you to think about a good reputation, people who love the defendant and things about him. He doesn't want you to think about the people who loved Charisse Christopher, her mother, and daddy who loved her. The people who loved little Lacie Jo, the grandparents who are still here. The brother who mourns for her every single day and wants to know where his best little playmate is. He doesn't have anybody to watch cartoons with him, a little one. These are the things that go into why it is especially cruel, heinous, and atrocious, the burden that child will carry forever.

The jury sentenced Payne to death on each of the murder counts. The Supreme Court of Tennessee affirmed the conviction and sentence. . . .

We granted certiorari . . . to reconsider our holdings in *Booth* . . . that the Eighth Amendment prohibits a capital sentencing jury from considering "victim impact" evidence relating to the personal characteristics of the victim and the emotional impact of the crimes on the victim's family. . . .

Under our constitutional system, the primary responsibility for defining crimes against state law, fixing punishments for the commission of these crimes, and establishing procedures for criminal trials rests with the States. The state laws respecting crimes, punishments, and criminal procedure are of course subject to the overriding provisions of the United States Constitution. . . .

Within the constitutional limitations defined in our cases, the States enjoy their traditional latitude to prescribe the method by which those who commit murder should be punished. . . . The states remain free, in capital cases, as well as others, to devise new procedures and new remedies to meet felt needs. Victim impact evidence is simply another form or method of informing the sentencing authority about the specific harm caused by the crime in question, evidence of a general type long considered by sentencing authorities. [The] *Booth* Court was wrong in stating that this kind of evidence leads to the arbitrary imposition of the death penalty. In the majority of cases, and in this case, victim impact evidence serves entirely legitimate purposes. In the event that evidence is introduced that is so unduly prejudicial that it renders the trial fundamentally unfair, the Due Process Clause of the Fourteenth Amendment provides a mechanism for relief. . . . Courts have always taken into consideration the harm done by the defendant in imposing sentence, and the evidence adduced in this case was illustrative of the harm caused by Payne's double murder.

We are now of the view that a State may properly conclude that for the jury to assess meaningfully the defendant's moral culpability and blameworthiness, it should have before it at the sentencing phase evidence of the specific harm caused by the defendant. "[T]he State has a legitimate interest in counteracting the mitigating evidence which the defendant is entitled to put in, by reminding the sentencer that just as the murderer should be considered an individual, so too the victim is an individual whose death represents a unique loss to society and in particular to his family." . . . By turning the victim into a "faceless stranger at the penalty phase of a criminal trial" . . . *Booth* deprives the State of the full moral force of its evidence and may prevent the jury from having before it all the information necessary to determine the proper punishment for a first-degree murder.

The present case is an example of the potential for such unfairness. The capital sentencing jury heard testimony from Payne's girlfriend that they met at church, that he was affectionate, caring, kind to her children. . . . Payne's parents testified that he was a good son, and a clinical psychologist testified that Payne was an extremely polite prisoner and suffered from a low IQ. None of this testimony was related to the circumstances of Payne's brutal crimes. . . . The Supreme Court of Tennessee in this case obviously felt the unfairness of the rule pronounced in *Booth* when it said "[i]t is an affront to the civilized members of the human race to say that at sentencing in a capital case,

a parade of witnesses may praise the background, character and good deeds of the defendant (as was done in this case), without limitation as to relevancy, but nothing may be said that bears upon the character of, or the harm imposed, upon the victims.". . .

We thus hold that if the State chooses to permit the admission of victim impact evidence and prosecutorial argument on that subject, the Eighth Amendment erects no per se bar.

♦

However, Georgia's new death penalty legislation was upheld in *Gregg v. Georgia*, 428 U.S. 153 (1976). The new law provided that the jury must find, in a sentencing hearing separate from the trial, an aggravating circumstance before the death penalty could be imposed. The statute enumerated possible aggravating circumstances. By requiring a jury to find an aggravating circumstance, arbitrariness is believed to be lessened.

Furman, Gregg, Locket, and their progeny stand for the principle that a sentencing statute cannot totally eliminate discretion, nor grant so much discretion that the death penalty can be imposed arbitrarily. These concepts of individualized sentencing and minimized discretion in sentencing are somewhat antithetical. The Supreme Court itself recognizes that a tension exists between the two goals and has struggled to establish procedures and standards to successfully implement them. "Experience has shown that the consistency and rationality promised in *Furman* are inversely related to the fairness owed the individual when considering a sentence of death. A step toward consistency is a step away from fairness."[9]

The death penalty issue has been divisive to the Court. Some Justices have so strongly believed that the death penalty is unconstitutional (either inherently or as administered) that they have refused to acquiesce to notions of *stare decisis* on the issue. Justice Thurgood Marshall, for example, dissented in every capital punishment case, including both denials of petitions of certiorari and cases under review, because of his firmly held belief that capital punishment was unconstitutional.

Until 1994, Justice Blackmun held that the death penalty was not inherently unconstitutional. However, in *Callins v. Collins*, he made the following statement.

Courts are in the very business of erecting procedural devices from which fair, equitable, and reliable outcomes are presumed to flow. Yet, in the death penalty area, this Court, in my view, had engaged in a futile effort to balance these constitutional demands, and now is retreating not only from the *Furman* promise of consistency and rationality, but from the requirement of individualized sentencing as well. Having virtually conceded that both fairness and rationality cannot be achieved in the administration of the death penalty . . . the Court has chosen to deregulate the entire enterprise, replacing, it would seem, substantive constitutional requirements with mere aesthetics, and abdicating its statutorily and constitutionally imposed duty to provide meaningful judicial oversight to the administration of death by the States. From this date forward, I no longer shall tinker with the machinery of death. For more than 20 years I have endeavored—indeed, I have struggled—along with a majority of this Court, to develop procedural and substantive rules that would lend more than the mere appearance of fairness to the death penalty endeavor. Rather than continue to coddle the Court's delusion that the desired level of fairness has been achieved and the need for regulation eviscerated, I feel morally and intellectually obligated simply to concede that the death penalty experiment has failed. It is virtually self-evident to me now that no combination of procedural rules or substantive regulations ever can save the death penalty from its inherent constitutional deficiencies. The basic question—does the system accurately and consistently determine which defendants "deserve" to die?—cannot be answered in the affirmative. It is not simply that this Court has allowed vague aggravating circumstances to be employed . . . relevant mitigating evidence to be disregarded . . . and vital judicial review to be blocked. . . . The problem is that the inevitability of factual, legal, and moral error gives us a system that we know must wrongly kill some defendants, a system that fails to deliver the fair, consistent, and reliable sentences of death required by the Constitution. . . . Perhaps one day this Court will develop procedural rules or verbal formulas that actually will provide consistency, fairness, and reliability in a capital-sentencing scheme. I am not optimistic that such a day will come. I am more optimistic, though, that this Court eventually will conclude that the effort to eliminate arbitrariness while preserving fairness "in the infliction of [death] is so plainly doomed to failure that it—and the death penalty—must be abandoned altogether." . . . I may not live to see that day, but I have faith that eventually it will arrive. The path the Court has chosen lessens us all. I dissent.[10]

THE DEATH PENALTY MORATORIUM MOVEMENT Although a majority of Americans support the death penalty, recent polling also reveals majority support for a moratorium until fairness issues are addressed. Specifically, concerns about wrongly convicted prisoners and a possible racial bias in the administration of the penalty have led many conservatives who support the death penalty to join with death penalty abolitionists in support of a moratorium. The movement has had moderate success. Illinois Governor Ryan imposed a moratorium on imposing death in 2000. In the same year, the New Hampshire legislature became the first state legislature to abolish the punishment since 1965. Although this bill was subsequently vetoed by the Governor, it is evidence of a new attitude about the death penalty. Death penalty abolitionist movements have come and gone in United States history. Why has the movement picked-up steam now?

SIDEBAR

According to Jeffrey Kirchmeier, many events are fueling this movement, including the following:

- Sister Helen Prejean's book and subsequent movie, *Dead Man Walking.* Kirchmeier likens the impact of this book on the death penalty to the impact Harriet Beecher Stowe's book, *Uncle Tom's Cabin,* had on the slavery abolition movement.
- The criticism of Supreme Court Justices Blackmun and Powell, as well as that of many other judges.
- The 1997 American Bar Association statement urging a moratorium on the death penalty.
- New technologies have led to the discovery of wrongly convicted and sentenced individuals. Between 1973–2002, 99 prisoners were released from death row after new technology proved their innocence or at least established the absence of proof beyond a reasonable doubt.
- New research indicating that innocent persons are executed.
- The economy was good and the crime rate declined during the 1990s.
- There was considerable media attention of cases where prisoners who had been sentenced to death were later set free.
- Many states added the possibility of life without parole.

Source: Another Place Beyond Here: The Death Penalty Moratorium Movement in the United States, 73 University of Colorado Law Review 1 (2002).

One of the decisions of the Court that bothered Justice Blackmun was *McCleskey v. Kemp,* 481 U.S. 279 (1987), wherein the Court refused to set aside a death sentence even though the defendant presented reliable statistical data supporting the conclusion that race continues to be a significant factor in the application of capital punishment. The Court held that statistical evidence could not be used to invalidate an entire sentencing scheme; rather, the burden falls on each individual defendant to prove that race was a factor in his or her sentence. Justice Blackmun argued that the Court was thereby abandoning the *Furman* requirement of consistency and rationality.

SIDEBAR

CAPITAL PUNISHMENT IN THE UNITED STATES   In 2002, the laws of thirty-eight states and the federal government authorized capital punishment. Alaska, Hawaii, Iowa, Maine, Massachusetts, Michigan, Minnesota, North Dakota, Rhode Island, Vermont, West Virginia, and Wisconsin were the states without the death penalty. Also, there was no death penalty in the District of Columbia.

By the end of 2001 there were more than 3,000 people awaiting execution. Hundreds of new inmates sentenced to death are added to the total every year. A total of sixty-five were executed in 2001. Between 1976 (Furman decision) and 2001, 749 people were executed in the United States. Texas leads in the number of people executed, where 265 people were executed between 1977 and mid-year 2002. Virginia executed 85 during that period. Interestingly, Delaware has the largest per capita execution rate—0.167 per 10,000 people.

Electrocution and lethal injection are the primary methods of execution, but state laws also provide for gassing, hanging, and firing squad. Among prisoners executed between 1977 and 1997, the average time between imposition of the most recent sentence and the execution was longer than nine years.

Source: Death Penalty Information Center and Amnesty International. *Capital Punishment* 1999 (Bureau of Justice Statistics, December 1998).

The definition of cruelty is an evolving concept. Electrocution, lethal injection, hanging, and shooting are all approved methods of executing a prisoner. Other methods, such as starvation, would not pass constitutional muster.

The Eighth Amendment has been interpreted to prohibit sentences that are disproportionate to the crime committed. In this vein, the Supreme Court has held that capital punishment may not be imposed for the crime of raping an adult woman.[11] Similarly, a person may not be put to death for aiding in a felony that results in murder, unless there was an intent to kill.[12]

In 1986, the Supreme Court stated that defendants who are incapable of understanding why they are being executed because of insanity may not be executed until they regain their faculties.[13] The Court applied similar reasoning to reach the same conclusion about individuals who are mentally retarded in *Atkins v. Virginia*.

 CASE

ATKINS V. VIRGINIA

122 S.Ct. 2242 (2002)

Those mentally retarded persons who meet the law's requirements for criminal responsibility should be tried and punished when they commit crimes. Because of their disabilities in areas of reasoning, judgment, and control of their impulses, however, they do not act with the level of moral culpability that characterizes the most serious adult criminal conduct. Moreover, their impairments can jeopardize the reliability and fairness of capital proceedings against mentally retarded defendants. Presumably for these reasons, in the 13 years since we decided *Penry v. Lynaugh*, 492 U.S. 302 (1989), the American public, legislators, scholars, and judges have deliberated over the question whether the death penalty should ever be imposed on a mentally retarded criminal. The consensus reflected in those

deliberations informs our answer to the question presented by this case: whether such executions are "cruel and unusual punishments" prohibited by the Eighth Amendment to the Federal Constitution.

Petitioner, Daryl Renard Atkins, was convicted of abduction, armed robbery, and capital murder, and sentenced to death. At approximately midnight on August 16, 1996, Atkins and William Jones, armed with a semiautomatic handgun, abducted Eric Nesbitt, robbed him of the money on his person, drove him to an automated teller machine in his pickup truck where cameras recorded their withdrawal of additional cash, then took him to an isolated location where he was shot eight times and killed. . . .

In the penalty phase, the defense relied on one witness, Dr. Evan Nelson, a forensic psychologist who had evaluated Atkins before trial and concluded that he was "mildly mentally retarded." His conclusion was based on interviews with people who knew Atkins, a review of school and court records, and the administration of a standard intelligence test which indicated that Atkins had a full scale IQ of 59. . . .

The jury sentenced Atkins to death, but the Virginia Supreme Court ordered a second sentencing hearing because the trial court had used a misleading verdict form. 257 Va. 160, 510 S. E. 2d 445 (1999). At the resentencing, Dr. Nelson again testified. The State presented an expert rebuttal witness, Dr. Stanton Samenow, who expressed the opinion that Atkins was not mentally retarded, but rather was of "average intelligence, at least," and diagnosable as having antisocial personality disorder. App. 476. The jury again sentenced Atkins to death.

The Supreme Court of Virginia affirmed the imposition of the death penalty. Atkins did not argue before the Virginia Supreme Court that his sentence was disproportionate to penalties imposed for similar crimes in Virginia, but he did contend "that he is mentally retarded and thus cannot be sentenced to death." The majority of the state court rejected this contention, relying on our holding in *Penry*. The Court was "not willing to commute Atkins' sentence of death to life imprisonment merely because of his IQ score."

The Eighth Amendment succinctly prohibits "excessive" sanctions. It provides: "Excessive bail shall not be required, nor excessive fines imposed, nor cruel and unusual punishments inflicted." In *Weems v. United States*, 217 U.S. 349 (1910), we held that a punishment of 12 years jailed in irons at hard and painful labor for the crime of falsifying records was excessive. We explained "that it is a precept of justice that punishment for crime should be graduated and proportioned to the offense." *Id.*, at 367. We have repeatedly applied this proportionality precept in later cases interpreting the Eighth Amendment. . . .

A claim that punishment is excessive is judged not by the standards that prevailed in 1685 when Lord Jeffreys presided over the "Bloody Assizes" or when the Bill of Rights was adopted, but rather by those that currently prevail. As Chief Justice Warren explained in his opinion in *Trop v. Dulles*,

356 U.S. 86 (1958): "The basic concept underlying the Eighth Amendment is nothing less than the dignity of man. . . . The Amendment must draw its meaning from the evolving standards of decency that mark the progress of a maturing society." . . .

Proportionality review under those evolving standards should be informed by " 'objective factors to the maximum possible extent,' " see *Harmelin*, 501 U. S., at 1000 (quoting *Rummel v. Estelle*, 445 U.S 263, 274–275 (1980)). We have pinpointed that the "clearest and most reliable objective evidence of contemporary values is the legislation enacted by the country's legislatures." *Penry*, 492 U.S., at 331. Relying in part on such legislative evidence, we have held that death is an impermissibly excessive punishment for the rape of an adult woman, *Coker v. Georgia*, 433 U.S. 584, 593–596 (1977), or for a defendant who neither took life, attempted to take life, nor intended to take life, *Enmund v. Florida*, 458 U.S. 782, 789–793 (1982). . . .

We also acknowledged in *Coker* that the objective evidence, though of great importance, did not "wholly determine" the controversy, "for the Constitution contemplates that in the end our own judgment will be brought to bear on the question of the acceptability of the death penalty under the Eighth Amendment. . . .

The parties have not called our attention to any state legislative consideration of the suitability of imposing the death penalty on mentally retarded offenders prior to 1986. In that year, the public reaction to the execution of a mentally retarded murderer in Georgia apparently led to the enactment of the first state statute prohibiting such executions. In 1988, when Congress enacted legislation reinstating the federal death penalty, it expressly provided that a "sentence of death shall not be carried out upon a person who is mentally retarded." In 1989, Maryland enacted a similar prohibition. It was in that year that we decided *Penry*, and concluded that those two state enactments, "even when added to the 14 States that have rejected capital punishment completely, do not provide sufficient evidence at present of a national consensus." 492 U.S., at 334.

Much has changed since then. Responding to the national attention received by the Bowden execution and our decision in *Penry*, state legislatures across the country began to address the issue. In 1990 Kentucky and Tennessee enacted statutes similar to those in Georgia and Maryland, as did New Mexico in 1991, and Arkansas, Colorado, Washington, Indiana, and Kansas in 1993 and 1994. In 1995, when New York reinstated its death penalty, it emulated the Federal Government by expressly exempting the mentally retarded. Nebraska followed suit in 1998. There appear to have been no similar enactments during the next two years, but in 2000 and 2001 six more States—South Dakota, Arizona, Connecticut, Florida, Missouri, and North Carolina—joined the procession. The Texas Legislature unanimously adopted a similar bill, and bills have passed at least one house in other States, including Virginia and Nevada.

It is not so much the number of these States that is significant, but the consistency of the direction of change. Given the well-known fact that anticrime legislation is far more popular than legislation providing protections for persons guilty of violent crime, the large number of States prohibiting the execution of mentally retarded persons (and the complete absence of States passing legislation reinstating the power to conduct such executions) provides powerful evidence that today our society views mentally retarded offenders as categorically less culpable than the average criminal. The evidence carries even greater force when it is noted that the legislatures that have addressed the issue have voted overwhelmingly in favor of the prohibition. Moreover, even in those States that allow the execution of mentally retarded offenders, the practice is uncommon. Some States, for example New Hampshire and New Jersey, continue to authorize executions, but none have been carried out in decades. Thus there is little need to pursue legislation barring the execution of the mentally retarded in those States. And it appears that even among those States that regularly execute offenders and that have no prohibition with regard to the mentally retarded, only five have executed offenders possessing a known IQ less than 70 since we decided *Penry*. The practice, therefore, has become truly unusual, and it is fair to say that a national consensus has developed against it.

To the extent there is serious disagreement about the execution of mentally retarded offenders, it is in determining which offenders are in fact retarded. In this case, for instance, the Commonwealth of Virginia disputes that Atkins suffers from mental retardation. Not all people who claim to be mentally retarded will be so impaired as to fall within the range of mentally retarded offenders about whom there is a national consensus. As was our approach in *Ford v. Wainwright*, with regard to insanity, "we leave to the State[s] the task of developing appropriate ways to enforce the constitutional restriction upon its execution of sentences." 477 U.S. 399, 405, 416–417 (1986).

As discussed above, clinical definitions of mental retardation require not only subaverage intellectual functioning, but also significant limitations in adaptive skills such as communication, self-care, and self-direction that became manifest before age 18. Mentally retarded persons frequently know the difference between right and wrong and are competent to stand trial. Because of their impairments, however, by definition they have diminished capacities to understand and process information, to communicate, to abstract from mistakes and learn from experience, to engage in logical reasoning, to control impulses, and to understand the reactions of others. There is no evidence that they are more likely to engage in criminal conduct than others, but there is abundant evidence that they often act on impulse rather than pursuant to a premeditated plan, and that in group settings they are followers rather than leaders. Their deficiencies do not warrant an exemption from criminal sanctions, but they do diminish their personal culpability.

In light of these deficiencies, our death penalty jurisprudence provides two reasons consistent with the legislative consensus that the mentally retarded should be categorically excluded from execution.

First, there is a serious question as to whether either justification that we have recognized as a basis for the death penalty applies to mentally retarded offenders. *Gregg v. Georgia*, 428 U.S. 153, 183 (1976), identified "retribution and deterrence of capital crimes by prospective offenders" as the social purposes served by the death penalty. Unless the imposition of the death penalty on a mentally retarded person "measurably contributes to one or both of these goals, it 'is nothing more than the purposeless and needless imposition of pain and suffering,' and hence an unconstitutional punishment." *Enmund*, 458 U.S., at 798.

With respect to retribution—the interest in seeing that the offender gets his "just deserts"—the severity of the appropriate punishment necessarily depends on the culpability of the offender. Since *Gregg*, our jurisprudence has consistently confined the imposition of the death penalty to a narrow category of the most serious crimes. For example, in *Godfrey v. Georgia*, 446 U.S. 420 (1980), we set aside a death sentence because the petitioner's crimes did not reflect "a consciousness materially more 'depraved' than that of any person guilty of murder." *Id.*, at 433. If the culpability of the average murderer is insufficient to justify the most extreme sanction available to the State, the lesser culpability of the mentally retarded offender surely does not merit that form of retribution. Thus, pursuant to our narrowing jurisprudence, which seeks to ensure that only the most deserving of execution are put to death, an exclusion for the mentally retarded is appropriate.

With respect to deterrence—the interest in preventing capital crimes by prospective offenders—"it seems likely that 'capital punishment can serve as a deterrent only when murder is the result of premeditation and deliberation,' "*Enmund*, 458 U.S., at 799. Exempting the mentally retarded from that punishment will not affect the "cold calculus that precedes the decision" of other potential murderers. *Gregg*, 428 U.S., at 186. Indeed, that sort of calculus is at the opposite end of the spectrum from behavior of mentally retarded offenders. The theory of deterrence in capital sentencing is predicated upon the notion that the increased severity of the punishment will inhibit criminal actors from carrying out murderous conduct. Yet it is the same cognitive and behavioral impairments that make these defendants less morally culpable—for example, the diminished ability to understand and process information, to learn from experience, to engage in logical reasoning, or to control impulses—that also make it less likely that they can process the information of the possibility of execution as a penalty and, as a result, control their conduct based upon that information. Nor will exempting the mentally retarded from execution lessen the deterrent effect of the death penalty with respect to offenders who are not mentally retarded. Such individuals are unprotected by the exemption and will continue to face the threat of execution. Thus, executing the mentally retarded will not measurably further the goal of deterrence.

The reduced capacity of mentally retarded offenders provides a second justification for a categorical rule making such offenders ineligible for the death penalty. The risk "that the death penalty will be imposed in spite of factors which may call for a less severe penalty," *Locket v. Ohio*, 438 U.S. 586, 605 (1978), is enhanced, not only by the possibility of false confessions,[25] but also by the lesser ability of mentally retarded defendants to make a persuasive showing of mitigation in the face of prosecutorial evidence of one or more aggravating factors. Mentally retarded defendants may be less able to give meaningful assistance to their counsel and are typically poor witnesses, and their demeanor may create an unwarranted impression of lack of remorse for their crimes. As *Penry* demonstrated, moreover, reliance on mental retardation as a mitigating factor can be a two-edged sword that may enhance the likelihood that the aggravating factor of future dangerousness will be found by the jury. 492 U.S., at 323–325. Mentally retarded defendants in the aggregate face a special risk of wrongful execution.

Our independent evaluation of the issue reveals no reason to disagree with the judgment of "the legislatures that have recently addressed the matter" and concluded that death is not a suitable punishment for a mentally retarded criminal. We are not persuaded that the execution of mentally retarded criminals will measurably advance the deterrent or the retributive purpose of the death penalty. Construing and applying the Eighth Amendment in the light of our "evolving standards of decency," we therefore conclude that such punishment is excessive and that the Constitution "places a substantive restriction on the State's power to take the life" of a mentally retarded offender. *Ford*, 477 U.S., at 405.

The judgment of the Virginia Supreme Court is reversed and the case is remanded for further proceedings not inconsistent with this opinion.

EXECUTIVE CLEMENCY, PARDONS, AND REPRIEVES   In most states and the federal government, the chief executive (i.e., the governor or the president) possesses several powers concerning criminal convictions and sentences. One such power is executive clemency. To forgive or, more commonly, to reduce a punishment is clemency. To reduce a prisoner's sentence from death to life imprisonment is clemency. The reduction of a sentence is also known as **commutation of sentence**. Commutation is used when the executive believes a person guilty, but also believes the sentence is too harsh. In 1993 the Supreme Court ruled that prisoners sentenced to death who claim to have new evidence of their innocence do not possess the right to federal review in all instances. The court indicated that executive clemency is the "fail-safe" to guard against unwarranted executions.

The **pardon** is similar to commutation of sentence in that both relieve a person of punishment. However, the pardon is different in one important respect: it also relieves the defendant of the conviction. With the pardon, the conviction is erased and treated as though it never occurred. Pardons are used when the executive believes there was an error concerning the defendant's guilt.

Finally, a **reprieve** is a stay or delay of execution of sentence. Reprieves are used to give the executive or a court the opportunity to further review the case.

The governor has the sole authority to grant clemency in thirty-one states. In ten states, clemency boards have the final authority. In seven states, clemency boards make recommendations to their respective governors. In Rhode Island, the governor can grant clemency only with the consent of that state's senate.

Sources: Janice Brown, "Note: The Quality of Mercy," 40 *U.C.L.A. L. Rev.* 327 (1992), citing Deborah Leavy, "Note, A Matter of Life or Death: Due Process Protection in Capital Clemency Proceedings," 90 *Yale L.J.* 889, 895–96 (1981).

SIDEBAR

commutation of sentence
Changing a criminal punishment to one less severe.

pardon
A president's or governor's release of a person from punishment for a crime.

reprieve
Holding off on enforcing a criminal **sentence** for a period of time after the sentence has been handed down.

Corporal/Physical Punishment.   The Eighth Amendment limits the use of physical punishment. Punishment is not, however, unconstitutional simply because it involves pain. The issue is whether the pain is excessive. Pain is excessive when it exceeds the quantity necessary to achieve a legitimate penological purpose, such as rehabilitation or retribution. Generally, hard labor is not per se cruel.[14] If the labor is beyond the physical limits of the inmate, or involves unnecessary pain, it is unconstitutional.

Whipping has been held both constitutional[15] and unconstitutional[16] by lower courts. The Supreme Court has not decided the issue.[17]

Solitary confinement may be used in some circumstances, such as when a prisoner is disruptive or is highly dangerous. The use of prolonged solitary confinement for other prisoners is of questionable constitutionality.

The basic medical and nutritional needs of inmates must be satisfied by the government. Deliberately disregarding the medical or nutritional needs of inmates, or in some other manner imposing cruel or unusual punishment, can lead to liability under 42 U.S.C. § 1983.

The Supreme Court has said that the Eighth Amendment is to be interpreted consistent with society's evolving standards of decency. Therefore, although some courts have approved sterilization, and many states are considering chemical castration of men who commit sexual assault, there is a possibility that such practices could be found inconsistent with the Eighth Amendment.

Incarceration.   Restraint is an effective method of dealing with dangerous persons. Incarceration serves this purpose, and in some cases the offender is also rehabilitated. Regrettably, because rehabilitation is rare and (contrary to popular belief) prison conditions are often poor, many offenders leave prison angry, no more educated or employable, and occasionally more dangerous.

Nevertheless, incarceration continues to be the most common method of punishing violent offenders. Offenders may be committed to prisons, camps, or local jails. Those sentenced to short terms (one year or less) are usually housed in a local jail. Individuals sentenced to longer terms are committed to prisons.

indeterminate sentence

A sentence having a minimum and maximum, with the decision of how long the criminal will serve depending on the criminal's behavior in prison and other things.

determinate sentence

An exact penalty set by law.

Indeterminate and Determinate Sentencing.   The **indeterminate** sentence gives corrections officials the greatest amount of control over an inmate's sentence. Under an indeterminate sentence, the judge sets a minimum and maximum period to be served and the corrections agency determines the actual date of release. Once common in the United States, indeterminate sentencing has fallen into disfavor.

In **determinate sentencing** schemes, the sentencing judge is given discretion to set a fixed sentence from within a range set by the legislature. The determinate sentence is fixed and there is no possibility of early release.

Definite and Indefinite Sentencing.   Unlike determinate sentencing, with definite sentencing the sentencing judge has no discretion. Rather, the legislature establishes the specific penalty to be imposed for each crime and there is no possibility of early release. Definite sentencing reduces sentencing disparity. However, it is criticized for not allowing the particular facts of each case to be taken into consideration.

Indefinite sentencing incorporates both judicial and corrections agency discretion. It is the antithesis of definite sentencing. The sentencing judge is given a range from which to impose sentence and the corrections agency is delegated the authority to grant early releases.

Presumptive Sentencing.   In many instances, when a legislature gives the sentencing judge discretion, it also establishes a *presumptive sentence*. That is, the legislature states what sentence should be imposed from within a range, absent **aggravating** or **mitigating circumstances.** Circumstances upon which the judge relies to increase the presumptive sentence are aggravating; those used to justify a sentence below a presumption are mitigating.

If a judge deviates from a presumptive sentence, the aggravating or mitigating circumstances justifying the departure must be made part of the record. For example, an assault statute may call for one to three years' punishment with a presumptive sentence of eighteen months. If the judge sentences the defendant to more or less than eighteen months, the reasons must be reflected on the record. Of course, even when deviating from a presumption, the sentencing judge must remain with the statutory limits.

What constitutes an aggravating or mitigating circumstance is often expressed in the statute. Examples of aggravating circumstances are injury, torture, or death of the victim; use of a weapon during commission of the crime; whether the crime involved a child; and whether the defendant violated a trust. Examples of mitigating circumstances are physical disability of the defendant; the defendant's having dependents; a crime committed in a nonviolent manner; and the defendant's acting in good faith.

Suspended Imposition of Sentence. For some misdemeanors and infractions, judges are sometimes permitted to *suspend imposition of sentence* (SIS), also known as *diversion*. SIS is one of many forms of community-based correction, a term that refers to several varieties of nonincarceration correctional programs, such as probation, restitution, halfway houses, and parole. (Some of these other forms of community-based correction are discussed later.)

SIS is different from suspended sentencing. In SIS, a judge not only withholds sentencing the defendant, but also refrains from entering a judgment of conviction until some future date. If the defendant complies with imposed conditions until that date, the prosecution is dismissed and the defendant is freed from having a criminal record. Suspended sentences, in contrast, involve conviction and imposition of sentence, but the defendant is relieved of actually serving the sentence so long as conditions are satisfied.

Where available, SIS is usually limited to nonviolent misdemeanors and infractions and is available to first-time offenders only.

Concurrent and Consecutive Sentencing. If a defendant is already serving a sentence for another crime, or is convicted of two related crimes, the sentencing judge may impose **concurrent** or **consecutive sentences.** If two sentences are concurrent, it is said that they "run together." That is, a defendant who receives two five-year sentences will actually spend five years incarcerated. If the sentences are consecutive, the defendant will spend a total of ten years incarcerated.

Parole. After committing a defendant to a correctional institution, the judge loses control and responsibility over that defendant, unless a statute provides otherwise. In many states, **parole** is available to prison inmates. *Parole*, an early release from prison, is used to encourage inmates to stay out of trouble and engage in rehabilitative efforts while in prison. Parole decisions are made by

aggravating circumstances
Actions or occurrences that increase the seriousness of a crime, but are not part of the legal definition of that crime.

mitigating circumstances
Facts that provide no justification or excuse for an action, but that can lower the amount of moral blame, and thus lower the criminal penalty or civil damages for the action.

concurrent sentences
Prison terms that run at the same time.

consecutive sentences
An additional prison term given to a person who is already convicted of a crime; the additional term is to be served after the previous one is finished.

parole
Early release from prison or jail. Parole is usually granted with conditions such as requiring the parolee to refrain from communicating with the victim of the crime that led to the confinement and remaining free of criminality while on parole. If the conditions of parole are violated, parole may be revoked and the parolee may be returned to confinement to complete the original sentence.

corrections officials (i.e., a parole board). Similar to probation, an offender must comply with certain conditions while on parole. Conditions routinely include not possessing a gun; not contacting witnesses, judge, jurors, or prosecutors associated with the offender's conviction; and not becoming involved in further criminal activity. Violation of a condition of parole may result in recommitment to prison.

Parole has fallen into disfavor in recent years. The result has been to limit the availability of parole in many situations. Parole has been eliminated for those convicted of crimes against the United States.

The Federal Guidelines. In November 1987, the Federal Sentencing Guidelines became effective. The guidelines are a milestone in federal criminal law. Their purpose is twofold: (1) to reduce sentencing disparity and (2) to achieve "honesty in sentencing."[18] Prior to the Guidelines, judges were given a large penalty range from which a defendant could be sentenced. The result of this discretion was that defendants similarly situated were often sentenced very differently. One goal of the Guidelines is to reduce such disparity in sentencing.

The second goal, honesty in sentencing, concerns parole. Prior to the Guidelines, defendants could be released on parole, in some cases, after only one-third of the imposed sentence had been served. In addition, prisoners complained that parole was arbitrarily and inconsistently applied. Accordingly, Congress eliminated parole, and the guidelines now reflect the time that will be served, less fifty-four days of good time that may be earned yearly (after the first year).

To achieve the first goal—the reduction of sentencing disparity—the Guidelines greatly limit the discretion of the judge in sentencing. To determine what sentence should be imposed, the offender's criminal history category and offense level must be determined. The criminal history category is simply determined by the number of prior convictions of the offender.

Finding an offender's offense level is more complex. First, the crime is assigned a base offense number. That number is then increased by "specific offense characteristics." Adjustments to this figure are then made for mitigating or aggravating circumstances. This final figure is the offense level.

Once the criminal history category and offense level are determined, the court looks to the sentencing table. This table provides a small range (the top figure never exceeds 25 percent of the bottom figure) from which the judge is to sentence the defendant. Only in rare instances may a judge deviate from the proscribed sentencing range.

The Guidelines continue to permit judges to suspend sentences to probation for offenses at the low end of the sentencing table. For offenses just above the probation cutoff, judges may sentence an offender to probation, provided some form of confinement is ordered, such as house arrest or community confinement. There is also a third layer of offenses for which the judge may order a "split sentence." This is where one-half or more of the sentence must be served in prison, and the remaining amount may be served in another form of confinement.

A SENTENCING STORY   Sentencing a defendant today is much different from
years ago, as evidenced by the following sentence imposed upon a defendant in
the Federal District of the Territory of New Mexico. The sentence was imposed
by a United States judge, sitting in Taos, in an adobe stable used as a temporary courtroom.

"Jose Manuel Miguel Xavier Gonzales, in a few short weeks it will be
spring. The snows of winter will flee away, the ice will vanish, and the air
will become soft and balmy. In short, Jose Manuel Miguel Xavier Gonzales,
the annual miracle of the year's awakening will come to pass—but you won't
be here.

"The rivulet will run its purling course to the sea, the timid desert flowers
will put forth their tender roots, the glorious valleys of this imperial domain will
blossom as the rose—still you won't be here to see.

"From every treetop some wild woods songster will carol his mating song,
butterflies will sport in the sunshine, the busy bee will hum happily as it pursues
its accustomed vocation, the gentle breeze will tease the tassels of the wild
grasses, and all nature—Jose Manuel Miguel Xavier Gonzales—will be glad but
you. You won't be here to enjoy it because I command the sheriff or some other
officer or officers of this country to lead you out to some remote spot, swing you
by the neck from a nodding bough of some sturdy oak, and let you hang until you
are dead.

"And then, Jose Manuel Miguel Xavier Gonzales, I further command that
such officer or officers retire quickly from your dangling corpse, that the vultures
may descend from the heavens upon your filthy body, until nothing shall remain
but the bare, bleaching bones of a cold-blooded, copper-colored, blood-thirsty,
throat-cutting, sheep-herding, murdering son of a bitch."

The Guidelines have been the subject of much controversy. Federal judges
themselves have been very critical of the Guidelines. Many contend that
the reason judges are complaining is simply their loss of authority. Though this
may be true, there also appear to be problems caused by the rigidity of the
Guidelines.

The drafters of the Guidelines knew that all factors that should be considered in sentencing could not be anticipated (or quantified). As such, provisions
are made permitting deviation from the Guidelines. However, deviation is
rarely permitted. This has led to some absurd results. For example, one twenty-
one-year-old honor student, with no prior record, was sentenced to ten years
in prison for his involvement in one drug transaction.[19] At least one federal
district judge has resigned because of dissatisfaction with the guidelines.
Whether the guidelines will become more flexible remains to be seen.

The federal government was not the first to enact guideline sentencing. At
least two states, Minnesota and Washington, were using guidelines when the
federal version became law. It is probable that more jurisdictions will contemplate similar reform in the future.

PRISONS IN THE UNITED STATES   Lack of space in United States prisons is an ever-increasing concern. Most prisons are overcrowded, often housing double or triple the intended capacity; this leads to serious problems for both prison administrators and inmates. If prison conditions are extremely bad, an inmate may succeed in an Eighth Amendment lawsuit against prison authorities.

The total number of local, state, and federal prisoners was 1,962,220 in 2001. In 1989, the number was approximately 700,000. A total of 4.7 million people were on probation or parole in 2001. There were 470 inmates per 100,000 people in 2001 as opposed to 292 per 100,000 in 1990.

Increases in imprisonment of women and blacks continue to outpace that of men and Caucasians. Incarceration for drug offenses is increasing more than any other crime. Stiffer penalties and mandatory prison time for drug cases are largely responsible for the increase in the federal system. In 1980, 22.7 percent of the federal prison population consisted of drug offenders. By 1990, this group made up 47.8 percent of the federal inmate population.

Blacks constitute 46 percent of jail population; whites, 36 percent; Hispanics, 16 percent; and others, 2 percent. In 2001, 470 of each 100,000 residents of the U.S. were sentenced to jail or prison.

Source: Bureau of Justice Statistics (2000).

Probation and Revocation.   A popular alternative to incarceration is probation (also known as a **suspended sentence**). Probation is not always an alternative and is rarely available for crimes that are punished with life imprisonment or death. While on probation, the defendant is released from custody, but must comply with conditions imposed by the court during the probationary period. Each defendant is placed under the supervision of a probation officer during this period. The probation officer is an officer of the court, not of the corrections system.

Typical conditions of probation include a requirement of steady employment, refraining from other unlawful conduct, not carrying a firearm or other weapon, and not leaving the jurisdiction of the court. A judge may tailor conditions to fit the circumstances of each case. For example, a child molester may be prohibited from obtaining employment that requires working around children.

Some judges make consent to search by a probation officer a condition of probation. This may include search of the person as well as property. In some cases, judges impose the search requirement independently; in others, the defendant and prosecutor stipulate to the searches through a plea agreement. In either situation, are there limits to this authority? May a probation officer search a probationer at any time, in any manner, and without any cause to believe that mischief is afoot? Further, can a defendant who is facing incarceration as an alternative give meaningful consent to such a condition? This is the subject of the *Consuelo-Gonzalez* case, in which the court decided that probationers are entitled to full Fourth Amendment protection as to law enforcement officers generally. Searches by police officers of probationers must satisfy the usual Fourth Amendment requirements.

suspended sentence

A sentence (usually "jail time") that the judge allows the convicted person to avoid serving (usually if the person continues on good behavior, completes community service, etc.).

CASE

UNITED STATES V. CONSUELO-GONZALEZ

521 F.2d 259
(9th Cir. 1975)

Consuelo-Gonzalez appeals from a conviction under 21 USC § 841(a)(1) for possession of heroin with intent to distribute. We reverse.

Between November 15, 1972, and December 18, 1972, agents of the Federal Bureau of Narcotics and Dangerous Drugs received information from four different sources that Virginia Consuelo-Gonzalez was actively engaged in the importation and sale of heroin. A check of the records at the United States Attorney's Office on December 12, 1972, revealed to the agents that Virginia Consuelo-Gonzalez had previously been convicted of heroin smuggling under the name of Virginia Cardenas and was currently on probation. At this time, the agents were also apprised that it was a condition of Consuelo-Gonzalez's probation that she submit her person and property to search at any time upon request by a law enforcement officer. On December 14, 1972, an independent verification was made of the fact that Virginia Cardenas and Virginia Consuelo-Gonzalez were one and the same person; and on December 19, 1972, the agents reconfirmed the probationary status and condition that she submit to search.

On the morning of December 19, 1992, . . . federal and local law enforcement officers approached the Consuelo-Gonzalez residence for purposes of conducting a search of the premises. When they arrived, they found the front door of the house ajar. The agents knocked on the door and waited for Consuelo-Gonzalez to appear. When she did so, the lead agent showed her his identification, informed her that he was aware of her probation and the conditions which had been attached to it, and indicated his intention to enter the residence and conduct a search. Consuelo-Gonzalez responded to his request by stepping back and saying "Sure, search my purse." Upon entering the house, the lead agent made a cursory search of her handbag to determine whether it contained

weapons. None were found. The handbag was then placed beside a chair in which Consuelo-Gonzalez was asked to sit.

A thorough search of Consuelo-Gonzalez's person and residence was then commenced. In the bedroom, the agents found a narcotics injection outfit in a dresser; and on a shelf in the living room they discovered a paper sack containing a bundle of notebook papers with brown debris on them. Both of these items were seized. A second search of Consuelo-Gonzalez's handbag revealed two coin purses, inside of which the agents found two white paper bindles and seven rubber condoms containing a total of 11.7 grams of brown powder, later proven to be heroin. This evidence was also seized, and subsequently used to provide the basis for the present conviction.

In a timely and appropriate manner, counsel for Consuelo-Gonzalez moved to suppress this evidence. However, the trial judge denied the motion to suppress, relying specifically upon the authorization to search which had been made a condition of the probation. . . . Thereafter, defendant was found guilty of possession of heroin with intent to distribute. . . .

In this appeal, defendant asserts that the trial court erred in failing to suppress the evidence on the ground that the condition of probation requiring her to "submit to search of her person or property at any time when requested by a law-enforcement" officer was improper and thus could not serve to make the search lawful. It is argued that the Fourth Amendment requires this result.

While we are not prepared to embrace the full reach of defendant's argument, we do believe that the condition employed in the instant case is not in keeping with the purposes intended to be served by the Federal Probation Act. It is our view that, even though the trial judge has very broad discretion in fixing the terms and conditions of probation, such terms must be reasonably related to the purposes of the Act. In determining whether a reasonable relationship exists, we have found it necessary to give consideration to the purposes sought to be served by probation, the extent to which the full constitutional guarantees available to those not under probation should be accorded probationers, and the legitimate needs of law enforcement. Having done so, we have concluded that Consuelo-Gonzalez could have been required to submit her person and property to search by a probation officer. We have further concluded that any search made pursuant to the condition included in the terms of probation must necessarily meet the Fourth Amendment's standard of reasonableness. . . .

Although it is doubtful that any formulation of a condition relating to the search of a probationer's person or property can be drafted that will provide unambiguous guidance to both the probationer and the probation officer, it is suggested that the following condition would properly reflect the views expressed herein:

> That she submit to search of her person or property conducted in a reasonable manner and at a reasonable time by a probation officer.

. . . [W]e hold that the search in this case was improper and that the motion to suppress should have been granted. . . .

The guiding principle which has emerged in construing the Probation Act is that the only permissible conditions are those that, when considered in context, can reasonably be said to contribute significantly both to the rehabilitation of the convicted person and to the protection of the public. . . .

This guiding interpretive principle plainly suggests the manner in which the Act's administration should be accommodated to the constitutional guarantees of the Bill of Rights. While it must be recognized that probationers, like parolees and prisoners, properly are subject to limitations from which ordinary persons are free, it is also true that these limitations in the aggregate must serve the ends of probation. . . . [I]t is necessary to recognize that when fundamental rights are curbed it must be done sensitively and with a keen appreciation that the infringement must serve the broad purposes of the Probation Act. This burden cannot be avoided by asserting either that the probationer has voluntarily waived his rights by not objecting in a proper manner to the conditions imposed upon him or that he must accept any condition the court "deems best" as a consequence of being "in custody."

Turning to the Fourth Amendment rights that Consuelo-Gonzalez insists were infringed, two things are obvious. The first is that some forms of search by probation officers are not only compatible with rehabilitation, but, with respect to those convicted of certain offenses such as possession and distribution of narcotics; are also essential to the proper functioning of a probationary system. The second is that the condition imposed on Consuelo-Gonzalez literally permits searches which could not possibly serve the ends of probation. For example, an intimidating and harassing search to serve law enforcement ends totally unrelated to either her prior conviction or her rehabilitation is authorized by the terms of the condition. Submission to such searches should not be the price of probation. A probationer, like the parolee, has the right to enjoy a significant degree of privacy. . . .

Probation authorities also have a special and unique interest in invading the privacy of probationers. This special and unique interest does not extend to law enforcement officers generally. . . . Inasmuch as the search of Consuelo-Gonzalez's residence and handbag occurred neither during the course of a probation visit by a probation officer nor pursuant to a proper warrant, the evidence must be suppressed.

. . . [I]t may well be necessary during the course of a probation visit to conduct a pat-down search for weapons or contraband, to examine the probationer's arms to ascertain whether drugs are being used, or take the probationer into custody. When done reasonably and humanely by probation officers, no question concerning the appropriateness of their actions should arise. Moreover, a thorough search of a probationer's residence incident to, or following, a probation visit is not dependent upon the establishment of probable cause. A reasonable belief on the part of the probation officer that such a search is necessary to perform properly his duties is sufficient. As we said [in a prior case], this belief may be based on a "hunch" having its origin in what the probation officer has learned or observed about the behavior and attitude of the probationer.

Probationers are also protected by the Fourth Amendment's reasonableness requirement in regard to searches by probation officers. However, the standards are lowered, as the public has a greater interest in searching the probationer and the probationer has a lessened expectation to privacy. Also, probation officers do have a penal objective; in fact, they should have the welfare of their probationers in mind.

Therefore, probation officers may search a probationer's person or property with reasonable grounds; no warrant is required, although the search must be conducted in a reasonable manner. These conclusions have also been reached by the Supreme Court.[20] As a condition of probation, a search condition must be reasonably related to the probation, or it is invalid. Therefore, if a person is convicted of embezzlement, a condition providing for searches of the person would be unreasonable. The result would, of course, be different if the offense were possession of a firearm or drugs.

Finally, any other condition of probation that encroaches upon a constitutional guarantee is suspect. For example, a condition that restricts free speech is unconstitutional in most circumstances.[21] However, the right to travel freely and to bear arms are examples of constitutionally preserved rights that are commonly restricted during probation and parole.

A defendant who violates a condition of probation may be disciplined. Generally, the decision about whether any action should be taken for a violation is made by the probation officer. If a violation is extreme, the probation officer may file a petition to revoke probation. The sentencing court then holds a **revocation hearing.** If granted, the defendant is taken off probation and incarcerated.

revocation hearing
The due process hearing required before the government can revoke a privilege it has previously granted.

At the revocation hearing, the defendant may be entitled to counsel. As a general rule, the right is not found in the Sixth Amendment, as the "critical stages" of trial have passed. In one rare case, the Supreme Court held that a Sixth Amendment right to counsel did exist at a revocation hearing. In *Mempa v. Rhay*, 389 U.S. 128 (1967), the trial judge withheld sentencing, placed the defendant on probation, and did not pronounce sentence until after the defendant violated his probation and then had it revoked. Because the revocation hearing turned out to be the defendant's sentencing hearing, where there is a right to counsel under the Sixth Amendment, the Court found that the Sixth Amendment applied.

The Due Process Clauses of the Fifth and Fourteenth Amendments may also provide a right to counsel at a revocation hearing. If a substantial question of law or fact must be resolved at the hearing, counsel must be appointed for the indigent defendant so that the issues can be fully explored and developed. If revocation is obvious, though, counsel need not be allowed.

Community Service. One alternative to incarceration for nonviolent offenders is community service. In such a program, a defendant's sentence is suspended and the completion of a stated number of community service hours is a condition of the defendant's probation.

In most instances, the probation officer works with the probationer to find an appropriate job. However, the judge may require that a specific job be performed.

The requirements of community service range from unskilled to professional. For example, a judge may require that a professional, such as a physician or attorney, work in a clinic that provides services to the poor. The same
person may be expected to pick up trash from local roads. Clearly, the former
makes best use of the defendant's skills and benefits the community the most.

Restitution.   The purpose of restitution is to compensate the victim, not to
punish the offender. As such, restitution is not a substitute for other forms of
punishment.

Restitution is limited to the actual amounts resulting from the offenses
convicted.[22] Said another way, restitution is limited to losses resulting from the
specific conduct that formed the basis of the conviction.[23] However, an agreement between the government and the defendant to pay a higher amount may
be constitutional.[24]

Restitution may be made a condition of probation. A probationer's refusal
to pay restitution can result in a revocation of probation. However, when a fine
or restitution is imposed as a condition of probation, and "the probationer has
made all reasonable efforts to pay . . . yet cannot do so through no fault of his
own, it is fundamentally unfair to revoke probation automatically without considering whether adequate alternative methods of punishing the defendant are
available."[25]

Fines.   Different from restitution, the purpose of a fine is to punish the
offender. Accordingly, restitution monies are paid to victims and fines end up
in the public treasury. Fines are a very common method of punishing misdemeanants. Serious crimes are frequently punished with both a fine and incarceration. Any fine imposed must be reasonable, that is, the amount must be
within the financial means of the offender. Excessive fines are prohibited by the
Eighth Amendment.

It is a violation of equal protection to sentence individuals without
means to pay a fine to longer periods of incarceration than those who can
pay a fine. In *Williams v. Illinois*,[26] a defendant was sentenced to a maximum
one year in prison and a $500 fine for petty theft. Illinois statute provided
that if at the end of the year, the fine (and court costs) were not paid, the
defendant was to remain in jail for a time to satisfy the debt. This was calculated at $5.00 per day. The Court found that because Williams was indigent,
the statute violated the Equal Protection Clause by improperly sentencing
defendants according to economic status. Of course, a defendant who has the
financial means to pay a fine, and does not, may have probation revoked or
incarceration increased.

Forfeiture.   Forfeitures are similar to fines, in that they involve the taking of
property and money to punish defendants. A forfeiture is, however, not
directed at the defendant's pocketbook in general, as is a fine. Rather, forfeiture
focuses on taking the property owned by a defendant that is in some manner
connected with the crimes. Automobiles, airplanes, or boats used to transport
drugs are an example. Forfeiture has become an increasingly popular tool
amongst law enforcement agencies.

Procedurally, forfeiture may occur within and as part of a criminal proceeding. In addition, many laws permit forfeiture to occur in a separative in rem civil proceeding. Most statutes allow law enforcement officers to make seizures based upon probable cause, to be immediately followed by the filing of a forfeiture proceeding.[27] Of course, seizure can also occur later in the proceedings. Under federal law, if a seizure was proper (i.e., based upon probable cause), the burden of proof falls on a claimant to establish that the property is not subject to seizure. The claimant must prove this by a preponderance of the evidence.[28]

Under federal law, forfeiture is provided for in several instances, including violations of the Racketeer Influenced and Corrupt Organizations Act (RICO) and under the so-called drug kingpin statute, the Continuing Criminal Enterprise law.[29]

There are limits to the use of forfeiture. In *United States v. James Daniel Good Real Property*,[30] the Supreme Court determined that the Due Process Clause requires the government to provide notice and a preseizure hearing when it intends to forfeit real property, unless exigent circumstances justify an immediate seizure. There is no requirement of preseizure notice in cases where property can disappear. The Court stated that in cases where property is movable, immediate seizure, without notice or a hearing, is necessary to "establish the court's jurisdiction over the property" and to guard against someone absconding with the property.

A critical issue concerns the relationship between the crime and the property forfeited. Forfeiture of all property associated with a crime can be troubling. Forfeiting a boat that was purchased with drug money and is used to transport drugs from Colombia to the United States is not problematic. But is it constitutionally sound to forfeit a home because one joint of marijuana is discovered inside? Does the Eighth Amendment's Excessive Fines Clause limit the use of forfeitures? In *Austin*, the Supreme Court examined this issue.

 CASE

AUSTIN V. UNITED STATES

113 S. Ct. 2801 (1993)

In this case, we are asked to decide whether the Excessive Fines Clause of the Eighth Amendment applies to forfeitures of property under 21 U.S.C. §§ 881(a)(4) and (a)(7). We hold that it does and therefore remand the case for consideration of the question whether the forfeiture at issue here was excessive.

On August 2, 1990, petitioner Richard Lyle Austin was indicted on four counts of violating South Dakota's drug laws. Austin ultimately pleaded guilty to one count of possessing cocaine with intent to distribute and was sentenced by the state court to seven years' imprisonment. On September 7, the United States filed an in rem action in the United States District Court for the District of South Dakota seeking forfeiture of Austin's mobile home and auto body shop under 21 U.S.C. §§ 881(a)(4) and (a)(7) [these laws provide for the forfeiture of property in drug cases]. Austin filed a claim and an answer to the complaint.

On February 4, 1991, the United States made a motion, supported by an affidavit from Sioux Falls Police Officer Donald Satterlee, for summary judgment. According to Satterlee's affidavit, Austin met Keith Engebretson at Austin's body shop on

June 13, 1990, and agreed to sell cocaine to Engebretson. Austin left the shop, went to his mobile home, and returned to the shop with two grams of cocaine which he sold to Engebretson. State authorities executed a search warrant on the body shop and mobile home the following day. They discovered small amounts of marijuana and cocaine, a .22 caliber revolver, drug paraphernalia, and approximately $4,700 in cash. In opposing summary judgment, Austin argued that forfeiture of the properties would violate the Eighth Amendment. The District Court rejected this argument and entered summary judgment for the United States.

The United States Court of Appeals for the Eighth Circuit "reluctantly agree[d] with the government" and affirmed. . . . Although it thought that "the principle of proportionality should be applied in civil actions that result in harsh penalties, . . . and that the Government was "exacting too high a penalty in relation to the offense committed . . . the court felt constrained from holding the forfeiture unconstitutional.". . .

Austin contends that the Eighth Amendment's Excessive Fines Clause applies to in rem civil forfeiture proceedings. . . . In [an earlier case] we held that the Excessive Fines Clause does not limit the award of punitive damages to a private party in a civil suit when the government neither has prosecuted the action nor has any right to receive a share of the damages. . . . The Court concluded that both the Eighth Amendment and § 10 of the Bill of Rights of 1689, from which it derives, were intended to prevent the government from abusing its power to punish . . . and therefore "that the Excessive Fines Clause was intended to limit only those fines directly imposed by, and payable to, the government." . . .

We found it unnecessary to decide . . . whether the Excessive Fines Clause applies only to criminal cases. . . . The United States now argues that

> any claim that the government's conduct in a civil proceeding is limited by the Eighth Amendment generally, or by the Excessive Fines Clause in particular, must fail unless the challenged action, despite its label, would have

been recognized as a criminal punishment at the time the Eighth Amendment was adopted.

* * *

It further suggests that the Eighth Amendment cannot apply to a civil proceeding unless that proceeding is so punitive that it must be considered criminal. . . .

Some provisions of the Bill of Rights are expressly limited to criminal cases. . . . The text of the Eighth Amendment includes no similar limitation.

Nor does the history of the Eighth Amendment require such a limitation. Justice O'Connor noted in *Browning-Ferris:* "Consideration of the Eighth Amendment immediately followed consideration of the Fifth Amendment. After deciding to confine the benefits of the Self-Incrimination Clause of the Fifth Amendment to criminal proceedings, the Framers turned their attention to the Eighth Amendment. There were no proposals to limit that Amendment to criminal proceedings. . . . "

The purpose of the Eighth Amendment, putting the Bail Clause to one side, was to limit the government's power to punish. . . . The Cruel and Unusual Clause is self-evidently concerned with punishment. The Excessive Fines Clause limits the Government's power to extract payments, whether in case or in kind, "as punishment for some offense." . . . "The notion of punishment, as we commonly understand it, cuts across the division between civil and criminal law." . . . "It is commonly understood that civil proceedings may advance punitive and remedial goals, and conversely, that both punitive and remedial goals may be served by criminal penalties." . . . Thus, the question is not, as the United States would have it, whether forfeiture . . . is civil or criminal, but rather whether it is punishment.

In considering this question, we are mindful of the fact that sanctions frequently serve more than one purpose. We need not exclude the possibility that a forfeiture serves remedial purposes to conclude that it is subject to the limitations of the Excessive Fines Clause. We, however, must determine that it can be explained as serving in part to punish. . . . We turn, then, to consider whether, at the time the Eighth Amendment was ratified, forfeiture was understood at least in part as punishment and whether forfeiture under §§ 881(a)(4) and (a)(7) should be so understood today.

Three kinds of forfeiture were established in England at the time the Eighth Amendment was ratified in the United States: deodand, forfeiture upon conviction for a felony or treason, and statutory forfeiture. . . . Each was understood, at least in part, as imposing punishment.

* * *

The First Congress passed laws subjecting ships and cargos involved in customs offenses to forfeiture. . . . Indeed, examination of those laws suggests that the First Congress viewed forfeiture as punishment. . . . It is also of some interest that "forfeit" is the word Congress used for fine. . . .

We turn next to consider whether forfeitures under 21 U.S.C. §§ 881(a)(4) and (a)(7) are properly considered punishment today. We find nothing in these provisions or their legislative history to contradict the historical understanding of forfeiture as punishment. . . .

The legislative history of § 881 confirms the punitive nature of these provisions. When it added subsection (a)(7) to § 881 in 1984, Congress recognized "that the traditional criminal sanctions of fine and imprisonment are inadequate to deter or punish the enormously profitable trade in dangerous drugs." . . . It characterized the forfeiture of real property as "a powerful deterrent." . . .

We therefore conclude that forfeiture under these provisions constitutes "payment to a sovereign as punishment for some offense," . . . and, as such, is subject to the limitations of the Eighth Amendment's Excessive Fines Clause.

The *Austin* Court held that the Eighth Amendment's Excessive Fines Clause applies to civil in rem forfeiture proceedings. Accordingly, a forfeiture must be proportional to the offense. A fine or forfeiture that is grossly larger than the underlying offense is excessive and violative of the Eighth Amendment. The fine at issue in *United States v. Bajakajian* is an example of an excessive fine.

 CASE

UNITED STATES V. BAJAKAJIAN

118 S.Ct. 2028 (1998)

Justice Thomas delivered the opinion of the Court:

Respondent Hosep Bajakajian attempted to leave the United States without reporting, as required by federal law, that he was transporting more than $10,000 in currency. Federal law also provides that a person convicted of willfully violating this reporting requirement shall forfeit to the government "any property . . . involved in such offense." 18 U.S.C. § 982 (a)(1). The question in this case is whether forfeiture of the entire $357,144 that respondent failed to declare would

violate the Excessive Fines Clause of the Eighth Amendment. We hold that it would, because full forfeiture of respondent's currency would be grossly disproportional to the gravity of his offense.

On June 9, 1994, respondent, his wife, and his two daughters were waiting at Los Angeles International Airport to board a flight to Italy; their final destination was Cyprus. Using dogs trained to detect currency by its smell, customs inspectors discovered some $230,000 in cash in the Bajakajians' checked baggage. A customs inspector approached respondent and his wife and told them that they were required to report all money in excess of $10,000 in their possession or in their baggage. Respondent said that he had $8,000 and that his wife had another $7,000, but that the family had no additional currency to declare. A search of their carry-on bags, purse, and wallet revealed more cash; in all, customs inspectors found $357,144. The currency was seized and respondent was taken into custody.

A federal grand jury indicted respondent on three counts. Count One charged him with failing to report, as required by 31 U.S.C. § 5316 (a)(1)(A), that he was transporting more than $10,000 outside the United States, and with doing so "willfully," in violation of § 5322 (a). Count Two charged him with making a false material statement to the United States Customs Service, in violation of 18 U.S.C. § 1001. Count Three sought forfeiture of the $357,144 pursuant to 18 U.S.C. § 982 (a)(1), which provides: "[A] person or an agent or bailee of the person shall file a report . . . when the person, agent, or bailee knowingly—" (1) transports, is about to transport, or has transported, monetary instruments of more than $10,000 at one time—"(A) from a place in the United States to or through a place outside the United States. . . . " 31 U.S.C. § 5316(a).

"The court, in imposing sentence on a person convicted of an offense in violation of § . . . 5316, . . . shall order that the person forfeit to the United States any property, real or personal, involved in such offense, or any property traceable to such property." 18 U.S.C. § 982 (a)(1).

Respondent pleaded guilty to the failure to report in Count One; the Government agreed to dismiss the false statement charge in Count Two; and respondent elected to have a bench trial on the forfeiture in Count Three. After the bench trial, the District Court found that the entire $357,144 was subject to forfeiture because it was "involved in" the offense. *Ibid.* The court also found that the funds were not connected to any other crime and that respondent was transporting the money to repay a lawful debt. Tr. 61–62 (Jan. 19, 1995). The District Court further found that respondent had failed to report that he was taking the currency out of the United States because of fear stemming from "cultural differences": Respondent, who had grown up as a member of the Armenian minority in Syria,

had a "distrust for the Government." *Id.*, at 63; see Tr. of Oral Arg. 30.

Although § 982 (a)(1) directs sentencing courts to impose full forfeiture, the District Court concluded that such forfeiture would be "extraordinarily harsh" and "grossly disproportionate to the offense in question," and that it would therefore violate the Excessive Fines Clause. Tr. 63. The court instead ordered forfeiture of $15,000, in addition to a sentence of three years of probation and a fine of $5,000—the maximum fine under the Sentencing Guidelines—because the court believed that the maximum Guidelines fine was "too little" and that a $15,000 forfeiture would "make up for what I think a reasonable fine should be." *Ibid.*

The United States appealed, seeking full forfeiture of respondent's currency as provided in § 982 (a)(1). The Court of Appeals for the Ninth Circuit affirmed. 84 F.3d 334 (1996). U.S. 524 U.S. 321 (1998), 117 S.Ct. 1841, 137 L.Ed.2d 1045 (1997).

II

The Eighth Amendment provides: "Excessive bail shall not be required, nor excessive fines imposed, nor cruel and unusual punishments inflicted." U.S. Const., Amdt. 8. This Court has had little occasion to interpret, and has never actually applied, the Excessive Fines Clause. We have, however, explained that at the time the Constitution was adopted, "the word 'fine' was understood to mean a payment to a sovereign as punishment for some offense." *Browning-Ferris Industries of Vt., Inc. v. Kelco Disposal, Inc.*, 492 U.S. 257, 265, 109 S.Ct. 2909, 2915, 106 L.Ed.2d 219 (1989). The Excessive Fines Clause thus "limits the government's power to extract payments, whether in cash or in kind, 'as punishment for some offense.' "*Austin v. United States*, 509 U.S. 602, 609–610, 113 S.Ct. 2801, 2805, 125 L.Ed.2d 488 (1993) (emphasis deleted). Forfeitures—payments in kind—are thus "fines" if they constitute punishment for an offense.

We have little trouble concluding that the forfeiture of currency ordered by § 982 (a)(1) constitutes punishment. The statute directs a court to order forfeiture as an additional sanction when "imposing sentence on a person convicted of" a willful violation of § 5316's reporting requirement. The forfeiture is thus imposed at the culmination of a criminal proceeding and requires conviction of an underlying felony, and it cannot be imposed upon an innocent owner of unreported currency, but only upon a person who has himself been convicted of a § 5316 reporting violation. Cf. *Austin v. United States, supra,* at 619, 113 S.Ct., at 2810 (holding forfeiture to be a "fine" in part because the forfeiture statute "expressly provide[d] an 'innocent owner' defense" and thus "look[ed] . . . like punishment.").

The United States argues, however, that the forfeiture of currency under § 982 (a)(1) "also serves important remedial purposes." Brief for United States 20. The Government asserts that it has "an overriding sovereign interest in controlling what property leaves and enters the country." *Ibid.* It claims that full forfeiture of unreported currency supports that interest by serving to "dete[r] illicit movements of cash" and aiding in providing the Government with "valuable information to investigate and detect criminal activities associated with that cash." *Id.,* at 21. Deterrence, however, has traditionally been viewed as a goal of punishment, and forfeiture of the currency here does not serve the remedial purpose of compensating the Government for a loss. . . . Although the Government has asserted a loss of information regarding the amount of currency leaving the country, that loss would not be remedied by the Government's confiscation of respondent's $357,144.

The United States also argues that the forfeiture mandated by § 982 (a)(1) is constitutional because it falls within a class of historic forfeitures of property tainted by crime. . . . "The thing is here primarily considered as the offender, or rather the offence is attached primarily to the thing; and this, whether the offence be malum prohibitum, or malum in se. . . . [T]he practice has been, and so this Court understands the law to be, that the proceeding in rem stands independent of, and wholly unaffected by any criminal proceeding in personam." *The Palmyra,* 12 Wheat., at 14–15, 6 L.Ed. 531.

Traditional in rem forfeitures were thus not considered punishment against the individual for an offense. . . . The forfeiture in this case does not bear any of the hallmarks of traditional civil in rem forfeitures. The Government has not proceeded against the currency itself, but has instead sought and obtained a criminal conviction of respondent personally. The forfeiture serves no remedial purpose, is designed to punish the offender, and cannot be imposed upon innocent owners.

§ 982 (a)(1) thus descends not from historic in rem forfeitures of guilty property, but from a different historical tradition: that of in personam, criminal forfeitures. Such forfeitures have historically been treated as punitive, being part of the punishment imposed for felonies and treason in the Middle Ages and at common law. See W. McKechnie, *Magna Carta* 337–339 (2d ed. 1958); 2 F. Pollock & F. Maitland, *The History of English Law* 460–466 (2d ed. 1909). Although in personam criminal forfeitures were well established in England at the time of the Founding, they were rejected altogether in the laws of this country until very recently.

The Government specifically contends that the forfeiture of respondent's currency is constitutional because it involves an "instrumentality" of respondent's crime. According to the Government, the unreported cash is an instrumentality because it "does not merely facilitate a violation of law," but is "the very sine qua non of the crime." . . .

Acceptance of the Government's argument would require us to expand the traditional understanding of instrumentality forfeitures. This we decline to do. Instrumentalities historically have been treated as a form of "guilty property" that can be forfeited in civil in rem proceedings. In this case, however, the Government has sought to punish respondent by proceeding against him criminally, in personam, rather than proceeding in rem against the currency. It is therefore irrelevant whether respondent's currency is an instrumentality; the forfeiture is punitive, and the test for the excessiveness of a punitive forfeiture involves solely a proportionality determination.

III

Because the forfeiture of respondent's currency constitutes punishment and is thus a "fine" within the meaning of the Excessive Fines Clause, we now turn to the question of whether it is "excessive."

A

The touchstone of the constitutional inquiry under the Excessive Fines Clause is the principle of proportionality: The amount of the forfeiture must bear some relationship to the gravity of the offense that it is designed to punish. See *Austin v. United States*, 509 U.S., at 622–623, 113 S.Ct., at 2812 (noting Court of Appeals' statement that "'the government is exacting too high a penalty in relation to the offense committed'". . . . Until today, however, we have not articulated a standard for determining whether a punitive forfeiture is constitutionally excessive. We now hold that a punitive forfeiture violates the Excessive Fines Clause if it is grossly disproportional to the gravity of a defendant's offense.

The text and history of the Excessive Fines Clause demonstrate the centrality of proportionality to the excessiveness inquiry; nonetheless, they provide little guidance as to how disproportional a punitive forfeiture must be to the gravity of an offense in order to be "excessive." Excessive means surpassing the usual, the proper, or a normal measure of proportion. See 1 N. Webster, *American Dictionary of the English Language* (1828) (defining excessive as "beyond the common measure or proportion"); S. Johnson, *A Dictionary of the English Language* 680 (4th ed. 1773) ("[b]eyond the common proportion"). The constitutional question that we address, however, is just how proportional to a criminal offense a fine must be, and the text of the Excessive Fines Clause does not answer it.

Nor does its history. The Clause was little discussed in the First Congress and the debates over the ratification of the Bill of Rights. As we

have previously noted, the Clause was taken verbatim from the English Bill of Rights of 1689. See *Browning-Ferris Industries of Vt., Inc. v. Kelco Disposal, Inc.*, 492 U.S., at 266–267, 109 S.Ct., at 2915–2916. That document's prohibition against excessive fines was a reaction to the abuses of the King's judges during the reigns of the Stuarts, *id.*, at 267, 109 S.Ct., at 2916, but the fines that those judges imposed were described contemporaneously only in the most general terms. See *Earl of Devonshire's Case*, 11 State Tr. 1367, 1372 (H.L. 1689) (fine of & pound;30,000 "excessive and exorbitant, against Magna Charta, the common right of the subject, and the law of the land"). Similarly, Magna Charta—which the Stuart judges were accused of subverting—required only that amercements (the medieval predecessors of fines) should be proportioned to the offense and that they should not deprive a wrongdoer of his livelihood:

"A Free-man shall not be amerced for a small fault, but after the manner of the fault; and for a great fault after the greatness thereof, saving to him his contenement; (2) and a Merchant likewise, saving to him his merchandise; (3) and any other's villain than ours shall be likewise amerced, saving his wainage." Magna Charta, 9 Hen. III, ch. 14 (1225), 1 Stat. at Large 6–7 (1762 ed.).

None of these sources suggests how disproportional to the gravity of an offense a fine must be in order to be deemed constitutionally excessive. We must therefore rely on other considerations in deriving a constitutional excessiveness standard, and there are two that we find particularly relevant. The first, which we have emphasized in our cases interpreting the Cruel and Unusual Punishments Clause, is that judgments about the appropriate punishment for an offense belong in the first instance to the legislature. See, *e.g., Solem v. Helm*, 463 U.S. 277, 290, 77 L.Ed.2d 637, 103 S. Ct. 3001 (1983) ("Reviewing courts . . . should grant substantial deference to the broad authority that legislatures necessarily possess in determining the types and limits of punishments for crimes"); see also *Gore v. United States*, 357 U.S. 386, 393, 2 L.Ed.2d 1405,

78 S. Ct. 1280 (1958) ("Whatever views may be entertained regarding severity of punishment, . . . these are peculiarly questions of legislative policy"). The second is that any judicial determination regarding the gravity of a particular criminal offense will be inherently imprecise. Both of these principles [*** 331]counsel against requiring strict proportionality between the amount of a punitive forfeiture and the gravity of a criminal offense, and we therefore adopt the standard of gross disproportionality articulated in our Cruel and Unusual Punishments Clause precedents. See, *e.g., Solem v. Helm, supra,* [**29]at 288; *Rummel v. Estelle,* 445 U.S. 263, 271, 63 L.Ed.2d 382, 100 S. Ct. 1133 (1980).

In applying this standard, the district courts in the first instance, and the courts of appeals, reviewing the proportionality determination *de novo,* n10 must compare [*2038]the amount of the forfeiture to the gravity of the defendant's offense. If the amount of the forfeiture is grossly disproportional to the gravity of the defendant's offense, it is unconstitutional.

B

Under this standard, the forfeiture of respondent's entire $357,144 would violate the Excessive Fines Clause. Respondent's crime was solely a reporting offense. It was permissible to transport the currency out of the country so long as he reported it. Section 982 (a)(1) orders currency to be forfeited for a "willful" violation of the reporting requirement. Thus, the essence of respondent's crime is a willful failure to report the removal of currency from the United States. Furthermore, as the District Court found, respondent's violation was unrelated to any other illegal activities. The money was the proceeds of legal activity and was to be used to repay a lawful debt. Whatever his other vices, respondent does not fit into the class of persons for whom the statute was principally designed: He is not a money launderer, a drug trafficker, or a tax evader. See Brief for United States 2–3. And

under the Sentencing Guidelines, the maximum sentence that could have been imposed on respondent was six months, while the maximum fine was $5,000. App. to Pet. for Cert. 17a (transcript of District Court sentencing hearing); United States Sentencing Commission, Guidelines Manual, § 5 (e) 1.2, Sentencing Table (Nov. 1994). Such penalties confirm a minimal level of culpability.

The harm that respondent caused was also minimal. Failure to report his currency affected only one party, the Government, and in a relatively minor way. There was no fraud on the United States, and respondent caused no loss to the public fisc. Had his crime gone undetected, the Government would have been deprived only of the information that $357,144 had left the country. The Government and the dissent contend that there is a correlation between the amount forfeited and the harm that the Government would have suffered had the crime gone undetected. See Brief for United States 30 (forfeiture is "perfectly calibrated"); *post,* at 2041 ("a fine calibrated with this accuracy"). We disagree. There is no inherent proportionality in such a forfeiture. It is impossible to conclude, for example, that the harm respondent caused is anywhere near 30 times greater than that caused by a hypothetical drug dealer who willfully fails to report taking $12,000 out of the country in order to purchase drugs.

Comparing the gravity of respondent's crime with the $357,144 forfeiture the Government seeks, we conclude that such a forfeiture would be grossly disproportional to the gravity of his offense. It is larger than the $5,000 fine imposed by the District Court by many orders of magnitude, and it bears no articulable correlation to any injury suffered by the Government. . . .

* * *

For the foregoing reasons, the full forfeiture of respondent's currency would violate the Excessive Fines Clause. The judgment of the Court of Appeals is Affirmed.

Similarly, even though forfeiture may be characterized as civil, the exclusionary rule applies to bar illegally seized evidence in quasi-criminal forfeiture cases.[31] This is contrary to the rule that the exclusionary rule is not applied in civil and administrative cases.

Modern Sentencing Alternatives.   In recent years, many new alternatives to incarceration have been developed. Such alternatives are actually forms of probation, and, as such, are administered by courts and probation officers.

For the nonviolent criminal, work release is an alternative. While in these programs the offender lives in a jail, but is permitted to leave jail to work. Work release has many advantages. The defendant continues to earn a living. This is particularly important if the defendant has dependents. Also, it is good for the self-esteem of offenders; they continue to feel a useful part of the community. The final advantage is true of many sentencing alternatives: the cost to the public is lower because the offender is often required to pay, in whole or part, for participation in the program.

For those convicted of some alcohol and drug offenses, courts have turned to alcohol and drug treatment over imprisonment. These programs vary greatly. For first-time drunk driving convictions, offenders may be required to do one or more of the following, in addition to traditional conditions of probation:

1. Participate in an alcohol treatment program, such as Alcoholics Anonymous.
2. Report for periodic urine or blood tests to detect the presence of alcohol.
3. Take Antabuse, a drug that makes a person ill if alcohol is ingested.
4. Participate in a defensive/safe-driving school.

If a defendant has a previous drunk driving conviction, he or she is likely to receive some "executed time" or jail time, in addition to some or all of the previously listed conditions. A few courts have tried a form of shock treatment. For example, a defendant may be required to meet with drunk drivers who are responsible for killing someone and discuss that experience. In another example, at least one judge has required that a drunk driver work in a hospital emergency room so that the defendant would be exposed to alcohol-related injuries and deaths.

First-time drug users may also be placed on probation, subject to conditions similar to those previously listed: periodic urinalysis or blood screening and drug counseling and treatment. This form of probation is not available to drug dealers.

Two other forms of probation that may be used independently or mixed with one or more of the others are house arrest and halfway houses. If a defendant is sentenced to house arrest, he or she may not leave the home without prior permission of the probation officer, except in emergencies.

Today, the use of electronic shackles makes enforcement of house arrests easier. These devices are attached to the probationer's leg, and through the transmission of a radio signal it can be determined if the defendant is at home.

Halfway houses are minimum security homes located in the community. Generally they serve two groups of offenders: those making the transition from prison to the community and those who need some confinement, but not jail or prison.

Halfway houses are commonly used in conjunction with work release programs. The residents are given some freedom to leave the home, but are restricted in their travel. Often such homes provide drug and alcohol counseling and treatment and vocational training.

Yet another community-based correction program is the boot camp or "shock incarceration" program. Boot camps are gaining in popularity as a method of reforming youthful offenders. As of early 1994, nearly thirty states were operating prison boot camps.[32]

The typical boot camp experience involves 90 to 180 days of "rigid military-training atmosphere followed by intensive community supervision." Boot camp programs are usually limited to first-time offenders who have been sentenced to a term of imprisonment. Most programs are designed to accommodate individuals sentenced to prison, but a growing number of jails are using boot camps as an alternative to traditional confinement.[33]

This is not by any means an exhaustive list of alternative punishments. The list is limited only by the Constitution and the imagination of judges. For example, one Florida judge required those convicted of drunk driving to place bumper stickers on their cars warning of their convictions. This requirement was upheld by the Florida Court of Appeals.[34]

Habitual Offender Statutes

The career criminal or repeat offender is now subject to extreme penalty in most jurisdictions. These statutes are referred to as *recidivist* or **habitual offender laws**.

Most statutes provide for an increased penalty if a defendant has been convicted of a stated number of felonies, often three, within a certain period of time, such as ten years. These are popularly known as the "three strikes and you are out" laws.

To prevent unfair prejudice to the defendant, the jury usually does not know about the habitual criminal charge until it has reached a verdict in the underlying charge. So, if Pam is charged with murder and of being a habitual criminal, the jury would initially know only of the murder charge. If the jury

halfway house
A facility in which persons recently discharged from a rehabilitation center or prison live for a time and are given support and assistance in readjusting to society at large.

habitual offender statutes
Laws that may apply to a person who has been convicted of as few as two prior crimes (often violent or drug-related crimes) and that greatly increase the penalties for each succeeding crime.

ANOTHER SENTENCING STORY Willie Smith was convicted of the extortion and assault of a 93-year-old woman confined to a wheelchair. He was also convicted of resisting arrest, counterfeiting food stamps, and mugging.

During sentencing, the trial judge told the defendant that he was irritated by the defendant's constant claims of police brutality and left the bench, approached the defendant, and punched him in the nose. While the defendant was on the floor of the courtroom, the judge kicked and punched him. The judge then returned to the bench and stated to the defendant, "That, Mr. Smith, is a sample of real, honest-to-goodness police brutality."

SIDEBAR

comes back with an acquittal, the habitual criminal charge is dismissed. If the verdict is guilty, the jury is then told that it must also determine if the defendant is an habitual criminal. This is known as a bifurcated procedure.

To prove the habitual criminal charge, the prosecutor will introduce court records reflecting the prior convictions and, in some instances, call the prosecutors involved in the prior convictions to attest that the defendant was indeed convicted.

Habitual criminal laws have been attacked as violative of the Double Jeopardy Clause. Such claims have not been successful, as they are not considered a second punishment of one of the earlier offenses. Rather, evidence of a criminal record provides a reason to increase the penalty for the most recent offense.

POSTCONVICTION REMEDIES

Technically, motions for new trials are postconviction remedies. Other than such motions, there are two major methods of attacking a conviction or other decision at the trial level: appeal and habeas corpus.

Appeal

The Constitution of the United States does not expressly confer a right to appeal.[35] Regardless, every state provides for appeal either through statute or constitution. Once a state establishes a right to appeal, the United States Constitution requires that appellate procedure not violate the Fourteenth Amendment's Due Process or Equal Protection Clauses.

Appeals from federal district courts go to the United States Courts of Appeals (circuit courts). From there, appeal is taken to the Supreme Court of the United States. In state cases, appeal is taken to the state intermediate appellate court, if any. Appeal from that court is taken to the state high court, usually named the Supreme Court of the state. All issues, federal and state, are heard by those courts. Issues of state law may not be appealed any further. If the defendant wishes to appeal a decision of the state high court concerning an issue of federal law, the appeal is taken to the United States Supreme Court.

Filing the Appeal.   Because the right to appeal is purely statutory, it may be lost if it is not timely filed. The federal rules require that appeals be filed within ten days of the date of judgment.[36] The government is given thirty days in those instances where it may appeal. Appeals from state courts to the United States Supreme Court must be filed within ninety days of the entry of judgment.[37]

Procedures vary, but it is common to require the appellant to file a number of documents to begin the appeal. The first document is a notice or petition of appeal. This simply informs all the parties, as well as the trial judge, that the case is being appealed. A designation of record will also be filed by the parties. Through this document, the parties select the portions of the trial record that they desire to be sent to the appellate court. A statement of issues that must be resolved on appeal may also be filed by the appellant. Finally, a filing fee must be paid. Appellants who cannot afford it may seek relief from the filing fee requirement.

After the necessary documents are filed, the parties brief the issues for the appellate court. The appellate court, in its discretion, may hear oral arguments.

Because the penalty for untimely filings is harsh (dismissal of the appeal), most courts recognize constructive filings. This is particularly true for incarcerated defendants who rely on counsel or prison officials in preparing or filing an appeal.

Note that most jurisdictions provide for the possibility of bail pending appeal. This is most often available in misdemeanor cases; however, it may be granted in felony cases also.

The Scope of Review. To avoid unnecessary delay, only **final orders** may be appealed. Therefore, erroneous pretrial decisions are not corrected until appeal is taken, after the case is completed. Orders that may not be reviewed until safter final judgment are those relating to the suppression of evidence, discovery, and the sufficiency of the charging instruments.

> **final judgment (order)**
> The last action of a court; the one upon which an appeal can be based.

There are a few exceptions to the final judgment rule. The most prominent exception is the collateral order doctrine. Under this doctrine, orders that are independent of the criminal case may be immediately appealed. The appeal proceeds concurrently with the underlying criminal case.

Appeals taken from ongoing litigation (where no final order has been issued) are called **interlocutory appeals.** Orders holding a defendant incompetent to stand trial, denying bail, and denying a defendant's double jeopardy claim have been held collateral and immediately appealable.[38] Certain orders that occur after judgment, such as revocation of probation, are also immediately appealable.

> **interlocutory appeal**
> The *Interlocutory Appeals Act* (28 U.S.C. 1292 (1948)) is a federal law that provides for an appeal while a trial is going on if the trial judge states in writing: 1) A legal question has come up that directly affects the trial. 2) There are major questions as to how that point of law should be resolved. 3) The case would proceed better if the appeals court answers the question.

Remember, cases are not retried on appeal. Appellate courts review the record for errors of law, not fact. That means the appellate court will not examine the evidence and substitute its judgment for that of the trial court (or jury). However, the court will examine the record to make sure that sufficient evidence exists to support the judgment. So long as sufficient evidence can be found, the appellate court will not reverse, even if it would have decided the case differently. Issues of law are reviewed anew (de novo).

Not every error warrants reversing the trial court. Only when an error prejudices the defendant is reversal required. An error is prejudicial if there is a possibility that it changed the outcome of the case. If not, it was **harmless error.** The appellant bears the burden of proving that he or she was prejudiced by the error of the trial court.

> **harmless error**
> A trivial mistake made by a judge in the procedures used at trial, or in making legal rulings during the trial.

Some error is so violative of the Constitution that it is irrebuttably presumed prejudicial, so reversal is automatic. An order denying defense counsel at trial is never harmless error.[39]

Prosecution/Defense Appeals. Because of the Double Jeopardy Clause, defendants have a broader right to appeal than does the government. A defendant who is tried and convicted is free to appeal any factual or legal error. However, this right may be limited by a requirement of *preservation*. To satisfy this rule, the defendant must raise the issue at the trial level. This gives the trial judge an opportunity to avoid error.

Failure to raise the issue results in a waiver. For example, a defendant who does not challenge the sufficiency of an indictment at the trial level may not raise the issue for the first time before the appellate court. The same is true of evidentiary matters. The defendant must object to the admission of evidence that he or she believes should be excluded, so as to preserve the issue for appeal.

The prosecution has a limited right to appeal. Because of the prohibition on trying a person twice for the same offense, the government has no right to appeal acquittals. However, most states permit the government to appeal certain orders issued before jeopardy attaches. Orders dismissing charging instruments, suppressing evidence prior to trial, and releasing the defendant before trial may be appealed. These interlocutory appeals do not violate the Fifth Amendment's Double Jeopardy Clause because jeopardy does not attach until a jury has been impaneled or the first witness is sworn in a nonjury trial. See Chapter 9 for a more thorough discussion of double jeopardy and appeals.

The Right to Counsel on Appeal.   There is no Sixth Amendment right to counsel on appeal. The Sixth Amendment right begins once a defendant is charged and continues, at all critical stages, through trial and sentencing. In some instances, it is in effect at probation revocation. It does not ever include appeals.

The right to counsel on appeal can be found, however, in the Equal Protection Clause of the Fourteenth Amendment. The Supreme Court said, in *Douglas v. California*,[40] that indigent defendants convicted of a felony have a right to appointed counsel on appeal, provided that the appeal is by right. *By right* means that the defendant's appeal must be heard by the appellate court. Most, if not all, states have provided for appeal by right.

If an appeal is discretionary, the Equal Protection Clause of the Fourteenth Amendment does not compel the state to provide counsel.

As is true at trial, the defendant is entitled to effective counsel. The appointed attorney has an ethical obligation to zealously pursue the defendant's appeal. Because of the large number of frivolous appeals, the Supreme Court has stated that an appointed attorney may be allowed to withdraw. However, the following must be done: first, the attorney must request withdrawal from the appellate court; second, a brief must be filed explaining why the attorney believes the appeal to be wholly without merit. In that brief, all potential issues must be outlined for the court's review. If the appellate court agrees that there are no valid issues, the attorney may withdraw. If the court finds an issue that has some merit, the lawyer must continue to represent the defendant.

Habeas Corpus

Both the states and federal governments have habeas corpus relief. Here we discuss federal habeas corpus relief, particularly federal habeas corpus in state criminal proceedings. Although habeas corpus relief is available at any stage of a criminal proceeding, most habeas corpus petitions are filed after conviction. The discussion here is limited to such postconviction petitions.

Through habeas corpus proceedings, an individual may attack the lawfulness of confinement, whether it be substantive or procedural in nature. Further, the conditions of confinement and the lawfulness of an imposed punishment may be reviewed by a habeas court.

History. Translated, habeas corpus means "you have the body." In action, the writ is used to order someone who has custody of another to bring that person before the court. Any person who believes that he or she is being detained illegally may use the writ to gain his or her freedom. Because of the significant power of the writ, it has come to be known as the "Great Writ of Liberty."

The writ has ancient origin, dating back as far as the twelfth century. Habeas corpus was often used to enforce provisions of the Magna Carta. The success of the writ in protecting liberty in England influenced the drafters of the American Constitution. The result is Article I, § 9, clause 2, which states: "The Privilege of the Writ of Habeas Corpus shall not be suspended unless when in Cases of Rebellion or Invasion the Public Safety may require it."

Federal habeas corpus is important in criminal law because it is used to challenge state court convictions. That is, if a defendant believes that his or her federal constitutional rights were violated in a state court, he or she may attack the conviction through federal habeas corpus.

Habeas corpus has had congressional authorization since 1789. The first statute made habeas corpus available only to federal prisoners. This was changed by the Habeas Corpus Act of 1867, which extended habeas corpus to any person "restrained of his or her liberty in violation of the constitution, or of any treaty or law of the United States." The 1867 act continues to be in effect, with some modifications.

Scope of Review. The current habeas corpus statutes are found at 28 U.S.C. §§ 2241–2255. Section 2254 provides habeas corpus relief to state prisoners. Under § 2255, federal prisoners are to move to vacate or set aside their sentences, in a procedure nearly identical to § 2254. Relief under this section must be sought before a federal prisoner can bring habeas corpus. Even then, the statute states that habeas corpus shall not be issued if the prisoner was unsuccessful with a § 2255 claim, unless that proceeding was "inadequate or ineffective." A biased judge is an example of when habeas corpus may be issued after a § 2255 motion has been denied.

The federal courts continued to have little involvement with state proceedings, even after the 1867 act extended the reach of federal habeas corpus to state prisoners. This was in large part due to Supreme Court decisions limiting the review of federal habeas corpus to questions of jurisdiction.

The scope of review was enlarged in *Brown v. Allen*, 344 U.S. 443 (1953), in which it was held that federal habeas corpus could be used to relitigate all issues of federal law. This decision significantly increased the power of federal habeas corpus and resulted in increased intervention of federal courts in state criminal proceedings.

The Supreme Court has since narrowed habeas corpus relief by decision. For example, a state prisoner may not use federal habeas corpus to relitigate Fourth Amendment claims (search and seizure), provided the defendant was provided a "full and fair litigation" in state court. Also, the Court has emphasized that the purpose of habeas corpus is to provide relief to persons imprisoned in violation of the laws of the United States, not to relitigate or correct factual errors. Accordingly, a claim of innocence, even when supported by new evidence, is not alone sufficient to confer habeas jurisdiction upon a court. An independent constitutional claim must be made for a court to examine such a petition.[41]

exhaustion of remedies
A person must usually take all reasonable steps to get satisfaction from a state government before going into federal court. This is called *exhaustion of state remedies.*

Exhaustion of Remedies.   Before a state prisoner can seek the aid of a federal court, he or she must satisfy certain procedural requirements. First, the defendant must use all means available in the state system to correct the alleged error. This is the doctrine of **exhaustion of remedies.** Section 2254(b) states:

> An application for a writ of habeas corpus in behalf of a person in custody pursuant to the judgment of a State court shall not be granted unless it appears that the applicant has exhausted the remedies available in the courts of the State, or that there is either an absence of available corrective process or the existence of circumstances rendering such process ineffective to protect the rights of the prisoner.

The remedies that must be exhausted depend on what is available in the state system, such as motions for new trial, state habeas corpus relief, and appeals. Of course, if no remedy is available, the defendant may immediately petition for habeas corpus relief.

If a remedy is available, but it would be futile to exhaust it, habeas corpus may be brought without exhaustion. For example, assume State Supreme Court has previously addressed the legal issue raised by the defendant, and its decision is contrary to the defendant's claim. Unless there is reason to believe that the court will reconsider its decision, there is no need to exhaust this remedy. Excessive delay in the state proceedings may also be a basis for bringing habeas corpus before the state remedies have been exhausted, provided the state does not have a remedy for such delays (e.g., mandamus).

The fact that a defendant has failed to timely appeal (or file a motion for new trial, etc.) does not mean that habeas corpus is unavailable. The question is: Are state remedies available? If a defendant has missed the right to appeal under state law, and no other remedy is available, then habeas corpus may be used to resolve his or her federal constitutional claims. However, defendants who deliberately bypass state procedures may be denied habeas relief.[42]

The Custody Requirement.   The Habeas Corpus Act speaks of prisoners "in custody." However, this has been interpreted to include all wrongful restraints of liberty. The Supreme Court has said that persons who are subject to "restraints not shared by the public generally" are entitled to habeas corpus protection, even though they may not be in the physical custody of the government.

Under this interpretation, persons placed on probation and parole have been held to be in custody, as have defendants released on bail.[43] Habeas corpus protection is also available to a defendant who has served his or her entire sentence, because the restraint of liberty includes not only incarceration but also collateral loss of civil liberties (e.g., right to carry a weapon), injury to reputation, and the possibility of an increased penalty for a later conviction.

A defendant who is lawfully detained may use habeas corpus to challenge his or her sentence if he or she believes it is excessive. Also, if he or she was convicted of several crimes and was sentenced to consecutive sentences, he or she need not wait until the lawful sentence expires before petitioning for habeas corpus. It appears that an invalid sentence may be attacked even though it runs concurrently with a valid sentence. Again, the collateral effects of the conviction are the rationale.

Procedure. The following rules were established by the United States Supreme Court to implement 22 U.S.C. § 2254.[44] The petition for habeas corpus relief is filed in the federal district within which the prisoner is being held. The petition shall name the person who has custody of the applicant as the respondent. Indigent persons may file a motion to proceed in forma pauperis, which relieves such persons from paying the filing fee.

Immediately after the petition is filed, the district judge will examine the petition. If the petition is "plainly" invalid, the court will dismiss it. If not, the court will direct the respondent to answer the petition.

Counsel may be appointed and discovery is available, with leave of the district court. After the petition has been answered and appropriate discovery conducted, the district court may hold an evidentiary hearing and issue an opinion or rule from the record without a hearing. Habeas corpus decisions may be appealed.

The Right to Counsel. To date, the Supreme Court has not found a constitutional right to the assistance of counsel in preparing and presenting a petition for habeas corpus.

In some instances the district court may have to hold an evidentiary hearing. It is possible that in such instances a due process right to counsel exists to assure that the hearing is fair. The issue is not of critical importance presently, because federal habeas corpus rules require the appointment of counsel for such hearings. Additionally, the rules give the district court the discretion to appoint counsel earlier, if necessary.

Although there may be no right to counsel, there is a right to "access to the courts." Therefore, prisoners must be furnished with paper, pens, stamps, and access to a law library. Further, unless a prison provides adequate legal assistance to its prisoners, so-called "jailhouse lawyers" may not be prohibited from assisting other inmates in the preparation of legal documents.

WEB LINKS

Punishment and Sentencing
Information and documents about trials, sentencing, appeals, and punishment can be found at http://courttv.com.
There is much information about the death penalty on the WWW. Here are a few sites:

http://www.deathpenaltyinfo.org/
http://www.prodeathpenalty.com/
http://www.aclu.org/death-penalty/
http://web.amnesty.org/rmp/dplibrary.nsf/index?openview

KEY TERMS

aggravating circumstances
commutation of sentence
concurrent sentences
consecutive sentences
determinate sentence
exhaustion of remedies
final judgment (order)

habitual offender statutes
halfway house
harmless error
indeterminate sentence
interlocutory appeal
mitigating circumstances
pardon

parole
reprieve
revocation hearing
suspended sentences
victim impact statement

REVIEW QUESTIONS

1. What is a presentence investigation? Who conducts the investigation and what is its purpose?
2. What are aggravating and mitigating circumstances in sentencing?
3. What is the final judgment rule?
4. Does a defendant have a right to appointed counsel on appeal?
5. What is habeas corpus?
6. Distinguish harmless from prejudicial error.
7. May victim impact evidence be considered by sentencing courts?

8. Which of the following punishments has been held to be inherently cruel and unusual by the Supreme Court?
   a. Death by hanging
   b. Death by starvation
   c. Flogging
   d. Solitary confinement
   e. Imprisonment without lighting or a bed
9. Differentiate a suspended imposition of sentence from a sentence suspended to probation.

REVIEW PROBLEMS

1–4. Kevin, an attorney, has been indicted for embezzlement. After his preliminary hearing, he filed a motion to suppress a confession he believes was illegally obtained. A hearing was conducted and the trial court granted his motion. The evidence was vital to the prosecution.

Kevin's attorney has also requested that the trial be continued because he claims that Kevin is not competent to stand trial. The judge ordered a mental evaluation, held a hearing, and found Kevin competent to stand trial.

The defense also requested that the court order a number of police officers to submit to depositions prior to trial. The court denied the motion.

At trial, the defendant objected to the introduction of a document that he believed was unconstitutionally obtained during a search of his office. The judge overruled the objection and admitted the confession into evidence.

Answer the following questions using these facts.

1. The prosecution strongly believes that the documents that were suppressed are admissible. The prosecutor objects on the record to the judge's order and then appeals the issue after

Kevin is acquitted. What should be the outcome on appeal?
2. Kevin disagrees with the trial court finding of competency. What is his remedy?
3. Believing that Kevin cannot have a fair trial without the depositions, his attorney filed an interlocutory appeal seeking an order from the appellate court requiring the trial judge to provide for the depositions. What should be the outcome?
4. Kevin appealed the trial court's decision denying his motion to suppress the document. The appellate court affirmed the trial court, and Kevin filed a habeas corpus petition in federal court claiming that his federal constitutional rights were violated by admission of the evidence. What should be the outcome?

END NOTES

1. The Supreme Court has not yet answered this question. *See also United States v. Rogers*, 921 F.2d 957 (10th Cir. 1990), *cert. denied*, 111 S. Ct. 113 (1991).
2. *United States v. Jackson*, 886 F.2d 838 (7th Cir. 1989).
3. Fed. R. Crim. P. 32(c)(1).
4. Fed. R. Crim. P. 32(c)(3).
5. *Apprendi v. New Jersey*, 530 U.S. 466 (2000).
6. *Eddings v. Oklahoma*, 455 U.S. 104 (1982).
7. *United States v. Watts*, 519 U.S. 148 (1997).
8. *Locket*, 438 U.S. at 604–05.
9. *Callins v. Collins*, 510 U.S. 1141 (1994) 114 S. Ct. 1127, 1132 (1994) (Blackmun, J., dissenting).
10. 114 S. Ct. at 1129–30.
11. *Coker v. Georgia*, 433 U.S. 584 (1977).
12. *Enmund v. Florida*, 458 U.S. 782 (1972).
13. *Ford v. Wainwright*, 477 U.S. 399 (1986).
14. *Pervear v. Commonwealth*, 72 U.S. (5 Wall) 475 (1867); *Wing Wong v. United States*, 163 U.S. 228

(1896); *Kehrli v. Sprinkle*, 524 F.2d 328 (10th Cir. 1975).
15. *Delaware v. Cannon*, 55 Del. 587, 190 A.2d 574 (1963).
16. *Jackson v. Bishop*, 404 F.2d 571 (8th Cir. 1968).
17. For a thorough discussion of the constitutionality of whipping, *see* Daniel E. Hall, "When Caning Meets the Eighth Amendment: Whipping Offenders in the United States," 4 *Widener J.* PS.L. 403 (1995).
18. Breyer, "The Federal Sentencing Guidelines and the Key Compromises Upon Which They Rest," 17 *Hofstra L. Rev.* 4 (1988).
19. Federal Judges Association, *In Camera* (Dec. 1990).
20. *Griffin v. Wisconsin*, 483 U.S. 868 (1987).
21. *Porth v. Templar*, 453 F.2d 330 (10th Cir. 1971).
22. *United States v. Green*, 735 F.2d 1203 (9th Cir. 1984).
23. *Hughey v. United States*, 495 U.S. 411 (1990).

24. *Phillips v. United States*, 679 F.2d 192 (9th Cir. 1982).
25. *Bearden v. Georgia*, 461 U.S. 660, 668–69 (1983).
26. 399 U.S. 235 (1970).
27. *See*, for example, 21 U.S.C. § 881.
28. 19 U.S.C. § 1615.
29. *See* 21 U.S.C. § 853.
30. 114 S. Ct. 492 (1993).
31. *One 1958 Plymouth v. Pennsylvania*, 380 U.S. 693 (1965).
32. *The Growing Use of Jail Boot Camps: The Current State of the Art* (National Institute of Justice, Oct. 1993).
33. Belinda McCarthy & Bernard McCarthy, *Community-Based Corrections* 128 (2d ed., Brooks/Cole 1991).
34. *Goldschmitt v. State*, 490 So. 2d 123 (Fla. Dist. Ct. App.), *review denied*, 496 So. 2d 142 (Fla. 1986).
35. *McKane v. Durston*, 153 U.S. 684 (1894).
36. Fed. R. Crim. P. 37.
37. Supreme Ct. R. 11.1.
38. LaFave & Israel, *Criminal Procedure* § 26.2(c) (Hornbook Series; St. Paul, Minn.: West, 1985).
39. *Gideon v. Wainwright*, 373 U.S. 335 (1963).
40. 372 U.S. 353 (1963).
41. *Herrera v. Collins*, 113 S. Ct. 853 (1993).
42. *Fay v. NOIA*, 372 U.S. 391 (1963).
43. *Jones v. Cunningham*, 371 U.S. 236 (1963); *Hensley v. Municipal Court*, 411 U.S. 345 (1973).
44. *See Rules Governing Section 2254 Cases in the United States District Courts* (Feb. 1989). These rules also contain the forms necessary to petition for habeas corpus relief in the district court of the United States.

The Constitution of the United States of America

We the People of the United States, in Order to form a more perfect Union, establish Justice, insure domestic Tranquility, provide for the common defence, promote the general Welfare, and secure the Blessings of Liberty to ourselves and our Posterity, do ordain and establish this Constitution for the United States of America.

ARTICLE I

Section 1. All legislative Powers herein granted shall be vested in a Congress of the United States, which shall consist of a Senate and House of Representatives.

Section 2. (1) The House of Representatives shall be composed of Members chosen every second Year by the People of the several States, and the Electors in each State shall have the Qualifications requisite for Electors of the most numerous Branch of the State Legislature.

(2) No Person shall be a Representative who shall not have attained to the age of twenty-five Years, and been seven Years a Citizen of the United States, and who shall not, when elected, be an Inhabitant of that State in which he shall be chosen.

(3) Representatives and direct Taxes shall be apportioned among the several States which may be included within this Union, according to their respective Numbers, which shall be determined by adding to the whole Number of free Persons, including those bound to Service for a Term of Years, and excluding Indians not taxed, three fifths of all other Persons. The actual Enumeration shall be made within three Years after the first Meeting of the Congress of the United States, and within every subsequent Term of ten Years, in such Manner as they shall by Law direct. The Number of Representatives shall not exceed one for every thirty Thousand, but each State shall have at Least one Representative; and until such enumeration shall be made, the State of New Hampshire shall be entitled to chuse three, Massachusetts eight, Rhode Island and Providence Plantations one, Connecticut five, New York six, New Jersey four, Pennsylvania eight, Delaware one, Maryland six, Virginia ten, North Carolina five, South Carolina five, and Georgia three.

(4) When vacancies happen in the Representation from any State, the Executive Authority thereof shall issue Writs of Election to fill such Vacancies.

(5) The House of Representatives shall chuse their Speaker and other Officers; and shall have the sole Power of Impeachment.

Section 3. (1) The Senate of the United States shall be composed of two Senators from each State, chosen by the Legislature thereof, for six Years; and each Senator shall have one Vote.

(2) Immediately after they shall be assembled in Consequence of the first Election, they shall be divided as equally as may be into three Classes. The Seats of the Senators of the first Class shall be vacated at the Expiration of the Second Year, of the second Class at the Expiration of the fourth Year, and of the third Class at the Expiration of the sixth Year, so that one third may be chosen every second Year; and if Vacancies happen by Resignation, or otherwise, during the Recess of the Legislature of any State, the Executive thereof may make temporary Appointments until the next Meeting of the Legislature, which shall then fill such Vacancies.

(3) No Person shall be a Senator who shall not have attained to the Age of thirty Years, and been nine Years a Citizen of the United States, and who shall not, when elected, be an Inhabitant of that State for which he shall be chosen.

(4) The Vice President of the United States shall be President of the Senate, but shall have no Vote, unless they be equally divided.

(5) The Senate shall chuse their other Officers, and also a President pro tempore, in the Absence of the Vice President, or when he shall exercise the Office of the President of the United States.

(6) The Senate shall have the sole Power to try all Impeachments. When sitting for that Purpose, they shall be on Oath or Affirmation. When the President of the United States is tried, the Chief Justice shall preside: And no Person shall be convicted without the Concurrence of two thirds of the Members present.

(7) Judgment in Cases of Impeachment shall not extend further than to removal from Office, and disqualification to hold and enjoy any Office of honor, Trust or Profit under the United States: but the Party convicted shall nevertheless be liable and subject to Indictment, Trial, Judgment and Punishment, according to Law.

Section 4. (1) The Times, Places and Manner of holding Elections for Senators and Representatives, shall be prescribed in each State by the Legislature thereof; but the Congress may at any time by Law make or alter such Regulations, except as to the Places of chusing Senators.

(2) The Congress shall assemble at least once in every Year, and such Meeting shall be on the first Monday in December, unless they shall by Law appoint a different Day

Section 5. (1) Each House shall be the Judge of the Elections, Returns and Qualifications of its own Members, and a Majority of each shall constitute a Quorum to do Business; but a smaller Number may adjourn from day to day, and may be authorized to compel the Attendance of absent Members, in such Manner, and under such Penalties as each House may provide.

(2) Each House may determine the Rules of its Proceedings, punish its Members for disorderly Behaviour, and, with the Concurrence of two thirds, expel a Member.

(3) Each House shall keep a Journal of its Proceedings, and from time to time publish the same, excepting such Parts as may in their Judgment require Secrecy; and the Yeas and Nays of the Members of either House on any question shall, at the Desire of one fifth of those Present, be entered on the Journal.

(4) Neither House, during the Session of Congress, shall, without the Consent of the other, adjourn for more than three days, nor to any other Place than that in which the two Houses shall be sitting.

Section 6. (1) The Senators and Representatives shall receive a Compensation for their Services, to be ascertained by Law, and paid out of the Treasury of the United States. They shall in all Cases, except Treason, Felony and Breach of the Peace, be privileged from Arrest during their Attendance at the Session of their respective Houses, and in going to and returning from the same; and for any Speech or Debate in either House, they shall not be questioned in any other Place.

(2) No Senator or Representative shall, during the Time for which he was elected, be appointed to any civil Office under the Authority of the United States, which shall have been created, or the Emoluments whereof shall have been encreased during such time; and no Person holding any Office under the United States, shall be a Member of either House during his Continuance in Office.

Section 7. (1) All Bills for raising Revenue shall originate in the House of Representatives; but the Senate may propose or concur with Amendments as on other Bills.

(2) Every Bill which shall have passed the House of Representatives and the Senate, shall, before it become a Law, be presented to the President of the United States; If he approve he shall sign it, but if not he shall return it, with his Objections to that House in which it shall have originated, who shall enter the Objections at large on their Journal, and proceed to reconsider it. If after such Reconsideration two thirds of that House shall agree to pass the Bill, it shall be sent, together with the Objections, to the other House, by which it shall likewise be reconsidered, and if approved by two thirds of that House, it shall become a law. But in all such Cases the Votes of both Houses shall be determined by Yeas and Nays, and the Names of the Persons voting for and against the Bill shall be entered on the Journal of each House respectively. If any Bill shall not be returned by the President within ten Days (Sunday excepted) after it shall have been presented to him, the Same shall be a Law, in like Manner as if he had signed it, unless the Congress by their Adjournment prevent its Return, in which Case it shall not be a Law.

(3) Every Order, Resolution, or Vote to which the Concurrence of the Senate and House of Representatives may be necessary (except on a question of Adjournment) shall be presented to the President of the United States; and before the Same shall take Effect, shall be approved by him, or being disapproved by him, shall be repassed by two thirds of the Senate and House of Representatives, according to the Rules and Limitations prescribed in the Case of a Bill.

Section 8. (1) The Congress shall have Power To lay and collect Taxes, Duties, Imposts and Excises, to pay the Debts and provide for the common Defence and general Welfare of the United States; but all Duties, Imposts and Excises shall be uniform throughout the United States;

(2) To borrow Money on the credit of the United States;

(3) To regulate Commerce with foreign Nations, and among the several States, and with the Indian Tribes;

(4) To establish an uniform Rule of Naturalization, and uniform Laws on the subject of Bankruptcies throughout the United States;

(5) To coin Money, regulate the Value thereof, and of foreign Coin, and to fix the Standard of Weights and Measures;

(6) To provide for the Punishment of counterfeiting the Securities and current Coin of the United States;

(7) To establish Post Offices and post Roads;

(8) To promote the Progress of Science and useful Arts, by securing for limited Times to Authors and Inventors the exclusive Right to their respective Writings and Discoveries;

(9) To constitute Tribunals inferior to the supreme Court;

(10) To define and punish Piracies and Felonies committed on the high Seas, and Offenses against the Law of Nations;

(11) To declare War, grant Letters of Marque and Reprisal, and make Rules concerning Captures on Land and Water;

(12) To raise and support Armies, but no Appropriation of Money to that Use shall be for a longer Term than two Years;

(13) To provide and maintain a Navy;

(14) To make Rules for the Government and Regulation of the land and naval Forces;

(15) To provide for calling forth the Militia to execute the Laws of the Union, suppress Insurrections and repel Invasions;

(16) To provide for organizing, arming, and disciplining, the Militia, and for governing such Part of them as may be employed in the Service of the United States, reserving to the States respectively, the Appointment of the Officers, and the Authority of training the Militia according to the discipline prescribed by Congress;

(17) To exercise exclusive Legislation in all Cases whatsoever, over such District (not exceeding ten Miles square) as may, by Cession of particular States, and the Acceptance of Congress, become the Seat of the Government of the United States, and to exercise like Authority over all Places purchased by the Consent of the Legislature of the State in which the Same shall be, for the Erection of Forts, Magazines, Arsenals, dock-Yards, and other needful Buildings;—And

(18) To make all Laws which shall be necessary and proper for carrying into Execution the foregoing Powers, and all other Powers vested by this Constitution in the Government of the United States, or in any Department or Officer thereof.

Section 9. (1) The Migration or Importation of such Persons as any of the States now existing shall think proper to admit, shall not be prohibited by the Congress prior to the Year one thousand eight hundred and eight, but a Tax or Duty may be imposed on such Importation, not exceeding ten dollars for each Person.

(2) The Privilege of the Writ of Habeas Corpus shall not be suspended unless when in Cases of Rebellion or Invasion the public Safety may require it.

(3) No Bill of Attainder or ex post facto Law shall be passed.

(4) No Capitation, or other direct, Tax shall be laid, unless in Proportion to the Census or Enumeration herein before directed to be taken.

(5) No Tax or Duty shall be laid on Articles exported from any State.

(6) No Preference shall be given by any Regulation of Commerce or Revenue to the Ports of one State over those of another; nor shall Vessels bound to, or from, one State, be obliged to enter, clear or pay Duties in another.

(7) No Money shall be drawn from the Treasury, but in Consequence of Appropriations made by Law; and a regular Statement and Account of the Receipts and Expenditures of all public Money shall be published from time to time.

(8) No Title of Nobility shall be granted by the United States: And no Person holding any Office of Profit or Trust under them, shall, without the Consent of the Congress, accept of any present, Emolument, Office, or Title, of any kind whatever, from any King, Prince or foreign State.

Section 10. (1) No State shall enter into any Treaty, Alliance, or Confederation; grant Letters of Marque and Reprisal; coin Money; emit Bills of Credit; make any Thing but gold and silver Coin a Tender in Payment of Debts; pass any Bill of Attainder, ex post facto Law, or Law impairing the Obligation of Contracts, or grant any Title of Nobility.

(2) No State shall, without the Consent of Congress, lay any Imposts or Duties on Imports or Exports, except what may be absolutely necessary for executing its inspection Laws: and the net Produce of all Duties and Imposts, laid by any State on Imports or Exports, shall be for the Use of the Treasury of the United States; and all such Laws shall be subject to the Revision and Controul of the Congress.

(3) No State shall, without the Consent of Congress, lay any Duty of Tonnage, keep Troops, or Ships of War

in time of Peace, enter into any Agreement or Compact with another State, or with a foreign Power, or engage in War, unless actually invaded, or in such imminent Danger as will not admit of Delay.

ARTICLE II

Section 1.   (1) The executive Power shall be vested in a President of the United States of America. He shall hold his Office during the Term of four Years, and, together with the Vice President, chosen for the same Term, be elected, as follows:

(2) Each State shall appoint, in such Manner as the Legislature thereof may direct, a Number of Electors, equal to the whole Number of Senators and Representatives to which the State may be entitled in the Congress: but no Senator or Representative, or Person holding an Office of Trust or Profit under the United States, shall be appointed an Elector.

The Electors shall meet in their respective States, and vote by Ballot for two Persons, of whom one at least shall not be an Inhabitant of the same State with themselves. And they shall make a List of all the Persons voted for, and of the Number of Votes for each; which List they shall sign and certify, and transmit sealed to the Seat of the Government of the United States, directed to the President of the Senate. The President of the Senate shall, in the presence of the Senate and House of Representatives, open all the Certificates, and the Votes shall then be counted. The Person having the greatest Number of Votes shall be the President, if such Number be a Majority of the whole Number of Electors appointed; and if there be more than one who have such Majority, and have an equal Number of Votes, then the House of Representatives shall immediately chuse by Ballot one of them for President; and if no Person have a Majority, then from the five highest on the List the said House shall in like Manner chuse the President. But in chusing the President, the Votes shall be taken by States, the Representation from each State having one Vote; a quorum for this Purpose shall consist of a Member or Members from two thirds of the States, and a Majority of all the States shall be necessary to a Choice. In every Case, after the Choice of the President, the Person having the greatest Number of Votes of the Electors shall be the Vice President. But if there should remain two or more who have equal Votes, the Senate shall chuse from them by Ballot the Vice President.

(3) The Congress may determine the Time of chusing the Electors, and the Day on which they shall give their Votes; which Day shall be the same throughout the United States.

(4) No Person except a natural born Citizen, or a Citizen of the United States, at the time of the Adoption of this Constitution, shall be eligible to the Office of President; neither shall any Person be eligible to that Office who shall not have attained to the Age of thirty-five Years, and been fourteen Years a Resident within the United States.

(5) In Case of the Removal of the President from Office, or of his Death, Resignation, or Inability to discharge the Powers and Duties of the said Office, the Same shall devolve on the Vice President, and the Congress may by Law provide for the Case of Removal, Death, Resignation or Inability, both of the President and Vice President, declaring what Officer shall then act as President, and such Officer shall act accordingly, until the Disability be removed, or a President shall be elected.

(6) The President shall, at stated Times, receive for his Services, a Compensation, which shall neither be increased nor diminished during the Period for which he shall have been elected, and he shall not receive within that Period any other Emolument from the United States, or any of them.

(7) Before he enter on the Execution of his Office, he shall take the following Oath or Affirmation:—"I do solemnly swear (or affirm) that I will faithfully execute the Office of President of the United States, and will to the best of my Ability, preserve, protect and defend the Constitution of the United States."

Section 2.   (1) The President shall be Commander in Chief of the Army and Navy of the United States, and of the Militia of the several States, when called into the actual Service of the United States; he may require the Opinion, in writing, of the principal Officer in each of the executive Departments, upon any Subject relating to the Duties of their respective Offices, and he shall have Power to grant Reprieves and Pardons for Offenses against the United States, except in Cases of Impeachment.

(2) He shall have Power, by and with the Advice and Consent of the Senate, to make Treaties, provided two thirds of the Senators present concur; and he shall nominate, and by and with the Advice and Consent of the Senate, shall appoint Ambassadors, other public Ministers and Consuls, Judges of the supreme Court, and all other Officers of the United States, whose Appointments are not herein otherwise provided for, and which shall be established by Law: but the Congress may by Law vest the Appointment of such inferior Officers, as they think

proper, in the President alone, in the Courts of Law, or in the Heads of Departments.

(3) The President shall have Power to fill up all Vacancies that may happen during the Recess of the Senate, by granting Commissions which shall expire at the End of their next Session.

Section 3. He shall from time to time give to the Congress Information of the State of the Union, and recommend to their Consideration such Measures as he shall judge necessary and expedient; he may, on extraordinary Occasions, convene both Houses, or either of them, and in Case of Disagreement between them, with Respect to the Time of Adjournment, he may adjourn them to such Time as he shall think proper; he shall receive Ambassadors and other public Ministers; he shall take Care that the Laws be faithfully executed, and shall Commission all the Officers of the United States.

Section 4. The President, Vice President and all Civil Officers of the United States, shall be removed from Office on Impeachment for, and Conviction of, Treason, Bribery, or other high Crimes and Misdemeanors.

ARTICLE III

Section 1. The judicial Power of the United States, shall be vested in one supreme Court, and in such inferior Courts as the Congress may from time to time ordain and establish. The Judges, both of the supreme and inferior Courts, shall hold their Offices during good Behaviour, and shall, at stated Times, receive for their Services, a Compensation, which shall not be diminished during their Continuance in Office.

Section 2. (1) The judicial Power shall extend to all Cases, in Law and Equity, arising under this Constitution, the Laws of the United States, and Treaties made, or which shall be made, under their Authority;—to all Cases affecting Ambassadors, other public Ministers and Consuls;—to all Cases of admiralty and maritime Jurisdiction;—to Controversies to which the United States shall be a party;—to Controversies between two or more States;—between a State and Citizens of another State;—between Citizens of different States;—between Citizens of the same State claiming Lands under Grants of different States, and between a State, or the Citizens thereof, and foreign States, Citizens or Subjects.

(2) In all Cases affecting Ambassadors, other public Ministers and Consuls, and those in which a State shall be Party, the supreme Court shall have original Jurisdiction. In all the other Cases before mentioned, the supreme Court shall have appellate Jurisdiction, both as to Law and Fact, with such Exceptions, and under such Regulations as the Congress shall make.

(3) The Trial of all Crimes, except in Cases of Impeachment, shall be by Jury; and such Trial shall be held in the State where the said Crimes shall have been committed; but when not committed within any State, the Trial shall be at such Place or Places as the Congress may by Law have directed.

Section 3. (1) Treason against the United States, shall consist only in levying War against them, or in adhering to their Enemies, giving them Aid and Comfort. No Person shall be convicted of Treason unless on the Testimony of two Witnesses to the same overt Act, or on Confession in open Court.

(2) The Congress shall have Power to declare the Punishment of Treason, but no Attainder of Treason shall work Corruption of Blood, or Forfeiture except during the Life of the Person attainted.

ARTICLE IV

Section 1. Full Faith and Credit shall be given in each State to the public Acts, Records, and judicial Proceedings of every other State. And the Congress may by general Laws prescribe the Manner in which such Acts, Records and Proceedings shall be proved, and the Effect thereof.

Section 2. (1) The Citizens of each State shall be entitled to all privileges and Immunities of Citizens in the several States.

(2) A Person charged in any State with Treason, Felony, or other Crime, who shall flee from Justice, and be found in another State, shall on Demand of the executive Authority of the State from which he fled, be delivered up, to be removed to the State having Jurisdiction of the Crime.

(3) No Person held to Service of Labour in one State, under the Laws thereof, escaping into another, shall, in Consequence of any Law or Regulation therein, be discharged from such Service or Labour, but shall be delivered up on Claim of the Party to whom such Service or Labour may be due.

Section 3. (1) New States may be admitted by the Congress into this Union; but no new State shall be formed or erected within the Jurisdiction of any other State; nor any State be formed by the Junction of two or more States, or Parts of States, without the Consent of the Legislatures of the States concerned as well as of the Congress.

(2) The Congress shall have power to dispose of and make all needful Rules and Regulations respecting the Territory or other Property belonging to the United States; and nothing in this Constitution shall be so construed as to Prejudice any Claims of the United States, or of any particular State.

Section 4. The United States shall guarantee to every State in this Union a Republican Form of Government, and shall protect each of them against Invasion; and on Application of the Legislature, or of the Executive (when the Legislature cannot be convened) against domestic Violence.

ARTICLE V

The Congress, whenever two thirds of both Houses shall deem it necessary, shall propose Amendments to this Constitution, or, on the Application of the Legislatures of two thirds of the several States, shall call a Convention for proposing Amendments, which, in either Case, shall be valid to all Intents and Purposes, as Part of this Constitution, when ratified by the Legislatures of three fourths of the several States, or by Conventions in three fourths thereof, as the one or the other Mode of Ratification may be proposed by the Congress; Provided that no Amendment which may be made prior to the Year One thousand eight hundred and eight shall in any Manner affect the first and fourth Clauses in the Ninth Section of the first Article; and that no State, without its Consent, shall be deprived of its equal Suffrage in the Senate.

ARTICLE VI

(1) All Debts contracted and Engagements entered into, before the Adoption of this Constitution, shall be as valid against the United States under this Constitution, as under the Confederation.

(2) This Constitution, and the Laws of the United States which shall be made in Pursuance thereof; and all Treaties made, or which shall be made, under the Authority of the United States, shall be the supreme Law of the Land; and the Judges in every State shall be bound thereby, any Thing in the Constitution or Laws of any State to the Contrary notwithstanding.

(3) The Senators and Representatives before mentioned, and the Members of the several State Legislatures, and all executive and judicial Officers, both of the United States and of the several States, shall be bound by Oath or Affirmation, to support this Constitution; but no religious Test shall ever be required as a Qualification to any Office or public Trust under the United States.

ARTICLE VII

The Ratification of the Conventions of nine States, shall be sufficient for the Establishment of this Constitution between the States so ratifying the Same.

ARTICLES IN ADDITION TO, AND AMENDMENT OF, THE CONSTITUTION OF THE UNITED STATES OF AMERICA, PROPOSED BY CONGRESS, AND RATIFIED BY THE SEVERAL STATES, PURSUANT TO THE FIFTH ARTICLE OF THE ORIGINAL CONSTITUTION

AMENDMENT I (1791)

Congress shall make no law respecting an establishment of religion, or prohibiting the free exercise thereof; or abridging the freedom of speech, or of the press; or the right of the people peaceably to assemble, and to petition the Government for a redress of grievances.

AMENDMENT II (1791)

A well regulated Militia, being necessary to the security of a free state, the right of the people to keep and bear Arms, shall not be infringed.

AMENDMENT III (1791)

No Soldier shall, in time of peace be quartered in any house, without the consent of the Owner, nor in time of war, but in a manner to be prescribed by law.

AMENDMENT IV (1791)

The right of the people to be secure in their persons, houses, papers, and effects, against unreasonable searches and seizures, shall not be violated, and no Warrants shall issue, but upon probable cause, supported by Oath or affirmation, and particularly describing the place to be searched, and the persons or things to be seized.

AMENDMENT V (1791)

No person shall be held to answer for a capital, or otherwise infamous crime, unless on a presentment or indictment of a Grand Jury, except in cases arising in the land or naval forces, or in the Militia, when in actual service in time of War or public danger; nor shall any person be subject for the same offence to be twice put in jeopardy of life or limb; nor shall be compelled in any criminal case to be a witness against himself, nor be deprived of

The Constitution of the United States of America

505

life, liberty, or property, without due process of law; nor shall private property be taken for public use, without just compensation.

AMENDMENT VI (1791)

In all criminal prosecutions, the accused shall enjoy the right to a speedy and public trial, by an impartial jury of the State and district wherein the crime shall have been committed, which district shall have been previously ascertained by law, and to be informed of the nature and cause of the accusation; to be confronted with the witnesses against him; to have compulsory process for obtaining witnesses in his favor, and to have the Assistance of Counsel for his defence.

AMENDMENT VII (1791)

In Suits at common law, where the value in controversy shall exceed twenty dollars, the right of trial by jury shall be preserved, and no fact tried by a jury, shall be otherwise re-examined in any Court of the United States, than according to the rules of the common law.

AMENDMENT VIII (1791)

Excessive bail shall not be required, nor excessive fines imposed, nor cruel and unusual punishments inflicted.

AMENDMENT IX (1791)

The enumeration in the Constitution, of certain rights, shall not be construed to deny or disparage others retained by the people.

AMENDMENT X (1791)

The powers not delegated to the United States by the Constitution, nor prohibited by it to the States, are reserved to the States respectively, or to the people.

AMENDMENT XI (1798)

The Judicial power of the United States shall not be construed to extend to any suit in law or equity, commenced or prosecuted against one of the United States by Citizens of another State, or by Citizens or Subjects of any Foreign State.

AMENDMENT XII (1804)

The Electors shall meet in their respective states and vote by ballot for President and Vice-President, one of whom, at least, shall not be an inhabitant of the same state with themselves; they shall name in their ballots the person voted for as President, and in distinct ballots the person voted for as Vice-President, and they shall make distinct lists of all persons voted for as President, and of all persons voted for as Vice-President, and of the number of votes for each, which lists they shall sign and certify, and transmit sealed to the seat of the government of the United States, directed to the President of the Senate;—The President of the Senate shall, in the presence of the Senate and House of Representatives, open all the certificates and the votes shall then be counted;—The person having the greatest number of votes for President, shall be the President, if such number be a majority of the whole number of Electors appointed; and if no person have such majority, then from the persons having the highest numbers not exceeding three on the list of those voted for as President, the House of Representatives shall choose immediately, by ballot, the President. But in choosing the President, the votes shall be taken by states, the representation from each state having one vote; a quorum for this purpose shall consist of a member or members from two-thirds of the states, and a majority of all the states shall be necessary to a choice. And if the House of Representatives shall not choose a President whenever the right of choice shall devolve upon them, before the fourth day of March next following, then the Vice-President shall act as President, as in the case of the death or other constitutional disability of the President—The person having the greatest number of votes as Vice-President, shall be the Vice-President, if such number be a majority of the whole number of Electors appointed, and if no person have a majority, then from the two highest numbers on the list, the Senate shall choose the Vice-President; A quorum for the purpose shall consist of two-thirds of the whole number of Senators, and a majority of the whole number shall be necessary to a choice. But no person constitutionally ineligible to the office of President shall be eligible to that of Vice-President of the United States.

AMENDMENT XIII (1865)

Section 1. Neither slavery nor involuntary servitude, except as a punishment for crime whereof the party shall have been duly convicted, shall exist within the United States, or any place subject to their jurisdiction.

Section 2. Congress shall have power to enforce this article by appropriate legislation.

AMENDMENT XIV (1868)

Section 1. All persons born or naturalized in the United States and subject to the jurisdiction thereof, are citizens of the United States and of the State wherein they reside. No State shall make or enforce any law which shall abridge the privileges or immunities of citizens of the United States; nor shall any State deprive any person of life, liberty, or property, without due process of law; nor deny to any person within its jurisdiction the equal protection of the laws.

Section 2. Representatives shall be apportioned among the several States according to their respective numbers, counting the whole number of persons in each State, excluding Indians not taxed. But when the right to vote at any election for the choice of electors for President and Vice-President of the United States, Representatives in Congress, the Executive and Judicial officers of a State, or the members of the Legislature thereof, is denied to any of the male inhabitants of such State, being twenty-one years of age, and citizens of the United States, or in any way abridged, except for participation in rebellion, or other crime, the basis of representation therein shall be reduced in the proportion which the number of such male citizens shall bear to the whole number of male citizens twenty-one years of age in such State.

Section 3. No person shall be a Senator or Representative in Congress, or elector of President and Vice-President, or hold any office, civil or military, under the United States, or under any State, who, having previously taken an oath, as a member of Congress, or as an officer of the United States, or as a member of any State legislature, or as an executive or judicial officer of any State, to support the Constitution of the United States, shall have engaged in insurrection or rebellion against the same, or given aid or comfort to the enemies thereof. But Congress may by a vote of two-thirds of each House, remove such disability.

Section 4. The validity of the public debt of the United States, authorized by law, including debts incurred for payment of pensions and bounties for services in suppressing insurrection or rebellion, shall not be questioned. But neither the United States nor any State shall assume or pay any debt or obligation incurred in aid of insurrection or rebellion against the United States, or any claim for the loss or emancipation of any slave; but all such debts, obligations and claims shall be held illegal and void.

Section 5. The Congress shall have power to enforce, by appropriate legislation, the provisions of this article.

AMENDMENT XV (1870)

Section 1. The right of citizens of the United States to vote shall not be denied or abridged by the United States or by any State on account of race, color, or previous condition of servitude.

Section 2. The Congress shall have power to enforce this article by appropriate legislation.

AMENDMENT XVI (1913)

The Congress shall have power to lay and collect taxes on incomes, from whatever source derived, without apportionment among the several States, and without regard to any census or enumeration.

AMENDMENT XVII (1913)

The Senate of the United States shall be composed of two Senators from each State, elected by the people thereof, for six years; and each Senator shall have one vote. The electors in each State shall have the qualifications requisite for electors of the most numerous branch of the State legislatures.

When vacancies happen in the representation of any State in the Senate, the executive authority of such State shall issue writs of election to fill such vacancies: *Provided,* That the legislature of any State may empower the executive thereof to make temporary appointments until the people fill the vacancies by election as the legislature may direct.

This amendment shall not be so construed as to affect the election or term of any Senator chosen before it becomes valid as part of the Constitution.

AMENDMENT XVIII (1919)

Section 1. After one year from the ratification of this article the manufacture, sale, or transportation of intoxicating liquors within, the importation thereof into, or the exportation thereof from the United States and all territory subject to the jurisdiction thereof for beverage purposes is hereby prohibited.

Section 2. The Congress and the several States shall have concurrent power to enforce this article by appropriate legislation.

Section 3. This article shall be inoperative unless it shall have been ratified as an amendment to the Constitution by the legislatures of the several States, as provided in the Constitution, within seven years from the date of the submission hereof to the States by the Congress.

AMENDMENT XIX (1920)

The right of citizens of the United States to vote shall not be denied or abridged by the United States or by any State on account of sex.

Congress shall have power to enforce this article by appropriate legislation.

AMENDMENT XX (1933)

Section 1. The terms of the President and Vice President shall end at noon on the 20th day of January, and the terms of Senators and Representatives at noon on the 3d day of January, of the years in which such terms would have ended if this article had not been ratified; and the terms of their successors shall then begin.

Section 2. The Congress shall assemble at least once in every year, and such meeting shall begin at noon on the 3d day of January, unless they shall by law appoint a different day.

Section 3. If, at the time fixed for the beginning of the term of the President, the President elect shall have died, the Vice President elect shall become President. If a President shall not have been chosen before the time fixed for the beginning of his term, or if the President elect shall have failed to qualify, then the Vice President elect shall act as President until a President shall have qualified; and the Congress may by law provide for the case wherein neither a President elect nor a Vice President elect shall have qualified, declaring who shall then act as President, or the manner in which one who is to act shall be selected, and such person shall act accordingly until a President or Vice President shall have qualified.

Section 4. The Congress may by law provide for the case of the death of any of the persons from whom the House of Representatives may choose a President whenever the right of choice shall have devolved upon them, and for the case of the death of any of the persons from whom the Senate may choose a Vice President whenever the right of choice shall have devolved upon them.

Section 5. Sections 1 and 2 shall take effect on the 15th day of October following the ratification of this article.

Section 6. This article shall be inoperative unless it shall have been ratified as an amendment to the Constitution by the legislatures of three-fourths of the several States within seven years from the date of its submission.

AMENDMENT XXI (1933)

Section 1. The eighteenth article of amendment to the Constitution of the United States is hereby repealed.

Section 2. The transportation or importation into any State, Territory or possession of the United States for delivery or use therein of intoxicating liquors, in violation of the laws thereof, is hereby prohibited.

Section 3. This article shall be inoperative unless it shall have been ratified as an amendment to the Constitution by conventions in the several States, as provided in the Constitution, within seven years from the date of the submission hereof to the States by the Congress.

AMENDMENT XXII (1951)

Section 1. No person shall be elected to the office of the President more than twice, and no person who has held the office of President, or acted as President, for more than two years of a term to which some other person was elected President shall be elected to the office of the President more than once. But this Article shall not apply to any person holding the office of President when this Article was proposed by the Congress, and shall not prevent any person who may be holding the office of President, or acting as President, during the term within which this Article becomes operative from holding the office of President or acting as President during the remainder of such term.

Section 2. This Article shall be inoperative unless it shall have been ratified as an amendment to the Constitution by the legislatures of three-fourths of the several States within seven years from the date of its submission to the States by the Congress.

AMENDMENT XXIII (1961)

Section 1. The District constituting the seat of Government of the United States shall appoint in such manner as the Congress may direct:

A number of electors of President and Vice President equal to the whole number of Senators and Representatives in Congress to which the District would be entitled if

it were a State, but in no event more than the least popu-
lous State; they shall be in addition to those appointed
by the States, but they shall be considered, for the purposes of the election of President and Vice President, to be
electors appointed by a State; and they shall meet in
the District and perform such duties as provided by the
twelfth article of amendment.

Section 2.   The Congress shall have power to enforce
this article by appropriate legislation.

AMENDMENT XXIV (1964)

Section 1.   The right of citizens of the United States to
vote in any primary or other election for President or
Vice President, for electors for President or Vice President, or for Senator or Representative in Congress, shall
not be denied or abridged by the United States or any
State by reason of failure to pay any poll tax or other tax.

Section 2.   The Congress shall have power to enforce
this article by appropriate legislation.

AMENDMENT XXV (1967)

Section 1.   In case of the removal of the President from
office or of his death or resignation, the Vice President
shall become President.

Section 2.   Whenever there is a vacancy in the office
of the Vice President, the President shall nominate a Vice
President who shall take office upon confirmation by a
majority vote of both Houses of Congress.

Section 3.   Whenever the President transmits to the
President pro tempore of the Senate and the Speaker of
the House of Representatives his written declaration
that he is unable to discharge the powers and duties of
his office, and until he transmits to them a written declaration to the contrary, such powers and duties shall be
discharged by the Vice President as Acting President.

Section 4.   Whenever the Vice President and a
majority of either the principal officers of the executive
departments or of such other body as Congress may by
law provide, transmit to the President pro tempore of

the Senate and the Speaker of the House of Representatives their written declaration that the President is
unable to discharge the powers and duties of his office,
the Vice President shall immediately assume the powers
and duties of the office as Acting President.

Thereafter, when the President transmits to the
President pro tempore of the Senate and the Speaker
of the House of Representatives his written declaration
that no inability exists, he shall resume the powers
and duties of his office unless the Vice President and
a majority of either the principal officers of the executive department or of such other body as Congress
may by law provide, transmit within four days to the
President pro tempore of the Senate and the Speaker
of the House of Representatives their written declaration that the President is unable to discharge the powers and duties of his office. Thereupon Congress shall
decide the issue, assembling within forty-eight hours
for that purpose if not in session. If the Congress,
within twenty-one days after receipt of the latter written declaration, or, if Congress is not in session, within
twenty-one days after Congress is required to assemble, determines by two-thirds vote of both Houses that
the President is unable to discharge the powers and
duties of his office, the Vice President shall continue
to discharge the same as Acting President; otherwise,
the President shall resume the powers and duties of
his office.

AMENDMENT XXVI (1971)

Section 1.   The right of citizens of the United States, who
are eighteen years of age or older, to vote shall not be
denied or abridged by the United States or by any State
on account of age.

Section 2.   The Congress shall have power to enforce
this article by appropriate legislation.

AMENDMENT XXVII (1992)

No law varying the compensation for the services of the
senators and representatives shall take effect, until an
election of representatives shall have intervened.

APPENDIX B

Selected Excerpts from the Model Penal Code

PART I GENERAL PROVISIONS

Article 1. Preliminary

§ 1.04. Classes of Crimes; Violations.

(1) An offense defined by this Code or by any other statute of this State, for which a sentence of [death or of] imprisonment is authorized, constitutes a crime. Crimes are classified as felonies, misdemeanors or petty misdemeanors.

(2) A crime is a felony if it is so designated in this Code or if persons convicted thereof may be sentenced [to death or] to imprisonment for a term which, apart from an extended term, is in excess of one year.

(3) A crime is a misdemeanor if it is so designated in this Code or in a statute other than this Code enacted subsequent thereto.

(4) A crime is a petty misdemeanor if it is so designated in this Code or in a statute other than this Code enacted subsequent thereto or if it is defined by a statute other than this Code which now provides that persons convicted thereof may be sentenced to imprisonment for a term of which the maximum is less than one year.

(5) An offense defined by this Code or by any other statute of this State constitutes a violation if it is so designated in this Code or in the law defining the offense or if no other sentence than a fine, or fine and forfeiture or other civil penalty is authorized supon conviction or if it is defined by a statute other than this Code which now provides that the offense shall not constitute a crime. A violation does not constitute a crime and conviction of a violation shall not give rise to any disability or legal disadvantage based on conviction of a criminal offense.

(6) Any offense declared by law to constitute a crime, without specification of the grade thereof or of the sentence authorized upon conviction, is a misdemeanor.

(7) An offense defined by any statute of this State other than this Code shall be classified as provided in this Section and the sentence that may be imposed upon conviction thereof shall hereafter be governed by this Code.

§ 1.05. All Offenses Defined by Statute; Application of General Provisions of the Code.

(1) No conduct constitutes an offense unless it is a crime or violation under this Code or another statute of this State.

(2) The provisions of Part I of the Code are applicable to offenses defined by other statutes, unless the Code otherwise provides.

(3) This Section does not affect the power of a court to punish for contempt or to employ any sanction authorized by law for the enforcement of an order or a civil judgment or decree.

§ 1.12. Proof Beyond a Reasonable Doubt; Affirmative Defenses; Burden of Proving Fact When Not an Element of an Offense; Presumptions.

(1) No person may be convicted of an offense unless each element of such offense is proved beyond a reasonable doubt. In the absence of such proof, the innocence of the defendant is assumed.

(2) Subsection (1) of this Section does not:
  (a) require the disproof of an affirmative defense unless and until there is evidence supporting such defense; or

(b) apply to any defense which the Code or another statute plainly requires the defendant to prove by a preponderance of evidence.

(3) A ground of defense is affirmative, within the meaning of Subsection (2)(a) of this Section, when:

(a) it arises under a section of the Code which so provides; or

(b) it relates to an offense defined by a statute other than the Code and such statute so provides; or

(c) it involves a matter of excuse or justification peculiarly within the knowledge of the defendant on which he can fairly be required to adduce supporting evidence.

(4) When the application of the Code depends upon the finding of a fact which is not an element of an offense, unless the Code otherwise provides:

(a) the burden of proving the fact is on the prosecution or defendant, depending on whose interest or contention will be furthered if the finding should be made; and

(b) the fact must be proved to the satisfaction of the Court or jury, as the case may be.

(5) When the Code establishes a presumption with respect to any fact which is an element of an offense, it has the following consequences:

(a) when there is evidence of the facts which give rise to the presumption, the issue of the existence of the presumed fact must be submitted to the jury, unless the Court is satisfied that the evidence as a whole clearly negatives the presumed fact; and

(b) when the issue of the existence of the presumed fact is submitted to the jury, the Court shall charge that while the presumed fact must, on all the evidence, be proved beyond a reasonable doubt, the law declares that the jury may regard the facts giving rise to the presumption as sufficient evidence of the presumed fact.

(6) A presumption not established by the Code or inconsistent with it has the consequences otherwise accorded it by law.

§ 1.13. General Definitions.

In this Code, unless a different meaning plainly is required:

(1) "statute" includes the Constitution and a local law or ordinance of a political subdivision of the State;

(2) "act" or "action" means a bodily movement whether voluntary or involuntary;

(3) "voluntary" has the meaning specified in Section 2.01;

(4) "omission" means a failure to act;

(5) "conduct" means an action or omission and its accompanying state of mind, or, where relevant, a series of acts and omissions;

(6) "actor" includes, where relevant, a person guilty of an omission;

(7) "acted" includes, where relevant, "omitted to act";

(8) "person," "he" and "actor" include any natural person and, where relevant, a corporation or an unincorporated association;

(9) "element of an offense" means (i) such conduct or (ii) such attendant circumstances or (iii) such a result of conduct as

(a) is included in the description of the forbidden conduct in the definition of the offense; or

(b) establishes the required kind of culpability; or

(c) negatives an excuse or justification for such conduct; or

(d) negatives a defense under the statute of limitations; or

(e) establishes jurisdiction or venue;

(10) "material element of an offense" means an element that does not relate exclusively to the statute of limitations, jurisdiction, venue or to any other matter similarly unconnected with (i) the harm or evil, incident to conduct, sought to be prevented by the law defining the offense, or (ii) the existence of a justification or excuse for such conduct;

(11) "purposely" has the meaning specified in Section 2.02 and equivalent terms such as "with purpose," "designed" or "with design" have the same meaning;

(12) "intentionally" or "with intent" means purposely;

(13) "knowingly" has the meaning specified in Section 2.02 and equivalent terms such as "knowing" or "with knowledge" have the same meaning;

(14) "recklessly" has the meaning specified in Section 2.02 and equivalent terms such as "recklessness" or "with recklessness" have the same meaning;

(15) "negligently" has the meaning specified in Section 2.02 and equivalent terms such as "negligence" or "with negligence" have the same meaning;

(16) "reasonably believes" or "reasonable belief" designates a belief which the actor is not reckless or negligent in holding.

ARTICLE 2. GENERAL PRINCIPLES OF LIABILITY

§ 2.01. Requirement of Voluntary Act; Omission as Basis of Liability; Possession as an Act.

(1) A person is not guilty of an offense unless his liability is based on conduct which includes a voluntary act or the omission to perform an act of which he is physically capable.

(2) The following are not voluntary acts within the meaning of this Section:
    (a) a reflex or convulsion;
    (b) a bodily movement during unconsciousness or sleep;
    (c) conduct during hypnosis or resulting from hypnotic suggestion;
    (d) a bodily movement that otherwise is not a product of the effort or determination of the actor, either conscious or habitual.

(3) Liability for the commission of an offense may not be based on an omission unaccompanied by action unless:
    (a) the omission is expressly made sufficient by the law defining the offense; or
    (b) a duty to perform the omitted act is otherwise imposed by law.

(4) Possession is an act, within the meaning of this Section, if the possessor knowingly procured or received the thing possessed or was aware of his control thereof for a sufficient period to have been able to terminate his possession.

§ 2.02. General Requirements of Culpability.

(1) *Minimum Requirements of Culpability.* Except as provided in Section 2.05, a person is not guilty of an offense unless he acted purposely, knowingly, recklessly or negligently, as the law may require, with respect to each material element of the offense.

(2) *Kinds of Culpability Defined.*
    (a) *Purposely.*
        A person acts purposely with respect to a material element of an offense when:
        (i) if the element involves the nature of his conduct or a result thereof, it is his conscious object to engage in conduct of that nature or to cause such a result; and
        (ii) if the element involves the attendant circumstances, he is aware of the existence of such circumstances or he believes or hopes that they exist.
    (b) *Knowingly.*
        A person acts knowingly with respect to a material element of an offense when:
        (i) if the element involves the nature of his conduct or the attendant circumstances, he is aware that his conduct is of that nature or that such circumstances exist; and
        (ii) if the element involves a result of his conduct, he is aware that it is practically certain that his conduct will cause such a result.
    (c) *Recklessly.*
        A person acts recklessly with respect to a material element of an offense when he consciously disregards a substantial and unjustifiable risk that the material element exists or will result from his conduct. The risk must be of such a nature and degree that, considering the nature and purpose of the actor's conduct and the circumstances known to him, its disregard involves a gross deviation from the standard of conduct that a law-abiding person would observe in the actor's situation.
    (d) *Negligently.*
        A person acts negligently with respect to a material element of an offense when he should be aware of a substantial and unjustifiable risk that the material element exists or will result from his conduct. The risk must be of such a nature and degree that the actor's failure to perceive it, considering the nature and purpose of his conduct and the circumstances known to him, involves a gross deviation from the standard of care that a reasonable person would observe in the actor's situation.

(3) *Culpability Required Unless Otherwise Provided.* When the culpability sufficient to establish a material element of an offense is not prescribed by law, such element is established if a person acts purposely, knowingly or recklessly with respect thereto.

(4) *Prescribed Culpability Requirement Applies to All Material Elements.* When the law defining an offense prescribes the kind of culpability that is sufficient for the commission of an offense, without distinguishing among the material elements thereof, such provision shall apply to all the material elements of the offense, unless a contrary purpose plainly appears.

(5) *Substitutes for Negligence, Recklessness and Knowledge.* When the law provides that negligence suffices to establish an element of an offense, such element also

is established if a person acts purposely, knowingly or recklessly. When recklessness suffices to establish an element, such element also is established if a person acts purposely or knowingly. When acting knowingly suffices to establish an element, such element also is established if a person acts purposely.

(6) *Requirement of Purpose Satisfied if Purpose Is Conditional.* When a particular purpose is an element of an offense, the element is established although such purpose is conditional, unless the condition negatives the harm or evil sought to be prevented by the law defining the offense.

(7) *Requirement of Knowledge Satisfied by Knowledge of High Probability.* When knowledge of the existence of a particular fact is an element of an offense, such knowledge is established if a person is aware of a high probability of its existence, unless he actually believes that it does not exist.

(8) *Requirement of Wilfulness Satisfied by Acting Knowingly.* A requirement that an offense be committed wilfully is satisfied if a person acts knowingly with respect to the material elements of the offense, unless a purpose to impose further requirements appears.

(9) *Culpability as to Illegality of Conduct.* Neither knowledge nor recklessness or negligence as to whether conduct constitutes an offense or as to the existence, meaning or application of the law determining the elements of an offense is an element of such offense, unless the definition of the offense or the Code so provides.

(10) *Culpability as Determinant of Grade of Offense.* When the grade or degree of an offense depends on whether the offense is committed purposely, knowingly, recklessly or negligently, its grade or degree shall be the lowest for which the determinative kind of culpability is established with respect to any material element of the offense.

§ 2.03 Causal Relationship Between Conduct and Result; Divergence Between Result Designed or Contemplated and Actual Result or Between Probable and Actual Result.

(1) Conduct is the cause of a result when:
  (a) it is an antecedent but for which the result in question would not have occurred; and
  (b) the relationship between the conduct and result satisfies any additional causal requirements imposed by the Code or by the law defining the offense.

(2) When purposely or knowingly causing a particular result is an element of an offense, the element is not established if the actual result is not within the purpose or the contemplation of the actor unless:
  (a) the actual result differs from that designed or contemplated, as the case may be, only in the respect that a different person or different property is injured or affected or that the injury or harm designed or contemplated would have been more serious or more extensive than that caused; or
  (b) the actual result involves the same kind of injury or harm as that designed or contemplated and is not too remote or accidental in its occurrence to have a [just] bearing on the actor's liability or on the gravity of his offense.

(3) When recklessly or negligently causing a particular result is an element of an offense, the element is not established if the actual result is not within the risk of which the actor is aware or, in the case of negligence, of which he should be aware unless:
  (a) the actual result differs from the probable result only in the respect that a different person or different property is injured or affected or that the probable injury or harm would have been more serious or more extensive than that caused; or
  (b) the actual result involves the same kind of injury or harm as the probable result and is not too remote or accidental in its occurrence to have a [just] bearing on the actor's liability or on the gravity of his offense.

(4) When causing a particular result is a material element of an offense for which absolute liability is imposed by law, the element is not established unless the actual result is a probable consequence of the actor's conduct.

§ 2.04. Ignorance or Mistake.

(1) Ignorance or mistake as to a matter of fact or law is a defense if:
  (a) the ignorance or mistake negatives the purpose, knowledge, belief, recklessness or negligence required to establish a material element of the offense; or
  (b) the law provides that the state of mind established by such ignorance or mistake constitutes a defense.

(2) Although ignorance or mistake would otherwise afford a defense to the offense charged, the defense

is not available if the defendant would be guilty of another offense had the situation been as he supposed. In such case, however, the ignorance or mistake of the defendant shall reduce the grade and degree of the offense of which he may be convicted to those of the offense of which he would be guilty had the situation been as he supposed.

(3) A belief that conduct does not legally constitute an offense is a defense to a prosecution for that offense based upon such conduct when:

(a) the statute or other enactment defining the offense is not known to the actor and has not been published or otherwise reasonably made available prior to the conduct alleged; or

(b) he acts in reasonable reliance upon an official statement of the law, afterward determined to be invalid or erroneous, contained in (i) a statute or other enactment; (ii) a judicial decision, opinion or judgment; (iii) an administrative order or grant of permission; or (iv) an official interpretation of the public officer or body charged by law with responsibility for the interpretation, administration or enforcement of the law defining the offense.

(4) The defendant must prove a defense arising under Subsection (3) of this Section by a preponderance of evidence.

§ 2.05. When Culpability Requirements Are Inapplicable to Violations and to Offenses Defined by Other Statutes; Effect of Absolute Liability in Reducing Grade of Offense to Violation.

(1) The requirements of culpability prescribed by Sections 2.01 and 2.02 do not apply to:

(a) offenses which constitute violations, unless the requirement involved is included in the definition of the offense or the Court determines that its application is consistent with effective enforcement of the law defining the offense; or

(b) offenses defined by statutes other than the Code, insofar as a legislative purpose to impose absolute liability for such offenses or with respect to any material element thereof plainly appears.

(2) Notwithstanding any other provision of existing law and unless a subsequent statute otherwise provides:

(a) when absolute liability is imposed with respect to any material element of an offense defined by a statute other than the Code and a conviction is based upon such liability, the offense constitutes a violation; and

(b) although absolute liability is imposed by law with respect to one or more of the material elements of an offense defined by a statute other than the Code, the culpable commission of the offense may be charged and proved, in which event negligence with respect to such elements constitutes sufficient culpability and the classification of the offense and the sentence that may be imposed therefor upon conviction are determined by Section 1.04 and Article 6 of the Code.

§ 2.06. Liability for Conduct of Another; Complicity.

(1) A person is guilty of an offense if it is committed by his own conduct or by the conduct of another person for which he is legally accountable, or both.

(2) A person is legally accountable for the conduct of another person when:

(a) acting with the kind of culpability that is sufficient for the commission of the offense, he causes an innocent or irresponsible person to engage in such conduct; or

(b) he is made accountable for the conduct of such other person by the Code or by the law defining the offense; or

(c) he is an accomplice of such other person in the commission of the offense.

(3) A person is an accomplice of another person in the commission of an offense if:

(a) with the purpose of promoting or facilitating the commission of the offense, he

(i) solicits such other person to commit it; or

(ii) aids or agrees or attempts to aid such other person in planning or committing it; or

(iii) having a legal duty to prevent the commission of the offense, fails to make proper effect so to do; or

(b) his conduct is expressly declared by law to establish his complicity.

(4) When causing a particular result is an element of an offense, an accomplice in the conduct causing such result is an accomplice in the commission of that offense, if he acts with the kind of culpability, if any, with respect to that result that is sufficient for the commission of the offense.

(5) A person who is legally incapable of committing a particular offense himself may be guilty thereof, if

it is committed by the conduct of another person for which he is legally accountable, unless such liability is inconsistent with the purpose of the provision establishing his incapacity.

(6) Unless otherwise provided by the Code or by the law defining the offense, a person is not an accomplice in an offense committed by another person if:

(a) he is a victim of that offense; or

(b) the offense is so defined that his conduct is inevitably incident to its commission; or

(c) he terminates his complicity prior to the commission of the offense and

(i) wholly deprives it of effectiveness in the commission of the offense; or

(ii) gives timely warning to the law enforcement authorities or otherwise makes proper effort to prevent the commission of the offense.

(7) An accomplice may be convicted on proof of the commission of the offense and of his complicity therein, though the person claimed to have committed the offense has not been prosecuted or convicted or has been convicted of a different offense or degree of offense or has an immunity to prosecution or conviction or has been acquitted.

§ 2.07. Liability of Corporations, Unincorporated Associations and Persons Acting, or Under a Duty to Act, in Their Behalf.

(1) A corporation may be convicted of the commission of an offense if:

(a) the offense is a violation or the offense is defined by a statute other than the Code in which a legislative purpose to impose liability on corporations plainly appears and the conduct is performed by an agent of the corporation acting in behalf of the corporation within the scope of his office or employment, except that if the law defining the offense designates the agents for whose conduct the corporation is accountable or the circumstances under which it is accountable, such provisions shall apply; or

(b) the offense consists of an omission to discharge a specific duty of affirmative performance imposed on corporations by law; or

(c) the commission of the offense was authorized, requested, commanded, performed or recklessly tolerated by the board of directors or by a high managerial agent acting in behalf of the corporation within the scope of his office or employment.

(2) When absolute liability is imposed for the commission of an offense, a legislative purpose to impose liability on a corporation shall be assumed, unless the contrary plainly appears.

(3) An unincorporated association may be convicted of the commission of an offense if:

(a) the offense is defined by a statute other than the Code which expressly provides for the liability of such an association and the conduct is performed by an agent of the association acting in behalf of the association within the scope of his office or employment, except that if the law defining the offense designates the agents for whose conduct the association is accountable or the circumstances under which it is accountable, such provisions shall apply; or

(b) the offense consists of an omission to discharge a specific duty of affirmative performance imposed on associations by law.

(4) As used in this Section:

(a) "corporation" does not include an entity organized as or by a governmental agency for the execution of a governmental program;

(b) "agent" means any director, officer, servant, employee or other person authorized to act in behalf of the corporation or association and, in the case of an unincorporated association, a member of such association;

(c) "high managerial agent" means an officer of a corporation or an unincorporated association, or, in the case of a partnership, a partner, or any other agent of a corporation or association having duties of such responsibilities that his conduct may fairly be assumed to represent the policy of the corporation or association.

(5) In any prosecution of a corporation or an unincorporated association for the commission of an offense included within the terms of Subsection (1)(a) or Subsection (3)(a) of this Section, other than an offense for which absolute liability has been imposed, it shall be a defense if the defendant proves by a preponderance of evidence that the high managerial agent having supervisory responsibility over the subject matter of the offense employed due diligence to prevent its commission. This paragraph shall not apply if it is plainly inconsistent with the legislative purpose in defining the particular offense.

(6) (a) A person is legally accountable for any conduct he performs or causes to be performed in the name of the corporation or an unincorporated association or in its behalf to the same extent as if it were performed in his own name or behalf.

(b) Whenever a duty to act is imposed by law upon a corporation or an unincorporated association, any agent of the corporation or association having primary responsibility for the discharge of the duty is legally accountable for a reckless omission to perform the required act to the same extent as if the duty were imposed by law directly upon himself.

(c) When a person is convicted of an offense by reason of his legal accountability for the conduct of a corporation or an unincorporated association, he is subject to the sentence authorized by law when a natural person is convicted of an offense of the grade and the degree involved.

§ 2.08 Intoxication.

(1) Except as provided in Subsection (4) of this Section, intoxication of the actor is not a defense unless it negatives an element of the offense.

(2) When recklessness establishes an element of the offense, if the actor, due to self-induced intoxication, is unaware of a risk of which he would have been aware had he been sober, such unawareness is immaterial.

(3) Intoxication does not, in itself, constitute mental disease within the meaning of Section 4.01.

(4) Intoxication which (a) is not self-induced or (b) is pathological is an affirmative defense if by reason of such intoxication the actor at the time of his conduct lacks substantial capacity either to appreciate its criminality [wrongfulness] or to conform his conduct to the requirements of law.

(5) *Definitions.* In this Section unless a different meaning plainly is required:

(a) "intoxication" means a disturbance of mental or physical capacities resulting from the introduction of substances into the body;

(b) "self-induced intoxication" means intoxication caused by substances which the actor knowingly introduces into his body, the tendency of which to cause intoxication he knows or ought to know, unless he introduces them

pursuant to medical advice or under such circumstances as would afford a defense to a charge of crime;

(c) "pathological intoxication" means intoxication grossly excessive in degree, given the amount of the intoxicant, to which the actor does not know he is susceptible.

§ 2.09 Duress.

(1) It is an affirmative defense that the actor engaged in the conduct charged to constitute an offense because he was coerced to do so by the use of, or a threat to use, unlawful force against his person or the person of another, which a person of reasonable firmness in his situation would have been unable to resist.

(2) The defense provided by this Section is unavailable if the actor recklessly placed himself in a situation in which it was probable that he would be subjected to duress. The defense is also unavailable if he was negligent in placing himself in such a situation, whenever negligence suffices to establish culpability for the offense charged.

(3) It is not a defense that a woman acted on the command of her husband, unless she acted under such coercion as would establish a defense under this Section. [The presumption that a woman, acting in the presence of her husband, is coerced is abolished.]

(4) When the conduct of the actor would otherwise be justifiable under Section 3.02, this Section does not preclude such defense.

§ 2.10. Military Orders.

It is an affirmative defense that the actor, in engaging in the conduct charged to constitute an offense, does no more than execute an order of his superior in the armed services which he does not know to be unlawful.

§ 2.11. Consent.

(1) *In General.* The consent of the victim to conduct charged to constitute an offense or to the result thereof is a defense if such consent negatives an element of the offense or precludes the infliction of the harm or evil sought to be prevented by the law defining the offense.

(2) *Consent to Bodily Harm.* When conduct is charged to constitute an offense because it causes or threatens bodily harm, consent to such conduct or to the infliction of such harm is a defense if:

(a) the bodily harm consented to or threatened by the conduct consented to is not serious; or

(b) the conduct and the harm are reasonably foreseeable hazards of joint participation in a lawful athletic contest or competitive sport; or

(c) the consent establishes a justification for the conduct under Article 3 of the Code.

(3) *Ineffective Consent.* Unless otherwise provided by the Code or by the law defining the offense, assent does not constitute consent if:

(a) it is given by a person who is legally incompetent to authorize the conduct charged to constitute the offense; or

(b) it is given by a person who by reason of youth, mental disease or defect or intoxication is manifestly unable or known by the actor to be unable to make a reasonable judgment as to the nature or harmfulness of the conduct charged to constitute the offense; or

(c) it is given by a person whose improvident consent is sought to be prevented by the law defining the offense; or

(d) it is induced by force, duress or deception of a kind sought to be prevented by the law defining the offense.

§ 2.13. Entrapment.

(1) A public law enforcement official or a person acting in cooperation with such an official perpetrates an entrapment if for the purpose of obtaining evidence of the commission of an offense, he induces or encourages another person to engage in conduct constituting such offense by either:

(a) making knowingly false representations designed to induce the belief that such conduct is not prohibited; or

(b) employing methods of persuasion or inducement which create a substantial risk that such an offense will be committed by persons other than those who are ready to commit it.

(2) Except as provided in Subsection (3) of this Section, a person prosecuted for an offense shall be acquitted if he proves by a preponderance of evidence that his conduct occurred in response to an entrapment. The issue of entrapment shall be tried by the Court in the absence of the jury.

(3) The defense afforded by this Section is unavailable when causing or threatening bodily injury is an element of the offense charged and the prosecution is based on conduct causing or threatening such injury to a person other than the person perpetrating the entrapment.

ARTICLE 3. GENERAL PRINCIPLES OF JUSTIFICATION

§ 3.01. Justification an Affirmative Defense; Civil Remedies Unaffected.

(1) In any prosecution based on conduct which is justifiable under this Article, justification is an affirmative defense.

(2) The fact that conduct is justifiable under this Article does not abolish or impair any remedy for such conduct which is available in any civil action.

§ 3.02. Justification Generally: Choice of Evils.

(1) Conduct which the actor believes to be necessary to avoid harm or evil to himself or to another is justifiable, provided that:

(a) the harm or evil sought to be avoided by such conduct is greater than that sought to be prevented by the law defining the offense charged; and

(b) neither the Code nor other law defining the offense provides exceptions or defenses dealing with the specific situation involved; and

(c) a legislative purpose to exclude the justification claimed does not otherwise plainly appear.

(2) When the actor was reckless or negligent in bringing about the situation requiring a choice of harms or evils or in appraising the necessity for his conduct, the justification afforded by this Section is unavailable in a prosecution for any offense for which recklessness or negligence, as the case may be, suffices to establish culpability.

§ 3.03. Execution of Public Duty.

(1) Except as provided in Subsection (2) of this Section, conduct is justifiable when it is required or authorized by:

(a) the law defining the duties or functions of a public officer or the assistance to be rendered to such officer in the performance of his duties; or

(b) the law governing the execution of legal process; or

(c) the judgment or order of a competent court or tribunal; or

(d) the law governing the armed services or the lawful conduct of war; or

(e) any other provision of law imposing a public duty.

(2) The other sections of this Article apply to:

(a) the use of force upon or toward the person of another for any of the purposes dealt with in such sections; and

(b) the use of deadly force for any purpose, unless the use of such force is otherwise expressly authorized by law or occurs in the lawful conduct of war.

(3) The justification afforded by Subsection (1) of this Section applies:

(a) when the actor believes his conduct to be required or authorized by the judgment or direction of a competent court or tribunal or in the lawful execution of legal process, notwithstanding lack of jurisdiction of the court or defect in the legal process; and

(b) when the actor believes his conduct to be required or authorized to assist a public officer in the performance of his duties, notwithstanding that the officer exceeded his legal authority.

§ 3.04. Use of Force in Self-Protection.

(1) *Use of Force Justifiable for Protection of the Person.* Subject to the provisions of this Section and of Section 3.09, the use of force upon or toward another person is justifiable when the actor believes that such force is immediately necessary for the purpose of protecting himself against the use of unlawful force by such other person on the present occasion.

(2) *Limitations on Justifying Necessity for Use of Force.*

(a) The use of force is not justifiable under this Section:

(i) to resist arrest which the actor knows is being made by a peace officer, although the arrest is unlawful; or

(ii) to resist force used by the occupier or possessor of property or by another person on his behalf, where the actor knows that the person using the force is doing so under a claim of right to protect the property, except that this limitation shall not apply if:

(1) the actor is a public officer acting in the performance of his duties or a person lawfully assisting him therein or a person making or assisting in a lawful arrest; or

(2) the actor has been unlawfully dispossessed of the property and is making a re-entry or recaption justified by Section 3.06; or

(3) the actor believes that such force is necessary to protect himself against death or serious bodily harm.

(b) The use of deadly force is not justifiable under this Section unless the actor believes that such force is necessary to protect himself against death, serious bodily harm, kidnapping or sexual intercourse compelled by force or threat; nor is it justifiable if:

(i) the actor, with the purpose of causing death or serious bodily harm, provoked the use of force against himself in the same encounter; or

(ii) the actor knows that he can avoid the necessity of using such force with complete safety by retreating or by surrendering possession of a thing to a person asserting a claim of right thereto or by complying with a demand that he abstain from any action which he has no duty to take, except that:

(1) the actor is not obliged to retreat from his dwelling or place of work, unless he was the initial aggressor or is assailed in his place of work by another person whose place of work the actor knows it to be; and

(2) a public officer justified in using force in the performance of his duties or a person justified in using force in his assistance or a person justified in using force in making an arrest or preventing an escape is not obliged to desist from efforts to perform such duty, effect such arrest or prevent such escape because of resistance or threatened resistance by or on behalf of the person against whom such action is directed.

(c) Except as required by paragraphs (a) and (b) of this Subsection, a person employing protective force may estimate the necessity thereof under the circumstances as he believes them to be when the force is used, without retreating, surrendering possession, doing any other act which he has no legal duty to do or abstaining from any lawful action.

(3) *Use of Confinement as Protective Force.* The justification afforded by this Section extends to the use of confinement as protective force only if the actor takes all reasonable measures to terminate the confinement as soon as he knows that he safely can, unless the person confined has been arrested on a charge of crime.

§ 3.05. Use of Force for the Protection of Other Persons.

(1) Subject to the provisions of this Section and of Section 3.09, the use of force upon or toward the person of another is justifiable to protect a third person when:
  (a) the actor would be justified under Section 3.04 in using such force to protect himself against the injury he believes to be threatened to the person whom he seeks to protect; and
  (b) under the circumstances as the actor believes them to be, the person whom he seeks to protect would be justified in using such protective force; and
  (c) the actor believes that his intervention is necessary for the protection of such other person.
(2) Notwithstanding Subsection (1) of this Section:
  (a) when the actor would be obliged under Section 3.04 to retreat, to surrender the possession of a thing or to comply with a demand before using force in self-protection, he is not obliged to do so before using force for the protection of another person, unless he knows that he can thereby secure the complete safety of such other person; and
  (b) when the person whom the actor seeks to protect would be obliged under Section 3.04 to retreat, to surrender the possession of a thing or to comply with a demand if he knew that he could obtain complete safety by so doing, the actor is obliged to try to cause him to do so before using force in his protection if the actor knows that he can obtain complete safety in that way; and
  (c) neither the actor nor the person whom he seeks to protect is obliged to retreat when in the other's dwelling or place of work to any greater extent than in his own.

§ 3.06. Use of Force for the Protection of Property.

(1) *Use of Force Justifiable for Protection of Property.* Subject to the provisions of this Section and of Section 3.09, the use of force upon or toward the person of another is justifiable when the actor believes that such force is immediately necessary:
  (a) to prevent or terminate an unlawful entry or other trespass upon land or a trespass against or the unlawful carrying away of tangible, movable property, provided that such land or movable property is, or is believed by the actor to be, in his possession or in the possession of another person for whose protection he acts; or
  (b) to effect an entry or re-entry upon land or to retake tangible movable property, provided that the actor believes that he or the person by whose authority he acts or a person from whom he or such other person derives title was unlawfully dispossessed of such land or movable property and is entitled to possession, and provided, further, that:
    (i) the force is used immediately or on fresh pursuit after such dispossession; or
    (ii) the actor believes that the person against whom he uses force has no claim of right to the possession of the property and, in the case of land, the circumstances, as the actor believes them to be, are of such urgency that it would be an exceptional hardship to postpone the entry or re-entry until a court order is obtained.
(2) *Meaning of Possession.* For the purposes of Subsection (1) of this Section:
  (a) a person who has parted with the custody of property to another who refuses to restore it to him is no longer in possession, unless the property is movable and was and still is located on land in his possession;
  (b) a person who has been dispossessed of land does not regain possession thereof merely by setting foot thereon;
  (c) a person who has a license to use or occupy real property is deemed to be in possession thereof except against the licensor acting under claim of right.
(3) *Limitations on Justifiable Use of Force.*
  (a) *Request to Desist.* The use of force is justifiable under this Section only if the actor first requests the person against whom such force is used to desist from his interference with the property, unless the actor believes that:
    (i) such request would be useless; or

(ii) it would be dangerous to himself or another person to make the request; or

(iii) substantial harm will be done to the physical condition of the property which is sought to be protected before the request can effectively be made.

(b) *Exclusion of Trespasser.* The use of force to prevent or terminate a trespass is not justifiable under this Section if the actor knows that the exclusion of the trespasser will expose him to substantial danger of serious bodily harm.

(c) *Resistance of Lawful Re-entry or Recaption.* The use of force to prevent an entry or re-entry upon land or the recaption of movable property is not justifiable under this Section, although the actor believes that such re-entry or recaption is unlawful, if:

(i) the re-entry or recaption is made by or on behalf of a person who was actually dispossessed of the property; and

(ii) it is otherwise justifiable under paragraph (1)(b) of this Section.

(d) *Use of Deadly Force.* The use of deadly force is not justifiable under this Section unless the actor believes that:

(i) the person against whom the force is used is attempting to dispossess him of his dwelling otherwise than under a claim of right to its possession; or

(ii) the person against whom the force is used is attempting to commit or consummate arson, burglary, robbery or other felonious theft or property destruction and either:

(1) has employed or threatened deadly force against or in the presence of the actor; or

(2) the use of force other than deadly force to prevent the commission or the consummation of the crime would expose the actor or another in his presence to substantial danger of serious bodily harm.

(4) *Use of Confinement as Protective Force.* The justification afforded by this Section extends to the use of confinement as protective force only if the actor takes all reasonable measures to terminate the confinement as soon as he knows that he can do so with safety to the property, unless the person confined has been arrested on a charge of crime.

(5) *Use of Device to Protect Property.* The justification afforded by this Section extends to the use of a device for the purpose of protecting property only if:

(a) the device is not designed to cause or known to create a substantial risk of causing death or serious bodily harm; and

(b) the use of the particular device to protect the property from entry or trespass is reasonable under the circumstances, as the actor believes them to be; and

(c) the device is one customarily used for such a purpose or reasonable care is taken to make known to probable intruders the fact that it is used.

(6) *Use of Force to Pass Wrongful Obstructor.* The use of force to pass a person whom the actor believes to be purposely or knowingly and unjustifiably obstructing the actor from going to a place to which he may lawfully go is justifiable, provided that:

(a) the actor believes that the person against whom he uses force has no claim of right to obstruct the actor; and

(b) the actor is not being obstructed from entry or movement on land which he knows to be in the possession or custody of the person obstructing him, or in the possession or custody of another person by whose authority the obstructor acts, unless the circumstances, as the actor believes them to be, are of such urgency that it would not be reasonable to postpone the entry or movement on such land until a court order is obtained; and

(c) the force used is not greater than would be justifiable if the person obstructing the actor were using force against him to prevent his passage.

§ 3.07. Use of Force in Law Enforcement.

(1) *Use of Force Justifiable to Effect an Arrest.* Subject to the provisions of this Section and of Section 3.09, the use of force upon or toward the person of another is justifiable when the actor is making or assisting in making an arrest and the actor believes that such force is immediately necessary to effect a lawful arrest.

(2) *Limitations on the Use of Force.*

(a) The use of force is not justifiable under this Section unless:

(i) the actor makes known the purpose of the arrest or believes that it is otherwise known by or cannot reasonably be made known to the person to be arrested; and

(ii) when the arrest is made under a warrant, the warrant is valid or believed by the actor to be valid.

(b) The use of deadly force is not justifiable under this Section unless:

(i) the arrest is for a felony; and

(ii) the person effecting the arrest is authorized to act as a peace officer or is assisting a person whom he believes to be authorized to act as a peace officer; and

(iii) the actor believes that the force employed creates no substantial risk of injury to innocent persons; and

(iv) the actor believes that:

(1) the crime for which the arrest is made involved conduct including the use or threatened use of deadly force; or

(2) there is a substantial risk that the person to be arrested will cause death or serious bodily harm if his apprehension is delayed.

(3) *Use of Force to Prevent Escape from Custody.* The use of force to prevent the escape of an arrested person from custody is justifiable when the force could justifiably have been employed to effect the arrest under which the person is in custody, except that a guard or other person authorized to act as a peace officer is justified in using any force, including deadly force, which he believes to be immediately necessary to prevent the escape of a person from a jail, prison, or other institution for the detention of persons charged with or convicted of a crime.

(4) *Use of Force by Private Person Assisting an Unlawful Arrest.*

(a) A private person who is summoned by a peace officer to assist in effecting an unlawful arrest, is justified in using any force which he would be justified in using if the arrest were lawful, provided that he does not believe the arrest is unlawful.

(b) A private person who assists another private person in effecting an unlawful arrest, or who, not being summoned, assists a peace officer in effecting an unlawful arrest, is justified in using any force which he would be justified in using if the arrest were lawful, provided that (i) he

believes the arrest is lawful, and (ii) the arrest would be lawful if the facts were as he believes them to be.

(5) *Use of Force to Prevent Suicide or the Commission of a Crime.*

(a) The use of force upon or toward the person of another is justifiable when the actor believes that such force is immediately necessary to prevent such other person from committing suicide, inflicting serious bodily harm upon himself, committing or consummating the commission of a crime involving or threatening bodily harm, damage to or loss of property or a breach of the peace, except that:

(i) any limitations imposed by the other provisions of this Article on the justifiable use of force in self-protection, for the protection of others, the protection of property, the effectuation of an arrest or the prevention of an escape from custody shall apply notwithstanding the criminality of the conduct against which such force is used; and

(ii) the use of deadly force is not in any event justifiable under this Subsection unless:

(1) the actor believes that there is a substantial risk that the person whom he seeks to prevent from committing a crime will cause death or serious bodily harm to another unless the commission or the consummation of the crime is prevented and that the use of such force presents no substantial risk of injury to innocent persons; or

(2) the actor believes that the use of such force is necessary to suppress a riot or mutiny after the rioters or mutineers have been ordered to disperse and warned, in any particular manner that the law may require, that such force will be used if they do not obey.

(b) The justification afforded by this Subsection extends to the use of confinement as preventive force only if the actor takes all reasonable measures to terminate the confinement as soon as he knows that he safely can, unless the person confined has been arrested on a charge of crime.

ARTICLE 4. RESPONSIBILITY

§ 4.01. Mental Disease or Defect Excluding Responsibility.

(1) A person is not responsible for criminal conduct if at the time of such conduct as a result of mental disease or defect he lacks substantial capacity either to appreciate the criminality [wrongfulness] of his conduct or to conform his conduct to the requirements of law.

(2) As used in this Article, the terms "mental disease or defect" do not include an abnormality manifested only by repeated criminal or otherwise antisocial conduct.

§ 4.02. Evidence of Mental Disease or Defect Admissible When Relevant to Element of the Offense; [Mental Disease or Defect Impairing Capacity as Ground for Mitigation of Punishment in Capital Cases].

(1) Evidence that the defendant suffered from a mental disease or defect is admissible whenever it is relevant to prove that the defendant did or did not have a state of mind which is an element of the offense.

[(2) Whenever the jury or the Court is authorized to determine or to recommend whether or not the defendant shall be sentenced to death or imprisonment upon conviction, evidence that the capacity of the defendant to appreciate the criminality [wrongfulness] of his conduct or to conform his conduct to the requirements of law was impaired as a result of mental disease or defect is admissible in favor of sentence of imprisonment.]

§ 4.03. Mental Disease or Defect Excluding Responsibility Is Affirmative Defense; Requirement of Notice; Form of Verdict and Judgment When Finding of Irresponsibility Is Made.

(1) Mental disease or defect excluding responsibility is an affirmative defense.

(2) Evidence of mental disease or defect excluding responsibility is not admissible unless the defendant, at the time of entering his plea of not guilty or within ten days thereafter or at such later time as the Court may for good cause permit, files a written notice of his purpose to rely on such defense.

(3) When the defendant is acquitted on the ground of mental disease or defect excluding responsibility, the verdict and the judgment shall so state.

§ 4.04. Mental Disease or Defect Excluding Fitness to Proceed.

No person who as a result of mental disease or defect lacks capacity to understand the proceedings against him or to assist in his own defense shall be tried, convicted or sentenced for the commission of an offense so long as such incapacity endures.

§ 4.05. Psychiatric Examination of Defendant with Respect to Mental Disease or Defect.

(1) Whenever the defendant has filed a notice of intention to rely on the defense of mental disease or defect excluding responsibility, or there is reason to doubt his fitness to proceed, or reason to believe that mental disease or defect of the defendant will otherwise become an issue in the cause, the Court shall appoint at least one qualified psychiatrist or shall request the Superintendent of the _____ Hospital to designate at least one qualified psychiatrist, which designation may be or include himself, to examine and report upon the mental condition of the defendant. The Court may order the defendant to be committed to a hospital or other suitable facility for the purpose of the examination for a period of not exceeding sixty days or such longer period as the Court determines to be necessary for the purpose and may direct that a qualified psychiatrist retained by the defendant be permitted to witness and participate in the examination.

(2) In such examination any method may be employed which is accepted by the medical profession for the examination of those alleged to be suffering from mental disease or defect.

(3) The report of the examination shall include the following: (a) a description of the nature of the examination; (b) a diagnosis of the mental condition of the defendant; (c) if the defendant suffers from a mental disease or defect, an opinion as to his capacity to understand the proceedings against him and to assist in his own defense; (d) when a notice of intention to rely on the defense of irresponsibility has been filed, an opinion as to the extent, if any, to which the capacity of the defendant to appreciate the criminality [wrongfulness] of his conduct or to conform his conduct to the requirements of law was impaired at the time of the criminal conduct charged; and (e) when directed by the Court, an opinion as to the capacity of the defendant to have a particular state of mind which is an element of the offense charged.

If the examination can not be conducted by reason of the unwillingness of the defendant to participate therein, the report shall so state and shall include, if possible, an opinion as to whether such unwillingness of the defendant was the result of mental disease or defect.

The report of the examination shall be filed [in triplicate] with the clerk of the Court, who shall cause copies to be delivered to the district attorney and to counsel for the defendant.

§ 4.08. Legal Effect of Acquittal on the Ground of Mental Disease or Defect Excluding Responsibility; Commitment; Release or Discharge.

(1) When a defendant is acquitted on the ground of mental disease or defect excluding responsibility, the Court shall order him to be committed to the custody of the Commissioner of Mental Hygiene [Public Health] to be placed in an appropriate institution for custody, care and treatment.

(2) If the Commissioner of Mental Hygiene [Public Health] is of the view that a person committed to his custody, pursuant to paragraph (1) of this Section, may be discharged or released on condition without danger to himself or to others, he shall make application for the discharge or release of such person in a report to the Court by which such person was committed and shall transmit a copy of such application and report to the prosecuting attorney of the county [parish] from which the defendant was committed. The Court shall thereupon appoint at least two qualified psychiatrists to examine such person and to report within sixty days, or such longer period as the Court determines to be necessary for the purpose, their opinion as to his mental condition. To facilitate such examination and the proceedings thereon, the Court may cause such person to be confined in any institution located near the place where the Court sits, which may hereafter be designated by the Commissioner of Mental Hygiene [Public Health] as suitable for the temporary detention of irresponsible persons.

(3) If the Court is satisfied by the report filed pursuant to paragraph (2) of this Section and such testimony of the reporting psychiatrists as the Court deems necessary that the committed person may be discharged or released on condition without danger to himself or others, the Court shall order his discharge or his release on such conditions as the Court determines to be necessary. If the Court is not

so satisfied, it shall promptly order a hearing to determine whether such person may safely be discharged or released. Any such hearing shall be deemed a civil proceeding and the burden shall be upon the committed person to prove that he may safely be discharged or released. According to the determination of the Court upon the hearing, the committed person shall thereupon be discharged or released on such conditions as the Court determines to be necessary, or shall be recommitted to the custody of the Commissioner of Mental Hygiene [Public Health], subject to discharge or release only in accordance with the procedure prescribed above for a first hearing.

(4) If, within [five] years after the conditional release of a committed person, the Court shall determine, after hearing evidence, that the conditions of release have not been fulfilled and that for the safety of such person or for the safety of others his conditional release should be revoked, the Court shall forthwith order him to be recommitted to the Commissioner of Mental Hygiene [Public Health], subject to discharge or release only in accordance with the procedure prescribed above for a first hearing.

(5) A committed person may make application for his discharge or release to the Court by which he was committed, and the procedure to be followed upon such application shall be the same as that prescribed above in the case of an application by the Commissioner of Mental Hygiene [Public Health]. However, no such application by a committed person need be considered until he has been confined for a period of not less than [six months] from the date of the order of commitment, and if the determination of the Court be adverse to the application, such person shall not be permitted to file a further application until [one year] has elapsed from the date of any preceding hearing on an application for his release or discharge.

§ 4.09. Statements for Purposes of Examination or Treatment Inadmissible Except on Issue of Mental Condition.

A statement made by a person subjected to psychiatric examination or treatment pursuant to Sections 4.05, 4.06 or 4.08 for purposes of such examination or treatment shall not be admissible in evidence against him in any criminal proceeding on any issue other than that of his mental condition but it shall be admissible upon that issue, whether or not it would otherwise be deemed a privileged communication [,unless such statement constitutes an admission of guilt of the crime charged].

§ 4.10. Immaturity Excluding Criminal Conviction; Transfer of Proceedings to Juvenile Court.

(1) A person shall not be tried for or convicted of an offense if:

    (a) at the time of the conduct charged to constitute the offense he was less than sixteen years of age [, in which case the Juvenile Court shall have exclusive jurisdiction]; or

    (b) at the time of the conduct charged to constitute the offense he was sixteen or seventeen years of age, unless:

        (i) the Juvenile Court has no jurisdiction over him, or,

        (ii) the Juvenile Court has entered an order waiving jurisdiction and consenting to the institution of criminal proceedings against him.

(2) No court shall have jurisdiction to try or convict a person of an offense if criminal proceedings against him are barred by Subsection (1) of this Section. When it appears that a person charged with the commission of an offense may be of such an age that criminal proceedings may be barred under Subsection (1) of this Section, the Court shall hold a hearing thereon, and the burden shall be on the prosecution to establish to the satisfaction of the Court that the criminal proceeding is not barred upon such grounds. If the Court determines that the proceeding is barred, custody of the person charged shall be surrendered to the Juvenile Court, and the case, including all papers and processes relating thereto, shall be transferred.

ARTICLE 5. INCHOATE CRIMES

§ 5.01. Criminal Attempt.

(1) *Definition of Attempt.* A person is guilty of an attempt to commit a crime if, acting with the kind of culpability otherwise required for commission of the crime, he:

    (a) purposely engages in conduct which would constitute the crime if the attendant circumstances were as he believes them to be; or

    (b) when causing a particular result is an element of the crime, does or omits to do anything with the purpose of causing or with the belief that it will cause such result without further conduct on his part; or

    (c) purposely does or omits to do anything which, under the circumstances as he believes them to be, is an act or omission constituting a substantial step in a course of conduct planned to culminate in his commission of the crime.

(2) *Conduct Which May Be Held Substantial Step Under Subsection (1)(c).* Conduct shall not be held to constitute a substantial step under Subsection (1)(c) of this Section unless it is strongly corroborative of the actor's criminal purpose. Without negativing the sufficiency of other conduct, the following, if strongly corroborative of the actor's criminal purpose, shall not be held insufficient as a matter of law:

    (a) lying in wait, searching for or following the contemplated victim of the crime;

    (b) enticing or seeking to entice the contemplated victim of the crime to go to the place contemplated for its commission;

    (c) reconnoitering the place contemplated for the commission of the crime;

    (d) unlawful entry of a structure, vehicle or enclosure in which it is contemplated that the crime will be committed;

    (e) possession of materials to be employed in the commission of the crime, which are specially designed for such unlawful use or which can serve no lawful purpose of the actor under the circumstances;

    (f) possession, collection or fabrication of materials to be employed in the commission of the crime, at or near the place contemplated for its commission, where such possession, collection or fabrication serves no lawful purpose of the actor under the circumstances;

    (g) soliciting an innocent agent to engage in conduct constituting an element of the crime.

(3) *Conduct Designed to Aid Another in Commission of a Crime.* A person who engages in conduct designed to aid another to commit a crime which would establish his complicity under Section 2.06 if the crime were committed by such other person, is guilty of an attempt to commit the crime, although the crime is not committed or attempted by such other person.

(4) *Renunciation of Criminal Purpose.* When the actor's conduct would otherwise constitute an attempt under Subsection (1)(b) or (1)(c) of this Section, it is an affirmative defense that he abandoned his

effort to commit the crime or otherwise prevented its commission, under circumstances manifesting a complete and voluntary renunciation of his criminal purpose. The establishment of such defense does not, however, affect the liability of an accomplice who did not join in such abandonment or prevention.

Within the meaning of this Article, renunciation of criminal purpose is not voluntary if it is motivated, in whole or in part, by circumstances, not present or apparent at the inception of the actor's course of conduct, which increase the probability of detection or apprehension or which make more difficult the accomplishment of the criminal purpose. Renunciation is not complete if it is motivated by a decision to postpone the criminal conduct until a more advantageous time or to transfer the criminal effort to another but similar objective or victim.

§ 5.02. Criminal Solicitation.

(1) *Definition of Solicitation.* A person is guilty of solicitation to commit a crime if with the purpose of promoting or facilitating its commission he commands, encourages or requests another person to engage in specific conduct which would constitute such crime or an attempt to commit such crime or which would establish his complicity in its commission or attempted commission.

(2) *Uncommunicated Solicitation.* It is immaterial under Subsection (1) of this Section that the actor fails to communicate with the person he solicits to commit a crime if his conduct was designed to effect such communication.

(3) *Renunciation of Criminal Purpose.* It is an affirmative defense that the actor, after soliciting another person to commit a crime, persuaded him not to do so or otherwise prevented the commission of the crime, under circumstances manifesting a complete and voluntary renunciation of his criminal purpose.

§ 5.03. Criminal Conspiracy.

(1) *Definition of Conspiracy.* A person is guilty of conspiracy with another person or persons to commit a crime if with the purpose of promoting or facilitating its commission he:
  (a) agrees with such other person or persons that they or one or more of them will engage in conduct which constitutes such crime or an attempt or solicitation to commit such crime; or

  (b) agrees to aid such other person or persons in the planning or commission of such crime or of an attempt or solicitation to commit such crime.

(2) *Scope of Conspiratorial Relationship.* If a person guilty of conspiracy, as defined by Subsection (1) of this Section, knows that a person with whom he conspires to commit a crime has conspired with another person or persons to commit the same crime, he is guilty of conspiring with such other person or persons, whether or not he knows their identity, to commit such crime.

(3) *Conspiracy With Multiple Criminal Objectives.* If a person conspires to commit a number of crimes, he is guilty of only one conspiracy so long as such multiple crimes are the object of the same agreement or continuous conspiratorial relationship.

(4) *Joinder and Venue in Conspiracy Prosecutions.*
  (a) Subject to the provisions of paragraph (b) of this Subsection, two or more persons charged with criminal conspiracy may be prosecuted jointly if:
    (i) they are charged with conspiring with one another; or
    (ii) the conspiracies alleged, whether they have the same or different parties, are so related that they constitute different aspects of a scheme of organized criminal conduct.
  (b) In any joint prosecution under paragraph (a) of this Subsection:
    (i)   no defendant shall be charged with a conspiracy in any county [parish or district] other than one in which he entered into such conspiracy or in which an overt act pursuant to such conspiracy was done by him or by a person with whom he conspired; and
    (ii) neither the liability of any defendant nor the admissibility against him of evidence of acts or declarations of another shall be enlarged by such joinder; and
    (iii) the Court shall order a severance or take a special verdict as to any defendant who so requests, if it deems it necessary or appropriate to promote the fair determination of his guilt or innocence, and shall take any other proper measures to protect the fairness of the trial.

(5) *Overt Act.* No person may be convicted of conspiracy to commit a crime, other than a felony of the

first or second degree, unless an overt act in pursuance of such conspiracy is alleged and proved to have been done by him or by a person with whom he conspired.

(6) *Renunciation of Criminal Purpose.* It is an affirmative defense that the actor, after conspiring to commit a crime, thwarted the success of the conspiracy, under circumstances manifesting a complete and voluntary renunciation of his criminal purpose.

(7) *Duration of Conspiracy.* For purposes of Section 1.06(4):

(a) conspiracy is a continuing course of conduct which terminates when the crime or crimes which are its object are committed or the agreement that they be committed is abandoned by the defendant and by those with whom he conspired; and

(b) such abandonment is presumed if neither the defendant nor anyone with whom he conspired does any overt act in pursuance of the conspiracy during the applicable period of limitation; and

(c) if an individual abandons the agreement, the conspiracy is terminated as to him only if and when he advises those with whom he conspired of his abandonment or he informs the law enforcement authorities of the existence of the conspiracy and of his participation therein.

§ 5.04. Incapacity, Irresponsibility or Immunity of Party to Solicitation or Conspiracy.

(1) Except as provided in Subsection (2) of this Section, it is immaterial to the liability of a person who solicits or conspires with another to commit a crime that:

(a) he or the person whom he solicits or with whom he conspires does not occupy a particular position or have a particular characteristic which is an element of such crime, if he believes that one of them does; or

(b) the person whom he solicits or with whom he conspires is irresponsible or has an immunity to prosecution or conviction for the commission of the crime.

(2) It is a defense to a charge of solicitation or conspiracy to commit a crime that if the criminal object were achieved, the actor would not be guilty of a crime under the law defining the offense or as an accomplice under Section 2.06(5) or 2.06(6)(a) or (b).

§ 5.05. Grading of Criminal Attempt, Solicitation and Conspiracy; Mitigation in Cases of Lesser Danger; Multiple Convictions Barred.

(1) *Grading.* Except as otherwise provided in this Section, attempt, solicitation and conspiracy are crimes of the same grade and degree as the most serious offense which is attempted or solicited or is an object of the conspiracy. An attempt, solicitation or conspiracy to commit a [capital crime or a] felony of the first degree is a felony of the second degree.

(2) *Mitigation.* If the particular conduct charged to constitute a criminal attempt, solicitation or conspiracy is so inherently unlikely to result or culminate in the commission of a crime that neither such conduct nor the actor presents a public danger warranting the grading of such offense under this Section, the Court shall exercise its power under Section 6.12 to enter judgment and impose sentence for a crime of lower grade or degree or, in extreme cases, may dismiss the prosecution.

(3) *Multiple Convictions.* A person may not be convicted of more than one offense defined by this Article for conduct designed to commit or to culminate in the commission of the same crime.

§ 5.06. Possessing Instruments of Crime; Weapons.

(1) *Criminal Instruments Generally.* A person commits a misdemeanor if he possesses any instrument of crime with purpose to employ it criminally. "Instrument of crime" means:

(a) anything specially made or specially adapted [sic] for criminal use; or

(b) anything commonly used for criminal purposes and possessed by the actor under circumstances which do not negative unlawful purpose.

(2) *Presumption of Criminal Purpose from Possession of Weapon.* If a person possesses a firearm or other weapon on or about his person, in a vehicle occupied by him, or otherwise readily available for use, it shall be presumed that he had the purpose to employ it criminally, unless:

(a) the weapon is possessed in the actor's home or place of business;

(b) the actor is licensed or otherwise authorized by law to possess such weapon; or

(c) the weapon is of a type commonly used in lawful sport.

"Weapon" means anything readily capable of lethal use and possessed under circumstances not manifestly appropriate for lawful uses which it may have; the term includes a firearm which is not loaded or lacks a clip or other component to render it immediately operable, and components which can readily be assembled into a weapon.

(3) *Presumptions as to Possession of Criminal Instruments in Automobiles.* Where a weapon or other instrument of crime is found in an automobile, it is presumed to be in the possession of the occupant if there is but one. If there is more than one occupant, it shall be presumed to be in the possession of all, except under the following circumstances:

(a) where it is found upon the person of one of the occupants;

(b) where the automobile is not a stolen one and the weapon or instrument is found out of view in a glove compartment, car trunk, or other enclosed customary depository, in which case it shall be presumed to be in the possession of the occupant or occupants who own or have authority to operate the automobile;

(c) in the case of a taxicab, a weapon or instrument found in the passenger's portion of the vehicle shall be presumed to be in the possession of all the passengers, if there are any, and, if not, in the possession of the driver.

§ 5.07. Prohibited Offensive Weapons.

A person commits a misdemeanor if, except as authorized by law, he makes, repairs, sells, or otherwise deals in, uses or possesses any offensive weapon. "Offensive weapon" means any bomb, machine gun, sawed-off shotgun, firearm specially made or specially adapted for concealment or silent discharge, any blackjack, sandbag, metal knuckles, dagger, or other implement for the infliction of serious bodily injury which serves no common lawful purpose. It is a defense under this Section for the defendant to prove by a preponderance of evidence that he possessed or dealt with the weapon solely as a curio or in a dramatic performance, or that he possessed it briefly in consequence of having found it or taken it from an aggressor, or under circumstances similarly negativing any purpose or likelihood that the weapon would be used unlawfully. The presumptions provided in Section 5.06(3) are applicable to prosecutions under this Section.

PART II DEFINITION OF SPECIFIC CRIMES

Offenses Involving Danger to the Person

ARTICLE 210. CRIMINAL HOMICIDE

§ 210.0. Definitions.
In Articles 210–213, unless a different meaning plainly is required:

(1) "human being" means a person who has been born and is alive;

(2) "bodily injury" means physical pain, illness or any impairment of physical condition;

(3) "serious bodily injury" means bodily injury which creates a substantial risk of death or which causes serious, permanent disfigurement, or protracted loss or impairment of the function of any bodily member or organ;

(4) "deadly weapon" means any firearm, or other weapon, device, instrument, material or substance, whether animate or inanimate, which in the manner it is used or is intended to be used is known to be capable of producing death or serious bodily injury.

§ 210.1. Criminal Homicide.
(1) A person is guilty of criminal homicide if he purposely, knowingly, recklessly or negligently causes the death of another human being.

(2) Criminal homicide is murder, manslaughter or negligent homicide.

§ 210.2. Murder.
(1) Except as provided in Section 210.3(1)(b), criminal homicide constitutes murder when:

(a) it is committed purposely or knowingly; or

(b) it is committed recklessly under circumstances manifesting extreme indifference to the value of human life. Such recklessness and indifference are presumed if the actor is engaged or is an accomplice in the commission of, or an attempt to commit, or flight after committing or attempting to commit robbery, rape or deviate sexual intercourse by force or threat of force, arson, burglary, kidnapping or felonious escape.

(2) Murder is a felony of the first degree [but a person convicted of murder may be sentenced to death, as provided in Section 210.6].[1]

---

1. The brackets are meant to reflect the fact that the Institute took no position on the desirability of the death penalty. . . .

§ 210.3. Manslaughter.

(1) Criminal homicide constitutes manslaughter when:
    (a) it is committed recklessly; or
    (b) a homicide which would otherwise be murder is committed under the influence of extreme mental or emotional disturbance for which there is reasonable explanation or excuse. The reasonableness of such explanation or excuse shall be determined from the viewpoint of a person in the actor's situation under the circumstances as he believes them to be.

(2) Manslaughter is a felony of the second degree.

§ 210.4. Negligent Homicide.

(1) Criminal homicide constitutes negligent homicide when it is committed negligently.

(2) Negligent homicide is a felony of the third degree.

§ 210.5. Causing or Aiding Suicide.

(1) *Causing Suicide as Criminal Homicide.* A person may be convicted of criminal homicide for causing another to commit suicide only if he purposely causes such suicide by force, duress or deception.

(2) *Aiding or Soliciting Suicide as an Independent Offense.* A person who purposely aids or solicits another to commit suicide is guilty of a felony of the second degree if his conduct causes such suicide or an attempted suicide, and otherwise of a misdemeanor.

§ 210.6. Sentence of Death for Murder; Further Proceedings to Determine Sentence.

(1) *Death Sentence Excluded.* When a defendant is found guilty of murder, the Court shall impose sentence for a felony of the first degree if it is satisfied that:
    (a) none of the aggravating circumstances enumerated in Subsection (3) of this Section was established by the evidence at the trial or will be established if further proceedings are initiated under Subsection (2) of this Section; or
    (b) substantial mitigating circumstances, established by the evidence at the trial, call for leniency; or
    (c) the defendant, with the consent of the prosecuting attorney and the approval of the Court, pleaded guilty to murder as a felony of the first degree; or
    (d) the defendant was under 18 years of age at the time of the commission of the crime; or
    (e) the defendant's physical or mental condition calls for leniency; or

    (f) although the evidence suffices to sustain the verdict, it does not foreclose all doubt respecting the defendant's guilt.

(2) *Determination by Court or by Court and Jury.* Unless the Court imposes sentence under Subsection (1) of this Section, it shall conduct a separate proceeding to determine whether the defendant should be sentenced for a felony of the first degree or sentenced to death. The proceeding shall be conducted before the Court alone if the defendant was convicted by a Court sitting without a jury or upon his plea of guilty or if the prosecuting attorney and the defendant waive a jury with respect to sentence. In other cases it shall be conducted before the Court sitting with the jury which determined the defendant's guilt or, if the Court for good cause shown discharges that jury, with a new jury empaneled for the purpose.

In the proceeding, evidence may be presented as to any matter that the Court deems relevant to sentence, including but not limited to the nature and circumstances of the crime, the defendant's character, background, history, mental and physical condition and any of the aggravating or mitigating circumstances enumerated in Subsections (3) and (4) of this Section. Any such evidence not legally privileged, which the Court deems to have probative force, may be received, regardless of its admissibility under the exclusionary rules of evidence, provided that the defendant's counsel is accorded a fair opportunity to rebut any hearsay statements. The prosecuting attorney and the defendant or his counsel shall be permitted to present argument for or against sentence of death.

The determination whether sentence of death shall be imposed shall be in the discretion of the Court, except that when the proceeding is conducted before the Court sitting with a jury, the Court shall not impose sentence of death unless it submits to the jury the issue whether the defendant should be sentenced to death or to imprisonment and the jury returns a verdict that the sentence should be death. If the jury is unable to reach a unanimous verdict, the Court shall dismiss the jury and impose sentence for a felony of the first degree.

The Court, in exercising its discretion as to sentence, and the jury, in determining upon its verdict, shall take into account the aggravating and mitigating circumstances enumerated in Subsections (3) and (4) and any other facts that it deems relevant, but it shall not impose or recommend sentence of death unless it finds one of the aggravating circumstances enumerated in Subsection (3) and further finds that there are no mitigating circumstances sufficiently substantial to call for leniency. When the issue is submitted to the jury, the Court shall so instruct and also shall inform the jury of the nature of the sentence of imprisonment that may be imposed, including its implication with respect to possible release upon parole, if the jury verdict is against sentence of death.

Alternative formulation of Subsection (2):

(2) *Determination by Court.* Unless the Court imposes sentence under Subsection (1) of this Section, it shall conduct a separate proceeding to determine whether the defendant should be sentenced for a felony of the first degree or sentenced to death. In the proceeding, the Court, in accordance with Section 7.07, shall consider the report of the presentence investigation and, if a psychiatric examination has been ordered, the report of such examination. In addition, evidence may be presented as to any matter that the Court deems relevant to sentence, including but not limited to the nature and circumstances of the crime, the defendant's character, background, history, mental and physical condition and any of the aggravating or mitigating circumstances enumerated in Subsections (3) and (4) of this Section. Any such evidence not legally privileged, which the Court deems to have probative force, may be received, regardless of its admissibility under the exclusionary rules of evidence, provided that the defendant's counsel is accorded a fair opportunity to rebut any hearsay statements. The prosecuting attorney and the defendant or his counsel shall be permitted to present argument for or against sentence of death.

The determination whether sentence of death shall be imposed shall be in the discretion of the Court. In exercising such discretion, the Court shall take into account the aggravating and mitigating circumstances enumerated in Subsections (3) and (4) and any other facts that it deems relevant but shall not impose sentence of death unless it finds one of the aggravating circumstances enumerated in Subsection (3) and further finds that there are no mitigating circumstances sufficiently substantial to call for leniency.

(3) *Aggravating Circumstances.*

    (a) The murder was committed by a convict under sentence of imprisonment.

    (b) The defendant was previously convicted of another murder or of a felony involving the use or threat of violence to the person.

    (c) At the time the murder was committed the defendant also committed another murder.

    (d) The defendant knowingly created a great risk of death to many persons.

    (e) The murder was committed while the defendant was engaged or was an accomplice in the commission of, or an attempt to commit, or flight after committing or attempting to commit robbery, rape or deviate sexual intercourse by force or threat of force, arson, burglary or kidnapping.

    (f) The murder was committed for the purpose of avoiding or preventing a lawful arrest or effecting an escape from lawful custody.

    (g) The murder was committed for pecuniary gain.

    (h) The murder was especially heinous, atrocious or cruel, manifesting exceptional depravity.

(4) *Mitigating Circumstances.*

    (a) The defendant has no significant history of prior criminal activity.

    (b) The murder was committed while the defendant was under the influence of extreme mental or emotional disturbance.

    (c) The victim was a participant in the defendant's homicidal conduct or consented to the homicidal act.

    (d) The murder was committed under circumstances which the defendant believed to provide a moral justification or extenuation for his conduct.

    (e) The defendant was an accomplice in a murder committed by another person and his participation in the homicidal act was relatively minor.

    (f) The defendant acted under duress or under the domination of another person.

    (g) At the time of the murder, the capacity of the defendant to appreciate the criminality [wrongfulness] of his conduct or to conform his conduct to the requirements of law was impaired as a result of mental disease or defect or intoxication.

    (h) The youth of the defendant at the time of the crime.

ARTICLE 211. ASSAULT; RECKLESS ENDANGERING; THREATS

§ 211.0. Definitions.

In this Article, the definitions given in Section 210.0 apply unless a different meaning plainly is required.

§ 211.1. Assault.

(1) *Simple Assault.* A person is guilty of assault if he:

    (a) attempts to cause or purposely, knowingly or recklessly causes bodily injury to another; or

(b) negligently causes bodily injury to another with a deadly weapon; or

(c) attempts by physical menace to put another in fear of imminent serious bodily injury.

Simple assault is a misdemeanor unless committed in a fight or scuffle entered into by mutual consent, in which case it is a petty misdemeanor.

(2) *Aggravated Assault.* A person is guilty of aggravated assault if he:

(a) attempts to cause serious bodily injury to another, or causes such injury purposely, knowingly or recklessly under circumstances manifesting extreme indifference to the value of human life; or

(b) attempts to cause or purposely or knowingly causes bodily injury to another with a deadly weapon.

Aggravated assault under paragraph (a) is a felony of the second degree; aggravated assault under paragraph (b) is a felony of the third degree.

§ 211.2. Recklessly Endangering Another Person.

A person commits a misdemeanor if he recklessly engages in conduct which places or may place another person in danger of death or serious bodily injury. Recklessness and danger shall be presumed where a person knowingly points a firearm at or in the direction of another, whether or not the actor believed the firearm to be loaded.

§ 211.3. Terroristic Threats.

A person is guilty of a felony of the third degree if he threatens to commit any crime of violence with purpose to terrorize another or to cause evacuation of a building, place of assembly, or facility of public transportation, or otherwise to cause serious public inconvenience, or in reckless disregard of the risk of causing such terror or inconvenience.

ARTICLE 212. KIDNAPPING AND RELATED OFFENSES; COERCION

§ 212.0. Definitions.

In this Article, the definitions given in section 210.0 apply unless a different meaning plainly is required.

§ 212.1. Kidnapping.

A person is guilty of kidnapping if he unlawfully removes another from his place of residence or business, or a substantial distance from the vicinity where he is found, or if he unlawfully confines another for a substantial period in a place of isolation, with any of the following purposes:

(a) to hold for ransom or reward, or as a shield or hostage; or

(b) to facilitate commission of any felony or flight thereafter; or

(c) to inflict bodily injury on or to terrorize the victim or another; or

(d) to interfere with the performance of any governmental or political function.

Kidnapping is a felony of the first degree unless the actor voluntarily releases the victim alive and in a safe place prior to trial, in which case it is a felony of the second degree. A removal or confinement is unlawful within the meaning of this Section if it is accomplished by force, threat or deception, or, in the case of a person who is under the age of 14 or incompetent, if it is accomplished without the consent of a parent, guardian or other person responsible for general supervision of his welfare.

§ 212.2. Felonious Restraint.

A person commits a felony of the third degree if he knowingly:

(a) restrains another unlawfully in circumstances exposing him to risk of serious bodily injury; or

(b) holds another in a condition of involuntary servitude.

§ 212.3. False Imprisonment.

A person commits a misdemeanor if he knowingly restrains another unlawfully so as to interfere substantially with his liberty.

§ 212.4. Interference with Custody.

(1) *Custody of Children.* A person commits an offense if he knowingly or recklessly takes or entices any child under the age of 18 from the custody of its parent, guardian or other lawful custodian, when he has no privilege to do so. It is an affirmative defense that:

(a) the actor believed that his action was necessary to preserve the child from danger to its welfare; or

(b) the child, being at the time not less than 14 years old, was taken away at its own instigation without enticement and without purpose to commit a criminal offense with or against the child.

Proof that the child was below the critical age gives rise to a presumption that the actor knew the child's age or acted in reckless disregard thereof. The offense is a misdemeanor unless the actor, not being a parent or person in equivalent relation to the child, acted with knowledge that his conduct would cause serious alarm for the child's safety, or in reckless disregard of a likelihood of causing such alarm, in which case the offense is a felony of the third degree.

(2) *Custody of Committed Persons.* A person is guilty of a misdemeanor if he knowingly or recklessly takes or entices any committed person away from lawful custody when he is not privileged to do so. "Committed person" means, in addition to anyone committed under judicial warrant, any orphan, neglected or delinquent child, mentally defective or insane person, or other dependent or incompetent person entrusted to another's custody by or through a recognized social agency or otherwise by authority of law.

§ 212.5. Criminal Coercion.

(1) *Offense Defined.* A person is guilty of criminal coercion if, with purpose unlawfully to restrict another's freedom of action to his detriment, he threatens to:

(a) commit any criminal offense; or

(b) accuse anyone of a criminal offense; or

(c) expose any secret tending to subject any person to hatred, contempt or ridicule, or to impair his credit or business repute; or

(d) take or withhold action as an official, or cause an official to take or withhold action.

It is an affirmative defense to prosecution based on paragraphs (b), (c) or (d) that the actor believed the accusation or secret to be true or the proposed official action justified and that his purpose was limited to compelling the other to behave in a way reasonably related to the circumstances which were the subject of the accusation, exposure or proposed official action, as by desisting from further misbehavior, making good a wrong done, refraining from taking any action or responsibility for which the actor believes the other disqualified.

(2) *Grading.* Criminal coercion is a misdemeanor unless the threat is to commit a felony or the actor's purpose is felonious, in which cases the offense is a felony of the third degree.

ARTICLE 213. SEXUAL OFFENSES

§ 213.0. Definitions.

In this Article, unless a different meaning plainly is required:

(1) the definitions given in Section 210.0 apply;

(2) "sexual intercourse" includes intercourse per os or per anum, with some penetration however slight; emission is not required;

(3) "deviate sexual intercourse" means sexual intercourse per os or per anum between human beings who are not husband and wife, and any form of sexual intercourse with an animal.

§ 213.1. Rape and Related Offenses.

(1) *Rape.* A male who has sexual intercourse with a female not his wife is guilty of rape if:

(a) he compels her to submit by force or by threat of imminent death, serious bodily injury, extreme pain or kidnapping, to be inflicted on anyone; or

(b) he has substantially impaired her power to appraise or control her conduct by administering or employing without her knowledge drugs, intoxicants or other means for the purpose of preventing resistance; or

(c) the female is unconscious; or

(d) the female is less than 10 years old.

Rape is a felony of the second degree unless (i) in the course thereof the actor inflicts serious bodily injury upon anyone, or (ii) the victim was not a voluntary social companion of the actor upon the occasion of the crime and had not previously permitted him sexual liberties, in which cases the offense is a felony of the first degree.

(2) *Gross Sexual Imposition.* A male who has sexual intercourse with a female not his wife commits a felony of the third degree if:

(a) he compels her to submit by any threat that would prevent resistance by a woman of ordinary resolution; or

(b) he knows that she suffers from a mental disease or defect which renders her incapable of appraising the nature of her conduct; or

(c) he knows that she is unaware that a sexual act is being committed upon her or that she submits because she mistakenly supposes that he is her husband.

§ 213.2. Deviate Sexual Intercourse by Force or Imposition.

(1) *By Force or Its Equivalent.* A person who engages in deviate sexual intercourse with another person, or who causes another to engage in deviate sexual intercourse, commits a felony of the second degree if:

(a) he compels the other person to participate by force or by threat of imminent death, serious bodily injury, extreme pain or kidnapping, to be inflicted on anyone; or

(b) he has substantially impaired the other person's power to appraise or control his conduct, by administering or employing without the knowledge of the other person drugs, intoxicants or other means for the purpose of preventing resistance; or

(c) the other person is unconscious; or

(d) the other person is less than 10 years old.

(2) *By Other Imposition.* A person who engages in deviate sexual intercourse with another person, or who causes another to engage in deviate sexual intercourse, commits a felony of the third degree if:

(a) he compels the other person to participate by any threat that would prevent resistance by a person of ordinary resolution; or

(b) he knows that the other person suffers from a mental disease or defect which renders him incapable of appraising the nature of his conduct; or

(c) he knows that the other person submits because he is unaware that a sexual act is being committed upon him.

§ 213.3. Corruption of Minors and Seduction.

(1) *Offense Defined.* A male who has sexual intercourse with a female not his wife, or any person who engages in deviate sexual intercourse or causes another to engage in deviate sexual intercourse, is guilty of an offense if:

(a) the other person is less than [16] years old and the actor is at least [4] years older than the other person; or

(b) the other person is less than 21 years old and the actor is his guardian or otherwise responsible for general supervision of his welfare; or

(c) the other person is in custody of law or detained in a hospital or other institution and the actor has supervisory or disciplinary authority over him; or

(d) the other person is a female who is induced to participate by a promise of marriage which the actor does not mean to perform.

(2) *Grading.* An offense under paragraph (a) of Subsection (1) is a felony of the third degree. Otherwise an offense under this section is a misdemeanor.

§ 213.4. Sexual Assault.

A person who has sexual contact with another not his spouse, or causes such other to have sexual conduct with him, is guilty of sexual assault, a misdemeanor, if:

(1) he knows that the conduct is offensive to the other person; or

(2) he knows that the other person suffers from a mental disease or defect which renders him or her incapable of appraising the nature of his or her conduct; or

(3) he knows that the other person is unaware that a sexual act is being committed; or

(4) the other person is less than 10 years old; or

(5) he has substantially impaired the other person's power to appraise or control his or her conduct, by administering or employing without the other's knowledge drugs, intoxicants or other means for the purpose of preventing resistance; or

(6) the other person is less than [16] years old and the actor is at least [four] years older than the other person; or

(7) the other person is less than 21 years old and the actor is his guardian or otherwise responsible for general supervision of his welfare; or

(8) the other person is in custody of law or detained in a hospital or other institution and the actor has supervisory or disciplinary authority over him.

Sexual contact is any touching of the sexual or other intimate parts of the person for the purpose of arousing or gratifying sexual desire.

§ 213.5. Indecent Exposure.

A person commits a misdemeanor if, for the purpose of arousing or gratifying sexual desire of himself or of any person other than his spouse, he exposes his genitals under circumstances in which he knows his conduct is likely to cause affront or alarm.

§ 213.6. Provisions Generally Applicable to Article 213.

(1) *Mistake as to Age.* Whenever in this Article the criminality of conduct depends on a child's being below the age of 10, it is no defense that the actor did not know the child's age, or reasonably believed the child to be older than 10. When criminality depends on the child's being below a critical age other than 10, it is a defense for the actor to prove by a preponderance of the evidence that he reasonably believed the child to be above the critical age.

(2) *Spouse Relationships.* Whenever in this Article the definition of an offense excludes conduct with a spouse, the exclusion shall be deemed to extend to persons living as man and wife, regardless of the legal status of their relationship. The exclusion shall be inoperative as respects spouses living apart under a decree of judicial separation. Where the definition of an offense excludes conduct with a spouse or conduct by a woman, this shall not preclude conviction of a spouse or woman as accomplice in a sexual act which he or she causes another person, not within the exclusion, to perform.

(3) *Sexually Promiscuous Complainants.* It is a defense to prosecution under Section 213.3, and paragraphs (6), (7) and (8) of Section 213.4 for the actor to prove by a preponderance of the evidence that the alleged victim had, prior to the time of the offense charged, engaged promiscuously in sexual relations with others.

(4) *Prompt Complaint.* No prosecution may be instituted or maintained under this Article unless the alleged offense was brought to the notice of public authority within [3] months of its occurrence or, where the alleged victim was less than [16] years old or otherwise incompetent to make complaint, within [3] months after a parent, guardian or other competent person specially interested in the victim learns of the offense.

(5) *Testimony of Complainants.* No person shall be convicted of any felony under this Article upon the uncorroborated testimony of the alleged victim. Corroboration may be circumstantial. In any prosecution before a jury for an offense under this Article, the jury shall be instructed to evaluate the testimony of a victim or complaining witness with special care in view of the emotional involvement of the witness and the difficulty of determining the truth with respect to alleged sexual activities carried out in private.

Offenses Against Property

ARTICLE 220. ARSON, CRIMINAL MISCHIEF, AND OTHER PROPERTY DESTRUCTION

§ 220.1. Arson and Related Offenses.

(1) *Arson.* A person is guilty of arson, a felony of the second degree, if he starts a fire or causes an explosion with the purpose of:

(a) destroying a building or occupied structure of another; or

(b) destroying or damaging any property, whether his own or another's, to collect insurance for such loss. It shall be an affirmative defense to prosecution under this paragraph that the actor's conduct did not recklessly endanger any building or occupied structure of another or place any other person in danger of death or bodily injury.

(2) *Reckless Burning or Exploding.* A person commits a felony of the third degree if he purposely starts a fire or causes an explosion, whether on his own property or another's, and thereby recklessly:

(a) places another person in danger of death or bodily injury; or

(b) places a building or occupied structure of another in danger of damage or destruction.

(3) *Failure to Control or Report Dangerous Fire.* A person who knows that a fire is endangering life or a substantial amount of property of another and fails to take reasonable measures to put out or control the fire, when he can do so without substantial risk to himself, or to give a prompt fire alarm, commits a misdemeanor if:

(a) he knows that he is under an official, contractual, or other legal duty to prevent or combat the fire; or

(b) the fire was started, albeit lawfully, by him or with his assent, or on property in his custody or control.

(4) *Definitions.* "Occupied structure" means any structure, vehicle or place adapted for overnight accommodation of persons, or for carrying on business therein, whether or not a person is actually present. Property is that of another, for the purposes of this section, if anyone other than the actor has a possessory or proprietory interest therein. If a building or structure is divided into separately occupied units, any unit not occupied by the actor is an occupied structure of another.

§ 220.2. Causing or Risking Catastrophe.

(1) *Causing Catastrophe.* A person who causes a catastrophe by explosion, fire, flood, avalanche, collapse of building, release of poison gas, radioactive material or other harmful or destructive force or substance, or by any other means of causing potentially widespread injury or damage, commits a felony of the second degree if he does so purposely or knowingly, or a felony of the third degree if he does so recklessly.

(2) *Risking Catastrophe.* A person is guilty of a misdemeanor if he recklessly creates a risk of catastrophe in the employment of fire, explosives or other dangerous means listed in Subsection (1).

(3) *Failure to Prevent Catastrophe.* A person who knowingly or recklessly fails to take reasonable measures to prevent or mitigate a catastrophe commits a misdemeanor if:

    (a) he knows that he is under an official, contractual or other legal duty to take such measures; or

    (b) he did or assented to the act causing or threatening the catastrophe.

§ 220.3. Criminal Mischief.

(1) *Offense Defined.* A person is guilty of criminal mischief if he:

    (a) damages tangible property of another purposely, recklessly, or by negligence in the employment of fire, explosives, or other dangerous means listed in Section 220.2(1); or

    (b) purposely or recklessly tampers with tangible property of another so as to endanger person or property; or

    (c) purposely or recklessly causes another to suffer pecuniary loss by deception or threat.

(2) *Grading.* Criminal mischief is a felony of the third degree if the actor purposely causes pecuniary loss in excess of $5,000 or a substantial interruption or impairment of public communication, transportation, supply of water, gas or power, or other public service. It is a misdemeanor if the actor purposely causes pecuniary loss in excess of $100, or a petty misdemeanor if he purposely or recklessly causes pecuniary loss in excess of $25. Otherwise criminal mischief is a violation.

ARTICLE 221. BURGLARY AND OTHER CRIMINAL INTRUSION

§ 221.0. Definitions.

In this Article, unless a different meaning plainly is required:

(1) "occupied structure" means any structure, vehicle or place adapted for overnight accommodation of persons, or for carrying on business therein, whether or not a person is actually present.

(2) "night" means the period between thirty minutes past sunset and thirty minutes before sunrise.

§ 221.1. Burglary.

(1) *Burglary Defined.* A person is guilty of burglary if he enters a building or occupied structure, or separately secured or occupied portion thereof, with purpose to commit a crime therein, unless the premises are at the time open to the public or the actor is licensed or privileged to enter. It is an affirmative defense to prosecution for burglary that the building or structure was abandoned.

(2) *Grading.* Burglary is a felony of the second degree if it is perpetrated in the dwelling of another at night, or if, in the course of committing the offense, the actor:

    (a) purposely, knowingly or recklessly inflicts or attempts to inflict bodily injury on anyone; or

    (b) is armed with explosives or a deadly weapon.

Otherwise, burglary is a felony of the third degree. An act shall be deemed "in the course of committing" an offense if it occurs in an attempt to commit the offense or in flight after the attempt or commission.

(3) *Multiple Convictions.* A person may not be convicted both for burglary and for the offense which it was his purpose to commit after the burglarious entry or for an attempt to commit that offense, unless the additional offense constitutes a felony of the first or second degree.

§ 221.2. Criminal Trespass.

(1) *Buildings and Occupied Structures.* A person commits an offense if, knowing that he is not licensed or privileged to do so, he enters or surreptitiously remains in any building or occupied structure, or separately secured or occupied portion thereof. An offense under this Subsection is a misdemeanor if it is committed in a dwelling at night. Otherwise it is a petty misdemeanor.

(2) *Defiant Trespasser.* A person commits an offense if, knowing that he is not licensed or privileged to do so, he enters or remains in any place as to which notice against trespass is given by:

    (a) actual communication to the actor; or

    (b) posting in a manner prescribed by law or reasonably likely to come to the attention of intruders; or

    (c) fencing or other enclosure manifestly designed to exclude intruders.

An offense under this Subsection constitutes a petty misdemeanor if the offender defies an order to leave personally communicated to him by the owner of the premises or other authorized person. Otherwise it is a violation.

(3) *Defenses*. It is an affirmative defense to prosecution under this Section that:
  (a) a building or occupied structure involved in an offense under Subsection (1) was abandoned; ors
  (b) the premises were at the time open to members of the public and the actor complied with all lawful conditions imposed on access to or remaining in the premises; or
  (c) the actor reasonably believed that the owner of the premises, or other person empowered to license access thereto, would have licensed him to enter or remain.

ARTICLE 222. ROBBERY

§ 222.1 Robbery.

(1) *Robbery Defined*. A person is guilty of robbery if, in the course of committing a theft, he:
  (a) inflicts serious bodily injury upon another; or
  (b) threatens another with or purposely puts him in fear of immediate serious bodily injury; or
  (c) commits or threatens immediately to commit any felony of the first or second degree.

An act shall be deemed "in the course of committing a theft" if it occurs in an attempt to commit theft or in flight after the attempt or commission.

(2) *Grading*. Robbery is a felony of the second degree, except that it is a felony of the first degree if in the course of committing the theft the actor attempts to kill anyone, or purposely inflicts or attempts to inflict serious bodily injury.

ARTICLE 223. THEFT AND RELATED OFFENSES

§ 223.0. Definitions.

In this Article, unless a different meaning plainly is required:

(1) "deprive" means: (a) to withhold property of another permanently or for so extended a period as to appropriate a major portion of its economic value, or with intent to restore only upon payment of reward or other compensation; or (b) to dispose of the property so as to make it unlikely that the owner will recover it.

(2) "financial institution" means a bank, insurance company, credit union, building and loan association, investment trust or other organization held out to the public as a place of deposit of funds or medium of savings or collective investment.

(3) "government" means the United States, any State, county, municipality, or other political unit, or any department, agency or subdivision of any of the foregoing, or any corporation or other association carrying out the functions of government.

(4) "movable property" means property the location of which can be changed, including things growing on, affixed to, or found in land, and documents although the rights represented thereby have no physical location. "Immovable property" is all other property.

(5) "obtain" means: (a) in relation to property, to bring about a transfer or purported transfer of a legal interest in the property, whether to the obtainer or another; or (b) in relation to labor or service, to secure performance thereof.

(6) "property" means anything of value, including real estate, tangible and intangible personal property, contract rights, choses-in-action and other interests in or claims to wealth, admission or transportation tickets, captured or domestic animals, food and drink, electric or other power.

(7) "property of another" includes property in which any person other than the actor has an interest which the actor is not privileged to infringe, regardless of the fact that the actor also has an interest in the property and regardless of the fact that the other person might be precluded from civil recovery because the property was used in an unlawful transaction or was subject to forfeiture as contraband. Property in possession of the actor shall not be deemed property of another who has only a security interest therein, even if legal title is in the creditor pursuant to a conditional sales contract or other security agreement.

§ 223.1. Consolidation of Theft Offenses; Grading; Provisions Applicable to Theft Generally.

(1) *Consolidation of Theft Offenses*. Conduct denominated theft in this Article constitutes a single offense. An accusation of theft may be supported by evidence that it was committed in any manner that would be theft under this Article, notwithstanding the specification of a different manner in the indictment or information, subject only to the power of the Court to ensure fair trial by granting a continuance or other appropriate relief where the conduct of the defense would be prejudiced by lack of fair notice or by surprise.

(2) *Grading of Theft Offenses.*

    (a) Theft constitutes a felony of the third degree if the amount involved exceeds $500, or if the property stolen is a firearm, automobile, airplane, motorcycle, motorboat or other motor-propelled vehicle, or in the case of theft by receiving stolen property, if the receiver is in the business of buying or selling stolen property.

    (b) Theft not within the preceding paragraph constitutes a misdemeanor, except that if the property was not taken from the person or by threat, or in breach of a fiduciary obligation, and the actor proves by a preponderance of the evidence that the amount involved was less than $50, the offense constitutes a petty misdemeanor.

    (c) The amount involved in a theft shall be deemed to be the highest value, by any reasonable standard, of the property or services which the actor stole or attempted to steal. Amounts involved in thefts committed pursuant to one scheme or course of conduct, whether from the same person or several persons, may be aggregated in determining the grade or the offense.

(3) *Claim of Right.* It is an affirmative defense to prosecution for theft that the actor:

    (a) was unaware that the property or service was that of another; or

    (b) acted under an honest claim of right to the property or service involved or that he had a right to acquire or dispose of it as he did; or

    (c) took property exposed for sale, intending to purchase and pay for it promptly, or reasonably believing that the owner, if present, would have consented.

(4) *Theft from Spouse.* It is no defense that theft was from the actor's spouse, except that misappropriation of household and personal effects, or other property normally accessible to both spouses, is theft only if it occurs after the parties have ceased living together.

§ 223.3. Theft by Unlawful Taking or Disposition.

(1) *Movable Property.* A person is guilty of theft if he unlawfully takes, or exercises unlawful control over, movable property of another with purpose to deprive him thereof.

(2) *Immovable Property.* A person is guilty of theft if he unlawfully transfers immovable property of another or any interest therein with purpose to benefit himself or another not entitled thereto.

§ 223.3. Theft by Deception.

A person is guilty of theft if he purposely obtains property of another by deception. A person deceives if he purposely:

(1) creates or reinforces a false impression, including false impressions as to law, value, intention or other state of mind; but deception as to a person's intention to perform a promise shall not be inferred from the fact alone that he did not subsequently perform the promise; or

(2) prevents another from acquiring information which would affect his judgment of a transaction; or

(3) fails to correct a false impression which the deceiver previously created or reinforced, or which the deceiver knows to be influencing another to whom he stands in a fiduciary or confidential relationship; or

(4) fails to disclose a known lien, adverse claim or other legal impediment to the enjoyment of property which he transfers or encumbers in consideration for the property obtained, whether such impediment is or is not valid, or is or is not a matter of official record.

The term "deceive" does not, however, include falsity as to matters having no pecuniary significance, or puffing by statements unlikely to deceive ordinary persons in the group addressed.

§ 223.4. Theft by Extortion.

A person is guilty of theft if he obtains property of another by threatening to:

(1) inflict bodily injury on anyone or commit any other criminal offense; or

(2) accuse anyone of a criminal offense; or

(3) expose any secret tending to subject any person to hatred, contempt or ridicule, or to impair his credit or business repute; or

(4) take or withhold action as an official, or cause an official to take or withhold action; or

(5) bring about or continue a strike, boycott or other collective unofficial action, if the property is not demanded or received for the benefit of the group in whose interest the actor purports to act; or

(6) testify or provide information or withhold testimony or information with respect to another's legal claim or defense; or

(7) inflict any other harm which would not benefit the actor.

It is an affirmative defense to prosecution based on paragraphs (2), (3) or (4) that the property obtained by threat of accusation, exposure, lawsuit or other invocation of official action was honestly claimed as restitution or indemnification for harm done in the circumstances to which such accusation, exposure, lawsuit or other official action relates, or as compensation for property or lawful services.

§ 223.5. Theft of Property Lost, Mislaid, or Delivered by Mistake.

A person who comes into control of property of another that he knows to have been lost, mislaid, or delivered under a mistake as to the nature or amount of the property or the identity of the recipient is guilty of theft if, with purpose to deprive the owner thereof, he fails to take reasonable measures to restore the property to a person entitled to have it.

§ 223.6. Receiving Stolen Property.

(1) *Receiving*. A person is guilty of theft if he purposely receives, retains, or disposes of movable property of another knowing that it has been stolen, or believing that it has probably been stolen, unless the property is received, retained, or disposed with purpose to restore it to the owner. "Receiving" means acquiring possession, control or title, or lending on the security of the property.

(2) *Presumption of Knowledge*. The requisite knowledge or belief is presumed in the case of a dealer who:

(a) is found in possession or control of property stolen from two or more persons on separate occasions; or

(b) has received stolen property in another transaction within the year preceding the transaction charged; or

(c) being a dealer in property of the sort received, acquires it for a consideration which he knows is far below its reasonable value.

"Dealer" means a person in the business of buying or selling goods including a pawnbroker.

§ 223.7. Theft of Services.

(1) A person is guilty of theft if he purposely obtains services which he knows are available only for compensation, by deception or threat, or by false token or other means to avoid payment for the service. "Services" includes labor, professional service, transportation, telephone or other public service, accommodation in hotels, restaurants or elsewhere, admission to exhibitions, use of vehicles or other movable property. Where compensation for service is ordinarily paid immediately upon the rendering for such service, as is the case of hotels and restaurants, refusal to pay or absconding without payment or offer to pay gives rise to a presumption that the service was obtained by deception as to intention to pay.

(2) A person commits theft if, having control over the disposition of services of others, to which he is not entitled, he knowingly diverts such services to his own benefit or to the benefit of another not entitled thereto.

§ 223.8. Theft by Failure to Make Required Disposition of Funds Received.

A person who purposely obtains property upon agreement, or subject to a known legal obligation, to make specified payment or other disposition, whether from such property or its proceeds or from his own property to be reserved in equivalent amount, is guilty of theft if he deals with the property obtained as his own and fails to make the required payment or disposition. The foregoing applies notwithstanding that it may be impossible to identify particular property as belonging to the victim at the time of the actor's failure to make the required payment or disposition. An officer or employee of the government or of a financial institution is presumed: (i) to know any legal obligation relevant to his criminal liability under this Section, and (ii) to have dealt with the property as his own if he fails to pay or account upon lawful demand, or if an audit reveals a shortage or falsification of accounts.

ARTICLE 224. FORGERY AND FRAUDULENT PRACTICES

§ 224.0. Definitions.

In this Article, the definitions given in Section 223.0 apply unless a different meaning plainly is required.

§ 224.1. Forgery.

(1) *Definition*. A person is guilty of forgery if, with purpose to defraud or injure anyone, or with knowledge that he is facilitating a fraud or injury to be perpetrated by anyone, the actor:

(a) alters any writing of another without his authority; or

(b) makes, completes, executes, authenticates, issues or transfers any writing so that it purports to be the act of another who did not authorize that act, or to have been executed at a time or place or in a numbered sequence other than was in fact the case, or to be a copy of an original when no such original existed; or

(c) utters any writing which he knows to be forged in a manner specified in paragraphs (a) or (b).

"Writing" includes printing or any other method of recording information, money, coins, tokens, stamps, seals, credit cards, badges, trademarks, and other symbols of value, right, privilege, or identification.

(2) *Grading.* Forgery is a felony of the second degree if the writing is or purports to be part of an issue of money, securities, postage or revenue stamps, or other instruments issued by the government, or part of an issue of stock, bonds or other instruments representing interests in or claims against any property or enterprise. Forgery is a felony of the third degree if the writing is or purports to be a will, deed, contract, release, commercial instrument, or other document evidencing, creating, transferring, altering, terminating, or otherwise affecting legal relations. Otherwise forgery is a misdemeanor.

§ 224.5. Bad Checks.

A person who issues or passes a check or similar sight order for the payment of money, knowing that it will not be honored by the drawee, commits a misdemeanor. For the purposes of this Section as well as in any prosecution for theft committed by means of a bad check, an issuer is presumed to know that the check or order (other than a postdated check or order) would not be paid, if:

(1) the issuer had no account with the drawee at the time the check or order was issued; or

(2) payment was refused by the drawee for lack of funds, upon presentation within 30 days after issue, and the issuer failed to make good within 10 days after receiving notice of that refusal.

§ 224.8. Commercial Bribery and Breach of Duty to Act Disinterestedly.

(1) A person commits a misdemeanor if he solicits, accepts or agrees to accept any benefit as consideration for knowingly violating or agreeing to violate a duty of fidelity to which he is subject as:

(a) partner, agent or employee of another;

(b) trustee, guardian, or other fiduciary;

(c) lawyer, physician, accountant, appraiser, or other professional adviser or informant;

(d) officer, director, manager or other participant in the direction of the affairs of an incorporated or unincorporated association; or

(e) arbitrator or other purportedly disinterested adjudicator or referee.

(2) A person who holds himself out to the public as being engaged in the business of making disinterested selection, appraisal, or criticism of commodities or services commits a misdemeanor if he solicits, accepts or agrees to accept any benefit to influence his selection, appraisal or criticism.

(3) A person commits a misdemeanor if he confers, or offers or agrees to confer, any benefit the acceptance of which would be criminal under this Section.

Offenses Against the Family

ARTICLE 230. OFFENSES AGAINST THE FAMILY

§ 230.1. Bigamy and Polygamy.

(1) *Bigamy.* A married person is guilty of bigamy, a misdemeanor, if he contracts or purports to contract another marriage, unless at the time of the subsequent marriage:

(a) the actor believes that the prior spouse is dead; or

(b) the actor and the prior spouse have been living apart for five consecutive years throughout which the prior spouse was not known by the actor to be alive; or

(c) a Court has entered a judgment purporting to terminate or annul any prior disqualifying marriage, and the actor does not know that judgment to be invalid; or

(d) the actor reasonably believes that he is legally eligible to remarry.

(2) *Polygamy.* A person is guilty of polygamy, a felony of the third degree, if he marries or cohabits with more than one spouse at a time in purported exercise of the right of plural marriage. The offense is a continuing one until all cohabitation and claim of marriage with more than one spouse terminates. This section does not apply to parties to a polygamous marriage, lawful in the country of which they are residents or nationals, while they are in transit through or temporarily visiting this State.

(3) *Other Party to Bigamous or Polygamous Marriage.* A person is guilty of bigamy or polygamy, as the case

may be, if he contracts or purports to contract marriage with another knowing that the other is thereby committing bigamy or polygamy.

§ 230.2. Incest.

A person is guilty of incest, a felony of the third degree, if he knowingly marries or cohabits or has sexual intercourse with an ancestor or descendant, a brother or sister of the whole or half blood [or an uncle, aunt, nephew or niece of the whole blood]. "Cohabit" means to live together under the representation or appearance of being married. The relationships referred to herein include blood relationships without regard to legitimacy, and relationship of parent and child by adoption.

§ 230.4. Endangering Welfare of Children.

A parent, guardian, or other person supervising the welfare of a child under 18 commits a misdemeanor if he knowingly endangers the child's welfare by violating a duty of care, protection or support.

§ 230.5. Persistent Non-Support.

A person commits a misdemeanor if he persistently fails to provide support which he can provide and which he knows he is legally obliged to provide to a spouse, child or other dependent.

Offenses Against Public Administration

ARTICLE 240. BRIBERY AND CORRUPT INFLUENCE

§ 240.0. Definitions.

In Articles 240–243, unless a different meaning plainly is required:

(1) "benefit" means gain or advantage, or anything regarded by the beneficiary as gain or advantage, including benefit to any other person or entity in whose welfare he is interested, but not an advantage promised generally to a group or class of voters as a consequence of public measures which a candidate engages to support or oppose;

(2) "government" includes any branch, subdivision or agency of the government of the State or any locality within it;

(3) "harm" means loss, disadvantage or injury, or anything so regarded by the person affected, including loss, disadvantage or injury to any other person or entity in whose welfare he is interested;

(4) "official proceeding" means a proceeding heard or which may be heard before any legislative, judicial, administrative or other governmental agency or official authorized to take evidence under oath, including any referee, hearing examiner, commissioner, notary or other person taking testimony or deposition in connection with any such proceeding;

(5) "party official" means a person who holds an elective or appointive post in a political party in the United States by virtue of which he directs or conducts, or participates in directing or conducting party affairs at any level of responsibility;

(6) "pecuniary benefit" is benefit in the form of money, property, commercial interests or anything else the primary significance of which is economic gain;

(7) "public servant" means any officer or employee of government, including legislators and judges, and any person participating as juror, advisor, consultant or otherwise, in performing a governmental function; but the term does not include witnesses;

(8) "administrative proceeding" means any proceeding, other than a judicial proceeding, the outcome of which is required to be based on a record or documentation prescribed by law, or in which law or regulation is particularized in application to individuals.

§ 240.1. Bribery in Official and Political Matters.

A person is guilty of bribery, a felony of the third degree, if he offers, confers or agrees to confer upon another, or solicits, accepts or agrees to accept from another:

(1) any pecuniary benefit as consideration for the recipient's decision, opinion, recommendation, vote or other exercise of discretion as a public servant, party official or voter; or

(2) any benefit as consideration for the recipient's decision, vote, recommendation or other exercise of official discretion in a judicial or administrative proceeding; or

(3) any benefit as consideration for a violation of a known legal duty as public servant or party official.

It is no defense to prosecution under this section that a person whom the actor sought to influence was not qualified to act in the desired way whether because he had not yet assumed office, or lacked jurisdiction, or for any other reason.

§ 240.2. Threats and Other Improper Influence in Official and Political Matters.

(1) *Offenses Defined.* A person commits an offense if he:

    (a) threatens unlawful harm to any person with purpose to influence his decision, opinion, recommendation, vote or other exercise of discretion as a public servant, party official or voter; or

    (b) threatens harm to any public servant with purpose to influence his decision, opinion, recommendation, vote or pecuniary benefit as consideration for exerting special influence upon a public servant or procuring another to do so. "Special influence" means power to influence through kinship, friendship or other relationship, apart from the merits of the transaction.

(3) *Paying for Endorsement or Special Influence.* A person commits a misdemeanor if he offers, confers or agrees to confer any pecuniary benefit receipt of which is prohibited by this Section.

ARTICLE 241. PERJURY AND OTHER FALSIFICATION IN OFFICIAL MATTERS

§ 241.0. Definitions.

In this Article, unless a different meaning plainly is required:

(1) the definitions given in Section 240.0 apply; and

(2) "statement" means any representation, but includes a representation of opinion, belief or other state of mind only if the representation clearly relates to state of mind apart from or in addition to any facts which are the subject of the representation.

§ 241.1. Perjury.

(1) *Offense Defined.* A person is guilty of perjury, a felony of the third degree, if in any official proceeding he makes a false statement under oath or equivalent affirmation, or swears or affirms the truth of a statement previously made, when the statement is material and he does not believe it to be true.

(2) *Materiality.* Falsification is material, regardless of the admissibility of the statement under rules of evidence, if it could have affected the course or outcome of the proceeding. It is no defense that the declarant mistakenly believed the falsification to be immaterial. Whether a falsification is material in a given factual situation is a question of law.

(3) *Irregularities No Defense.* It is not a defense to prosecution under this Section that the oath or affirmation was administered or taken in an irregular

manner or that the declarant was not competent to make the statement. A document purporting to be made upon oath or affirmation at any time when the actor presents it as being so verified shall be deemed to have been duly sworn or affirmed.

(4) *Retraction.* No person shall be guilty of an offense under this Section if he retracted the falsification in the course of the proceeding in which it was made before it became manifest that the falsification was or would be exposed and before the falsification substantially affected the proceeding.

(5) *Inconsistent Statements.* Where the defendant made inconsistent statements under oath or equivalent affirmation, both having been made within the period of the statute of limitations, the prosecution may proceed by setting forth the inconsistent statements in a single count alleging in the alternative that one or the other was false and not believed by the defendant. In such case it shall not be necessary for the prosecution to prove which statement was false but only that one or the other was false and not believed by the defendant to be true.

(6) *Corroboration.* No person shall be convicted of an offense under this Section where proof of falsity rests solely upon contradiction by testimony of a single person other than the defendant.

§ 241.2. False Swearing.

(1) *False Swearing in Official Matters.* A person who makes a false statement under oath or equivalent affirmation, or swears or affirms the truth of such a statement previously made, when he does not believe the statement to be true, is guilty of a misdemeanor if:

    (a) the falsification occurs in an official proceeding; or

    (b) the falsification is intended to mislead a public servant in performing his official function.

Offenses Against Public Order and Decency

ARTICLE 250. RIOT, DISORDERLY CONDUCT, AND RELATED OFFENSES.

§ 250.1. Riot; Failure to Disperse.

(1) *Riot.* A person is guilty of riot, a felony of the third degree, if he participates with [two] or more others in a course of disorderly conduct:

    (a) with purpose to commit or facilitate the commission of a felony or misdemeanor;

(b) with purpose to prevent or coerce official action; or

(c) when the actor or any other participant to the knowledge of the actor uses or plans to use a firearm or other deadly weapon.

(2) *Failure of Disorderly Persons to Disperse Upon Official Order.* Where [three] or more persons are participating in a course of disorderly conduct likely to cause substantial harm or serious inconvenience, annoyance or alarm, a peace officer or other public servant engaged in executing or enforcing the law may order the participants and others in the immediate vicinity to disperse. A person who refuses or knowingly fails to obey such an order commits a misdemeanor.

§ 250.2. Disorderly Conduct.

(1) *Offense Defined.* A person is guilty of disorderly conduct if, with purpose to cause public inconvenience, annoyance or alarm, or recklessly creating a risk thereof, he:

(a) engages in fighting or threatening, or in violent or tumultuous behavior; or

(b) makes unreasonable noise or offensively coarse utterance, gesture or display, or addresses abusive language to any person present; or

(c) creates a hazardous or physically offensive condition by any act which serves no legitimate purpose of the actor.

"Public" means affecting or likely to affect persons in a place to which the public or a substantial group has access; among the places included are highways, transport facilities, schools, prisons, apartment houses, places of business or amusement, or any neighborhood.

(2) *Grading.* An offense under this section is a petty misdemeanor if the actor's purpose is to cause substantial harm or serious inconvenience, or if he persists in disorderly conduct after reasonable warning or request to desist. Otherwise disorderly conduct is a violation.

§ 250.4. Harassment.

A person commits a petty misdemeanor if, with purpose to harass another, he:

(1) makes a telephone call without purpose of legitimate communication; or

(2) insults, taunts or challenges another in a manner likely to provoke violent or disorderly response; or

(3) makes repeated communications anonymously or at extremely inconvenient hours, or in offensively coarse language; or

(4) subjects another to an offensive touching; or

(5) engages in any other course of alarming conduct serving no legitimate purpose of the actor.

§ 250.5. Public Drunkenness; Drug Incapacitation.

A person is guilty of an offense if he appears in any public place manifestly under the influence of alcohol, narcotics or other drugs, not therapeutically administered, to the degree that he may endanger himself or other persons or property, or annoy persons in his vicinity. An offense under this Section constitutes a petty misdemeanor if the actor has been convicted hereunder twice before within a period of one year. Otherwise the offense constitutes a violation.

§ 250.6. Loitering or Prowling.

A person commits a violation if he loiters or prowls in a place, at a time, or in a manner not usual for law-abiding individuals under circumstances that warrant alarm for the safety of persons or property in the vicinity. Among the circumstances which may be considered in determining whether such alarm is warranted is the fact that the actor takes flight upon appearance of a peace officer, refuses to identify himself, or manifestly endeavors to conceal himself or any object. Unless flight by the actor or other circumstances makes it impracticable, a peace officer shall prior to any arrest for an offense under this Section afford the actor an opportunity to dispel any alarm which would otherwise be warranted, by requesting him to identify himself and explain his presence and conduct. No person shall be convicted of an offense under this Section if the peace officer did not comply with the preceding sentence, or if it appears at trial that the explanation given by the actor was true and, if believed by the peace officer at the time, would have dispelled the alarm.

ARTICLE 251. PUBLIC INDECENCY

§ 251.1. Open Lewdness.

A person commits a petty misdemeanor if he does any lewd act which he knows is likely to be observed by others who would be affronted or alarmed.

(1) *Prostitution.* A person is guilty of prostitution, a petty misdemeanor, if he or she:

(a) is an inmate of a house of prostitution or otherwise engages in sexual activity as a business; or

(b) loiters in or within view of any public place for the purpose of being hired to engage in sexual activity.

"Sexual activity" includes homosexual and other deviate sexual relations. A "house of prostitution" is any place where prostitution or promotion of prostitution is regularly carried on by one person under the control, management or supervision of another. An "inmate" is a person who engages in prostitution in or through the agency of a house of prostitution. "Public place" means any place to which the public or any substantial group thereof has access.

(2) *Promoting Prostitution*. A person who knowingly promotes prostitution of another commits a misdemeanor or felony as provided in Subsection (3). The following acts shall, without limitation of the foregoing, constitute promoting prostitution:

(a) owning, controlling, managing, supervising or otherwise keeping, alone or in association with others, a house of prostitution or a prostitution business; or

(b) procuring an inmate for a house of prostitution or a place in a house of prostitution for one who would be an inmate; or

(c) encouraging, inducing, or otherwise purposely causing another to become or remain a prostitute; or

(d) soliciting a person to patronize a prostitute; or

(e) procuring a prostitute for a patron; or

(f) transporting a person into or within this state with purpose to promote that person's engaging in prostitution, or procuring or paying for transportation with that purpose; or

(g) leasing or otherwise permitting a place controlled by the actor, alone or in association with others, to be regularly used for prostitution or the promotion of prostitution, or failure to make reasonable effort to abate such use by ejecting the tenant, notifying law enforcement authorities, or other legally available means; or

(h) soliciting, receiving, or agreeing to receive any benefit for doing or agreeing to do anything forbidden by this Subsection.

(3) *Grading of Offenses Under Subsection (2)*. An offense under Subsection (2) constitutes a felony of the third degree if:

(a) the offense falls within paragraph (a), (b) or (c) of Subsection (2); or

(b) the actor compels another to engage in or promote prostitution; or

(c) the actor promotes prostitution of a child under 16, whether or not he is aware of the child's age; or

(d) the actor promotes prostitution of his wife, child, ward or any person for whose care, protection or support he is responsible.

Otherwise the offense is a misdemeanor.

(4) *Presumption from Living off Prostitutes*. A person, other than the prostitute or the prostitute's minor child or other legal dependent incapable of self-support, who is supported in whole or substantial part by the proceeds of prostitution is presumed to be knowingly promoting prostitution in violation of Subsection (2).

(5) *Patronizing Prostitutes*. A person commits a violation if he hires a prostitute to engage in sexual activity with him, or if he enters or remains in a house of prostitution for the purpose of engaging in sexual activity.

(6) *Evidence*. On the issue whether a place is a house of prostitution the following shall be admissible evidence; its general repute; the repute of the persons who reside in or frequent the place; the frequency, timing and duration of visits by non-residents. Testimony of a person against his spouse shall be admissible to prove offenses under this Section.

§ 251.3. Loitering to Solicit Deviate Sexual Relations.

A person is guilty of a petty misdemeanor if he loiters in or near any public place for the purpose of soliciting or being solicited to engage in deviate sexual relations.

§ 251.4. Obscenity.

(1) *Obscene Defined*. Material is obscene if, considered as a whole, its predominant appeal is to prurient interest, that is, a shameful or morbid interest, in nudity, sex or excretion, and if in addition it goes substantially beyond customary limits of candor in describing or representing such matters. Predominant appeal shall be judged with reference to ordinary adults unless it appears from the character of the material or the circumstances of its dissemination to be designed for children or other specially susceptible audience. Undeveloped photographs, molds, printing plates, and the like, shall be deemed obscene notwithstanding that processing or other acts may be required to make the obscenity patent or to disseminate it.

(2) *Offenses*. Subject to the affirmative defense provided in Subsection (3), a person commits a misdemeanor if he knowingly or recklessly:

(a) sells, delivers or provides, or offers or agrees to sell, deliver or provide, any obscene writing, picture, record or other representation or embodiment of the obscene; or

(b) presents or directs an obscene play, dance or performance, or participates in that portion thereof which makes it obscene; or

(c) publishes, exhibits or otherwise makes available any obscene material; or

(d) possesses any obscene material for purposes of sale or other commercial dissemination; or

(e) sells, advertises or otherwise commercially disseminates material, whether or not obscene, by representing or suggesting that it is obscene.

A person who disseminates or possesses obscene material in the course of his business is presumed to do so knowingly or recklessly.

(3) *Justifiable and Non-Commercial Private Dissemination.* It is an affirmative defense to prosecution under this Section that dissemination was restricted to:

(a) institutions or persons having scientific, educational, governmental or other similar justification for possessing obscene material; or

(b) non-commercial dissemination to personal associates of the actor.

(4) *Evidence; Adjudication of Obscenity.* In any prosecution under this Section, evidence shall be admissible to show:

(a) the character of the audience for which the material was designed or to which it was directed;

(b) what the predominant appeal of the material would be for ordinary adults or any special audience to which it was directed, and what effect, if any, it would probably have on conduct of such people;

(c) artistic, literary, scientific, educational or other merits of the material;

(d) the degree of public acceptance of the material in the United States;

(e) appeal to prurient interest, or absence thereof, in advertising or other promotion of the material; and

(f) the good repute of the author, creator, publisher or other person from whom the material originated.

Expert testimony and testimony of the author, creator, publisher or other person from whom the material originated, relating to factors entering into the determination of the issue of obscenity, shall be admissible. The Court shall dismiss a prosecution for obscenity if it is satisfied that the material is not obscene.

Glossary

accessory　A person who helps commit a crime without being present. An *accessory before the fact* is a person who, without being present, encourages, orders, or helps another to commit a crime. An *accessory after the fact* is a person who finds out that a crime has been committed and helps to conceal the crime or the criminal.

actus reus　(Latin) An act. For example, an *"actus reus"* is a "wrongful deed" (such as killing a person) which, if done with mens rea, a "guilty mind" (such as *"malice aforethought"*), is a crime (such as *first degree* murder).

admission　An *"admission"* is a voluntary statement that a fact or a state of events is true.

adversary system　The system of law in the U.S. The judge acts as the decision maker between opposite sides (between two individuals, between the state and an individual, etc.) rather than acting as the person who also makes the state's case or independently seeks out evidence.

affirmative defense　A defense that is more than a simple denial of the charges. It raises a new matter that may result in an acquittal or reduction of liability. It is a defense that must be affirmatively raised, often prior to trial or it is lost.

aggravating circumstances　Actions or occurrences that increase the seriousness of a crime, but are not part of the legal definition of that crime.

alibi　(Latin) "Elsewhere"; the claim that at the time a crime was committed a person was somewhere else. [pronounce: al-eh-bi]

appellate court　A higher court that can hear appeals from a lower court.

arraignment　The hearing at which a defendant is brought before a judge to hear the charges and to enter a plea (guilty, not guilty, etc.)

arrest　The official taking of a person to answer criminal charges. This involves at least temporarily depriving the person of liberty and may involve the use of force. An arrest is usually made by a police officer with a warrant or for a crime committed in the officer's presence.

arson　The malicious and unlawful burning of a building.

assault　An intentional threat, show of force, or movement that could reasonably make a person feel in danger of physical attack or harmful physical contact. It can be a crime or tort.

attempt　An effort to commit a crime that goes beyond preparation and that proceeds far enough to make the person who did it guilty of an *"attempt crime."* For example, if a person fires a shot at another in a failed effort at murder, the person is guilty of *attempted murder*.

bail　The money or property given as security for a defendant's appearance in court. The money, often in the form of a bail bond, may be lost if the defendant released does not appear in court.

battered woman syndrome　Continuing abuse of a woman by a spouse or lover, and the resulting physical or psychological harm.

battery　An intentional, unconsented to, physical contact by one person (or an object controlled by that person) with another person. It can be a crime or a tort.

beyond a reasonable doubt　The level of proof required to convict a person of a crime. For a jury to be convinced *"beyond a reasonable doubt,"* it must be fully satisfied that the person is guilty. This is the highest level of proof required in any type of trial.

bill of attainder　A legislative act pronouncing a person guilty (usually of treason) without a trial and sentencing the person to death and attainder. This is now prohibited by the U.S. Constitution.

bill of particulars   A detailed, formal, written statement of charges or claims by a plaintiff or the prosecutor (given upon the defendant's formal request to the court for more detailed information).

Bill of Rights   The first ten amendments (changes or additions) to the U.S. Constitution.

breach of the peace   A vague term for any illegal public disturbance; sometimes refers to the offense known as "disorderly conduct." It is defined and treated differently in different states.

bribery   The offering, giving, receiving, or soliciting of anything of value in order to influence the actions of a public official.

burden of going forward (production)   The requirement that one side in a lawsuit produce evidence on a particular issue or risk losing on that issue.

burden of persuasion   The requirement that to win a point or have an issue decided in your favor in a lawsuit you must show that the weight of evidence is on your side, rather than "in the balance" on that question.

burden of proof   The requirement that to win a point or have an issue decided in your favor in a lawsuit you must show that the weight of evidence is on your side, rather than "in the balance" on that question.

burglary   Unlawfully entering the house of another person at night with the intention of committing a felony (usually theft).

certiorari   (Latin) "To make sure." A request for *certiorari* (or "cert." for short) is like an appeal, but one which the higher court is not required to take for decision. It is literally a writ from the higher court asking the lower court for the record of the case.

chain of custody   The chronological list of those in continuous possession of a specific physical object. A person who presents physical evidence (such as a gun used in a crime) at a trial must account for its possession from time of receipt to time of trial in order for the evidence to be "admitted" by the judge. It must thus be shown that the *chain of custody* was unbroken.

challenge for cause   A formal objection to the qualifications of a prospective juror or jurors.

civil liberties   Political liberties guaranteed by the Constitution and, in particular, by the Bill of Rights, especially the First Amendment.

clear and present danger   A test of whether or not speech may be restricted or punished. It may be if it will probably lead to violence soon or if it threatens a serious, immediate weakening of national safety and security.

co-conspirator's rule   The principle that statements by a member of a proven conspiracy may be used as evidence against any of the members of the conspiracy.

common law   The legal system that originated in England and is composed of caselaw and statutes that grow and change, influenced by ever-changing custom and tradition.

commutation of sentence   Changing a criminal punishment to one less severe.

compensatory damages   Damages awarded for the actual loss suffered by a plaintiff.

complaint   A *criminal complaint* is a formal document that charges a person with a crime.

concert of action rule   The rule that, unless a statute specifies otherwise, it is not a conspiracy for two persons to agree to commit a crime if the definition of the crime itself requires the participation of two or more persons. Also called *Wharton Rule* and *concerted action rule*.

concurrent jurisdiction   Two or more courts having the power to adjudicate the same class of cases or the same matter.

concurrent sentences   Prison terms that run at the same time.

confession   A voluntary statement by a person that he or she is guilty of a crime.

consecutive sentences   An additional prison term given to a person who is already convicted of a crime; the additional term is to be served after the previous one is finished.

consent   Voluntary and active agreement.

conspiracy   A crime that may be committed when two or more persons agree to do something unlawful (or to do something lawful by unlawful means). The agreement can be inferred from the persons' actions.

constructive   Inferred, implied, or presumed from the circumstances.

contempt   A willful disobeying of a judge's command or official court order. Contempt can be *direct* (within the judge's notice) or *indirect* (outside the court and punishable only after proved to the judge). It can also be *civil contempt* (disobeying a court order in favor of an opponent) or *criminal contempt*.

contract   An agreement that affects or creates legal relationships between two or more persons. To be a *contract*, an agreement must involve at least one promise, consideration, persons legally capable of making binding agreements, and a reasonable certainty about the meaning of the terms.

conversion   Any act that deprives an owner of property without that owner's permission and without just cause.

corporate liability   The liability of a corporation for the acts of its directors, officers, shareholders, agents, and employees.

corpus delicti   (Latin) "The body of the crime." The material substance upon which a crime has been committed; for example, a dead body (in the crime of murder) or a house burned down (in the crime of arson).

court of general jurisdiction   Another term for trial court; that is, a court having jurisdiction to try all classes of civil and criminal cases except those that can be heard only by a court of limited jurisdiction.

court of limited jurisdiction   A court whose jurisdiction is limited to civil cases of a certain type, or which involve a limited amount of money, or whose jurisdiction in criminal cases is confined to petty offenses and preliminary hearings.

court of record   Generally, another term for trial court.

criminal law   Branch of the law that specifies what conduct constitutes crime and establishes appropriate punishments for such conduct.

criminal procedure   The rules of procedure by which criminal prosecutions are governed.

culpable   Blamable; at fault. A person who has done a wrongful act (whether criminal or civil) is described as "culpable."

damages   Money that a court orders paid to a person who has suffered damage (a loss or harm) by the person who caused the injury (the violation of the person's rights).

deadly weapon   Any instrument likely to cause serious bodily harm under the circumstances of its actual use. Such things as a fan belt used to choke a man and a fire used to burn an occupied house have been called *deadly weapons* by courts.

deposition   The process of taking a witness's sworn out-of-court testimony. The questioning is usually done by a lawyer, with the lawyer from the other side given a chance to attend and participate.

detainer   A warrant or court order to keep a person in custody when that person might otherwise be released. This is often used to make sure a person will serve a sentence or attend a trial in one state at the end of a prison term in another state or in a federal prison.

deter   To discourage; to prevent from acting.

determinate sentence   An exact penalty set by law.

diminished capacity   The principle that having a certain recognized form of *diminished mental capacity* while committing a crime should lead to the imposition of a lesser punishment or to lower the degree of the crime.

discovery   The formal and informal exchange of information between the prosecution and the defense.

discretion   The power to act within general guidelines, rules, or laws, but without either specific rules to follow or the need to completely explain or justify each decision or action.

DNA printing   Comparing body tissue samples (such as blood, skin, hair, or semen) to see if the genetic materials match. It is used to identify criminals by comparing their DNA with that found at a crime scene and used to identify a child's parent. Most states allow its use as evidence.

double jeopardy   A second prosecution by the same government against the same person for the same crime (or for a lesser included offense) once the first prosecution is totally finished and decided. This is prohibited by the U.S. Constitution.

Due Process Clause   The *due process clauses* of the Fifth and Fourteenth Amendments to the U.S. Constitution require that no person be deprived of life, liberty, or property without having notice and a real chance to present his or her side in a legal dispute.

duress   Unlawful pressure on a person to do what he or she would not otherwise have done. It includes force, threats of violence, physical restraint, etc.

Durham rule   The principle, used in *Durham v. U.S.* (214 F.2d. 862 (1954)), that a defendant is not guilty of a crime because of insanity if he or she was "suffering from a disease or defective mental condition at the time of the act and there was a causal connection between the condition and the act."

element   A basic part. For example, some of the *elements* of a cause of action for battery are an intentional, unwanted physical contact. Each of these things ("intentional," "unwanted," etc.) is one *"element."*

embezzlement   The fraudulent and secret taking of money or property by a person who has been trusted with it. This usually applies to an employee's taking money and covering it up by faking business records or account books.

entrapment   The act of government officials (usually police) or agents of inducing a person to commit a crime that the person would not have committed without the inducement.

ex post facto law   (Latin) After the fact. An *ex post facto law* is one that retroactively attempts to make an action a crime that was not a crime at the time it was done, or a law that attempts to reduce a person's rights based on a past act that was not subject to the law when it was done.

exclusionary rule   *"The exclusionary rule"* often means the rule that illegally gathered evidence may not be used in a criminal trial. The rule has several exceptions, such as when the evidence is used to impeach a defendant's testimony and when the evidence was gathered in a good faith belief that the process was legal.

exhaustion of remedies   A person must usually take all reasonable steps to get satisfaction from a state government before going into federal court. This is called *exhaustion of state remedies*.

extortion   To compel, force, or coerce; for example, to get a confession by depriving a person of food and water. To get something by illegal threats of harm to person, property, or reputation. The process is called *extortion*.

extradition   One country (or state) giving up a person to a second country (or state) when the second requests the person for a trial on a criminal charge or for punishment after a trial.

false imprisonment   The unlawful restraint by one person of the physical liberty of another.

false pretenses   A lie told to cheat another person out of his or her money or property. It is a crime in most states, though the precise definition varies.

federalism   A system of political organization with several different levels of government (for example, city, state, and national) co-existing in the same area with the lower levels having some independent powers.

felony-murder rule   The principle that if a person (even accidentally) kills another while committing a felony, then the killing is murder.

fighting words   Speech that is not protected by the First Amendment to the U.S. Constitution because it is likely to cause violence by the person to whom the words are spoken.

final judgment (order)   The last action of a court; the one upon which an appeal can be based.

first-degree murder   The most serious form of a particular crime that has more than one type. For example, *first degree* murder includes premeditation or extreme atrocity or cruelty, or is done in the commission of a major felony.

foreseeable   The degree to which the consequences of an action *should* have been anticipated, recognized, and considered beforehand. *Not* hindsight.

forfeiture   A deprivation of money, property, or rights, without compensation, as a consequence of a default or the commission of a crime.

forgery   Making a fake document (or altering a real one) with intent to commit a fraud.

fruit of the poisonous tree doctrine   The rule that evidence gathered as a *result* of evidence gained in an illegal search or questioning cannot be used against the person searched or questioned even if the later evidence was gathered lawfully.

grand jury   Persons who receive complaints and accusations of crime, hear preliminary evidence on the complaining side, and make formal accusations or indictments.

habitual offender statutes   Laws that may apply to a person who has been convicted of as few as two prior crimes (often violent or drug-related crimes) and that greatly increase the penalties for each succeeding crime.

halfway house   A facility in which persons recently discharged from a rehabilitation center or prison live for a time and are given support and assistance in readjusting to society at large.

harmless error   A trivial mistake made by a judge in the procedures used at trial, or in making legal rulings during the trial.

hearsay   A statement about what someone else said (or wrote or otherwise communicated). *Hearsay evidence* is evidence, concerning what someone said outside of a court proceeding, that is offered in the proceeding to prove the truth of what was said. The *hearsay rule* bars the admission of hearsay as evidence *to prove the hearsay's truth* unless allowed by a hearsay exception.

hung jury   A jury that cannot reach a verdict (decision) because of disagreement among jurors.

in limine   (Latin) "At the beginning"; preliminary. A motion *in limine* is a (usually pretrial) request that prejudicial information be excluded as trial evidence.

independent source   The general rule that if new evidence can be traced to a source completely apart from the illegally gathered evidence that first led to the new evidence, it may be used by the government in a criminal trial.

indeterminate sentence   A sentence having a minimum and maximum, with the decision of how long the criminal will serve depending on the criminal's behavior in prison and other things.

indictment   A sworn written accusation of a crime, made against a person by a prosecutor to a *grand* jury.

inevitable discovery rule   The principle that even if criminal evidence is gathered by unconstitutional methods, the evidence may be admissible if it definitely would have come to light anyway.

inference   A fact (or proposition) that is *probably* true because a true fact (or proposition) leads you to believe that the *inferred* fact (or proposition) is also true.

inferior court   A court with special, limited responsibilities, such as a probate court.

information   A formal accusation of a crime made by a proper public official such as a prosecuting attorney.

injunction   A judge's order to a person to do or to refrain from doing a particular thing.

intentional   Determination to do a certain thing.

interlocutory appeal   The *Interlocutory Appeals Act* (28 U.S.C. 1292 (1948)) is a federal law that provides for an appeal while a trial is going on if the trial judge states in writing: 1) A legal question has come up that directly affects the trial. 2) There are major questions as to how that point of law should be resolved. 3) The case would proceed better if the appeals court answers the question.

interpret   Studying a document *and* surrounding circumstances to decide the document's meaning.

interrogation   Questioning by police, especially of a person suspected or accused of a crime. A *custodial interrogation*

involves a restraint of freedom, so it requires a Miranda warning. A routine *investigatory interrogation* involves no restraint and no accusation of a crime.

intervening cause   A cause of an accident or other injury that will remove the blame from the wrongdoer who originally set events in motion.

irresistible impulse   The loss of control due to insanity that is so great that a person cannot stop from committing a crime.

judicial review   A higher court's examination of a lower court's decision.

jurisdiction   The geographical area within which a court (or a public official) has the right and power to operate. Or, the persons about whom and the subject matters about which a court has the right and power to make decisions that are legally binding.

kidnapping   Taking away and holding a person illegally, usually against the person's will or by force.

knowingly   With full knowledge and intentionally; willfully.

larceny   Stealing of any kind. Some types of larceny are specific crimes, such as *larceny by trick* or grand larceny.

legal cause   The proximate cause of an injury; probable cause; cause that the law deems sufficient.

legal impossibility   A person who is unable to commit a crime because of legal impossibility cannot be convicted of a crime he or she intends or attempts.

legislative history   The background documents and records of hearings related to the enactment of a bill.

lineup   A group of persons, placed side-by-side in a line, shown to a witness of a crime to see if the witness will identify the person suspected of committing the crime. A *lineup* should not be staged so that it is suggestive of one person.

M'Naghten rule   A test employed in a number of jurisdictions for determining whether a criminal defendant had the capacity to form criminal intent at the time he or she committed the crime of which he or she is accused. The M'Naghten rule is also referred to as the right-wrong test.

malicious (criminal) mischief   The criminal offense of intentionally destroying another person's property.

manslaughter   A crime, less severe than murder, involving the wrongful but non-malicious killing of another person.

mayhem   The crime of violently, maliciously, and intentionally giving someone a serious permanent wound. In some states, a type of aggravated assault. Once, the crime of permanently wounding another (as by dismemberment) to deprive the person of fighting ability.

mens rea   (Latin) A state of mind that produces a crime.

merger of offenses   When a person is charged with two crimes (based on the exact same acts), one of which is a lesser included offense of the other. The lesser crime *merges* because, under the prohibition against double jeopardy, the person may be tried for only one of them.

mitigating circumstances   Facts that provide no justification or excuse for an action, but that can lower the amount of moral blame, and thus lower the criminal penalty or civil damages for the action.

Model Penal Code   A proposed criminal code prepared jointly by the Commission on Uniform State Laws and the American Law Institute.

motion   A request that a judge make a ruling or take some other action.

motive   The reason why a person does something.

National Crime Information Center   Computerized records of criminals, warrants, stolen vehicles, etc.

necessity   *Necessity* often refers to a situation that requires an action that would otherwise be illegal or expose a person to tort liability.

negligence   The failure to exercise a reasonable amount of care in a situation that causes harm to someone or something.

nolle prosequi   (Latin) The ending of a criminal case because the prosecutor decides or agrees to stop prosecuting. When this happens, the case is *"nolled," "nollied,"* or *"nol. prossed."*

objection   A claim that an action by your adversary in a lawsuit (such as the use of a particular piece of evidence) is improper, unfair, or illegal, and asking the judge for a ruling on the point.

omission   Failing to do something that should be done.

ordinances   A local or city law, rule, or regulation.

overbreadth doctrine   A law will be declared void for *overbreadth* if it attempts to punish speech or conduct that is protected by the Constitution and if it is impossible to elim-

inate the unconstitutional part of the law without invalidating the whole law.

pardon   A president's or governor's release of a person from punishment for a crime.

parole   Early release from prison or jail. Parole is usually granted with conditions such as requiring the parolee to refrain from communicating with the victim of the crime that led to the confinement and remaining free of criminality while on parole. If the conditions of parole are violated, parole may be revoked and the parolee may be returned to confinement to complete the original sentence.

peremptory challenge   The automatic elimination of a potential juror by one side before trial without needing to state the reason for the elimination.

perjury   Lying while under oath, especially in a court proceeding. It is a crime.

plain view doctrine   The rule that if police officers see or come across something while acting lawfully, that item may be used as evidence in a criminal trial even if the police did not have a search warrant.

plea   The defendant's formal answer to a criminal charge. The defendant says "guilty," "not guilty" or "nolo contendere" (no contest).

plea bargain (plea agreement)   Negotiations between a prosecutor and a criminal defendant's lawyer, attempting to resolve a criminal case without trial.

police power   The government's right and power to set up and enforce laws to provide for the safety, health, and general welfare of the people.

polling the jury   Individually asking each member of a jury what his or her decision is. This is done by the judge, at the defendant's request, immediately after the verdict.

precedent   Prior decisions of the same court, or a higher court, which a judge must follow in deciding a subsequent case presenting similar facts and the same legal problem, even though different parties are involved and many years have elapsed.

preliminary hearing   The first court proceeding on a criminal charge, in federal courts and many state courts, by a magistrate or a judge to decide whether there is enough evidence for the government to continue with the case and to require the defendant to post bail or be held for trial.

presumption   A *presumption of law* is an automatic assumption required by law that whenever a certain set of facts shows up, a court must automatically draw certain legal conclusions.

principal   A person directly involved with committing a crime, as opposed to an accessory.

principle of legality   The procedural side of due process which requires that criminal laws (and punishments) be written and enacted before an act may be punished.

probable cause   The U.S. constitutional requirement that law enforcement officers present sufficient facts to convince a judge to issue a search warrant or an arrest *warrant*, and the requirement that no warrant should be issued unless it is more likely than not that the objects sought will be found in the place to be searched or that a crime has been committed by the person to be arrested.

prostitution   A person offering her (in most states, his or her) body for sexual purposes in exchange for money. A crime in most states.

provocation   An act by one person that triggers a reaction of rage in a second person. *Provocation* may reduce the severity of a crime.

proximate cause   The "legal cause" of an accident or other injury (which may have several actual causes). The *proximate cause* of an injury is not necessarily the closest thing in time or space to the injury and not necessarily the event that set things in motion because "proximate cause" is a legal, not a physical concept.

punitive damages   Damages that are awarded over and above compensatory damages or actual damages because of the wanton, reckless, or malicious nature of the wrong done by the plaintiff.

purposely   Intentionally; knowingly.

quash   Overthrow; annul; completely do away with. *Quash* usually refers to a court stopping a subpoena, an order, or an indictment.

Racketeer Influenced and Corrupt Organizations Act   (19 U.S.C. 1961). A broadly applied 1970 federal law that creates certain "racketeering offenses," which include participation in various criminal schemes and conspiracies, and that allows government seizure of property acquired in violation of the act.

rape   The crime of a man imposing sexual intercourse by force or otherwise without legally valid consent.

receiving stolen property   The criminal offense of getting or concealing property known to be stolen by another.

recklessness   Indifference to consequences; indifference to the safety and rights of others. Recklessness implies conduct amounting to more than ordinary negligence.

record on appeal   A formal, written account of a case, containing the complete formal history of all actions taken, papers filed, rulings made, opinions written, etc.

regulation   A rule that is put out by a local government or an administrative agency to regulate conduct.

reprieve   Holding off on enforcing a criminal sentence for a period of time after the sentence has been handed down.

retreat to the wall   The doctrine that before a person is entitled to use deadly force in self defense, he or she must attempt to withdraw from the encounter by giving as much ground as possible.

revocation hearing   The due process hearing required before the government can revoke a privilege it has previously granted.

robbery   The illegal taking of property from the person of another by using force or threat of force.

rules of court   Rules promulgated by the court, governing procedure or practice before it.

scienter   (Latin) Knowingly; with guilty knowledge. [pronounce: si-*en*-ter]

second-degree murder   Murder without premeditation.

self-defense   Physical force used against a person who is threatening the use of physical force or using physical force.

separation of powers   The division of the federal government (and state governments) into legislative (law making), judicial (law interpreting), and executive (law carrying-out) branches.

shield laws   A state law that prohibits use of most evidence of a rape (or other sexual crime) victim's past sexual conduct, or that protects the victim's identity.

showup   A pretrial identification procedure in which only one suspect and a witness are brought together.

sidebar   An in-court discussion among lawyers and the judge that is out of the hearing of witnesses and the jury. Sidebar conferences are usually *on the* record.

sodomy   A general word for an "unnatural" sex act or the crime committed by such act. While the definition varies, *sodomy* can include oral sex, anal sex, homosexual sex, or sex with animals.

solicitation   Asking for; enticing; strongly requesting. This may be a crime if the thing being urged is a crime.

sovereign immunity   The government's freedom from being sued. In many cases, the U.S. government has waived immunity by a statute such as the Federal Tort Claims Act.

specific intent   An intent to commit the exact crime charged, not merely a general intent to commit some crime or merely a generally guilty mind.

stalking   The crime of repeatedly following, threatening, or harassing another person in ways that lead to a legitimate fear of physical harm. Some states define *stalking* more broadly as any conduct with no legitimate purpose that seriously upsets a targeted person, especially conduct in violation of a protective order.

standing   A person's right to bring (start) or join a lawsuit because he or she is directly affected by the issues raised. This is called "standing to sue."

stare decisis   (Latin) The doctrine that judicial decisions stand as precedents for cases arising in the future.

statute   A law passed by a legislature.

statute of limitation   Federal and state statutes prescribing the maximum period of time during which various types of civil actions and criminal prosecutions can be brought after the occurrence of the injury or the offense.

statutory construction   Determining the meaning of a statute.

statutory rape   The crime of a man having sexual intercourse with a girl under a certain state-set age (whether or not the girl consents.)

strict liability   Guilt of a criminal offense even if you had no criminal intention (mens rea).

strict liability   The legal responsibility for damage or injury, even if you are not at fault or negligent.

strict liability crimes   Crimes or offenses in which mens rea or criminal intent is not an element. Such offenses include regulatory crimes, petty offenses, and infractions.

subornation of perjury   The crime of asking or forcing another person to lie under oath.

suspended sentence   A sentence (usually "jail time") that the judge allows the convicted person to avoid serving (usually if the person continues on good behavior, completes community service, etc.).

tax evasion   The deliberate nonpayment or underpayment of taxes that are legally due. Criminal tax evasion has higher fines than civil fraud and the possibility of a prison sentence upon the showing of "willfulness."

tax fraud   The deliberate nonpayment or underpayment of taxes that are legally due.

tort   A civil (as opposed to a criminal) wrong, other than a breach of contract.

transactional immunity   Freedom from prosecution for all crimes related to the compelled testimony, so long as the witness tells the truth.

transferred intent   The principle that if an unintended illegal act results from the intent to commit a crime, that act is also a crime.

trial court   A court that hears and determines a case initially, as opposed to an appellate court; a court of general jurisdiction.

use immunity   Freedom from prosecution based on the compelled testimony and on anything the government learns from following up on the testimony.

vagueness doctrine   The *vagueness doctrine* is the rule that a criminal law may be unconstitutional if it does not clearly say what is required or prohibited, what punishment may be imposed, or what persons may be affected. A law that violates due process of law in this way is *void for vagueness*.

vicarious liability   Legal responsibility for the acts of another person because of some relationship with that person.

victim impact statement   At the time of sentencing, a statement made to the court concerning the effect the crime has had on the victim or on the victim's family.

voir dire examination   (French) "To see, to say"; "to state the truth." The preliminary in-court questioning of a prospective witness (or juror) to determine competency to testify (or suitability to decide a case). [pronounce: vwahr deer]

Index

Abortion, 102
  privacy and, 267
Absolute immunity, 294
Accessory to a crime, 210
  defined, 210
Accomplices, 210
  Model Penal Code and, 210
Accusatorial system, 276, 277
Acquired immunodeficiency syndrome. *See* AIDS.
Acquittal, judgment of, 452
Acquitted crimes, punishing, 460
Acts,
  omissions as, 70–72
  personal status as, 68–69
  possession as, 69
  thoughts and statements as, 66, 68
Actual possession, 69
Actus reus, 66–79
  defined, 66
Administrative law, 38–39, 40
Admission, 380
  at common law, 380
  defined, 380
Adultery, 99
Adversarial hearing, 413, 459
Adversary hearing, 412
Adversary system, 276–277
  defined, 276
Advocacy of unlawful conduct, 168, 170
Aerial surveillance, 348–349
Affirm court decision, 10
Affirmative defense, 222
  defined, 222
Affray, 168

Aggravated assault and battery, 106–107
Aggravating circumstances, 473
  defined, 473
Aguilar v. Texas, 323, 329
  two prongs of, 323–324
AIDS (acquired immunodeficiency syndrome),
  and murder, 96–97
  as deadly weapon, 97
  intentional passing on of, 96
  transmission of, 96
Air pollution, 200
Al Qaeda, 192
Alabama v. Shelton, 446–447
Alcohol-related crimes, 175–177
  driving while under the influence, 176
  minimum drinking age, 176
Alcohol treatment, 488
Alibi, 241
  defined, 241
Alien and Seditions Acts, 191
Allen charge, 453
Allen v. United States, 453
American Bar Association's Model Rules of
  Professional Conduct, 291
American government, basic structure of, 4–7
American Library Association v. Pataki, 166
Anarchy, 25
Andersen, Arthur, 61–62
Antagonistic defense, 428
Antiterrorism and Effective Death Penalty Act of
  1996, 191
Appeal, 490–492
  defense, 491–492
  filing, 491–492

Appeal *continued*
 prosecution, 491–492
 right to counsel on, 492
 scope of review for, 491
Appellate courts, 10, 12
 defined, 10
 levels of, 10
Appointed counsel, 446
Appreciable gap, 91
Argersinger, 449
Arizona v. Fulminante, 390
Arraignment, 421–422
 defined, 421
Arrest, 362–375, 406
 by citizens, 237–238
 by law enforcement officers, 235–237
 defined, 362, 406
 executing warrants for, 371–372
 for misdemeanor, 366–369
 illegal, 372
 in protected areas, 365–366
 Model Penal Code and resisting, 186, 235
 probable cause for, 363
 protective sweep and, 369–371
 protective sweep during, 345–346
 resisting unlawful, 235
 search incident to, 369–371
 summary of rules and exceptions, 374
 use of force during, 234–235
 versus investigatory detention, 342
 search incident to, 345–346
 warrant for, 364–365
 warrant preference for, 363
Arrest warrant,
 executing, 371–372
 preference for, 363
 protective sweep, 369–370
 search incident to, 369–370
 summary of rules and exceptions, 374
Arson, 124, 145
 common law definition, 124
 defined, 124
 Model Penal Code and, 124
Ashcroft v. Free Speech Coalition, 162–166
Asportation
 of kidnapping victim, 115
 of property, 128, 129

Assault, 105–106, 136
 aggravated, 106–107
 apprehension of imminent battery, 105–106
 attempted battery as, 106
 defined, 105
Assault and battery, 105–107
 aggravated, 106–107
Assisting suicide, 102
Assumption of duty, 71
 express, 71
Atkins v. Virginia, 467–471
Attempt, 211–214
 acts that might constitute, 213
 defined, 212
 Model Penal Code and, 212
Attempted battery, 106
Attorney General, 280
Attorneys, court appointed, 290
Atwater v. City of Lago Vista, et al., 366–369
Austin v. United States, 481–483
Automobiles summary of Fourth Amendment
 issues and, 358–359

Bad-check statutes, 132–133
Bail, 411
 defined, 411
 excessive, 412
 posting, 406, 411
Barker v. Wingo, 443, 445
Barnes v. Glen Theater, Inc., 158
Battered woman syndrome, 232
 defined, 232
Battery, 105–106
 aggravated, 106–107
 attempted as assault, 106
 defined, 105
 intentional, 105
 Model Penal Code and, 105
 negligent, 105
Bell v. Wolfish, 362
Betts due process standard, 446
Beyond a reasonable doubt, 443
 defined, 443
Bhopal, India, 204
 Union Carbide in, 201
Bill of Attainder, 252
 defined, 252

Bill of particulars, 423
  defined, 423
Bill of Rights, 26
  defined, 26
Blackmail, 137
Blood tests, identification by, 393, 397–399
Body searches, real suspicion for, 350
Bond v. United States, 319
Booking defendant, 406
Boot camp, 489
Booth v. Maryland, 459, 460
Border searches, 349–350
Bowers v. Hardwick, 156–157, 270
Brady, James, 226
Brady Doctrine, 425–426
Brady Handgun Violence Prevention Act of 1993,
  174
Brady v. Maryland, 425
Breach of contract, 17
Breach of the peace, 167
  defined, 167
Break-in, actual, 125
Breaking and entering, 125
Bribery, 133, 183
  common law and, 183
  defined, 183–184
  in business activities, 183
  surveillance for, 391
Briggs v. Maryland, 145, 146–149
Brown v. Allen, 493
Burden of going forward (production), 222
  defined, 222
Burden of persuasion, 222
  defined, 222
Burden of production for insanity defense, 227
Burden of proof, 222, 442–443
  defined, 222
Bureau of Alcohol, Tobacco, and Firearms, 279
Burglary, 125–126, 145
  defined, 125
  graded, 126

Callins v. Collins, 464
Capital crimes, 417
Capital punishment, 461–471
  in United States, 466–467
  methods of applying, 467

Carroll v. United States, 357
Casey v. Planned Parenthood, 267, 268–269, 270
Castration,
  chemical, 114
  surgical, 114
Causation, 72–79
  factual, 72
  legal, 72
Cause in fact, 72
Caveat emptor, 131
Cavity search, 349
  clear indication of illegality, 349
Certiorari, 12
  defined, 12
Chain of custody, 401
  defined, 401
Challenge for cause, 450
  defined, 450
Change of venue, motion for, 427–428
Cheek v. United States, 185–186
Chemical castration, 114
Chernobyl, 204
Child abuse cases, 442
Child exploitation, 113
Child molesting, 111
Child Online Protection Act, 162
Child pornography, 160
Child Pornography Prevention Act, 162
Child seduction, 113
Child solicitation, 113
Childnapping, 115, 117
Children, sex offenses against, 111–113
  exploitation, 113
  molesting, 111
  seduction, 113
  solicitation, 113
  vicarious sexual gratification through, 112–113
Chimel v. California, 345, 346–347
Church of Lukumi Babalu Aye, Inc. v. Hialeah, 253–256
Citizens' arrest, 237–238
City of Indianapolis v. Edmonds, 352–357
City of Little Falls v. Edwin George Witucki, 168, 169–170
Civil contempt, 188
Civil law,
  compared with criminal law, 16–20
  definition of, 16
  Louisiana and, 276

Civil liberties, 26, 118
  and state constitutions, 305
  defined, 26
Civil rights crimes, 118–119
Civil rights laws,
  federal, 293
  state, 293
Clean Air Act (CAA), 201, 202
Clean Water Act (CWA), 201, 202
Clear and present danger, 170, 259
  defined, 170
Clear indication of illegality, 349
Clemency, 471
Clinton, William J., 181–182
Closed-circuit television, testifying via, 442
Closing arguments, 453
Coast Guard, 201, 279
Co-conspirator hearsay rule, 218
  defined, 218
Code of Judicial Conduct, 288
Collateral order doctrine, 491
Color of law, 118
Commercial bribery, Model Penal Code
  and, 183
Commissioners on Uniform Laws, 177
Commitment,
  of criminally insane, 227
  mandatory, 229
Common law, 30–34, 36–37
as source of criminal law, 45
  defined, 30
  uses of, 36,
Common-law crimes, 31, 32
Common system, 276
Commonwealth v. Edmunds, 308–309
Commonwealth v. Hughes, 115, 116
Commonwealth v. Schnopps, 99
Communications Decency Act of 1996, 118,
  162, 166
Community-based correction, 473
Community service, 479–480
Commutation of sentence, defined, 471
Compensatory damages, 18
  defined, 18
Complaint, 18, 406–410
  defined, 406
  examples, 408–410

Comprehensive Environmental Response,
  Compensation, and Liability Act
  (CERCLA), 202
Comprehensive Forfeiture Act of 1984, 179
Computer Abuse Amendments Act of 1994, 148
Computer crimes, 145–149
  viruses, 145
Computer Fraud and Abuse Act, 145
Computers,
  as targets, 145
  as tool in commission, 145
Concert of action rule (Wharton's Rule), 216
  defined, 216
Concurrence, 78
Concurrent jurisdiction, 5
  defined, 5
Concurrent sentence, 473
  defined, 473
Concurring opinion, 33
Confession, 380
  at common law, 380
  defined, 380
  voluntariness requirement, 390
Confinement in kidnapping, 115
Confrontation, right to, 442
Confrontation Clause of Sixth Amendment, 442, 452
Consecutive sentence, 473
  defined, 473
Consent, 241, 334
  defined, 241, 334
Consent searches, 334, 337–338
Consolidated theft statutes, 139–140
Conspiracy, 214, 216–218
  defined, 214
  specific intent for, 217
  withdrawal from, 217
Constitution of the United States, 25, 499–508
Constitutional interpretation, 300
Constitutional law, 43–44
Constitutionalization of criminal procedure, 305
Constitutions as source of criminal law, 44
Constructive breaking, 125
Constructive filing of appeal, 491
Constructive intent, 52
  defined, 52
Constructive possession, 69, 129
Contemporaneous objection, 301

Contempt, 187–189
    cited by legislature, 189
    defined, 187
    direct, 187
    indirect, 187
Continuing Criminal Enterprise (CEE), 179,
    218, 481
Contraband, 340
Contract, 17
    defined, 17
    duty by, 71
Contract law, 17
Conversion, 130
    defined, 130
Coolidge v. New Hampshire, 338, 339, 340
Cooper v. Oklahoma, 229
Cooperative federalism, 6
Coram nobis, 454
Corporal punishment, 471–472
Corporate crime, 61–62
Corporate liability, 61
    defined, 61
    Model Penal Code and, 61
Corpus delicti, 104
    defined, 104
Counsel,
    effective assistance of, 447–448
Counsel, right to, 277, 445–449
    appointed, 446
    at grand jury, 413
    at lineups, 394
    at showups, 394
    beginning of, 449
    effective assistance of, 447–448
    for habeas corpus, 495
    indigency, 445–447
    invoking, 387
    on appeal, 492
    scope of, 449
    to self-representation, 449
    waiving, 389
County of Riverside v. McLaughlin, 411,
    413, 416
Court of general jurisdiction, 12
    defined, 12
Court of limited jurisdiction, 12
    defined, 12

Court rules, 41
    as source of criminal law, 45
    defined, 41
Court system, structure of, 9–13
Courts of record, 12
    defined, 12
Creating danger, 72
Crime against the public, defining, 154
Crime control model, 278
Crime statistics, 85
Crimes,
    alcohol-related, 175–177
    capital, 417
    drug, 175–176
    inchoate, 210, 211–218
    infamous, 417
    parties to, 210–211
    tax, 184–186
Crimes against administration of government,
    180–189
    bribery, 183–184
    perjury, 180–182
Crimes against environment, 200–205
Crimes against habitation, 124, 125
Crimes against public morality, 155–167
    deviate sexual conduct, 155–159
    indecent exposure, 158
    lewdness, 158
    obscenity, 158–161
    prostitution, 155
    regulating Internet, 161–167
    solicitation, 155
Crimes against sovereignty and security, 189–200
    espionage, 191
    sedition, 191
    terrorism, 191–200
    treason, 189
Crimes against the public order, 167–180
    alcohol, 175–177
    disturbing the peace, 168
    drug, 175–176, 177–178
    incitement/advocacy of unlawful conduct, 168
    involving firearms, 173–175
    riot and unlawful assembly, 167
    threats, 170
    vagrancy and panhandling, 170–172
Crimes involving firearms, 173–175

Criminal adjudications, 276
Criminal cases, removal of, 431
Criminal contempt, 187–189
Criminal justice system, 276–277, 278
Criminal law,
    compared with civil law, 16–20
    defined, 24
    purpose of, 16
    sources of, 30–45
    versus criminal procedure, 24
Criminal law violators, purposes of punishing,
        27–30
    incapacitation, 28
    rehabilitation, 28–29
    retribution, 29–30
    specific and general deterrence, 27–28
Criminal mischief, 144–145
    defined, 144
Criminal procedure, constitutionalization of, 305
    defined, 24, 276
    versus criminal law, 24
Criminal record of defendant, discovery of, 423
Criminally insane,
    commitment of, 227
    disposition of, 227
    Model Penal Code approach, 227
Cross-examination, right to, 442
Culpability, 20
    defined, 20
Curtilage, 348
Custodial interrogation requirement, 380
Custody determination, 385
Custody requirement for habeas corpus, 494–495
Customs, 279
Cuyler v. Sullivan, 447
Cyberstalker, 118

Damages, 17, 18
    defined, 17
Danger, creating, 72
Dangerous words, 259
Daubert v. Merrell Dow Pharmaceuticals, 397
Deadly force, use under Model Penal Code, 234
Deadly weapon, 93
    defined, 93
    doctrine, 93, 95
    Modal Penal code definition, 93, 95

Death With Dignity Act, 104
Declaration of Independence, 25
Defendant, 276
    criminal record of, 423
    statements of, 423
    trial rights of, 436–449
    See also Trial rights of defendants.
Defense, 222–242
    affirmative, 222
    affirmative defined, 222
    appeals, 491–492
    defined, 222
    infancy as, 238–239
    use-of-force, 231–238
Defense attorneys, 288–291
    court appointed, 290
    ethics of, 288
    legal assistants to, 291
Defense case, 452
Defense of others, 100, 233
    at common law, 233
Defense of property and habitation, 233–234
    at common law, 233
    use of deadly force, 233
Deferred sentencing, 178
Definite sentencing, 472
Defraud, intent to, 132
Defrauding insurance carrier, 124
Delaware v. Prouse, 357, 359–360
Deliberate, 91
Delinquency proceedings, 436–437
Deoxyribonucleic acid. See DNA.
Department of Human Resources v. Smith, 252, 256
Department of the Interior, 201
Deposition, discovery of, 424
    defined, 424
Destruction of property, 144–145
Detainer, 430–431
    defined, 430
Detention, pretrial, 412–413
Deter, 27–28
    defined, 27
Determinate sentencing, 472
    defined, 472
Deterrence,
    general, 28
    specific, 27–28

Deviate sexual conduct, 155–159
Diminished capacity, 223
  defined, 223
Direct contempt, 187
Directed verdict, 452
Discovery, 422–427
  bill of particulars, 423
  criminal record of, 423
  defined, 422
  deposition, 424
  documents, 424
  freedom of information laws, 426–427
  scientific reports and tests, 424
  statements of defendant, 423
  tangible objects, 424
  witness statements, 424
Discretion, 281
  defined, 281
  prosecutorial, 281
Discrimination, 249–250
Disease of the mind, 224
Dismiss, motion to, 427
Dismissal with prejudice, 443
Disorderly conduct, 168
Dissenting opinion, 33
District attorney, 281
Disturbing the peace, 168
Diversion, 473
DNA printing, 400
  defined, 400
DNA tests, identification by, 393, 399–400
Documents, discovery of, 424
Double jeopardy, 7, 246–247
  defined, 246
  Model Penal Code and, 247
Double Jeopardy Clause, 246–247, 419, 490, 491
Douglas v. California, 492
Driving while under the influence, 176–177
Drug crimes, 175–176, 177–178
  Continuing Criminal Enterprise (CEE) and, 179
  deferred sentencing for, 178
  Model Penal Code and, 177
  possession of paraphernalia, 180
  Racketeer Influenced and Corrupt
    Organizations Act (RICO) and, 179
  surveillance for, 391
Drug Enforcement Administration, 279

Drug kingpin statute, 481
Drug paraphernalia, possession of, 180
Drug sales, 133
Drug treatment, 488, 489
Drunk driver, 100
Drunk driving, 177
  conviction, 488
Dual federalism, 6
Dual sovereignty, 4
Due process, 249–251
  law enforcement officers, 279–280
  participants in, 279–293
  procedural, 250
  substantive, 250
Due Process Clause, 36, 249, 250, 449, 479, 481, 490
  defined, 36
  in Fourteenth Amendment, 298, 299
Due Process Model, 278
  participants in, 279–293
Duress, 230
  defined, 230
Durham rule, 225
  defined, 225
Durham v. United States, 225
Duty,
  assumption of, 71
  by contract, 71
  by relationship, 70
  imposed by statute, 70

Edwards, 389
Eighth Amendment, 172, 229, 250, 412, 458, 461, 467, 471, 472, 483
Eisenstadt v. Baird, 270
Electronic communications, interception of, 391
  minimizing irrelevant information, 391
Electronic surveillance, 390–393
  court-ordered, 391
Element, 63, 84
  analysis, 63–64
  defined, 63, 84
  of a crime, 63, 84
  of larceny, 63
Embezzlement, 130–131, 135, 139, 144
  conversion, 130
  creation of, 128, 129

Embezzlement *continued*
   defined, 130
   intent to defraud, 130
Emergency Planning and Community Right-to-
   Know Act, 202, 204
Emergency responses by police, 347–348
Endangered Species Act (ESA), 201, 202, 204
Enron, 61
Entrapment, 240–241
   defined, 240
   objective test for, 241
   subjective test for, 240–241
Environment, crimes against, 200–205
Environmental Protection Agency (EPA), 201, 203
Equal protection, 249–251
Equal Protection Clause, 250, 449, 490, 492
Escobedo v. Illinois, 380
Espionage, 191
   surveillance for, 391
Estes v. Texas, 437
Ethics of prosecutors, 287
Euthanasia, 104
Evidence,
   falsified, 287
   perjured, 287
   preservation of, 346, 347
Ex Parte hearing, 406, 407
Ex post facto law, 36, 251
   defined, 251
Excessive bail, 412
Excessive Fines Clause, 483
Excessive noise, 168
Exclusionary rule, 300–303, 312
   and exceptions, 303
   defined, 300
Exculpatory evidence, 287
Execution, methods used for, 467
Executive branch of government, 8
Exhaustion of remedies, 494
   defined, 494
Exigent circumstances, 334, 366
Expansion, 300
Expansion of rights, 300
Express assumption of duty, 71
Extortion, 133, 135, 137–138, 139
   defined, 137
   surveillance for, 391

Extradition, 429–430
   defined, 429
   waiving, 429
Eyewitness identifications, 393

Facially invalid warrant, 328, 329
Facially valid warrant, 328, 329
Factual causation, 72, 73
Factual guilt, 278
Factual impossibility, 213
Failure to disperse, 167
Fairness right in lineup, 394–396
   self-incrimination and, 396
Fairness right in showup, 394–396
   self-incrimination and, 396
False imprisonment, 117
   defined, 117
False pretenses, 131–135, 139, 144
   creation of, 128
   defined, 131
   defraud intent to, 132
   forgery, 134–135
   fraudulent checks, 132–133
   intent to defraud, 132
   larceny by trick, 132
   mail fraud, 133
   material, 131
   material representation, 131–132
   present fact, 132
   Racketeer Influenced and Corrupt
      Organizations Act (RICO), 133–134
Falsified evidence, 287
Faretta v. California, 449
Federal Bureau of Investigation, 279
Federal civil rights statutes, 293
Federal Counterfeit Access Device and Computer
   Fraud and Abuse Act, 145
Federal crimes, 6
Federal district courts, 12
Federal government, 4
Federal habeas corpus, 493
Federal Insecticide, Fungicide, and Rodenticide
   Act (FIFRA), 202, 204
Federal judges, lifetime appointment of, 14
Federal Kidnapping Act, 114
Federal Rules of Evidence, 452
Federal Sentencing Guidelines, 474–475

Federal Tort Claims Act (FTCA), 294
Federal Wiretap Act, 390–393
Federalism, 4–7
  defined, 4
Felony,
  second-degree, 101
  third-degree, 101
Felony-murder doctrine, 87–90
Felony-murder rule, 87–89
  defined, 87
Felony-murder statutes, elements to establish, 88
Fences, 135
Fetus, 101, 102
  viability of, 102
Fifth Amendment, 172, 229, 246, 247, 248, 249,
    250, 251, 266, 282, 298, 300, 303, 380, 386,
    395, 397, 400, 401, 416, 417, 419, 427, 443,
    445, 449, 479
Fighting words, 168, 259
  defined, 168
Final instructions to jury, 453
Final judgment, 491
  defined, 491
Fines, 480
Fingerprinting, identification by, 393, 397
Firearms,
  crimes involving, 173–175
  possession, sale and transfer laws, 174
  registration and licensing of, 175
  use laws, 174–175
First Amendment, 158, 172, 251, 266
  and hate crime legislation, 261–262
  and religion, 252–258
  and speech, 259–266
  free speech, 118, 119
  protection, 68
First-degree murder, 89, 90–93
  defined, 90
Flag burning, 259
Florida v. J. L., 324–326
Florida v. Royer, 342
Foreign Intelligence Surveillance Act of 1978
    (FISA), 191
Foreseeability, 72
  defined, 72
Forfeiture, 133, 480–488
  defined, 133

Forgery, 134–135, 143, 145
  defined, 134
Formal charge, 416–421
Fourteenth Amendment, 172, 229, 247, 249,
    250, 251, 266, 267, 270, 298, 303, 380, 395,
    443, 445, 449, 479, 490, 492
  Due Process Clause in, 298, 299
Fourth Amendment, 235, 266, 282, 303, 304,
    312–328, 390, 396
  emergency exception to, 348
  frisking and, 341
  hot pursuit exception to, 348
  interrogation and, 342
  privacy, 312–319
  probable cause, 319–328
  questioning and, 342
Fourth Amendment issues and automobiles,
    summary of, 358–359
Fourth Amendment problems, analyzing,
    372–374
Fraudulent checks, 132–133, 139
Freedom, 25
Freedom of Information Act (FOIA), 426
  discovery through, 426
Freedom of information laws, discovery through,
    426–427
Frisbie v. Collins, 430
Frisk, 340–343
  probable cause to, 342
Fruit of the poisonous tree, 303–304
  doctrine defined, 303
Fry v. United States, 396–397
Fundamental fairness, 299
Furman v. Georgia, 461, 464, 466

General deterrence, 28
General intent, 51, 52, 53
Genetic fingerprinting, 400
Gideon v. Wainwright, 446, 448, 449
Good faith reliance on warrant, 328
Government,
  basic structure of American, 4–7
  liability of, 293–294
Government administration, crimes against,
    180–189
Government officials, liability of, 293–294
Graham v. Connor, 235, 236–237

Grand jury, 413, 416–417
  defined, 416
  hearings, 280
  indictment by, 281, 417, 419
  procedures of, 416–417
  purpose of, 416
Great Writ of Liberty, 493
Gregg v. Georgia, 464
Griswold v. Connecticut, 266, 267
Guilty, but mentally ill verdict, 228
Guilty but mentally ill defense (GBMI), 226
Guilty mind, 50
Guilty plea, 421
  voluntary, 421
Gun Control Act of 1968, 174

*H. J. Inc. v. Northwestern Bell Telephone
    Co.*, 134
Habeas corpus, 492–495
  custody requirement for, 494–495
  exhaustion of remedies, 494
  federal, 493
  history of, 493
  procedure for, 495
  relief, 493
  right to counsel for, 495
  scope of review for, 493–494
  writ of, 429
Habeas Corpus Act of 1867, 493
Habitation,
  crimes against, 124, 125
  defense of, 233–234
Habitual offender statutes, 489–490
  defined, 489
Halfway house, 473, 488–489
  defined, 489
Harassing, 117
Harassment, 118
Harmless error, 491
  defined, 491
Hate crime legislation and First Amendment,
    261–262
Hate crimes laws, 119
Hazardous materials, regulating, 203
Hearsay, 218
  defined, 218

Hearsay evidence, 323, 442
  probable cause and, 416
  two-prong test for, 323
Heat of passion manslaughter, 98
Hinckley, John, 226
Homeless persons, 172
Homicide, 84–104
  and AIDS, 96–97
  and common law, 86–90
  common law definition of, 86–87
  Model Penal Code approach to, 101
  statutory approaches to, 90–97
Horizontal division of power, 7
Horton v. California, 340
Hot pursuit by police, 348
  arrest after, 366
House arrest, 488
Hung jury, 453
  defined, 453
Identification,
  by photographs, 396
  exclusion of improper, 401–402
  eyewitness, 393
  in-court, 402
  pretrial procedures, 393
  scientific procedures for, 396–401

Identification procedures, scientific. *See* Scientific
    identification procedures.
Identity theft, 140–143
Identity Theft and Assumption Deterrence Act of
    1998, 143
Illegal arrests, 372
Illinois v. Gates, 323
Illinois v. Wardlow, 341
Immunity, 248–249
  from prosecution, 417
  of governmental officials, 293–294
  transactional, 248
  use, 248
Imperfect self-defense, 234
Impoundment, 361
In camera review of evidence, 428
In limine motion, 452
  defined, 452
Incapacitation, 28

Incarceration, 472
Incest, 111
Inchoate crimes, 210, 211–218
    attempt, 211–214
Incitement of unlawful conduct, 168, 170
Incompetence, establishing, 229
Incorporation, 298
In-court identification, 402
Indecent exposure, 158
    Model Penal Code and, 158
Indefinite sentencing, 472
Independent content approach, 299
Independent source, 304
    defined, 304
Indeterminate sentencing, 472
    defined, 472
Indictment, 417–419
    by grand jury, 281, 417, 419
    sealed, 443
    waiver of, 417, 418
Indictment of Zacarias Moussaoui, 192–200
Indigency, 445–447
Indirect contempt, 187
Inevitable discovery doctrine, 304
Infamous crimes, 417
Infancy as defense, 238–239
Inference, 64
    defined, 64
Inferior courts, 12
    defined, 12
Informant, 323
Information, 416
    defined, 416
Informations, charging for crime by, 421
Initial appearance, 411
    with warrantless arrest, 411
Injunction, 61
    defined, 61
Innocence, presumption of, 277, 442–443
Inquisitorial system, 277
Insanity at time of trial, 229
    mistrial, 229
Insanity defense, 223–229
    at time of trial, 229
    burden of production for, 227
    clear and convincing evidence, 227

disease of the mind, 224
    guilty but mentally ill, 226
    irresistible impulse test, 223, 225
    M'Naghten test, 223, 224
    Model Penal Code test for, 223, 225–226
    procedures of, 226–227
    psychiatric examination for, 226
Insanity plea, 65
Intelligible principle, 39
Intent,
    objective, 64
    subjective, 64
Intent murder, 73
Intent to defraud, 130, 132
Intent to do serious bodily harm, 93
Intentional, 17
    defined, 17
Intentional battery, 105
Intentional tort, 17
Interlocutory appeals, 491
    defined, 491
International Association of Chiefs of Police
    (IACP), 279
Internet, regulating the, 161–167
Interpret, 14
    defined, 14
Interrogation, 380
    defined, 380
    Miranda applied to, 385
    multiple, 386–387
Interstate Agreement on Detainers, 430
Intervening cause, 73
Intoxication, 239
    involuntary, 239
    voluntary, 239
Inventory search of vehicle, 361
Inventory searches, 361
Investigatory detention versus arrest, 342
Involuntary manslaughter, 100–101
Irrebuttable presumptions, 65, 238
Irresistible impulse test, 223, 225
    defined, 225

Jacobellis v. Ohio, 159
Jake's Law, 431
Janet A. Carson, appellant v. United States, ap

Jencks Act, 424, 426
JNOV. *See* Judgment notwithstanding the
	verdict.
Johnson v. Zerbst, 446
Judge, 276, 287–288
	code of ethics of, 288
Judge-made law, 30
Judgment notwithstanding the verdict
	(JNOV), 454
Judgment of acquittal, 452
Judicial branch of government, 6, 9
	duties and power of, 14–15
Judicial Conference, 41
Judicial immunity, 294
Judicial opinions, 33
Judicial review, 14–15
	defined, 14
	power of, 8, 37
Judiciary, 287
Jurisdiction, 5
	defined, 5
Jury,
	as factfinder, 437
	final instructions to, 453
	preliminary instructions to, 450
Jury deliberations, 453
Jury selection, 450
Jury trial, right to, 277, 436–437
Juvenile court, 436–437
Juvenile court system, 238
	common law and, 238
	purpose of, 238–239

Kansas v. Hendricks, 114
Katz decision, 392
Katz v. United States, 312, 313–314, 390
Keeler v. Superior Court, 33, 34–36, 102
Ker v. California, 371
Kevorkian, Dr. Jack, 102–104
Kidnapping, 114–117, 133
	defined, 114
	elements of, 115
	federal, 115–117
	sentence for, 391
	Kelsey, 118, 293
	Kogan, 67

Knock-and-announcement requirement, 372
Knowingly,
	act, 62–63
	defined, 62
Kyllo v. United States, 314–315, 316

Labelle v. State, 95–96
Larcenies, 135
Larceny, 128–130, 136, 139, 144
	by trick, 132
	common-law elements of, 128
	constructive possession, 129, 130
	creation of, 127
	defined, 128
Law enforcement agencies,
	federal, 8
	state, 8
Law Enforcement Code of Ethics, 279–280
Law enforcement officers, 279–280
	discretion of, 279
	ethics of, 279–280
Legal assistants, 291
	ethical guidelines for, 291
Legal causation, 72
Legal cause, 72
	defined, 72
Legal guilt, 278
Legal impossibility defense, 213
	defined, 213
Legality principle, 32–33, 250
Legislative branch of government, 8, 38
Legislative contempt, 189
Legislative history, 58
	defined, 58
Lewdness, 158
Liability of government officials, 293–294
Liability of governments, 293–294
Libelous statements, 259
Lie detection testing, 400–401
Lineup, 393
	defined, 393
	fairness right in, 394
Locket v. Ohio, 461, 464
Logan Act, 191
Love Canal, 201
Lying in wait, 117

M'Naghten test, 223, 224, 239
  defined, 224
Mahoney, Larry, accident, 27
Mail fraud, 133
Malicious (criminal) mischief, 144–145
  defined, 144
Malum in se, 55, 57, 90
Malum prohibitum, 90
Manifest necessity for mistrial, 246
Manslaughter, 98–101
  common law and, 98
  defined, 98
  provocation for, 98–100
Mapp v. Ohio, 300, 301, 302–303
Marbury v. Madison, 15
Marine Mammal Protection Act (MMPA), 204–205
Marital rape exception, 108
Maryland v. Buie, 345, 369, 370–371
Material representation, 131–132
Materiality in perjury, 181
Maum prohibitum, 55, 57
Mayhem, 107
McCeskey v. Kemp, 466
McNabb-Mallory rule, 380
McVeigh, Timothy, death certificate for, 190
Megan's Laws, 113–114
Mempa v. Rhay, 479
Mens rea, 50–65
  and common law, 50–53, 55–56
  current approaches to, 62–64
  defined, 50
  proving, 64–65
Merger doctrine, 84
Merger of offenses, 84
  defined, 84
Michigan State Police v. Sitz, 352
Michigan v. Jackson, 389
Military Commission Order 1, 192
Military Order 1, 192
Military trial, 436
Miller test, 160, 161, 162
Miller v. California, 159–160
Mincey v. Arizona, 347–348
Minnesota v. Carter, 316–319
Minnesota v. Dickerson, 343–345
Minnesota v. Olson, 316

Minnick v. Mississippi, 387–388
Miranda, 307, 380–389
  elements of warning, 388–389
  exceptions to, 386
  public safety interests and, 386
  routine questions and, 386
  undercover officers and, 386
  violating, 389
  volunteered statements and, 386
  waiver of, 389
Miranda v. Arizona, 300, 380, 381–382
Mischief, 144
Misdemeanor manslaughter, 90, 100
Mistake of fact, 239–240
Mistake of law, 239–240
Mistrial, 229, 246
  manifest necessity for, 246
Mitigating circumstances, 473
  defined, 473
Model Code of Professional Responsibility, 287, 291
Model Penal Code, 43, 50, 74
  accomplices and, 210
  and corporate liability, 61
  and double jeopardy, 247
  and obscenity, 160–161
  and states of mind, 62–64
  approach to homicide, 101
  arson and, 124
  as source of criminal law, 45
  attempt and, 212
  commercial bribery and, 183
  consolidation of theft offenses, 143
  defined, 43
  drug crimes and, 177
  excerpts from, 509–542
  failure to disperse and, 167
  indecent exposure and, 158
  possession and, 69
  prostitution and, 155
  rape, 108, 109
  resisting arrest and, 235
  retreat provision in, 232
  riot and, 167
  test for insanity defense, 223, 225–226
  use of deadly force under, 234
  voluntariness and, 66

Model Rules of Professional Conduct, 287
Morissette v. United States, 58
Motion, 419
  defined, 419
  to quash, 419
Motion in limine, 428
Motion practice, 427–429
  for change of venue, 427–428
  for severance, 428
  in limine, 428
  to dismiss/quash, 427
  to suppress, 427
Motive, 65
  defined, 65
Moussaoui, Zacarias, indictment of,
    192–200
Mug shot, 396
Murder, 101, 133
  common law definition of, 86–87
  surveillance for, 391

Narcotics, 176
National Association of Legal Assistants (NALA)
    Code of Ethics, 291
National Crime Information Center
    (NCIC), 149
  defined, 149
National Crime Victimization Survey
    (NCVS), 85
National Federation of Paralegal Organizations
    Code of Ethics, 291
National Firearms Act, 174, 175
National government, 4
National Incident Based Reporting System
    (NIBRS), 85
National Instant Background Check System
    (NICS), 174
Necessity, 230
  defined, 230
Negligence, 17
  defined, 17
Negligent, 101
Negligent battery, 105
Negligent homicide, 100, 101
Negligent tort, 17
New federalism, state constitutions and, 305–309

Nighttime searches, 334
Ninth Amendment, 266, 270
No-knock warrants, 334, 372
Nolle prosequi, 281, 292, 421
  defined, 281
Nolo contendere plea, 421, 422
Nonforcible rape, 109–110
North Carolina v. Butler, 389
Not guilty by reason of insanity, 227
Not guilty plea, 421, 422
Notice, 33
Nucleotide bases, 399

Objections, 452
  defined, 452
Objective intent, 64
Obscenity, 158–161
  Model Penal Code and, 160–161
Obstruction of justice, 186
Occupational Safety and Health Act
    (OSHA), 203
Offense analysis, 63
Omissions,
  as acts, 70–72
  defined, 70
Omnibus Crime Control Act and Safe Streets Act
    of 1968, 191, 390
  Title III of, 390–393
Open fields doctrine, 348–349
Opening statements, 451
Ordinances, 37–38
  as source of criminal law, 45
  defined, 37
Osborne v. Ohio, 160
Overbreadth doctrine, 251
  defined, 251
Oyler v. Boles, 282

Panhandling, 170, 172
Papachristou v. City of Jacksonville, 172
Paralegals, 291
Pardon, defined, 471
Parental kidnapping, 115–117
Parental Kidnapping Prevention Act, 116
Parole, 473–474
  defined, 473

Parole board, 474
Parties to crimes, 210–211
Patriot Act, 191
    conditions of, 191–192
Payne v. Tennessee, 460, 461–464
Payton v. New York, 366
People v. Alicia Troiano, 59–60
People v. Belge, 289–290
People v. Dioguardi, 138–139
People v. Murray, 213, 214
People v. Warner-Lambert Co., 74–75
Peremptory challenge, 450
    defined, 450
Perjured evidence, 287
Perjury, 72, 180–182, 290
    common law and, 180
    defined, 180
    materiality in, 181
    subornation of, 181
    suborning, 291
    traps, 240
Personal harassment, 118
Personal recognizance, 412
Personal status as act, 68–69
Petit juries, 416
Petty offenses, 436
Photographs, identification by, 396
Physical punishment, 471–472
Physician-assisted suicide, 104
Picketing, 259
Pickpocket, 136
Pimps, 155
Plain feel doctrine, 343–345
Plain view doctrine, 338–340
    defined, 338
Plea, 421
    defined, 421
Plea agreement, defined, 421
Plea bargain, 419, 421
    defined, 421
Police, 279
    emergency responses by, 347–348
    hot pursuit by, 348
Police Code of Conduct, 279, 280
Police officers, qualified immunity
    for, 294

Police power, 6
    defined, 6
Polling the jury, 453
    defined, 453
Polygraph tests, 400
Possession,
    actual, 69
    as an act, 69
    constructive, 69
Postconviction remedies, 490–495
    appeal, 490–492
*Posters 'N' Things, Ltd. v. United
    States*, 180
Powell v. Alabama, 445, 446
Precedent, 30–31
    defined, 30
Preliminary examination, 416
Preliminary hearing, 413–416
    defined, 413
Preliminary instructions to jury, 450
Premeditated, 91
Present fact, 132
Presentence investigation, 458–459
    no right to counsel during, 458
Presentence report, 459
    review of, 459
Preservation, 491–492
of evidence, 346, 347
Presumption, 65
    defined, 65
    irrebuttable, 65
    of innocence, 277
Presumptive sentencing, 472–473
Pretrial activity, 422–429
    discovery, 422–427
Pretrial conference, 429
Pretrial detention, 412–413
Pretrial identification procedures, 393
Pretrial release, 411–412
Primary evidence, 303
Principal in a crime, 210
    defined, 210
Principle of legality, 32–33, 250
    defined, 250
Prison boot camp, 489
Prisoners, searches of, 361–362

Privacy, 312–328
  as hotel guests, 319
  reasonable expectation of, 312, 313
  right to, 305
Privacy Act, 426–427
Privacy rights, 266–270
  abortion and, 267
Pro se, 449
Probable cause, 319–328
  at preliminary hearing, 413
  defined, 319
  sources to establish, 323–327
  with hearsay evidence, 416
Probable cause hearing, 411
Probable desistance, 212–213
Probation, 473, 476–480
Probation officer, presentence interview by,
  458–459
Procedural due process, 250
Procedural law, 24
Profiles, 349–350
  drug courier, 357
  illegal alien, 357
Proof, burden of, 442–443
Property and habitation, defense of, 233–234
Property bond, 412
Prosecution,
  immunity from, 417
  improper, discriminatory, 282
Prosecution appeals, 491–492
Prosecution's case in chief, 451–452
Prosecutor, 9, 276, 280–287
  discretion of, 281–291
  ethics of, 287
  legal assistants to, 291
Prosecutorial discretion, 281–291
Prostitution, 155
  defined, 155
  Model Penal Code and, 155
Protective sweep, 345–346
  arrest and, 369–370, 371
Provocation, 98–100
  defined, 98
Proximate cause, 72
  defined, 72

Proximity test, 212
Public drunkenness, 176
Public indecency, 158
  Model Penal Code and, 158
Public offenses, 57
Public official, bribery of, 183
Public order, crimes against, 167–180
Public safety issues, *Miranda* and, 386
Public servant, bribery of, 183
Public trial, right to, 437
Punishing acquitted crimes, 460
Punishment, forms of, 460–489
  capital, 461–471
  community service, 479
  concurrent sentencing, 473
  consecutive sentencing, 473
  corporal, 471–472
  definite sentencing, 472
  determinate sentencing, 472
  federal guidelines for, 474
  fines, 480
  forfeiture, 480–488
  incarceration, 472
  indefinite sentencing, 472
  indeterminate sentencing, 472
  modern alternatives, 488–489
  parole, 473–474
  physical, 471–472
  presumptive, 472–473
  probation, 476
  restitution, 480
  revocation, 476
  suspended imposition of sentence, 473
  suspended sentence, 476
Punitive damages, 18
  defined, 18
Purposely,
  act, 62–63
  defined, 62

Qualified immunity, 294
Quash, 419
  defined, 419
  motion to, 419, 427
Quasi-judicial acts by prosecutors, 294

Questioning and *Miranda,*
  routine, 386
  spontaneous, 386

R.A.V. v. City of St. Paul, 262–263
Racial profiling controversy, 350–351
Racketeer Influenced and Corrupt
    Organizations Act (RICO), 133–134, 179,
    218, 481
  defined, 133–134
Racketeering activity, pattern of, 133
Rap sheet, 459
Rape, 108–109
  common-law definition, 108
  defined, 108
  elements of, 109
  marital exception, 108
  shield laws, 111
Rape shield laws, 111, 292, 442
Reagan, Ronald, 226
Reasonability of deadly force, 235, 237
Reasonable person, 98
Reasonable person standard, 64
Rebuttable presumptions, 65, 238
Rebuttal, 452
Receiving stolen property, 135–136, 139, 143
  defined, 135
Recidivist laws, 489
Reckless homicide, 74, 101
Recklessness, 63
  defined, 63
Record on appeal, 10
  defined, 10
Regulations, 38
  as source of criminal law, 45
  defined, 38
Regulatory offenses, 57
Rehabilitation, 28–29
Reinterrogation, 387
Relationship, duty imposed by, 70
Release, pretrial, 411–412
Religion, First Amendment and, 252–258
Remand, 10
Removal of criminal cases, 431
Reno V. ACLU, 162

Reprieve, defined, 471
Res ipsa loquitur test, 212
Resisting arrest, 186
  Model Penal Code and, 186
Resource Conservation and Recovery Act
    (RCRA), 202, 203
Restitution, 473, 480
Restraining orders, 117
Restraint, 28
Retreat doctrine, 232
  Model Penal Code and, 232
Retreat to the wall, 232
  defined, 232
Retribution, 29–30
Reverse court decision, 10
Revocation hearing, 479
  defined, 479
Rhode Island v. Innis, 385–386
Richards v. Wisconsin, 335–337
Richardson v. United States, 137
RICO. *See* Racketeer Influenced and Corrupt
    Organizations.
Right to counsel,
  at pretrial lineups, 394
  at pretrial showups, 394
  invoking, 387
  waiving right to, 389
Right to privacy, 305
Right-wrong test, 224
Rights, expansion of, 300
Riot, 167–168
  Model Penal Code and, 167
Roadblocks for motor vehicles, 351–360
  occupants of vehicles at, 359
  searches at, 357
  stops at, 351
Robbery, 135, 136–137, 143, 145
  as assault, 136
  as larceny, 136
  defined, 136
  surveillance for, 391
Robinson v. California, 68
Roe v. Wade, 102, 267
Rogers v. Tennessee, 76–78
Roth v. United States, 159

Routine questions, *Miranda* and, 386
Routine traffic stops, *Miranda* and, 386
Rules, 38
Rules of court, 41
    defined, 41

Schmerber v. California, 398–399
Scienter, 51, 101, 211
    defined, 51
Scientific identification procedures, 396–401
    blood testing, 397–399
    chain of custody, 401
    DNA testing, 399–400
    fingerprinting, 397
    polygraph tests, 400–401
    validity and reliability of, 396–397
    voice tests, 400
Scientific reports and tests, discovery of, 424
Scottsboro case, 445
Search-incident-to-arrest doctrine, 369
Search warrants, 312, 316, 319
    description of items in, 329
    description of location in, 333
    exceptions to requirements, 334–362
    executing, 333–334, 335–337
    facially invalid, 328, 329
    facially valid, 328, 329
    good faith reliance on, 327–328
    "no-knock," 334
    requirements for, 328–334
    scope of, 333
Search warrants, exceptions to,
    aerial surveillance, 348–349
    border searches, 349–350
    consent searches, 334, 337–338
    emergency, 347–348
    hot pursuit, 348
    motor vehicles and roadblocks, 351–360
    open fields, 348–349
    plain view doctrine, 338–340
    profiles, 349–350, 357
    stop and frisk, 340–343
    Terry standard, 340–343
Searches,
    at roadblocks, 357
    consent, 334, 337–338
    incident to arrest, 345–346

    inventory, 361
    of prisoners, 361–362
    probable cause for, 342
    reasonable, 329
    Supreme Court definition of, 313
    third-party consent to, 338
    voluntary, 334, 337–338
Searches and seizures, 328–362
    exceptions to warrant requirement, 334–362
    warrant requirement for, 328–334
Second Amendment, 173
Second-degree felony, 101
Second-degree manslaughter, 100
Second-degree murder, 89, 90–93
    defined, 90
Secret Service, 279
Securities fraud, 133
Security, crimes against, 189–200
Sedition, 191
Selective incorporation doctrine, 299, 300
Self-defense, 231–233
    defined, 231
    imperfect, 100, 234
    in battered woman syndrome, 232
    retreat doctrine, 232
Self-incrimination, 247–248
    freedom from, 277
Self-representation, right to, 449
Seling v. Young, 114
Sentencing, 458–490
    community service, 479
    concurrent, 473
    consecutive, 473
    definite, 472
    determinate, 472
    federal guidelines for, 474
    fines, 480
    forfeiture, 480–488
    indefinite, 472
    indeterminate, 472
    modern alternatives for, 488–489
    presumptive, 472–473
    probation, 476
    restitution, 480
    revocation, 476
    suspended imposition of, 473
    suspended sentence, 476

Sentencing hearing, 459–460
   punishing acquitted crimes, 460
   right to counsel during, 459
   victim impact statement, 459
Sentencing procedure, 458–460
   presentence investigation, 458–459
   sentencing hearing, 459–460
Separation of powers, 7–9
   defined, 7
Severance, motion for, 428
Sex crimes, 107–114
   against children, 111–113
   incest, 111
   rape, 108–109
   sodomy, 110–111
   statutory rape, 109–110
Sex offenders, 109, 113
Sexual offenders, 113–114
   recidivism by, 108
Sexually oriented expression, 159
Shield laws, 111
   defined, 111
Shock incarceration program, 489
Showup, 393
   defined, 393
   fairness right in, 394
Sidebar, 452
   defined, 452
Simmons v. United States, 304
Sine qua non test, 72
Sixth Amendment, 250, 288, 291, 303, 380, 436,
     437, 442, 443, 445, 446, 447, 448, 449, 459,
     479, 492
   Miranda and, 389
Slanderous statements, 259
Sobriety checkpoint, 352
Social welfare agencies, 38
Societal vengeance, 29
Sodomy, 110–111
   defined, 110
Solicitation, 218
   defined, 218
   for prostitution, 155
Solitary confinement, 472
Sovereign immunity, 294
   defined, 294
Sovereignty, crimes against, 189–200

Special prosecutor, 281
Specific deterrence, 27–28
Specific intent, 51–52, 53, 62, 91
   defined, 51
Speech, 305
   and First Amendment, 259–266
   protection of, 68
Speedy trial, right to, 443–445
Speedy Trial Act of 1974, 443, 444, 445
Split sentence, 474
Spontaneous questioning, *Miranda* and, 386
"Spoofing," 118
Stalking, 117–118
   defined, 117
   public awareness of, 117
Standby counsel, 449
Standing, 304–305
   defined, 304
Stansbury v. California, 382–385
Star Chamber, 212
Stare decisis, 30
   defined, 30
State attorney, 281
State civil rights laws, 293
State constitutions,
   and new federalism, 305–309
   civil liberties and, 305
State governments, 4
State of Illinois v. Gerry Lockett, 126, 127
State trial courts, 10
State v. Baldwin, 141–142
State v. David Fierro, 102, 103
State v. Haines, 213, 214–216
State v. Hodges, 256, 257–258
State v. Losey, 89–90
State v. Snowden, 91, 92, 93
State-law crimes, 6
Statements as acts, 66, 68
Statements of defendant, 423
Statutes, 8
   as source of criminal law, 44–45
   defined, 8
   duty imposed by, 70
   power to invalidate, 15
Statutes of limitation, 241–242
   defined, 241
   common law and, 242

Statutory construction,
    canons of, 59
    defined, 59
    strict liability and, 58
Statutory crimes, robbery, 136
Statutory law, 37
Statutory rape, 109–110, 113
    defined, 109
Stolen property, receiving, 135–136
    defined, 135
Stop and frisk, 340–343
    probable cause to, 342
Stoval v. Denno, 394–395
Strict liability, 18, 56–57, 58–59
    and statutory construction, 58–59
    defined, 18, 56
Strict liability crimes, 56–57
    defined, 56
Strip search, 349
    clear indication of illegality, 349
Subjective intent, 64
Subornation of perjury, 181
    defined, 181
Subpoena, examples of, 414–415
Subpoena documents by grand jury, 417
Substance of tort law, 24
Substantial capacity test, 225
Substantial step to completion test,
    213, 214
Substantive contract law, 24
Substantive criminal law, 24
Substantive due process, 250
Substantive law, 24
Suicide, 102–104
    as common law crime, 102
    assisting as crime, 102
Superfund, 202
Suppress, motion to, 427
Suppression hearings, 427
Supremacy Clause of Article VI, 5
Surgical castration, 114
Suspended imposition of sentence (SIS),
    178, 473
Suspended sentence, 476
    defined, 476

Tangible objects, discovery of, 424
Tax crimes, 184–186
    evasion, 184
    fraud, 184–185
Tax evasion, 184, 185, 187
    defined, 184
Tax fraud, 184, 185, 187
    defined, 184
Telephone harassment, 118
Tennessee v. Garner, 235, 237
Terrorism, 191–200
Terry stops, 349, 350, 351
Terry v. Ohio, 341, 342, 362
Texas v. Gregory Lee Johnson, 259–261
Theft, 126–148
    by deception, 143
    by extortion, 143
    by receiving stolen property, 143
    by taking, 143
    by use of automobile, 143
    common-law, 128
    conversion of funds, 143
    identity, 140–143
    of mislaid property, 143
    of professional services, 143
Theft statutes, consolidated, 139–140
    Model Penal Code and, 143
Third-degree felony, 101
Thomas v. Commonwealth of Kentucky, 170, 171–172
Thoughts as acts, 66, 68
Threat, 168, 170
Threatening, 117
Three Mile Island, 204
Title III of Omnibus Crime Control Act, 390–393
    execution of orders for, 391–392
    exceptions to, 392–393
Tolling, 242
Tort, 17–18
    defined, 17
Tort law, 17
    substance of, 24
Tortfeasor, 17
Toscanino claim, 372
Total incorporation, 267, 299
Total incorporation plus, 299

Touby v. United States, 41–43
Toxic Substances Control Act (TSCA), 203
Toxic waste, 200
Toxins, exposure to, 200
Traffic stops, *Miranda* and routine, 386
Traffic violations, 407
Transactional immunity, 248
    defined, 248
Transferred intent, 55–56
    defined, 56
Treason, 189
    surveillance for, 391
Trespass, 125
Trial court, 9
    defined, 9
Trial procedure, 450–454
    by combat, 436
    by compurgation, 436
    by ordeal, 436
    closing arguments, 453
    defense case, 452
    final instructions, 453
    jury deliberations, 453
    opening statements, 451
    preliminary instructions to jury, 450
    prosecution's case in chief, 451–452
    rebuttal, 452
    verdict, 453–454
    voir dire, 450
Trial rights of defendants, 436–449
    to confrontation and cross-examination, 442
    to counsel, 445–449
    to jury trial, 436–437
    to public trial, 437
    to speedy trial, 443–445
Tribe, Lawrence, 392

U.S. Constitution, important dates in history
    of, 44
U.S. Marshals, 279
Undercover officers, *Miranda* and, 386
Unequivocality test, 212
Uniform Controlled Substance Act, 177
Uniform Crime Reports (UCR), 85
Uniform Interstate Criminal Extradition Act, 429

United and Strengthening America by Providing
    Appropriate Tools Required to Intercept and
    Obstruct Terrorism Act of 2001 (Patriot
    Act), 191
    conditions of, 191–192
United States Attorney, 9
United States Congress, 8
United States Constitution, 5–6, 8
United States Courts of Appeals, 10
United States District Courts, 9
United States Supreme Court, 6, 10
United States v. Armstrong, 282–286
United States v. Bajakajian, 483–487
United States v. Brignoni-Ponce, 350
United States v. Calley, 230, 231
United States v. Consuelo-Gonzalez, 476, 477–478
United States v. DeLuca, 437, 438–441
United States v. Dunn, 348
United States v. Gordon, 319, 320–323
United States v. Grimaud, 39–40
United States v. Jackson, 437
*United States v. James Daniel Good Real
    Property*, 481
United States v. Leon, 307, 327–328, 329
United States v. Lewis, 174
United States v. Ludwig, 326–327
United States v. Matlock, 338
United States v. Miller, 173, 174
United States v. Moore, 96
United States v. Robinson, 345
United States v. Scheffer, 401
United States v. Sun Myung Moon, 186, 187
United States v. Toscanino, 374–375
United States v. Wade, 394–395
United States v. Watson, 363
United States v. Watts, 460
Unlawful assembly, 167–168
Unlawful disclosure of tax information, 185
Unlawful entry, 125
Use immunity, 248
    defined, 248
Use-of-force defenses, 231–238
    during arrests, 234–238
    imperfect self-defense, 234
    of others, 233

Use-of-force defenses *continued*
  of property and habitation, 233–234
  self-defense, 231–232
Uttering, crime of, 135

Vagrancy, 68, 170, 172
  common law and, 170
Vagueness doctrine, 251
  defined, 251
Validity of scientific identification procedures,
    396–397
Vehicular homicide, 100
Venue, motion for change of, 427–428
Verdict, 453–454
  directed, 452
Vertical division of power, 4
Vicarious liability, 61–62, 87
  defined, 61
Victim assistance organizations, 293
Victim compensation programs, 293
Victim impact statement, 292, 459–460
  defined, 292, 459
Victims, 292–293
  effect on criminal adjudications, 292
  protection of, 292–293
  statements by, 323
Victims' rights, 292
Violent crime in United States, 104–105
Viruses, computer, 145
Voice tests for identification, 400
Voir dire, 450
Voir dire examination, defined, 450
Voluntariness, 66
  confession requirement, 390
  Model Penal Code and, 66

Voluntary manslaughter, 100
Volunteered statements, *Miranda* and, 386

Wade, 402
Waiver of indictment, 417, 418
Warrantless arrest, 363, 411
Warrantless searches, 357, 358
Warrants. *See* Search warrants; Arrest warrants.
Washington v. Glucksberg, 104
Wharton's Rule, 216
Whipping, 472
White slave traffic, 133
Whren v. United States, 357
Willful, 90–91
Williams v. Illinois, 480
Winston v. Lee, 399
Wire fraud, 133
Wiretap, roving, 192
Wisconsin v. Mitchell, 263–266
Witness protection, 292–293
Witness statements, discovery of, 424
Witness tampering, 186
Witnesses, statements by, 323
Work release, 488–489
Writ of error coram nobis, 454
Writ of habeas corpus, 429

"Year-and-a-day rule," 75–76
Youk, Thomas, 103
Young case, 443
Young v. Callahan, 444